The
International Critical Commentary

on the Holy Scriptures of the Old and

New Testaments

UNDER THE EDITORSHIP OF

THE REV. CHARLES AUGUSTUS BRIGGS, D.D.

Edward Robinson Professor of Biblical Theology,
Union Theological Seminary, New York;

THE REV. SAMUEL ROLLES DRIVER, D.D.

Regius Professor of Hebrew, Oxford;

THE REV. ALFRED PLUMMER, M.A., D.D.

Master of University College, Durham.

The International Critical Commentary

on the Holy Scriptures of the Old and New Testaments.

EDITORS' PREFACE.

THERE are now before the public many Commentaries, written by British and American divines, of a popular or homiletical character. *The Cambridge Bible for Schools*, the *Handbooks for Bible Classes and Private Students*, *The Speaker's Commentary*, *The Popular Commentary* (Schaff), *The Expositor's Bible*, and other similar series, have their special place and importance. But they do not enter into the field of Critical Biblical scholarship occupied by such series of Commentaries as the *Kurzgefasstes exegetisches Handbuch zum A. T.;* De Wette's *Kurzgefasstes exegetisches Handbuch zum N. T.;* Meyer's *Kritisch-exegetischer Kommentar;* Keil and Delitzsch's *Biblischer Commentar über das A. T.;* Lange's *Theologisch-homiletisches Bibelwerk;* Nowack's *Handkommentar zum A. T.;* Holtzmann's *Handkommentar zum N. T.* Several of these have been translated, edited, and in some cases enlarged and adapted, for the English-speaking public; others are in process of translation. But no corresponding series by British or American divines has hitherto been produced. The way has been prepared by special Commentaries by Cheyne, Ellicott, Kalisch, Lightfoot, Perowne, Westcott, and others; and the time has come, in the judgment of the projectors of this enterprise, when it is practicable to combine British and American scholars in the production of a critical, comprehensive

Commentary that will be abreast of modern biblical scholarship, and in a measure lead its van.

Messrs. Charles Scribner's Sons of New York, and Messrs. T. & T. Clark of Edinburgh, propose to publish such a series of Commentaries on the Old and New Testaments, under the editorship of Prof. C. A. BRIGGS, D.D., in America, and of Prof. S. R. DRIVER, D.D., for the Old Testament, and the Rev. ALFRED PLUMMER, D.D., for the New Testament, in Great Britain.

The Commentaries will be international and inter-confessional, and will be free from polemical and ecclesiastical bias. They will be based upon a thorough critical study of the original texts of the Bible, and upon critical methods of interpretation. They are designed chiefly for students and clergymen, and will be written in a compact style. Each book will be preceded by an Introduction, stating the results of criticism upon it, and discussing impartially the questions still remaining open. The details of criticism will appear in their proper place in the body of the Commentary. Each section of the Text will be introduced with a paraphrase, or summary of contents. Technical details of textual and philological criticism will, as a rule, be kept distinct from matter of a more general character; and in the Old Testament the exegetical notes will be arranged, as far as possible, so as to be serviceable to students not acquainted with Hebrew. The History of Interpretation of the Books will be dealt with, when necessary, in the Introductions, with critical notices of the most important literature of the subject. Historical and Archæological questions, as well as questions of Biblical Theology, are included in the plan of the Commentaries, but not Practical or Homiletical Exegesis. The Volumes will constitute a uniform series.

THE INTERNATIONAL CRITICAL COMMENTARY.

THE following eminent Scholars are engaged upon the Volumes named below:

THE OLD TESTAMENT.

Genesis	The Rev. JOHN SKINNER, D D., Professor of Old Testament Language and Literature, College of Presbyterian Church of England, Cambridge, England.
Exodus	The Rev. A. R. S. KENNEDY, D.D., Professor of Hebrew, University of Edinburgh.
Leviticus	J. F. STENNING, M.A., Fellow of Wadham College, Oxford.
Numbers	G. BUCHANAN GRAY, D.D., Professor of Hebrew, Mansfield College, Oxford. [Now Ready.
Deuteronomy	The Rev. S. R. DRIVER, D.D., D.Litt., Regius Professor of Hebrew, Oxford. [Now Ready.
Joshua	The Rev. GEORGE ADAM SMITH, D.D., LL.D , Professor of Hebrew, Free Church College, Glasgow.
Judges	The Rev. GEORGE MOORE, D.D., LL. D., Professor of Theology, Harvard University, Cambridge, Mass. [Now Ready.
Samuel	The Rev. H. P. SMITH, D.D., Professor of Biblical History, Amherst College, Mass. [Now Ready.
Kings	The Rev. FRANCIS BROWN, D.D., D.Litt., LL.D., Professor of Hebrew and Cognate Languages, Union Theological Seminary, New York City.
Chronicles	The Rev. EDWARD L. CURTIS, D D., Professor of Hebrew, Yale University, New Haven, Conn.
Ezra and Nehemiah	The Rev. L. W. BATTEN, Ph.D., D.D., Rector of St. Marks Church, New York City, sometime Professor of Hebrew, P. E. Divinity School, Philadelphia.
Psalms	The Rev. CHAS. A. BRIGGS, D.D., D.Litt., Professor of Biblical Theology, Union Theological Seminary, New York.
Proverbs	The Rev. C. H. TOY, D.D., LL D., Professor of Hebrew, Harvard University, Cambridge, Mass. [Now Ready.
Job	The Rev. S. R. DRIVER, D.D., D.Litt., Regius Professor of Hebrew, Oxford.
Isaiah	Chaps. I-XXXIX. The Rev. S. R. DRIVER, D.D., D.Litt., Regius Professor of Hebrew, Oxford.
Isaiah	Chaps. XL-LXVI. The late Rev. Prof. A. B. DAVIDSON, D.D., LL.D.
Jeremiah	The Rev. A. F. KIRKPATRICK, D.D., Master of Selwyn College, Regius Professor of Hebrew, Cambridge, England.
Ezekiel	By the Rev. G. A. COOKE, M.A., Fellow Magdalen College, and the Rev. CHARLES F. BURNEY, M.A., Fellow and Lecturer in Hebrew, St. Johns College, Oxford.
Daniel	The Rev. JOHN P. PETERS, Ph.D., D.D., sometime Professor of Hebrew, P. E. Divinity School, Philadelphia, now Rector of St. Michael's Church, New York City.
Amos and Hosea	W. R. HARPER, Ph.D., LL D., President of the University of Chicago, Illinois. [In Press.
Micah to Malachi	W. R. HARPER, Ph.D., LL D., President of the University of Chicago.
Esther	The Rev. L. B. PATON, Ph.D., Professor of Hebrew, Hartford Theological Seminary.

The International Critical Commentary.

Ecclesiastes	Prof. GEORGE A. BARTON, Ph.D., Professor of Biblical Literature, Bryn Mawr College, Pa.
Ruth	Rev. CHARLES P. FAGNANI, D.D., Associate Professor of Hebrew, Union Theological Seminary, New York.
Song of Songs and Lamentations	Rev. CHARLES A. BRIGGS, D.D., D.Litt., Professor of Biblical Theology, Union Theological Seminary, New York.

THE NEW TESTAMENT.

St. Matthew	The Rev. WILLOUGHBY C. ALLEN, M.A., Fellow of Exeter College, Oxford.
St. Mark	The late Rev. E. P. GOULD, D.D., sometime Professor of New Testament Literature, P. E. Divinity School, Philadelphia. [*Now Ready.*
St. Luke	The Rev. ALFRED PLUMMER, D.D., sometime Master of University College, Durham. [*Now Ready.*
St. John	The Very Rev. JOHN HENRY BERNARD, D.D., Dean of St. Patrick's and Lecturer in Divinity, University of Dublin.
Harmony of the Gospels	The Rev. WILLIAM SANDAY, D.D., LL.D., Lady Margaret Professor of Divinity, Oxford, and the Rev. WILLOUGHBY C. ALLEN, M.A., Fellow of Exeter College, Oxford.
Acts	The Rev. FREDERICK H. CHASE, Norissonian Professor of Divinity, President of Queens College and Vice-Chancellor, Cambridge, England.
Romans	The Rev. WILLIAM SANDAY, D.D., LL.D., Lady Margaret Professor of Divinity and Canon of Christ Church, Oxford, and the Rev. A. C. HEADLAM, M.A., D.D., Principal of Kings College, London. [*Now Ready.*
Corinthians	The Right Rev. ARCH. ROBERTSON, D.D., LL D., Lord Bishop of Exeter, and the Rev. RICHARD J. KNOWLING, D.D., Professor of New Testament Exegesis, Kings College, London.
Galatians	The Rev. ERNEST D. BURTON, D.D., Professor of New Testament Literature, University of Chicago.
Ephesians and Colossians	The Rev. T. K. ABBOTT, B.D., D.Litt., sometime Professor of Biblical Greek, Trinity College, Dublin, now Librarian of the same. [*Now Ready.*
Philippians and Philemon	The Rev. MARVIN R. VINCENT, D.D., Professor of Biblical Literature, Union Theological Seminary, New York City. [*Now Ready.*
Thessalonians	The Rev. JAMES E. FRAME, M.A., Associate Professor in the New Testament, Union Theological Seminary, New York.
The Pastoral Epistles	The Rev. WALTER LOCK, D.D., Warden of Keble College and Professor of Exegesis, Oxford.
Hebrews	The Rev. A. NAIRNE, M.A., Professor of Hebrew in Kings College, London.
St. James	The Rev JAMES H. ROPES, D.D., Bussey Professor of New Testament Criticism in Harvard University.
Peter and Jude	The Rev. CHARLES BIGG, D.D., Regius Professor of Ecclesiastical History and Canon of Christ Church, Oxford. [*Now Ready.*
The Epistles of St. John	The Rev. S. D. F. SALMOND, D.D., Principal of the United Free Church College, Aberdeen.
Revelation	The Rev. ROBERT H. CHARLES, M.A., D.D., Professor of Biblical Greek in the University of Dublin.

SAMUEL

HENRY PRESERVED SMITH

A

CRITICAL AND EXEGETICAL COMMENTARY

ON

THE BOOKS OF SAMUEL

BY

HENRY PRESERVED SMITH

PROFESSOR OF BIBLICAL HISTORY AND INTERPRETATION
IN AMHERST COLLEGE

NEW YORK

CHARLES SCRIBNER'S SONS

1904

Norwood Press
J. S. Cushing & Co. — Berwick & Smith
Norwood Mass. U.S.A.

TO MY WIFE

Anna Macneale Smith

WHOSE CONFIDENCE AND AFFECTION HAVE BEEN MY HELP

IN THIS AS IN ALL MY WORK

AND TO THE MEMORY OF OUR BELOVED

Neale

SO EARLY CALLED TO HIGHER SERVICE THAN WE

ARE YET PERMITTED TO RENDER

PREFACE.

———◆———

THE plan and purpose of this series of commentaries are so well illustrated by the volumes that have preceded this — the one on Deuteronomy by Professor Driver and the one on Judges by Professor Moore — that further statement would be superfluous. In preparing the present number of the series I have constantly had occasion to admire the work of these predecessors, and I shall be gratified if the present volume shall be found worthy of a place by the side of theirs.

The historical importance of the Books of Samuel must be evident to the least attentive reader. In them we have the only sources of information concerning the origin of the monarchy in Israel. How much this implies will be seen if we suppose the names of Samuel, Saul, and David blotted out of our history of Israel. Besides the direct information which we receive from their narrative, these books throw great light upon the manners, customs, and religion of Israel, not only for the period of which they professedly treat, but also for the times in which the various authors lived and wrote.

An understanding of these books is therefore a first necessity to the scholar who would correctly apprehend the history of Israel. Such an understanding is not so easy to attain as appears upon the surface. For one thing, the Hebrew text has come to us much corrupted in transmission — imperfect to a greater degree than that of any other part of the Old Testament, with perhaps one exception. The difficult and delicate task thus thrown upon the exegete will appear to the careful student of this volume. In the second place, these books present peculiar problems for the so-called higher criticism. Nowhere are the phenomena of a complex literary process more obvious, and yet nowhere are these phenomena more difficult to interpret.

The expositor is encouraged in the face of these difficulties by the fact that excellent work has already been done in both these departments of study. The criticism of the text was seriously undertaken (though with inadequate apparatus) by Thenius in 1842, and since that time the problem has been attacked by Wellhausen, Klostermann, Driver, and Budde. In the department of the higher criticism so much cannot be said. Yet even here the books before us have had as much attention as any part of the Old Testament, except the Pentateuch and the Book of Isaiah.

Originality can hardly be claimed by one who follows in such a train. I can only claim that I have carefully considered every suggestion of my predecessors and have tried to judge it on its merits. With regard to the text, the emendations of Thenius and Wellhausen have become a part of exegetical tradition.

In my anxiety to be helpful to the beginner I have sometimes explained that which the more advanced student will find to be sufficiently clear in itself. So far as I know, I have passed no difficulty by in silence. That the consideration of many passages results in a *non liquet* will probably not be found surprising.

The preparation of the commentary, after being begun, was interrupted for about two years by causes beyond my control. For the greater part of the time in which I was engaged upon it, no good library was within my reach. My friend Professor Briggs and the librarians of Union, Lane, and Hartford Theological Seminaries generously relieved this difficulty by granting me the use of a number of volumes — a courtesy which it gives me pleasure here to acknowledge.

AMHERST, MASS., *July* 20, 1898.

CONTENTS

———◆———

INTRODUCTION.

§ 1. *The Title.*

THE two books are one book in Hebrew manuscripts. The division into two was first made by the Greek translators or by the Greek copyists. As we know from classic writers, the rolls on which Greek and Latin works were written were of certain conventional sizes. Biblical books (Samuel, Kings, Chronicles) were divided into two in order to conform to this rule of the trade. The division passed over into the Latin Bible, but invaded the Hebrew copies only with the first Rabbinical Bible of Bomberg.* The original state of the case is still indicated, in editions of the Hebrew, by the Massoretic summary which gives the number of verses only at the end of the second book, thus treating the two as one. In this summary we find also the phrase *Book of Samuel* used, and are told that the middle verse is the one numbered by us 1 S. 28²⁴. Origen is quoted by Eusebius † as affirming specifically that the first and second *Books of the Kingdoms* form one book among the Hebrews, and that this bears the name of Samuel. A Greek MS. also remarks ‡ at the close of 1 S. that Aquila *following the Hebrews* does not divide but makes the two one book. Jerome in the Prologus Galeatus (printed in the authorized editions of the Vulgate) names as third in the list of the Prophets, *Samuel, quem nos Regum primum et secundum dicimus.* With this agrees the Talmud, which names Judges, Samuel, Kings, § as though each were but a single book.

---

* Published at Venice, 1516. Cf. Ginsburg, *Introduction to the Massoretico-Critical Edition of the Hebrew Bible* (1897).

† *Hist. Eccles.* VI. 25, as cited by Kl.

‡ Field, *Hexap. Orig.* I. p. 543.

§ The passage (*Baba Bathra*, 14 *a*) is translated in Briggs, *Biblical Study* (1883), p. 175 ff., and Briggs, *General Introduction to the Study of Holy Scripture* (1899), p. 252 f.

The title of the book (or books) is in the Hebrew Canon *Samuel*, apparently because Samuel is the leading character in the earlier chapters. The name is unfortunate, as Samuel ceases to be prominent after the middle of the first book, and David occupies the narrator's whole attention from that point on. The infelicity is removed by the Greek translators who count the two books as First and Second *Books of the Kingdoms*, the two following counting Third and Fourth of the series. The Latin adopted a modification of this form, counting four books of Kings (*Regum*). In at least one printed edition of the Hebrew text, this name has been introduced by the side of the other.

In the more accurate editions of the Hebrew text 2 S. has no heading, and is separated only by a space of three words' breadth from the preceding book. The note at the end of 2 S. begins סכום פסוקי דספר שמואל, the verses of the two books together being reckoned 1506. The edition which introduces ספר ראשון (שני) מהמלכים along with שמואל א׳ (ב׳) is the edition of Plantin, 1680. In 𝕲 we find βασιλειῶν πρώτη, δευτέρα, represented in some Latin MSS. by *Regnorum* instead of *Regum*. In 𝕾 *Kethâbhâ dashmu'il nebhiyâ*.

§ 2. *Contents.*

The Books of Samuel form a part of the continuous history of Israel which begins with the conquest of Canaan and ends with the Exile, or, if we include the Pentateuch as is apparently the design of the collectors of the books, which begins with the Creation and ends with the Exile. This part of the history is, however, less closely connected with the Book of Judges, which precedes, than with the First Book of Kings, which follows. For, while there is every reason to believe that the Philistine oppression, from which Samson began to deliver Israel, is the same which afflicted the people in the time of Samuel, we have no certain means of deciding how long a time had elapsed from the death of Samson until the events narrated in 1 S. 1; while at the conclusion of 2 S. the unfinished life of David is immediately continued in the opening chapters of 1 K.

The period covered by these books may be estimated at about a hundred years. It was evidently one of the most important centuries in the life of Israel, for in it was effected the transition from the tribal form of government (if government it may be

called) to the settled monarchy of David. At the opening of the
period the prominent figures (Eli, Samuel) are classed by the
author with the heroes of the Book of Judges. Saul is the first
who attempts to cement the people together by the monarchy.
Although his experiment ended in disaster, there is no reason to
doubt that his failure paved the way for David's success. In the
long struggle against the Philistine oppressor the nation realized
its own unity, learned its own strength, and prepared to play its
part in the history of the world. What light we have upon this
time of storm and stress, of heroic struggle and high achievement,
comes from the Books of Samuel.

In accordance with what has just been said, the subject-matter
divides itself readily under the three heads : Samuel, Saul, and
David. But as the three are contemporaneous for some years, the
sections overlap, and the transition period of Saul falls within
the time allotted to Samuel on the one hand or to David on the
other. Such seems to have been the mind of the author (or final
redactor) of the Books, to whom Saul was of minor importance.
This is sufficiently indicated by the fact that Samuel is the real
authority after Saul is anointed, and that so soon as Saul is
rejected David is anointed. To the theocratic view, the history
belongs to Samuel and to David, and its two sections are 1 S. 1–15,
the life of Samuel ; and 1 S. 16–2 S. 24, the life of David. The
life of David, however, consists of two well-marked sections, the
first, the period of struggle, is described in 1 S. 16–2 S. 1 ;
the second, his reign over Israel, occupies 2 S. 2–24.

The plan of the Book is of course the plan of the final editor. The remarks
just made concerning the minor importance of Saul apply to the view of this
editor alone. For it is evident that the work embodies documents whose view
of Saul is much more favourable. To the earlier writer Saul is one of the
heroic figures in the history of Israel, and this writer would doubtless have
made the story of Saul equally important with the story of David. The manner
in which his work is now interrupted by sections of a different tenor makes it
difficult to form a distinct scheme of the Book. But the following schedule
will show the subjects treated :

A. 1 SAMUEL 1–15. THE LIFE OF SAMUEL.

    1–7. Samuel as Judge.
      1^1–4^{1a}. Birth, consecration, and call.
      4^{1b-22}. The house of Eli.

§ 3. *Composition of the Book.*

As is now well known, the Hebrew historians whose works have come down to us made free use of previously existing documents. Their method is abundantly exemplified in the Books of Chronicles, where we are able to compare the result and the sources. Where the earlier documents, or sources of compilation, have perished, as is the case in the books we are now considering, the demonstration is not so striking. But even here the phenomena are sufficiently plain, and enable us to say with practical certainty that the method was the same. The first thing that attracts our attention in reading the story of Samuel and David is the obvious *duplication of certain incidents*. Two denunciations of Eli's course are related, either one of which abundantly answers the author's purpose. There are two accounts of Saul's rejection, and the second makes no allusion to the earlier. The two (or three) accounts of Saul's appointment as king are probably another example. Two accounts of David's coming to court have long given trouble to the harmonist. We have two sets of negotiations for Saul's daughter, the later being ignorant of the earlier one. There are at least two accounts of David's flight from court, two of his having Saul in his power, two of his seeking refuge with Achish, two of the death of Saul. The difficulty of working these into one history increases with each additional incident. The simplest way to account for them is to suppose that they are real duplicates, — variant accounts of the same series of events, put together by a compiler who wished to preserve for us whatever he found of interest in both (or all) his sources.

Equally convincing is the *difference in style and point of view*, which is noticed as we pass from one section to another. In one place Samuel appears as the theocratic ruler of the people, comparable to Moses, and to Moses alone among the heroes of Israel. He administers the government as the representative of Yahweh. The whole people gather at his call, and he rebukes and commands with more than kingly authority. In another place he is the seer of a small town, respected as one who blesses the sacrifice and presides at the local festival, but known only as a clairvoyant, whose information concerning lost or strayed property is reliable. Even thus he is unknown to Saul, whose home is only a few miles away. With this difference of view goes a difference of political theory. In one account Saul is chosen as king by God, is welcomed by Samuel, is assured that God is with him and encouraged to act as he finds opportunity. His election by God is an act of grace; for God has looked upon the affliction of his people, and now promises that Saul shall deliver them from the hand of the Philistines. But in other sections of the narrative the desire of the people for a king is an act of rebellion against Yahweh. Their act is an act of apostasy parallel to all their rebellions of earlier times. No wonder; for to this narrator the Philistine oppression has already been relieved by Samuel. By spiritual weapons these enemies have been vanquished so that they come no more into the territory of Israel, and even surrender the territory which they had taken away. So great a discrepancy, not in details of the narrative only, but also in the whole view of the same period, is not conceivable in one author. It can be accounted for only on the hypothesis that various works have been combined in one.

§ 4. *Analysis of 1 Samuel i.–xv.*

As already remarked, these chapters form a distinctly marked section of the work before us. Within this section we can easily select certain paragraphs which have a common tone. In these

Samuel appears as the theocratic ruler of Israel. The most striking instance is chapter 7³ff.. In this section Samuel's influence
suffices to make the people put away their false gods as by
a common impulse. At his command they gather at Mizpah.
Their assembly is a religious convocation. The Philistine attack
finds the people apparently undefended. But the prevailing
prayer of Samuel is stronger than earthly weapons. Throughout
the chapter, Samuel reminds us of Moses. Like the great Law-
giver, Samuel rebukes the people, judges them, intercedes for
them. Their victory over the enemy is due to his prayers, as
the victory over Amalek in the Wilderness is due to the upraised
hands of Moses.

The parallel continues in the next chapter (ch. 8). Here the
people rebel against their prophet, and in so doing rebel against
Yahweh himself. Their action is as ungrateful as was their murmuring in the Wilderness. Their hearts are incorrigible. Even
the fact that Samuel's sons do not walk in his ways is not allowed
to mitigate their guilt. The position of Samuel as Yahweh's
vicegerent is impregnable.

The continuation of the story is 10¹⁷⁻²⁵. The choice of a king
by lot follows immediately on the people's demand. In handling
the lot Samuel appears not exactly as another Moses, but at least
as another Joshua. Like Joshua also he delivers a farewell address,
now contained in chapter 12. This originally followed at once on
the election of Saul. Its resemblance to Jos. 24 is obvious. In
it Samuel still appears as the executive officer of the theocracy.
He holds up to the people their revolt against Yahweh, and con-
vinces them that they have sinned in asking a king. The conviction leads to no attempt to undo what has been done, and people
and king are allowed to go on on sufferance. But they are solemnly warned that, if they do ill, they and their king will perish.

The forebodings which thus cast their shadows over Saul's
inauguration are realized in chapter 15. Although Samuel has
resigned the supreme power, the king is still subject to his order ;
and he commands Saul to exterminate the Amalekites. Saul obeys
only in part, and for his sin is peremptorily deposed — *de jure*
deposed, for the prophet consents to pay him outward honour.
But to the author's view, the experiment with Saul has turned out

a failure; and Samuel pronounces the divine sentence to this effect.

The common tone of these chapters will be admitted by the attentive reader, and their contrast with the sections now inter-polated between them will scarcely be denied. And, reading them in connexion, we discover that they form an unbroken nar-rative. Their author told in them all that he cared to tell of the life of Saul. But we naturally suppose that he told more of Samuel, who was to him the important figure. And it is altogether likely that he introduced him at an earlier stage of life than that in which he here appears — already at the height of his power. It is not improbable, therefore, that the account of Samuel's birth and youth form part of the same document. And in the account of this which we find in 1 there is nothing inconsistent with the sup-position that it is a part of the same history. With this we naturally take the call of the prophet as narrated in 3. As the text now stands, chapter 4 belongs in the same connexion, for it is the sequel of 3.

Provisionally, then, we may restore a life of Samuel which was once a separate document and which embraced what we now read as chapters 1, 3, 4, 7^{3-17}, 8, 10^{17-25}, 12, 15. I will designate it *Sm*. We next examine the parts which do not belong to this source, and our attention is attracted by $9^{1}-10^{16}$. This is a continuous, and, for the most part, homogeneous, narrative, contrasting re-markably with the one we have been examining. It begins like a separate book, introducing persons hitherto unknown. When Samuel appears, it is in a very different character from the one he wears in Sm. This story has little of the theological character of the other account, though the author shows piety of another stamp. Chapters 11, $13^{2}-14^{52}$, agree so well in their tone with 9, 10, that we have little difficulty in joining them together. As in the other case, they belong to a single document, and are apparently continuous.* This document is a life of Saul, as truly as the other is a life of Samuel, and we may call it *Sl*.

There are considerable portions which have not yet been as-

---

* Some minor sections, which do not at first sight agree with the context in which they are found, will be considered later.

signed to either of our two sources. The most marked in its individuality is the account of the Ark in the country of the Philistines, 5^1–7^1. It contains no references to Samuel or Saul, so that we are quite at a loss to place it. Our only clue is that it presupposes the capture of the Ark, the account of which is now contained in 4. We therefore put it in Sm., but its individuality is so marked that we may suspect it to have been embodied in that document from some source now lost to us. Chapter 2, which next claims our attention, is made up of several distinct paragraphs. First is Hannah's Psalm. This is now universally conceded to be an independent composition inserted in the text from some poetical collection like our own Book of Psalms. We next find an account of the wickedness of Eli's sons, 2^{12-17}, followed by a panegyric of Samuel $^{18-21}$. The next four verses take up Eli's sons again, while v.^{26} recurs to Samuel. Finally, we have a denunciation of Eli (2^{27-36}) by an anonymous man of God who reminds us of the similar character in 1 K. 13^1.

By experiment we discover that the paragraphs concerning Eli's sons and the weakness of their father, with the message of the man of God, can be put together without the references to Samuel. But the references to Samuel do not stand together (if taken by themselves), and seem to have been inserted into the other account when it was already complete. The case is not like that of the references to Eli in chapter 1, for those references are so wrought into the narrative that we cannot suppose them ever to have been independent of it, nor it ever to have existed without them. The riddle will be solved if we suppose that Sm. took from an earlier source the account of the wickedness of Eli's sons, the rebuke of the anonymous prophet, and the account of the capture and restoration of the Ark. This material he wrought into his life of Samuel in the usual method of the Hebrew historiographer.

The analysis given above, so far as the separation of the documents is concerned, is the one now the common property of criticism. The only point at which I have ventured to diverge from my predecessors is in regard to the denunciation of punishment contained in 2^{27-36}. This is generally taken to be a sheer intrusion made by a very late hand, after the virtual completion of our present Book. The argument is, that it duplicates chapter 3 and takes away its point. The truth in this is that 4 is the sequel either of 2^{27-36} or of 3. One of the two denunciations is superfluous. But I find it more probable that an author in writing the life of Samuel should add 3 to the denunciation already in the text, than that one should put 2^{27-36} into a text which already has the message to Samuel. The author of Sm. must give the honour to Samuel even if he found the anonymous already there. And that the anonymous is presupposed is evident from 3^{12}, for in this verse Yahweh says: *In that day I will execute upon Eli all that I have spoken against his house*. The palpable reference is to what the man of God has said in the preceding chapter.

The earlier document which I here postulate consists of $2^{12\ 17.\ 22-25.\ 27-36}\ 4^{1b}-7^1$. It also contained originally some further account of Eli and of Shiloh which the author could not use. One indication of this is the fact that Eli steps upon the scene in 1^3 without introduction. As a Philistine oppression of forty years is known to the author of Judges (13^1), from which Samson only *began* to deliver Israel (Jd. $13^{5.\ 25}$), it is not unlikely that this Eli document was once read in that connexion. The argument that 2^{27-36} is of later date than the context has no weight in the face of the difficulty we meet in assigning a definite date to either of our documents.

So far as Saul is concerned, the two narratives which we have separated cover the same ground. Each has an account of his election, both make Samuel the instrument of his anointing, each gives an exploit of his, each narrates his rejection. They must have existed as separate histories before they were combined in our present text. Of the two, Sl. is evidently the older document. It is more primitive in its religious ideas. It has a near and clear view of the personages and of the progress of events. We may class it with the stories of Gideon, of Jephthah, and of Samson, which form the groundwork of the Book of Judges. The other account, so far as it is original with the author whom we call Sm., is less concrete. It idealizes persons and events. It is dominated by a theological idea. It is, in fact, in line with the latest redactor of the Book of Judges, who embodied the Deuteronomistic theory of history in the framework of that book. There is reason to suppose, therefore, that Sm. designed to replace the older history by one of his own which would edify his generation. This design and this method are indications of a comparatively late date — perhaps in or after the Exile.

The historical method which joins together two or more documents, narrating the same events or treating the same subject, is so well illustrated in the Pentateuch that I need not stop to argue the probabilities in its favour in the

Books of Samuel. The original independence of the document which we have called Sl. accounts for the insertion of one section which has puzzled the critics. I refer to 13⁸⁻¹⁵ᵃ, the first account of Saul's rejection or of the breach between him and Samuel. The paragraph is an evident duplicate of 15 and its insertion in the completed book is unaccountable. Yet the critics generally assume that it is a late insertion by an editor or scribe to whom Saul's rejection in 15 came too late. As the reason why the other events of Saul's life are duplicated is that they are narrated once in each document, there is a presumption that the same is true in this case. The section 13⁸⁻¹⁵ᵃ was Sl.'s account of Saul's rejection and was inserted into his history before Sm. was written. The argument is briefly: (1) that this section was closely inwoven into Sl. by the preparatory verse 10⁸. This could hardly be called the method of a mere interpolator; (2) historical fidelity called for some account of this kind. The fact was notorious that Saul's kingdom did not endure. This was as well known to the writer of Sl. as it is to us. Though far from the pragmatism of Sm. he would yet find the reason for this in the will of Yahweh and his prophet; (3) this account is as mild as it well could be. It does not blame Saul but leaves us in doubt whether he was really at fault. In this respect, certainly, the paragraph does not show dependence on 15, where a high-handed act of disobedience is narrated. The gentler treatment of Saul would naturally come earlier in time; (4) only by supposing this to have preceded can we account for the geographical location of 15. As is well known, the centre of Samuel's public activity, according to Sm., is Mizpah. It is here that he calls the people together on solemn occasions, and it is here that Saul would most naturally bring the people for his festivities. Why then do we find the festivities and the rejection of 15 at Gilgal? Only because the author had before him an account which already made Gilgal the site.*

It remains to inquire whether either of the two documents was complete in itself, or whether one or the other contained more than the life of a single hero. The probability is in favour of each one's being part of a larger history. The life of David was so important in the eyes of any Israelitic writer (we may feel sure) that the life of Saul or of Samuel would be treated as an intro-

---

* In order to show the state of the discussion I have here assumed that the paragraph in question is exactly 13⁸⁻¹⁵ᵃ, which is its extent according to the analysis of Wellhausen, Budde, and others. The exact boundaries of the insertion however are not absolutely certain, as the reader will see by turning to the exposition in the body of the book. I myself think it begins with v.⁴. It should be remarked also that though the section was in the history of Sl. before it was joined to Sm., it is nevertheless an addition to the earliest text of Sl. It fits so badly in its present context that it shows itself to be an insertion. My only contention is that it is an *early* insertion.

duction to the story of David. This is confirmed by the phenomena before us. Chapter 15, which is as far as we have traced
Sm., is continued in 16^{1-13}, while 14^{52} certainly prepares the way
for 16^{14ff}. The paragraph 14^{47-51} is indeed a concluding summary
such as we find elsewhere at the end of an important reign or
period. But it is probable that the author of Sl. would at least
give us some account of his hero's death. As he has no more
exploits to tell, it is not improper for him to insert his summary
here. Still it is possible that these verses are a later insertion or
have been transferred hither from some other place.

Redactional alterations, made to fit the documents together,
are not numerous. The most marked is 11^{12-14} where the proposition to *renew* the kingdom is a concession to the other document.
Some other minor alterations or insertions will be considered in
the course of the exposition.

This is the place to consider whether the two streams of narrative so plainly discernible in 1 Sam. 1–15 belong to the Pentateuchal (Hexateuchal) authors commonly known as J and E.
The affirmative has been maintained by recent critics.* The
document which I have called Sm. these scholars identify with E,
and the other history they attribute to J. Repeated examination
of the points of resemblance has failed to convince me of the
identity which is claimed. Details may be left until we come to
the exposition ; but here it may be allowed to say that Sm. shows
quite as many resemblances to D, or the Deuteronomic school,
as it shows to E. For Sl. it seems enough to say that its affinities seem to be with the stories that form the basis of the Book
of Judges rather than with the traditions of the Patriarchs told us
by J.

§ 5. *Analysis of 1 Samuel xvi.–2 Samuel i.*

The problems presented by this section of the history are more
complicated than those just considered. The confusion and in-

---

* The theory that the Pentateuchal sources extend into the historical books is as
old as Gramberg's *Kritische Geschichte* (1830) and was elaborated by Schrader in
the eighth edition of De Wette's *Einleitung* (1869). It has recently been revived
by Budde and Cornill, with the qualified approval of Professor Moore (*Judges*, p.
xxxiii f.). A judicious review of the arguments of Bu. and Co. is given by Kittel,
SK. 1891, p. 44 ff.

consistencies of the narrative, and the evident duplicates which it contains, show that it is composite.   But as Saul and David appear in both accounts, and as Samuel is in the background, it is more difficult to separate the documents.   Chapter 16 encourages us to make a beginning, for it introduces David to us twice.   In the first half of the chapter he is a shepherd boy not old enough to be called to the family sacrifice.   In the second half he is a warrior of experience and of approved valour.   The two sections cannot come from the same hand, and each of them fits admirably to one of the two documents we have traced hitherto.   For vv.[1-13] are the logical sequel to 15 (Sm.) ; since the rejection of Saul must be followed by some provision for his successor.   The other account 16[14-23] continues 14[52] (Sl.), as has already been pointed out.

The first definite clue in what follows seems to be 18[13] where we read that Saul removed David from his presence (מעמו) by giving him a command of troops engaged in service away from the court.   This points back to 16[21] where David had been made his armour-bearer ; 18[6-13] therefore belongs with 16[14-23].   It did not follow immediately on that paragraph, however, because the song of the women 18[6] which is the occasion of Saul's distrust must have been preceded by some exploit of David's which called forth the eulogy.   Such an exploit is indeed found in 17.   But that chapter agrees more nearly (in its representation of David's youth) with the other document.   We must assume that the original paragraph has been omitted, or else that it has been worked over so that we no longer recognize it.*

The chapter now under consideration gives an account of two of Saul's daughters, each of which Saul offers to David as a wife. The two accounts are evidently independent, and one of them shows reference to Sm.   It is natural to find in the other 18[20-29a] a continuation of Sl., with which it agrees in representing Saul as hoping to get David out of the way by the hand of the Philistines. In this hope he is disappointed and the marriage takes place. The account concludes with the statement that *Saul feared David*

---

* The question whether the recension of 𝔊 is to be preferred to that of 𝔐 in 17 and 18 will be discussed in the commentary.   The presumption is in favour of the shorter text, which is that of 𝔊.

still more. This would properly introduce one of the attempts upon David's life. Among several that offer themselves, the one which fits most naturally in the story is 19^{11-17} where Saul sets guards about the house of David. The night in which this took place is the wedding night, a time when David would be least suspicious. The evident sequel is the flight to Nob, 21^{2-10}, and the conclusion to this is the massacre of the priests $22^{1.\ 2.\ 6-23}$.

The most striking duplicate in what follows is 23^{19}–24^{23} compared with 26. It is altogether probable that one of these should be assigned to each of our documents. If so, 26 is the one which belongs with Sl. because in it David appears as the daring warrior who invades the enemy's camp. The intervening matter offers 23^{1-14} which seems to belong in the same stream. The story of Nabal in 25 and the account of David's service with Achish 27. 29. 30 also go well in this connexion. 2 S. 1 seems to be the continuation of the same document.

Without denying the subjective nature of such an analysis, I venture to think that we have a consistent narrative in the sections thus put together, to wit: 16^{14-23} $18^{6-13.\ 20-29a}$ 19^{11-17} 21^{2-10} $22^{1.\ 2.\ 6-23}$ 23^{1-14} 25. 26. 27. 29. 30. 2 S. 1. What is left is not so homogeneous, though for the most part the fragments fit together fairly well. It makes David, the shepherd lad secretly anointed by Samuel, come to the camp of Saul where he slays the Philistine champion. His introduction to Saul is followed by Jonathan's pledge of friendship (18^{1-5}). Saul, on the other hand, is his enemy at once and tries to pin him to the wall (18^{14-16}) — the evident reference to 16^{14-23} does not necessarily prove the coherence of the two paragraphs. We had reason to believe in the earlier period that Sm. was dependent to some extent on Sl. The same seems to be true here. The evil spirit which Sl. made the occasion of introducing David to the court, becomes in Sm. the divine inciter of Saul against David. Yahweh is with David to protect him, while Saul is the incarnation of all villainy. So in 18^{17-19}, Merab is promised to David, being his by right on account of the defeat of Goliath, but taken from him by a flagrant breach of faith, and given to another. Soon after, Saul orders Jonathan to slay David, but a temporary reconciliation is effected, 18^{30}–19^7. But at the next exhibition of prowess Saul tries again to murder

David with his own hand, 19^{8-10}. David escapes and comes to Samuel at Ramah, where he is miraculously saved from Saul's various attempts to take him, 19^{18-24}. This, it should be noticed, is a duplicate account of what we have in 10^{10-12}, and as that belongs to Sl., this is naturally attributed to Sm., where we have already placed it. The natural continuation is 21^{11-16}, David's flight to Achish, with which we may perhaps connect 22^{3-5}. It has already been pointed out that $23^{19}-24^{26}$ belongs in this document. Its tone agrees with this, for David is saved by an interposition of Providence, 23^{26}, and his enemy is delivered into his hand by the same power. The distinct recognition of David's kingly future on the part of Saul, 24^{21-23}, seems to point in the same direction. Further, 23^{15-18} should perhaps be taken with this narrative, though it may be a later interpolation. Samuel appears for the last time in 28, where, although dead, he plays the part assigned to him in the earlier chapters of this source, and his message is vindicated in 31, the story of Saul's despair and suicide.

Reading continuously 16^{1-13} 17^1-18^5 (in the text of ⑮) 18^{14-19} $18^{30}-19^{10}$ 19^{18-24} 21^{11-16} 22^{3-5} $23^{11}-24^{26}$ 28. 31 we shall find no insuperable objection to considering them one history. We have thus accounted for all our text except 20 (including 21^1). This seems impossible to fit into either of our sources. It is the account of Jonathan's device for sounding his father and acquainting David with the result. In the composite text it comes after Saul's repeated attempts upon David's life, when it is simply ludicrous to have Jonathan deny that David is in danger. But it is equally out of place in either of the separate sources. In one it comes immediately after David's flight to Samuel, which, with Saul's pursuit, must have been known to all the world. In the other it would follow David's escape from his own house, in connexion with which Saul's animus must have been revealed to the court and to his own immediate family. The only place where it would seem possible is after Saul's first manifestation of hostility, which is the first attempt with the spear, 18^{9-11}. But when we place it here we are at once brought into difficulty by the fact that at the end of the interview David leaves the court for good — which contradicts the subsequent tenor of both documents. There seems to be nothing left except to suppose we have here a fragment from another source. The obvious purpose of the story is to prepare for David's treatment of Jonathan's son Meribbaal (Mephibosheth) in 2 S.[9] and it is possible that that story and this originally stood in connexion. It should be noted that in this chapter there is an assumption that it was not safe for David to be seen with Jonathan, something which is not intimated in either of our sources.

Here, as in the analysis of 1–15, I cannot claim originality in discovering the paragraphs which belong together. Earlier critics, however, have been obliged to assume a number of fragmentary insertions which do not seem to me probable. In claiming that the book is made up of two fairly continuous histories, I do not mean to assert that these are not themselves composite. There is every probability in favour of this being the case. It is perhaps sufficient for the present to show the first stage of the critical process. There is evidently much yet to be done. Some minor interpolations will be discussed in the commentary.

§ 6. *Analysis of 2 Samuel ii.–xxiv.*

The narrative here shows few duplicate sections such as we meet in the earlier book. It is now generally conceded that we have in 9–20 a block of homogeneous matter from an old and well-informed source. It reaches a period with the description of David's court in 20[23-26]. A similar description is given in 8[16-18]. It seems natural to suppose that in the latter place the paragraph was intended to serve the same purpose as in the earlier ; and, in fact, chapter 8 is a compendium of David's wars, designed to take the place of the more extended history in 9–20. Chapters 5 and 7 seem to belong with 8, for their author emphasizes the religious ideas of Israel's unity and of David's significance with reference to the Messianic hope. The tone of these chapters would agree with Sm., while there seems no objection to making 9–20 a part of Sl. Chapters 2–4 will then belong with the latter, while 6 represents matter belonging to both. At least, it is impossible to suppose either to have lacked an account of the capture of Jerusalem such as is here given.

The curious appendix, 21–24, contains pieces of widely different origin. The two calamities recounted in 21[1-14] and 24 seem to belong together, and to have been originally continuous. Between them was first inserted an old catalogue of exploits and of heroes, 21^{15-22} 23^{8-39}. This was in turn rent asunder by the two Psalms, 22 and 23^{1-7}. It is possible that some of this material belongs to the documents already separated, and there seems no internal reason why we should not make 21^{1-14} and 24 a part of the history from which came 9–20. But how they came to be dislocated from the main body is difficult to say. It should be noted that the whole section, 21–24, separates what belongs together, for 1 Kings 1 is the original continuation of 1 Sam. 20.

Spinoza in the *Tractatus Theologico-Politicus* sets forth the theory that all the books from Genesis to Kings are the work of a single historian. He does not discuss the Books of Samuel in detail, but probably held that they (like the Pentateuch) contain fragments of different dates. Richard Simon likewise does not discuss the composition of these books in detail, but is content to assert that the historical books of the Bible are all compiled from ancient records by way of abridgment. He cites the opinion of Abarbanel that Samuel and Kings were compiled by Jeremiah out of the records of Samuel, Nathan, Gad, and other prophets or public writers who lived before him. He also quotes other opinions to the same effect, and remarks that there are in these books several ways of speaking which clearly demonstrate that the last collection was not made until a long time after most of these prophets had lived.*

The first attempt at detailed analysis of the Books of Samuel seems to have been made by Eichhorn, in whose Introduction † we find a comparison of the matter common to 2 Samuel and 1 Chronicles. This he supposes to be taken from a common source, a compendious life of David. He further points out that 1 S. 24 and 26 are duplicates, and that 16^{14-23} and 17^{11-32} are inconsistent. The last-mentioned paragraph he strikes out of the text, on the ground of its omission by ⅅ. He points out also that 1 S. 1–3 and 7 are later than the adjacent matter.

Eichhorn's hypothesis of a brief life of David which furnished the matter common to Samuel and Chronicles was ably refuted by De Wette in his *Beiträge* (II. p. 14 ff.). The same scholar ‡ gives the evidence of compilation, beginning with the contradiction between 16^{14-23} and $17^{12ff. 55}$. He adds that these last are not consistent with $17^{31-40. 54}$. Besides other inconsistencies, he points out the duplicate nature of $23^{19}-24^{23}$ and 26, recognizes that 2 S. 21–24 is an appendix, and that the poetic sections are inserted from a book of songs.

---

* Richard Simon, *A Critical History of the Old Testament*, translated into English by H. D., London, 1682; pp. 4, 22, 62.

† *Einleitung in das Alte Testament*, Fünfte Auflage, Göttingen, 1823, III. pp. 464–533.

‡ In his *Einleitung in das Alte Testament*, Vierte Auflage, Berlin, 1833.

He does not make a thoroughgoing analysis, and contents himself with refuting Bertholdt, whose work is now antiquated.

Gramberg * with genuine critical insight calls attention to the resemblance between the pragmatism of 1 S. 7 and that of the framework of the Book of Judges. He also recognizes that 1 S. and the early part of 2 S. consist of two narratives which relate the same events in different ways. He disentangles the two documents, beginning with 1 S. 9 and following them through 16. From that point on, his analysis is not so successful.

Ewald † divides the historical books Judges to 2 Kings among six different authors. He supposes the earliest materials to have been statistical, like 2 S. 23^{8-39}, and that these were taken from the public records — it is unfortunate that he should class with them 1 Chr. 11^{10-47} and 12^{1-22}. Next to these was a narrative, near the events in point of time, which embraced such sections as 1 S. 13. 14 and 30^{26-31}. Then came an extended work, the Prophetical Book of Kings, which is the source of a large part of the material in Samuel and Kings (down to 2 K. 10). Another writer, of less vigorous style, covered the same period — a specimen of his work is 1 S. 5–8, and another is 1 S. 31. Later fragments inserted into the history are 1 S. 12. 15–17. 24. 26. 28. The work thus compiled was Deuteronomically edited, brief insertions indicating the point of view of the editor, like 1 S. $8^{3. 4}$ and parts of 12. The final redactor lived in the Exile, but the changes made by him in our books were slight, the insertion of 1 S. $2^{27 ff.}$ being the only one mentioned.

The analysis made by Schrader ‡ assigns the greater part of the books to two writers whom he distinguishes as the theocratic and the prophetic narrator, and whom he identifies (as already mentioned) with the two authors of the Pentateuch now generally known as E and J. The details of his analysis however do not bear examination, as he classes together sections palpably inconsistent.

The problem was taken in hand afresh by Wellhausen. § With great clearness of vision he separates the two main sources of 1 S., though he is not always positive concerning the intricacies of 19 and 20. In 2 S. he makes 6. 9–20 parts of a life of David, while pointing out the various elements which are put together in the rest of the Book. His conclusion is that the bulk of 2 S. is a literary unit, and that 1 S. 14^{52}–2 S. 8^{18} is another literary unit, " in which however the continuous thread is frequently interrupted by foreign matter. These later insertions are doubtless supplements which attach themselves to the older connexion, or put a new elaboration in the place of a

---

* *Kritische Geschichte der Religionsideen des Alten Testament*, Berlin, 1830, p. 71 ff.

† *Gesch. des Volkes Israel* 3, I. pp. 193–244; ETr. I. pp. 133–168.

‡ In De Wette's *Einleitung*, Achte Auflage, 1869.

§ In his edition of Bleek's *Einleitung*, the fourth, published in 1878. This section is not contained in the later editions of Bleek, but is reprinted in the book entitled *Composition des Hexateuchs und der historischen Bücher*, Berlin, 1889.

genuine member of the older document." In 1 S. 1–14, finally, he unites three pieces which belong to each other but which have not sprung from the same point of view (*Comp.* p. 265).

Budde * marks an advance by showing how complete each of the two documents in 1 S. 1–14 is in itself. He seems to exaggerate however in declaring that neither can be shown to be dependent on the other. In the second half of 1 S. he finds the continuation of the same two histories but with considerable supplementary insertions, and he follows the two documents down to 2 S. 7. As already remarked, he believed them to be identical with the Pentateuchal sources E and J, having come to this conclusion independently of Schrader.† 2 S. 8 he supposes to be a compendious conclusion to the history of David designed to replace 9–20, which an editor sensitive to David's reputation left out of the history, but which one with more historic sense afterwards reinserted. This scholar's textual and higher criticism is embodied in his edition of the text. ‡ The student will readily convince himself that the analysis in this book is not always correct, that the colouring is sometimes certainly wrong, and further, that his rearrangement of the chapters in 2 S. creates a book which in fact never had any earlier existence. But the work is nevertheless indispensable, and a distinct advance on anything which had been done before.

Kuenen (*HCO²*.) comes to substantially the same conclusion with Wellhausen. A careful statement of the phenomena is given by Driver, *LOT*⁶. pp. 172–185. While agreeing with Budde that one of the two sources shows affinity with E, he points out the considerable differences between the other and J. Cornill (*Einleitung*⁴) seems to add little to the results of his predecessors.

§ 7. *The Text and Versions.*

All existing copies of the Hebrew Bible represent a single recension of the text. Extravagant views of the integrity and perfection of this text prevailed among Jewish scholars, and passed over into the Church. These views were formulated into a dogma in at least one instance ; and, with few exceptions, Protestant scholars were dominated by them down to the present century. The integrity of the Massoretic text was mildly ques-

---

* *Die Bücher Richter und Samuel*, 1890.

† Budde's book was preceded by a study entitled "Saul's Königswahl und Verwerfung," *ZATW*. 1888. Cornill treated the same subject under the title "Ein Elohistischer Bericht über die Entstehung des Israel. Königtums," *ZKWKL*. 1885, and in the *Königsberger Studien*, 1887, and *ZATW*. 1890. His discussion seems to have been of material help to Budde.

‡ Part 8 of Haupt's *SBOT*. Baltimore, 1894.

tioned by Cappel, and roughly attacked by Morin ; but these are only the exceptions that prove the rule. The true state of the case with reference to the Books of Samuel has been recognized for about half a century. The text of these books in the current Hebrew recension is more corrupt than the text of any other part of the Old Testament, unless it be the Book of Ezekiel. From what has been said of Hebrew MSS. and editions, it will be seen that variations of these among themselves give little help in the work of emendation. In some few instances, however, the MSS. show a better reading than is found in the printed copies.

The greater part of this commentary was prepared on the basis of Baer's edition (Lipsiae, 1892), with frequent reference to the editions of Jablonski, 1699, and Michaelis, 1720. In the final revision I have carefully gone over the edition of Ginsburg (London, 1894). I have also noted the various readings of De Rossi in his *Variae Lectiones Veteris Testamenti*, Parma, 1785. Ginsburg gives a large number of corrections in his margin, taken apparently from the versions. I have in no case depended upon these, though in a few instances they have called my attention to a reading whose possibility had not occurred to me.

In the absence of light from the MSS., we must seek the help of the ancient versions. And among these the Greek easily takes the first place, owing to its age and to the fact that it had a Hebrew original very different from the one known to us. If we had 𝕲 in its earliest form, it would be equivalent to a Hebrew codex of the first Christian century, or even of earlier date. Unfortunately the copies of 𝕲 now in our possession have suffered manifold corruption. Logically, we should wait until their faults have been removed, and the uncorrupt original has been restored, before proceeding to the correction of the Hebrew text.

For this we cannot wait, as such an edition is not likely to be published for many years to come. Until it appears, we may provisionally make use of the material at hand. Various editions of 𝕲 are known to us, and with due care they may help us to valuable improvements in our text. The copies most accessible to us are based with a greater or less degree of accuracy on the celebrated Codex Vaticanus (ᴮ). Excessive claims have sometimes been made for this MS., as though it transmitted the original Septuagint, or were free from Hexaplar influence. These claims cannot be substantiated. Codex [B] represents one recension of the text of 𝔊, and one recension only. But from the number of MSS. which are generally found agreeing with it, we may conclude that it represents that type with considerable fidelity.

A second group is represented by the Codex Alexandrinus ([A]). That this also represents a recension — that is, a form of the text modified by the work of an editor — must be evident to every reader. For, on comparison of [A] with [B], the former is seen to have been systematically corrected by a Hebrew copy resembling the one now current. Typical of a third group is the edition of Lagarde ([L]). This also has been frequently corrected by a Hebrew copy or by one of the other Greek translations.* But with almost equal frequency, this copy has retained the earlier reading along with the correction.

The great divergence of these several types of text shows the complexity of the problem which confronts the editor of the Septuagint. For the corrector of the Hebrew it is not quite so serious. It allows him to argue that where these three copies agree they represent a very early type of text. Where they agree in a reading different from that preserved in 𝕳, this reading deserves to be considered on its merits, as if it were the reading of a very ancient Hebrew copy. Internal probability should decide between them.

We may go farther than this. Where our Greek copies differ among themselves, we may assume that the variation has arisen in one of two ways, — either there has been corruption of one or more by the ordinary accidents of Greek transmission, or else one or two have been corrected by a Hebrew copy. The skilful critic will be able to distinguish the cases. And in any case he may consider the reading most remote from the present Hebrew as a possible variant of the autotype. To ascertain the weight of probability in each particular case is undoubtedly a delicate business. But it is along these lines that criticism must proceed. Preceding commentators have worked along these lines, and have

---

* In the Books of Samuel it shows no special affinity with the fragments of Aquila, Symmachus, and Theodotion that have come down to us. Its agreement with the current text of 𝔖 is remarked by Dr. and others. Cf. Stockmayer in *ZATW.* XII. p. 218 f.

made many undoubted improvements in the text. Their arguments and results have been attentively considered in the present work.

Hexaplar diacritical marks have been preserved for us in only a few instances in the Books of Samuel. The same is true of the readings of the ancient Greek versions attributed to Aquila, Symmachus, and Theodotion. For these I have depended on Field, *Hexaplorum Origenis quae Supersunt*, London, 1875.

The most complete apparatus for 𝕲 is the well-known edition begun by Holmes and continued by Parsons (*HP.*), Oxford, 1798–1827. The Books of Samuel (Kings) are contained in the second volume of this work. I have consulted it on all difficult passages. Repeated attempts to group the MSS. as presented in this work have given no results in which I have confidence, and I have fallen back upon the rule formulated above. My citation of 𝕲, therefore, must be taken to mean only that 𝕲^{ABL} agree in a particular reading. The text of ᴮ is reproduced in Swete's *Old Testament in Greek*, I. Cambridge, 1887, with some corrections by Nestle in the appendix to Vol. II. The variations of ᴬ are given in the margin of the same edition. The edition of Lagarde (which the editor supposed to represent the recension of Lucian) is entitled, *Librorum Veteris Testamenti Canonicorum Pars Prior*, and was published in Göttingen, 1883.

The translation of the Bible into Latin made by Jerome (𝕷) has little independent value for the correction of the text. The standard edition of the Roman Catholic Church does indeed frequently depart from the meaning of the current Hebrew. But careful examination shows that this is due to contamination from the preceding Latin version, or versions, made from Greek prototypes. When Jerome's own work is cleared from these admixtures it is found to represent a copy closely resembling 𝕳. In preparing this commentary I have examined 𝕷 by means of the apparatus given in Vercellone's *Variae Lectiones* (Rome, 1864), and have cited as 𝕷 only what is confirmed by such examination.

The readings of the Old-Latin (𝕴) sometimes throw light on the Greek text from which they are derived. I have therefore examined the fragments contained in Sabatier's *Bibliorum Sacrorum Latinae Versiones Antiquae* (1743), and also those given by Vercellone from the margin of a codex of Leon — *Codex Gothicus Legionensis*.

The Syriac version known as the Peshiṭta has apparently undergone a revision under ecclesiastical authority. Its testimony to a Hebrew original is therefore open to suspicion — for the importance of the Greek Old Testament in the Church influenced the revisers, if not the translators, of 𝕾. Where this version differs materially from 𝔐 we cannot be sure that the variation is not due to Greek influence. The difficulty of using this translation in criticism of the Hebrew is enhanced by the state of its own text. The only printed edition within reach is that of Lee, which was a reprint of the Syriac part of Walton's Polyglott, which in its turn was taken from the Paris Polyglott, resting finally upon a single MS. — of late date and slender authority. The edition published at Oroomiah in connexion with a rendering in Modern Syriac differs very slightly from that of Lee, and it is not yet certain that it can be called an independent witness. Where I have adduced a reading of 𝕾 I mean the edition of Lee. In a few instances this testimony seems to have some value.*

The other translation which throws light upon the text is the Jewish Aramaic version known as the Targum (𝕿). It conforms in general to the type of Hebrew current among us. But not infrequently it shows an apprehension of the text different from that embodied in the Massoretic punctuation, and occasionally it tacitly corrects even the consonants of the traditional copies. I have collated the edition of Lagarde, which reproduces the old and good *Codex Reuchlinianus*, and which was published in 1872.

§ 8. *Religious Ideas of the Books of Samuel.*

In turning our attention to the religious ideas expressed or implied in the Books of Samuel, we are first impressed by the variety of view in different parts of the work. In some places we have a glimpse of the most primitive stage of Israel's religion. An instance of this is the treatment of the Teraphim (1 S. 19). We cannot doubt that this was an image in human form and that

---

* The need of a critical edition of 𝕾 is great. But there is no evidence that such an edition will influence our view of the Hebrew text to any considerable extent. On the editions and MSS. the reader may consult an article by Rahlfs in *ZATW.* IX. pp. 161-210, and the volume by Barnes, *An Apparatus Criticus to Chronicles*, Cambridge, 1897.

it was an object of worship. It is mentioned as being in the house of David, with no explanation of its coming there and with no betrayal of surprise. We are warranted in inferring that it was a part of the ordinary furniture of the Israelite house. The author of the story had no idea that the use of such an image was contrary to the command of Yahweh, or that it was inconsistent with complete loyalty to him. The worst enemy of Saul never accused him of being anything but a true worshipper of Yahweh, and David is, if possible, even more free from suspicion. To understand the position of the author we must remember that the prophet Hosea also mentions the Teraphim, without special remark, as coexisting with the worship of Yahweh, Hos. 3[4].

The narrative we are considering reminds us of another passage, Gen. 31[19. 30-35] (E), where Rachel steals the Teraphim of her father. Here also the presence of the Teraphim in the family of Israel gives the author no offence. Yet we can hardly avoid seeing that he views them with something of contempt. They are carried off by a woman, and when they must be concealed they are ignominiously thrust under her camel saddle and sat upon. This author has a touch of sarcasm in his tone, from which the narrator in Samuel is free. The story of David and Michal therefore represents an earlier stage of thought than that of E.

It is rather striking that the only other reference to the Teraphim in Samuel is at the opposite pole of religious thought. In this (1 S. 15[22]) the Teraphim are classed with idolatry and witchcraft as an abomination to Yahweh.

We shall probably not be wrong in seeing a survival of preprophetic religion in the account of the witch of Endor (1 S. 28). The narrative, however, does not stand in the same relation to its material as in the case just considered. The author condemns necromancy (at least as we now read) and makes Saul in his better days to have cut off its devotees from the land. But through the story we are able to see the spiritistic ideas which once prevailed in Israel. The spirits of the dead are classed with the gods. They possess superhuman knowledge. They can be induced by magical means to reveal the secrets of the future. This was once religion. From the time of Isaiah it was distinctly proscribed.

That Yahweh is the God of Israel is the faith of all parts of the Old Testament. In the older parts of our book however this is taken in the literal sense — his jurisdiction does not extend beyond the land of his people. David says in evident good faith (1 S. 26[19]): *They have driven me forth from union with the heritage of Israel, saying: Go, serve other gods!* According to this, the exile is no longer under the protection of his own god, but is obliged to seek help from the gods of the land where he sojourns. There is here no trace of the later conviction that Yahweh is the only God, and that the gods of the nations are naught.

But, as in the case already considered, the diversity of view in different parts of the Book is so marked as to constitute contradiction. In the Deuteronomic sections there can be no doubt that the author has the exclusive view, according to which the gods of the nations are no gods. This is in fact distinctly asserted in one passage (1 S. 12[21]), which however may be a late expansion of the text. The way is prepared for this universalism by the account of Dagon before the Ark. Here the god of the Philistines is not regarded as a nonentity, but his inferior power when brought into conflict with Yahweh is made evident.

No stress can be laid upon the use of the name Baal in proper names, as it proves only the appellative application of the title (*Lord*) to Yahweh. Nor, in the present state of the narrative, can we argue conclusively that the ephod used in consulting the oracle was an image of Yahweh. It is in the representation of the character of Yahweh, that we see the primitiveness of Israel's religion at this time. Yahweh is a God inscrutable in his actions — a God of moods we might almost call him. He instigates Saul against David for no reason of which the latter is conscious. Yet by inhaling the fragrance of a sacrifice, it is probable that he may be placated and thus his good humour be restored. At a later time he instigates David to commit a sin, apparently in order that he may punish him, just as he hardened the hearts of Eli's sons in order that he might destroy them.

Yahweh may be pleased by extraordinary efforts or by extraordinary self-denial. For this reason, Saul adjures the people to abstain from food the whole day, confident that he will be granted a victory. Unfortunately the sequel was not, in this case, a happy one, because the injunction was violated. But this does not make the adjuration less meritorious in itself considered.

Nevertheless Yahweh is a righteous God. He watches over oaths and vows, and punishes their violation. This is curiously illustrated in the case just alluded to. Saul's adjuration is unwittingly violated by Jonathan. Yahweh is wroth and refuses to answer when approached in the use of the oracle. He unerringly points out the offender and would apparently insist upon his death. It is something extraordinary that the people interfere and ransom Jonathan. Another instance of Yahweh's vindicative justice is given in the matter of the Gibeonites. Israel has sworn to spare them. But Saul in his zeal for Israel breaks the covenant. Blood therefore rests upon himself and upon all his house. Yahweh becomes the avenger, and the blood is purged by the death of seven descendants of Saul "before Yahweh." Thus (as in the case of Eli's house also) the iniquities of the fathers are visited upon the children.

Yahweh is a God who reveals himself to his people. Even the individual (it would appear) may seek an omen from casual things, as did Jonathan from the words of the Philistines. But more distinctly the divine will is revealed in certain appointed ways. One of these is the Urim and Thummim which we may identify with the sacred lot. The oracle given by the Ephod probably expressed itself in the same way. Most distinctly, Yahweh speaks to (and through) his prophets, sometimes apparently by dreams, sometimes in waking visions. He sends the Spirit also, which produces extraordinary effects in those who are seized by it. They experience exaltation of feeling so that they join in religious dances, rave, fall down in a cataleptic state. In other cases, the Spirit drives to deeds of heroic courage, or prepares the Anointed of Yahweh for his work as a ruler ; and again it produces morbid jealousy, melancholy, and deeds of frenzy.

The extermination of the enemies of Israel is a religious duty, for they are the enemies of Yahweh also. The method of dealing with them is set forth in the account of Saul and Amalek. The objects of attack are solemnly dedicated to Yahweh, so that to leave any alive is to commit sacrilege. We can hardly be wrong in supposing that their extermination was pleasing to him, as the "devotion" of Israel was pleasing to Chemosh. The author of this section of our history is possessed by the idea of the author of Deuteronomy — to leave the enemies of Yahweh alive is sinful. It is some relief to think that his history is here the reflection of his idea.

The pragmatism which shows itself in the Book of Judges is carried over into the first section of 1 Samuel. This is a philosophy of history, according to which when Israel was faithful to Yahweh it was prospered and kept in safety. When it forgot him it was delivered over to the power of its enemies. Thus the Philistine oppression comes because the people have forsaken Yahweh and served Baal and Astarte. When they repent and seek their God, he delivers them by the hand of Samuel. As an expression of belief in the justice of God in dealing with the nations, this view deserves all respect. The mechanical way in which it is carried out, however, gives a one-sided view of the course of Israel's history.

§ 9. *Commentaries.*

Among the Fathers, Theodoret possesses considerable acumen, and his *Questiones in Libros Regum* (Migne, Tom. 80) will always be of value. The commentary of Procopius of Gaza is now proved to have been mainly taken from Theodoret.* The *Questiones Hebraicae in Libros Regum* printed in Jerome's works are known to be spurious. They are occasionally interesting however for their embodiment of Jewish tradition.

The merits of the Rabbinical commentators Rashi (Isaaki), Kimchi (Kamchi) and Levi ben Gerson are perhaps less conspicuous in their treatment of the Books of Samuel than elsewhere, because of their dependence on the traditional text. Besides these, which are contained in Buxtorf's Rabbinical Bible, I have consulted Abarbanel in the edition of 1686, and the portions of Tanchum's Arabic commentary published by Haarbrücker (1844).

Among the Roman Catholic expositors I know only Cornelius à Lapide, in the edition of Venice, 1700, and those who are cited by Poole in his Synopsis, or by Schmid in his commentary.

---

* Cf. Eisenhofer, *Procopius von Gaza*, Freib. 1897.

Among the Protestant scholars of the seventeenth century a high place must be accorded to Sebastian Schmid of Strasburg. His commentary on the Books of Samuel (two volumes, quarto, 1687, 1689) is a monument of solid and judicious learning. The author shares the prejudice of his time in favour of the received text, and the theological questions which he discusses at length have to us lost a large part of their interest. But, so far as the text on which he comments is uncorrupt, the author's judgment is sound, and much that is of value in recent conservative commentaries is derived from him. Among Reformed theologians Clericus (Le Clerc) is much esteemed. His commentary on Samuel appeared in 1708. The often suggestive *Annotationes* of Grotius are embodied in the *Biblia Illustrata* of his Lutheran opponent Calov. Of this I have used the second edition (1719).

The questions of textual criticism which have come to the front in recent years were first fairly discussed by Thenius. He undertook systematically to correct the text by comparison of the ancient versions. His commentary forms part of the *Kurzgefasstes Exegetisches Handbuch.** Thenius sometimes goes too far in his preference for the reading of ⅏, but this should not make us undervalue his really pioneer work. The next step was taken by Wellhausen in his *Text der Bücher Samuelis* (1871). The author's well-known brilliancy and balance are manifest in this early work, and all succeeding commentators are indebted to it. The only criticism to be made upon it is that it is not always sufficiently appreciative of the work accomplished by Thenius. Keil alone, of recent expositors, holds on to a conception of the Hebrew text inherited from the seventeenth century, and his commentary (second edition, 1875) refuses to recognize the most evident gains of recent scholarship. The exposition of Erdmann in Lange's *Bibelwerk* is accessible in an English translation (1877). The author can hardly be said to be in advance of Keil, but his American editor (Professor Toy) has enriched the work with notes which show a scholarship abreast of the times. The great work of Reuss, *La Bible, Traduction Nouvelle* (Paris, 1874), contains in its first

---

* The first edition was published in 1842; the second in 1864; a third, edited by Löhr, has just appeared (1898).

volume a lucid translation of the historical books, with brief but luminous notes. The translation and notes of Klostermann are always original and ingenious. His treatment of the text is free from bias and often suggestive. The majority of his conjectural emendations, however, have not commanded general assent. His work is a part of the *Kurtzgefasster Kommentar* of Strack and Zöckler, and was published in 1887. Budde's *Richter und Samuel* (1890) has already been alluded to. It contains valuable notes on the text. The edition of the text in *SBOT.* by the same author also deserves mention here as well as among the introductory works.

In English the only help to the understanding of this part of the Bible which deserves mention is Driver's *Notes on the Hebrew Text of the Books of Samuel* (1890). The book has a valuable introduction on Hebrew palaeography, and discusses with great fulness questions of textual criticism. As the author confesses his frequent dependence on Wellhausen, so I do not hesitate to avow that I have frequently adopted an explanation from him.

In addition to the books mentioned, I have had constantly by me Kittel's translation in Kautzsch's *Heilige Schrift des Alten Testaments*. I have examined also a number of programmes, dissertations, and pamphlets, some of which will be referred to in the notes.

A list of abbreviations will be found at the end of the volume.

A COMMENTARY ON THE BOOKS OF SAMUEL.

A COMMENTARY ON THE BOOKS OF SAMUEL.

1 SAMUEL I.–XV. THE LIFE OF SAMUEL DOWN TO THE REJECTION OF SAUL.

As the final redactor of the Books regarded it, this section makes one division of his work. The legitimate rule of Samuel was succeeded by the legitimate rule of David ; Saul played but a subordinate part. That this was not the mind of one of his sources is evident from what has been said in the Introduction (see above p. xviii).

I. 1–IV. 1ª. Samuel's birth and call. — Hannah, the childless wife of Elkanah, grieves over her privation and prays for a son. Her prayer is answered, and in accordance with the vow made in her prayer she dedicates her son to the service of Yahweh. He is therefore brought to the sanctuary at Shiloh when yet a boy. Here his behaviour is in marked contrast to that of the hereditary priests, the sons of Eli. While yet a lad (as it would seem) he becomes a prophet by the divine call, and the first revelation which he receives is a denunciation of punishment on Eli for his indulgence of his sons. This revelation is followed by others, which establish Samuel's reputation as a prophet throughout Israel.

The piece begins like the stories appended to the history of the Judges, Jd. 17¹ 19¹ (cf. 13²). The place to which it introduces us is Shiloh, where we find the Ark of God under the guardianship of Eli and his family, and where there is a temple for it. The time is not far from that commemorated by the story of Samson, as the Philistines are the prominent enemies of Israel. Probably

3

the author of the Book of Judges had in mind the story of Eli or of Samuel, or even of Saul, when he credited Samson with only the beginning of deliverance (Jd. 13⁵). Shiloh appears as the sanctuary of Israel in the Book of Joshua in at least one passage ascribed to JE (18⁸⁻¹⁰) as well as in others of later date, also in Jd. 18³¹ in an insertion which is classed with E. The prominence given to this sanctuary in our present account makes it probable that the various documents are in some way connected.

Our account, however, is not a unit. It has received at least one insertion from an extraneous source in the Song of Hannah. Again, the warning of Eli by an anonymous man of God (2²⁷⁻³⁶) unpleasantly duplicates the message revealed to Samuel in the next chapter. One of the two is superfluous. Against the opinion of most critics which sees in 2²⁷⁻³⁶ a barefaced insertion, I have given reasons above (Introduction, p. xix f.) for supposing that it was already a part of the account of Eli's sons which the author used in writing the life of Samuel.

That the earlier part of 1 Sam. properly belongs in the period of the Judges has often been pointed out. That there was ever a separate book of Judges which included 1 Sam. 1-12 cannot be certainly asserted. Graf * claims that Jd. 17 18 19-21 and 1 Sam. 1-7²ᵃ are from the same source. But no one seems to have followed him in this, and the character of the documents is quite dissimilar. If the assertion had been limited to Jd. 17 18 and 1 Sam. 3-6, more could be said in its favour. Graf also points out that the speech of Samuel in 1 Sam. 12 marks the close of the period of the Judges, as Joshua's farewell address marks the close of the period of conquest. To this Kuenen † adds the obvious argument that both Eli and Samuel are called Judges, 1 Sam. 4¹⁸ 7¹⁵⁻¹⁷. The latter passage, however, uses the term *judge* in a different sense from that which it has in the Book of Judges. That at some time Eli was counted among the Judges of Israel is possible. But it seems impossible to fit both him and Samuel into the scheme of the author of the present Book of Judges. At the same time it must be admitted that the point of view of the author of 1 Sam. 7²⁻¹⁷ was very similar to his. ‡

1–18. Hannah's prayer. — The story introduces us at once to the principal characters : *There was a man of the Ramathites, a*

---

* *Gesch. BB.* p. 98. I have not seen the dissertation *De Templo Silonensi* to which he refers.

† *HCO².* I. p. 337.

‡ Cf. Bu., *RS.* p. 201, Ki. *GH.* II. pp. 29–32.

Zuphite of the hill country of Ephraim whose name was Elkanah]
cf. similar openings, Jd. 13², 1 S. 9¹. There has possibly been
conflation in the description. That he was a *Ramathite* would
be enough to indicate that he was *of the hill country of Ephraim*,
without the addition of those words. Ramah is a common Old
Testament name, designating at least eight different places. Four
localities have been identified with the Ramah of Elkanah and
Samuel. These are *Beit Rima* thirteen miles northeast of Lydda,
Ram Allah nine miles north of Jerusalem, *Er-Ram* four miles
nearer that city, and *Neby Samwil* about four miles northwest of
it. The first of these seems too near the Philistine territory, the
last two are in Benjamin. The Biblical data are not sufficient to
decide the question with certainty, but my own mind inclines to
Ram Allah as having the probability on its side. *Zuph* occurs
again as the name of the district in which Saul finds the home of
Samuel, 9⁵. The genealogy given seems to leave no doubt that
Elkanah was an Ephraimite by blood. — **2.** As in some other
cases where a man had two wives, sorrow was caused by the fact
that one was blessed with children, while the other *had no child* —
so we should read here with 𝕲. She would not have grieved,
had she had even one. The case of Rachel before the birth of
Joseph will occur to every one. The name *Hannah* corresponds
to the English name *Grace*, and *Peninnah* means *Coral* or *Pearl*.
— **3.** Elkanah *used to go up year by year to worship and to sacrifice to Yahweh Sebaoth in Shiloh*] the institution of the pilgrimage
is apparently as old as the existence of shrines. That Elkanah
went *once a year* seems to point to a time when the three yearly
festivals were not yet regarded as obligatory. The divine name
Yahweh Sebaoth occurs in Samuel eleven times, and all seem to
belong to the later strata of the book. The meaning of the name
has been much discussed. To our conception Yahweh is appropriately called *God of the hosts of heaven*, understanding by the *hosts*
either the stars or the angels. But to the earlier thought of Israel,
the angels were unknown. *God of the armies of Israel* is favoured
by the fact that צבאות does designate these armies in many passages (Ex. 7⁴ 12¹⁷ Num. 1³, al.). It should be noted, however, that
Amos, the earliest writer to whom we can trace the appellation,
seems to have been especially impressed by the fact that Yahweh

uses the armies of the heathen for the accomplishment of his ends, Am. 3¹³ᶠ· 4¹³ 5¹⁵. He is therefore God of the nations, not of Israel alone. *Shiloh* is the modern *Seilun*, and its situation is described in Jd. 21¹⁹ as *north of Bethel, east of the road which goes up from Bethel to Shechem*. There was a yearly festival there in the time of the judges, Jd. 21¹⁹ᶠᶠ·. In order to an understanding of what follows, the narrator adds : *And Eli and his two sons, Hophni and Phinehas, were there priests to Yahweh*] the text is that of 𝔊.

1. מן־הרמתים] The pointing makes the name of the place *Ramathaim*. This name (that is, the dual form, later *Arimathaea*) does not appear elsewhere in the Old Testament, but even in this same account (v.¹⁹) is given as a singular. We., *TBS.*, p. 35, therefore supposes an attempt made in this instance to substitute a more modern form for the older, which, however, did not extend beyond this single case. It seems simpler with Kl. to point הרמתים, for which we may cite הרמתי 1 Chr. 27²⁷. — הרמתים צופים] is grammatically impossible. For the second word we have Σειφά 𝔊ᴮ, which indicates sufficiently that the ם has come from the following word. 𝔗 seems to feel the difficulty in the received text, for it renders מתלמידי נביא. The restoration of We. is now generally adopted, as above. — ירחם] 𝔊 renders ירחמאל, but 1 Chr. 6¹⁹ seems to go back to 𝔥. — אפרתי] seems to have been originally equivalent to *Ephraimite*, Jd. 12⁵ 1 K. 11²⁶. In this place, however, 𝔊 has ἐν Νασείβ Εφφράιμ, so that the original may have been בן צוף אפרים as suggested by We. — **2.** אחת] a number of MSS. have האחת. — אין ילדים] οὐκ ἦν παιδίον 𝔊 seems more forcible. — **3.** ועלה] the perfect with Waw Consecutive is used of customary action, Dr., *Tenses*³, § 120; Dav., *Syntax*, § 54; König, *Syntax*, 367 *h*. — האיש ההוא מעירו] 𝔊ᴮ has simply ὁ ἄνθρωπος; the shorter text has the presumption in its favour. — מימים ימימה] Ex. 13¹⁰ Jd. 11⁴⁰ 21¹⁹, cf. Kön., *Syntax*, 266 *a*. יהוה צבאות — besides the Bible Dictionaries the student may consult *ZATW*. VI. p. 17; *PRE*.², article Zebaoth; Smend, *Alttest. Religionsgeschichte*, p. 185 ff. On the pronunciation of the name of Israel's God, *ZATW*. III. p. 280 f., IV. p. 21 ff. שני בני־עלי] 'Ηλεὶ καὶ οἱ δύο υἱοὶ αὐτοῦ 𝔊. It is necessary that Eli should be mentioned because he appears in the immediate sequel. There is every reason to adopt the reading of 𝔊 therefore. Even if Eli had been mentioned in some preceding part of this history now lost, it would be quite as appropriate to mention him here as to mention his sons alone. The change to 𝔥 may possibly have been made to shield Eli from the blame afterwards pronounced upon his sons. We. and Dr. decide against 𝔊, while Bu. supposes that the original was simply ושם עלי כהן. The name *Phinehas* is said to mean *negro* in Egyptian (Lauth, *ZDMG*. XXV. p. 139).

4–8. The point of interest is the behaviour of Hannah. The author, therefore, means to say that on one occasion *Hannah*

wept and could not eat.   But the connexion is broken by a long
sentence, which gives an account of Peninnah's habitual scornful
treatment of her rival.   The result is awkward, and we must concede the possibility that the text has been interpolated.   As it
stands, we must make a long parenthesis : *It came to pass on one
occasion that Elkanah sacrificed* (*now he used to give portions to
Peninnah and her children, but to Hannah one portion though he
loved her, and her rival would vex her . . .*) *and she wept and
would not eat.*   The words are plain enough in themselves, with
the exception of אפים, which will be discussed in the critical note.
— **6**. The received text asserts that *her rival vexed her,* taunting
her with her barrenness.   The expression is somewhat confused,
however, and it is noticeable that 𝔊 in its primitive form only
asserts that she (Hannah) was greatly troubled.   There is reason
to suspect the text. — **7**.   The received text must mean : *So he
would do year by year*] making Elkanah the subject.   In this case
we must (by a change of the points only) read : *as often as he
came up to the house of Yahweh.*   The next clause is either an interpolation or corrupt.   Conjecturally we may read : *But Hannah covered her face and wept and would not eat.* — **8**.   Elkanah
endeavours to comfort her : *Why wilt thou weep and wilt not eat,
and why does thy heart reproach thee ?*]   The rhetorical question
is followed by another : *Am I not better to thee than ten sons ?*]
The answer would have been in the affirmative, but it was for his
sake that she wished children, so the attempt at consolation
rather opened the springs of grief afresh.

4. The author begins ויהי היום ויזבח אלקנה as though he were going to relate
what happened on one particular occasion.   He then drops into the frequentative tense ונתן as though what followed was a common experience, and this
is kept up until the end of v.[7], where we find והבכה which would naturally
connect with ויזבח.   The result is an obscure sentence, and 𝔊 unfortunately
gives little help. — ויהי היום] I S. 14[1] 2 K. 4[8. 11. 18] Job 1[6].   There seems no
reason to separate the phrase from others like ויהי בעת ההיא, cf. also ויהי החרש
I S. 20[24], Ges.[26] 126 *q*. — ונתן] one is tempted to change to ויתן, which is
apparently favoured by 𝔊.   But this would involve change of the following
verbs. — ולכל־בניה ובנותיה] 𝔊[B] has simply καὶ τοῖς υἱοῖς αὐτῆς, which is original.
The expansion of such phrases by a scribe is too common to call for remark.
— **5**. אפים] is impossible; πλὴν ὅτι 𝔊[B] points to אפס־כי, cf. Num. 13[28] Dt.
15[4] Jd. 4[9] Am. 9[8], where it evidently means *nevertheless*.   It is awkward, how-

ever, to say: *Nevertheless he loved Hannah and Yahweh had shut her womb.*
We expect the author either to say *only* one portion (לברה) in contrast to
Peninnah, or else to say that he distinguished her in some way as: he gave
her a portion *before them.* The latter alone would be accounted for by the
following כי. There is reason to suppose, therefore, that the corruption is
incurable in the present state of our knowledge: κατὰ πρόσωπον 𝔊ᴸ; *tristis*
𝔏 seem to be attempts to render the text of 𝔥. — בחיר 𝔗 gives a good sense,
but cannot be got out of the present text, and it is difficult to suppose that this
translator had another reading before him. Bu. supposes that the original
may have been מר אפים. But the point of the narrative is that Hannah wept
because of the contrast between herself and her co-wife, not because of anything in her husband's mien. — **6.** The verse is removed by Bu. to the margin
of his text as a later insertion, but without sufficient reason. As it stands we
must render *and her rival provoked her.* — צרה] the co-wife, as is shown with
abundant learning by Lagarde, *Mittheilungen,* I. 125 ff. In this place, however,
𝔊ᴮ renders κατὰ τὴν θλίψιν αὐτῆς, evidently reading בצרתה. This would join
very well to the preceding clause of 𝔊ᴮ. 'For the Lord had not given her a
son *like her rival.'* But, on the other hand, it does not join well with what follows. A further difficulty is made by הרעמה, an abnormal form, Ges.²⁶ § 22 s. The
verb in the Hiphil is always *to thunder,* in the Qal *to roar* (Ps. 96¹¹). The
word is probably corrupt here, as neither of these meanings is appropriate.
After בעבור we expect mention of the cause of Hannah's grief — בעבור חרפתה
would give a good sense. 𝔊ᴮ seems to have read בעבור זה. — **7.** יעשה] must have
Elkanah in mind as the actor, which indeed he was. There seems to be no
reason for changing to תעשה (Dr.). The עלתה which follows must be עלתה of
course, though 𝔏 seems to favour עלתם; בבית] should be בית. The words
כן תכעסנה ותבכה make a difficulty by their abrupt change of subject. It is not
unlikely therefore that חנה is represented in the last three letters of the first
verb. Kl.'s proposal to read ותכס חנה, *and Hannah covered her face* in sign
of grief, is attractive. 𝔊 seems to have read ותכעס, καὶ ἠθύμει. With מדי
עלתה cf. מדי צאתה I S. 18³⁰. **8.** After חנה 𝔊 introduces καὶ εἶπεν αὐτῷ ᾽Ιδοὺ
ἐγώ, κύριε· καὶ εἶπεν αὐτῇ. This is entirely appropriate, but if original it is difficult to see how it was lost. For למה 𝔊 has: τί ἐστί σοι ὅτι, which has no claim
to be more original, but probably goes back to a variant Hebrew text. — ירע
לבבך] τύπτει σε ἡ καρδία σου, which indicates יכך לבבך. This is more appropriate, for ירע לב' is used of the heart that hardens itself against its neighbour,
Dt. 15¹⁰. Hannah no doubt *reproached herself* with her shortcoming, though
it was not voluntary. Her husband exhorts her not to blame herself, which is
precisely what she was doing — *her heart smote her* is the natural expression
in the case.

9–11. The vow. — Hannah presents herself before Yahweh:
She rose after they had eaten, and stood before Yahweh] the reading is that of 𝔊. The condition of things is described in the fol-

lowing clause : *Eli the priest was sitting at the time on his chair
at the door posts of the temple of Yahweh*] the structure seems to
have been a solid building, otherwise it could not be called *a
temple ;* the same word is afterwards applied to the temple of Solomon, I K. 6⁵. — **10.** *She was greatly distressed*] lit. *bitter of soul,*
cf. 2 K. 4²⁷, where it is said of the woman who has lost her only
son that her soul is bitter. — **11.** The prayer culminates in a vow :
*Yahweh Sebaoth! If thou wilt indeed look upon the affliction of
thy maidservant and wilt give thy maidservant a man child, then I
will give him to Yahweh all the days of his life*] she means that he
should become a temple servant, a *nethin*, Num. 8¹⁹. A vow is a
promise to give something to Yahweh, or to perform something
for him, in case he grants a prayer. An example is Jacob's vow,
Gen. 28²⁰⁻²² (E) : *If Yahweh God will be with me and protect me
on this journey . . . then this stone shall be to me a house of God,
and all that thou shalt give me I will tithe for thee.* The devotion
of human beings in this way is illustrated by Jephthah, and is presupposed in the elaborate provisions of the law for redemption,
Lev. 27. Our author does not seem to be troubled by the question whether Hannah had a right to make a vow of this kind without the consent of her husband. The point which most interests
us is that the author cannot have thought of Samuel (or Elkanah)
as a Levite, for in that case the vow would have been unmeaning.
But that he also loses sight of the ancient regulation that every
male that opens the womb is already the property of Yahweh,
seems evident. The statement in the text : *a razor shall not
come upon his head* reads like a later addition. But it is readily
accounted for by the view of a scribe that Samuel was to be a
Nazirite — a lifelong Nazirite like Samson. 𝕲 carries the like-
ness to Samson further by adding : *and wine and fermented
liquor he shall not drink*] cf. Jd. 13⁵. *And wilt remember me*]
reads like a reminiscence of Gen. 30²², where God *remembers*
Rachel in giving her a son.

9. ויקם חנה אחרי אכלה בשלה] the last word is unnecessary, and difficulty is
found in accepting אכלה, because *she* had not eaten. The latter is somewhat
relieved by reading אכלם with 𝕲. The objection that she finds the family still
at their meal in v.¹⁸ is hardly cogent in view of the state of the text there.
Still it is not impossible that there has been scribal expansion. We. points

בְּשֵׁלָה, which is possible, only I should take a letter from the preceding word אחרי אכל הבשרה = *after the eating of the boiled flesh*, 2[13]. The conjecture of Kl. ותנח אחריה אכלה בלשכה, which is adopted by Bu., seems too remote from any external testimony. It seems necessary, however, to insert with 𝔊 ותיצב לפני יהוה (Th., We., al.). — ישב . . . וְעֵלִי] a circumstantial clause. מזוזת is elsewhere used in the plural, and should, perhaps, be so pointed here, with 𝔊. — 10. וּבָכֹה תִבְכֶּה] the emphatic adverbial infinitive. The imperfect tense indicates continued action : *she kept weeping bitterly*. — 11. ולא־תשכח את־אמתך is superfluous and is also lacking in 𝔊[B]; we may disregard it. — זרע אנשים] does not occur again. That she means *a male child* is evident.

12–18. Eli's rebuke, followed by a blessing. — As Hannah prolonged her prayer, Eli, who saw the movement of her lips, but heard no sound, *took her for a drunken woman*] that excess in wine was not an infrequent concomitant of religious feasts seems indicated by the readiness with which the suspicion is entertained here.   For the construction cf. Job 13[24] : *why dost thou reckon me thine enemy ?* — 14. The rebuke : *How long wilt thou show thyself drunken*] seems to emphasize the disgracefulness of the spectacle. *Put away thy wine and go from the presence of Yahweh*] the second half is found in 𝔊 only, but seems to be original.   In 𝔊 Eli's *servant* is made to utter the rebuke, an evident attempt to shield the priest from the charge of harshness. — 15. Hannah repels the charge : *No, my Lord ; an afflicted woman am I, and I have not drunk wine or intoxicating drink*] the two are often mentioned together.   *But I poured out my soul before* Yahweh, cf. Ps. 62[9] (*pour out the heart*), 42[5]. — 16. *Do not take thy servant to be a vile woman*] lit. *a daughter of belial*.   The corresponding phrase *sons of belial* is frequent and evidently means *vile men*, Jd. 19[22], 1 Sam. 2[12].   The derivation of the word *belial*, however, is obscure, and recent discussions are inconclusive.   The Greek translators render *men of belial*, or *sons of belial*, by adjectives like *vile, ungodly, senseless, contrary*.   A satisfactory Hebrew etymology has not been found.   The older commentators propose *without yoke*, for which they cite Jer. 2[20].   Other conjectures, *that rises no more* (after falling), *that profits not*, are equally precarious.   The word is possibly a foreign word, but the Babylonian derivation does not as yet seem unequivocally established.   *For on account of the greatness of my grief have I continued until now.*   The soft answer turns away wrath. — 17.   Eli not only dismisses her in peace, but

adds a prayer that her petition may be granted. — **18**. Her prayer is that she may *stand well with him*] lit. *find favour in his eyes*, a frequent Old Testament phrase. The historian adds : *So the woman went her way, and her face was no more sad*] for the text see the critical note.

12. וֹהִיה] is possible, as one of the rare cases of the perfect with weak ו (so Dr., *Notes*, and *Tenses*[3], § 133). But it is more likely that it is the mistake of a scribe who thought the verb continued the preceding sentence. Restore ויהי (Bu.). — הרבתה להתפלל] the main verb expresses the idea which we express adverbially : *she prayed much*. Similar cases are הטיב לעשות : *he did well;* מהר לעשות : *he did quickly*. ועלי introduces the circumstantial clause : she continued praying *while Eli was observing her mouth*. — **13**. והנה היא] the *casus pendens : As for Hannah, she was speaking in her heart; only her lips were moving, but her voice was not heard*]* the whole sentence is explanatory of what Eli was observing. The name of Hannah is here omitted by 𝕲[BL]. — ויחשבה] resumes the story introduced by the ויהי at the beginning of v.[12]. — שכרה] on the form of the adjective, Ges.[26] § 84 *b*, 24. — **14**. תשתכרין] one of the few cases of the old feminine ending, Ges.[26] § 47 *o*. — מעליך] 𝕲 substitutes καὶ πορεύου (καὶ ἄπελθε L) ἐκ προσώπου Κυρίου. The clause seems to me one likely to be changed, to avoid the seeming identification of Yahweh with the Ark. — **15**. קשת־רוח] *harsh of spirit* seems impossible. Most modern scholars have adopted Th.'s emendation to קשת יום : ἡ σκληρὰ ἡμέρα 𝕲, cf. Job 30[25], where קשה יום is *one in misfortune*. — שכר] *fruit-wine* or *cider*, cf. Benzinger, *Hebr. Archäologie*, p. 96. — **16**. אל תתן . . . לפני] would naturally mean *do not give . . . into the power of*, which cannot be correct. What Hannah desires is that she may not be *reckoned to be* a vile woman. In this sense we find נתן followed by כ, and we should probably emend to כבת, throwing out לפני. Kl.'s לפי does not occur with this verb, and Dr.'s ל is also without parallel. Cf. Gen. 42[30]: ויתן אתנו כמרגלים : *and took us for spies.* — בליעל] is an obscure word, cf. BDB. *s.v.*, Moore on Judges 19[22], Baudissin in *PRE.*[3] II. p. 548 f., Cheyne, in the *Expositor*, 1895, and in the *Expository Times*, June, 1897, with Baudissin's reply, *ibid.*, Nov. 1897, and Jensen's remarks, *ibid.*, Apr. 1898. — שיחי וכעסי] 𝕲 seems to have found but one of the two words, probably שיחי which was not definite enough for a Hebrew scribe, so that an explanatory word was added. — דברתי] decidedly less forcible than ἐκτέτακα 𝕲, probably הארכתי. — **17**. שלתך for שאלתך, cf. Ges.[26] § 23 *c*. — **18**. ותאכל] is lacking in seven Hebrew MSS., and although this is rather a slender basis on which to erect a theory, I suspect the word to be an insertion. The sense is perfectly good without it, as is seen in the translation given above. It is a question whether the author would have said *she went her way* if he meant simply that she returned to the chamber imme-

---

* 𝕲[L] adds here : *But the Lord heard her.* The example is instructive as showing how a text grows.

diately adjoining the temple. The text of 𝔊: *and came into the chamber and
ate with her husband and drank* will be a further expansion. If original, we
cannot account for its abbreviation. — [ופניה לא־היו־לה] καὶ τὸ πρόσωπον αὐτῆς
οὐ συνέπεσεν 𝔊. The only parallel cited for 𝔐 (Job 9²⁷) is of doubtful integrity.
It seems better therefore to correct היו־לה to נפלה, which is quite in accord
with Hebrew usage.

19–28. The prayer answered, and the vow performed. —
The division between this and the preceding is artificial. The
narrative continues without a break. After paying their respects
at the temple the next morning the family returned to their home
in Ramah. *And Elkanah knew Hannah his wife*] cf. Gen. 4¹.
And Yahweh remembered her] as he remembered Rachel Gen.
30²². — **20.** *And it came to pass at the end of a year that she bare
a son*] about the time of the yearly festival. *And called his name
Samuel: For from Yahweh I have asked him*] the last words evidently give her reason for the choice of this name. The etymology
does not bear out the intention. — **21.** At the usual time Elkanah
went up to Shiloh *to offer the yearly sacrifice*] as we have heard
nothing of *his vow*, which is added in the received text, the words
are probably the insertion of a scribe. — **22.** Hannah excuses herself from the present journey in the words : *When the boy is weaned
then I will bring him*] for two years she would keep him at home,
for this was the usual time, and is still the case in the East, cf.
Koran, 2²³³. Some commentators have thought it impossible that
the boy could be actually delivered to the priest at so early an
age, and have tried to interpret the verb *weaned* in a figurative
sense. But this seems uncalled for. *Then we shall see the face
of Yahweh, and he shall dwell there forever*] where the last clause
means of course *all his life*. — **23.** Elkanah consents, adding :
Only Yahweh establish thy word] a wish that their lives may be
spared to do as she purposes. — **24.** At the time set, *she brought
him up with a three year old bullock*] an unusually valuable sacrifice. The received text has *three bullocks* by an error of transcrip-
tion. *And an ephah of flour and a skin of wine*] the abundance
of provision was in order to invite many to " eat and drink and
rejoice before Yahweh " with them. The *ephah of flour* is Gideon's
offering also, Jd. 6¹⁹. " The quantity according to the smallest
computation was over a bushel " (Moore). — **25.** After sacrificing

the bullock *they brought the lad to Eli*] that the whole family was present is quite in accord with the fitness of things. — **26.** She recalls herself to his remembrance: *By thy life, Sir, I am the woman that stood near thee here to pray to Yahweh!* — **27.** The answer to her prayer; *Concerning this boy I prayed and Yahweh granted what I asked*] lit. *my request which I asked of him.* — **28.** The return she proposes to make: *Now I, on my part, have given him to Yahweh. All the days that he shall live he is given to Yahweh*] is Hannah's devotion of her son only a revival of the ancient law which claimed all the first born for Yahweh? At the end of the verse 𝔐 adds *and he bowed to Yahweh.* If this refers to Samuel, it seems appropriate enough. It is, however, lacking in 𝔊ᴮ, which inserts a clause not found in 𝔐 at the end of the Song which follows. The probable explanation is that the Song was inserted in the two texts at different points. The original text seems to have said, after Hannah's presentation of the lad, *so she left him there and went to Ramah.* The Song was inserted in 𝔐 between the two halves of this sentence; in 𝔊 it comes before the first half.

20. ותהר חנה — .* [לתקפות הימים] similarly לתקפת השנה Ex. 34²² 2 Chr. 24²³.* — [ותלד] 𝔊 puts καὶ συνέλαβεν at the end of v.¹⁹. The word has been interpolated in both recensions. Before בי, 𝔊 and 𝔗 insert *and she said;* a case of explicative expansion. — [כי מיהוה שאלתיו] as Kimchi sees, the theory of the author is that שמואל is a contraction of שאול מאל. But such contraction is unheard of elsewhere. There is an exegetical tradition in favour of שמועאל as the original form of the word, but, as shown by Dr. (*Notes,* in loc.), this also is without analogy. The most natural derivation, making it mean, *Name of God,* is attributed to St. Gregory by Schm. — **21.** [ואת־נדרו] Jewish tradition sees in this a vow made for the birth of a son. But the only vow of which the narrative gives us any knowledge is Hannah's vow. There is reason to suppose the words an addition to the original text therefore. The tendency to such expansion is seen in 𝔊 here, which reads, καὶ τὰς εὐχὰς αὐτοῦ καὶ πάσας τὰς δεκάτας τῆς γῆς αὐτοῦ. — **22.** [עד יגמל] a parallel case is Jd. 16², so that there is no need to insert οὐκ ἀναβήσομαι 𝔊ᴸ. — [ונראה] apparently intended by the punctuators as a Niphal. It is better to read it as the Qal imperfect on account of את־פני which follows — perhaps the well-known cohortative with weak ו: *I will bring him up that we may see the face of Yahweh.* — **23.** [את־דברו] must be understood of some promise. The only one of which

---

* According to these passages we should expect the singular תקפת here, and the ו is, in fact, omitted in many MSS.

we have record is Eli's wish that Hannah should have a son — which might be construed as a word of Yahweh. But this is already fulfilled in the birth of Samuel. It seems better therefore to read דברך with 𝕲 τὸ ἐξελθὸν ἐκ τοῦ στόματός σου. — **24.** [בפרים שלשה] ἐν μόσχῳ τριετίζοντι 𝕲 = בפר משלש; cf. Gen. 15⁹. The reading of 𝕲 is to be restored. At the end of the verse הנער, נער is unintelligible; καὶ τὸ παιδάριον μετ' αὐτῶν 𝕲 is superfluous, though 𝕲ᴸ helps it by reading καὶ εἰσῆλθον for ותבאהו. In the present state of our knowledge we must be content to omit the words; *the boy was young* is an impossible rendering, and besides, the sentence is superfluous. Dr. conjectures that the words והנער עמה belong at the end of v.²⁵, and he is followed by Bu. — **25.** I see no reason for departing from the received text. The consent of Eli was necessary to make the act valid, and it was entirely appropriate that both parents should present the lad at the sanctuary, though the mother takes the leading part. If we are to change at all, we must read ותבא אם הנער אל עלי — **26.** [כי ארני] והנער עמה a phrase claiming the favourable notice of the one addressed, Jd. 6¹⁵. — **28.** For the גם *correlativum* (Th. after Clericus) cf. Gen. 20⁵, גם־היא *she for her part.* השאיל is to encourage a person to ask by granting his request, then *to give* without a previous request. — [אשר היה seems impossible: אשר חי seems indicated by 𝕲𝕿𝕾 and is found in one codex. — [וישתחו שם ליהוה] some MSS. have וישתחו. The whole clause is lacking in 𝕲ᴮᴬ which give a substitute at the beginning of 2¹¹. It is represented in 𝕲ᴸ in both places.

II. 1–10. The song of Hannah.

— The author or the final redactor here puts into the mouth of Hannah a song of praise. Careful examination shows that it has no particular reference to her circumstances. The assertion that *the barren has borne seven while the prolific mother grows faint* is made only as an example of God's sovereign dealings with his creatures. Possibly this couplet may have drawn the editor's attention, and made him think the psalm appropriate for this place. But this sentence, with the rest of the composition, is too general to give us light on the situation of the author. The expressions used are those common to the songs gathered in the Psalter. Like many of them, it voices the faith of the pious in Yahweh as ruler over the destinies of men.

The structure of the poem is very simple. Four stanzas may be marked off: (1) The believer's doxology; (2) Warning to the arrogant; (3) Yahweh's government; (4) Confidence for the future. The metre regularly shows three accents to a line, except in one or two instances, where the text is probably at fault.

A translation is given by Professor Briggs in his *Messianic Prophecy* (N.Y., 1886), p. 124 f., and with critical notes in the *Presbyterian Review*, 1885, p. 112 f.

1–2. The opening stanza is one of praise, expressive of the singer's state of mind in view of Yahweh's glory.

> Glad is my heart in Yahweh,
> My horn is exalted in my God,
> My mouth is enlarged over my enemies,
> For I rejoice in thy salvation.
> There is none holy like Yahweh,
> For there is none righteous like our God,
> And there is no rock besides thee.

1. ותתפלל חנה ותאמר] 𝔊[B] has simply καὶ εἶπεν, which is enough. — [עלץ ἐστερεώθη 𝔊 may go back to אמץ; but as this verb with לב might convey the meaning of obstinacy (cf. Dt. 2[30]), it seems better to adhere to 𝔐. The elevation of the horn and the widening of the mouth are familiar figures in Hebrew poetry, Ps. 92[11] Is. 57[4]. The second ביהוה should doubtless be באלהי with 𝔊 and 28 MSS. — **2.** The second member is כי אין בלתך. Evidently something has been lost; and as 𝔊 has δίκαιος, we cannot do better than to insert it. But having followed 𝔊 in this, it seems better to go with it also in the interchange of בלתך and כאלהינו. The parallelism is thus improved. For צור, cf. Ps. 18[32].

3–5. Warning to the opposers.

> Do not speak haughtily,
> Or let arrogance come from your mouth,
> For a God of knowledge is Yahweh,
> And a God who weighs men's deeds.
>
> The bow of the mighty is broken,
> And the weak are girded with might.
> Those who had plenty do lack,
> But the famished inherit the land.
> For the barren has borne seven,
> And the mother of many languishes.

3. The first member is unmanageably long. It seems probable, therefore, that תרבו תדברו are duplicates, and that the same is true of the double גבהה. It answers every purpose to read אל תרברו גבהה. For עתק, cf. Ps. 31[19]. — אל דעות] Job 36[4]. The plural is probably emphatic, and might be rendered *all-knowing* (Briggs). — [ולא נתכנו עללות *et les crimes ne passent pas impunis* (Reuss) is hardly justified. At least the עללות should be described, in order that we may understand that crimes are meant. The *Qrê*, reading ולו (also in the text in some copies), makes a possible sense: *And by him actions are weighed*. But 𝕲, reading καὶ θεὸς ἑτοιμάζων ἐπιτηδεύματα αὐτοῦ, makes us suspect the original to have been ואל הכן עללות (SS). — **4.** חתים] Th. and Dr. cite Is. 21[17] in favour of the reading. But it seems simpler to correct to חתה: ἠσθένησε 𝕲. — **5.** נשכרו] *hire themselves out* would be appropriate, but the verb is nowhere found in this stem, and הסרו, suggested by 𝕲, is preferable. — חרלו] needs something to complete the sense. Briggs takes ער from the beginning of the next verse, and translates *keep holiday forever*. But in order to mean *keep holiday*, the verb needs something to complete the sense — cease *from labour*. Reifmann, cited by Dr., proposes חרלו עבד, which is adopted by Bu.: παρῆκαν γῆν 𝕲 does not seem to help us, but *habitaverunt* 𝕴 points to παρῴκησαν, which is also confirmed by the Armenian (according to HP). I have, therefore, ventured to restore יֵרשו ארץ, cf. Ps. 25[13]. — ער] could undoubtedly be spared. 𝕾 omits, but 𝕲 represents it by ὅτι. — אמללה] Ges.[26] § 55 d.

6–8. Yahweh's government.

> Yahweh kills and gives life,
> Brings down to Sheol and brings up.
> Yahweh makes poor and makes rich,
> Brings low and also sets on high.
>
> He raises the poor from the dust,
> From the dung-hill he raises the needy,
> To make him sit with nobles of the people,
> And gives him in possession a glorious throne.
> [For to Yahweh belong the pillars of the earth,
> And he has set the world upon them].

6. The second half is synonymous with the first — Sheol the abode of the dead. — **7.** אף] is represented by καί alone in 𝕲: *et* 𝕴. — **8.** דל and אביון are parallel, Ps. 72[13]. — מאשפת] Many codd. have ומאשפת, which is also the reading of 𝕲𝕴. The אשפת is the mound of rubbish which accumulates near an Oriental town. Beggars often spend the night upon it in default of a lodging. — נריבים] δυναστῶν λαῶν 𝕲[B]: δυναστῶν λαοῦ 𝕲[L], evidently reading נריבי־עם, which seems more vigorous. The couplet in brackets is not found in 𝕲, and is therefore probably not original. In place of it we find: διδοὺς εὐχὴν τῷ εὐχομένῳ, καὶ εὐλόγησεν ἔτη δικαίου, which seems an endeavour to adapt the psalm more nearly to Hannah's circumstances.

9, 10. The confidence of the believer.

> The feet of his friends he will guard,
> But the wicked shall perish in darkness,
> (For not by strength is a man mighty).

> Yahweh will shatter his enemies,
> Upon them ne will thunder in the heavens.
> Yahweh will judge the ends of the earth;
> He will give strength to his king,
> And will exalt the horn of his anointed.

9. ⅏ omits the first two members of the verse. These seem, however, more in accord with the context than the third. — **10.** יחתו] read יֵחַת with ⅏. — מריבו] is confirmed by ⅏, but is of course to be taken collectively: מריביו *Qrê.* — עליו *Qrê.* Bu. proposes עֶלְיוֹן, which would not be out of place. In this verse ⅏ inserts six lines from Jer. 9²²ᶠ. For יהוה in line 3 ⅏ has simply αὐτός. — משיחו] as a title of the king (and we can hardly understand it otherwise here) this word is another indication of comparatively late date.

11. The verse is the conclusion of the account of Samuel's dedication and originally read : *And she left him there before Yahweh and went to Ramah ; but the boy continued ministering to Yahweh in the presence of Eli the priest.*

11. καὶ κατέλιπεν αὐτὸν ἐκεῖ ἐνώπιον κυρίου ⅏ is represented in 𝔐 by the last three words of 1²⁸. It is scarcely possible to doubt that ⅏ has the original, and that its proper place is here. — וילך אלקנה הרמתה] can scarcely be original, as Hannah has been the prominent character in what precedes. We should read וילכו הרמתה or ותלך הרמתה. The words על־ביתו are lacking in ⅏ᴮ and superfluous. — משרת] is often used of priestly service.

12–17. The corruption of the existing priesthood. — The author describes the conduct of Eli's sons in a manner to point the contrast afforded by Samuel, and also to prepare for the catastrophe that is to overtake their house. The crime of which they are accused is arrogance in demanding a share of the sacrifice and in not contenting themselves with the portions assigned by custom or by law.

The paragraph separates itself so neatly from what precedes and follows, that we naturally suppose it to belong to an older document which the author of the life of Samuel wove into his narrative.

12. The sons of Eli were *wicked men*] the phrase used, *sons of belial*, is parallel to *daughter of belial* used in 1¹⁶. We must be careful not to assume that belial was at this time a proper name. Whatever its origin, it denotes extreme depravity. *They knew not*

C

Yahweh] in any such sense as would lead them to do his will, *nor the priest's due from the people*] this clause from the next verse seems to belong here. — **13, 14.** *Whenever a man sacrificed, the priest's servant would come, at the boiling of the flesh, with his three-pronged fork in his hand, and would strike it into the pot or the pan or the kettle*] the method could scarcely be more offensive. *All that the fork brought up the priest would take for himself*] by the hand of his servant, that is. This violence was not exercised in isolated cases only, but was practically universal — *to all Israel that came to sacrifice to Yahweh in Shiloh.* — **15.** Worse is to follow : *Moreover, before they burned the fat, the priest's servant used to come and say to the offerer : Give roasting-flesh for the priest — he will not take boiled flesh from thee, but raw*] this amounted to sacrilege, as nothing ought to intervene between the presentation of the offering and the burning of the part belonging to Yahweh. The expostulation of the worshipper to this effect only led to fresh insult : *Should the offerer say : They are going to burn the fat at once, then take whatever you please, he would reply : No ! You shall give it at once or I will take it by force.* — **17.** The greatness of the sin consisted in this, that these priests *despised the offerings of Yahweh.*

13. ומשפט הכהנים את] 𝔊 had משפט מאת; this is confirmed by 9 MSS. and seems preferable. The nearest parallel is Dt. 18³ — משפט הכהנים מאת. It is extremely difficult to decide whether this clause belongs with the preceding verse or whether it should begin a new sentence : *the custom of the priest . . . was that his servant would come.* The decisive consideration is the use of the phrase in Dt. 18³, where it certainly means the *due of the priests from the people.* On this account it belongs with the preceding, though we expect an את to precede משפט. For שלש השנים We. and Dr. read שלשה שנים. — **14.** והכה doubtless should be the pointing, with 𝔊. Instead of four vessels 𝔊 has but three. — כו] should be corrected to לו with 𝔊𝔖𝔗. — שם בשלה] the tautology is relieved by 𝔊ᴮ θῦσαι κυρίῳ ἐν Σηλώμ, and this should be restored. It is not certain that שם should be retained with this reading (Kl., Bu.). — **15.** וגם] evidently introduces the climax. — יקח] λάβω 𝔊𝔖. The reading of 𝔥 seems more likely to be original. — **16.** ויאמר] as pointed by 𝔐 would describe a single case. It seems better to point ויאמר and to understand it as stating a hypothesis. — אליו is not represented in 𝔊. — לו Kt.] לא Qrê and in 19 codd., besides 𝔊𝔖. — לקחתי] is justified by analogy, cf. Dr. *Tenses,*³ § 136γ; but it is smoother to change to ולקחתי (Kl.). — **17.** את־פני יהוה, which is inserted in different places in different recensions of 𝔊, is possibly not original, as it is superfluous and may have crept in from the next verse. — האנשים] lacking in 𝔊, seems to be an insertion intended to lighten the categorical assertion that the *priests* treated the offerings with contumely.

18–21. The narrative returns to Samuel who *continued serving Yahweh*] lit. *the face of Yahweh*, which means Yahweh himself. Samuel is described as *a lad girded with a linen ephod*] where the ephod is evidently a priestly garment, 22[18] 2 S. 6[14]. Baudissin* points out that linen garments were worn by the Egyptian priests. Direct influence cannot be proved. — **19.** *And his mother used to make him a little robe*] no English word exactly corresponds to the Hebrew. The garment was worn over the tunic. There seems no reason to find fault with the statement on the ground that as the boy grew it would no longer be a *little* robe. The narrator has the earlier years especially in mind. Doubtless the cloth was spun and woven by his mother, as well as the robe cut and sewed by her. — **20.** The blessing of Eli: *Yahweh repay thee with seed from this woman for the gift which she gave to Yahweh*] the received text is obscure, but the reference must be to 1[28], where Hannah expressly says she has given him to Yahweh. **21.** *And Yahweh visited Hannah*] as he did Sarah, Gen. 21[1], *so that she gave birth to three sons and two daughters*] in addition to Samuel. *But the lad Samuel grew up in the presence of Yahweh.*

19. ומעיל קטן] the מעיל was the outer garment worn by well-to-do people. It was usually sleeveless, as we may judge from the emphasis laid upon those with sleeves. For קטן Kl. proposes כתון, *cotton*, which, however, occurs nowhere in Biblical Hebrew. — **20.** ישם] would perhaps answer our purpose. But ἀποτίσαι 𝔊[B] indicates ישלם as does ἀνταποδώσει 𝔊[L]. — שאל ליהוה] cannot be right, though the attempt is made to translate it, *which one asked of Yahweh*. But there is no reason for the indefinite verb here: Eli would certainly have said שאלה or שאלת and would also have used מן. On the basis of 1[28] we naturally restore השאילה (Bu.). 𝔊 has ἔχρησας which is evidently השאלת, cf. Ex. 12[36]. But it seems unfair to give the merit to Elkanah. — והלכו למקמו] better to make the suffix plural as in some codd.; 𝔊 however makes the verb singular. — **21.** כי־פקר] seems without motive: ויפקר 𝔊𝔖 should be restored. — ותהר] is lacking in 𝔊[B], cf. 1[20], which shows how easily such insertions are made. After ותלד insert עור 𝔊[B].

---

* *Geschichte des Alttestamentlichen Priesterthums*, Leipzig, 1889, p. 70, referring to Herodotus, II. 37. Compare, also, Nowack, *Hebr. Archäologie*, II. p. 116.

22-25. Eli's ineffectual rebuke. — The paragraph joins directly to v.[17], and, as already indicated, was probably part of a source which treated the sin and punishment of Eli's sons without reference to Samuel. — **22.** Although Eli was a very old man, *yet he used to hear what his sons were doing*] the reference is to the sins already laid to their charge. The impurity predicated of them in the second half of the verse was not in the mind of the original author. — **23.** The rebuke : *Why will you do the like of these things which I hear from the mouth of all the people ?*] this, which is an abbreviated text, seems to convey all that he meant to say. — **24.** *No, my sons ! Not good is the report which I hear . . . the people of Yahweh*] the text is suspicious, and perhaps originally contained a prohibition. — **25.** The motive is the difficulty of finding a mediator when Yahweh is the offended party : *If a man sin against a man, God will mediate*] cases of this kind could be brought before God as umpire, and the oracle would decide between the parties. *But if against Yahweh one sin, who shall act as mediator ?* No higher power exists to whom the case can be submitted. The conclusion is, that the offended party will take his revenge. The expostulation was fruitless, *for Yahweh was minded to slay them*], and on that account incited them to sin, as he afterwards incited David to take the census, 2 S. 24[1].

26. Samuel is again brought in, in contrast. He *kept growing larger and better in the estimation of Yahweh, and in the estimation of men.*

22. כל] is lacking in 𝕲[BL]. The second half of the verse brings as an additional accusation against the priests that they *used to lie with the women who ministered at the gate of the Tent of Meeting*] the sentence is suspicious; first, because it is lacking in 𝕲[B]. In the second place the original narrator has stated his accusation above and this should have been made a part of that accusation. Finally, the whole narrative, except in this verse, is ignorant of *women who ministered* and of the *Tent of Meeting* as established at Shiloh. The language is borrowed from the Priestly document of the Pentateuch, Ex. 38[8]. For these reasons the half verse is to be regarded as a late interpolation (We., Kl., Dr., Bu.). — **23.** את־דבריכם רעים] is lacking in 𝕲[B] and difficult to construe : *for I hear of your evil dealings* (RV.) cannot be the meaning. It seems better to leave the words out. — מאת] ἐκ στόματος 𝕲 is more vivid. — העם אלה] is impossible. The אלה has come in by false duplication of the following אל. 𝕲 has κυρίου which perhaps represents אלהים; but notice the phrase עם יהוה at the end of the next verse. — **24.** אשר אנכי שמע מעברים] seems unintelligible: *which I hear the people circulating* 𝔗 would require העם to be expressed before the participle: *You make the people transgress* would require the addition of אתם, and the same is true of Kimchi's proposal: *You make the people forsake* [*the sanctuary*]. If a word of this kind can be used here at all, it is better to correct to העברתם or האברתם, *ye lead astray*. But אל at the beginning of the verse suggests a negative command, in which case there has been radical corruption. — **25.** פללו] as the direct object is without analogy we may read ופלל לו; We., Bu., al., point ופללו. — **26.** וגדל] is lacking in 𝔊ᴮ.

27–36. The Threat of Punishment upon Eli.

— An unnamed prophet comes to Eli and rehearses the benefits he and his house have received from Yahweh. The ingratitude with which he has treated his benefactor is pointed out, and the removal of his house from the priesthood is foretold, with the consequent impoverishment of his descendants.

The piece reminds us of similar sections elsewhere, Jd. 6[7ff.] 1 K. 13[1ff.], where a prophet is sent with a rebuke, and of others, Jd. 2[1-5] 10[11-16], where Yahweh himself (or his Angel) delivers the rebuke. All such sections are of comparatively late date, and the present one is no exception. The only question which is raised concerning it is whether it is an insertion made after the narrative of Samuel's life was completed. In answering this we need to note that the account of the priests' wickedness, ending at 1[25], might be continued perfectly well by the account of the capture of the Ark beginning at 4[1]. The oldest historian would then have left us to draw the moral ourselves. It seems on the whole probable that this was the case. But an editor, not content with this form of the story, inserted our section on purpose to point out the lesson. This may very well have been done before the story of Samuel was inserted in the narrative, as the author of that story had abundant reason to tell us of his hero's call even if 2[27-36] were already in his text, while the interpolator would have no motive to insert 2[27-36] if 3 was already a part of the history.

We. (*Comp.*, p. 239 f.) treats this section as an interpolation into the narrative similar to the Song of Hannah, though of earlier date, "yet scarcely older than Deuteronomy and the reform of Josiah." Bu., *RS.* p. 200, thinks the section in place but "Deuteronomistically recast," with which Cornill agrees *Einleitung*[3], p. 99; and Driver takes substantially the same view, *LOT.*[6],

p. 174. I can see no evidence of the recasting, and if the piece is not much later than Josiah, there is no reason why it may not have existed before the incorporation of the story of Samuel into this context.

27. *A man of God*] the phrase is frequently used of a prophet, especially in the Books of Kings; it is twice used of an angel, Jd. 13⁶, ⁸, in a passage ascribed to J. by Prof. Moore, once applied to Moses in Deuteronomy (33¹, E), and once also in Joshua (14⁶, a passage Deuteronomistically coloured). *Thus saith Yahweh*] is a standing phrase in the prophetic books. *I certainly revealed myself to thy father's house, while they were in Egypt, servants to the house of Pharaoh*] the *father's house* was probably the clan of Levi. Parallel to this election by Yahweh as a reason for obedience, is the frequent argumentation from his choice of Israel as his people. — **28**. *And I chose him from all the tribes of Israel as my priest, to offer on my altar, to burn sacrifices and to bear an ephod*] whether we should translate *to bear* an ephod, or *to wear* an ephod depends upon the meaning of the word ephod, concerning which this passage leaves us wholly in the dark. *And I gave thy father's house all the offerings of the sons of Israel for food*] the last two words are omitted by 𝔥, but found in 𝔊. They seem necessary to the sense, for the point of the rebuke is that Eli's sons were dissatisfied with the provision made for them. It seems clear that the writer has in mind either the tribe of Levi or the house of Aaron which was chosen to the priesthood in Egypt, and that therefore he lived before the descent of Zadok (who displaced the descendants of Eli) was traced either to Levi or to Aaron.* — **29**. *Why then dost thou look with an evil eye on my sacrifices and on my offerings and dost honour thy sons above me, in fattening them with the first-fruits of all the offerings of Israel my people?* The Hebrew text is obscure and this restoration is only provisional. It seems to express the mind of the writer — that Eli allowed his sons to seize as their own the portion that belonged of right to God. — **30**. A change of purpose is declared : *I had thought that thy house and thy clan should continue in my presence forever*] lit. *should walk to and fro before me.* The figure is that

---

* Cf. Baudissin, *Geschichte des Alttestamentlichen Priesterthums*, Leipzig, 1889, p. 197 f.

of a courtier who lives in his sovereign's favour, basks in the light
of his countenance. *But now, saith Yahweh, far be it from me ;
for them that honour me I will honour, and they that despise me
shall be lightly esteemed.* — **31**. The prediction to which this leads
up : *I will cut off thy seed*] a man has hope in the survival of his
posterity, long after he himself is gone. *So that there shall not be
an old man in thy family*] premature death is a sign of the divine
displeasure. — **32**. *And thou shalt look, being in straits and with
envious eyes, upon all with which I favour Israel*] as a punishment for the present greedy behaviour. The text must be confessed to be very uncertain. — **33**. *And the man of thine whom I
do not cut off from my altar shall be spared in order to consume his
eyes and to starve his soul, and all the increase of thy house shall
die by the sword of men*] one is tempted to see a reference to the
slaughter of the priests by Saul. — **34**. An earnest of the calamity
should be the death of Eli's sons : *on the same day both shall die.* —
35. In contrast with Eli there shall be a faithful priest : *All that is
in my heart and in my desire he will do, and I will build him an
enduring house*] that is, a continuous posterity, cf. 2 S. 7[11], *Yahweh
makes known to thee that Yahweh will build thee a house.* This
priest, in person or in his descendants, *shall walk before mine
Anointed for all time*] lit. *all the days.* The *Anointed* is of course
the king of Israel, and the writer seems to look back upon a long
line of kings. There can be no doubt therefore that the *faithful
priest* is Zadok, who was made priest by Solomon in place of
Abiathar (Eli's great-grandson). This is expressly stated to be
the fulfilment of the prophecy, I K. 2[27]. The family of Zadok
maintained themselves in the sanctuary of Jerusalem until the
final destruction of the temple. — **36**. Eli's family shall be so
reduced as to seek the menial offices of the sanctuary for the
pittance that might thus be earned. *And the one that is left of thy
house shall come to do him obeisance for a bit of money or a loaf
of bread*] the contrast is between the regularly installed priesthood
which lives of the altar, and the hangers-on of the sanctuary who
are willing to earn an occasional penny or an occasional meal by
menial services. The ambition of the latter is to be put into one
of the priests' places *in order to eat a morsel of the bread of Yahweh*]
the state of things is that which we find after the reform of Josiah,

when the priests of the Bamoth were obliged to content themselves with what subordinate places there were in the service of the
Jerusalem sanctuary.

27. הנגלה] the interrogative ה is out of place, for it would call for a
negative answer. It has come on to this word by duplication of the next preceding letter. — לבית פרעה] might in connection with בהיותם mean *belonging
to the house of Pharaoh.* But 𝕲 is probably right in inserting δούλων; read,
therefore, 'עברים לבית פ. — **28.** ונחר] as an infinitive absolute representing a
finite verb, the word might pass. But it is simpler to restore ואבחר with 𝕲𝕷.
The scribe probably thought he was going to begin the verse with בחרתי
corresponding to נגליתי above; ונחר בחרתי seems to stand for להעלות or
to be corrupted from it. — לשאת] probably ולשאת with 𝕲𝕷. At the end of
the verse εἰς βρῶσιν 𝕲 should be restored. — **29.** למה] prefix ו with 𝕲. —
תבעטו] the verb occurs only Dt. 32¹⁵, where it means *to kick.* But whether it
would take ב in the meaning *to kick at* is not certain. 𝕲 evidently read תביט
which makes good sense. — אשר צויתי מעון] is unintelligible in this context:
ἀναιδεῖ ὀφθαλμῷ 𝕲 may represent מעין 18⁹ (Kl.). This makes good sense,
and we must suppose אשר צויתי inserted to help out the unintelligible מעון
after the מעין had become mutilated. — להבריאכם] may be conjecturally
altered to להבריא אתם, for it is Eli's indulgence to his sons that is rebuked:
ἐνευλογεῖσθαι 𝕲 would be לְהִבָּרֵךְ. For לעמי we should perhaps read לעיני
(Bu.) although it is equally good simply to leave off the ל as a duplicate
of the preceding letter. — **30.** אמור אמרתי] only the second word is indicated
by 𝕲. The contrast may be between Yahweh's former *declaration* and his
present one. But it seems more forcible to make אמר denote the thought
of his mind, as frequently. — נאם־יהוה] is frequent in the prophets. —
31. זרעך] τὸ σπέρμα σου 𝕲. The latter alone seems to be justified by the
concluding words of the verse (contra Dr., Kl.). את־זרע should be made to
conform to the word just discussed. — **32.** The verse, down to בביתך, is
omitted by 𝕲ᴮ, whence some have supposed it not original. But the omission can be accounted for by homeoteleuton, and the verse is represented in
most MSS. of 𝕲 and also in Ḷ. But to make sense of it is another matter. —
והבטת צר מעון] is nonsense; Kl. is probably right in seeing a reference to
the מעון which we have changed to מעין above (very possibly the form may
have been מְעֹן). In that case, the simplest correction will be to read ומעין
instead of מעון. For ייטיב I have ventured, in so desperate a passage, to put
אישיב. — **33.** עיניך] read עינו 𝕲. — ולאריב] is pointed as a Hiphil with the
ה dropped. The reference to Dt. 28⁶⁵ is so evident, however, that the correction to להראיב seems obvious. — נפשך] read נפשו 𝕲. — אנשים cannot mean
cum ad virilem aetatem venerit 𝕷. Read with 𝕲 בחרב אנשים. — **34.** אל־חפני
ופנחס] is superfluous and perhaps a gloss. — **35.** בית נאמן] cf. 25²⁸. — **36.** כל]
is lacking in 𝕲ᴮ and superfluous. — וככר־לחם] also lacking in 𝕲ᴮ. — לחם] 𝕲𝕷
adds τοῦ κυρίου, confirmed by Ḷ, and doubtless original.

III. 1–21. The revelation to Samuel. — Samuel while sleeping in the sanctuary hears a voice calling him.   Supposing that it is Eli, he waits upon him thrice.   Eli at last perceives the nature of the call and instructs the lad how to reply.   The sequel is a revelation of Yahweh's determination to destroy the house of Eli. On hearing the message the aged priest resigns himself to the divine will.   The significance of the revelation is that it opens Samuel's career as a prophet, and his reputation soon becomes known throughout Israel.

The chapter seems to be a unit.   Doubts have been expressed as to the originality of [11-14]; but these seem not to be well founded.   The necessity of the account in a life of Samuel is evident.   The fact that this section duplicates the warning of the anonymous man of God in the preceding chapter does not make it the less necessary that Samuel should be accredited as a prophet.   And no more appropriate credential could be found than a prediction of the destruction of the house of Eli.   The tone and style agree well with ch. 1.

1–10. Samuel hears a voice calling him in the night, and the voice proves to be the voice of Yahweh.   The account opens with a restatement of Samuel's position in the temple service, and then tells us that *the word of Yahweh was rare in those days, there was no . . . vision*] the qualifying word may mean *public* or *widespread*, but there is reason to suppose that the original reading is lost. — **2, 3.** After the opening clause, the thread of the narrative is interrupted to describe the condition of things at the time when the event took place, and is resumed in v.[4].   So the sentence is : *It came to pass in that day, when Eli . . . that Yahweh called Samuel.*   The circumstantial clause is complicated ; three of its items tell of the condition of things at the moment, the other gives us information of the state of Eli's physical vision.   It is difficult to see how this clause bears on the present history.   But taking the text as it stands we may render by inserting a parenthesis : *When Eli was lying in his place (now his eyes had begun to grow dim, he could not see) and the lamp of God had not yet gone out, Samuel also was lying in the Temple of Yahweh where the Ark of God was.*   But the originality of the words in parenthesis is difficult to maintain. The other items are important for the picture they present of the sanctuary. It is evident that Eli and Samuel slept in adjoining rooms, if not in the same room. Samuel, at least, lay in the apartment in which the Ark stood. The difference between this arrangement and that provided in the traditional Tabernacle is evident. That a lamp should burn all night before Yahweh is in accordance with the fitness of things. The early Israelites in providing Yahweh a dwelling were careful to furnish it with articles of use and luxury according to their ideas. Of any typical or symbolical meaning such as later attached itself to this furniture we find no trace in our narrative. We may assume, however, that the lamp burned all night in the sanctuary, as was later expressly provided, Ex. 27^{21}, cf. 2 Chr. 13^{11}, and therefore that the time of Samuel's call was in the early morning. The sanctuary is here called a *temple* as in 1^9. The sleeping of an attendant near the Ark, as a servant sleeps near the monarch so as to serve him, seems to show preëxilic custom, but how it shows this account to be pre-Deuteronomic * I do not see. The belief that sleepers in the sanctuary receive revelations in dreams was common in antiquity and seems not yet to have died out, as there are traces of it among the Moslems to the present time. *The Ark of God* is here mentioned for the first time. It is evidently the same which was afterwards transferred to his citadel by David, and which was the sacred object in the Temple of Solomon. But we have no description of it by an early writer. See below, on 4^3. — **4.** The text must be restored at this point, where we expect the most detailed account, so as to read : *Yahweh stood and called : Samuel! Samuel!* The repetition of the name is one of the marks of E among the Pentateuchal documents, Gen. 22^{11} 46^2 Ex. 3^4. — **5.** Answering what he supposed was the call of Eli, Samuel is bidden to return to his place. — **6.** Yahweh calls again : *Samuel! Samuel!* with the same result as before. — **7.** The remark that *Samuel did not yet know Yahweh, and the word of Yahweh had not yet been revealed to him,* is added to explain how it was that he did not recognize the voice of the speaker. — **8.** At the third experience Eli *perceived that Yahweh was calling the*

---

* As affirmed by Kittel, *GH.* II. p. 33.

lad. — **9.** Hence his instruction : *Go and lie down ; and if one call thee thou shalt say : Speak ! for thy servant is listening.* As the subject is left indefinite in the clause *and if one call thee*, it is probable that the name of Yahweh was not mentioned in what follows.   Eli will let the lad discover who the speaker is. — **10.** When the call comes again, Samuel replies as he has been directed.

This single passage is not enough to give us an Old Testament doctrine of revelation.   But it conveys with great clearness its author's conception.   He does not describe a dream, because he makes Samuel rise and run to Eli after each call.   He conceived of the prophet as hearing a voice physically audible.   This voice enunciated in articulate words the message which the prophet was to receive.   The experience is therefore not parallel to that of Jacob, who saw and heard God in a dream.

1. נפרץ] seems to give no good meaning. פֹּרֵץ, which We. substitutes, is too violent in meaning for this place, though it is possible that the נ has come from the preceding word. — **2.** ועיניו] should be read with the *Qrê.* — החלו כהות] We. seems to be wrong in insisting that the second word cannot be an infinitive, on the ground that a ל would be required.   Cf. אחל תת Dt. 2^{25. 31}, אחל גדלך Jos. 3⁷.   It is better, therefore, to point כהות. — לא] should perhaps be ולא (𝔊). — **3.** טרם is usually construed with the imperfect tense as here, Dr., *Tenses*[3], 27 β. — **4.** ויקרא] In v.¹⁰ we read that Yahweh *stood and called as before.*   It seems necessary, therefore, that the opening account should contain this particular, and so we find in 𝔊^L καὶ κατέστη καὶ ἐκάλεσε κύριος. The omission of ויתיצב may be accounted for by its anthropomorphism.   That it was not omitted below only shows, what we know from other passages, that a correction of this kind is rarely carried far. — אל־שמואל] should be שמואל שמואל as below, and here also in 𝔊. — **5.** הנני] the regular answer when one's name is called. — **6.** ויקם] is lacking in 𝔊^{BL}.   By its omission we lose nothing, and the second call is made uniform with the first. — **7.** טרם] ἐδούλευε πρὶν ἤ 𝔊^L seems to be a case where a Greek editor tried to make sense out of a text he did not understand.* — ידע] should be pointed as an imperfect after טרם (Böttcher, followed by Th.). — **9.** אליך] 𝔊^L adds ὁ καλῶν, which is a correct interpretation of the writer's meaning. — דבר יהוה] 𝔊^B has simply λάλει, which is what Samuel actually says in v.¹⁰.   It seems to me more likely that the name is a later insertion than a later omission. — **10.** כפעם־בפעם] cf. Jd. 16²⁰.   From what has already been said it is evident that the narrative cannot be made to illustrate the *incubation* common among

---

* The reading, however, is found in I *serviebat antequam*, Cod. Goth. Leg. *apud* Vercellone.

Egyptians, Greeks, and Romans. But there is probably a similar idea at the basis; namely, that the sanctuary is a favourable place to receive revelations. Cf. Seyffert, *Dictionary of Classical Antiquity*, p. 435, Friedländer, *Darstellungen aus d. Sittengesch. Roms*[6], III. p. 571 ff.

11–14. The message. — The contents are of such a nature that Samuel could no longer be in doubt as to the personality of the speaker : *Behold I am about to do a thing in Israel such that the ears of every one that hears it shall ring*] cf. 2 K. 21[12] Jer. 19[3], both describing the effect of news of calamity. The verb is used once of the trembling of the lips from fear (Hab. 3[16]). — **12.** *In that day I will fulfil upon Eli all that I have spoken against his house from beginning to end*] lit. *beginning and ending;* the adverbial infinitives express the completeness of the punishment. — **13.** *And thou shalt tell him*] a slight change from the received text — *that I will punish his house forever for the guilt of his sons, in that his sons were blaspheming God, and he did not rebuke them*] the text has been purposely obscured to shield the reader from pronouncing the words *blaspheming God*, but the original has fortunately been preserved in 𝕲. — **14.** *Therefore have I sworn to the house of Eli that the guilt of the house of Eli shall not be expiated*] the technical term can best be translated thus, though Hebrew and Greek ideas of expiation must not be confused. *By sacrifice or by offering forever*] the expression seems to be made very general in order to emphasize the impossibility of placating the offended deity by any of the methods known to the ritual. In ordinary cases of his anger he might be appeased by *smelling an offering*, 26[19].

It has been supposed by some that the revelation to Samuel was originally of a different tenor, predicting the doom of Shiloh and appointing Samuel as Eli's successor. But the reasons advanced to sustain this thesis are not convincing, and the tone of the verses seems quite homogeneous with the rest of this document. The fact that there is an allusion in v.[12] to the preceding message to Eli has already been pointed out, as has the bearing of this fact upon the comparative age of the whole chapter.

11. עשׂה] on the use of the participle in divine announcements, cf. Dr., *Tenses*[3], § 135, 3. — **12.** אל] in the first occurrence at least we should read על. The interchange of the two prepositions is so common as scarcely to call

for remark. — **13.** והגדתי לו] cannot mean *for I have told him* (RV.), but must be *and I will make known to him*. This seems unnecessary, and the conjecture of Kl. (adopted by Bu.) that we should read והגדְתָ לו is taken as the basis of the translation above; for the object of this revelation is to warn Eli of the impending doom of his house. — בעון] the construct, governing the clause which follows, is doubtless possible, Ges.²⁶ § 130 c. It seems awkward here, however, and the word is left out by Bu. on conjecture. As it seems better to have some authority, I prefer to emend according to 𝔊ᴬᴮ which reads בעון בניו but omits אשר־ידע. — מקללים להם] cannot mean *made themselves vile*, AV., or *bring a curse upon themselves*, RV. All the analogies are in favour of מקללים אלהים which was read by 𝔊. The passage is one of those altered by the scribes (*tiqqunê sopherim*), cf. Geiger, *Urschrift und Uebersetzungen*, p. 271. — כהה] is used in the sense of *restrain* only here, so that there may be an error of the text. — **14.** נשבע] is regularly followed by אם giving the oath a negative force, or by אם־לא where the force is affirmative. — יתכפר] this stem is found here only, but there can be no doubt of the meaning. The Piel is the technical term for removing by a ritual act anything which is offensive in the sight of God and would therefore make his worshippers unacceptable to him, cf. Dr., *Deuteronomy*, p. 425, BDB., *s.v.*

15–18. The message delivered. — Samuel lay until the morning, when he rose *and opened the doors of the house of Yahweh*] a part of his regular work as servant of the sanctuary. That he was *afraid to make the vision known* is easily understood. — **16, 17.** Eli's adjuration, *so may God do to thee and more too, if thou conceal from me a word of all that he spoke to thee*] induces a response. The formula *so may God do to thee* is an imprecation originally connected with the ceremony of slaying an animal at the taking of an oath. The parties pray that the fate of the victim may be theirs. The fact that the formula is used only in Samuel and Kings is an argument against attributing these books to the Pentateuchal authors E and J, who had abundant opportunity to use the expression in their histories. The omission of the subject of the verb shows Eli's dread of the divine sentence. At Samuel's report, the old man resigns himself : *It is Yahweh, let him do what is good in his sight*] compare David's expression in 2 S. 15²⁶.

15. After הבקר, add וישכם בבקר which has fallen out of 𝔐 on account of the resemblance of הבקר and בבקר; it is preserved by 𝔊. The *doors* here mentioned are another evidence that the House of Yahweh was not a tent. — **16.** את־שמואל] some MSS. have אל־ש׳. — **18.** ממנו] 𝔊ᴸ adds ῥῆμα (= דבר), which seems necessary to the sense. — בעינו] the *Qrê* substitutes בעיניו as usual. With the phrase *the good in his eyes,* compare *the right in his eyes, the evil in his eyes.* Strictly parallel with the present passage are Gen. 16[6] 19[8] (both J) and Jd. 19[24] (late). But we find הישר והטוב once in Dt. (6[18]) and ככל־הטוב in Jd. 10[15] (E). Exactly like the text are 1 S. 12[3] 14[36. 40] 2 S. 19[28], representing both the main streams of narrative from which our history is made up.

III. 19–IV. 1[a]. The sequel is, that Samuel becomes widely known as a prophet. The verses are, however, not necessary to the connexion, and may be an editorial insertion.

19. As Samuel grew up he continued to enjoy the favour of Yahweh. *Yahweh was with him and let none of his words fall to the ground*] that is, he confirmed them, so that they were not useless. — **20.** *And all Israel knew, from Dan to Beersheba*] cf. Jd. 20[1] 2 S. 3[10] 17[11]; *that Samuel was authenticated as a prophet of Yahweh*] the evident idea of the author is that the people came to the sanctuary to consult the prophet. — **21, IV. 1[a].** The verse as it stands is tautological. By the change of a single word, we get an excellent continuation of the preceding : *And Israel again appeared in Shiloh because Yahweh revealed himself to Samuel, and the word of Samuel came to all Israel*] the sanctuary had been deserted because of the wickedness of Eli's sons, and because God did not reveal himself to them. All this was changed by the establishment of Samuel as prophet. At the end of this paragraph 𝔊 adds : (*and Samuel was established as a prophet from one end of the land to the other*) *but Eli was exceeding old and his sons kept on doing worse and worse before Yahweh*] what is here in parenthesis is duplication of [20b], but the rest is possibly original.

19. For הפיל] 𝔊 may have read נפל, cf. Jos. 21[43] 2 K. 10[10]. — **21.** Bu. proposes to interchange this verse and the following, partly on the ground of 𝔊, and partly because that order seems more natural. The difficulty, however, is caused by ויסף יהוה להראה which, as it now stands, only says that Yahweh appeared again in Shiloh, and thus duplicates the second half of the verse. By the single change of יהוה to ישראל the difficulty is avoided, and the verses fall into a natural order. — להראה is an unusual form for an infinitive construct, but occurs Jd. 13[21], cf. Ges.[26] 75 *c*, Stade, *Gram.* 622 *b.* — [בשלה בדבר יהוה is lacking in 𝔊 and probably later expansion. — **IV. 1[a].** The division into chapters has cut off this clause from the paragraph to which it belongs. The addition adopted above is found in the MSS. of 𝔊, apparently without exception.

IV. 1ᵇ–VII. 1. War with the Philistines; defeat of Israel and capture of the ark; the experiences of the Philistines with the ark and its return to the land of Israel.

The three chapters form a closely connected whole. They show no trace of acquaintance with Samuel, but form a natural continuation of the history of Eli and his sons. They are now generally supposed to belong to an older stratum of the narrative than that which has preceded. In spite of their unity of scope, there are indications that they are from a composite history like that of JE.

IV. 1ᵇ–22. The great disaster. — The author tells us of the first repulse in few words. The original opening of the account, however, is mutilated in 𝔋 by the same cause which made the last words of 3²¹ illegible. Restoring the reading from 𝔊, we get: *And it came to pass in those days that the Philistines gathered for war against Israel*] the Philistines appear as the oppressors of Israel in the time of Samson. We know very well that they occupied the great maritime plain from Joppa southwards to the border of Egypt. They appear as a confederacy of five cities, each with a chief magistrate (in some places called a king) bearing the title of *Seren*. That they were immigrants was known to Amos (9⁷), who derives them from *Caphtor*. Cf. Dt. 2²³ Jer. 47⁴. At the opening of this campaign the Israelites camped at Ebenezer. According to 7¹² the place did not receive the name until later. But the historical accuracy of that account is open to question. The Philistine camp was at *Aphek*, probably the same with the *Aphek in Sharon* of Jos. 12¹⁸ (𝔊). Sharon was the natural continuation of the Shephela. The place cannot now be certainly identified. — **2.** When battle was joined, *Israel was smitten before the Philistines*] and their loss is put at four thousand men *in the ranks in the field*. This calls attention to the fact that the Israelites did not flee, but suffered heavy loss while holding their ground.

IV. 1. Having given the first clause to the preceding paragraph, we find this one beginning with ויצא, which gives no explanation of the reason why Israel went out. This is supplied by 𝔊 which begins καὶ ἐγενήθη ἐν ταῖς ἡμέραις ἐκείναις καὶ συναθροίζονται ἀλλόφυλοι εἰς πόλεμον ἐπὶ Ἰσραήλ. This is now generally adopted as the original beginning of the section. It seems to be found in all MSS. of ⑥. — לקראת פלשתים] should probably be לקראתם ⑥. On the Philistines, Ebers, *Aegypten und die Bücher Mosis* (1868), pp. 130–237; Max-Müller, *Asien und Europa* (1893), pp. 387–390. — האבן העזר] cannot be right. The first word must be אבן (We.). — אפק] We. (*Comp.*, p. 254) identifies this with the Aphek of 29¹ 1 K. 20²⁶ 2 K. 13¹⁷. Cf. Buhl, *Geog.*, p. 212. — **2.** ויערכו לקראת] cf. 2 S. 10⁹· ¹⁰. — ותטש] gives no suitable sense here : καὶ ἔκλινεν ⑥ points to ותט (adopted by We. al.). It should be noticed, however, that נטה is nowhere used of a battle, so that the emendation is doubtful; והקש would give a good meaning and would easily be corrupted into ותטש, cf. 2 S. 2¹⁷. — וישראל] prefix איש with ⑥ (Bu.).

3–11. The bringing of the Ark to the camp does not deliver the Israelites; on the contrary the Ark itself falls into the hands of the enemy.

— As usual *the Sheikhs* determine what is to be done. They recognize that *Yahweh has smitten them*] the defeat of course could not be because their God was less powerful than the deities of the enemy. *Let us bring to us from Shiloh the Ark of our God that he may go out in the midst of us and save us from our enemies.* The Ark was taken into battle on other occasions, as in the Ammonite war, 2 S. 11¹¹. The cry which was raised when the Ark set out at the head of the people was (Num. 10³⁵) : *Rise, Yahweh, and let thine enemies be scattered, and let thy haters flee before thee* — a war-cry on the face of it. That the Ark went before the people at the invasion of the country and the siege of Jericho (Jos. 3, 4) is significant in the same connexion. The present account identifies Yahweh and the Ark very closely, but it does not describe the sacred object. From the name we infer that it was a chest, for the same word is used of the sarcophagus of Joseph, Gen. 50²⁶, and of the box set by the side of the altar to receive the money contributions of the worshippers, 2 K. 12¹⁰. The author of Deuteronomy (10³) describes it so far as to say that it was of acacia wood, and made to contain the two tables of the Covenant. Hence his name for it is *Ark of Yahweh's Covenant*, and this usage prevails in Deuteronomistic passages in other books. The priestly writer of Ex. 25 gives us the exact dimensions, and covers it with gold after his manner. He also makes it contain the tables of the Law which he calls *the Testimony*. So that his name for it is *Ark of the Testimony*. He also gives an elaborate description of its lid or cover, to him the most important part of the sacred object, something of which we do not hear in earlier writers.   Jeremiah alludes to it once under the name given it by the Deuteronomist, but in terms which show that he attached no great importance to it, Jer. 3[16].   The commoner name in the historical books is *Ark of Yahweh* or *Ark of God*.   In some cases this designation has been obscured by interpolation, a scribe having inserted the word *Covenant* to conform to his own usage, as is illustrated in the passage before us.

3. ארון ברית יהוה] τὴν κιβωτὸν τοῦ θεοῦ ἡμῶν 𝔊[B]; both readings are combined in 𝔊[L].   The original is evidently ארון אלהינו, for which a scribe substituted the Deuteronomic phrase.   We must judge in the same way of the insertion of ברית in v.[4] (twice) and in v.[5].   So far the revision was carried and then given up.   In all these cases the testimony of 𝔊[B] is against the insertion.   The problem of the nomenclature of the Ark is, however, somewhat complicated.   No less than twenty-two various designations are found for it.   Of these, ארון ברית with its expansions, are Deuteronomistic, and ארון העדות belongs to P.   The original name must have been simply ארון יהוה, for which might be substituted ארון אלהים or ארון האלהים.   The only one of these used in the Hexateuch is ארון יהוה, which occurs in Jos. 3, 4, 6, and 7, always in the narrative of JE, and (curiously) in both elements, J and E. The occurrence of ארון האלהים in the present chapter would, therefore, militate against its assignment to either of the Hexateuchal sources.

It remains to notice, however, that the interchange of the two names in the chapters before us cannot well be explained except on the ground of two different hands having been concerned in the composition of the narrative. The facts are as follows:

1. ארון ברית יהוה in vv.[3-5] is the result of interpolation, as already noted, and so is ארון ברית האלהים, which occurs in v.[4b].

2. ארון אלהי ישראל which is used in 5[7. 8. 10. 11] 6[3], in the mouth of the Philistines is the natural expression for them to use.

3. ארון יהוה is used 4[6]; it then gives place to ארון האלהים, but is resumed 5[3. 4], interrupted by 5[10], but again resumed in 6[1], being used throughout the rest of the chapter and in 7[1], which belongs with it.

4. ארון אלהים is used only once (4[11]); but ארון האלהים characterizes 4[13]–5[2], in which it occurs eight times.   It recurs again twice in 5[10].

The verse 5[10] can well be spared and is probably an insertion.   The section 4[11-22] forms a distinct section of the narrative, being concerned with the reception of the news by Eli and the effect upon him and his house.   Nothing stands in the way of our assigning it to a different hand from the one that wrote the rest of the account.   The two verses 5[1. 2] are, in part, a necessary introduction to what follows.   But they are over full, and probably have suffered redactional accommodation to their present place.

Notice that ויבא should be ויצא, which was read by 𝔊.

D

4. The proposition is adopted and the Ark is brought from Shiloh ; *and also the two sons of Eli with the Ark of God*] they would naturally accompany it, but the author calls attention to their presence because their fate is involved. If this were part of the document which makes Samuel so prominent, his name would certainly have been mentioned here either to explain his escape or to account for his absence. — **5.** When the Ark reached the camp *all Israel shouted a great shout and the earth resounded*] cf. Jos. 6⁵·²⁰ (E). — **6.** The Philistines inquire the cause of *this noise of shouting in the camp of the Hebrews*] so the Israelites are named ordinarily by foreigners. They ascertain that *the Ark of Yahweh has come to the camp.* — **7.** The fear of the Philistines is motived by the thought : *These are their gods ; they have come to them to the camp*] the text is that of $\mathfrak{G}^B$. *Woe to us, for it has not been thus heretofore*] indicates that the palladium had not usually been taken to war in this period. — **8.** The question of desperation : *Who shall deliver us from the hand of these mighty gods ?* is followed by the historical reason : *These are the gods which smote the Egyptians with every sort of plague and with pestilence*] the received text has *with every sort of plague in the wilderness.* This might be condoned in the mouth of the Philistines, but it would hardly occur to an Israelitic writer to impute the inaccuracy to them. — **9.** *Take courage*] Jd. 20²²; *and be men*] lit. *and become men* if you never were men before. In case of defeat they could expect only to become slaves of the Hebrews ; *as they have been slaves to you.* **10.** The result was the courage of despair on the part of the Philistines, so that in the battle which ensued *Israel was defeated, and fled each to his tents*] 2 S. 18¹⁷ 19⁹. The slaughter in Israel is given as *thirty thousand footmen*] cf. Jd. 20² 1 S. 15⁴ 2 S. 10⁶. —**11.** The climax : *The Ark of God was taken and the two sons of Eli died*] so the sentence pronounced by Samuel was executed.

---

4. The Ark is here called in 𝔐 ארון ברית־יהוה צבאות ישב הכרבים of which $\mathfrak{G}^B$ omits צבאות and ברית. The presumption is in favour of the shorter form, and it is probable that ישב הכרבים also is a later insertion, for no reason can be given why the author should so describe Yahweh here, cf. 2 S. 6². —וישם] is inappropriate. The word עם is not represented in $\mathfrak{G}$. —ונב proposed by Kl. would not be out of place. But on the testimony of $\mathfrak{G}$ it seems better to read simply the ʾ. The names *Hophni and Phinehas* read like an afterthought. — **5.** ברית]

is to be omitted, with 𝔊.—וַתֵּהֹם] on the form Ges.[26] § 72 h, who makes it
Qal.— 6. קוֹל הַתְּרוּעָה] cf. קוֹל הַצְּעָקָה v.[14].—מֶה] on the pointing, Ges.[26] § 37 f.
— 7. The speech of the Philistines varies somewhat in the different recensions
of 𝔊, and all differ from 𝔐. The latter has simply בא אלהים. But it must be evident that אליהם is the appropriate word. As this is rendered by 𝔊 we naturally
adopt it, and with it the context as translated above. The reading of 𝔊^L οὖτος ὁ
θεὸς αὐτῶν seems to be a correction of the phrase in 𝔊^B. — בא] should be read
באו with 𝔊^B. — אוי לנו] 𝔊 adds ἐξελοῦ ἡμᾶς, Κύριε, σήμερον, which is of course
impossible in the mouth of the Philistines. If original, it is part of a speech
attributed to the Israelites, which it is now impossible to reconstruct. — אתמל
שלשם] cf. Ex. 5[7f.] 1 S. 14[21] 19[7]. — 8. הָאַדִּירִים] στερεῶν 𝔊^B seems to render הָאַבִּירִים,
which is more appropriate, so Cappellus, Notae Criticae, p. 433. — בַּמִּדְבָּר] has
been supposed to indicate a tradition which made the Egyptians follow the
Israelites into the desert and there to be smitten by the plagues. But the text
is uncertain, 𝔊 reading καὶ ἐν τῇ ἐρήμῳ. This is of course ungrammatical, but
may conceal ובדבר as conjectured by We. and adopted by Dr., Bu., al. —
9. The two imperatives are continued by two perfects with waw consecutive,
Dr., Tenses[3], § 112. —וּנְלַחְתֶּם] 𝔊 seems to render וְנִלְחֲמְתּוּ.— 10. וַיִּלָּחֲמוּ] as
𝔊^B omits the Philistines, it is altogether probable that both parties are thought
of as subjects — they fought. — 11. The names Hophni and Phinehas read
again as if an afterthought.

12–21. The effect of the tidings. — *There ran a Benjamite
from the ranks] Rabbinical tradition makes him to have been Saul,
who had rescued the tables of the Law from the hands of Goliath.
With his clothes rent and earth on his head] the usual signs of
grief, 2 S. 1[2] 15[32]. — 13. The verse is difficult to understand.
The received text (*Qrê*) makes Eli sit *by the side of the road,
watching*] the road would naturally be the one leading to the
scene of battle. Yet the fugitive apparently comes first to the
town and afterwards to Eli. A change of pointing would make
Eli's station to be *beside the Mizpah road,* but this does not relieve
the difficulty. We are forced therefore to read with 𝔊 *by the side
of the gate watching the road*] where the gate is evidently the gate
of the sanctuary, at which he was accustomed to sit, 1[9]. Though
he was blind, his mind was intent upon the road along which news
must come — *for his heart was trembling for the Ark of God.*
The bearer of tidings comes first to the town, which *shrieks* at the
news. — 14. Eli hears the outcry before the messenger reaches him,
but the latter does not delay — *he hastened and came and told Eli.*
— 15. The verse, which speaks of his age and blindness, inter-

rupts the narrative and is apparently a redactional insertion. If
original, it belongs after the first clause of v.¹⁴. — **16.** *I am he that
is come from the ranks*] the speaker takes for granted that some
one was expected. — **17.** To Eli's question the answer is given in
four particulars : *Israel fled before the Philistines ; there was a
great slaughter of the people ; thy two sons are dead ; and the Ark
of God has been captured*] the four form an ascending scale to
Eli, reaching the climax in the capture of the Ark. — **18.** When
the messenger *mentioned the Ark*] the special object of Eli's solici-
tude, the old man *fell from his seat backward by the side of the
gate, and his neck was broken, and he died*] the author adds in explanation that *the man was old and heavy*. The additional remark : *he had judged Israel forty years* is evidently designed to
bring Eli into the same class with the Judges whose story is given
in the Book of Judges.

12. [איש־בנימין] is possible, but more natural is איש בנימיני, which is
favoured by 𝕲. — **13.** יד [ידך, *Qrê* and some MSS., is undoubtedly correct.
It seems unnecessary to change to ביר or ליד, however, as is done by some
commentators. — [דרך מצפה] would naturally be interpreted the *Mizpah road*.
But the punctuators give us מִצְפֶּה, which is confirmed by 𝕲. This version,
however, reads παρὰ τὴν πύλην σκοπεύων τὴν ὁδόν = יד השער מצפה הדרך, which
is restored by Th. — **14.** המון is the confused noise made by a crowd of people.
— **15.** The verse is expanded in 𝕲 by the repetition (substantially) of the
greater part of v.¹⁴. This indicates that its original place was different from
the one in which we now find it ; and, as a rule, such dislocations are proof of
later insertion. For *ninety-eight* years 𝕲 has *ninety*. — [ועינין קמה] for which the
Orientals give קמו *Qrê*, seems harsh in spite of the parallels adduced by Dr.
Notes. The confusion of ה and ו is so easy that it seems better to restore the
plural here. Cf. 1 K. 14⁴. Twelve codd. read קמה ועינו here. — **16.** If the
preceding verse be omitted, we may also omit האיש אל־עלי with 𝕲ᴬᴮ. For
the first המערכה 𝕲 seems to have read המהנה. — **17.** [המבשר] the original meaning was *one that made another change colour*, therefore a bringer of important
tidings, whether good or bad. In actual Hebrew usage it generally means a
bringer of good tidings. For לפני read מפני with 16 MSS. and probably 𝕲.
The successive stages of the disaster are emphasized by יום. The names of
the two sons are omitted by 𝕲ᴮᴸ. — **18.** [כהזכירו] some MSS. have בהזכירו.
The two prepositions are not infrequently confused. — [בעד יד] can hardly be
right. Probably an original ביד was corrupted into בעד, and then the יד was
inserted in the endeavour to make sense : ἐχόμενος 𝕲ᴬᴮ, ἐχόμενα 𝕲ᴸ elsewhere represent ביד or אל־יד, Ps. 141⁶ 1 S. 19³. — [מפרקתו] here only. It means
the neck as dividing (פרק) the head and trunk.

19. The effects in the family of Eli are set forth. *His daugh-ter-in-law, the wife of Phinehas, was with child*] the phrase used here does not occur elsewhere : it seems to mean *pregnant and near the time of childbirth.* The news of the capture of the Ark and the death of her father-in-law brought on the pangs of labour. —**20.** At the moment of her giving birth, *the women standing about her said to her : fear not, for thou hast given birth to a son*] a message which should give her comfort in her sorrow. *But she neither answered nor heeded*] lit. *set her heart*, Ex. 7²³ Prov. 27²³. —**21, 22.** The account is over-full, probably by conflation, ²² being almost an exact duplicate of a part of ²¹. Leaving out the latter we get : *And they called the boy Ichabod, saying : the glory from Israel is taken captive — because of the capture of the Ark of God and because of her father-in-law and her husband*] the sub-ject is the women standing about her, for she was already uncon-scious.

19. חרה ללת] the nearest parallel is Is. 26¹⁷ : כמו הרה תקריב ללדת. On the form ללה, König, *Gram.* I. p. 402, Ges.²⁶ § 69 *m.* The form here may be a simple scribal error, no parallel to the contraction having been pointed out except אחת for אחרה. After אל־הלקח we should expect וימת, which should there-fore probably be restored for ומת. Still an infinitive may have been intended, 6 MSS. read ואל מת. With צריה cf. Is. 21³. נהפך על is found in the sense of being *poured suddenly upon*, Is. 60⁶. — **20.** וכעת מותה] in itself gives good sense, but the reading of 𝕲 καὶ ἐν τῷ καιρῷ αὐτῆς ἀποθνήσκει : וכעתה מרה which seems to fit the case better. — **21.** ותקרא] the subject evidently cannot be the mother, for she was already unconscious; so that we must suppose the subject is indefinite — *one called.* The verb is feminine because the writer has in mind the women standing about. — אי כבוד] *Inglorious* is the evident intention of the writer — ἀδοξία (Josephus). The only instance that can be cited for אי as an equivalent of אין is Job 22³⁰, where the text is doubtful. 𝕲 seems to point to אוי as the first member. — אל] should probably be על. — **22.** The verse is omitted (on grounds already stated) by We., and is put into the margin by Bu.

V. 1–12. The devastation wrought by the Ark. — First, the god of the Philistines is smitten : then they themselves suffer. The trophy is brought *from Eben-ha-ezer to Ashdod*] one of the five chief cities of the Philistines. It lay near the coast about midway between Joppa and Gaza. A village on the site still bears the name *Esdūd.* The tautology in this verse and the next indicates that this was originally the conclusion of the preceding section.   After the account of the family of Eli the author adds : *But as for the Philistines,* etc.   He then begins his specific account of the fortunes of the Ark. — **2.**   As we should expect in the case of so remarkable a trophy, *they brought it to the temple of Dagon and set it up by the side of Dagon*] the national god of the Philistines if we may argue from his prominence here.   The temple here alluded to existed until the time of the Maccabees, 1 Macc. 10[83f.] 11[4].

The nature and attributes of Dagon are wholly unknown.   He is a god of the Philistines in whose honour a great feast is held, Jd. 16[23].   According to Schrader, *COT.* I. p. 170, the name is found in Assyrian.   If the name be Semitic, it may be related either to דג *fish* or to דגן *corn.*   The adoration of a fish-god in Syria is well attested, and on the other hand the *god of corn* would be at home in the fine grain-growing land of the Shephela.   For *Beth-Dagon* (two places of the name are mentioned in the Old Testament) Jerome gives us *domus tritici,* while for *Dagon* he allows *piscis tristitiae* (*OS.* pp. 25, 32).   Isaaki and Kimchi suppose that the figure of Dagon was half man and half fish.   The combination with Atargatis (Derketo) is uncertain, see Moore's note on Jd. 16[23], Baudissin in *PRE*[3]. II. p. 171, Movers, *Phönizier,* I. p. 590.   For *the god of the harvest* Sanchuniathon is cited by Movers.   Cf. Wellhausen, *Skizzen,* III. p. 170, n. 2.

3.   The next day, *the Ashdodites rose, and came to the house of Dagon and looked*] the latter clause is lacking in 𝕲, but is probably original.   They found *Dagon prostrate on his face on the ground*] cf. Jd. 3[25], Gen. 17[3. 17] ; the narrator evidently means that Dagon was doing obeisance to Yahweh.   Without learning the lesson of Yahweh's superiority, the Ashdodites raised their god *and returned him to his place.* — **4.**   The next lesson was a severer one.   The following morning they not only find him prostrate, but *the head of Dagon and his hands were cut off upon the threshold, only his trunk was left of him*] the received text has *only Dagon was left,* which is manifestly impossible. — **5.**   The narrator traces a peculiar custom of the worshippers at this temple to this event — *therefore the priests of Dagon and all who enter the house of*

Dagon do not tread on the threshold of Dagon in Ashdod until this day, but step over it] the last words are not in 𝔥 but seem to be original.   The threshold, having been the resting place of the hands and head of Dagon, is consecrated, so that it must not be touched.   We find *every one who leaps over the threshold* (or *upon the threshold*) alluded to, Zeph. 1⁹, but we cannot be sure that there is any connexion between the passages, or that the custom is the same in the two cases.   Various threshold ceremonies are cited by Schm. p. 132.

1. On the location of Ashdod, Robinson, *BR*². II. p. 33; GASmith, *Geog.*³ p. 192. — **2.** ויציגו] elsewhere of *setting upright* as Gen. 30³⁸ Jd. 8²⁷.   It seems to imply that worship was to be offered to the captive God as well as to Dagon. — **3.** ממחרת] is lacking in 𝔊ᴮ, which, however, reads καὶ εἰσῆλθον εἰς οἶκον Δαγών, καὶ εἶδον lacking in 𝔥.   Probably 𝔊 is right in both respects, the ממחרת can be spared here though it is needed in v.⁴. — נפל] the participle describes the state of the idol. — לפניו] would mean *before it*, which is superfluous.   על־פניו should be restored, following 𝔊 (We). — ויקחו] καὶ ἤγειραν 𝔊 points to ויקימו, which alone is in place. — ויישיבו] καὶ κατέστησαν 𝔊 indicates ויציבו, which, however, would scarcely be followed by למקומו.   At the end of the verse 𝔊ᴬᴮ I add a sentence taken from v.⁶, but which here interrupts the sequence. — **4.** וישכמו] 𝔊 seems to have read ויהי כי השכימו, adopted by Bu.   But the wording in 𝔊 may be due simply to free translation. — לפניו] should doubtless be על־פניו as above. — רק דגון] πλὴν ἡ ῥάχις Δαγών 𝔊: Dagon solus truncus 𝔏.   The emendation גוו for דגון is due to Lagarde, *Prophetae Chald.* p. li.   𝔗 has גופיה and 𝔖 ודרונן וגשמה; and Ew., *GVI*³. II. p. 586 (English Trans. II. p. 415), had already proposed to insert גוף or גויה before דגון.   We. suggests רגו, which does not seem natural without some explanation. — **5.** At the end of the verse 𝔊 adds: ὅτι ὑπερβαίνοντες ὑπερβαίνουσιν.   We. admits that this is correct description, but re fuses to admit the words to the text, because we cannot account for their omission.   To which the obvious reply is, that the archetype of 𝔥 was evidently illegible in many places and so very possibly here.

To the references concerning Dagon given above may be added Scholz, *Götzendienst und Zauberwesen bei den alten Hebräern*, Regensburg, 1877, pp. 238–244.   His endeavour to identify Dagon with various fish-gods should, however, be viewed with reserve.

6–12. A plague breaks out in the city and follows the Ark wherever it is carried. — 6. *And the hand of Yahweh was heavy on the Ashdodites*] a phrase elsewhere used of oppression by a ruling caste or people, Jd. 1³⁵.   *And he wasted them*] in Hos. 2¹⁴ the same verb is used for destroying the vines and fig trees ; *and* *smote them with tumours*] we can hardly go astray in seeing a description of the bubonic plague. The same word is used Dt. 28[27] in connexion with *the boil of Egypt,* cf. Driver, *Dt.,* p. 310. At the end of the verse 𐤈 adds epexegetically *Ashdod and her borders,* probably a late insertion. — **7.** *Let not the Ark of the God of Israel remain with us, for his hand is severe upon us*] cf. *the hand of a severe master,* Is. 19[4]. — **8.** A council of the *Tyrants of the Philistines* is held. These officers bear a special title. Whether they were kings (as Jeremiah calls them, 25[20]) or more like the *Suffetes* of the Carthaginians cannot now be determined. It does not appear that Achish, king of Gath, was also a *Seren.* The conclusion : *To Gath let the Ark of Israel go around*] Gath, one of the chief cities of the Philistines, cannot now be identified. — **9.** But when the Ark was brought to Gath *the hand of Yahweh was heavy upon them, and he smote the men of the city both small and great, and tumours broke out upon them*] the rendering of the last clause is conjectural only, as the verb used occurs only here. But it is evident that the plague is the same as the one described above. — **10.** The Ark is next sent to Ekron, but the people cry out at its coming ; *They have brought the Ark of the God of Israel to me to slay me and my people*] the pronouns represent the speech of each individual man. For *Ekron* 𐤂 has *Ashkelon* in this verse. Ekron was nearest of the Philistine cities to the land of Israel. — **11.** Another council of the chiefs is called, and the people pray : *Send away the Ark of the God of Israel that it may return to its place*] only thus can they hope to escape extermination. The author adds in explanation : *For there was a deadly panic*] the ·word is used of the tumult of a routed army, Dt. 7[23], Is. 22[5], 𐤈 adds: *the hand of God was exceeding heavy there,* but 𐤂 asserts that *the panic was violent when the Ark of God came there.* Possibly both forms are later expansions of the text. — **12.** The tumult was caused not merely by fear of death, but by actual suffering : *The men who did not die were smitten with tumours, and the cry of the city went up to heaven*] cf. Ex. 2[23].

6. בעפלים] The word עפלים occurs only in this passage and in Dt. 28[27], though the singular occurs as a proper name עֹפֶל. The root seems to mean *to swell,* and so the word would appropriately be used of any tumour or boil. In later Hebrew it seems to have been applied only to hæmorrhoids, and to have become a vulgar word. No other reason can be given for the Massoretic substitution of מחרים in the *Qrê*, than that the latter was a more decent name for the same affliction. The copies of 𝕲 show much variation καὶ ἐξέζεσεν αὐτοῖς εἰς τὰς ναῦς ᴮ: καὶ ἐξέβρασαν εἰς τὰς ναῦς αὐτῶν ᴸ. The *ships* seem out of place here, so that we are unable to accept this reading. 𝕲ᴸ has, along with the rendering just quoted: καὶ ἐπάταξεν αὐτοὺς εἰς τὰς ἕδρας αὐτῶν, which shows the earliest meaning given to עפלים, cf. 𝕷 *et percussit in secretiori parte natium*. Josephus has the same idea when he says: "they died of dysentery, a sore disease and one that brought the most painful death; before their soul could be released by an easy death they brought up their bowels eaten away and destroyed by the disease." The same interpretation of עֳפָלִים may have been in the mind of the author of Ps. 78⁶⁶; cf. also 𝕲ᴮ in its rendering of Dt. 28²⁷ εἰς τὴν ἕδραν. Whether ναῦς in the passage before us (𝕲) is equivalent to ἕδρα, as supposed by Schleusner, must be decided by a Greek scholar. — את־אשדור ואת־גבוליה] is evidently superfluous, and, as it is not rendered by 𝕲, we may safely omit it.

𝕲 in its turn has an addition: καὶ μέσον τῆς χώρας αὐτῆς ἀνεφύησαν μύες· καὶ ἐγένετο σύγχυσις θανάτου μεγάλη ἐν τῇ πόλει. The mention of *mice* here is consistently carried on by similar additions in v.¹⁰ (lacking in 𝕲ᴸ but confirmed by I) and in 6¹. In 6⁴·¹¹·¹⁸ the mice appear also in 𝕳. It is evident that we must choose one consistent recension — either adopting 𝕲 throughout or else striking out the mice altogether. In favour of the latter alternative is the general rule that the shorter text is more likely to be original; secondly, the text of 𝕳 reads with perfect smoothness up to the point where the golden mice are first mentioned, and where they are mentioned they read like interpolations; and thirdly, the explicit assertion in 6⁴ *one plague was upon you all*, could not have been made in this form if the author had known that two plagues had been sent. I conclude on these grounds that the mice, wherever they appear, are the result of late redactional insertion. — **7.** ואמרו] seems to be a mistake for ויאמרו. The phrase ארון אלהי ישראל is appropriate in the mouth of the Philistines, as has been remarked above. — **8.** כל] is lacking in 𝕲. — סרני] is evidently the native name, Jos. 13³ Jd. 3³. Conjectures as to their powers are found in Stark, *Gaza*, p. 136 ff. — גת] cf. GAS., *Geog.* p. 194 f. — יסב] We also speak colloquially of *coming around* to a place even where no circuit is necessary. 𝕲 adds εἰς Γέθθα at the end of the verse. — **9.** אחרי הסב אתו] 𝕲 seems to have read אחרי הסב אתו or אחרי הפכו, but the construction of 𝕳 is not without analogies. — ורהי יד־יהוה בעיר מהומה גדולה מאד] is confused, and Kl. (followed by Bu.) proposes to omit יד יהוה. It seems to me more probable that the words מהומה גדולה מאד are secondary. The *panic* is here premature. — וישתרו] the verb is found only here. The corresponding Arabic word means *to have a cracked eyelid*. — **10.** It has already been pointed out that the verse is possibly an intruder. — עקרון] on the site, cf. Robinson, *BR²*. II. 228; GAS. *Geog.* p. 193; Buhl, *Geog.* p. 187. — רסבו] τί ἀπεστρέψατε 𝕲 is more animated, and perhaps original. — **11.** וישב] 𝕲 points וישׁב. For מהומת־מות 𝕲 has only מהומה and is perhaps right, for *a death-dealing* *panic* would hardly be accurate — מות might arise from duplication of the two letters just preceding. — [כברה] is abruptly introduced; we should expect כי כברה or ורכבר. 𝕲 omits יד and connects כברה with מהומה. For the rest of the verse, also, 𝕲 has a different reading: ὡς εἰσῆλθεν κιβωτὸς θεοῦ 'Ισρ. ἐκεῖ. This may have arisen by the corruption of כברה מאד יד into כבא ארון, or the reverse may have taken place. But the sense is complete at העיר without either of the additions. — **12.** This verse joins very well on to the preceding in the shorter form that has been suggested. For והאנשים אשר לא־מתו: καὶ οἱ ζῶντες καὶ οὐκ ἀποθανόντες 𝕲. — [השמים] השמימה 17 codd. (DeR.).

VI. 1–VII. 1. The return of the Ark. — The Philistines after taking council as to the proper method, send the Ark back to its own country with a votive offering. The returning palladium is received at Beth Shemesh, but there also works disaster. It is therefore transferred to Kirjath Jearim, where it finds a resting place.

The section is evidently connected with what precedes. But it is possible that we have not the complete narrative. We look for the conclusion of the account concerning Ekron (or Gath, if Ekron is not original), but instead are simply told how long the Ark was in the *field* of the Philistines. The actors who consult the necromancers here are not the Tyrants who had been called to help the Ekronites, but the people as a whole. While therefore we concede the coherence of the narrative in its general features, we must admit that these differences point to its composite nature. With them coincides the change from the hand of *God* 5¹², to the Ark of *Yahweh*, 6¹.

1. *The Ark of Yahweh was in the field of the Philistines*] David dwelt *in the field of the Philistines* while in possession of Ziklag 27⁷·¹¹, so that we cannot here claim *the field* as the open country in distinction from the cities, cf. Jd. 5⁴. At the end of the verse 𝕲 adds : *and their land swarmed with mice*, which is adopted by Bu. as a part of the text. Reasons against this have been given above. — **2.** The Philistines seek advice from *the priests and the diviners*] who, as conversant with divine things, would know how to placate the offended deity. The diviners are elsewhere coupled with the soothsayers or the prophets, Is. 3² Jer. 27⁹ 29⁸. Balaam is called a diviner Jos. 13²². Micah speaks of the priests as *giving an oracle*, and the prophets as *divining* (3¹¹). In Arabic also the *kahin* (the same word is in Hebrew the *priest*) is a diviner. *Tell us with what we shall send it to its place*] the demand shows that they expect to offer a present of some kind. — **3**. The reply emphasizes the need of the trespass offering : *If ye are sending the Ark away*] the participle treats the future action as already begun in the intention of the actors, cf. Jer. 31⁸, Is. 65¹⁷. *You must not send it away empty*] the phrase is elsewhere used of sending one away with empty hands, Job 22⁹ Gen. 31⁴² Dt. 15¹³. What is meant is at once explained : *for you shall surely repay him a reparation*] the verb is used of giving back or taking back what has been wrongfully taken away, Gen. 14¹⁶ 20⁷ 2 S. 9⁷. The transition is easy to the requiting of a wrong either by punishment, Jd. 9⁵⁷, or by reparation, Ex. 21³⁴. The endeavour of the Philistines is to recompense Yahweh for the wrong done him. The remainder of the verse as it stands in 𝕳 says : *then you shall be healed and it shall be known to you why his hand does not turn from you*] which must be interpreted as meaning that the hand of Yahweh would be heavy upon them so long as they refused this acknowledgment. But the text may not be sound. To the question as to the nature of the required present the answer is : *the number of the Tyrants of the Philistines, five golden tumours, for one plague was upon you and your Tyrants*] the bearing of this upon the question of the *mice* which are here introduced (as *golden* mice) by 𝕳 has already been noted. It should be remarked that Budde, who is large-hearted enough to admit the mice in v.¹, finds it impossible to retain them here. In fact, they and the tumours cannot both have been original in this place. They are, besides, lacking in 𝕲.

The ingenious hypothesis of Hitzig should be noticed : that the mice were symbols of the pestilence, so that the votive offerings were five golden mice simply, and the misunderstanding of this led to the confusion in the text. Wellhausen came to the same conclusion independently of Hitzig. There seems to be no Hebrew analogy to strengthen this supposition, and it seems pretty certain that if the earliest author of this account had known of the assumed symbolism he would have indicated it in some way.

5. *And you shall* [thus] *give glory to the God of Israel*] recognizing his power as God, Jer. 13¹⁶. *Perchance he will lighten his hand*] which had been heavy upon them. The first half of the verse, which duplicates the preceding verse, is best omitted. —

6. The priests exhort the Philistines not to be obstinate in their opposition to Yahweh, putting their exhortation in the form of rhetorical questions : *Why will you harden your hearts*] after the manner of the Egyptians, who furnish a frightful example : lit. *make your hearts heavy.* The same verb is used Ex. 8¹¹, ²⁸ 9³⁴ (J). *Was it not after he made sport of them that they let them go ?*] the subject of the first verb is Yahweh, cf. Ex. 10² (J). — **7.** Instructions as to the proper way of sending the Ark back to its people. A *new cart* should be made, for one that had been used would have been already profaned. The animals to draw the cart were to be *two milch cows upon which the yoke had not come*] they were to be unbroken, for the same reason that the cart must be new. Th. calls attention to the fact that the *red heifer* must be one that had never been yoked, Num. 19², and cites from Ovid : *nullum passa jugum.* In order to test the will of Yahweh the cows were to be yoked to the cart, *but you shall leave their calves behind them in the house*] so that the natural inclination of the mothers would keep them from going away. — **8.** They are to place the Ark on the cart : *and the golden objects which you shall have repaid him as a reparation*] the construction shows that the matter, being determined upon, is certain to be done — *you shall place in a box at its side*] the word translated *box* occurs only in this account. — **9.** The behaviour of the cattle would show whether Yahweh wished to return to his own land : *If it goes on the way to its own border, to Beth Shemesh, then he has done us this great harm*] the identification of Yahweh and the Ark is complete and we might equally well translate : *If he goes on his way to his own border,* etc. *But if not, then we shall know that it was not his hand that smote us — it was an accident that came to us*] the way is left open in case the behaviour of the Ark should not be what they expect. Beth Shemesh was probably the nearest Israelite town to Ekron. It was counted to Judah, 2 K. 14¹¹ Jos. 15¹⁰, and lay on one of the natural roads from the Shephela to the hill country.

1. After חרשים καὶ ἐξέζεσεν ἡ γῆ αὐτῶν μύας 𝔊. — **2.** On the kind of divination practised by the קסם we have light in Ezek. 21²⁶. Cf. also Stade, *GVI.* I. p. 505; Wellhausen, *Skizzen*, III. p. 126 f.; Driver on Dt. 18¹⁰. — הורדענו] with two syllables written *defective* to prevent the accumulation of vowel letters. —

רַמֶּה] on the pointing Ges[26]. § 102 k. — **3.** מְשֻׁלָּחִים] we should add אתם with 7 MSS. 𝕲𝕾 (Dr.). — איעב] the meaning of the word seems sufficiently evident from the examples given above. We may add Gen. 26[10], where Abimelech says that Isaac had nearly brought upon him *a fine*. In the legal system the *trespass-offering* is an endeavour to compensate Yahweh for infringement of his rights, cf. BDB. *s. v.* אשם. — הרפאו] as the priests were not yet certain that Yahweh was the sender of the plague (cf. vs.[9]) the assurance seems premature that they should be healed. One is tempted to read הרא or רבחנו. For ונודע לכם, 𝕲 renders καὶ ἐξιλασθήσεται ὑμῖν and then reads the rest as a question : *why should not his hand turn from you?* This is favoured by the tense of the verb. But the probability does not seem sufficient to establish the reading of 𝕲 rather than 𝕳. — **4.** וחמשה עכברי זהב [עפלי זהב] which is added by 𝕳, is lacking in 𝕲 and therefore suspicious. — לכלם] some MSS. לכלכם : 𝕲𝕾 represent simply לכם. — **5.** The half verse (down to הארץ) duplicates the preceding verse and is therefore superfluous. The sense is perfectly good without it, and part of it is lacking in 𝕲. We regards it as a gloss. — לאלהי ישראל] τῷ Κυρίῳ 𝕲 may be original, having been changed so as not to have the most sacred name in the mouth of the uncircumcised. — **6.** התעלל] the verb in this stem seems to mean *he amused himself with another*, or *at the expense of another*. Saul fears that the Philistines will amuse themselves by torturing him, 31[4], cf. Jer. 38[19]. The anthropomorphism need cause no surprise in view of such a passage as Ps. 2[4]. — **7.** קחו עשו] does not seem to occur elsewhere without designation of the material. — עגלה] as the vehicle had two wheels, the word is properly rendered *cart*. The word is used Gen. 45[19], where it designates the 'wagon' used for the transport of persons, and Num. 7[8], where it designates the vehicle on which the various parts of the Tabernacle (though not the most sacred) are to be carried. It recurs in the account of the transfer of the Ark to Jerusalem in the time of David. According to Erman (*Life in Ancient Egypt*, p. 491) the word was adopted in Egyptian as the name of the baggage wagon (or cart) drawn by oxen, in distinction from the *chariot* drawn by horses. — עלות] is the participle of עול *to give suck*, cf. Is. 40[11]. — אסר] the verb is used of harnessing to the chariot, Gen. 46[29] 2 K. 9[21]. — בן is used of the young of animals, Job 39[4] and elsewhere. — ביתה] the house of the family is also the home of the cattle. — **8.** אל] is so evidently a mistake for אל that we wonder at any one's making it. The interchange is frequent in precisely those books which have a badly transmitted text, so that it is to be attributed to careless scribes rather than to the authors. It is in fact difficult to believe that the two words could be confused, so long as Hebrew was a living language. Cf. BDB. *s. v.*, *note 2.* — כלי] is a word of very wide meaning; implements, instruments, vessels, ornaments are all included under it. — השבתם] the perfect indicates that in intention they have already given the recompense. — בארגז] pointed with the article, which, however, may mean no more than *the* box which was necessary for the purpose. On the other hand, the punctuators may have supposed the ארגז a necessary part of every cart. The word is generally taken to mean *box* or *chest*, though some suppose *a bag* intended. Bochart makes it a Philistine word, *Hierozoicon*, II. 36. The versions evidently have no more light than we, 𝔊ᴮ ἐν θέματι βερεχθάν, where the last word is probably an attempt to transfer the Hebrew word, ἐν θέματι being the translation. θέμα represents מערכה, in Lev. 24⁶ and elsewhere, and something might be said in favour of setting the votive offerings *in a row* by the side of the Ark. But the evidence is not sufficient to assure us of a variant reading here. 𝔖 ברגזחא evidently has the root רגז in mind and makes the sense *put them in reverence by its side*, for which some might argue. But if the author wished to give a warning of this kind he would connect it with the handling of the Ark, not with the votive offerings alone. It should be noted that the word ארגז occurs in vs.¹¹·¹⁵ both of which are late insertions into the narrative. — מצדו] the Torah roll was also to be put *by the side* of the Ark, Dt. 31²⁶. — **9.** דרך גבולו] *in the direction of his own territory*, cf. Ex. 13¹⁷ Num. 21³³ I S. 13¹⁸. On the site of Beth Shemesh, the modern *Ain Shems*, cf. GAS. *Geog.* p. 219, Lagarde, *OS.* p. 237; Rob. *BR²*. II. p. 233 ff.

10. The advice adopted ; the cart is made and the kine are yoked. — **11.** *And they placed the Ark of Yahweh on the cart*] the rest of the verse seems to be a late insertion. The variations in the text of 𝔊 show that different attempts were made to conform its text to 𝔚. The interest of the original narrator is in the behaviour of the cattle, and he passes over the subordinate matters. — **12.** *And the kine took a straight course on the Beth Shemesh road ; in the highway they went, lowing as they went, and did not turn to the right hand or the left*] the apparent redundancy is due to the author's desire to make the miracle plain. The lowing of the kine shows their natural desire to return to their calves. The Tyrants followed as far as the Beth Shemesh line. — **13.** At this time the people of Beth Shemesh were engaged in *harvesting the wheat in the valley* up which the Ark came. At such times the whole village goes forth to the field. *They lifted up their eyes and saw*] a form of detailed description common in Hebrew. *And came rejoicing to meet it*] should be read with 𝔊. — **14.** The Ark came *to the field of Joshua the Beth-shemshite and stood still*] this is an important item, as the stopping indicated the will of Yahweh as to his abiding place. For the next clause we should probably read : *and they set there a great stone*] as an altar, *and they split the wood of the cart and offered the kine as a burnt-offering to Yahweh*] an appropriate welcome. Araunah also offers the implements of the oxen for wood, and the oxen themselves as sacrifices, 2 S. 24²². — **15.** The

verse is superfluous, [16] joins directly to [14]. The Ark has already
been lifted from the cart — this we know because the cart has been
burnt. The burnt offering has been offered. The only reason for
the verse is found in the mention of the *Levites*. A late editor or
scribe could not reconcile the free handling of the Ark by the
men of Beth Shemesh with the legal prescription, and therefore
inserted the Levites. These are utterly foreign to our whole narrative up to this point. Yet they alone (on the later theory) were
empowered to touch the sacred things, not only the Ark but the
chest and its contents. Hence the insertion. It is possible also
that the author did not like the *great stone*, and so made it in this
verse only the pedestal for the Ark. — **16**. The five Tyrants
having seen their object attained *returned to Ekron the same day.*
— **17**. The verse (with [18a]) is another late insertion, a recapit-
ulation after the method of the Priestcode and the Chronicler.
It is free with its gold, according to the precedent set by these
writers, for it is doubtful whether the original author contemplated golden mice for all the cities, towns, and hamlets of the
Philistines. — **18**. The first half should be omitted with the preceding verse. The rest seems to affirm : *Witness is the great
stone by which they set the Ark of Yahweh ; to the present day it is
in the field of Joshua the Beth-shemshite*] other memorial stones,
Gen. 31[52] Jos. 24[27].

11. אל] for על as so often. — [ואת הארגז . . . טחריהם the half verse is not
objectionable on the ground of Hebrew style as is shown by Dr., *Notes*. But
comparison of the copies of 𝕲 shows so many variations, in the words and in
their arrangement, that we must suppose the original 𝕲 to have been supplemented in various ways to bring it into harmony with 𝕳. טחריהם in the text
is also an indication of interpolation, for the original narrative has עפליכ as the
name of the plague; though some MSS. here conform to the usage elsewhere,
reading עפליהם in the *Kt*. We. strikes out all but ואת הארגז; Bu. remands the
whole to the margin. — **12**. The construction is not free from difficulty. —
[וישרנה older form of the third person feminine plural, Ges[26]. § 47 *k*; Böttcher
sees in it a dual, *Lehrbuch*, § 931 *B*. The form is Qal with assimilation of the י.
This stem, however, means *to be straight* or *to be right*, whereas to *go in a
straight path* is expressed in Hebrew by a Piel or Hiphil, Prov. 9[15] 15[21]. It
does not seem violent therefore to change here to וַיְשַׁרְנָה, though analogous
verbs are followed by the direct object or by the infinitive with ל, cf. Ex. 8[24]
2 S. 15[14]. Possibly בדרך is an error for דרכן which we expect. — [כמסלה אחת
the *one* highway implies that various others were within reach. A מסלה is a

road made by throwing up the earth. — הלך וגעו] the adverbial clause describing continuous action, Gen. 8⁵ 12⁹ Jos. 6⁹ 2 S. 3¹⁶. — **13.** בית שמש is here put for the inhabitants and followed by the plural, cf. Hos. 5⁸, הריעו בית און.— ויצאו את־עיניהם ויראו] the phrase occurs in the Hexateuch several times, always in JE, but in both J and E, e.g., Gen. 13¹⁰·¹⁴ (J) 31¹⁰·¹² (E), also in Jd. 19¹⁷ (assigned to J) 2 S. 18²⁴ Jer. 3² 13²ᵛ Is. 49¹⁸ 60⁴ Zech. 5¹·⁵. The prophetic passages are all in the imperative, in which the detailed expression is easily accounted for. — לראות] εἰς ἀπάντησιν αὐτῆς 𝕲 points to לקראתו which should be restored, cf. Jd. 19³ (We.). — **14.** והעמר שם ושם] καὶ ἔστησαν ἐκεῖ παρ' αὐτῇ 𝕲ᴮ evidently renders ויעמידו שם עמה. It is not impossible that the original had both verbs : _it stayed and they placed there by it_ = ותעמד ויעמידו שם עמו, and that one verb dropped from one recension and the other from the other — or is שם ושם an original שם שם וישימו which became illegible?— אבן גדולה] it is conjectured by Bu. that the stone was set up as a _maççebah_. But the immediate context favours an altar. The proximity of the Ark and the necessity of offering sacrifices in its honour argue for an altar. Doubtless a _maççeba_ would be set up as soon as the dwelling of Yahweh should be arranged. A case strictly parallel does not occur. Jacob's stone was a _maççeba_ according to E (Gen. 28¹⁸·²²), but it was destined to mark a permanent sanctuary, and the same is true of the _maççeba_ in Gilead, Gen. 31⁴⁵ (E). A memorial stone was raised by Joshua, 24²⁶ᶠ·, and the same was done by Samuel at Ebenezer according to a late passage, 1 S. 7¹². Saul's altar, 14³³, is more like the account in our text than any other mention of a stone. Various heaps of stones are mentioned as memorials, but present no close resemblance, at least in the recension of the Old Testament which is in our hands. — **15.** The glossatory character of the verse is pointed out by We. —אל] 16 MSS. have על which alone is in place. — **17.** כחרי] is evidence of interpolation, as already shown. — **18.** וְעַד אבל] makes no sense. The _meadow_ (if it were allowable to translate so) in which the Ark rested could not be one of the villages of the Philistines. For אבל read אבן, with 𝕲, and point the other word וְעַד as was first suggested by We. The emendation is accepted by so valiant a defender of the traditional text as Keil. The insertion of the article before אבן seems to be unnecessary.

19. The verse affirms that Yahweh smote some of the people. The received text seems to give as a reason that _they looked upon the Ark._ There is, however, no other indication that this author thought it sinful to look upon the Ark. Had he thought so, he would have shown what precautions were taken by the Israelites before the battle to prevent this profanation, and would for this cause have aggravated the plague sent upon the Philistines. 𝕲 has a whole clause which has fallen out of 𝔐 and which relieves the difficulty : _The sons of Jeconiah did not rejoice with the men_ *of Beth Shemesh when they looked upon the Ark of Yahweh*] by adopting this we avoid the awkward repetition of the word translated *and he smote*, which in 𝔥 comes at the beginning of the verse, as well as at the beginning of the next clause : *And he smote among them seventy men*] the anger of Yahweh was not always easy to account for. Such an occasion for it as the indifference of the sons of Jeconiah is not stranger than some others of which we have a record. To the *seventy* men, the present text adds ungrammatically *fifty thousand men* — doubtless a gloss. The various attempts to explain the words scarcely deserve attention. The oldest is that of the Targum, which renders *seventy men of the elders and fifty thousand of the congregation*. Kimchi represents the traditional interpretation to be *seventy men, of the worth of fifty thousand*. Kimchi's own theory is that asyndetically the expression means simply fifty thousand and seventy men. — **20.** The people ask two questions, the first indicative of their fear — *who is able to stand before Yahweh this holy God ?* The holiness of Yahweh is his apartness from the world. This makes it impossible to approach him except after special ceremonial preparation, and his displeasure is fatal to those who approach him without that preparation (consecration). The question of the Beth-Shemshites shows their despair of meeting Yahweh's requirements. They regard his presence as a constant source of danger to them. The second question is a practical one : *To whom shall he go up from us ?*] the verb indicates that some place in the hill country was to be chosen. — **21.** The place chosen is *Kirjath Jearim*. The name evidently means *City of Thickets*. It is mentioned in Jos. 15⁹, where it is identified with Baalah ; in Jos. 15⁶⁰ it is called Kirjath Baal, cf. 18¹⁴. Eusebius * places it ten (or nine) miles from Jerusalem on the road to Lydda. It is not yet certainly identified with any existing site. Probably the name Kirjath Baal indicates that the town was already a sanctuary. On this account the men of Beth Shemesh chose it as the place of the Ark, and the people of Kirjath Jearim found it natural that they should have such an offer made them. — **VII. 1.** They therefore came and brought up the Ark, *and*

---

* *OS.* 234, 95 and 271, 40.

E

brought it to the house of Abinadab] of whom we know nothing further. The house was situated *on the hill* on which the town was built. To provide an appropriate attendant, *they consecrated Eleazar his son to keep the Ark*] nothing is said of his belonging to the priestly family or tribe.

19. ויך] anticipates unpleasantly the next clause: καὶ οὐκ ἠσμένισαν οἱ υἱοὶ Ἰεχονίου 𝕲. As the Greek verb does not occur elsewhere in the Old Testament, we are left to surmise its original. Kl.'s conjecture ולא הדו בני יכניהו is probably correct (adopted by Bu.), cf. Ex. 18⁹ Ps. 21⁷. — בעם] should be corrected to בהם with 𝕲. — חמשים אלף איש] the words are a late insertion, apparently unknown to Josephus, and recognized as a gloss by Keil. Whether they were a marginal note, intended to remind the reader of the later plague (2 S. 24) where seventy thousand fell, cannot be determined. — ויתאבלו] Gen. 37³⁴ Ex. 33⁴ (E). הכה מכה גדולה occurs Jos. 10¹⁰ Jd. 11³³ (also ascribed to E). — **20.** On the idea of holiness, cf. WRSmith, *Religion of the Semites*, p. 135, Smend, *Alttestamentliche Religionsgeschichte*, p. 333, Duhm's *Commentary on Isaiah*, 1⁴. — **21.** On the site of Kirjath Jearim, Moore on Jd. 18¹², GAS. *Geog.* p. 226. The essay of Poels, *Le Sanctuaire de Kirjath-Jearim* (Louvain, 1894), is a harmonistic attempt to identify Kirjath Jearim, Gibeon, Gibeah, and Mizpah, and so to show that the law of a single sanctuary was in force in the time of Samuel.

VII. 2–17. Samuel delivers the people. — During the time of the sojourn of the Ark at Kirjath Jearim, Samuel turns the attention of the people to the need of repentance. At his exhortation they put away the strange gods. A great assembly is called at Mizpah, where the people openly confess their sins. The Philistines take occasion to invade the country, but at Samuel's prayer Yahweh interferes and throws them into confusion; so they become an easy prey to Israel. The victory, which is commemorated by a memorial stone, is so complete that the Philistines do not invade the country again all the days of Samuel. Samuel is established as supreme magistrate of the people.

The contradiction between the statements here made and what we know of the actual history is complete. The conquests of Saul and David are here attributed to Samuel, who occupies the position of the theocratic ruler — comparable only to Moses. The author's theory of history is like that of the Deuteronomistic editor of the Book of Judges — if possible more mechanical than his. The people are enslaved because they have worshipped

strange gods.   No sooner do they return to Yahweh than he
returns to them and delivers them.   The deliverance is accomplished by a miraculous intervention.   No human warrior (like
the Judges) is needed.   For this reason we may assume that the
section is even later than the pragmatic framework of the Book of
Judges.   That it is later than the preceding chapters of the life of
Samuel seems evident.   The call of Samuel, at any rate, is
designed to establish him as a prophet rather than as judge and
ruler.   That this chapter was composed with a view to what precedes seems, however, plain enough ; and equally plain that it
was originally designed to ignore Saul altogether.

In Jer. 15¹ we find Yahweh saying: "Though Moses and Samuel should
stand before me, my soul would not be towards this people."   Co. (*Einl*³. p.
99) argues that Jeremiah has our present account in mind and the reasoning
is adopted by Bu. (*RS.* p. 178) and Dr. (*LOT*⁶. p. 178).   The coördination
of Moses and Samuel is undoubtedly striking.   But Jeremiah's conception of
them seems to be that they were prophets like himself — for it is his own
intercession which is rejected and the rejection justified by the mention of his
predecessors.   The passage does not prove more than the existence of a tradition of Samuel's prophetic activity.   The present narrative seems to represent
a more advanced stage of theocratic theory.

2. The intention of the verse is evidently to say that from the
time of the Ark's return the people received a new impulse.
Unfortunately the main verb is obscure and probably corrupt.
We should probably read : *From the day the Ark dwelt at Kirjath
Jearim all the house of Israel turned after Yahweh*⌉ the inserted
clause : *the days were many and became twenty years* is probably
secondary. — **3.** *If with all your heart*⌉ the clause is put first for
emphasis. The passages in which it occurs are comparatively late,
Dt. 11¹³ 13⁴ Jos. 22⁵ 1 Sam. 12²⁴ Jer. 29¹³ Joel 2¹². *You are* [now]
returning to Yahweh⌉ the expression betrays the same conception
which is contained in the phrase *strange gods* which follows, cf. Dt.
31¹⁶ Jer. 5¹⁹ Jos. 24²⁰. *The Ashtaroth* seem an afterthought here,
as in some other passages. The word is the plural of the name
which in the Old Testament is vocalized (probably wrongly) as
Ashtoreth. The well-known goddess of the Canaanites (properly
Astarte) is elsewhere associated with Baal.   An Astarte of the
Philistines is mentioned 1 Sam. 31¹⁰.   *And prepare your heart*

towards Yahweh your God] a late formula, 2 Chr. 12¹⁴ 20³³ 30¹⁹ Ezr. 7¹⁰. *And serve him*] that is *worship him*, in this sense the word is Deuteronomic. *That he may deliver you*] the form of the verb indicates that this is the purpose of the preceding imperatives. — **4.** The preaching is effectual : *The Sons of Israel put away the Baals*] the word is used as equivalent to the *foreign gods* above. — **5.** Samuel announces a general assembly at *Mizpah*] doubtless the same place afterwards occupied by Gedaliah as the capital of the country, Jer. 40. It is identified, since Robinson, with *Neby Samwil*, a prominent hill five miles north of Jerusalem. The place is a sanctuary (or *the* sanctuary) also in Jd. 20¹. — **6.** The assembly engages in public expression of sorrow for sin : *They drew water and poured it before Yahweh*] a rite not elsewhere mentioned. It must be symbolical of contrition. Fasting, which is the second, observance mentioned, is elsewhere expressive of sorrow. *We have sinned in relation to Yahweh*] Dt. 1⁴¹ Jd. 10¹⁰. That Samuel *judged* the people in Mizpah is probably to be taken in the sense in which other rulers are said to *judge*. He heard the cause of the oppressed and secured their rights.

2. ויֵרְבּוּ הַיָּמִים וַיִּהְיוּ עֶשְׂרִים שָׁנָה] the only way we can fit the words into the present text is by making them a parenthesis, and even then it is more natural to say הַיָּמִים רַבּוּ וגו׳. It seems that the whole sentence is a gloss, not merely וַיִּהְיוּ עֶשְׂרִים שָׁנָה (Bu.). Possibly, however, it is a corruption of something which cannot now be recovered. 𝔊ᴸ ἐν εἰρήνῃ is confirmed by Ḷ, and may point to some statement about Shiloh. — וַיִּנָּהוּ] gives no suitable meaning. The verb means *to lament for the dead*, Mic. 2⁴ Ez. 32¹⁸. But the return of Yahweh could not be an occasion for such mourning. 𝔊ᴬᴮ has ἐπέβλεψεν, 𝔊ᴸ καὶ ἐπέστρεψε, both which point to וַיִּפֶן. 𝕮 conjectures only, as is shown by Dr., and 𝔖𝕷 seem to have read וַיֵּנַחוּ (Cappel, *Critica Sacra*, p. 364). It seems best, with Ew., Bu., to adopt the reading of 𝔊. — **3.** אִם־בְּכָל־לְבַבְכֶם] the phrase occurs in D frequently, usually with the addition of וּבְכָל נַפְשׁ. On the literary usage which shows לֵבָב (not לֵב) to be the form characteristic of E, D, and Deuteronomistic editors, cf. BDB.; *s. v.* — הָסִירוּ אֶת־אֱלֹהֵי הַנֵּכָר] the phrase occurs Gen. 35² Jos. 24²³ Jd. 10¹⁶, all which are assigned to E² by recent editors, cf. also 2 Chr. 33¹⁵. — אֱלֹהֵי הַנֵּכָר are *gods of foreign countries*, like בְּנֵי הַנֵּכָר *men of foreign countries*. — **4.** הַבְּעָלִים] cf. Jd. 2¹¹. ¹³, where also the Baals and Astartes are the gods and goddesses of the heathen, see Moore's note. On Baal, Baudissin in *PRE*³. II. p. 323 ff., WRS., *Rel. Sem.* p. 92 ff. The god and goddess are mentioned together by Eshmunazar in his inscription, l. 18. On Astarte, Baudissin, *PRE*³. II. p. 147 ff., and of the older literature, Selden, *De Diis Syris*, II. 2. — **5.** המצפתה] the name, which means *the watchtower*, generally has the article. On the identification, cf. Robinson, *BR²*. I. p. 460, Buhl, *Geog.* p. 168. — **6.** וישפכו] 𝔊 adds *on the ground*. Such phrases are easily inserted, and therefore suspicious. — שם] lacking in 𝔊𝔖 must be exscinded for the same reason.

7. *The Philistines heard that Israel had assembled*] the opportunity for plundering an unwarlike company was not to be lost. Josephus correctly understands that the people had come without arms. — **8.** Israel has recourse to spiritual weapons : *Do not be silent, so as not to cry to Yahweh thy God*] cf. Ps. 28¹ Job 13¹³; *thy God* 𝔊 seems more appropriate than *our God* 𝔐. Several MSS. of 𝔊 add at the end of the verse : *And Samuel said : Far be it from me to refrain from crying to Yahweh my God for you.* — **9.** In his worship Samuel *took a sucking lamb*] no emphasis is to be laid (as some have supposed) on the comparative insignificance of the offering. A lamb of the first year is enjoined as the regular burnt offering in Ex. 29³⁸ᶠᶠ· Lev. 23¹² Num. 6¹⁴. *And offered it as a whole burnt offering to Yahweh*] the burnt offering is the present with which one approaches the divine king. To Samuel's prayer, Yahweh *answers* by audible voice, as is more fully set forth in the next verse, cf. Ex. 19¹⁹. — **10.** While Samuel *was engaged in offering the burnt offering*, the Philistines advanced to the attack. *But Yahweh thundered with a great voice that day against the Philistines and routed them*] cf. Jd. 4¹⁵ and its poetical parallel, 5²⁰· ²¹. In the present passage the interference of Yahweh is so pronounced that the rout begins before any active effort is made by Israel. At the battle of Bethhoron, where Yahweh routed the Canaanites by casting great stones from heaven upon them (Jos. 10¹¹), the Israelites were an armed force, as they were at the Kishon. The interference of Yahweh for his people by thunder and lightning is a not uncommon feature of poetic theophanies, 2 S. 22¹⁴ 1 S. 2¹⁰ Is. 66⁶. Cf. also Ps. 68³⁴ 77¹⁹. — **11.** The people had only to pursue the flying foe, which they did *till below Beth Car*] the place is nowhere else mentioned, and the text has possibly suffered. — **12.** A memorial stone is set up *between Mizpah and Yeshana*] see the note on 6¹³. The name Yeshana here is restored from 𝔊 and 𝔖. The name in 𝔐 is probably corrupt. What follows in 𝔐 makes, further, a double difficulty, for

it says simply : *Hitherto has Yahweh helped us,* whereas it was
not only to this point that Yahweh had helped them, but beyond
it ; and, moreover, there is no declaration concerning the object
of setting up the stone.   Conjectural emendation gives us : *This
is a witness that Yahweh has helped us,* which alone is appropriate
in the context. — **13.** The Philistines *were subdued and came no
more into the border of Israel*] the extravagance of the statement
is evident. — **14.** *The cities which the Philistines had taken from
Israel were restored, from Ekron to Gath*] these two were nearest
the territory of Israel.   The author evidently means to include
Ekron and Gath in the list of those restored.   *The territory of
these* was also recovered, *and there was peace between Israel and
the Amorite*] that is, the Canaanitish peoples. — Samuel's reign
(as we may call it) lasted as long as he lived. — **16.** His custom
was to go about to the principal places, — Bethel, Gilgal, and
Mizpah, all known as sanctuaries, — and *administer justice.* —
17. He officiated also at Ramah, his home, *and there he built an
altar to Yahweh*] the author does not take the view of the Priestcode as to the legitimacy of one sole altar.   To the Deuteronomic
view the one legitimate sanctuary was not chosen until the time
of Solomon.

7. התקבצו] with pluperfect force. — אל] is doubtless to be read or understood as על, which is the proper word when a hostile attack is described. —
8. מזעק] for the force of the preposition cf. his eyes were dim *from seeing,* i.e.,
so as not to see, Gen. 27¹. — **9.** טלה] a rare and apparently late word, Is. 40¹¹
65²⁵. — ויעלהו is doubtless to be read, with the *Qrê.* — כליל] describes the burnt
offering as *wholly consumed* upon the altar, Dt. 33¹⁰ Lev. 6¹⁵ f. — **10.** ויהי שמואל
מעלה] cf. the similar construction 2 K. 13²¹ 19³⁷. — ויהמם] the verb is used of
' striking with panic terror ' (Moore on Jd. 4¹⁵). — **11.** בית כר; 𝕿 reads *Beth
Sharon;* 𝕾 has *Beth Yeshan* as in v.¹²; Kl. suggests *Beth Horon.* — **12.** השן]
the word is appropriate for a sharp rock or peak.   In connection with Mizpah
we rather expect the name of a town, and this is given by 𝕲𝕾 who read הישנה,
evidently the Benjamite town mentioned 2 Chr. 13¹⁹.   This reading is adopted
by Graetz (*Gesch. der Juden,* I. p. 157) followed by most recent expositors. —
עד־הנה] is not explicit enough, whether the הנה be taken of space or time.
Wellhausen seems first to have discovered that the first word must be עד.   He
therefore restores עד היא כי, for which Bu. substitutes עדה תהי כי, which seems no
improvement. — **13.** ויכנעו] cf. Jd. 3³⁰ 11³³. — ולא־יספו עוד לבוא] 15³⁵ Jd. 13²¹.
— **14.** ותשבנה] there is no other instance of the active voice with *cities* as
the subject; perhaps we should read ותושבנה which is favoured by 𝕲, cf.

Jer. 27¹⁶. — *From Ekron to Gath*] 𝔊ᴮ has *from Ashkelon to Azob*. In *Azob* We. sees an allusion to Zeph. 2⁴. — **15**. וישפט] the allusion to the function of the judge as described in the Book of Judges is palpable. This author describes the activity in detail in what follows. — **16**. והלך] of customary action, Dav., *Syntax*, § 54 *R*, 1. — מדי שנה בשנו] is heavy, but is supported by Zech. 14¹⁶. סבב is used of going about to various places in order, 2 Chr. 17⁹. — את־ישראל את כל וגו׳] is tautological. It is probable that the scribe had in mind the את־ישראל of the verse below and inserted it here. — המקומות] 𝔊 had המקדש ס, which may possibly be original (Cappel, *Notae Criticae*, p. 434). — **17**. שפט] the pausal form seems unexplained, Ges²⁶. § 29 *i*, note.

VIII. **The demand for a king**. — In Samuel's old age he makes his sons judges, but they do not follow his example in their administration of the office. The people thereupon demand a king. The demand is offensive to Samuel and also to Yahweh, who describes it as rebellion against him and as in line with the people's customary depravity. Without hope of converting them, but as a testimony against their folly, Samuel describes the manner in which the king is likely to carry on his office. As was expected, the people persist in their demand, and Samuel is commanded to accede to it. The account as it now stands concludes with the dismission of the people, but was originally continued by the choice of a king by lot as now read in 10¹⁷⁻²⁷.

The section is homogeneous down to ²²ᵇ and directly continues the preceding account. It is also of late date. In fact, it is hardly conceivable that the conception of the monarchy as essentially evil and in itself a revolt from the theocracy could have arisen before the fall of Jerusalem. For, however bad the individual kings of the house of David might be, there was always a hope (well illustrated by Isaiah) that the ideal government would come to view in the reign of a righteous king. The phrase *manner of the kingdom* used in this passage has reminded most critics of the similar phrase in Deuteronomy (17¹⁴⁻²⁰), and some have argued that this passage was anterior to that. But on comparison it is seen that the abuses held up by Samuel here are not touched upon in Deuteronomy. Nothing is there said about impressing the people for forced labour and taking their property without compensation, which are the evils here made prominent. Had the author of Deuteronomy known our passage, he could hardly have refrained from legislating against these abuses. And it cannot be argued, on the other hand, that our author, if later, would have shown his dependence on Deuteronomy, for the abuses there forbidden — multiplying horses, taking many wives, and accumulating treasure — could not be effective as an argument with the people.

Stade places the section later than Jeremiah and Ezekiel. Wellhausen gives the argument summarized above in favour of a date posterior to the Judaic monarchy (*Comp.* p. 246). Bu. argues for priority of this as compared with Deut. (*RS.* p. 184), and is followed by Co. at least in the earlier editions of his *Einleitung*.

1–5. The occasion of the demand. — When Samuel became old, *he appointed his sons judges for Israel.* — **2**. That both should be settled at Beersheba is surprising, and two places were probably named originally. Josephus gives *one in Bethel and one in Beersheba.* — **3**. The common experience of Orientals was illustrated : *they turned aside after gain and took bribes and wrested justice]* so far there seems ground for the complaint of the people. — **4**. The Sheikhs act for the people, as in 4³ Num. 16²⁵. — **5**. The desire for a king is here motived by the maladministration of justice. In v.²⁰ it is due to a desire for a leader in war.

6–9. The demand is sinful. — The view of the author is evidently that the theocracy is the divinely appointed constitution for Israel, and that the substitution of another form is treason to God. He does not seem to recognize that Samuel was chargeable with fault in not correcting the abuses of his sons' government, nor does he tell us how Yahweh would give them relief. Yahweh's prejudgment is on the side of Samuel, whose anger he shares. — **7**. The grievance of Samuel is adopted by Yahweh : *Hearken to the voice of the people according to what they keep saying]* the tense implies importunity. *For it is not thou whom they have rejected, but it is I whom they have rejected from being king over them]* the pronouns are made emphatic by their position. — **8**. The main sentence says : *Like all the deeds they have done to me . . . have they done to thee.* Parenthetically the deeds are described : *they have forsaken me and served other gods]* Jd. 2¹³ 10¹³ 1 K. 9⁹ (apparently Deuteronomistic). — **9**. The people are, however, to be left without excuse : *Thou shalt solemnly testify]* Gen. 43³

Jer. 11⁷ — *the method of the king who shall rule over them*] that
is, *his customary behaviour.* Yahweh will allow him, perhaps
authorize him, so to act.

1. שים is used of appointing officers, Dt. 17¹⁵ 2 S. 8¹⁴. — **2.** The statement
of Josephus cited above (*Ant.* VI. 32) is adopted by Graetz and Ewald. —
3. ברדכו *Kt,* ברדכיו *Qrê.* There seems no reason for preferring the latter except that usage is on the side of the plural. — ויטו] *turned aside from its
proper course,* Dt. 16¹⁹. בצע is generally used of unrighteous gain, Ex. 18²¹
Jer. 6¹³. — **4.** כל] is lacking in 𝕲ᴮ, which reads ἄνδρες for זקני. — **6.** וירע הדבר]
Gen. 21¹¹·¹² (E) 1 S. 18⁸ 2 S. 11²⁵·²⁷. — ויתפלל] cf. Jer. 32¹⁶ 42⁴. — **7.** For
לכל אשר we should perhaps read כאשר with 𝕲. — כי] assigns a reason why
Samuel should not hesitate — it was not a personal concern. — **8.** עשו] 𝕲
adds לי, which is adopted by most recent commentators. — ויעזבני] specifies the
acts intended by עשו.

10–18. The king's method. — Samuel repeated all the words
of Yahweh *to the people who were asking of him a king*] as though
he had one in his possession. — **11.** *This is the way of the king
who shall rule over you: Your sons he will take and place in his
chariots and among his horsemen, and they shall run before his
chariots*] the runners before the chariot continue in the East
down to the present day, and their office is an honourable one.
— **12.** *And he shall make them captains of thousands and captains
of hundreds*] reading with 𝕲. The author counts on very small
military ambition in Israel, a view which would argue for a late
date. The people would also be forced to plough and reap for the
king, *and to make his arms and his chariot furniture.* — **13.** The
women would not be exempt from conscription, but would be
compelled to serve *as perfumers*] perhaps we should read *as
embroiderers* with 𝕊 ; *and as cooks and as bakers*] of which the
king's kitchen would need many. — **14.** Oppression will affect
not only persons but also property ; fields and vineyards will be
seized and given to the king's servants. — **15.** Heavy taxes will be
laid : *Your grain fields and your vineyards he will tithe and give
the proceeds to his eunuchs and to his servants*] the Oriental thinks
of the king as wealthy enough to dispense with such methods of
raising money, which are therefore hated and resented. — **16.** He
would exact the service of their slaves and their *best cattle*] so
is to be read. — **17.** The tithing will be extended to sheep and
goats ; and the Israelites will be slaves instead of freemen. —

18. The result : *You shall cry out in that day on account of the king which you shall have chosen for yourselves*] the sting is in the fact that their misery will be self-inflicted. For this reason also, Yahweh will not answer.

10. ויאמר] is not frequent with the accusative, as here. — **11.** וירצו] for which 𝔊 seems to have read ירציכ, is doubtless original. — **12.** ולישום] the periphrastic infinitive is illustrated by Dr., *Tenses*[3], § 206 and and Dav., *Syntax*, § 94, R. 4. It should be noted that several of the examples cited are of suspicious integrity, the ו having arisen by duplication of a preceding י. In the present case, however, the reading seems to be confirmed by 𝔊. We assume an ellipsis of היו, the full form being היו לשום . *Captains of fifties* in 𝔐 is replaced by *captains of hundreds* in 𝔊, while 𝔖 has both, and adds *and captains of tens*. 𝔊 seems original. — **13.** לרקחות] *preparers of unguents*, of which the Orientals are notoriously fond. 𝔖 seems to translate לרקמוה, which would be equally appropriate. — לטבחוה] the cook is also the butcher. — **14.** ועבדיו־] Graetz conjectures (*Gesch. der Juden*, I. p. 164) that we should read יכניו, as the servants are spoken of in the next verse. There is, however, no external evidence for the reading. — **16.** ובחוריכם] καὶ τὰ βουκόλια ὑμῶν 𝔊, pointing to ובקריכם, which is undoubtedly original. The correction was made by Cappellus (*Critica Sacra*, p. 247). — ועשה למלאכתו] the only parallels are Lev. 7[24] Ez. 15[5]. We should expect לעשות במלאכתו, cf. I K. 5[30] 9[23]. The unusual construction led a scribe to substitute ועשר, which was read by 𝔊. — **17.** צאן is small cattle in distinction from neat cattle (בקר). — **18.** 𝔊 adds at the end of the verse : *Because you chose a king for yourselves*. This is at least correct interpretation.

19–22. The expostulation was fruitless : *The people refused to listen to the voice of Samuel and said : No ! But a king shall be over us*] this obstinacy is parallel to their treatment of Moses. — **20.** The reason here assigned for their desire is the example of foreign nations. *Our king shall judge us*] possibly in the sense of *vindicating* them, or of *delivering* them from their enemies. But as the account begins with the miscarriage of civil justice, the author may have this still in mind. The administration of justice was always a prominent function of the king. Fighting his people's battles was also his work. This author seems to forget that Samuel had secured them peace. — **21, 22ᵃ.** When the report of the people's continued demand is brought to Yahweh, he consents to gratify them : *Hearken to their voice and make a king rule over them.* — **22ᵇ.** The half verse is a later insertion. The original account joined 10[17] directly to 8[22a]. The compiler was obliged to dismiss the people to their homes, in order to insert the following incident taken from another source.

19. On the Dagesh in לּא cf. Ges.[26], § 20 *g*, and Baer's dissertation *De primarum vocabulorum literarum dagessatione* prefixed to *Liber Proverbiorum*, ed. Baer et Delitzsch (1880). Some MSS. have לו in the text, while 𝕲 seems to have read לו לא. — **20.** וישפטנו] on the force of the verb cf. Moore's note on Jd. 3[10]. — מלחמתינו] is given by Ginsburg. Many editions and MSS. have מלחמתנו. For the phrase *go out before us* cf. Jd. 4[14]. — **22.** והמלכת] is the perfect with waw consecutive continuing the imperative. The second half of this verse, in which Samuel dismisses the people to their homes, is inserted to allow the inclusion of the following account in the narrative. The document we have just read originally made Samuel at once call an assembly at Mizpah, where a king is chosen by lot. This is recognized by most recent scholars.

IX. 1–X. 16. The adventure of Saul. — Saul, the son of Kish, is sent by his father to seek the asses which have strayed. He does not find them, but comes into contact with Samuel, who anoints him (secretly) as king over Israel.

After what has been said in the Introduction, it is needless to point out that we have here the beginning of a separate document, — a life of Saul, — which differs in all respects from the one we have just been considering. It is the earliest and most reliable of the sources which relate the origin of the monarchy in Israel.

1–4. Introduction of Saul, and occasion of the journey. — There was a man *of Gibeah of Benjamin*] so we should probably read. The place should be mentioned at the outset. Kish is described as a man of some position in the community : *a mighty man of valour* is more than the Hebrew intends to say. — **2.** He had a son named Saul *in the prime of life and goodly*] the words do not imply that he was in his adolescence ; and the same may be said of his position in the household, it does not imply immaturity. So long as his father lived he would be under his authority, and there is no necessary contradiction between the language used here and the later account, according to which Saul had a son already grown. The name of Saul is probably abbreviated from a longer form meaning *Asked-of-God*. The clause at the end of this verse is probably a late insertion. —

3. The asses belonging to Kish have strayed, and Saul is sent with one of the servants to seek them. — **4.** Correcting the number of the verbs by the versions, we get : *They passed through Mt. Ephraim and crossed into the land of Shalisha and did not find them, and they crossed into the land of Shaalim and they were not there, and they crossed into the land of Benjamin and did not find them]* the districts of Shalisha and Shaalim are not identified.

1. מבן־ימין] the fact that he was a Benjamite is related again at the end of the verse, and We.'s conjecture that we should read מגבעת בנימין is plausible. — בן־איש ימיני] is not without analogy, at least איש ימיני is found 2 S. 20¹ Est. 2⁵. But it is unusual to terminate a genealogy by saying *son of a Benjamite*. It is probable that בן is the error of a scribe who expected to continue the genealogy. — גבור חיל] the phrase seems to mean no more than *a man well to do;* cf. BDB., *s.v.* חיל. — **2.** משכמו וגו׳] the clause recurs in 10²³, where it is entirely appropriate (at Saul's first appearance in public). Here it seems to have come in from there by a late hand (Bu.). — **3.** האתנות] the she-asses seem to have been especially prized, Job 1³. — לקיש] cf. Dav., *Syntax,* § 28, R. 5. — נא] after the imperative softens the command. — את־אחד] is unusual, perhaps a scribal error; but a precisely similar instance is found Num. 16¹⁵. אחד is pointed in both cases as a construct and might be regarded as made definite by this relation, König, *Syntax,* § 288 f.; cf. also Dav., *Syntax,* 72, R. 4. — נערים is used of servants not infrequently. At the end of this verse 𝕲ᴸ𝕾 add : *and Saul arose and took one of the servants of his father and went to seek the asses of Kish his father* — one of the rather numerous instances of agreement of 𝕲ᴸ with 𝕾. — **4.** The verbs which are partly singular and partly plural in 𝕳 should be all plural as in 𝕲. For *Shalisha* and *Shaalim* the versions give a confusing variety of equivalents, but none which help us to a better text. A *Baal Shalisha* is mentioned in the region of Samaria 2 K. 4⁴². *Shaalim* has been conjectured to be an error for *Shaalabim* mentioned in connection with Beth Shemesh, Jd. 1³⁵ 1 K. 4⁹. It seems easier to combine with the ארץ שועל of 13¹⁷.

5. The verse indicates that they had planned further search when Saul suddenly proposes to abandon the effort : *They had come into the land of Zuph]* a part of Benjamin — *when Saul said . . . : Let us return, lest my father cease thinking of the asses and be anxious about us]* the verb means *to have fears,* Jer. 17⁸ 38¹⁹ 42¹⁶ Is. 57¹¹. — **6.** The servant has a different idea : *There is a man of God in this city; and the man is honoured, all that he says surely comes true]* the title *man of God* is frequent in the account of Elijah and Elisha. The commendation of the seer is to induce Saul to apply to him for an indication : *Perchance he may tell us the way on which we came out*] the journey is not yet complete, and we may yet be rightly directed. What they want is guidance in order to complete the mission on which they have started. — **7.** Saul objects that to approach a great man a present is necessary, and this is not at hand : *And suppose we go, what shall we bring the man ?* The question is raised which confronts them if they agree to carry out the plan of the servant. *The bread is gone from our sacks*] this would suffice if there were any, cf. 10⁴. The rest of the verse is obscure. — **8.** The servant relieves the difficulty. He has *a quarter of a shekel of money*] a small coin containing about sixty grains of silver, but proportionately much more valuable then than now. *And thou shalt give it to the man of God*] a slight change of the text is necessary, as Saul must be the giver. — **9.** The verse tells us that the *prophet of to-day was formerly called a seer.* It interrupts the connexion here, however, and seems to be a marginal note which has crept into the text. — **10.** The objection being met, Saul consents : *And they went to city where the man of God was*] the city is intended by the editor to be Ramah. The original account, however, may have named another place.

5. צוּף] cf. 1¹. 𝕿 connects it fancifully with צפה and translates: *the land in which was the prophet.* — **6.** הנה־נא] cf. Gen. 12¹¹ 1 K. 22¹⁸; the phrase invites favourable consideration of the proposition which follows. — For the imperfects of repeated experience cf. Dav., *Syntax*, § 44 a, Dr., *Tenses*³, § 33 a. — **7.** והנה] the case at first sight seems to be one where we should expect הן *if.* But cf. BDB. *sub voce.* — תשורה] occurs only here; the versions are at a loss, and the word is possibly corrupt. Cappellus (*Notae Criticae*, p. 435) supposes 𝕾 to have read השארה. We expect *and we have nothing else to bring.* But this cannot be got out of the text. — מה אתנו] also is abrupt and awkward (some Hebrew editions have ומה). I therefore suspect corruption too deep-seated to be healed. — **8.** ונתתי] 𝕾 seems to have read ונתתָ, but it is better to correct to ונתתו (Kl.), which will more readily account for the corruption. — **9.** In v.⁶ Samuel has been called איש אלהים, on which see the note to 2²⁷. The verse now before us calls him a Seer (ראה), a word used twice by Isaiah (28⁷ 30¹⁰), elsewhere only in this passage and in Chronicles (1 Chr. 9²² 26²⁸ 29²⁹, dependent on the account before us, and 2 Chr. 16⁷· ¹⁰ where it is applied to Hanani). The rarity of the word led a scribe to insert this verse as an explanation, which, however, has fallen into the wrong place; it belongs after v.¹¹. The conception of the prophet (נביא) which it betrays

is that of a clairvoyant to whom one may come for the discovery of lost articles.   On the bearing of the gloss on questions of criticism cf. Briggs, *Higher
Criticism of the Hexateuch*[2], p. 150. — לפנים] occurs Dt. 2[10]. — יקרא] the
tense indicates what was customary in the past.

11. *As they were going up the ascent of the city*] cf. 2 S. 15[30],
they met maidens coming out to draw water] the usual duty of the
young women of the village, as we see from the case of Rebecca
Gen. 24[15f.]   One well or spring supplied the whole village. —
12. To the inquiry of Saul whether the Seer is here, they answer :
He is ! Behold he is before you. Just now he came to the city.
The rest of the verse explains the situation more distinctly : *For
the people have a sacrifice today on the Bamah*] at this period of
Israel's history each town had its sanctuary on a hill in the vicinity.   Hence the name *high-place.*   This one had a building for
the accommodation of the worshippers. — **13.** *As soon as you
come to the city you shall find him, before he goes up to the Bamah
to eat*] the sacrifice is a feast — " the essential rite was eating the
flesh of the victim at a feast in which the god of the clan shared
by receiving the blood and fat pieces " (BDB).   The importance
of Samuel is such that *the people will not eat until he comes, for he
is to bless the sacrifice*] it should be noted, however, that blessing
the sacrifice is not a priestly function, and there is no ritual necessity for Samuel's presence. — **14.** The two strangers follow the
advice ; but as they come into the city gate Samuel comes out
towards them on his way to the Bamah. — **15.** The verse is a
digression, showing how Samuel had been prepared for the interview : Yahweh had told Samuel] lit., *had uncovered his ear*, cf.
20[12f.] 22[8. 17] 2 S. 7[27]. — **16.** *About this time to-morrow*] Ex. 9[18] (J)
I K. 19[2] 20[6].   *Thou shalt anoint him prince over my people Israel*]
the word translated *prince* (נגיד) is not used in Hexateuch or
Judges, but is found several times in Samuel and Kings, I S. 10[1]
13[14] 25[30] 2 S. 5[2] 6[21] 7[8] I K. 1[35], etc.   It is also found in Chronicles,
which is probably influenced by the earlier books, and in some
other late passages.   The passages in Samuel seem to belong to
the same stream of narrative, except 2 S. 7[8].   *And he shall save
my people from the hand of the Philistines*] the sentence is a
direct contradiction of 7[11ff.].   *For I have seen the affliction of my
people*] the text of 𝕲.   The evident view of the author is that

the king is a gift of God, and not that there is sin in asking such a gift : *For their cry is come to me*] Ex. 3⁹. We may note that anointing is a rite of consecration for things, as Jacob's *maç-çebah*, Gen. 31¹³ (E), the Tabernacle, Ex. 40⁹ (P), as well as persons, 1 K. 19¹⁶ (prophets). There is no reason to suppose the significance any different in the case of kings. — **17.** When Samuel saw Saul *Yahweh answered him*] that is, the question raised in his mind : *Behold the man of whom I said to thee : He shall rule over my people.* — **18, 19.** Saul questions Samuel : *Where is the house of the Seer?* Samuel replies to the intent of the question rather than its form : *I am the Seer : go before me to the Bamah*] he politely gives Saul precedence. *In the morning I will dismiss thee*] the guest goes away with the permission of his host. *All that is in thine heart*] implies that Saul had more questions to ask than those about the asses ; moreover, this one is answered at once, without waiting for the morrow. — **20.** Saul's mind is set at rest *concerning the asses that strayed now three days ago*] and more important matters are hinted at : *To whom belong the desirable things of Israel? Is it not to thee and to thy father's house?* The meaning cannot be called certain. But it does not seem out of place that Saul's ambition should be raised to the office within his reach. — **21.** Saul's answer shows becoming modesty : *Am I not a Benjamite, of the least of the tribes of Israel, and is not my clan the least of all the clans of the tribe of Benjamin?* The assertion (put in the form of a question) must not be taken too literally. Saul's father, as we have already seen, was a man of standing in the community.

11. עלים הַמָּה] the circumstantial clause, Dav., *Syntax* § 141. In some cases the clause is followed by והנה, which is read by 𝔊ᴸ here. — בָזֶה] *in this place* as Ex. 24¹⁴ (E). — **12.** לִפְנֶיךָ מהר] why they should *hasten* is not clear. As pointed out by Lagarde (*Anm. zur Griechischen Uebersetz d. Proverbien*, p. iii) 𝔊 read לפניכם, which he supposed to imply that מהר was made up of the final letter of לפניכם and the first two of הראה. This last word, however, is not represented in 𝔊, and it seems better to read לפניכם הוא (Bu.). — כִּי הַיוֹם] better כהיום, with 𝔊 (We.) cf. Gen. 25³¹ 1 Sam. 2¹⁶. — **13.** אחרי־כן] some MSS. and edd. prefix ו. — כהיום] the form we have restored above. On the repetition of the accusative cf. Dr., *Tenses* ³, § 197. 6. Of the examples cited, 2 K. 9²⁷ seems the only exact parallel. — **14.** באים . . . יצא] the participles indicate the flow of events — they were *just coming* into the city gate when Samuel met them. בתוך העיר was conjecturally emended to בתוך השער by Th., and the emendation is adopted by most moderns, being confirmed by v.[18]. The received text makes no difficulty, as the village was probably small and compact and the two men would soon reach the centre of it. But as it is necessary to read alike in the two verses it seems better to restore השער here than העיר in v.[18] (Kl.). — **15.** גלה] with pluperfect force, Dr., *Tenses*[3], § 76, *Obs.;* Dav., *Syntax*, § 39 c. — **16.** ראיתי את־עמי] 𝔊𝔗 read ראיתי את־עני עמי, which is evidently original, cf. Ex. 3[7] (E) 2 K. 14[26]. On the meaning of the verb משח cf. an article by Meinel, *ZATW*. XVIII. p. I ff. — **17.** אשר אמרתי] *concerning whom I said;* a similar expression in v.[23] Gen. 3[17] Jd. 7[4]. — עצר] the verb nowhere else has the meaning *to rule*. It means to *shut up* (the heavens) Dt. 11[17], *to restrain* (an animal) 2 K. 4[24], *to check* (one's words) Job 4[2]. But such a meaning seems inappropriate here, and we must suspect the text. Kl. proposes ישר on the ground of ἄρξει 𝔊[AB]: καταρξει 𝔊[L], cf. Jd. 9[22] Is. 32[1]. — **18.** את־שמואל] the verb is generally found with אל, — unless Num. 4[19] be an exception, — and this preposition should probably be restored here. — אי־זה] seems to imply that the object sought is in the immediate vicinity, cf. I K. 13[12]. — **19.** 𝔊 has *I am he* instead of *I am the Seer*. — ואכלתם] the preceding verb is in the singular, addressed to Saul alone, so that we should restore ואכלת here. — **20.** הימים] We. and Bu. omit the article. But as the prophet has in mind the particular three days which have just elapsed, the article seems in place. Cf. Lev. 25[21]: *it shall produce a crop sufficient for the three years* — לשלש השנים — where we must understand *the three years you have in mind*, for they have not been described. — **20.** כל] is omitted both times by 𝔊. — חמדת] the two possible translations are represented in *the desire* of Israel (AV.) and [all] *that is desirable in Israel* (RV.). The latter is favoured by 𝔊 and adopted by Kl., Dr., Ki., and by the analogy of Hag. 2[7], where, however, we should read a plural (and so possibly here). — **21.** מקטני] occasional instances occur of an ancient construct ending in י (Jd. 20[12] cited by We.). Such a form may be represented in the second שבטי (instead of שבט). "The construction with מן is sometimes virtually a superlative." Dav., *Syntax*, § 34. R. 4.

22-25. Saul is Samuel's guest. — The *room* into which they are brought is apparently a hall built for the express use of worshippers at the Bamah, in their sacrificial feasts. Saul and his servant are given the place of honour *at the head of the guests*. The simplicity of manners is indicated by the equal treatment of Saul and his servant. There were present about thirty men, probably the heads of families or the freemen of the village. — **23.** Saul's coming had been anticipated, as we see by Samuel's command to the cook : *Bring the portion which I gave to thee, concerning which I said to thee : Set it by thee*] in Arabia also it was customary to set aside a choice portion for an honoured guest.* — **24.** In obedience to the command the cook *lifted the leg and the rump*] the choice part of the sacrifice, and the one still regarded as the portion of honour by the fellahin. The rest of the verse is obscure and apparently corrupt. It says : *Behold what is left*] but it is almost certain that the guests had not begun the meal until Samuel appeared. And the clause : *For it was kept for thee to the time appointed, saying, the people I have called*] is nonsense. With due reserve I propose below an emendation which gives the sense : *Behold, the meal is served! Eat! For to the appointed time we have waited for thee to eat with the guests*] if this, or something like it, were the original reading, we see that Samuel had directed the villagers to wait for his coming, which was of course politeness to his guest. — **25.** After the feast, *they came from the Bamah to the city, and they spread a bed for Saul on the roof, and he lay down*] the text of the last clause 𝔐 is here also unintelligible (in this context), and must be corrected by 𝔊. For sleeping on the roof, we have abundant examples in modern Oriental life, though no other Old Testament example has come under my observation. The verse-division should include the first word of the following verse with this.

22. לשכתה] the לשכה is a chamber in a palace, Jer. 36¹², or in the temple, Jer. 35²⁻⁴; one was also in use at Shiloh according to 1 Sam. 1¹⁸ 𝔊. — הקרואים] *those invited, the guests.* — כשלשים] ὡσεὶ ἑβδομήκοντα 𝔊. The larger number is the less likely to be original. — **23.** לטבח] cf. 8¹³. — המנה] 1⁴. — אשר אמרתי] as in v.¹⁷. — **24.** העליה] the intention is to read the preposition עלי with the article and pronominal suffix. No other instance of such a construction has been pointed out (Dr., *Notes*) ; and if the construction were allowable, it would not be appropriate here, for השוק is, of course, *the leg with the flesh upon it.* The slight change into האליה seems first to have been proposed by Geiger, *Urschrift*, p. 380, and has everything to commend it. The reading is apparently suspected by the Talmud, for the Gemara asks (Aboda Zara, 25ᵃ) : What was it that was upon the leg? to which Rabbi Johanan answers, *it was the leg and the rump.* Other passages from Talmud and Midrash are cited by Dr. The parallel in the custom of the fellahin of to-day is noticed by Nestle, *Marginalien und Materalien*, p. 13. If האליה was the original reading, as accepted by We., Bu., Dr., Brown (Lexicon), we can see a reason for the mutilation of the word, for the אליה was to be burned

---

* Wellh., *Skizzen,* III. p. 114.

F

upon the altar. The editors supposed it impossible for Samuel to be ignorant of this "Mosaic" ordinance. Kl. proposes הכליה, which seems to have no superiority to the reading just considered. The difficulty of the rest of the verse is admitted. The people do not ordinarily eat until Samuel comes, much less would they proceed without him when he had made preparations for a guest; הנשאר therefore cannot be right. — [לאמר העם קראתי] seems absolutely unintelligible in the context. For קראתי ... כי למועד 𝕲 gives ὅτι εἰς μαρτύριον τέθειταί σοι παρὰ τοὺς ἄλλους · ἀπόκινζε (𝕲ᴸ has παρατέθεικά σοι παρὰ τοῦ λαοῦ). This is better than 𝕳, but, as pointed out by Dr., קרץ, which we should assume as the original of ἀποκνίζε (so Ew. and We.), is not used in biblical Hebrew in the sense of taking food; and after Saul has been exhorted to eat, it is superfluous to add *fall to*. The conjectures of the commentators scarcely call for attention, except that of Bu., who restores at the end שמרו לך לאכל עם הקראים. More radical treatment seems to be necessary. What we expect is a polite invitation to Saul as the guest of honour to begin the meal, because the guests were waiting his lead. First, then, it seems necessary to read השאר for הנשאר, שאר being flesh prepared for the table, Ex. 21¹⁰ Ps. 78²⁰. Samuel says : *Behold the meat is set before thee,* as we should say, *the meal is served.* For שמור־לך I would substitute אהרנו לך, *we have waited for thee,* in which case מועד would be the time to which Samuel and the other guests had agreed to wait for the expected stranger. — לאכל עם הק I adopt from Bu. in place of the useless לאמר העם קראתי. — 25. וישכמו: ויורבר עם־שאול על־הגג] is evidently out of joint, for they certainly did not rise in the morning until after *Samuel called Saul,* which follows; καὶ διέστρωσαν τῷ Σαοὺλ ἐπὶ τῷ δώματι καὶ ἐκοιμήθη 𝕲 evidently represents ויורברו לשאול על הגג וישכב. The text is corrected accordingly by recent expositors from Schleusner down. Keil alone hardens his heart.

IX. 26-X. 8. Saul is anointed by Samuel. — He also receives signs confirmatory of the prophetic commission, and is encouraged, after the signs shall have been fulfilled, to act according to his own judgment. *At the rising of the dawn Samuel called to Saul on the roof*] for the time of day cf. Gen. 19¹⁵ 32²⁵ ²⁷ Jos. 6¹⁵. The original text seems to have added only : *and they went out into the street*] all three together, as is evident from the next verse. — **27.** *They were going down in the edge of the city when Samuel said*] the construction is similar to v.¹¹. *Say to the lad that he pass on*] the addition of 𝕳 : *and he passed on* breaks the connexion, and must be exscinded. *But thou stand here that I may tell thee the word of God*] which for the present concerns Saul alone. — **X. 1.** *The vial of oil* is described by the same word which is used in the description of another prophet's anointing of

a king, 2 K. $9^{1.3}$. *And poured it upon his head*] the act of anointing could not be more clearly described. *And kissed him*] an evidence of personal affection, for kissing is nowhere an act expressive of fealty to a king; the kissing of an idol 1 K. 19^{18} Hos. 13^2
can hardly be called parallel. A part of Samuel's words have fallen
out of 𝔥, and the whole must be restored as follows : *Has not
Yahweh anointed thee as prince over his people Israel? And thou
shalt reign over the people of Yahweh and shalt save them from the
hand of their enemies round about. And this shall be the sign
that Yahweh has anointed thee over his heritage as prince*] it is
possible that theological prejudice has had something to do with
the mutilation of the text, for, to the later view, Saul did not actually save Israel from their enemies. — **2.** As Saul has no reason
for delaying longer, we may suppose that the signs which follow
occur on the road from Ramah to Gibeah (Saul's home). Unfortunately we are not able to identify either Ramah or the other
points mentioned, except Bethel. *When thou goest from me to-day
thou shalt meet two men at the tomb of Rachel in the boundary of
Benjamin*] the boundary here mentioned must be the boundary
between Ephraim and Benjamin, for the district of Zuph was in
Ephraim. It is impossible therefore to identify the *Tomb of
Rachel* here mentioned with the traditional site south of Jerusalem. As Jeremiah hears *Rachel weeping for her children* in
Ramah (31^{15}), and as her children are Joseph and Benjamin, we
naturally suppose her tomb located in the boundary of their
respective territories. To make Samuel's home in Judah in order
to bring Saul home by the traditional Tomb is to violate all the
probabilities. The next word is unintelligible. The men would
tell him : *Thy father has dismissed the matter of the asses and is
anxious for you, saying: What shall I do for my son?*] the state
of things anticipated by Saul, 9^5. — **3.** The second sign : *Thou
shalt pass on thence and come to the Oak of Tabor*] supposed by
some to be identical with the tree of Deborah, between Ramah
and Bethel, Jd. 4^5. This can hardly be called probable. The
grave of Deborah (Rebecca's nurse) is also put in this region by
Gen. 35^8 and associated with it is an oak — the Oak of Weeping.
In the number of sacred trees which once abounded in the
country, there is no need to merge these three into one. The

three men he should meet *going up to God at Bethel,* the ancient sanctuary, would have their offerings with them : *one carrying three kids, one carrying three baskets of bread*] the reading is conjectural, based on the paucity of the *three loaves* in 𝕳. Twenty loaves are easily carried by a man, 2 K. 4⁴², and would be no more than the equivalent of *the skin of wine* borne by the third member of the party. — **4.** The men should be so impressed by Saul's bearing that they would *salute* him and give him *two loaves,* an earnest of the *backsheesh* to be paid later to the king. — **5.** The third sign : *Afterwards thou shalt come to Gibeah of God*] apparently the full name of Saul's home, for he goes directly to his house after meeting with the prophets. *Where is the Resident of the Philistines*] evidently the same mentioned in 13⁸, though the location there given is Geba. *And it shall be at thy coming thither thou shalt meet a band of prophets coming down from the Bamah with a lyre and tambourine and flute and harp before them while they engage in prophesying*] it must be evident that we have here a company of dervishes engaged in their religious exercises. The enthusiastic nature of these exercises is evident from the later narrative and from the parallel account, 19¹⁸⁻²⁴. — **6.** *And the Spirit of Yahweh will rush upon thee*] the same verb is used to describe the enthusiasm which seized the earlier heroes of Israel, Jd. 14⁶, etc. *And thou shalt prophesy with them and be turned into another man*] it is worth remarking that in the later account, 16¹³, the Spirit comes as a result of the anointing. The verb used to describe the transformation effected in Saul is the same found in Ex. 7¹⁵ (E), where the rod is changed into a serpent and Ex. 7¹⁷·²⁰ (E), where the waters are turned into blood. — **7.** The coming to pass of the signs will justify Saul in doing *whatever the occasion demands*] cf. Jd. 9³³ — for he will be sure of the divine help. — **8.** The verse is an evident interpolation into the earliest narrative, but not necessarily late. It commands Saul to go down to Gilgal and to wait there seven days for Samuel.

26. וישכימן] is a corruption of וישכב, originally the conclusion of the preceding verse. — כעלות] some copies have בעלות (Ginsb.). — הנגה] *Qrê* is doubtless correct. — שניהם] lacking in 𝕲, is superfluous. Probably the original text was without explicit subject (Bu. omits הוא ושמואל following We.). חוץ is whatever is outside the house. — **27.** ויעבר] gives the purpose of the

command. — ויעבר] is superfluous and is lacking in 𝔊𝔖. — כיום] it seems unnecessary to tell him to stand *this very minute*, whereas in contrast to the *passing on* of the servant it would be natural to tell him to stand *here*. We should
probably emend to הלום with Kl. — **X. 1.** For kissing the king, Gen. 41⁴⁰
and Ps. 2¹² might be cited, but the text in both is suspicious. — הלא כי־משחך]
the construction is apparently smooth. But as in the next verse Samuel goes
on to give the signs which are to come to pass, it is evident that something is
missing. 𝔊 inserts after הלא the sentence given above, and this is adopted as
original by Th., We., Kl., Dr., Bu., Ki., and Ginsb. (margin). It has dropped
out by homeoteleuton. — נחלתו] cf. 26¹⁹ 2 S. 14¹⁶ 21³ Jer. 16¹⁸. — **2.** We
have assumed that Samuel's home was at Ramah, though this document nowhere so affirms. If the assumption be correct, Ramah can hardly be identified with *Er-Ram*, which is only three miles away from Gibeah. GASmith
suggests *Beit Rima* on the western edge of Mt. Ephraim, while Ew. (*GVI*³.
III. p. 31, E. Tr. III. p. 21) puts it at *Ram Allah*, about ten miles north of
Jerusalem. The tradition which puts Rachel's tomb near Bethlehem seems
to go back to Gen. 35¹⁹ (E) 48⁷ (J), but must be later than Jeremiah, as
shown above. The present text of Genesis seems to be interpolated in these
two passages. — בצלצח] is intended to contain the name of a place — *in
Zelzach*. But the definition is already precise enough. The name of the
place from which the men were coming would be appropriate, in which case
from Zelah, the burial place of Kish in a later passage 2 S. 21¹⁴, might be
conjectured. 𝔊 has a confused variety of readings, one of them possibly
going back to צלחים, *leaping*, which is adopted by Ew. *in grosser Eile;* another (𝔊ᴸ) seems to reproduce צהרים *meridie* 𝔏. — ואנ־] should probably be
pointed as the participle (Bu.). — **3.** וחלפת] the verb is used of the quick
motion of the whirlwind, Hab. 1¹¹, once apparently of *transgressing* the commandment, Is. 24⁵. It does not seem especially appropriate here, therefore,
and the text may not be sound. — אלון תבור] the conjecture which identifies this with the *Palm of Deborah* is due to Ew. (*GVI.* III. p. 31, E. Tr. III.
p. 21). — ככרות] for reasons given above, the conjecture of Kl. כלובי is plausible and adopted by Bu., but כלי seems more likely, cf. 9⁷. — **4.** שתי־לחם]
δύο ἀπαρχὰς ἄρτων 𝔊 evidently had בכורי, probably a corruption of an original
ככרות. — **5.** אל] found in the current editions is lacking in almost all MSS.
(De Rossi) and omitted by Ginsb. — נצבי] we should read נציב with 𝔊𝔏.
The word means (1) *an officer* or *prefect;* (2) *a garrison* of soldiers; (3) *a
pillar*. As Jonathan *smote* the one in question it seems most likely to have
been a single officer stationed by the Philistines as representative of their
authority. — ויהי] the form is unexpected; Dr. compares 2 S. 5²⁴ where also
a divine message is given. But there the message is a command and naturally employs the jussive, which is inappropriate here. It seems necessary,
therefore, to correct to והיה. The verb פגע means *he came suddenly upon*
something. — חבל] *a string*, but, as we use *band*, not necessarily a company
in single file. — ולפניהם וגו] the whole is a circumstantial clause. The names
of the musical instruments here mentioned are translated, as nearly as may

be, in the foregoing. An elaborate discussion is found in Weiss., *Die Musi-*
kalische Instrumente in d. Heiligen Schr. des Alten Testamentes, Graz. 1895.
— **7.** Bu. inserts כל before אשר on the ground of Ⓖ. But this does not
seem necessary. — **8.** That the verse does not belong to the original narrative
should be evident. It flatly contradicts the preceding command to Saul, to
act according to his own judgment and the leadings of Providence. It evidently prepares for the paragraph 13⁸⁻¹⁵ which also is an interruption to the
flow of the narrative. The interpolation is recognized as such by We. (*Comp.*
245, 248), Stade (*GVI.* I. p. 211), Co., Bu. I have given reasons in the
introduction for thinking the insertion not so late as is generally supposed. —
Seven days shalt thou wait . . . then I will tell thee] on the construction cf.
Moore, *Judges*, p. 350.

9–16. The return of Saul.

— The author condenses his account,
dwelling only on the third of the three expected signs. Possibly
the narrative was once fuller. He now says that as Saul turned
to go from Samuel *God gave him another understanding*] the
words do not seem inappropriate here, though they do not exactly correspond to the place of Saul's ' conversion ' in the prediction, v.⁶. It is psychologically quite comprehensible that the
impulse should anticipate the predicted order of events. — **10.** *He
came thence to Gibeah*] seems to be the correct reading. The
rest of the verse is sufficiently clear from v.⁵. — *And he played the
prophet in the midst of them*] the verb is apparently denominative.
— **11.** The result in the minds of the people is : *that every one
who knew him in times past and saw him raving with the prophets said each to his fellow : What now has come upon the son of
Kish ?* The Hebrew sentence is awkward, and perhaps should
be emended, but the general sense is clear. The question is
repeated in another form : *Is Saul also among the prophets*] the
implication is that his former life had been of a very different
kind from theirs. — **12.** The first clause is perfectly plain in
meaning in itself considered, but entirely unintelligible in this
context : *And a man from there answered and said : And who is
their father ?* As generally interpreted, the question is intended
to say : *the son of Kish is as much to be expected among them as
any one else ; prophetic inspiration does not depend upon parentage.*
But this is so patent a fact that it seems needless to call attention
to it. The question *what has happened to the son of Kish ?* does
not mean that Saul's *parentage* was such that he could not be

expected to prophesy, but that his known individual character was such that his prophesying was a surprise. On this theory the question *who is their father* is indeed pia quidem vox sed quae ipsi questioni non satisfecit (Schm.). Such an answer could hardly be composed by our author. The original reading seems to be lost. Because of this incident a proverb circulated in the form : *Is Saul also among the prophets?* The Rabbinical expositors see in the question of v.¹¹ an expression of surprise that the son of so lowly a man as Kish should be found in such distinguished company. The reverse is more likely, for Kish has been described as a well-to-do man, and it is evident from some passages in the historical books that the prophets did not stand high in the estimation of the people. — **13.** After a time Saul ceased prophesying *and went down to the house*] on the reading see the note below. — **14.** Saul's uncle asks about the journey. — **15, 16.** His further question as to Samuel's word only brought out the reply : *Why! he told us that the asses were found.*

9. והיה] should be ויהי. The scribe was misled by the preceding series of verbs (Dr.). — כהפנתו] Jer. 48³⁹ is the nearest parallel. — ויהפך] Zeph. 3⁹, cited by Dr., protects the verb here (contra Kl.). — לב] our word *heart* hardly expresses the idea, which is that his *mind* was illuminated, cf. BDB. *s.v.* — **10.** ויבאו שם] καὶ ἔρχεται ἐκεῖθεν 𝕲. As the servant has been lost sight of for some time 𝕲 seems to be correct. But if we adopt משם it seems clear that something has dropped out. — **11.** ויהי כל־יודעו] the nearest parallel seems to be 2 S. 2²³ where we have ויהי כל־הבא followed by ויעמרו in the apodosis. But the point is here not that *all who knew him saw him*, but that *all who knew him and saw him asked* the question. It seems better and more vigorous therefore to make ויאמר begin the apodosis and omit העם with 𝔏. For the construction cf. Nu. 21⁸, where however the other tense is used. — מה־זה] on the form of the question BDB. *s.v.* זה. — **12.** מישם] seems to have been read מהם by 𝕲. — אביהב] πατὴρ αὐτοῦ 𝕲𝕾 𝕴 seems to give no help. 𝕮 interprets : *and who is their master?* — which seems as irrelevant as the ordinary translation. — **13.** הבמה] As Saul met the prophets coming from the Bamah he would probably not go on thither but to his home. We. therefore conjectures הביתה. There he would meet his uncle who appears in the next verse. — **14.** The uncle on the father's side would have almost a father's claim. — **16.** הגד הגיד] the adverbial infinitive strengthens the verb: *he told us, sure!* The second half of the verse is relegated to the margin by Bu. perhaps correctly. It really adds nothing to the sense. — אשר אמר שמ׳] is lacking in 𝕲ᴮ.

ON THE MEANING OF נביא. — The word is obscure and we can do little more than note the bounds of our ignorance. The word does not seem to be

Hebrew in its origin, as the verb exists only in the denominative forms. It is however a good Semitic form, like קָצִיר *a harvester*, פָּקִיד *an overseer*. As these examples show, nouns of this form usually describe a person who devotes himself steadily to the particular action indicated by the root. The only clue to the root meaning of נבא is in Arabic where it means: (1) *he uttered a low voice or sound*, (2) *he was elevated*, (3) *he went from a land to another land*. Hoffmann (*ZATW*. III. p. 87) explains (2) to be *he rose into view, he comes from another region, where we cannot see him, into our own*. He therefore supposes the נביא to be *one who rises* [is roused] *from his sluggishness under the influence of a divine inspiration*. This seems rather forced, however, and as the organs of supernatural communication notoriously chirp, or mutter, or give forth a murmuring sound, it seems most likely that the *nabi* was originally *the mutterer*. Later we find Saul מהנבא under the influence of an evil spirit, where the utterance of inarticulate sounds would probably be one of the phenomena. The prophet is elsewhere called insane — מְשֻׁגָּע — where also the utterance of incoherent sounds is probably one of the symptoms, 2 K. 9[11] Jer. 29[26]. The account of the *nebiim* in the text reminds us strongly of the priests of the Syrian goddess described by Lucian. The 'prophets' of Baal, also, *rave* about the altar, 1 K. 18[29].

17-27. The public choice and anointing of Saul. — Samuel calls the people to Mizpah and by the sacred lot selects a king. The lot falls upon Saul who is found after some search and anointed. He is received by some with enthusiasm while others are indifferent.

The account continues 8[22a] directly. Having expostulated with the representatives of the people at Ramah, Samuel is finally directed to yield to their desires. He therefore (in this paragraph) calls an assembly of the whole people to the sanctuary at Mizpah. If the whole intervening story is left out, the narrative is without a break. The style is homogeneous; Mizpah is the place of assembly here and in 7; the author here, as in 8, expresses the idea that the monarchy is a rejection of Yahweh.

Our paragraph seems to be homogeneous down to [25a]. After this, we may suspect that the dismission of the people to their homes is intended to prepare the way for 11 — the original continuation of [25a] being 12[1]. I find no reason for suspecting 17-19a, with Cornill, or [25a], with Budde. The evidences for a comparatively late date are the same here as in other parts of the same document. In accordance with his general theory Bu. derives the paragraph from E.

17. A general assembly of the people is called at Mizpah as in 7. The reason for the choice of Mizpah may be the same that influenced the author of Jd. 20. — **18.** Yahweh again reproaches the people with ingratitude : *I brought you up from Egypt and delivered you from the hand of Egypt, and from the hand of all the kingdoms that were oppressing you*] the construction is unusual, and it is possible that the passage has been interpolated. — **19.** Their sin is rejection of Yahweh ; *who has been your saviour*] the same word is used of the judge, Jd. 3¹⁵. The author has the idea which is illustrated in the occurrence described in 7⁷⁻¹⁴. *And ye said : No ! but a king shalt thou place over us*] the reference is evidently to 8¹⁹. In order to the fulfilment of their desire he commands them to station themselves before Yahweh (who would choose among them) : *by your tribes and by your thousands*] the *thousand* is a subdivision of a tribe Jd. 6¹⁵. — **20, 21.** The choice is made by the sacred lot, each tribe coming by its representatives before the oracle and receiving the answer *yes* or *no,* until the proper one is found. The account is parallel to Jos. 7¹⁶⁻¹⁸, where however there are four stages instead of three. In the first stage *the tribe of Benjamin* is taken. This tribe was brought *by its clans and the clan of the Matrite was taken*] the name occurs nowhere else, and some have supposed an error. One of the sons of Benjamin in Gen. 46²¹ is *Beker,* which may be the original here.* We should now insert with 𝕲 : *and he brought near the clan of Matri man by man*] the clause has fallen out of 𝔥 but is necessary to the sense. Kish would represent the household now chosen. Among his sons the name of Saul finally came out, but the man himself was not to be found. — **22.** To the question : *Did the man come hither?*] the oracle replied : *He is hidden in the baggage*] out of modesty of course. Slight changes in the text of this and the following verse will be noted below. — **23.** *One ran and fetched him thence and as he stood among the people he was taller than all the people from his shoulder upward*] a head taller, as we should say. A Lapide quotes from the *Aeneid :* cunctis altior ibat (of Anchises), and : toto vertice supra est (of Turnus), and similar language from Pliny concerning Trajan. Before the invention of firearms, personal strength was essential in a leader, as indeed it is still among the Arabs.† — **24.** At the

---

* Ew., *GVI*³. III. p. 33 (E. Tr. III. p. 23).   † Doughty, II. p. 27 sq.

presentation to the people, they shout : *May the king live !* the usual greeting to a ruler, 2 S. 16¹⁶ 1 K. 1²⁵. ³¹ 2 K. 11¹². The Emir of Hayil in Central Arabia is saluted with : O, long of days ! and his subjects in speaking of him say : God give him long life ! * Whether this account originally added that Samuel anointed Saul is not certain, but this is rendered probable by the language of 15¹. — **25ᵃ**. *Samuel recited before the people the custom of the kingdom and wrote it in a book and deposited it before Yahweh*] it seems impossible to understand this of anything else than the *custom of the king* already recited in 8⁹⁻¹⁸. This was threatened as the penalty of the people's choice. As they have persisted in their choice, the threat will be carried out. The document is laid up before Yahweh as a testimony, so that when they complain of tyranny they can be pointed to the fact that they have brought it upon themselves.

25ᵇ–27. The original document seems to have joined 12¹ (Samuel's farewell) directly to ²⁵ᵃ. The rest of this chapter is inserted to give room for 11 in which Saul appears still as a private citizen. In the theory of the editor he did not assume kingly power at once, because the people did not recognize him, or at least a considerable part did not recognize him, as king. When Samuel dismissed the people there went with Saul only *the brave men whose heart God had touched*] the phrase does not occur elsewhere (Jer. 4¹⁸ is different) but the meaning is sufficiently evident. *But the base men*] lit. *sons of belial*, Jd. 19²², *said : How shall this fellow save us ?*] with a touch of contempt in the form of the question. In consistency *they brought him no present*] cf. 9⁷. There is no thought as yet of fixed taxes. The two words at the end of this verse in 𝕲 belong to the next section.

17. יצק] the Hiphil only here, but הזעיק is found in the meaning *he called out the warriors*, 2 S. 20⁵ Jd. 4¹⁰. ¹³. — **18**. כה־אמר יהוה] the usual beginning of a prophetic speech as 2²⁷. — העליתי] of the deliverance from Egypt, usual in E but not confined to him. — הממלכות הלחצים] the disagreement in gender may be accounted for by supposing the participle to be construed *ad sensum*. But I suspect the original had only הממלכות which a scribe found too sweeping and tried to correct by insertion. The verb לחץ is used Jd. 2¹⁸ 4³ al., usually

* Doughty, II. pp. 55, 226.

in Deuteronomistic passages. — **19.** מאסתם] of the people's rejection of Yahweh 8[7] Num. 11[2)] cf. 14[31] (late). — לו] in the received text is replaced by לא by the Qrê and in a number of MSS., as well as in 𝕲𝕾𝕿𝕷. — התיצבו לפני יהוה] Jos. 24[1]. — **20.** ויקרב] exactly as in Jos. 7[17]. — **21.** למשפחתיו *Kt.*: למשפחתו *Qrê*. As the next verse begins with ו the original may have been simply למשפחות (𝕲). After המטרי, 𝕲[AB] adds: καὶ προσάγουσιν τὴν φυλὴν Ματταρεὶ εἰς ἄνδρας, 𝕲[L] has an equivalent, but does not agree verbally. Probably a clause of this significance has dropped out of 𝕳 — so all recent scholars suppose. — **22.** וישאלו] καὶ ἐπηρώτησεν Σαμουήλ 𝕲[B] 𝕾. Probably the original was simply וישאל. For the next clause הבא עוד הלם איש, 𝕲[B] has: εἰ ἔρχεται ὁ ἀνὴρ ἐνταῦθα. This alone corresponds to the answer which follows, and we restore (with Th., al.) הבא הלם האיש. The baggage of an army is הכלים, 17[22] 25[13]. — **23.** וירצו] read the singular with 𝕲; the unexpressed personal subject with the singular is appropriate here. — **24.** הראיתם] with *daghesh dirimens* Ges.[26] § 22 *s.* — בו] 𝕲 reads יו, but בחר ב׳ is found 16[8. 9. 10] 2 S. 6[21] Dt. 18[5] 21[5]. — בכל העם] ἐν πᾶσιν ὑμῖν 𝕲. The case is difficult to decide; בכלכם is perhaps more likely to have been changed (under the influence of the כל־העם which precedes and follows) than the reverse. — וירעו] καὶ ἔγνωσαν 𝕲[B]; the Hebrew seems to be original. Before וירעו Bu. inserts by conjecture וימשחהו למלך, while Co. would apparently insert the same words at the end of the verse. It is possible, however, that this author supposed Saul not to have been anointed, and that the allusion in 15[1] is an interpolation. The command to Samuel in 8[22] says nothing of anointing. — **26.** החיל] *the army* is out of place here; read בני החיל with 𝕲 (Th., al.). — אשר־נגע אלהים בלבם] no similar phrase has been pointed out. — **27.** זה] is used in contempt, 21[16] 25[21] 2 S. 13[17], cf. BDB. *s.v.* — ויהי כמחריש] the words are a corruption of two which originally opened the following paragraph.

Chapter XI. The Ammonite invasion, the part taken by Saul, and the effect on his fortunes. — Nahash the Ammonite besieges Jabesh Gilead, and the people offer to submit to him. But he will put scorn upon them and upon all Israel, by putting out every man's right eye. His contempt for Israel is seen in the confidence with which he allows the Jabeshites to seek help from their kinsmen. The messengers come to Gibeah, where the people are moved to pity, but also to despair. Saul alone is aroused by the message, and by the Spirit of God, to heroic measures. At his peremptory summons the people march to the relief of the beleaguered city. The Ammonites are taken completely by surprise, and the deliverance is equally complete. In recognition of Saul's kingly qualities, the people make him king at Gilgal with religious rejoicing.

The piece is a part of the narrative which we left at 10^{16}. The tone is entirely different from that of 10$^{17-27}$. The author is in ignorance of the public appointment of Saul as king. The messengers from Jabesh come to Gibeah, not to seek Saul, but to appeal to the people. No one thinks it necessary to send for Saul to the field. He comes home at the regular time, and then has to inquire before he is told what is the matter. More complete disregard of what is related as having taken place at Mizpah could not be imagined. On the other hand, the entire consonance of this chapter and 9^1–10^{16} is evident, and the author seems to have foreshadowed this event when he says : *do as the occasion serves, for God is with thee* (10^7).

The resemblance between this passage and some of the early narratives of the Book of Judges is plain. The integrity of the piece has suffered in vv. $^{12-14}$, as will be shown.

1–3. The invasion and the terms offered. — *It came to pass in about a month*] the reading is that of ⅁. — *Nahash the Ammonite*] he is called later, *king of the Bnê Ammon*. The name means *Serpent*, cf. 2 S. 17^{25} and *Nahshon*, Ex. 6^{23}. This Nahash lived until some time after David was settled in Jerusalem, 2 S. 10^2. The Ammonites were kindred of Israel (Gen. 19$^{31-38}$), but always troublesome neighbours, cf. Moore on Jd. 11^4. In the theory of the Israelitic writers they occupied the desert east of Gilead, Dt. 2$^{16-25.\ 37}$, but they are represented as claiming the territory as far as the Jordan. Probably they were not scrupulous about an ancestral title, but like the Bedawin of the present day asserted themselves wherever they had the power. — *And besieged Jabesh Gilead*] lit. *encamped upon*. But where the Bedawin encamp upon a territory they destroy it ; and while unable to undertake a formal siege, they quickly reduce a walled town to submission by depriving it of supplies, 2 K. 25^1. Jabesh is mentioned Jd. 21 1 S. 31^{11} 2 S. 2$^{4.\ 5}$ 21^{12} and in Chronicles. It is placed by Eusebius six miles from Pella on the road to Gerasa, and is now generally identified with *Ed-Deir* on the *Wady Yabis*, which appears to preserve the ancient name. The men of Jabesh are willing to become tributaries. — *Make terms with us that we may serve thee*] the Bedawin frequently reduce the towns of the oases to the condition here in mind, receiving a percentage of all crops. The case of Khaibar when it surrendered to Mohammed is in point. The *covenant* here asked is evidently imposed by the stronger party, cf. Jos. 9 ; but it naturally binds him to cease from further molestation when it has once been ratified. — **2.** The reply of Nahash : *On this stipulation I will make terms with you : the boring out of every man's right eye*] lit. *by boring out for you every right eye.* Josephus supposes the intention to be to make them unfit for war. But the Bedawy's motive is probably no deeper than the pleasure of insulting an enemy : *Thereby I will put ignominy on all Israel*] the disgrace of Jabesh would be a gibe in the mouth of all Israel's enemies, cf. 17¹⁰. — **3.** A respite of seven days is asked : *That we may send messengers through all the territory of Israel, and if there be none to save us we will come out to thee.* At the end of the verse 𝔊ᴸ adds that they sent out the messengers, but such complementary insertions are not infrequent.

1. Καὶ ἐγενήθη ὡς μετὰ μῆνα 𝔊ᴬᴮ; καὶ ἐγένετο μετὰ μῆνα ἡμερῶν 𝔊ᴸ evidently represents a variant of ויהי כמחריש which is found in 𝔥 at the end of the preceding verse and there supposed to mean: *and he was like one holding his peace,* that is, in reference to the scoffs of the crowd. But it is difficult to see why the author should make a comparison when it would be more natural to say directly *and he held his peace.* The reading of 𝔊 is restored in the form ויהי כמהדיש by Th. and adopted by most later scholars. The form כמחריש is possible, as we see from Gen. 38²⁴ כמשלש, but as the מן is superfluous I think כמו חדש more probable. On the identification of Jabesh Gilead, Eusebius in *O.S.* 268; Moore, *Judges,* p. 446, who cites the recent authorities. — כרת-לנו בריח] the usual formula, Jos. 9¹⁵ 24²⁵ 2 S. 5³ 2 K. 11⁴. The term seems to have originated in the cutting apart of a victim, cf. WRSmith, *Rel. Sem.* pp. 297, 461; Doughty, II. p. 41; Valeton in *ZATW.* 12, p. 227 ff.; and Kraetschmar, *Die Bundesvorstelling im AT.* (1896). — **2.** בזאת] apparently the ב of price. After לכם 13 MSS. and 𝔊ᴮᴸ add בריח. But the omission makes no difficulty. — בנקור לכם] ἐν τῷ ἐξορύξαι ὑμῶν 𝔊ᴮᴸ. That they should do the mutilating themselves would be a refinement of cruelty. But the Bedawy might not so regard it. — נקר is used of the ravens picking out the eye, Prov. 30¹⁷; the Piel in the same sense Jd. 16²¹. — וישמתיה] 𝔊ᴬᴮ seems to omit the suffix. — כל] omitted by 𝔊ᴮ. — **3.** וזקני] ἄνδρες 𝔊; the latter is favoured by Bu. on the ground of v.¹. But the conformity is more likely to be the result of correction by a scribe than the dissimilation. — הרף לנו] cf. 2 K. 4²⁷. The protasis with ואם־אין is followed by perfect with waw consecutive as in Ex. 22² Num. 27⁹. The fact that אין has a participle under its government does not make the sentence different from those cited. — מושיע] with the accusative, as in 14³⁹ Jd. 6³⁶.

4–7ᵃ. The reception of the message by Saul. — The messengers came *to Gibeah of Saul*] the town seems to have gone by this name later, Is. 10²⁹. There were several other towns which bore the name Gibeah. ⅏ has, *to Gibeah to Saul*, which is contradicted by what follows. — *The people wept aloud*] Jd. 2⁴ 21² 1 S. 30⁴ 2 S. 13³⁶. — **5.** *Saul was just coming after the oxen from the field*] as already noticed, the messengers made no inquiry for Saul, no care was taken to send for him, no special attention was paid to him when he came in sight, but he was left to find out the cause of the commotion by questioning the people. All this shows that it was not on account of Saul that the messengers came to Gibeah. — **6.** *And the Spirit of Yahweh*] so is probably to be read with ⅏ and some MSS. of 𝔚, favoured also by 𝕮. — *And his wrath became very hot*] in Jd. 14¹⁹ also the Spirit of Yahweh is the efficient cause of wrath. — **7ᵃ.** *And he took a yoke of oxen and cut them in pieces*] the verb is used of cutting up a sacrificial victim, 1 K. 18²³·³³ and elsewhere; in one instance it describes the cutting up of a human body Jd. 19²⁹ 20⁶. In this latter case also the pieces are sent throughout all Israel. The threat conveyed is: *Whoever comes not forth after Saul, so shall his oxen be treated*] Ewald's theory that the oxen were slain as a sacrifice is without support in the text. The clause, *and after Samuel*, is probably a later insertion.

5. נא] is apparently the participle. — בקר] is the ploughing cattle, so that Saul had been tilling his field. Classic parallels for the king cultivating his own fields are given in Poole, *Synopsis.* — **6.** ותצלח] the same verb in 10⁶. — אלהים] some MSS. have יהוה which is favoured also by ⅏. כשמעו *Kt.*, כשמעו *Qrê;* the latter is more vigorous. — ואחר שמואל] is a redactional insertion (Co.).

7ᵇ–11. The deliverance. — *A terror from Yahweh fell upon the people and they gathered as one man*] the terror was *a terror of Yahweh* in that he sent it. Its object was Saul; the people were afraid to disobey. For *they gathered* ⅏, *they went out* is given by 𝔚. — **8.** *Bezek*, the place of muster, is identified with *Khirbet Ibzik*, " thirteen miles northeast from Shechem on the road down to Bethshan " (G. A. Smith, *Geog.* p. 336). The location is well suited to be the starting-point in this expedition, being nearly opposite Jabesh Gilead. The enormous numbers — *the Bnê*

Israel 300,000 *and the men of Judah* 30,000 — are to be judged
like similar data elsewhere, cf. Jd. 20². — **9.** *And he said*] Saul is
the subject (𝕲): *To-morrow deliverance will come to you when the
sun grows hot*] Saul had detained the messengers until he could
give a definite answer. The people of Jabesh naturally rejoiced
at receiving the assurance. — **10.** To keep the besiegers in false
security, the men of Jabesh promise to come out to them on the
next day : *And you shall do to us whatever you please*] lit. *according to all that is good in your eyes,* cf. 3¹⁸ 14³⁶. ⁴⁰ 2 S. 10¹² Jd. 19²⁴. —
11. The morrow began at sunset of the day on which the message
was sent, so the army doubtless marched all night as Josephus says.
Saul divided his troops into three columns as did Gideon, Jd. 7¹⁶,
and Abimelech Jd. 9⁴³. The advantage of attacking on different
sides at the same time is obvious. — *And they came into the midst
of the camp*] the attack was not discovered until the Israelites
were already in the midst of the scattered camp. The *morning
watch* is mentioned also Ex. 14²⁴ ; the night was divided into
three watches, notice the *middle* watch, Jd. 7¹⁹. — *And they smote
Ammon until the heat of the day and there was . . .*] the word is
probably corrupt. What we expect is a statement that there was
a great slaughter or a great panic. *They scattered and there were
not left two together.*

NOTE. — The reason for rejecting the numbers in v.⁸ is that in the time of
Deborah the total fighting strength was 40,000 men, Jd. 5⁸, and under great
stress Barak was able to bring only ten thousand into the field. There is no
reason to suppose that Israel had greatly increased since that time; the
Philistine oppression indicates the reverse. The later account of Saul's campaigns makes the impression that he at no time commanded a large force. On
the other hand, the ease with which numbers increase in size on paper is seen
from 𝕲 here which doubles the 300,000 of 𝕳, while Josephus raises it to
700,000.

7b. ויצאו] does not give a bad sense, but as 𝕲 renders ויצעקו, this is restored
by We., al.; the phrase כאיש אחד is used with verbs meaning *to gather,* Jd. 20¹
Ezra 3¹ Neh. 8¹; nowhere with יצא. — **8.** A *Bezek* is mentioned in Jd. 1⁴
where it would be supposed to be in Judah. 𝕲 seems to have read *in
Ramah,* which however was early corrupted to *Bamah* or *Bala* (I). The
identification of our Bezek with *Khirbet Ibzik* is as old as the fourteenth
century, cf. Moore on Jd. 1⁵. — **9.** ויאמרו] καὶ εἶπεν 𝕲ᴬᴮ is apparently correct.
— בחם [כחם *Qrê* fixes the point of time more exactly. — **10.** ויאמרו אנשי יבש]
𝕲 adds *to Nahash the Ammonite* and something of the kind seems necessary.

But I suspect the original reading to have been only ויאמרו לנחש and that the second word was corrupted to אנשי. For כבל־חשב, 𝕲^AB gives simply τό ἀγαθόν, and the shorter reading is to be preferred. — **11.** ראשים] of the divisions of the army, Jd. 7¹⁶ 9³⁴·⁴³ I S. 13¹⁷. On the double accusative, Dav., *Syntax*, § 76. For *Ammon* 𝕲 gives *sons of Ammon* which accords with almost uniform usage. — חנשארים] can be construed (cf. 10¹¹ 2 S. 2²³), but it is extremely awkward. Some relief is given by changing ויהי to ויהם, but the corruption is probably deeper.

12-15. The installation of Saul. — The people demand Saul as king, and, going down to Gilgal, they celebrate a feast of coronation — except that we hear nothing of a crown.

The paragraph has been worked over to fit the present composite narrative. Samuel probably had no place in the original document — the related section, 9¹–10¹⁶, makes him only the seer of a single town. There is no reason why he should accompany Saul to the war or why he should officiate at his public recognition. But in vv.¹²⁻¹⁴ we find Samuel acting as leader and recognized authority. There is reason to suppose, therefore, that these verses in their present shape are the redactional bonds between the two streams of narrative. Verse ¹⁵, on the other hand, may be a fragment of the original narrative, but something must have stood between it and v.¹¹.

12-15. The evidences of adaptation to the present situation found in vv.¹²⁻¹⁴ are emphasized by We. (*Comp.* p. 243) and Stade (*GVI.* I. p. 212). The three verses are regarded as an interpolation by Co. (*Einl³.* p. 100), and Bu. (*RS.* p. 173). Driver specifies only v.¹⁴ as redactional (*LOT⁶.* p. 176).

12. *Who is he who says : Saul shall not reign over us ?*] the negative is omitted in the current Hebrew, but found in 𝕲𝕾𝕿 as well as some MSS. — **13.** *And Saul said*] the traces of a reading *and Samuel said* are of no value. Saul's magnanimity is the point of the reply. — *Not a man shall be put to death*] the verb in this form is generally used of inflicting death as a penalty. — **14.** Samuel proposes to go to Gilgal *and renew the kingdom there*] there is no reason to suppose that the Gilgal here mentioned is any but the well-known sanctuary in the Jordan valley, not far from Jericho (Jos. 4¹⁹·²⁰ Jd. 2¹). The word *renew* the kingdom is a palpable allusion to the preceding account, and therefore redactional. On the other hand, Gilgal seems to belong to the

main stratum, for otherwise the people would have been invited
again to Mizpah. — **15**. *They made Saul king*] the verb is the
same used in 8²². — *There before Yahweh in Gilgal*] the repeated
mention of Gilgal seems superfluous, but is perhaps intended to
bring out the importance of the occasion. — *They sacrificed there
sacrifices, peace offerings*] the phrase *sacrifices of peace offerings*
is more common. The rendering *peace offerings* is conventional,
as the original meaning of the word is unknown. It designates
the offerings in which the greater part of the flesh forms a sacrificial meal. The *rejoicing before Yahweh* is a prominent element
in early worship.

12. שאול ימלך] may possibly be a question without the interrogative particle,
but of the examples cited as parallel some, at least, do not belong here. Either
the ה or the negative has dropped out; and as the latter has external authority
(𝕲𝕾𝕿) it seems best to restore it. Kl.'s conjecture: *Rather let Sheol rule
over us !* may be cited as a curiosity. — **13**. שאול] Σαμουήλ 𝕲ᴮ is a mere clerical error. — **14**. *Gilgal* in this passage might be supposed to be the Gilgal in
Mt. Ephraim, 2 K. 2¹. But elsewhere in the Books of Samuel the Gilgal in the
Jordan valley is intended. So in 10⁸ where ירדת is appropriate only to the
lower site, cf. 13¹². The name (usually written or pointed with the article)
means *the circle* and designated a circle of sacred stones, a cromlech, cf. Dr.
on Dt. 11³⁰, Moore on Jd. 2¹. For the location we have Jos. 4¹⁹· ²⁰, Eusebius
OS. p. 243, Baedeker *Pal*². p. 167. — ונחדש] the Piel seems to occur in late
passages. Kl. tries to make it mean *let us inaugurate* the kingdom, so
avoiding reference to the earlier anointing. But this is not supported by any
other passage. — **15**. וימלכו] 𝕲 reads: καὶ ἔχρισεν Σαμουὴλ ἐκεῖ [τὸν Σαοὺλ]
εἰς βασιλέα. The shorter text seems original. — שלמים] may be the offerings
which show the undisturbed relations which exist between God and the worshipper, Stade, *GVI.* I. p. 496. 𝕲 inserts καί before the word here.

XII. Samuel's farewell address. — Samuel addresses the people, protesting his integrity during a long career. The people
bear him witness. He then reviews Yahweh's dealings with Israel
from the time of Moses, and enumerates their backslidings, the
punishments which had followed, and the deliverances which
came when they cried to Yahweh. In spite of this experience
they had not trusted Yahweh in the recent danger from Nahash,
but had demanded a king. If they and their king should fear
Yahweh, it might yet be well. But if they should be rebellious,
king and people would be destroyed. In evidence of the truth

of his words he offers a miracle, and Yahweh sends it in the shape
of a thunderstorm, though the season is wheat harvest. The
people are terrified, and confess that the demand for a king is
another in their list of sins. Samuel encourages them that Yahweh
will not reject them, but repeats his warning against defection.

The contrast in thought and style between this section and the
preceding is obvious, and equally obvious is its resemblance to
7, 8, and 10¹⁷⁻²⁴. Outside the Books of Samuel the nearest parallel is Jos. 24 — Joshua's farewell address. The present chapter
seems to be less original than that, and is possibly framed after it
as a model. The thought and language remind us of the framework of the Book of Judges, and there is no violence in the supposition that this address once closed the account of the period
of the Judges, as Joshua's farewell address closed the account of
the conquest of Canaan. In this case the author who set forth
his scheme of history in Jd. 2¹¹–3⁶, and repeated it in Jd. 10⁶⁻¹⁸,
closed his book (or this section of the history of Israel) with this
chapter as a retrospect.

On the relation between this section and the framework of the Book of
Judges, see Moore, *Judges*, p. xxiii. Graf's theory that this was the closing
section of the pre-Deuteronomic Judges seems disproved by the style and
vocabulary, as does Bu.'s (*RS.* p. 182) that it belongs to E² which he puts
before 650 B.C. The question is important enough to warrant a somewhat
detailed examination of the usage of the section. We should first notice that
Bu. strikes out a number of clauses as Deuteronomistic expansions. But there
seems to be no evidence for such a working over of the chapter as this would
imply. Leaving these in the text we note the following affinities: **1.** שמעתי
[בקולכם] frequent in D. — **2.** [מתהלך לפניכם] Gen. 48¹⁵ (E). — **3.** [משיח] frequent
in Sam. and Psalms. — [עשקתי] Lev. 19¹³ Dt. 24¹⁴ 28²⁹, frequent in Ezek. and
the second Isaiah. — [רצתי] in connexion with עשק in Dt. 28³³ Am. 4¹ and in
many confessedly late authors. — [לקח כפר] Num. 35³¹ᶠ· (P) Am. 5¹². — אעלים
[עיני] Lev. 20⁴. — **4.** [מאומה] Gen. 39²³ 40¹⁵ (J) Num. 22³⁸ (E) Dt. 13¹⁸. —
5. [עד יהוה] occurs nowhere else, but nearly parallel are those passages in
which a sacred object is made witness to a declaration, as Jos. 22²⁷ (P)
Gen. 31⁴⁴ (JE). — **6.** [עשה] of appointing men to a work, 1 K. 12³¹ 2 K. 21⁶
Is. 28¹⁵ Eccl. 2⁸. — *Moses and Aaron*] usually associated in P and Chr.,
nowhere in the historical or prophetical books except here — *Moses, Aaron,
and Miriam* stands by itself (Mic. 6⁴). — [העלה] of the deliverance from Egypt
in E, D, Hos. 12¹⁴ Jer. 16¹⁴ 23⁷ al. and in redactional passages. — **7.** [התיצבו]
Ex. 14¹³ (J) 1 S. 10¹⁹. — [ואשפטה] in this sense Jer. 2³⁵ Ezek. 20³⁵ᶠ· Joel 4² and
other late passages. — [צדקות יהוה] Jd. 5¹¹ and, with a different shade of mean-

ing, Mic. 6⁵. — **8.** בא יעקב מצרים] Gen. 46⁶ Ex. 1¹ (both P). — ויזעקו אל־יהוה]
a standing phrase of the Deuteronomistic redactor of Jd.; cf. 1 S. 7⁸· ⁹ 8¹⁸. —
וישיבום] Lev. 23⁴³ Ezek. 36¹¹· ³³. — **9.** וימכר ביד] Jd. 2¹⁴ 3⁸ 4² 10⁷. — **10.** חטאנו
כי עזבנו] Jd. 10¹⁰. עזב is used for forsaking the true God, Jd. 10¹⁰· ¹³ Dt. 28²⁰
31¹⁶ Jer. 16¹¹ and often in Kings. — הבעלים] Jd. 2¹¹, cf. 2¹³ where the Ashtaroth
are brought in as here. — **11.** מיד איביכם] 2 K. 17³⁹. — איביכם מסביב] Dt. 12¹⁰
25¹⁹ Jos. 23¹ Jd. 2¹⁴ 8³⁴. — ותשבו בטח] Dt. 12¹⁰. — **12.** ויהוה מלככם] Is. 33²² 43¹⁵.
— **14.** אם־תיראו את־יהוה] Dt. 6²· ¹³ 10²⁰ Jos. 24¹⁴. — המרו את־פי יהוה] Num. 20²⁴
27¹⁴ (P) Dt. 1²⁶· ⁴³ 9²⁸ 1 K. 13²¹· ²⁶. — **15.** והיתה יד־יהוה בכם] Ex. 9³ (J) Dt. 2¹⁵
Jd. 2¹⁵ 1 S. 7¹³. — **16.** עשה לעיניכם] Dt. 1³⁰ 4³⁴ 29¹ Ex. 7²⁰ (E). — **17.** ויתן קלות]
Ex. 9²³ (E). — אשר עשיתם לשאול] the infinitive with ל, specifying more nearly
what is meant by a preceding noun, is found Gen. 18¹⁹ (R) Dt. 9¹⁸ Jd. 9⁵³ (E)
2 S. 13¹⁶ 1 K. 16¹⁹ Neh. 13⁷. — **19.** החפלל בער] Gen. 20⁷ (E) Dt. 9²⁰, frequent
in Jer. — **20.** אל־תסורו מאחרי] 2 K. 18⁶ 2 Chr. 34³³. — **21.** תהו] notoriously a
late word, applied to false gods in Is. 41²⁹. — לא־יועילו] Is. 44¹⁰ Jer. 2⁸ al. —
22. יטש יהוה] Jd. 6¹³ Is. 2⁶ Jer. 12⁷ Ps. 94¹⁴. — בעבור שמו] cf. Jos. 7⁹ Is. 48⁹
Ezek. 20⁹· ¹⁴· ²². — הואיל יהוה] 2 S. 7²⁹ and the parallel 1 Chr. 17²⁷ Job 6⁹. —
To make you a people for himself] does not occur elsewhere in this exact
wording, but the idea is frequent in Dt. — **23.** והוריתי בדרך] Ps. 25⁸ 27¹¹ 32⁸.
— **24.** The first half of the verse is nearly the same as Jos. 24¹⁴ᵃ. — *With all
your heart*] Jer. 29¹³ Joel 2¹², frequent in Dt. with the addition *and with all
your soul.* — הגדיל עמכם] Ps. 126²· ³. — **25.** הרע תרעו] 1 Chr. 21¹⁷. — תספו]
Gen. 19¹⁵· ¹⁷ 1 S. 26¹⁰ 27¹ Num. 16²⁶.

It must be evident that the passage shows dependence on Dt. and acquaintance with Jer., Ezek., and possibly later writers. The identification with E²
does not therefore seem well grounded, and Graf's theory also falls to the
ground. That the author is acquainted with 11 is seen from his allusion to
Nahash.

1–5. Samuel resigns his office. — He opens his speech by stating the situation : *I have hearkened to your voice . . . and have
appointed a king over you: Now, behold! the king is walking
before you*] the king is thought of as a shepherd walking before
his flock. A paraphrase is Num. 27¹⁶ᶠ· (P). The kingless people
are *sheep without a shepherd*. The Homeric parallel is well
known. — *But as for me I am old and gray and my sons are
among you*] already mature men who show that their father is
advancing in years. Any other reason cannot be imagined for
the mention of the sons here. — *And I have walked before you
from youth until this day*] as Saul is now to do — the people
walk at the heels of the leader, 25²⁷. — **3.** A challenge as to his
own fidelity : *Here am I ! Testify against me*] the phrase is
generally used of a witness who testifies to a crime. The ques-

tions which follow are, perhaps purposely, cast in rhythmical form
with assonance at the end :

> *Eth shōr mi lakáhti*
> *Wa-hamōr mi lakáhti*
> *We-eth mi 'ashákti*
> *Eth mi raççóthi*
> *U-miyyad mi lakáhti kópher.*

The tendency of the prophets to cast their oracles in poetic form
is illustrated elsewhere. The questions all refer to judicial honesty, which has always been rare in the East. Frequent enactments and exhortations in the Old Testament testify to the venality
of the judges in Israel. Samuel asks : *Whose ox have I taken?
Or whose ass have I taken?* He then puts the more general
questions : *Whom have I oppressed? Whom have I maltreated?*
The verbs are elsewhere joined to describe the oppression of the
weak by the powerful. *Or from whose hand have I taken a gift,
that I might blind my eyes with it?* The different reading of ⑮
will be discussed below. The verb meaning *blind* is found Lev. 20⁴
2 K. 4²⁷ Is. 1¹⁵ Ezek. 22²⁶. That a gift *blinds the clear-sighted* is
declared Ex. 23⁸, cf. Dt. 16¹⁹. *Testify against me, and I will restore
it to you!* Such seems the best reading. *And I will answer you,*
which has been proposed, does not seem appropriate, and would
require an additional word. — **4.** The people acquit Samuel, in
the words which he himself has used. — **5.** He solemnly concludes
his attestation by making Yahweh and the king witness : *Yahweh
is witness and his anointed is witness*] the king as the *anointed of
Yahweh* meets us in several instances in the later history. Doubtless the anointing has consecrated the king so that he is appropriately introduced in this connexion. — *That ye have not found in
my hand anything*] that would be a cause of accusation. — *And
they said: He is witness*] confirmatory of what Samuel has just
said. The assertion is made of Yahweh only, who is the principal
person.

1. ‏לכל אשר־אמרתם לי‎] is superfluous, but this author is diffuse throughout.
— **2.** ‏מהלך‎] is lacking in ⑤. — ‏ואני‎] is somewhat emphatic — *Saul is now
your leader, but I for my part have been your leader a long time.* — **3.** ‏ענו בי‎]
Ex. 20¹³ Num. 35³⁰ Dt. 19¹⁶. Before each clause of the second couplet ⑤
inserts the conjunction *or* (= ‏ו‎). — ‏ואעלים עיני בו‎] seems to be perfectly good

Hebrew. 𝕲^{AB} reads καὶ ὑπόδημα; ἀποκρίθητε κατ' ἐμοῦ. As pointed out by
Cappellus (*Critica Sacra*, p. 265), this must represent ונעלים ענו בי. This is
adopted as original by Th., We., Dr., Ki., and has influenced Sirach (46¹⁹),
as pointed out by Schleusner, *Thesaurus*, s.v. ὑπόδημα (the reading is found
in the newly discovered Hebrew fragments). A shoestring is proverbial for a
thing of little worth, Gen. 14²³, as it is in Arabic (Goldziher in *Jour. Assyr.*
VII. p. 296). But the coördination כפר ונעלים for *a bribe even a pair of shoes*
seems strange. We should expect at least גם נעלים, or ואף נעלים (Kl.). For
this reason it seems best to retain 𝕳. It has been supposed that the *pair of
shoes* in Am. 2⁶ is a symbol of transfer of real estate, in which case כפר ונעלים
might mean *gifts of money or deeds of real estate;* and this may be the origin
of the Syriac text of Sirach quoted by Dr., *gift or present*. After עיני בו we
may, however, restore ענו בי (Bu.), the phrases being so much alike that
one was easily lost; 𝕴 is conflate. — **5.** At the end of the verse ויאמר *Kt.* would
be possible, but to the solemn adjuration we should expect the whole people
to reply. The margin of the Massoretic edition, therefore, emends to ויאמרו,
which is found in the text of some editions, and is represented in 𝕲𝕾𝕷𝕿.

6–12. The historical retrospect. — Samuel recites the benefits
received from Yahweh and the people's ingratitude in return.
The beginning of the paragraph is obscure from corruption of
the text. We find in 𝕳 only *Yahweh who appointed Moses and
Aaron*, which is then left without predicate. Fairly satisfactory
is the reading of 𝕲 : *Witness is Yahweh*, though it may not be
the original. — *Who appointed Moses*] is the accepted translation, though *who wrought with Moses* is possible, and is perhaps
favoured by the following verse. — **7.** *And now take your stand
that I may plead with you concerning all the just deeds of Yahweh*]
this, the text of 𝕳, seems to give a good sense. The expanded
text of 𝕲, *that I may plead with you and make known to you*
(generally adopted), seems to be secondary. The reading of 𝕳
is supported by Ezek. 17²⁰. — **8.** The historical sketch proper now
begins, taking the sojourn in Egypt as the starting-point : *When
Jacob came to Egypt the Egyptians oppressed them*] the second
clause has dropped out of 𝕳, but is preserved in 𝕲. — *And your
fathers cried to Yahweh and Yahweh sent Moses and Aaron to
bring out your fathers, and made them dwell in this place*] this is
to be preferred to *and they made them dwell* 𝕳, " which is just
what Moses and Aaron did not make them do " (Dr.). — **9.** The
deliverance was followed by ingratitude : *They forgot Yahweh their
God, and he sold them into the hand of Sisera*] the phrase is often

used of God's delivering over his people into the power of their enemies. It is evidently connected with the prophetic view of Israel as Yahweh's spouse whom for her adulteries he sold into slavery. The list of oppressors here, *Sisera, the Philistines, the king of Moab,* does not pretend to follow the order of the Book of Judges. — **10.** The repentance and confession, followed by a prayer for forgiveness, make use of the language of Jd. 10¹⁰. On the Baals and the Astartes, cf. above, 7³. — **11.** Yahweh had sent as deliverers *Jerubbaal and Barak and Jephthah and Samuel*] *Barak* is adopted from 𝕲 instead of the Bedan of 𝔥, a name not otherwise known except in the genealogical list 1 Chr. 7¹⁷. As the present passage is wholly dependent on the Book of Judges, it is unlikely that it has preserved for us the name of a deliverer otherwise unknown. Rabbinical ingenuity has identified Bedan with *Jair,* Jd. 10³, and *Samson.* The introduction of Samuel into the list occasions no surprise, for the author makes him no whit below the greatest of the judges ; and the very point of the argument is that they had just rebelled against him. There is, therefore, no reason for changing the text at this point. — *And delivered you from the hand of your enemies round about and you dwelt in security*] almost exactly as in Dt. 12¹⁰. The point of view is palpably the same as that of 7¹³. — **12.** The author is so dominated by his idea that he represents the attack of Nahash as the occasion of the demand for a king : *You saw that Nahash king of Ammon came against you*] Bu. thinks the words a later insertion, but they seem necessary to the sense. — *And you said to me : No ! but a king shall rule over us, when Yahweh your God is your king*] the point of view distinctly affirmed.

6. יהוה] so isolated cannot be right : λέγων μάρτυς κύριος 𝕲 represents לאמר עד יהוה which is now generally adopted. 𝔖 has *Yahweh alone is God* and 𝕲ᴸ adds ὁ θεός to κύριος. It is possible therefore that the original was יהוה הוא האלהים which is more appropriate to this fresh start in the speech. — עשה את] the verb is unusual in the sense of appointing to a work, but the combination occurs just below of *working with* one. The rendering of 𝕿 : *who did great things by the hand of Moses* is probably only a paraphrase. — **7.** את כל־צדקות] 𝕲 prefixes καὶ ἀπαγγελῶ ὑμῖν on the ground of which most recent editors insert ואגידה לכם. But the case seems to be one in which the more difficult reading should be retained. The *plus* is lacking in 𝖑 (*Cod. Goth. Leg.* apud Vercellone). — **8.** מצרים] 𝕲 adds καὶ ἐταπείνωσεν αὐτοὺς Αἴγυπτος =

ויענם מצרים which is probably original (Dr., al.), as the omission can be accounted for by homeoteleuton. On the other hand *Jacob and his sons* 𝕲, instead of the simple *Jacob*, seems to be a scribe's expansion. — ויוציאו] as the emphasis is laid upon Yahweh's activity all through, ἐξήγαγεν 𝕲ᴬᴸ may be right. More attractive however is the simple change of pointing to ויציאו (We.) which makes the verb subordinate to the preceding. — ויושיבום] here the singular is decidedly to be preferred (We.), supported by 𝕲𝕾. — **9.** For *Hazor* 𝕲 has *Jabin king of Hazor*, adopted by We., Bu. The latter is in accordance with Jd. 4⁷, but the other is not so entirely without analogy as We. supposes; cf. 1 K. 2³². — **10.** ויאמר *Kt.*: read ויאמרו *Qrê* and versions. — העשתרות] τοῖς ἄλσεσιν 𝕲 as in 7³· ⁴. — **11.** וירבעל] as Jd. 8²⁹; *Deborah* is read here by 𝕾 which inserts *Gideon* later. — ברן] has given the exegetes much trouble. 𝕿 renders it שמשון on the theory that it represents בן דן, as is given by some of the Rabbinical expositors and set forth by Pseudo-Hieronymus in his *Questiones* (*Hier. Op.* Ed. Vallarsi, III. 814). *Barak* 𝕲𝕾 which is read by most recent scholars (including Keil) is the most suitable name. Ew. (*GVI*³. II. p. 514, Engl. Tr. II. p. 364) revived an old conjecture mentioned by Clericus and Michaelis that *Abdon* is the original name (cf. Jd. 12¹³). — שמואל] *Samson* 𝕲ᴸ𝕾 which is adopted by Kl., owes its place to the theory that Samuel would not put his own name here. But the writer found in Samuel the climax of the address, and there is no reason for changing the text or supposing ואת־שמואל to be a later insertion (Bu. and apparently Dr.). — בטח] the accusative of condition, Dav. *Syntax*, § 70 *b*. — **12.** ויהוה אלהיכם מלככם] the clause is lacking in 𝕲. The view which it expresses is found also in Jd. 8²³ (cf. Moore's note) and 1 S. 8⁷.

13-18. The threat of punishment upon people and king in case they turn aside from Yahweh, and its attestation by a miracle. — **13.** *And now*] frequently marks a turn in the discourse or draws a conclusion from what precedes, Jos. 24¹⁴· ²³ Jd. 9¹⁶. *Behold the king which you have chosen*] the received text adds *which you asked*, lacking in 𝕲ᴮ. Even without it the verse is overfull. *And behold! Yahweh has set over you a king*] the desire has been fulfilled. — **14.** The promise in case of obedience : *If you fear Yahweh . . . then you shall live*] on the reading see the critical note. — **15.** The alternative threat uses the same expressions : *hearken to the voice, rebel against the mouth.* The penalty threatened is : *then the hand of Yahweh will be against you and your king to destroy you*] the text of 𝕳 has *and against your fathers* which is absurd. — **16.** In confirmation of the prophet's word the people are to see *the great thing which Yahweh is about to do*] namely, send a thunder-storm in summer. — **17.** *Is it not*

wheat harvest to-day ?] the wheat is ripe after the barley, the first of which is cut at Passover. In this season rain rarely falls in Palestine.* *I will call upon Yahweh and he will send thunder and rain*] lit. *voices and rain.* The thunder is the voice of Yahweh, Ps. 18[14] 29[3]. The result will be their conviction of the great sin they had committed in *asking a king.* — **18.** The event was as Samuel had predicted. At his prayer the voices and the rain came : *and all the people feared Yahweh and Samuel.*

13. אשר שאלתם] omitted in 𝔊[B] but represented in 𝔊[AL] with a ו prefixed, as is the case in many MSS. of 𝔥. The words are an insertion made to counteract the impression that the people themselves had *elected* the king. The shorter text is noted by Capp. *Notae Criticae*, p. 436, and is adopted by most recent critics. — והנה] the ו is omitted by 9 MSS. (DeR.) and 𝔖, but the latter is free in its treatment of the conjunctions. — **14.** The text of 𝔥 is usually taken as " a protasis ending with an aposiopesis " (Dr. *Notes*) : *If ye fear Yahweh . . . and follow . . . after Yahweh your God* — the conclusion is left to the thought of the hearer. But the protasis is unconscionably long, and there is no such reason for the abrupt breaking off as we readily discover in Ex. 32[32] (Moses' impassioned intercession). To begin the apodosis with והיתם is grammatically the correct thing to do, but it makes an identical proposition : *if you fear Yahweh . . . then you will follow Yahweh.* 𝔊[L] feels the difficulty, for it adds at the end of the sentence καὶ ἐξελεῖται ὑμᾶς, which, however, has no other authority. We. gives והיתם as the reading of certain Hebr. MSS. and in one recension of 𝔗 we find ויתחוון, though DeR. denies the manuscript authority and finds that of the version slight. As a conjecture the reading recommends itself, even without any external authority. I have therefore adopted it, omitting the clause אחר יהוה אלהיכם, which was probably added after the corruption to והיתם had taken place (so Kl.). That the people *may live* is frequently given as the end of obedience, Dt. 4[1] Am. 5[14]. — **15.** ובאבתיכם] is evidently unsatisfactory : καὶ ἐπὶ τὸν βασιλέα ὑμῶν 𝔊[B] is what we require. But 𝔊[L] is probably right in adding ἐξολοθρεύσαι ὑμᾶς = להאבידכם, for this alone could give rise to the corrupt reading. The text of 𝔊[L] is adopted by Kl., Bu. Tanchum and Kimchi make ובאבתיכם mean *and upon your kings*, but this is forced. 𝔗𝔖 translate : *as it was upon your fathers*, and are followed by EV. — but this does violence to the Hebrew. — **16.** גם־עתה] is used for variety, ועתה having been twice used. — **17.** ודעו] the imperative expressing the consequence of the preceding verb, cf. Gen. 20[7], König, *Syntax*, 364 *i.* — לשאול] where we should say *in asking.* This construction is not uncommon in Hebrew, cf. König, *Syntax*, 402 *x.* The clause *which ye have done in the eyes of Yahweh* is lacking in 𝔖. — **18.** מאד] is differently placed in 𝔥 and 𝔊, and

---

* Jerome, in his commentary on Amos 4[7], is cited by Clericus, but he says only that he has never seen rain in the latter part of June or in July.

therefore suspicious. We have had occasion to notice that such words are of easy insertion.

19-25. The people's confession and Samuel's concluding exhortation. — The people, in fear of death because of this crowning sin, beseech Samuel's intercession : *Pray for thy servants to Yahweh thy God*] that Samuel stands in a special relation to Yahweh is evident from the language. — **20.** He encourages them : *Ye, indeed, have done this evil, only do not turn aside from following Yahweh*] 2 Chr. 25²⁷ 34³³. — **21.** *And do not turn aside after the nothings*] the word must be taken collectively on account of the verbs which follow : *Which do not profit and do not deliver, for they are nothing*] the language is that of Second Isaiah. — **22.** They have reason to be hopeful : *For Yahweh will not cast away his people for the sake of his great name*] for the verb cf. Jd. 6¹³ : *and now Yahweh has cast us off.* That Yahweh will save his people *for his name's sake* is a comparatively late conception, Jos. 7⁹ (P). That his reputation will suffer if he rejects them is evident : *For Yahweh has undertaken to make you a people for himself*] on the main verb cf. Moore, *Judges*, p. 47. — **23.** The prophet will do his part : *For my part—far be it from me that I should sin against Yahweh, that I should cease to pray for you*] to neglect his mediatorial opportunity would be to sin against both parties. — **24.** The condition is that they should serve Yahweh with steadfastness : *For you see what a great thing he has wrought in your presence*] not *for you*, as in EV. The reference is to the miracle just witnessed. — **25.** In case of persistence in evil they and their king *shall be destroyed;* the verb is used of being killed in battle 1 S. 26¹⁰ 27¹ and probably looks forward to Saul's death at Gilboa.

19. רעה] καὶ κακίας ἡμῶν 𝕲ᴸ; we expect rather הרעה הזאת. — **20.** כל] is lacking in 𝕲ᴸ. — **21.** כי] is entirely meaningless (We., Dr.) and is not represented in the versions. A scribe may have written מאחרי under the influence of the preceding verse and afterwards tried to make it fit here by changing the first letter to כי. — **22.** הואיל] *juravit* 𝕷 indicates האלה, but no change is necessary. — **23.** גם אנכי] the *casus pendens*, Dr. *Tenses*[8], § 196, Dav. *Syntax*, § 106. — חלילה לי מן] is a common construction : *it is too profane a thing for me to do*, cf. Jos. 24¹⁶. — והוריתי אתכם בדרך] cf. Ps. 25⁸. ¹² 32⁸ Prov. 4¹¹. — בדרך] should probably be pointed with the article (Kl., Bu.). — **24.** ויראו] on the form Stade, *Gram.* 111, 2. — **24.** *With all your heart;* 𝕲 prefixes *and.* — כי ראו] ὅτι εἴδετε 𝕲 = כי ראיתם, is certainly smoother.

XIII. and XIV. The revolt against the Philistines and the first successful attack. — Jonathan, Saul's son, opens the war for independence by slaying the resident of the Philistines. The enemy immediately invade the country and take up a strong position whence they ravage the land. Saul's force melts away until he has only six hundred men left and does not feel able to attack. At this juncture, Jonathan with his adjutant makes a foolhardy assault upon a detached post of the Philistines. His success throws their main camp into confusion. The commotion is visible to Saul who, without waiting for the answer of the oracle (which he has begun to consult), musters his men and leads them against the foe. He is reënforced by deserting Hebrews from the Philistine camp, and the day is spent in pursuing and plundering. The success is less pronounced than it might have been, because Saul lays a taboo on the eating of food. Thereby the people become too faint for successful pursuit, and, when the day ends, fall upon the captured cattle in such haste as to eat with the blood. Saul therefore commands a large stone to be used as an altar, and the animals are slain at it without further ritual offence.

The sequel is unexpected to Saul, for, on consulting the oracle with reference to a night attack, he receives no reply. He understands that Yahweh is angry because of the violation of the taboo. The guilty party is sought by the sacred lot and discovered to be Jonathan. He confesses that he ate a little honey in ignorance of his father's objurgation, and avows his willingness to die. But the people intervene and redeem him. There is by this time no thought of further warfare, and the campaign terminates without decisive advantage to either side.

This is the main narrative. It is interrupted (besides minor interpolations) by two digressions ; one (13^{4-15}) gives us at Gilgal an interview between Samuel and Saul in which the latter is informed of his rejection ; the second (13^{19-22}) describes the disarmed condition of Israel. At the end of the section (14^{47-51}) we find a general summary of Saul's activity which may have been added by a later hand. Aside from these, the story is clear and connected, and we have no difficulty in identifying it as a part of the life of Saul which began in 9^1–10^{16}.

There is substantial unanimity in the analysis,* and in the connexion of the main stream of the narrative with the earlier account of Saul's election. The reason for regarding the sections separated above as of later date than the rest of the story, lie on the surface, but will be pointed out in detail in the course of the exposition. The student may be referred to We., *Comp.* pp. 246–248, *Prol*[3]. pp. 266–272; Stade, *GVI.* I. p. 215 ff.; Kuenen, *HCO*[2]. pp. 371, 381; Budde, *RS.* pp. 191 f., 204–208, and his text in *SBOT.;* Cornill, *Einl*[3]. p. 97 f., *ZATW.* X. p. 96 f.; Kittel, *GH.* II. p. 28 (the results in his translation in Kautzsch, *HSAT.*); Driver, *LOT*[6]. p. 175; W. R. Smith, *OTJC*[2]. p. 134.

1. The verse as it stands in 𝕳 is meaningless and evidently a late insertion. — **2.** There seems no difficulty in connecting this verse directly with 11[15]. As soon as Saul was made king he recruited an army of three thousand men : *and two thousand were with Saul in Michmash and in Mount Bethel*] we naturally suppose each place garrisoned with a thousand. Michmash still bears its ancient name, and is a village on the north side of a narrow valley south of which lies Geba. The location is given by Eusebius and Jerome as nine miles from Jerusalem near Ramah. The sides of the wady on which it is located are still very steep. Bethel, now *Beitîn*, the well-known sanctuary, was, like Michmash, a stronghold. Both were occupied by armies in the Maccabean wars. The two places are mentioned together, Ezr. 2[27f.] Neh. 7[31] 11[31]. — *And the rest were with Jonathan his son in Geba of Benjamin*] the confusion of Gibeah and Geba is so obvious in this chapter that I have corrected to the one form throughout. Geba was the village just across the pass from Michmash, and the two together must be held in order to command the pass. For the location cf. Is. 10[29] which, however, makes evident that in Isaiah's time *Geba* and *Gibeah of Saul* were two different places, for after Michmash it mentions in order Geba, Ramah, and Gibeah of Saul. That Geba is intended in our narrative is evident from its mention in the immediate sequel. After the choice of his soldiers, Saul dismissed the rest of the people to their homes. — **3.** Jonathan *smote the Resident of the Philistines*] the verb seems to imply that it was a person, not a trophy or pillar, that was smitten. The rest of the verse : *And the Philistines heard; and Saul blew the trumpet in all the land, saying: Let the Hebrews hear!*] puts the

---

* I should state that I have differed from the consensus in regard to the extent of the insertion which ends at v.[15a].

name *Hebrews* in Saul's mouth, which cannot be correct. The clause *and the Philistines heard* presents a further difficulty because Saul's blowing of the trumpet should follow immediately on Jonathan's deed. For the last two words of the verse 𝕲 renders *the slaves have revolted* in which the verb at least seems to be original. But in this form, or in the form *the Hebrews have revolted*, the clause must represent the report that came to the Philistines. We are tolerably safe in restoring therefore : *and the Philistines heard* [the report] *saying: The Hebrews have revolted*] the intermediate clause will then be suspicious, as a probably late insertion. It is in fact superfluous, and the original narrative probably described a prompt movement of the Philistines upon Michmash, making Saul retreat to Geba, where we find him with six hundred men in v.[16]. This original datum has been expanded into the exaggerated statement of v.[5].

1. The verse as given in 𝔥 can mean only one thing: *Saul was a year old when he began to reign and he reigned two years over Israel*] this is palpably absurd. The earliest endeavour to give the words a sense seems to be recorded in 𝕿 : *Saul was innocent as a child a year old when he began to reign.* This is followed by Theod., and the earlier Rabbinical tradition, including the spurious Jerome in the *Questiones*. Isaaki thinks it possible to render *in the first year of Saul's reign . . . he chose*. RLbG. supposes that a year had passed since his first anointing. Tanchum however knows of interpreters bold enough to assume that a number has dropped out of the text. This has very slight Greek authority on its side, as two MSS. of HP read *Saul was thirty years old*. The whole verse is lacking in the most important MSS. of 𝕲 (𝐀 is defective here) and is therefore suspicious. The suspicion is not relieved by noticing that the sentence is cast in the form of the chronological data found in later parts of the history. It seems tolerably evident that a scribe, wishing to make his chronology complete, inserted the verse *without the numbers*, hoping to be able to supply these at a later date, which however he was unable to do. This applies both to the years of Saul's life and to the years of his reign, for ושתי שנים cannot be correct, and not improbably ושתי is corrupt duplication of the following word (We.). Extended discussion of the verse in the older expositors, Cornelius â Lapide, Schm., Pfeiffer (*Dubia Vexata*) have now only an antiquarian interest. The whole verse should be stricken out. — **2.** אלפים] should be followed by איש as indicated by 𝕲𝕾. On *Michmash*, cf. Baedeker, *Palestine*[2], p. 119, Furrer in Schenkel's *Bibel Lexikon*, IV. p. 216. *Mount Bethel* occurs only here according to 𝔥. On the now generally accepted identification of Bethel with *Beitin* cf. Moore, *Judges*, p. 42. The importance of the two places here mentioned is noted by

GASmith, *Geog.*³ pp. 250, 290. As *Jonathan* has not been mentioned before, the addition *his son* made by 𝔖 has much in its favour.—[בגבעת בנימין] in regard to the place here intended, we may note that Jonathan's deed in the next verse is performed at *Geba*. Moreover, the possession of Geba is important to him who would control the road leading up from the Jordan valley. In v.¹⁶ Saul and Jonathan are occupying Geba, which nevertheless is called *Gibeah of Benjamin* in 14¹⁶. It seems evident that *Geba* is intended throughout this narrative. In the time of Isaiah however as already noted, *Gibeah of Saul* was distinguished from Geba.—[איש לאהליו] the phrase dates back to the time when the people were nomads or at least tent-dwelling *fellahin*.—
3. [ויך] the verb is used nearly always of smiting living beings, once of striking the rock, Ex. 17⁶. But Jonathan would do more than *strike* a pillar, trophy, or triumphal monument; he would *overthrow* it, for which some other verb would be used; Am. 9¹, which is cited as an example of this verb used for the overthrow of columns, is obscure and probably corrupt. This reasoning leads to the conclusion that נציב is an officer or a garrison.—וישמעו פלשתים העברים . . .] is one of the *cruces criticorum*. The somewhat violent treatment advocated above proceeds on the theory that for the words וישמעו העברים: ἠθετήκασιν οἱ δοῦλοι 𝔊 we should restore פשעו העברים (Bu.). If so the words (with or without לאמר) should follow immediately on פלשתים (Bu.). But in that case the intermediate clause is suspicious. The full reason for its omission will be seen only after considering the next verse.

4–15ᵃ. That this paragraph (at least the main part of it) is from a different source is universally conceded. It is characterized by having Gilgal as its scene instead of Geba. But Saul's movement from Geba to Gilgal would be, from the military point of view, an insane step. The highlands were Israel's stronghold. To recover them when once abandoned would be practically impossible. In v.¹⁶ we find Saul and Jonathan still in Geba with their small force. The journey to Gilgal and back is made only to accommodate the compiler. The change of scene is accompanied by a remarkable change of tone in the narrative. In the opening verses Saul and Jonathan act as real rulers of the people. In the following chapter they continue to act in the same way, with no apparent consciousness that their kingdom has been rejected. In the intervening paragraph Samuel appears as the theocratic authority, and Saul is rebuked for having acted independently. Even when he has waited seven days in accordance with Samuel's injunction, and when the cause of Israel is in jeopardy because of the delay, he is chided for taking a single step without Samuel's presence and consent.

The paragraph has usually been supposed a duplicate of ch. 15 and dependent upon that. It seems to me more probable that this is the earlier and therefore the original, the first reason being that it is more closely knit with the older narrative. Besides the phenomena of v.$^{4f.}$, it is distinctly prepared for in 10^8. Only by supposing this to be the earlier narrative can we account for Gilgal as the scene of 15. For the author of that chapter assuredly would have made Samuel depose Saul at Mizpah, the sanctuary where he chose him, had he not found another locality specified by history. It hardly seems likely, moreover, that an author who knew the impressive and implacable narrative of 15 would feel any obligation to compose the one before us. On the other hand, as we have seen, the narrative of which 15 is a part was composed to replace this one, and the author had every reason to duplicate this section as he duplicated other scenes of the older story. It would be desirable to him also (as he is much more distinctly a preacher than the earlier author) to make clear the reason of Saul's rejection, which is, to say the least, only obscurely set before us in the present narrative.

If it be taken as proved that we have here a separate document, the question arises: Exactly where does it begin? Its lower limit is evidently ^{15a}. But the upper limit is not so plain. It is generally assumed to be ^{7b} as we find in Budde's text. To this there seem grave objections. In the first place the gathering of the people is already said to be at Gilgal in v.^{4}. This, to be sure, may be corrected to Geba, or omitted. But Gilgal, as a place of mustering the whole people, seems too natural so to be set aside. Again we have the enormous numbers of the Philistines in v.^{5}, which clearly do not comport with the main narrative — in which Saul operates with only six hundred men, and puts the enemy to flight. In fact the author, having gathered all Israel, is obliged to make them disperse to the caves and dens and carry with them a large part of Saul's standing army. That this could be supposed possible before a single skirmish had taken place does not seem credible in the author who exalts the valour of Jonathan. To this we may add that the *Gilgal* of v.^{4} is confirmed by the opening words of ^{7b} which do not say that Saul came down to Gilgal, but that he was *still there*. For these reasons I suppose

that the original narrative told : that Jonathan smote the resident
of the Philistines and that the Philistines heard of the Hebrew
revolt (^{3}) ; that the Philistines came up in force (^{5a}) ; and then
that Saul mustered the force at his command and found it to be
six hundred men (^{15b}). The promptness with which the Philistines acted was such that there was no time to call out the militia.

4–7. The situation of the people. — Probably the clause we
have cast out of v.^{3} may be prefixed here : *Saul blew the trumpet
in all the land* (^{4}) *and all Israel heard saying: Saul has smitten
the Resident of the Philistines*] it is probably not hypercritical to
see in the change from Jonathan to Saul an evidence of change
of author. — *And also Israel has made itself of ill odour with the
Philistines*] cf. Gen. 34^{30} Ex. 5^{21} 2 S. 10^6 16^{21}. That Gilgal is the
place of muster to this author has already been noticed, and correction or excision of the word is unnecessary. — **5**. The force of
the Philistines is given as *thirty thousand chariots* for which $\mathfrak{G}^{\mathrm{L}}$ $\mathfrak{S}$
have *three thousand*. This is favoured by Bochart and others,
but is still absurdly large. Egypt only mustered six hundred
chariots, Ex. 14^7, and other notices show that this was the scale
for large armies. But our author is prodigal of numbers. Syrian
experience later showed that chariots could not be used in the
hill country of Palestine. — *And people*] that is foot soldiers, *like
the sand which is on the shore of the sea for multitude*] cf. Jd. 7^{12}
2 S. 17^{11}. The Arab's hyperbole is similar : 'like the sand of the
desert.' — *They came up and camped in Michmash, east of Beth
Aven*] Michmash lies about southeast from Bethel, which by a
stretch of the imagination might be described as it is described in
the text. *Beth Aven* seems to be a scribe's distortion of *Bethel*.
In any case, the author who had just spoken of Michmash and
Bethel together (v.^{2}) would hardly have felt it necessary to be so
explicit here. — **6**. *And the men of Israel saw that they were in
a strait for they were hard pressed*] the diffusiveness shows the
writer's difficulty in accounting for the unaccountable dispersion
of the people. — *And the people hid themselves in caves and in
holes and in rocks and in tombs and in pits*] the list is an amplifi-
cation of what we find in 14^{11}, where however the sarcastic remark
of the Philistines does not imply that this elaborate statement has

preceded. — **7.** *And much people*] the reading is conjectural — *crossed the Jordan to the land of Gad and Gilead*] well-known districts in the possession of Israel. — *But Saul was yet in Gilgal . . .*] the latter part of the verse cannot now be restored with any certainty.

4. שמע] is lacking in 𝕾 which joins וכל־ישראל to the preceding verse. — נבאש] *to give intense provocation*, 2 S. 10⁶ 16²¹. — ויצעקו] καὶ ἀνέβησαν 𝕾ᴮ is apparently inner Greek corruption of ἀνεβόησαν which is found in several MSS. (HP). — הגלגל] supported by the versions, is exscinded by Bu., changed into הגבעתה by Co. (*ZKW.* 1885, p. 123). — **5.** Bochart's reduction of the chariots to three thousand, in which he includes the baggage wagons (*Hierozoicon*, Pars. I. Lib. II. Cap. IX.), though only a halfway measure, is adopted by We., Dr., al. — בית און] 𝕾 has *Beth Horon*, 𝕾 has *Bethel*. Nearly all the passages in which the name occurs have a suspicious text. Certainly the author who just wrote בית־אל would have no motive to use a different form here; for *Beth Aven* is another name for *Bethel*. — **6.** ראו] Bu. corrects to ראה on the ground of 𝕾, which, however, can hardly be taken so literally in a case like this. — כי נגש העם] omit העם with We., al.; 𝕾ᴮ has ὅτι στενῶς αὐτῷ μὴ προσάγειν αὐτόν. It is possible that the text is corrupt, though what Hebrew original is implied by 𝕾ᴮ is hard to discover. The verb נגש is used of an overseer's driving his slaves. — ובחוחים] is doubtless a corruption of ובחרים as first suggested by Ew. — צריחים] the word is used (as pointed out by Dr.) in the inscriptions of Medain Salih, for sepulchres hewn in the rock. — **7.** ועברים עברו] καὶ οἱ διαβαίνοντες διέβησαν 𝕾. I am not certain that the suggested reading וְעֹבְרִים עָבְרוּ is not correct. But as the participle in such cases usually follows the verb, I have followed Bu. in adopting Kl.'s conjecture, ועם רב עברו. We. proposed ועברו מעברות which was syntactically improved by Dr. into ויעברו מעברות. The final clause of the verse cannot be correct. Nor does We.'s emendation of אחריו to מאחריו on the basis of 𝕾ᴸ meet the difficulty. The flight of the people has already been described; what we now want to know is who remained. Kl. conjectures העם הרדף אחריו which is favoured by 𝕷. I should prefer העם יירד אחריו but do not feel certain that either is correct.

8–15ᵃ. Saul's rejection.

— He waited in Gilgal *seven days for the appointed time which Samuel had set*] the reference is to 10⁸ where, as we have already seen, Samuel directs him to go down to Gilgal and wait seven days for his coming. When Samuel did not appear *the people scattered away from him*] as we should expect, especially in a levy of undisciplined troops without commissary. — **9.** Saul orders the offering to be brought and himself *offered the burnt offering*] war was initiated with religious cere-

monies, as is indicated by the phrase *consecrate war* Jer. 6⁴, al. —
10. As Saul finished the ceremony *Samuel came and Saul went
out to greet him*] with the customary : *Blessed be thou !* is intimated by the word used, cf. 2 K. 4²⁹. — **11.** To Samuel's question :
What hast thou done ? he replies : *I saw that the people were
scattering away from me, and thou didst not come at the appointed
term and the Philistines were gathering at Michmash*] everything
seemed to call for prompt action ; "non solum se excusat sed
omnes, quotquot potest, accusat." * — **12.** *And I said*] he means
he said to himself : *Now will the Philistines come down to me to
Gilgal and the face of Yahweh I have not appeased*] by a gift, Ps.
45¹³ ; the phrase is also used of approaching Yahweh with entreaty,
Ex. 32¹¹ 1 K. 13⁶. — *And I constrained myself*] elsewhere in the
sense of restraining one's emotions, Gen. 43³¹ 45¹ Is. 42¹⁴. The
intimation is that he would have waited still longer, but the circumstances forced his hand. — **13.** The reply of Samuel : *Thou hast
acted foolishly ! If thou hadst kept the commandment of Yahweh
thy God which he commanded thee, then would Yahweh have established thy kingdom over Israel forever*] for changes in the pointing
of 𝕳 see the critical note. — **14.** *But now*] adversatively as in
2³⁰ cf. 24²¹, *thy kingdom shall not stand.* That the language and
behaviour of Samuel are less stern and damnatory here than in 15
will be generally conceded ; the fact makes for the priority of this
account. — *Yahweh has sought out a man according to his heart*]
the divine purpose is already a fixed fact. — *And Yahweh has set
him as Leader over his people*] still the consecutive tense, in view
of the divine purpose. — **15ᵃ.** The verse as it stands in 𝕳 tells us
of Samuel's going up *to Geba.* But as we hear nothing more of
him there, this is evidently a mistake. A clause has fallen out by
homeoteleuton which is preserved in 𝕲 and which should be
restored as follows : *And Samuel arose and went up from Gilgal
and went his way, and the rest of the people went after Saul to
meet the men of war and came from Gilgal to Geba of Benjamin*]
the eye of the scribe fell upon the second Gilgal instead of the
first.

What was Saul's sin in this matter is nowhere expressly set down,

---

* Mendoza, cited in Poole's *Synopsis.*

H

and it is difficult to discover anything in the text at which Samuel could justly take offence. The original command was to wait seven days, and this Saul did. In the circumstances he might well plead that he had been too scrupulous. It would not be impertinent to ask why Samuel had waited so long before appearing. No reason is given for his delay, and in the mind of the narrator there seems to have been no reason except that Samuel wished to put Saul to the test. It cannot be said that Saul usurped priestly prerogatives in offering with his own hand. The narrator would certainly have let us know this had it been his conception. Whatever may have been the priestly rights at this time, we may well suppose that the author thought of Saul as no more intruding upon them than did David and Solomon when they sacrificed. The language of Samuel's rebuke speaks of disobedience to a command of Yahweh, which however can only be the command of 10^8 which Saul literally obeyed. The only conclusion to which we can come is that the author glorifies the sovereign will of Yahweh who rejects and chooses according to his own good pleasure. Samuel is the embodiment of this sovereign will. The straits of the commentators are evident. Keil interprets Samuel's language not as a rejection of Saul, but as an announcement of the brevity of his reign. But this is contrary to the sense. Ewald says: "The ruler who prematurely and out of mere impatience lays his hand on that from which he should have refrained, trifles away his real power and his best success." * But the condemnation of Saul as acting 'prematurely' and 'out of mere impatience' is not warranted by anything in the text. Clericus also is obliged to read something into the text: "Forte citius aequo Sacra facturus, contemptim de Samuele aut cogitavit aut etiam loquutus est." Thenius also frames hypotheses for which there is no warrant in the narrative.

8. וייחל] is intended to be Piel, a not uncommon form, Stade, *Gram.* p. 278. It seems unnecessary to change to ויחל *Qrê.* מועד is an appointed time or place, cf. למועד דוד 20^{35}. — אשר שמואל] is impossible; we must either strike out אשר with 𝔖 or insert a word; אמר is inserted by Th., We., Bu. on the ground of 𝔊𝔗; שם is preferred by Kl., Dr., and might easily have been lost before שמואל. 6 Hebr. MSS. insert אמר; 5 insert שם (DeR.), cf. Ex. 9^5.

* Ew., *GVI*[3]. III. p. 46, E. Tr. III. p. 32.

[ויפץ —] cf. 2 S. 20²². — **9.** [והעלה] out of the several animals that were offered, the *'ola* was the one specially set apart for Yahweh. — **10.** [ככלתו . . . והנה] marks the appearance of Samuel just as the burnt offering was completed. — **11.** [כי] is probably to be taken as *כי recitativum* (Dr.), but it may also answer Samuel's unspoken question as to *why* Saul had acted as he had. — [נפּ֥ל] is probably to be pointed so (Bu.), cf. v.⁸, from which we see that the verb is [פוץ. — **12.** [ופני יהוה לא חליתי] the sentence is generally used of conciliating God. — **13.** [לא] is the pointing of the received text, but we should quite certainly read לֻ֥א, that is לוא, proposed by Hitzig (as stated by We. who, however, gives no reference, apparently depending upon Th., who gives Zeller, *Theol. Jahrb.* 1843, II. 278 ff.). The particle לו in a hypothesis contrary to reality, is followed in the apodosis by כי עתה, as here, in Num. 22²⁹ I S. 14³⁰ Job 6². Dr. inclines to retain the pointing of 𝔐, cf. also Dav., *Syntax*, § 131, R. 2. — [עתה] has lost its temporal force and become logical (Dav.). For: *the commandment of Yahweh thy God which he commanded thee*, we find in 𝔊 *my commandment which Yahweh commanded thee*. — **14.** [בקש] on the use of this tense, Dr., *Tenses*³, §§ 13, 14, Dav., *Syntax*, § 41. — [לו] the dative of advantage, Dav., *Syntax*, § 101, R. 1 *b*. — [כלכבו] the only exact parallel seems to be Jer. 3¹⁵, but cf. 2 S. 7²¹. — [ויצוהו לנגיד] 25³⁰ 2 S. 6²¹, the verb is used of appointing the Judges 2 S. 7¹¹, cf. Num. 27¹⁹. — **15.** The plus of 𝔊 is already noted by Mendoza (in Poole's *Synopsis*). — [מן־הגלגל] according to 𝔊ᴸ (from which the words passed into the current recension of 𝔏) we should add: וילך לדרכו ויתר העם עלה העם אחרי שאול לקראת עם המלחמה ויבאו מן הגלגל. The correction is adopted by all recent scholars (except Keil). Probably ויעל of 𝔏 is not original (not represented in 𝔊) and was inserted after the loss of this sentence. In addition to the commentaries on this passage, the reader may be referred to Graetz, *Gesch. d. Juden*, I. p. 175, and Ew., *GVI*³. p. 45, E. Tr. III. p. 32.

15ᵇ. The half verse tells us that *Saul numbered the people that were with him, about six hundred men.* As we find the same number given in 14², it is possible that it is an insertion here. We are even tempted to suppose the whole sentence an effort of the redactor to fit together the two discordant sections of his narrative.

16–18. The Philistine raid. — The first verse describes the condition of things which followed Jonathan's first stroke. The Philistines were in virtual possession of the country. The Hebrews only maintained themselves in one post: *Saul and Jonathan his son, and the people that were with them, were abiding in Geba of Benjamin*] the addition made by 𝔊 seems uncalled for. — **17.** The Philistine policy is to reduce the people to submission by devastating the country far and wide. The plunderers were in three divisions : *One division turned to the Ophrah road*] apparently the Ophrah mentioned among the towns of Benjamin, Jos. 18[23]. It was identified by Robinson * with *Taiyibeh,* five miles northeast of Bethel. The location would suit the present narrative. *The land of Shual* seems to be nowhere else mentioned. — **18.** The second band turned west from Michmash towards *Beth Horon,* a well-known town west of Michmash. As the Philistine force came from the west, there seems no reason why they should send foragers out in that direction. But perhaps the author thinks of them as having come up by a more northerly road. The third band went eastward : *towards the hill which overhangs the valley of Zeboim*] the description points to one of the heights which overlook the Ghor. The author thinks of a Philistine force settled at Michmash which employed itself in punishing the country, not looking for serious opposition. The *valley of Zeboim* is of course one of the wadys of which the region is full. A place, Zeboim in Benjamin, is mentioned after the exile, Neh. 11[34]. Verse [18] is continued directly by v.[23]; what is between is a later insertion.

16. After בנימין, 𝔊[B] adds καὶ ἔκλαιον, which is adopted by Graetz (*Gesch.* I. p. 175) and Kl. But it is hardly likely that the little band of soldiers would so give way to grief before they had tried conclusions with the enemy. — **17.** המשחית] the verb is used of laying a land waste, as the Bedawin do by pasturing cattle on the growing crops, Jd. 6[4], or, more seriously, by cutting down the fruit trees, a custom forbidden in Dt. 20[19f.] as it is by Arabic common sense. — שלשה ראשים] accusative of condition, Dr., *Notes,* Dav., *Syntax,* § 70, R. 1. — אחד] where we should expect האחד. A similar instance is found in I[2], cf. König, *Syntax,* § 334 *s.* — יפנה] the tense shows repeated action. The *land of Shual* is combined by Th., Erdm., with *the land of Shaalim* 9[4]. Robinson's identification of Ophrah is accepted by GASmith, *Geog.* p. 291, Note 1, but rejected by Dillmann (*Num. Lev. Jos.* p. 551 f.) on the ground that it is too far north for a Benjamite town. But it is not unlikely that the author in Jos. (P) made it a Benjamite town because he found it in this Benjamite history; cf. also Buhl, *Geog.* p. 177. — **18.** הגבול] Γαβεέ 𝔊 points to הגבעה, and, as We. remarks, it is only a *hill* that can be said to overhang a valley. — גי הצבעים] *Hyena Gorge* is still the name (*Wady abu Duba'*) of a valley north of *Wady Kelt* according to Ges., *WB*[12]., but Buhl (*Geog.* p. 98) makes it one of the side valleys of the latter, or even the *Wady Kelt* itself. — המדברה] is omitted by 𝔊 and looks like an explanatory insertion.

---

* *BR*[2]. I. p. 447.

19-22. The lack of arms in Israel. — The paragraph intends to represent Israel as having been disarmed by the Philistines, but its wording is obscure owing to corruption of the text. The disarmament is nowhere indicated in the rest of the narrative, and as the four verses can be cut out without injuring the connexion, we are safe in assuming that they are an interpolation. Schmid, who feels the inconsistency of this with the rest of the narrative, supposes the disarmament confined to Gibeah and its vicinity.

19. There was no smith in all the land of Israel ; *for the Philistines said : Lest the Hebrews make sword or spear*] the motive is expressed in the words of the actors, as in Gen. 32^{21} 42^4 2 S. 16^3 18^{18}. — **20.** The result was that all Israel was compelled to go to the land of the Philistines : *that every man might sharpen his ploughshare and his coulter and his axe and his pickaxe*] work necessary to the peasant. Most recent scholars give the *oxgoad* as the fourth instrument. But however formidable the spike in the end of the oriental oxgoad may be, it can scarcely be supposed that it must be taken to the smith to be sharpened. The author of the verse meant to name those tools which need to be set and tempered by the smith. — **21.** The verse is admitted to be hopelessly corrupt by Th., We., Dr., Bu., Ki. What we expect is either a further account of the oppressive regulations, or else a consequence such as is drawn in v.^{22}. The former is in the mind of the Greek translators when they say (as it would seem) that the price of the smith's work on each tool was three shekels. The latter is the conjecture of Jerome who speaks of the *bluntness* which affected all the tools of the farmer on account of the difficulty of getting them sharpened. A third conjecture is found in 𝕿 and has passed over into the English version in the form : *yet they had a file for the mattocks*. But this is as impossible to get out of the text as either of the others. — **22.** The results of the Philistine policy : *So it came to pass in the day of the battle of Michmash, that none of the people with Saul and Jonathan had either sword or spear — but Saul and Jonathan had them*] the original narrative seems to know nothing of this when it gives Saul a standing army of three thousand men.

23. The verse takes up the account of the Philistine position. In v.¹⁷ᶠ· the plunderers are described. Here we are told that *the garrison,* or the permanent guard left in the camp, pushed forward to the edge of the pass of Michmash.

19-22. The secondary nature of the paragraph is recognized by We., *Comp.* p. 248, Bu., *RS.* p. 205 (he includes v.²³), Co., *Einl*³. p. 97, and Ki. in Kautzsch, *HSAT*. — **19**. חרש] is used of a worker in wood, stone, or metal; τέκτων σιδήρου 𝕲 may point to חרש ברזל (cf. Is. 44¹²), or it may be simply an attempt to render the word as the context requires. — אמר] is changed to אמרו by the *Qrê* unnecessarily. — **20**. הפלשתים] the conjecture of Dr. Weir (given by Dr.) that we should read ארצה פלשתים is confirmed by 𝕲𝕿. — ללטש] *to beat out,* as the blacksmith does in reforging worn tools. Of the four implements here mentioned, the first and third seem to be tolerably certain, though tradition, as represented by the versions, is not uniform.   מחרשה is most naturally the *ploughshare,* though 𝕲ᴬᴮ has the *sickle,* with which 𝕾 agrees, while 𝕿 renders *oxgoad.* — אתו] should be pointed אִתּוֹ according to the form in Is. 2⁴ (Mic. 4³) Joel 4¹⁰. Beyond the fact that it is a tool of some kind, we cannot go with certainty. 𝕲 gives σκεῦος simply; Symmachus translates σκάφιον, which is the *mattock* (Procop. Gaz. *Com.* in loco). The passages in Isaiah and Joel speak of beating the את into a sword, or *vice versa.* This would fit the *coulter,* a knife fastened to the plough-beam to cut the sod before the ploughshare turns it. But we do not know whether the Hebrew plough had such an appendage. 𝕾 renders *ploughshare,* and 𝕿 *the pin of the yoke.* — קרדם is quite certainly the *axe,* Jd. 9⁴⁸. The fourth tool differs (in the received text) from the first by the pointing only. This identity is suspicious, and we probably have the mistake of a scribe to deal with. But what we should restore is doubtful. We. and others propose דרבנו, influenced by the occurrence of this word in v.²¹ and the rendering δρέπανον 𝕲, which word occurs also in v.²¹ 𝕲, though דרבן is nowhere else so rendered. But in the confusion of the text of v.²¹, it is difficult to allow much weight to the argument; for until we know what that verse means, we cannot be sure that it gives the same list of tools with this. The versions give the further choice of the *mattock* (Sym.), the *spade* 𝕾, the *adze* 𝕿, τριόδους (Aq.), *sarculum* 𝕷, and the *axe* (Ar.). To such variety it may be impertinent to add the conjecture of Ew. (*GVI*³. III. p. 47, E. Tr. III. p. 33), who reads חריצו, though his translation, the *threshing sledge,* will hardly do. According to Hoffmann (*ZATW.* II. p. 66), חריץ is the stonemason's pick, from which we may conjecture that the *pickaxe* would be called by the same name. This is an indispensable tool to the peasant in a rocky country like Palestine, and could scarcely be kept in shape without the services of a blacksmith. I have therefore ventured to insert it in my translation of the verse. — **21**. The difficulties of the verse seem to be insurmountable. — והיתה הפצירה פים] is ungrammatical, and unintelligible even if we try to correct the grammar. — ולשלש קלשון] is without analogy in Biblical Hebrew (on both phrases, cf. Dr., *Notes*). — והציב] coördinated as it is (or seems to be) with names of tools, makes no sense. For the opening clause we find καὶ ἦν ὁ τρυγητὸς ἕτοιμος τοῦ θερίζειν ⅏ = ויהי הקציר נכון לקצר, which is not very remote from ⅏. But this promising beginning is left incomplete. If we were told that *when the harvest was ready to reap* the Philistines came up and plundered it, or that the war broke out, we could fit the statement into this context. But what ⅏ actually adds is : τὰ δὲ σκεύη ἦν τρεῖς σίκλοι εἰς τὸν ὀδόντα, which is supposed to mean that *the tariff fixed for the tools was three shekels apiece*, though it takes violent treatment to get this meaning from the words. The final clause in ⅏ moreover, which affirms that the same arrangement held for the axe and the sickle, is superfluous. Th., reading הפציר הפים, translates *and the sharpening of the edges* (for the ploughshares and the spades) *was three shekels apiece*. But the meaning proposed for הפציר and for הפים is without authority, and the meaning *apiece* for לשן is also unparalleled. *Retusae itaque erant acies vomerum* 𝕷 is an attempt to make sense out of the text of ⅏, but is contrary to grammar, and provides no suitable preface to the final clause *usque ad stimulum corrigendum*. Another attempt is made by ℭ, which apparently supposes הפצירה to mean a file, for it translates: *and they had a file to sharpen the dulness of the iron tools*. ⅏ also has the file (if, indeed, שופינא רפתא be the file), though it understands that the Hebrews in their necessity used their large files for ploughshares (?) and for other tools. This is more fully developed by Ar., which says in so many words: *they fashioned the broad file into a pruning-hook, and took pegs from the harrows for picks*. These differences of interpretation show the impossibility of making sense of the text as it stands, or even of finding a plausible emendation. The final clause ולהציב הדרבן seems to connect most naturally with ללטש of the preceding verse. But the sentence is long and awkward unless we assume with Toy (in Erdm.) that the verse is mainly an erroneous duplication of the preceding. For this hypothesis there is some colour in the repetition of several of the same words. But when written in parallel lines, the correspondence is not very striking. — הדרבן] for the pointing, cf. Stade, *Gram.* 52 *a*. — **22.** והיה] should probably be made ויהי. After מלחמת (on the face of it a construct form) we should probably insert מכמש with ⅏ (Ew.). Toy proposes to read מכמש instead of מלחמת : *in the day of Michmash* would naturally mean *in the day of the battle of Michmash*. — **23.** מצב means in 14 the soldiers who were in occupation of the camp, in distinction from those who went out on the various expeditions. Here however it may mean the outpost which was thrown forward to protect the main camp from surprise. — מעבר] it is unnecessary to change the pointing to מֲעֲבַר with Ewald. What is meant is the *pass* from the highlands to the Jordan valley, which ran down the wady. The village of Michmash lay a little back from the ravine; the Philistine outpost was stationed on its very edge.

XIV. 1. Jonathan proposes an attack. — The main stream of the narrative here recurs, and tells of Jonathan's proposal to his

adjutant. A digression is made to describe the scene more exactly. —*It came to pass on that day*] that is, the particular day of which we are to speak, as in 1⁴—*that Jonathan ben Saul said to his armour-bearer*] it is proper that Jonathan should be given his full name at the beginning of so important a paragraph. The name does not imply that he has not been mentioned before, cf. 23¹⁶. The *armour-bearer* was the man chosen by a leader or prominent officer to be his trusty attendant, aid, adjutant, *armiger*, or squire. Jonathan proposes a surprise of the enemy's post, but does not let his father know, doubtless fearing to be forbidden the fool-hardy attempt. — **2**. The situation is described: first, with refer-ence to Saul, who *was sitting in the uttermost part of Geba*] so we must read, to be consistent, *under the pomegranate tree which is in the threshing-floor*] for the reading, see the critical note. The force with him was the *six hundred men* already mentioned. — **3**. An important member of the camp is the priest who has charge of the sacred lot. He is mentioned here in order to prepare us for the part he is afterwards to take. — *Ahijah ben Ahitub, brother of Ichabod*] the mention of Ichabod is possibly the work of the redactor. Ahimelech ben Ahitub, mentioned in the later history, may be the same as this Ahijah, the names being synonymous. The priest is described as *bearing the ephod*] in the correct text of v.¹⁸ we learn that Saul commanded the ephod to be brought, cf. also 23⁹ 30⁷. In these cases the ephod can hardly be the priest's garment. Beyond the fact that it was the instrument of the oracle, however, we know nothing about it. The description of things in Saul's camp closes with the state-ment: *the people did not know that Jonathan and his armour-bearer had gone*] they were therefore surprised when the commo-tion made itself visible in the opposing camp. — **4**. The locality of the exploit is described to us: *Between the ravines by which Jonathan sought to cross*] that is, side valleys running into the main wady. As we can readily see, these would leave projecting points, two of which are now described: *a tooth of rock on one side and a tooth of rock on the other*] cf. Job 39²⁸ and the well-known *Dent du Midi*. The names of the two rocks in question were *Bozez* and *Seneh*. We may conjecture that Bozez, *the shin-ing*, was the one facing the south, Seneh, *the thorny*, the one facing

the north.* — **5.** The description is completed by the statement
that *one rock was on the north in front of Michmash, the other on
the south in front of Geba*] each hill is defined by the village
nearest to it, to which it served as a fortification. Notice that 𝔊
has *Geba* here.

1. ויהי היום] the same expression 1⁴, cf. Ges.²⁶ § 126 *s.* — נשא כליו] Abimelech had such an attendant and so apparently had Gideon, Jd. 9⁵⁴ 7¹⁰. —
מעבר] Num. 32¹⁹ Jos. 22⁷ Jd. 7²⁵. The passages show that the word means
simply *beyond.* — הלז] cf. Dr. in BDB. *sub voce*, with his reference, Wright,
Comp. Gram. p. 117.⚡ בקצה הגבעה] as *Geba* is the town overlooking the pass,
it must be meant here. For בקצה describing a position on the outskirts of the
town cf. 9²⁷. — הרמון] evidently a well-known tree. מגרון is meant by 𝔊 as a
proper name, and in fact there is a *Migron* not far away, Is. 10²⁸. But as it
lies north of Michmash it will not answer our author's purpose. The versions
make a proper name of the word here, but do not agree in the form. As the
location is already given with some exactness a proper name is superfluous. On
this account We. proposes מֻרֶן with the meaning of גרן *a threshing-floor.* A
threshing-floor is usually located on a bare open hill and so would be excellent
for Saul's purpose — to prevent surprise and keep watch of the enemy's movements. — **3.** אחיה] in 21² 22⁹ we find the priest at Nob called אחימלך and he
also is a son of Ahitub. It is not unlikely therefore that the two names
designate the same individual, the original אחימלך having been changed to
avoid the suggestion of *Molech.* The identification is cited by Schm. from
Sanctius. On the assumed meaning *my brother is Yahweh,* or *brother of
Yahweh,* cf. Jastrow, *JBL.* XIII. p. 101 ff., and Barton, *ibid.* XV. p. 168 ff.
Keil is at pains to calculate the age of Ahijah to show that he could have had
a son old enough to accompany David after Saul's massacre of the priests. —
אי־כבוד] Ἰωχαβήλ 𝔊ᴬᴮ. — פינחס] is written פנחס 1³ (by the occidentals only).
Nestle (*Am. Jour. Sem. Lang.* XIII. p. 173) follows Lauth in supposing the
name (borne also by a son of Aaron) to be Egyptian and to mean *negro.* —
נשא אפוד] there seems to be no clear instance where נשא means *to wear* an
article of dress. In Ex. 28¹², ²⁹ however it describes the High Priest as bearing (or wearing) the names on the breastplate. The use of נשא would therefore be against the theory that the ephod was an article of clothing. On the
other hand, Samuel and David are *girded* with an ephod (2¹⁸ 2 S. 6¹⁴) which
would indicate that it could be worn. See Moore on Judges 17⁵, with the
extended list of authorities there given. — **4.** המעברות] on the daghesh cf. Stade,
Gram. § 317. The form is construct, governing the clause which follows,
Ges.²⁶ § 130 *c*; Dav., *Syntax,* § 25. 𝔊 however connects the first two words
of the verse with the preceding: *the people did not know that Jonathan had
gone to the pass.* — מהעבר] occurs only here and with מזה seems superfluous;

---

* So GASmith, *Geog.* p. 250.

one of the two words is omitted by 𝕲. — בוצץ] the attractive conjecture of GASmith as to the meaning of the word goes back apparently to Gesenius, *Thesaurus*, p. 229: appellativa significatio videtur *splendens*. Later lexicons take no notice of this. The form in 𝕲 is Βαζέθ or Βαζές. — חֶנֶה] is thus pointed by Ginsburg; the editions vary. The word is doubtless the same with סְנֶה, *the thorn*, as for example, the burning bush Ex. 3²⁻⁴, cf. Dt. 33¹⁶. The word has been transferred from Arabic to English in the name of the medicinal *senna;* 𝕲 has Σεννάρ. The two names are rendered by 𝕿, *Slippery* and *Inaccessible.* — 5. It is a question whether מצוק gives a suitable sense. Besides this passage it is used in 2⁸ only, and there it is used of the pillars which support the earth. But it will hardly do to say of a hill that it is *a column on the north.* In modern Hebrew ציק is the peak or summit of a hill (Levy, *NHWB.*). But what is required here is a word like בצור, which however seems to be applied specifically to cities or walls. As מצוק is not represented in 𝕲, it may be an intruder corrupted from the מצפון which follows. Were it original we should expect it to be repeated in the second half of the verse. It is exscinded by Th., Dr., Bu.; while Kl. goes his own way as usual. With מי מול defining a location, compare Ex. 34³ Dt. 4⁴⁶.

6–12. Jonathan suggests an omen. — The account takes up the speech of Jonathan, which was interrupted by the digression concerning the scene of the exploit. He first proposes to go against the enemy, and receives a hearty assurance of support from his squire. He then reveals his plan, which is, that they show themselves at the bottom of the valley. They would then notice the words used by the Philistines, and take from them a sign to indicate whether they should go further or stand still. The older commentators are confident that Jonathan, in proposing this test of the divine will, as well as in making the expedition, was acting under divine inspiration. See the question discussed at length by Schmid.

6. *Come, let us go over to the garrison of these uncircumcised*] the Philistines are frequently so stigmatized, Jd. 14³ 15¹⁸ 1 S. 18²⁴⁻²⁷ 31⁴ 2 S. 1²⁰. Jonathan's hope of doing something is a hope in God: *Perchance Yahweh will act for us*] there seems no reason to question the construction. — *For Yahweh finds no hindrance to his saving power in the many or the few*] that is, whether many be opposed, or few be on his side. — **7.** By emendation we get: *Do all to which thy heart inclines: behold, I am with thee; as thy heart so is my heart*] the text of 𝕳 is awkward, and it is doubtful

whether it will bear the meaning given it in EV. — **8–10.** Indication of the divine will is to be found in the conduct of the enemy :
See we will cross over to the men, and show ourselves to them] by
coming into the open at the bottom of the ravine, where the
Philistine sentinels would see them. — **9.** *If they say thus to us :
Stand still until we can reach you ! then we will stand still in our
place*] the mind of the enemy to attack might be a reason for
caution.　But we can hardly say that the challenge to come up
was a sign of cowardice, as is affirmed by Th. : ironiam ex con-
sternato animo profectam esse existimamus, Schm. — **10.** If, on
the other hand, the Philistines should invite them to come up,
they would make the attempt : for in that case *God will have
given them into our hand*] we cannot help seeing in this the arbitrary selection of an omen.　The nearest parallel is the *sign* prayed
for by Abraham's servant, whereby he might know the predestined
wife of Isaac, Gen. 24[14]. — **11.** The Philistines discover the advent-
urers, and say to each other : *See ! Hebrews are coming out of the
holes where they hid themselves !*] the expression does not necessarily presuppose the account in 13[6]. — **12.** The Philistines then
cry out to Jonathan and his armour-bearer : *Come up to us that
we may tell you something !*　The light language is simply a challenge, probably a banter.　It is not necessary to inquire what the
speakers expected to tell the strangers.　The words used do not
admit of being understood : *we will show you how to fight.*
Jonathan accepts the omen, and calls to his armour-bearer to
climb up after him, adding : *For Yahweh has given them into the
hand of Israel*] the victory is, in the divine purpose, already
obtained.

6–12. In this paragraph, except 12[b], we find the name of the hero spelled
יהונתן whereas elsewhere in these two chapters we have יונתן.　The fuller form
reappears in 18–20 and in 2 S.　The change of form just here may be explained
by supposing this paragraph the work of a different hand.　The incident is
one which might be interpolated by a pious scribe who wished to magnify
Jonathan's faith and dependence on God.　But it is skilfully wrought into the
narrative and cannot well be spared.　For a discussion of the names which
begin with יהו and יו see Bonk in *ZATW.* XI. pp. 125–156.

6. ונעברה] 𝔊 omits the ו. — אולי] expresses a hope, as in Gen. 32[21]. —
יעשה יהוה לנו] has an analogy in Jd. 2[7]; the object מעשה is contained in the
verb : *perchance Yahweh will do a deed for us* (Schm.).　Some have ques-

tioned whether the text is sound, and Kl. proposes to emend to יושיע לנו.
But this seems unnecessary. — מעצור] the noun occurs nowhere else, but the
verb is not infrequent in the meaning *to shut up, to keep back*. — [כרב או במעט
is logically connected with מעצור. — **7**. The received text is awkward, and it
is a question whether it can be translated.   נטה certainly does not belong in
a sentence where it must be made to mean *go on*.   𝕲 seems to have had
another text : ποίει πᾶν ὃ ἐὰν ἡ καρδία σου ἐκκλίνῃ would represent עשה כל אשר
לבבך נטה לו, and this preserves the natural meaning of נטה, cf. Jd. 9⁸.   This
text, suggested by Ew., has been accepted by most recent scholars. — [כלבבך
𝕲 adds καρδία μοῦ, which also is generally accepted since Ew. — **8**. [עברים
the participle is used of action in the immediate future and is carried on by
וננלינו. — **9**. For המו, *be still*, cf. Jer. 47⁶, and, of the sun's standing still, Jos.
10¹²ᶠ.   For הגיענו 𝕲 has ἀπαγγείλωμεν, perhaps reading הגידנו. — [תחתינו] *in
our tracks* is a colloquial equivalent, cf. Ex. 16²⁹ Jd. 7²¹. — **10**. [ויאמרו] +πρὸς
ἡμᾶς 𝕲 with which 𝕾 agrees.   But no great stress can be laid upon the
evidence for so easy an insertion. — [עלינו] πρὸς ἡμᾶς is the rendering of 𝕲,
as in v.¹² where 𝕳 has אלינו, which should probably be read here. — [בירנו] a
number of codd. have בידינו, but cf. Gen. 43²¹ Dt. 32²⁷. — [וזה] the ו is lacking in 𝕲𝕾𝕷 and may have come from erroneous duplication of the preceding
letter. — [עברים] in the mouth of the Philistines as elsewhere ; here without the
article : *some Hebrews*, not *the Hebrews* as in 𝕲.   According to We., Hitzig
conjectured עכברים, *mice*. — **12**. [המצבה] is doubtless to be corrected to המצב,
the form elsewhere used in this narrative.

13–16. The attack. — When Jonathan and his armour-bearer

accept the challenge, the garrison is thrown into confusion, and
the confusion soon becomes a panic. — **13**.   The two Hebrews
climb up on their hands and on their feet.   We must suppose that
while climbing the cliff they were hidden from the view of the
post at the top ; otherwise there would have been no surprise. —
And they turned before Jonathan and he smote them] this is the
reading of 𝕲 and on the whole the better, though the case is
particularly difficult to decide.   𝕳 reads : *and they fell before
Jonathan*.   In any case, Jonathan felled them to the ground, *and
his armour-bearer kept despatching them after him*] notice the
force of the participle. — **14**.   *The first slaughter*] distinguished
from the general carnage which came with the panic.   The latter
part of the verse is obscure.   What we expect is either a comparison with some similar event : 'like Gideon's slaughter of
Midian' for example, or else a definite location of the deed : 'in
the field which lies before Michmash,' or something like that.
𝕲 finds an account of the weapons used ; 𝕾 gives a comparison

of the activity of the heroes with that of the day labourer. A satisfactory text does not seem yet to have been constructed. — **15.** The terror aroused by Jonathan's onset spread to the whole force of the Philistines and became a panic. The force was divided (as noted above) into *the garrison* and *the raiders*. The account seems to assume that these latter were returning to the camp when they met the flying garrison; or else the attack was in the early morning when the raiders had not yet set out. — *So there came a terror in the camp and in the field . . . and even the plunderers trembled*] the intervening clause is difficult to place. — *And the earth quaked*] is evidently to be taken literally; Yahweh intervened directly to increase the fear, which thus became *a divinely sent panic*] lit., *a terror of God*. — **16.** The commotion was so great that Saul's sentinels in Geba saw: *And behold a tumult was surging hither and thither*] the remarkable thing was a mob moving purposelessly to and fro in its mad impulse.

13. ויפלו לפני יונתן] seems a little too abrupt. We expect the attack or the terror to be asserted. 𝕲 enables us to restore ויפנו לפני יונתן ויכם. Ew. seems to have been the first to adopt part of this, though he makes it mean *they looked him in the face*, being paralyzed by fear. As Jonathan was " swifter than an eagle," there seems no difficulty in supposing that the Philistines started to flee, but were quickly overtaken. — **14.** The verse is perfectly plain down to איש. After that it is now generally considered to be hopelessly corrupt. Tradition is represented by *in media parte jugeri quam par boum in die arare consuevit* 𝓛, and this has passed into the modern versions. But the objections to it are of the most serious kind. כבחצי has a combination of prepositions very rare, occurring in only two expressions, both defining a point of time (Dr., *Notes*); מענה in the meaning *furrow* occurs in one late passage, Ps. 129³ *Kt.*, where the text is not above suspicion. It is difficult, moreover, to see how Jonathan could slay twenty men *in half a furrow*, which indeed is nonsense. If it said *as in a furrow*, we should think of the slain as lying along in a row. In late Hebrew מענה is said to mean the amount of ground which a ploughman takes in hand at one time, Ges., *HWB*¹²., referring to Wetstein in Delitzsch, *Psalmen*³, which I have not seen, also Levy, *NHWB*. The Arabic usage is readily traced; *ma'na* is simply *the intention*, as is מענה in Hebrew, and so applied to *the task* which a man sets himself or intends to do. But to suppose that the word now applied by the *fellahin* to their task of ploughing had the same application in Biblical Hebrew is too violent. Nor are the difficulties yet over. צמד is undoubtedly *a yoke* of oxen, and then possibly as much land as a yoke of oxen can plough in a day — *an acre*, roughly speaking. Is. 5¹⁰, which is usually urged for this meaning, is not free from difficulty.

But assuming it provisionally, we cannot yet make an intelligible sentence: *as in half a furrow* (?) *an acre of field* is redundant and ungrammatical. The versions testify to the corruption, but unfortunately without helping to correct it. 𝕲^L has ἐν βολίσι καὶ ἐν πετροβόλοις καὶ ἐν κόχλαξι τοῦ πεδίου, with which I agrees (*Cod. Goth. Leg.*); 𝕲^{AB} omits from this καὶ ἐν πετροβόλοις, which Th. (followed by We.) had already conjectured to be a gloss. The reasoning of We. is plausible, though the testimony of I shows that the insertion must have been early. 𝕲 seems to have had at least בחצבים . . . השדה, and between came בצרי or באבני; it should be noted that צור is nowhere used of *stones as a weapon*, but it is more likely than אבן to be the original of צמד. If we restore בצרי השדה we should translate *among the rocks of the field*, which would not be out of place. On the basis of 𝔖 we might restore כחצים וכנהגי צמד השדה *like hewers of stone, or like drivers of oxen in the field*. The repeated blows of a man hewing stone would not be an inappropriate comparison, and possibly the Syrian ploughmen urge on their oxen with violent blows; but the language seems rather obscure. Ew. tries to translate 𝕳, making it mean that the slaughter was 'like a yoke (?) of land being ploughed' (*GVI*³. III. p. 48, E. Tr. III. p. 34). But the figure does not seem to fit. The reader who is interested in defending tradition may, as usual, consult Keil. — **15.** The text is not easy to interpret, though so smooth in appearance: *There came a terror on the camp in the field and upon all the people*] but why should a distinction be made between *the camp in the field* and *all the people?* The people here meant are the people of the Philistine camp, and the sentence is redundant. Or if we divide so as to read, *on the camp, both on the field and on all the people*, why should the camp be summed up under these two heads? 𝕲 seems to have read במחנה ובשדה *both in the camp and in the field*, as if to distinguish between the fortified (?) camp and the open country. So much is adopted by Kl., Bu., and may pass in default of something better. For the next clause, 𝕲 connects as follows: *and all the people, both garrison and raiders trembled*, and this again may pass; but we must certainly strike out נס־המה which now becomes intolerable. 𝕲^B reads καὶ αὐτοὶ οὐκ ἤθελον ποιεῖν, with which we can do nothing; and I suspect the verse has been freely interpolated. Perhaps the original was only ותהי חרדה במחנה ובשדה והמשחית חררו נס־המה. With ותרגז הארץ compare Am. 8⁸ Joel 2¹⁰; the verb is used of the mountains, 2 S. 22⁸ Is. 5²⁵. Th. and Keil try to understand the words here of the commotion produced by the panic, but this is rationalistic weakening of the author's meaning. — לחררת אלהים] cf. the divinely sent fear, חתת אלהים, which came upon the Canaanites, Gen. 35⁵. — **16.** הצפים] the sentinels regularly stationed on the walls of a city, 2 S. 13³⁴ 18²⁴. — גבעת] *Geba* should be read, as heretofore. — ההמון] 𝕲 renders המחנה. But as המון is the less common word, it is to be preferred; and it seems to give an excellent sense here, cf. Jd. 4⁷ and v.¹⁹ in this chapter. The first ה, however, is a duplicate, and we should read והנה המון. What they saw was a *tumult surging.* — וילך והלם] is impossible, and to be corrected according to 𝕲 הלם והלם. For נמוג We. suggests the meaning *surge*, commended by Dr.

17-23. The discomfiture of the Philistines. — On discovering the state of the enemy's camp, Saul inquires who is missing from his own force. He then takes the first steps towards ascertaining the will of Yahweh. But before the reply of the oracle is given, the state of the enemy so obviously invites attack, that the king marches forth without waiting further. At the scene of battle he finds the Philistines fighting each other. The Hebrew slaves from their camp join with him, and he is reënforced by the Israelites who have been in hiding. The result is a decided victory.

17. Saul says to the soldiers : *Search*] the verb is used of inspecting the troops, 13^{15}, and also of inquiring for one absent, 20^6 : *And see who is gone from us*] the result is to show the absence of Jonathan and his attendant. — **18.** The text of 𝔊, which is to be adopted unconditionally, reads : *And Saul said to Ahijah : Bring hither the Ephod, for he carried the Ephod that day before Israel*] similar language is used in other cases where the Ephod is consulted, 23^9 30^7. We. supposes that the remark concerning Ahijah cannot be by the author of v.^{3}. But the explanation of the general situation there need not prevent the reminder here, where there is particular occasion for it. The text of 𝔥 inserts *the Ark of God* here. Historically we could hardly object that the presence of the Ark at Kirjath Jearim would decide against this text, because our author may not have known of its detention at Kirjath Jearim. But the *Ephod* is elsewhere the means of giving the oracle, and if original here may have been displaced by a scrupulous scribe who was aware of its dangerous resemblance to an image. — **19.** The answer of the oracle is not yet given, when Saul sees the necessity of immediate action. The state of the Philistine camp gives plain enough indication of the will of God : *While Saul was yet speaking, the tumult kept on increasing*] on the text see the critical note. The act of consulting the oracle fell into two parts ; the king (or other inquirer) asked a question ; the priest gave the answer of Yahweh. In the case before us Saul interrupted his own question, saying to the priest : *Draw back thy hand !*] that is, the hand which was stretched out to take the lot. The verb is the same used of *drawing up* the feet into the bed, Gen. 49^{33}. — **20.** Saul and his men march to the scene : *Then*

Saul and all the people with him raised the war cry] such is the
natural interpretation of the words.   When they came to the camp
of the Philistines : *the sword of each was turned upon his fellow,
an exceeding great confusion*] as in the camp of Midian where also
friend was taken for foe, Jd. 7²². — **21.** The appearance of Saul
with an orderly band of soldiers gave disaffected allies of the
Philistines a rallying point : *The Hebrews who were on the side
of the Philistines heretofore, who had come with them into the camp,
they also turned to be with Saul*] Schm. compares the case of
David who followed Achish to Gilboa. — **22.** The noise and the
news spread rapidly, *and all the men of Israel who were in hiding
in the hill country of Ephraim*] although occupied by the tribe
of Benjamin, the district bore the name of Ephraim. — *They also
pursued them in the battle*] joining with the forces of Saul. —
23. The author sums up the day's work, before proceeding to a
more detailed account of one episode : *So Yahweh delivered Israel
that day and the battle went beyond Beth Horon*] a well-known
town on the western edge of the highlands.   The name is corrected on the basis of 𝔊ᴸ.   *Beth Aven*, the reading of 𝔥, seems
unsuitable.

17. אין] denies the presence of the subject, Gen. 37²⁹ Ex. 2¹². — **18.** הגישה
ארון האלהים] the difficulty in retaining the words is *prima facie* a historical
one.   The Ark had been settled at Kirjath Jearim, and if brought to Saul we
should have been told of the transfer.   Graetz speaks of a tradition to the
effect that there were two arks (*Gesch. d. Juden*, I. p. 160) and supposes that
one was made to supply the loss of the other.   But the tradition probably arose
from a desire to save the historicity of this passage.   Even if we suppose this
author not to know of the detention of the Ark at Kirjath Jearim, it remains
true that we nowhere else hear of it in connexion with Saul, and the presumption is therefore against it here.   The second difficulty is that, so far as we
know, the Ark was not used in consulting the oracle.   All the indications,
therefore, point to the correctness of 𝔊 προσάγαγε τὸ ἐφούδ.   The Rabbinical
commentators are aware that the Urim and Thummim are intended (Isaaki
and Kimchi *in loc.*).   For the rest of the verse we must also adopt the reading
of 𝔊, because 𝔥 is evidently the worse and at its close unintelligible.   כי הוא
נשא האפוד ביום ההוא לפני ישראל is an exact translation of 𝔊 and gives a perfectly
good sense.   It is adopted in substance by all recent expositors.   Dr., followed by Bu., prefers היה נשא instead of the simple נשא and לפני בני for לפני.
His reason in the latter case is that לפני ישראל is bald and against the usage of
Hebrew prose.   On this it is sufficient to remark that לפני בני ישראל is found
in the books Joshua, Judges, and Samuel four times, and that all four (Jos. 4¹²

8^{32} 10^{12} Jd. 8^{28}) come from a redactional hand; whereas לפני ישראל occurs in six places besides this (Jos. 10^{10} 11^6 20^{35} I S. 7^{10} 2 S. $10^{15. 19}$) representing three different documents. This verse is one of those in which Keil concedes the superiority of 𝕲. — **19.** עד דבר] the verb should be pointed as an infinitive, cf. Jd. 3^{26} Ex. 33^{22}; the more usual construction is ויהי עד מדבו. For the tense in וילך, cf. Dr., *Tenses*[3], § 127 *a*; but the emendation to הלך (Kl.) is attractive. — הלוך ורב] "double absolute object, the second being an adjective" (Moore, on Jd. 4^{24}), cf. 2 S. 5^{10} 18^{25}, Dav., *Syntax*, § 86, R. 4. — **20.** ויזעק] here pointed as a Niphal; but this is used of the people who are summoned to war, not of the leader who summons them. For the latter we find the Hiphil, Jd. $4^{10. 13}$ 2 S. $20^{4. 5}$. If we point ויזְעֵק however, we must change וכל to אֶת־כָּל. But the people had already been mustered, in order to discover who was missing, and it was not necessary to call them together. With all due reserve, therefore, I have pointed ויזָעֵק and suppose the shout of those who go into battle to be intended — though the verb is nowhere else used in that sense. 𝕲^A has ἀνεβόησε for which ^{BL} have ἀνέβη. — מהומה] is used of the panic produced in the Philistine cities by the plague, 5^9. — **21.** The verse division is disregarded by 𝕾 which makes the tumult to be *Hebrews against Philistines.* — והעברים] καὶ οἱ δοῦλοι 𝕲. The latter is plausible, for the slaves of the Philistines might well take advantage of such an opportunity. On the other hand, it is pretty certain that the camp would contain a large number of Hebrews impressed for the purpose of carrying away the booty, or who were seeking to ingratiate themselves with the enemy. Such *Hebrews* might well be contrasted, as here, with the *Israel with Saul.* For היו it is almost necessary to read אשר היו with Ew., cf. Dr., *Notes.* — עמם] is not represented in 𝕲. — סביב ונם] should be emended to סבבו גם (Th.) with 𝕲𝕾. — **22.** איש] is not represented in 𝕲, and the sense is good without it. — וירדבקו] is abnormally pointed, cf. Stade, *Gram.* § 529 *a*, Ges.²⁶ § 53 n.; the same form is found in 31^2 (1 Chr. 10^2). There seems to be no doubt that a Hiphil is intended, Jd. 18^{22} 20^{45} 2 S. 1^6 (lacking י as here). — **23.** בית־און] was corrected by Th. to בית חרן, and the conjecture is confirmed by 𝕲^L I.

24–35. Saul's taboo and Jonathan's violation of it.

— Saul lays a curse upon the eating of food before sundown. The people are mindful of the execration and go fasting, though thereby they grow faint. The only exception is Jonathan who, because of his absence from the main body of troops, is not informed of the adjuration, and eats of some honey which he finds. On being informed, he condemns his father's act as having weakened the people. At sunset the famished people rush upon the spoil and eat without due care to separate the blood from the flesh. Saul, informed of this, orders a great stone to be taken for an altar and at this the animals are slain.

I

The paragraph is obscure in places owing to the state of the text — possibly because later editors could not reconcile themselves to the religious views which lie at the basis of the narrative. It seems plain that Saul's purpose was to impose what is known in other religions as a *taboo*. As the confusion of the enemy showed, Yahweh was already working. Saul desired a continuance of his favour. The extraordinary privation laid upon the people was to secure this. Fasting is in itself one means of placating the divinity. And Yahweh as the God of Battles had a special claim upon the booty. It was in fact sacred, and it would be unsafe for individual Israelites to appropriate it until the first fruits had been set apart for Yahweh. If the people had set out (as is likely) without supplying themselves with provisions from their own stores, there would be all the more need of special precautions.

So far from Saul's vow being rash, ill-advised, or arbitrary, therefore, we see that it was the logical expression of his carefulness for divine things. From the practical point of view, Jonathan was no doubt right. The success of the day would have been greater without this extraordinary precaution. But this was a mere worldly consideration — Saul was moved by care for religion which would not take account of lower advantages or arguments. That he was entirely justified by the light of the times is probable ; for the author has no hesitation in narrating Yahweh's confirmation of the curse by his offended silence after its violation. The supposition that Saul was moved by fear lest the troops should be detained by the booty is inadequate to account for the form of the objurgation. It is not taking booty that is the object of the curse, but eating food of any kind.

24. The introductory clause must be taken from ⑮, which describes the situation as it was during the day, and therefore before the conclusion just reached. — *So Israel was with Saul about ten thousand men and the fighting was scattered over all the hill country of Ephraim*] on the reading, see the critical note. — *And Saul vowed a vow in that day, and Saul laid an oath on the people*] the restoration is partly conjectural. If it be correct, the author does not condemn Saul ; he only gives the facts as elsewhere. Other cases of the vow, Jd. 11[30f.] Gen. 28[20-22]. A vow of abstinence is attributed to David, Ps. 132²ᶠ. Saul's vow is imposed upon the people in the form of a curse, *saying: Cursed is the man who shall eat food until evening and [until] I avenge myself on my enemies*] the older commentators (followed by Keil) saw in the form of the oath — *my* enemies — an overweening desire for personal revenge ; but this is foreign to the author's idea. The Philistines were Saul's enemies because they were enemies of Israel. Another example of a curse assumed by the people as a whole is found in Jd. 21¹⁸. The result of this one was that *none of the people tasted food*, though they were tempted. — **25, 26.** The text has suffered and cannot be certainly restored. Recent authorities agree in making it mean : *And there was honey [or honeycomb] on the face of the ground, and the people came to the honeycomb whence the bees had gone, but no one put his hand to his mouth, for the people feared the oath of Yahweh*] the sense is obviously that the people were steadfast in the midst of special temptation. But the sentence is awkwardly constructed, and we may well doubt whether the ingenuity of the critics has yet recovered the original text. Why the bees should have deserted the comb, we are left to conjecture. That the Philistines had made spoil of honey and had thrown it away is possible, but the author would have told us if he had known this to be the fact. — **27.** Jonathan, having been absent from the army, *had not heard when his father adjured the people*] he therefore ate of the honey, dipping the end of his club in it. The refreshment experienced is described in the words, *and his eyes were lightened*] the eyes of the weary man do not see clearly — the world grows dark before him. — **28.** *One of the people answered*] that is, spoke as the occasion suggested, telling Jonathan of the oath. The last two words in the verse as they stand in 𝕳 — *and the people were weary* — disturb the sense, whether they be attributed to the author of the narrative or to Jonathan. We should emend so as to read : *and the people testified*, that is, *accepted the oath ;* or else in another way, joining to the beginning of the next verse, making it read : *So he left off, and said*. A third possibility is to strike the words out as a gloss. — **29.** Jonathan gives his opinion of his father's action and its effects on the people : *My father has brought disaster on the land*] relatively, he means. For the verb used here cf. Moore, *Judges*,

p. 301.   Jonathan's opinion is based on his own experience : *See how I am refreshed, just because I tasted a bit of honey !*   The refreshment is again presented as a clearing of the eyes from their dulness. — **30, 31**. The two verses belong together and their sense is : *If only the people had eaten today of the spoil of their enemies the slaughter of the Philistines would have been great and the people would have been smitten the Philistines from Michmash to Aijalon*] this cannot, to be sure, be got out of the present text. An alternative would be to make Jonathan's speech end (though abruptly) with v.[30], and to throw out the greater part of v.[31].   That the pursuit actually extended to Aijalon, as apparently asserted in 𝔥, we have no reason to believe, for such a success would have been all that the most sanguine could expect.   Aijalon (the modern *Yalo*) lay below Beth Horon well down towards the Philistine plain.   The last three words of the verse are plain enough of themselves, but not easy to fit in the present context. — **32**. The famished people *rushed upon the booty*] as a bird of prey rushes upon the quarry.   The booty in such raids consists largely of cattle, and these the people *slew to the earth* wherever they happened to find them.   The consequence was that *they ate with the blood*] the blood was the part of Yahweh, and for man to eat it was sacrilegious.   This idea runs through the history of Israel and is embodied in the various prohibitions of the Law, Dt. 12[16] Lev. 19[26]. — **33**. Word is brought to Saul that *the people are sinning against Yahweh in eating with the blood*] the definition of the sin leaves nothing to be desired, and Saul at once takes active measures against the sacrilege : *Roll hither a great stone*] the only way in which this would correct the evil would be by making the stone an altar on which the blood could be poured.   As we know from Arabic heathenism, the original Semitic sacrifice was the application of the blood (without fire) to the altar or sacred stone.* — **34**. Those present are ordered to *disperse among the people* and command them : *Let each man bring to Yahweh his ox or his sheep and slay it here*] on the original reading, see below.   The method was successful : *All the people brought each what he had in his hand, to Yahweh and slew it there*] another

---

* Cf. WRSmith, *Kinship*, pp. 223, 311.

slight change in the reading is adopted here. We also may speak
of having an animal or a herd *in hand.* — **35.** *So Saul built an
altar to Yahweh*] cf. 7[17]. The only reason for the statement in
this connexion is that the altar was the stone just mentioned.
With it he made a beginning of his altar-building to Yahweh, cf.
Gen. 10[8]. The author has it in mind to tell of other altars built
by Saul, but his narrative is now lost.

24. ואיש־ישראל נגש ביום ההוא] is an unexpected opening to the new paragraph. נגש, 13[6], is used to describe the straits in which the people found
themselves under the Philistine invasion. But we are here in the midst of
the deliverance, and although the deliverance was less complete than it might
have been, the people could hardly now be described as *oppressed by a task-
master,* or *driven away,* or *crowding each other,* which are the only meanings
to be got out of the verb. Saul's vow, though it increased the weariness,
could hardly be said to oppress the people, and if the author had meant to
connect this assertion with the vow he would have constructed his sentence
differently. ᵹ has an entirely different reading: καὶ Ἰσραὴλ ἦν μετὰ Σαούλ,
ὡσεὶ δέκα χιλιάδες ἀνδρῶν, καὶ ἦν ὁ πόλεμος διεσπαρμένος εἰς ὅλην τὴν πόλιν ἐν
τῷ ὄρει Ἐφράιμ ᵹ[L] with which [AB] agree nearly. This gives an admirable
opening for the new paragraph, and one that would not readily occur to redactor or scribe. It had probably become illegible in the archetype of 𝔐 and
a scribe substituted a phrase suggested by 13[6], returning to the oppression of
the people as the new point of departure. With We., it is proper to suppose
that *every city* has come in by duplication — בכל עיר from בכל הר. The scattered fighting would be in the open country rather than in the towns. The
impossibility of 𝔐 was discovered by Ew. (from Th.?) who besides adopting
ᵹ emends 𝔐 by conjecture. The reading of ᵹ is also adopted by Th. with
the silent correction of עיר to יער. The retranslation of ᵹ[AB] by We. is adopted
by Dr., Bu., al. I have chosen *the Israel with Saul* ᵹ[L] rather than *all the
people with Saul* ᵹ[AB], because it probably refers to the *Israel with* Saul of v.[22].
Et erant cum Saul quasi decem millia virorum, found in the authorized edition
of 𝔏, is no part of Jerome's translation but has crept in from 𝔩. The narrative is continued in ᵹ by: καὶ Σαοὺλ ἠγνόησεν ἄγνοιαν μεγάλην ἐν τῇ ἡμέρᾳ
ἐκείνῃ confirmed by 𝔩. Since We. this has been supposed to represent ושאול
שגה שגגה ביום ההוא. But it is not certain that the author could so have expressed himself. As confessed by We., שגגה occurs only in the Hexateuch
and Eccles. It is besides a technical term conveying a distinction not emphasized before the Priestcode; nor is it certain that שגגה is the original of the
Greek word found here which represents in various passages six different
Hebrew words. In this uncertainty the conjecture of Kl. adopted by Bu.
becomes attractive, to wit: that the original Greek phrase was: καὶ Σαοὺλ
ἤγνισεν ἀγνείαν. Bu. restores in his text ושאול הזיר נזר, citing Num. 6[1ff.]. But,
as he himself says, usage would favour ושאול נדר נדר (or better וידר שאול נדר

cf. 2 S. 15⁸ Is. 19²¹. — ויאל] is pointed as if from יאל, *he behaved foolishly*. But this does not agree with the context, so that we should read וַיֹּאֶל from אלה: *he caused the people to swear*, like השביע below. — ארור האיש] Dt. 27¹⁵ Jer. 11³. — ונקמתי] generally with ב, as in 18²⁵ Jd. 15⁷; with מן Is. 1²⁴. In the latter case the vengeance is a satisfaction taken *from* the enemy. On the tense cf. Dr., *Tenses³*, p. 134. — **25.** The text is corrupt, probably beyond restoration. — וכל־הארץ באו ביער] is impossible, whether we understand יער of a *forest* or of a *honeycomb*, for the simple reason that הארץ is never used for *the people of the land*;* — וכל־הארץ] may be a corruption of וכל־העם though it is difficult to see how a scribe could make this mistake here. If so, the words will be a duplicate of the כל־העם in the preceding verse; 𝕲 καὶ πᾶσα ἡ γῆ ἠρίστα seems to duplicate the whole preceding clause except the negative, and this is represented in 𝕴. The only thing which is in place is a statement that *all the land produced honey* or that *all the land flowed with honey*. But none of the efforts to put this into the text are satisfactory. We., Bu., Dr., Ki. leave out the whole clause, making the verse consist only of ויער היה על־פני השדה, *and there was honeycomb on the face of the field*. This is perhaps the best that can be done. — **26.** והנה הלך דבש] must be intended to mean *and there was a flow of honey;* but הלך in the only other passage in which it occurs means a *wayfarer*, 2 S. 12⁴. The change of pointing to הָלָך (Th.) is now generally adopted, and as its consequence the further emendation of דבש to דברו, *its bees*, evidently the original of λαλῶν 𝕲. That the honey was deserted of its bees made it especially tempting to the hungry people. It is not yet explained, to be sure, why the bees should have deserted their post. משיג is to be read משיב with 𝕲𝕿, cf. v.²⁷ (Kl.). — השבעה] perhaps to be corrected to שבעת יהוה with 𝕲. — **27.** יערת] the *nomen unitatis* of יער is יערה ותראנה *Kt.*: ותארנה *Qrê;* the latter is evidently to be preferred, cf. ארו v.²⁹. — **28.** ויעף העם] can mean only: *the people were exhausted*, a statement that interrupts the sense, whether supposed to be spoken to Jonathan, or an explanation by the author. If anything is in place here it is something completing the information given, like ויער העם, *the people testified* to the oath when Saul laid it upon them, perhaps by saying *amen*. Or we might read ויער בעם, *and he called the people to witness*, that is, Saul did (cf. 1 K. 2⁴²), when he laid the objurgation upon them. Something like this seems to have been the idea of Josephus (*Ant.* VI. VI. 3), when he says that Jonathan did not hear the curse *nor the approbation the multitude gave it*. 𝕲 reads וירד, an easy corruption of ויער. The two words are thrown out, as a marginal gloss which has crept into the text, by We., al. Another reading suggested by Josephus is ויִרֶף טעם, *he left off eating*, which would be entirely in place at the beginning of the next sentence. 𝕲 also connects its καὶ ἔγνω ['Ιωναθάν] with the following. — **29.** עכר] Gen. 34³⁰ Jos. 6¹⁸ 7²⁵ Jd. 11³⁵. — ראו] read ראה with 𝕲 (We.). — **30.** אף כי] emphatic introduction to what follows, making a climax: 'I have been re-

---

* Dr. points to one instance, 2 S. 15²³: *all the land was weeping aloud*. But there also it is doubtful whether the text is sound.

freshed by eating a little honey; *how much more* if the people had eaten
would they have been refreshed.' He changes the construction, however, and
instead of saying 'they would have been refreshed' states the consequence of
the refreshment 'there would have been great slaughter.'—[כי עתה] introduces the apodosis after לוא. But in this case we must omit the לא which
follows, and in this we have the authority of 𝕲. The change to הלא makes an
awkward sentence. Or possibly לא represents the affirmative particle of which
we have traces elsewhere.—[מכה] read המכה 𝕲, notice the ה which precedes.
— **31.** The first half of the verse is difficult as it stands, because it seems to
speak of a success such as even Jonathan would approve. But the narrator
would hardly contradict himself so directly. The only way of fitting the words
into the context is to throw out ביום ההוא (or correct it to היום) and make the
sentence a part of Jonathan's speech: *and they would have smitten the Philistines* [to-day] *from Michmash to Aijalon*. The only alternative seems to be
to throw out the whole clause (We., *Comp.* p. 248). 𝕲 relieves us of the difficulty so far as to omit Aijalon and to read בכמש for ממכש. But the narrator
hardly supposes the whole day's fighting to be confined to Michmash. Bu.
adopts this, and also adopts from Kl. עד הלילה for אילנה. But in this case it
would be better to take over the whole of Kl.'s conjecture מחם השמש עד הלילה.
The insecurity of our footing must be obvious. On the site of Aijalon, Robinson, *BR²*, III. p. 145, GASmith, *Geog.* pp. 210, 250 f., Buhl, *Geog.* p. 198 who
refers to Guérin, *Judée*, I. 290. Cf. also Moore, *Judges*, p. 53 f. — [ויעף העם]
pointed as if from עיף,cf. Jd. 4²¹, the more usual form is ייעף, and we should
probably point ויעף. The clause resumes the narrative. — **32.** [ויעש *Kt.:*] ויעט
Qrê is doubtless to be preferred, cf. 15¹⁹. Kl. defends the *Kt.* deriving it from
עיש a rare verb of uncertain meaning; καὶ ἐκλίθη 𝕲ᴮ points to ויט which favours
the *Qrê*, which is also directly rendered by 𝕲ᴸ. The verb is perhaps denominative from עיט *a bird of prey.* [שלל *Kt.:*] השלל *Qrê*, again to be preferred. — ויחטו
[ארצה] cf. אכנה ארצה 2 S. 2²². — [על־הדם] is probably the original phrase, Lev.
19²⁶ Ex. 12⁸, and אל־הדם v.³⁴ is to be corrected accordingly. אה־הדם proposed
by Th. is not superior though we can hardly call it un-Hebraic, cf. Lev. 17¹⁰.
— **33.** [ויגידו] the undefined subject is המגידים. [חטאים] on the pointing Ges.²⁶
§ 74 *i.* חטים is given by Ginsburg as the *Qrê.*—[לאכל] for this gerundial construction cf. Dav., *Syntax*, §93, other examples are 12¹⁷. ¹⁹ 19⁵ 20²⁰. — [בגדתם] *you
deal treacherously* does not seem to be the verb called for. 𝕲 finds the name of
a place *Gittaim*, of which we have no other trace in this region. Perhaps למגידים
would be in place. Kl.'s reconstruction is too ingenious. — [היום] must be corrected to הלם with 𝕲 (Th.). — **34.** This command is evidently directed to those
immediately about the king and strengthens the case for למגידים in the preceding verse. For [אלי : ἐνταῦθα 𝕲]; Kl. conjectures אל יהוה for which much may be
said and I have adopted it. — [בזה] can hardly be *upon this stone;* more probably *in this place.* — [ואכלתם] seems wanting in 𝕲 and is in fact superfluous. —
[איש שורו בידו] we should expect the sheep to be added as above; read איש אשר
בידו with 𝕲 (Th., al.). — [הלילה] lacking in 𝕲ᴮ, inserted by 𝕲ᴸ at the end of
the verse. Kl. followed by Bu. corrects to ליהיה, which is, in fact, what we

need. Some reader zealous for the Law changed it as in 𝔥, while another left it out as in 𝔊. — **35.** The appropriateness of this addition to the narrative is apparent only if we identify the altar here spoken of with the great stone already mentioned. Had the author meant to make it something additional he would have said Saul built *there* an altar (as is actually rendered by 𝔖). The building of altars is a mark of piety in the patriarchs, Gen. 8^{20} 12^7 13^{18} 26^{25} (all J) and 35^7 (E). We have no reason to interpret otherwise in the case of Saul. The supposition that the altar was built as a monument — non cultus causa, honoris ergo — is excusable in Schm., but hardly so in Keil. — אתו] must be circumstantial: *with it he began the building of altars.* — לבנות מזבח] the plural of the noun is not required, cf. Gen. 10^8: *he was the first to become a tyrant,* and probably Gen. 9^{20}: *Noah was the first husbandman.*

36-46. The penalty of the broken taboo. — Saul proposes to renew the attack on the Philistines, but at the priest's suggestion first seeks counsel of Yahweh. The oracle is silent; whereupon Saul concludes that the vow laid upon the people has been broken, and he takes measures to discover the guilty party. The sacred lot is cast first between Saul with his house on one side, and the people on the other; then between Saul and his son. Jonathan is discovered to be the guilty person, and is condemned to death by Saul. But the people, recognizing that the victory of the day is owing to Jonathan, revolt against the decision and ransom him. This closes the incident.

The section is the necessary conclusion of what precedes. There the vow has been registered and its violation recorded. Jonathan confesses his guilt in the terms already used in describing his unwitting trespass. In fact, the culmination of the story is found in Saul's Brutus-like sentence of his own son, and in Jonathan's noble willingness to die. The older commentators were much exercised by the question whether Jonathan was really bound by an adjuration of which he was ignorant. In the sense of the Biblical writer, he was so bound. Nor can we seriously question that, to the Biblical writer, the reason for Yahweh's refusal to answer Saul was his anger at Jonathan's transgression — though the commentators have ingeniously avoided this conclusion, and have tried to shift the guilt from Jonathan to Saul.

36-46. Doubts have been expressed as to the section being a part of the original narrative, and it is true that v.^{35} reads like the conclusion of a chapter in the history. But the account of the vow of Saul and of Jonathan's transgression is not complete without the present sequel. If necessary to choose, it would be better to strike out v.[35] than to dispense with [36–46]. We., who holds this to be foreign to the genuine context (*Comp.* p. 248), is well answered by Bu. (*RS.* p. 206).

36. Saul makes a proposition : *Let us go down after the Philistines by night and smite them*] reading with Bu. ; the received text, *let us plunder among them*, is weak. The people agree, but the priest advises consultation of the oracle : *let us draw near hither to God*] Ex. 16[9] Zeph. 3[2]. The initiative of the priest may be accounted for by his knowledge of the transgression. The emendation of the text to make Saul the subject is arbitrary, though Josephus gives the initiative to the king. — **37**. Saul *asks of God* in the customary form — here a double question, but one that admits only the answer *yes* or *no*, cf. 30[8]. From the form of the question it is probable that the oracle answered by the sacred lot. — *But he did not answer him that day*] how the priest discovered Yahweh's refusal to answer, we are not told. — **38**. Saul, with his usual promptness, takes immediate steps to discover the occasion of the divine wrath. He issues the order : *Come hither, all the cornerstones of the people!*] the chief men are called by this name Jd. 20[2] Is. 19[13]. — *And know and see wherein is this sin to-day*] or more probably *in whom* is this sin. Abstractly considered, the fault might be in a thing as well as in a person, but as Saul's measures look towards the discovery of a person, it is natural that he should express himself accordingly. — **39**. Saul solemnly protests that the offender shall not be spared : *By the life of Yahweh who delivers Israel*] that is, who is habitually Israel's deliverer ; *though it be I or Jonathan my son, he shall be put to death*] the conjectural reading represented here will be defended in the critical note. The silence of the people shows that they appreciate the gravity of the situation. — **40**. Arrangements are made for casting the lot by the division of all present into two parties. On one side are the people at large, on the other Saul and Jonathan, they being the only members of the royal family who are present. The arrangement, proposed by Saul, is consented to by the people. — **41**. The sacred lot is cast in accordance with Saul's prayer preserved for us in ᕮ : *And Saul said : Yahweh, God of Israel, why hast thou not answered thy servant this day ? If the guilt be in*

*me or in Jonathan my son, Yahweh, God of Israel, give Urim ; but
if thus thou say : It is in my people Israel; give Thummim.* The
arguments for adopting this text are : (1) the improbability of its
being invented by a late author ; (2) the difficulty of making
sense of the received text ; (3) the loss by homeoteleuton is very
probable ; (4) the word תמים alone would not suggest the insertion ; (5) only by supposing something of this kind to have been
originally in the text, can we account for the statement that Saul
and Jonathan *were taken.* If, as these considerations make extremely probable, this is a part of the original text of Samuel, it
is one of the most important contributions of 𝔊 to the restoration
of that text, and to our knowledge of Hebrew antiquity. The
Urim and Thummim were known by name to the post-exilic
writers, but the method of their use had been forgotten. The
only early references are 1 S. 28[6] where Urim is mentioned as one
method of revelation, and Dt. 33[8] where Urim and Thummim are
attributed to the tribe of Levi. The present text describes them
more exactly than any of these. Urim and Thummim were two
objects used in the lot — perhaps stones of different colours — one
of which gave the affirmative, the other gave the negative answer
to a question put in the form already indicated. In this case :
Saul and Jonathan were taken and the people escaped. — **42.** The
text seems to have suffered here also : *And Saul said : Cast
between me and Jonathan my son ; and Jonathan was taken*] the
abruptness of the statement is contrary to analogy. 𝔊 again comes
to our help and may plead the presumption that the same cause
which mutilated the preceding verse affected this also. It reads :
*And Saul said : Cast between me and Jonathan ! Whom Yahweh
shall take shall die. And the people said to Saul : It shall not be
so ! But Saul prevailed over the people, and they cast the lot
between him and Jonathan his son, and Jonathan was taken*] the
added feature of the protest of the people is too original to be a
Greek expansion of the text. — **43.** Jonathan confesses in response
to his father's question : *I did indeed taste a bit of honey with the
end of the staff which I carried. Here I am ! I am ready to die*]
the last words are not a complaint at his fate, but express a heroic
willingness to meet it. So Josephus correctly understands it :
" Jonathan was not dismayed at this threat of death, but submit-

ting nobly and magnanimously, he said : I do not ask you to spare me, Father ; death is all the sweeter to me, coming in connexion with your piety and after a brilliant victory." * Jonathan's spirit is comparable to that displayed by Jephthah's daughter, Jd. 11³⁶. — **44**. Saul pronounces the sentence, confirming it by an oath : *So do God to me and so again — thou shalt die, Jonathan!*] the impreca-tion as in 3¹⁷. — **45**. The people interfere and deliver Jonathan : *Shall Jonathan die who has wrought this great deliverance for Israel?* Jonathan's bold attack upon the enemy was the beginning of the victory, and without it the victory would not have been ob-tained. *By the life of Yahweh, there shall not fall a hair of his head*] 1 K. 1⁵², cf. 2 S. 14¹¹. — *For he has wrought with God*] the sense is, apparently, that if God was so well pleased with Jonathan as to give him the victory, he cannot now require his death. As this is a *non sequitur*, possibly the text has been obscured. — *The people ransomed Jonathan*] by substituting one of themselves — so Ew. and We. suppose. Driver points out that ransom by an animal substitute was allowed by comparatively early laws, Ex. 13¹³· ¹⁵ 34²⁰, so that we cannot be absolutely certain. — **46**. Of further pursuit there could be no thought. Hence *Saul went up from pursuing the Philistines, and the Philistines went to their own country*] the narrative reaches a pause with this verse, but the same document is continued in v.⁵².

36. נבזה] on the form, Ges.²⁶ § 67 *dd*; Stade, *Gram.* § 137 *a*, 584 *c*. This verb, however, is not the one we expect here, as Saul evidently means more than plundering, for he does not want to *leave one remaining*. As 𝕲 renders the same word we are thrown upon conjecture; and of the various conjectures the simplest is ונכה (Bu.), cf. 11¹¹ Jos. 11¹⁴. — נשאר] pointed as a jussive (a rare instance), Dr., *Tenses*³, § 50, Obs.; Ges.²⁶ § 48 *g*, note 2, 109 *d*; cf. 2 S. 17¹². The space after עשה, remarked in the Massoretic note, is probably a trace of a different verse division. — ויאמר הכהן וגו'] Bu. proposes to restore ויאמר לכהן הקרבה הלם את האפוד (making Saul the subject), constructed after the analogy of the restored v.¹⁸. But 𝕲 agrees with 𝔚, and the sense is good. If any change is needed, the clause might be stricken out, with 𝕊. Against its originality may be urged קרב (instead of נגש, used elsewhere in this narra-tive). — **37**. ענהו] 𝕲ᴸ adds κύριος. — **38**. נגשו] the form occurs three times; recession of the accent on account of the following monosyllable (? cf. Ges.²⁶ 66 *c*). 𝕲 seems to have read הגישו. — פנות] φυλάς 𝕲ᴸ. — במה] probably to be

---

* Joseph., *Antiq.* VI. VI. 5.

emended to במי with ⅏, Th., We., Bu., Kl., Dr., Ki. — **39.** חי־יהוה] the distinction made by the punctuators between חַי and חֵי in such expressions is artificial, and intended to disguise the fact that men swore by the life of Yahweh, cf. 20³, 2 S. 15²¹, where the two forms are found side by side. — ישנו] is confessedly a difficult form. It occurs Dt. 29¹⁴, where the analogy of איננו in the second half of the verse suggests that we should point ישנו, also 1 S. 23²⁸ Est. 3⁸. In the present passage Th. proposes to read ישנה, on the ground that the antecedent is החטאת, and this seems confirmed by ἀποκριθῇ ⅏, which would represent יענה. But the analogy of the following verses suggests that the original was יש בי או, a combination that might give rise to 𝔐 if one or two letters became illegible. This is the conjecture of Kl., and ב is quite in place as the *beth essentiae*. — **40.** לעבד] εἰς δουλείαν ⅏ is an obvious error, but shows a Hebrew original. — **41.** אל] is an erroneous insertion, יהוה being part of the vocative. — הבה תמים] all attempts to make sense of the words as they stand are vain : *Give a perfect* (*lot*) would be impertinent; *show the right* does violence to the words. The text of ⅏, apparently best preserved by ⅏ᴸ, retranslated into Hebrew gives : יהוה אלהי ישראל למה לא ענית את־עבדך היום אם בי או בבני בני העון יהוה אלהי ישראל הבה אורים ואם כה תאמר בעם העון הבה תמים The only difficulty with this is, that the eye of a scribe would not be so likely to mistake the second הבה for the first, as if the same word preceded both. The reading of ᴮ in the second half of the verse is confused, but it supplies ישראל before the second הבה, so that the probable reading was בעמי ישראל, instead of the simple בעם given above. After Ewald, who directs in general to ' complete the text from the LXX ' (*GVI.*³ III. p. 51, E. Tr. III. p. 36), this reading is accepted by Th., We., Dr., Bu., Ki. We. conjectures ואם ישנו בעמך ישראל as the opening of the second half of the sentence, and is followed by Dr., Bu., Ki. Absolute conformity of the two parts of the prayer is, however, not necessary, and אם כה תאמר seems more vivid, and therefore more likely to be original. Keil, followed by Erdm., argues against the whole insertion, and so does Kl. — **42.** The plus of ⅏ in this verse is contained, with slight variations, in ᴬᴮᴸ, and is testified by the asterisk of Origen. one of the few cases in which the Hexaplar signs have come down to us in the Books of Samuel. The retroversion of Bu. needs no correction unless (with ᴸ and Hex.) we read כדבר הזה instead of הדבר הזה. (For κ. κατακράτησε Σ. τοῦ λαοῦ either מהעם . . . ויחזק, cf. 17⁵⁰, or ויחזק בעם, Dt. 22²⁵.) Insert therefore after בני the words את אשר ילכד יהוה ימות ויאמר העם אל־שאול לא יהיה כדבר הזה ויחזק שאול בעם ויפילו בינו ובין יונתן בנו. The resemblance between יונתן בני and יונתן בנו accounts for the omission. The emendation, made by Th., is rejected by We., on the ground that to interrupt the decision of Yahweh is irreligious and the uncertainty intolerable. But the people may well have seen that the result could be only the loss either of Jonathan or of Saul, and have been willing rather to bear the wrath of Yahweh than to face this certain loss. The emendation is accepted by Kl., Bu.; not noticed by Dr. and Ki. — **43.** טעם טעמתי] the adverbial infinitive throws emphasis upon the root idea of the verb ' I *tasted* a little honey.' As it is here a confession of transgression, in which there was no question of less or more, we should probably understand it to be an out-and-out affirmation, and not intended to contrast *tasting* with *eating*, as though in mitigation. — הנני] 𝔊ᴸ and 𝔏 read והנני. — **44.** כה יעשה] must have after it לי, as indicated by 𝔊𝔏𝔖. The omission was probably made from superstitious dread on the part of the scribe who would not write an imprecation upon himself (We., who cites 25²², where an imprecation upon David has been obscured for the same reason). So the Arab writer changes a denunciation of the person present (in his narrative) to a denunciation of 'the remote.' The formula is found in 3¹⁷. At the end of the verse יונתן 𝔚: σήμερον 𝔊ᴬᴮ; σήμερον Ιωναθαν 𝔊ᴸ. The unusual place of the vocative is an argument against 𝔚, and it might also be pleaded that the determination of Saul to placate the deity at once is something that should be brought out. But the pathos of the sentence is greater as read in 𝔚, and the change to היום more likely than the reverse. The case is a difficult one to decide, but on the whole 𝔚 has the advantage (so We., Bu., Kl.). — **45.** הישועה] would be sufficient without qualification, as is felt by 𝔖, which reads simply: *who hath wrought deliverance for Israel.* — חלילה] is lacking in 𝔊ᴮ. The insertion is easily accounted for by the context (Kl., Bu.), and superfluous. — אם] is used in oaths with the negative sense. — משערת] the use of מן is explained by Dr., *Notes*, p. 91. It would not be extravagant hyperbole (to the Oriental mind) to take it as partitive: 'There shall not fall [even a fraction] of a hair.' — כי עם אלהים עשה] should mean in this context: *for on the side of God he wrought.* The construction is, however, awkward, and 𝔊 had a different text: ὅτι ἔλεον θεοῦ ἐποίησεν 𝔊ᴸ: ὅτι ὁ λαὸς τοῦ θεοῦ ἐποίησεν 𝔊ᴬᴮ. One of these is probably corrupted from the other, and possibly both go back to the pronunciation עַם for עִם. *For God will be gracious this day* is nearly what we require: כי ינחם אלהים היום. Kl. proposes כי נחם אלהים—*for the mercy of God hath made this day.* But it is difficult to justify this by the facts, for *this day* is not the day of the battle but the day following. — ויפדו] means *they ransomed:* καὶ προσηύξατο 𝔊 would point to ויפלל. There can scarcely be a doubt that 𝔚 is original.

47–51. Summary of Saul's activity.

— The paragraph is a summary such as we find in 2 S. 20²³⁻²⁶. The latter paragraph seems to have been originally the conclusion of one history of David. It should be noted that our section does not make any chronological attempt, such as we find in the framework of the Books of Kings. For this reason we should probably date it early, as compared with other redactional insertions. The author's idea of Saul's conquests also points to a time before the figure of David had received the prominence which it has in the greater part of the historical books. Not improbably this section was the conclusion of the life of Saul, from which came chapters 9. 10. 11. 13. 14

in their original form.   In this case it may have stood after 16²³,
from which place it was removed by the editor who wished to
conclude the account of Saul's successes before going on to relate
his rejection.

47–51. As to the character of the section, the critics are agreed; as to its
age there is some difference of opinion.   The similar closing formula for the
life of Samuel (7¹³⁻¹⁵) reminds us of those we find in the Book of Judges.   In
regard to David we have like data given 2 S. 3²⁻⁵ and 5¹³⁻¹⁶, both which give
the names of David's family, as well as 2 S. 20²³⁻²⁶ which originally closed an
account of David's life.   For Solomon also we can point out a much more
extended panegyric, but one which is in substance equivalent to our section,
in 1 K. 4¹–5¹⁴.   There seems to be no inherent improbability in the supposition
that such a panegyric was composed by the author who has just given the
account of Saul's piety (cf. Kuenen, *HCO²*. p. 381).   The theory of We.
(*Comp.* 247) is that the panegyric marks (in the mind of the editor) the close
of Saul's rightful reign, and this is adopted by Co., *Einl³*. p. 100.   This is
probably the reason for the *insertion* of the section in this place.   But we can
hardly suppose that an editor who knew no more of Saul's successes than is
contained in what has preceded, and who moreover regarded him as rejected
of Yahweh, could write such a panegyric.   The resemblance to the ' pragmatic ' sections of the Book of Judges affirmed by Bu. (*RS.* p. 206 f.) seems
less marked than he would make it.   Bonk (*De Davide*, p. 53, and *ZATW.*
XI. p. 143) finds here a fragment from a source which has not appeared up to
this point — a history of the family of Saul.   Ki. (*GH.* II. p. 29) declares for
an independent but late source, cf. also Dr., *LOT'⁶*. p. 173.

Properly there are two paragraphs, — one giving a summary of
Saul's wars, the other containing the names of his family. — **47.** *So
Saul took the kingdom over Israel and fought on all sides against
all his enemies*] the enemies *of Israel* seem to be in the author's
mind.   The enumeration of them gives the same names which we
find in the account of David's wars, 2 S. 8 and elsewhere : *Moab
and the Bnê Ammon, and Edom and Beth Rehob*] as 𝕲 author-
izes us to read. — *The king of Soba*] seems also natural, as in 𝕲,
rather than *the kings of Soba* 𝔐.   Beth Rehob and Soba were
both Aramaean states in the Lebanon region.   Rather curiously
the Philistines come last in the list. — *And wherever he turned
he was victorious*] on the emendation, see the critical note. —
48. Especial mention of the expedition against Amalek : *And he
gathered an army and smote Amalek*] the translation rather forces
the text.   In case it is not accepted, we must join the opening

clause with the preceding, making it read : *And wherever he turned
he was victorious and did valiantly.* The next sentence will then
be : *And he smote Amalek and delivered Israel from the hand of
his plunderer*] it is evident that the author has present stress
rather than a historic occasion in mind as furnishing a motive for
Saul. This shows the difference between his point of view and
that of chapter 15. — **49.** The family of Saul is brought before
us : first, his sons : *Jonathan and Ishbaal*] so we are authorized
to correct, the name in 頂 having been mutilated for religious
reasons. The first name means *Yahweh gave;* the second, *Man
of the Lord*, Baal having been used quite innocently for Yahweh
in this period. The third also contains a name of Yahweh
(*Melek*), though the second element is obscure. All three testify
to the piety of Saul. Of the daughters' names *Merab* is obscure,
Michal possibly the same which appears elsewhere as *Michael.* —
50. His wife was *Ahinoam daughter of Ahimaaz*] the names occur
elsewhere. The general of the army was *Abner,* who plays a more
prominent part after the death of Saul than before. He was *son
of Ner, uncle of Saul.* As the word translated *uncle* is of somewhat wide meaning, the author proceeds to define more exactly.
— **51.** *Kish the father of Saul and Ner the father of Abner were
sons of Abiel*] so we read on conjecture.

52. The verse joins closely to v.[46], and prepares the way for
16[14], where David is received into Saul's staff. — *The war was
severe against the Philistines all the days of Saul*] the author
guards against the impression that the late indecisive campaign
was the only one. — *And whenever Saul saw any powerful man
or any vigorous man, he would attach him to himself*] as in the
case of David which follows.

47. וישאול לכד] the order of the words indicates the opening of a new section. After Edom 𝕲[L] adds: καὶ εἰς τὸν βαιθροώβι, evidently intending the
Beth Rehob mentioned in connexion with Sobah, 2 S. 10[6]. The name has
been corrupted in 𝕲[B] to βαιθεώρ. The text is emended to conform to 𝕲[L] by
Kl., and the emendation is adopted by Bu. — במלכי] the singular number was
found by 𝕲 and is doubtless original. — ירשיע] seems to give no proper sense
in this connexion, though We. compares Syr. חיב. Hebrew usage allows
only the meanings *to convict* of guilt, or *to act wickedly.* 𝕲 ἐσώζετω points to
יׇיׇ ׇ which was first suggested by Cappellus (*Critica Sacra*, p. 261), and is

now generally adopted. — **48.** ויעש חיל] *and he wrought mighty deeds* as in Num. 24[18] Dt. 8[18]. Both 𝔖 and 𝔗 understand the expression to mean *he gathered an army* and this is a more appropriate introduction to the mention of Amalek. קבץ חיל occurs 1 K. 20[1], and it is possible that ויעש ח' may be interpreted in this sense, cf. Ezek. 28[4], *thou didst acquire might.* — שכסהו] cf. 23[1] Jd. 2[14] with Moore's note. — **49.** וישוי] occurs also Gen. 46[17] and is evidently a corruption of אשיו ישוי) = איש יהוה. This is the equivalent of *Ishbaal* which has been altered in the other direction into *Ishbosheth*. The actual name was Ish baal — *the man of the Lord*. The identity of the name in the text with Ishbosheth was affirmed by Ewald (*GVI*[3]. III. p. 148, E. Tr. III. p. 108), who also reconstructed ישוי from 𝔊. The exact state of the case was demonstrated by We., who is followed by Dr. (with some reserve), Bu., Ki. 𝔊[L] adds καὶ Ἐισβάαλ at the end of the list. — מלכישוע] Μελχισεδδι 𝔊[L]. Instead of three sons, four are ascribed to Saul in 31[2] (where three are slain) and 1 Chr. 8[33] 9[39]. — מיכל] Μελχόλ 𝔊 and מלכיל 𝔖 would point to מלכיאל, cf. G. 46[17]. — **50.** The first two names are compounded with אח (brother) like so many which have come down to us. — אבינר] occurs elsewhere in the shorter form אבנר. — **51.** בן־אביאל] should obviously be read בני־אביאל as is indicated by Josephus, and pointed out by Th. (followed by Kl., Dr., Ki., Bu.). Only thus do we get what belongs here, for that Kish was the father of Saul is already known to us, and that Ner was a son of Abiel throws no light on the situation unless we know who Abiel is.

52. וראה] the tense indicates what was repeatedly or habitually done, Dr., *Tenses*[3], §§ 120, 148, 1. With ויאספהו the author falls back into the narrative tense, having the particular instance in mind rather than the frequent repetition.

XV. The rejection of Saul. — The word of Yahweh is brought by Samuel to Saul, commanding the extermination of Amalek on the ground of what that people did to Israel in the Desert. Saul therefore gathers an army, and makes the campaign. But he succumbs to the temptation of the booty, and himself spares the king of Amalek, besides conniving at the people's taking the best of the spoil for themselves. Samuel is divinely informed of the disobedience, goes to meet Saul, and rebukes him. Giving no weight to the king's excuses, he formally announces that Yahweh has rejected him. Saul confesses his sin, but Samuel persists in his sentence; and when his garment rends in the grasp of Saul, he interprets the event as a sign of the divine decision to take away the kingdom. Nevertheless he consents to pay outward respect to the king, bowing with him in worship. Samuel then calls for Agag, whom he puts to death before Yahweh.

The first thing that strikes us in reading this account is, that it makes no mention of an earlier rejection of Saul. The author does not intimate that this is a second test. There is no hint that he supposes Saul to have repented of his former sin — a repentance such as the earlier commentators postulated, in order to harmonize the two accounts. This chapter, like 13^{4-15}, reads as if it were the only account of Saul's rejection. But the common features are striking. Gilgal is the scene of both. In each, Saul receives a command from Samuel. In each he disobeys (though the exact manner of the disobedience in 13^{4-15} is obscure) ; in each he is informed that his kingdom is taken from him ; in each the kingdom is said to have been given to another. The conclusion is obvious : though the two accounts are taken from two separate documents, and though each formed, in the history of which it was a part, the sole account of the rejection of Saul, yet they are derived from a common tradition, or one is dependent on the other.

Of the affiliations of the present section we can have no doubt. It belongs with chapters 1–3. 7. 8. 10^{17-25}. 12. The position of Samuel is the same as in those sections. Although retired, he is still the organ of the theocratic administration. Saul is still under obligation to obey his commands. Disobedience to Samuel is disobedience to God, and is punished by deposition. This identity of view is accompanied by resemblance of language. God is *Yahweh Sabaoth* (15^2, cf. $1^{3.11}$). There is distinct reference to the people's *coming up* out of Egypt (15^6 8^8 10^{18}) ; Samuel *cries to Yahweh* (15^{11} 7^9 12^8) ; Saul, like the people, is reproached with having *rejected the word of Yahweh* (15^{23} 8^7). Other similarities will show themselves in the detailed examination of the passage. We must suppose the story to belong with the chapters already named. Taking them as forming a single history, we see that this is really the climax. The document gives a life of Samuel, in which Saul has a prominent part to be sure, but a part which serves to set off the glory of Samuel. The author reckons Samuel as one of the divinely appointed judges. Saul's election was a mistake from the beginning. The real succession passed to David. The rebellious demand for a king was acceded to only under a protest on the part of Yahweh and his prophet. An unhappy

K

issue was looked for from the start. Nor was it long delayed.
The very first time that Saul was put to the test he failed.

We might, indeed, suppose that the author originally gave more
of Saul's exploits than have been preserved to us. But, as he has
already ascribed the Philistine victory to Samuel, he probably had
little else to give. In fact, his interest in Saul was not such as to
make him give more. As we have already seen, he was probably
dependent on the other (and earlier) document. His account of
Saul's rejection is a free reconstruction and expansion of 13^{8-15},
designed to take the place of that narrative, and to make it teach
a theocratic lesson.

XV. The critical questions are treated in the works already frequently
cited. I confess my inability to see why this chapter should be made 'intermediate between the two streams of narrative already considered' (We.,
Comp. p. 248, Dr., *LOT*[6]. p. 178, Ki., *GH.* II. p. 25). The character and
position of Samuel as here portrayed agree closely with his picture as drawn
in the life of Samuel, chapters 7. 8. 12, unless it is easier to unmake a king
than to make him, which will hardly be asserted. So far from "occupying a
position midway between prophets like Elijah or Elisha and those like Amos
or Hosea" (Ki.), Samuel as here represented is more autocratic than any of
these. No one of them, even in the stories which are told of them, ever stood
out so distinctly and frankly the superior of a king of Israel, as is the case
with Samuel in the section before us. The section agrees fully in this respect
with 7. 8. and 12.

The majority of critics draw a sharp line between this and the following
chapter (16^{1-13}). The reason is not apparent. On the contrary, the logical
sequence of this chapter is found in that paragraph. Saul is rejected in order
that David may be anointed. It may be said that Samuel's fear of Saul in the
second section is inconsistent with the autocratic position which he here occupies. But it should be remembered that the motive of the author in making
Samuel dissimulate is to account for the secresy of the transaction. He knew
that no hint of an anointing of David appears in any other document. To
account for this fact, he must make Samuel keep his errand secret. The
obvious device was to make his concealment motived by fear of Saul.

1–3. The command and its motive. — Samuel comes to Saul
with the Word of Yahweh. The hostility of Amalek shown in the
Wilderness is yet unpunished. Saul is therefore to devote them
to utter destruction. The historicity of the incident is open to
grave doubts. Saul's kingdom was over Benjamin, and there he
had all he could do to keep back the Philistine attack. Judah

was separated from him by the Jebusite fortress, and its loyalty could never have been very warm. The claim on Amalek was outlawed by some centuries. So far from this people being exterminated by Saul, they were engaged in active feud with David very soon after the supposed attack by Saul. Finally, no trace of this attack has survived in any passage of the Old Testament except the one before us. — **1.** The command seems to follow immediately on the farewell address of Samuel in 12. It begins with the statement : *Me did Yahweh send to anoint thee*] the pronoun is put first for emphasis. The statement is made in order to call attention to Samuel's right to command. — *Now hear the sound of the words of Yahweh*] the circumlocution is chosen to avoid anthropomorphism, and shows a comparatively late date. — **2.** *Thus saith Yahweh Sebaoth*] a standing formula with the prophets. This divine name has already been met in the account of Samuel's life, 1³·¹¹ 4⁴, cf. also 17⁴⁵. — *I have resolved to punish*] this seems to be the only way in which we can understand the words ; the translation *I remember* seems not justified by usage. *Amalek* was a clan of Bedawin inhabiting the Wilderness of the Wandering. They inhabited also the *Negeb*, Nu. 13²⁹. — *What Amalek did to Israel, in that he opposed him in the way when he came up out of Egypt*] the construction is difficult, but the historical reference is evident. In Ex. 17⁸⁻¹⁶ we find that Amalek made war with Israel in Rephidim. Again, they opposed Israel's entrance to Canaan from the south, Num. 14⁴⁵. In Deuteronomy also (25¹⁷⁻¹⁹) we find Amalek stigmatized as having met Israel *in the way* and having cut off their weary and faint stragglers. The phrase *in the way* would indicate that the present account depends upon Deuteronomy. Further instances of hostility between Amalek and Israel are found in Jd. 7¹² and in David's life, 1 S. 30. The comparatively late text 2 S. 8¹² speaks of their spoil having been consecrated by David, so that the present account can hardly have been known to the author of that verse. Had the vow recorded in Ex. 17¹⁴ been in this writer's mind he would have made some reference to it. — **3.** *Go and smite Amalek and devote him and all which belongs to him*] such solemn devotion to Yahweh (and therefore to destruction) is well known from Dt. 7² 20¹⁷, where it is commanded as the duty of Israel in dealing with the Canaanites, and from Jos. 6²¹, where it is described as actually carried out. By this act of consecration, a city or nation with all its property became Yahweh's. Indestructible objects of value (gold and silver) came into the treasury of the sanctuary, Jos. 6¹⁹. Everything else must be destroyed, including the human beings, as is made clear by this verse : *And do not spare him, but slay man and woman, child and babe, ox and sheep, camel and ass*] so at Jericho the ban covered man and woman, youth and aged, ox and ass, Jos. 6²¹; cf. Dt. 20¹⁶, where Israel is forbidden to leave alive *anything that breathes*. That Mesha devoted the Israelites to Chemosh in the same way is expressly said by himself (*Inscription*, l. 17).

1. The verse fits well on to the end of ch. 12, and Bu.'s supposition that it has been expanded is unnecessary. The solemn reminder would be especially appropriate if the commission were the first with which the new made king was charged. — אֹתִי] is emphatic by position. — שָׁלַח] is inexact, for in none of the documents was Samuel *sent* to anoint Saul. But we can probably not insist on verbal accuracy in our author. — לִמְלֹךְ] Jd. 9¹⁵ 2 S. 2⁴. — עַל־עַמּוֹ] is lacking in 𝔊ᴮ, whereas עַל־יִשְׂרָאֵל is not represented in 𝔊ᴸ. — לְקוֹל דִּבְרֵי] Dt. 4¹² 5²⁵. — **2.** פָּקַדְתִּי] this tense is quite justified in the meaning *I have determined* to do thus, Dr., *Notes*, referring to Jd. 15³, and *Tenses*³, § 13. The attempt to make the verb here mean *I remember* AV. or *I have* [mentally] *marked* RV. Erdm., Keil, is based (as alleged) upon Ex. 3¹⁶ Jer. 23² Ps. 8⁵. But examination shows that none of the passages sustain the assumed meaning. The oldest tradition for this passage is voiced in the rendering νῦν ἐκδικήσω, or νῦν ἐκδικῶ 𝔊 and is undoubtedly correct. With sound feeling Schm. renders : *visitare constitui*. — עֲמָלֵק] is connected with Edom in the genealogy, Gen. 36¹². ¹⁶. Balaam predicted their destruction, Num. 24²⁰. — אֲשֶׁר־שָׂם לוֹ] is supposed to mean *how he laid wait for him* AV., or *how he set himself against him* RV. But the supposed parallels 1 K. 20¹² Ezek. 23²⁴ both have עַל and both have an object supplied by 𝔊. 2 K. 10²⁴ seems similar to our text, but there לוֹ is dative of advantage and the verb has an object expressed; שִׂית, which is urged as an analogon, also requires עַל, Ps. 3⁷. It is probable that ἀπήντησεν 𝔊 points to a different reading, though what it is, is difficult to make out. Dt. 25¹⁸ has אֲשֶׁר קָרְךָ בַּדֶּרֶךְ, but this is not sufficiently explicit for our passage. For the verb here Kl. suggests שָׂטַן. If conjectures be in order, I would change to אֲשֶׁר צַר לוֹ, the crime being aggravated (as Dt. more explicitly states) by the fact that it was committed when *he* (Israel) *was in trouble*. But I have not ventured to introduce this into my translation, as the reasons for choosing it are not decisive. — בַּעֲלֹתוֹ מִמִּצְרָיִם] Gen. 13¹ (J) Ex. 17³ (E) Num. 21⁵ (J) 32¹¹ (P). The imperative לֵךְ is followed by the perfect consecutive as is customary. — וְהַחֲרַמְתֶּם] the plural is unexpected and we should probably restore והחרמתו as read by ⅏, making the next word ואת instead of את (We.). The verb seems to occur nowhere in Samuel except in this chapter. It is used by all the Pentateuchal sources. — תחמל] Dt. 13⁹ Ex. 2⁶. — מאיש עד אשה] cf. 22¹⁹ Jos. 6²¹. For עד (Ginsb.) many editions have ועד.

4–9. Saul's disobedience. — This consists in making important exceptions to the completeness of the destruction. — He first *called out the people and mustered them in Telam*] a town in the south of Judah, Jos. 15²⁴. The number given, *two hundred thousand footmen*, is to be judged like similar data elsewhere. The *ten thousand, the men of Judah*, seem to be an afterthought. — 5. *And he came to the city of Amalek*] the absence of a name for the city shows the author's vagueness of geographical knowledge. Cities there can hardly have been in that desert region, though a fortified village might by courtesy be so denominated. The reading *cities* ⅏ is plainly incorrect. Only one engagement is thought of. — *And lay in wait in the wadi*] a favourite move in Hebrew strategy, Jos. 8² Jd. 20²⁹. — 6. The *Kenites* whom Saul warned were old allies of Israel, represented in one document as the tribe of Moses' father in law, Jd. 4¹¹. After sharing the desert wanderings of Israel and entering Palestine, they preferred the nomad life in the Negeb, where they dwelt with Amalek according to the original text of Jd. 1¹⁶. The author does not seem to have questioned whether the warning to the Kenites would not frustrate the purpose of Saul in regard to Amalek. The reason of Saul's considerate treatment of the Kenite is given in his message to them in the circumstantial clause : *cum tu tamen misericordiam feceris cum omnibus filiis Israelis* (Schm.). The Kenites withdrew as warned. — 7. *And Saul smote Amalek from* —] the name of the place is now lost ; *Havilah*, which is given by our documents, is impossible. — *As far as Shur which is before Egypt*] " Shur is originally the *wall* which ran from Pelusium through Migdol to Hero " (We.).* — 8. *And he took Agag the king of Amalek alive*] cf. Jos. 8²³. — *But all the people he slew with the sword*] lit. *consecrated according to the mouth of the sword*, cf. Moore on Jd. 1²⁵. —

---

* The description of this wall, or line of fortifications, is given by Wiedemann, *Herodot's Zweites Buch* (Leipzig, 1890), p. 88, with references to Diodorus Siculus and the Egyptian sources.

9. *Saul and the people spared Agag and the best of the small and large cattle, the fatlings and the lambs*] a slight emendation of the received text is necessary. The wealth of Amalek must have been mainly in cattle. The motive of Saul in sparing Agag (pride, hope of ransom, an ill-timed emotion of pity, respect of persons) was much discussed by the older commentators (cf. Schm., *Quaestio* VI. ad Cap. XV.). An *Agag* is mentioned Num. 24⁷, where he is made the symbol of great exaltation, but it is not yet clearly made out whether there is a reference to this passage. On *the vile and refuse* which were destroyed, see the critical note.

4. וישמע] the Piel is used only here and 23⁸, where also Saul calls out the people to war. In both places it is possible that we should point a Hiphil, 1 K. 15²² Jer. 50²⁹ 51²⁷. — בטלאים] the name of a place is no doubt intended — *quasi agnos* 𝔏 is, of course, impossible. But ἐν Γαλγάλοις 𝔊 is not appropriate. Most recent critics find in the text only an orthographic variation of טלם a town mentioned Jos. 15²⁴. For *two hundred thousand* we find *four hundred thousand* 𝔊. The ten thousand of Judah are omitted by 𝔊ᴸ, but increased to thirty thousand by 𝔊ᴮ. — **5.** עיר] πόλεων 𝔊. — וירב] is intended for ויארב (ἐνήδρευσεν 𝔊) as is seen by Kimchi and Schm. Kautzsch (Ges.²⁶ § 68 *i*) takes it to be Hiphil, but ארב occurs nowhere else in this stem. — **6.** לכו סרו רדו] 𝔊 omits רדו, perhaps correctly. On the daghesh in רדו cf. Ges.²⁶ 20 *g*. — עמלקי] as we expect the author to be consistent, it seems best to restore עמלק here, the form which we find at the end of the verse. — אַסָּפְּךָ] should probably be pointed (Lag., *Proph. Chald.* p. li), cf. Gen. 18²³· ²⁴ 1 S. 12²⁵. This is much more forcible than the received pointing. — כל] is superfluous and therefore suspicious — lacking in 𝔊ᴮᴸ. — קיני] should certainly be קין or הקיני, probably the latter, because that form is elsewhere used in this passage; We., Bu., Ki., choose קין. — **7.** חוילה] elsewhere the name of some point or district in Arabia. It occurs once in a phrase similar to the one in the text — *from Havilah to Shur*, Gen. 25¹⁸. It there bounds the territory of the Ishmaelites, of which Havilah should be the eastern boundary. It would consequently be far from the scene of Saul's exploit. Still there is a possibility that our author, whose geography is not very distinct, borrowed the whole phrase from Genesis. We. conjectures *Telam* to be the original reading. But this does not commend itself, because Saul had advanced beyond Telam when the attack was made. Glaser (as cited by BDB. *sub voce*) proposes to read חכילה which is mentioned 1 S. 23¹⁹ 26¹· ³. But this hill in the Desert of Judah was hardly a part of the Amalekite territory. *Non liquet.* — בואך שור] cf. 27⁸ (where מטלם seems to have stood in connexion with it). — על־פני] *in front of* is frequently used of the east side, and would be appropriately so understood here. — **8.** העם] may mean the soldiery (Ki.), but as there is no record of any human being being spared except Agag, it is better to make it general. — ‫[החרים לפי־חרב‬ Jos. 6²¹ cf. Dt. 13¹⁶. — **9.** ‫[מיטב‬ only in the Book of the Covenant, Ex. 22⁴, and P, Gen. 47⁶· ¹¹. — ‫[והמשנים‬ is supposed to be the lambs of the second birth. The word is, however, a mistake for ‫השמנים‬ (Th., We., Dr., Bu., Ki.), and the adoption of this carries with it the erasure of ‫על‬ which follows. ‫השמנים והכרים‬ defines the *best of the cattle*. Kl. proposes *women and children* for which there is no support. ‫כרים‬, as delicacies, Dt. 32¹⁴. ‫כרמים‬ 𝕲 is adopted by Ew. ‫אגג‬ here and ‫אגו‬ in Nu. 24⁷ are the same name. From the reference in Numbers we conclude that an Agag had been an object of terror or of admiration to the Israelites — it should be noted, however, that 𝕲ᴬᴮᴸ has *Gog* there. — ‫[אבו‬ Ex. 10²⁷ (E), Dt. 2³⁰ 10¹⁰ I S. 31⁴. — ‫[נמבזה ונמס‬ is impossible. The first word is a *monstrum* (Dr.) caused by the stupidity of a scribe. The second is apparently for ‫נמאס‬, for we require a feminine form. Part of this original was wrongly spaced and formed part of the word which 𝕳 now reads as ‫א.ה.‬, the ‫ה‬ being duplication from the following word. The true text is therefore ‫וכל מלאכה נבזה ונמאס‬ with omission of ‫אתה‬. The word ‫מלאכה‬ is used for *property* in general, Ex. 22⁷· ¹⁰ (E), and for *cattle* Gen. 33¹⁴. We may compare ‫פעלה‬ used for flocks Is. 40¹⁰. Trumbull came to the conclusion (independently of We.) that *Shur* is the frontier fortification of Egypt, and the same is the view of Brugsch, as cited by Buhl and Socin (Ges. *WB*¹². *sub voce*).

10–23. The prophet's rebuke. — Samuel, divinely informed of Saul's transgression, goes to seek him, and meets him at Gilgal. Saul at first declares that he has carried out the commandment of Yahweh. When convicted by circumstantial evidence, he throws the blame on the people. The prophet cuts his protestations short, and when Saul attempts further argument, pronounces the final word of rejection. — **10.** *The word of Yahweh came to Samuel*] the context implies that it was in a vision of the night. — **11.** *I repent that I made Saul king*] Gen. 6⁶· ⁷ (J). The dogmatic attempt to explain the anthropomorphism may be read in Schm., *Quaestio* VII. Yahweh does not explain the nature of his emotion, but goes on to give its occasion : *For he has turned from following me and has not carried out my command*] lit. *my word;* the Hebrew has *my words*, but the reference is to one particular revelation. — *And Samuel was angry*] there seems to be no reason for changing the text. The violent emotion of the Oriental at the frustration of his hopes must not be judged by our standard of propriety. — *And cried to Yahweh all night*] in protest and expostulation. Schm. compares Moses' grief for Israel. — **12.** The entreaty fails to change the purpose of Yahweh, and

Samuel starts in the early morning to deliver his message. He is told : *Saul came to Carmel*] the Carmel in Judah, well known from the history of David. It lay nearly south of Hebron, and would be in Saul's path. — *And behold he has set up a trophy*] the noun means *a monument* in 2 S. 18¹⁸. The words *and turned and passed by* are difficult to understand in this connexion. Probably there is some confusion in the text. — *And went down to Gilgal*] must conclude the information concerning Saul's movements. The object of going to Gilgal was evidently to offer thank offerings, as indeed 𝕲 asserts. — **13.** *Blessed be thou of Yahweh*] the form of the salutation shows that it was originally a prayer. Saul's sweeping claim — *I have fulfilled the word of Yahweh* — is in flat contradiction to Yahweh's revelation to Samuel, v.¹¹. The author's purpose is to paint Saul as one hopelessly hardened in sin. The older commentators note his hypocrisy, tum in excusando, tum in confitendo et poenitendo (Schm.). — **14.** Samuel at once convicts him by present phenomena : *Then what is this bleating of sheep in my ears, and this lowing of cattle which I hear?* The inconsistency was palpable. — **15.** Saul's confession of the fact is so frank as to be impudent, and equally offensive is his intimation that the religious purpose in view was sufficient justification : *From Amalek I brought them : for the people spared the best of the sheep and the oxen to sacrifice to Yahweh thy God*] the designation may possibly intimate that Samuel was to profit by the sacrifice. Still, as he does not appear to be a priest, much emphasis can hardly be laid upon this ; and it is more natural to suppose that the author betrays here his theory that Yahweh was the God of Samuel, but hardly the God of Saul. — **16.** Samuel cuts the speech short : *Stop! and let me tell thee what Yahweh said to me this night*] in our mode of speaking it would be *last night*. — **17, 18.** Receiving permission to proceed, Samuel begins his rebuke : *Art thou not, though little in thine own eyes, chief of the tribes of Israel?* The question seems to be a rebuke of Saul's self-confessed subservience to the people. The next clause belongs with v.¹⁸, which should read : *And Yahweh anointed thee king over Israel and sent thee a journey.* The close collocation favours the view already advanced that in this document the command was given immediately after the coronation. — *Go and* *exterminate the sinners, Amalek, and fight against them until they are completely destroyed*] 2 S. 22³⁸ 1 K. 22¹¹. Amalek is called *sinners* because of the ancestral offence against Israel. — **19.** The situation has thus been described: the rebuke follows in the form of a question: *And why didst thou not obey the voice of Yahweh, and didst swoop upon the booty, and didst that which is evil in the eyes of Yahweh?*] Jd. 2¹¹ 3⁷. **21.** Saul's further protest only convicts himself. He now calls what was spared *the firstfruits of that which was devoted*, which is of course an absurdity. — **22, 23.** The reply of Samuel is rhythmical in form:

> *Does Yahweh delight in offerings and sacrifices*
> *As in obedience to the voice of Yahweh?*
> *Behold, obedience is better than sacrifice,*
> *And to hearken than the fat of rams.*
> *For rebellion is the sin of soothsaying,*
> *Obstinacy is the iniquity of Teraphim.*
> *Because thou hast rejected the word of Yahweh,*
> *He has rejected thee from ruling over Israel.*

The passage is a summary of later Jewish theology, cf. Ps. 50⁹ 51¹⁸. The author's remoteness from the times of Saul is evident from the horror with which he views the Teraphim. His verse seems to have been trimeter in construction, though transmission has obscured the original reading in some cases.

11. [המלכתי] 8²² 12¹. — [שב מאחרי] Num. 14⁴³ 32¹⁵ (P) Jos. 22¹⁶·¹⁸ (P). — [דברי לא הקים] Dt. 27²⁶ Jer. 34¹⁸. — [ויחר] is emended to ויצר by Bu., Ki., following a suggestion of Dr.; 𝔊 has καὶ ἠθύμησε which Dr. supposes to point to וימר. But it should be noted that in two other passages, 2 S. 6⁸ and its parallel* 1 Chr. 13¹¹, ויחר is rendered in the same way. In these passages David is said to have been *angry* at Yahweh's breaking out upon Uzzah, in which we find a close analogy to the present experience of Samuel. — [ויזעק] of crying to God in distress, Ex. 2²³ (P) Jd. 3⁹ 6⁶ (D) 1 S. 7⁹ 12⁸. — **12.** [הכרמלה] 25²·⁵·⁷·⁴⁰, mentioned as one of the cities of Judah, Jos. 15⁵⁵. The place would lie near Saul's road from the Negeb to Gilgal. The ruins still bear the name *Kurmul* (GASmith, *Hist. Geog.* p. 306 note). — [והנה מציב] is wrong, because it implies that Saul is still engaged at the work. Read והנה הציב with 𝔊 (which had even ויצב), We., Dr., Bu. — [יד] of the pillar of Absalom 2 S. 18¹⁸, and of a memorial of some kind Ex. 17¹⁶ (if the text is sound), cf. Is. 56⁵. — [ויסב] is in place only if, with 𝔊, we make Samuel the subject — *then he turned*

---

* The parallel passage weighs as much for the usage of 𝔊 as if it were independent of the other.

about — for Saul certainly did not need to turn. But what the context requires
is a continuation of the information about Saul, for Samuel wants to know
where he now is. ויסב has come in by mistake and should be omitted. The
text of 𝕲 has suffered here from the confusion of the names Saul and Samuel,
as is evident from 𝕲ᴮ which reads: and it was told *Saul* that *Samuel* came to
Carmel (corrected in ᴬᴸ). For ויסב ויעבר: καὶ ἀπέστρεψε τὸ ἅρμα [αὐτοῦ] 𝕲.
At the end of the verse 𝕲 reads: *and he came down to Gilgal to Saul, and
behold he offered a burnt offering to the Lord, the firstfruits of the spoil* which
he brought from Amalek. But, as remarked by We., this can hardly be original, as Samuel would take some notice of the sacrifice. — **13.** ברוך אתה לי׳]
23²¹ 2 S. 2⁵ Ruth 2²⁰. — **14.** הזה] defines the קול of course. — **15.** הביאם]
ἤνεγκα 𝕲 is more forcible and I have adopted it. אשר] is impossible to
reproduce except by a causal particle, cf. Davidson, *Syntax*, p. 198. Of the
examples cited there, only Gen. 30¹⁸ 1 K. 3¹⁹ 2 K. 17⁴ seem to hold, and it
should be remembered that even in such cases אשר does not define the cause
as כי would. — החרמנו] should be corrected to החרמתי according to 𝕲. —
16. הרף] *desine garrire multum,* Schm. In Dt. 9¹⁴ it expresses God's desire
not to hear entreaty or intercession from Moses. — ויאמרו *Kt.*] is doubtless to
be corrected to ויאמר with the *Qrê.* — **17.** The translation of the text as it
stands is attempted above. As the sentence is somewhat involved (for
Hebrew) there is room for suspicion as to the correctness of transmission.
𝕲ᴸ seems to have expanded, influenced by Saul's own confession of his
humble station in 9²¹, reading: *Art thou not* [too] *small in thine own eyes to
be ruler, coming from the tribe of Benjamin, the least of the tribes of Israel?
Yet Yahweh anointed thee king over all Israel;* where the contrast is between
Saul's own tribe and *all* Israel. This, however, is artificial and far-fetched for
an occasion like this. 𝕲ᴮ seems to find a sarcastic question in the words:
*Art thou not small in his eyes, O Ruler of the tribes of Israel? Yet Yahweh
anointed thee,* etc. In the uncertainty, and as 𝔚 might have given rise to the
other readings, it seems safest to adhere to the received text. — **18.** יהוה] is
superfluous if the sentence really begins with וימשחך. — והחרמתה] confirms the
text adopted in v.³. — החטאים] 𝕲 adds εἰς ἐμέ. — עד־כלותם אתם] can hardly be
correct. 𝕲 seems to have had עד כלותך אתם which would do. But it seems
simpler to omit the last word as an erroneous repetition (We., Dr., al.). —
19. ותעט] see on 14³². — ותעש הרע וגו׳] a standing Deuteronomistic phrase.
— **20.** אשר] as equivalent to כי *recitativum,* cf. Dr., *Notes,* and Ges.²⁶ 157 *c*;
but אכן is conjectured by Bu. — **21.** ראשית] elsewhere of the firstfruits of
vegetable products, Ex. 23¹⁹ 34²⁶ Num. 15²⁰ Dt. 18⁴. — **22.** החפץ] 1 S. 18²⁵;
the word is found in late writers. — כשמע] where the comparison would be
fully expressed by כבשמע. Such an ellipsis needs no justification. ולהקשיב
= 𝕲. The ו is lacking in 𝔚. Grammatically speaking there is an ellipsis of
טוב in the last clause. — בקול יהוה] 𝔖 and 𝕲ᴸ render בקולו, not being constrained by the metre. — **23.** The verse is obscure, and the versions do not
give much help. The writer intends to say, evidently, that Saul's sin is as bad
as the soothsaying and idolatry for which the heathen are condemned. His

sin is מרי — rebellion against the command of God, for which Ezekiel rebukes Israel, cf. Num. 17²⁵ Dt. 31²⁷. This sin is compared with the soothsaying from which (ideally) Israel is free Num. 23²³, but which was rife in the time of Jeremiah (14¹⁴), Ezek. 21²⁶, cf. Dt. 18¹⁰. The second member of the verse must be parallel with this. — ואון ותרפים] cannot therefore be right. *The guilt of* idolatry is what we require, and this would be עון הרפים for which we may claim Symmachus ἡ ἀνομία τῶν εἰδώλων. — הפצר] pausal form of a Hiphil, which, however, occurs nowhere else. The Qal means to *urge one* with persistent entreaty, Gen. 19³⋅ ⁹ 33¹¹ Jd. 19⁷. It is difficult to get from this any meaning that will fit our passage. A too insistent entreaty of God was not Saul's fault. 𝕲 seems to have read הפיצו. The natural parallel to מרי would be a derivative of סרר if we may judge by Dt. 21¹⁸ Jer. 5²³. Perhaps we might assume סררה, cf. סרה Dt. 13⁶. Or, on the ground of Jos. 22²², מרר would be in place. In fact several words suggest themselves, but none that would easily be corrupted to הפצר, Sym. τὸ ἀπειθεῖν, cf. Field. Kl. suggests חפץ רע; but this destroys the rhythm. — ממלך] at the end of the verse is abrupt, and as 𝕲 adds ἐπὶ Ἰσραήλ, we should probably restore על ישראל. Ew. suggests לו, which would agree better with the metre (*G VI*³. III. p. 55, E. Tr. III. p. 39).

24–31. Saul confesses his sin, and asks forgiveness. In his earnestness he lays hold of the prophet's tunic, which rends, so that Samuel uses the incident to point his sentence of rejection. Nevertheless, at Saul's further entreaty, he consents to join outwardly in worship.

There is some doubt whether the paragraph is by the author of the foregoing. It expressly contradicts the assertion of Yahweh's repentance, compare v.²⁹ and v.¹¹. Its representation of Samuel's outward loyalty to Saul, even after his rejection, seems inconsistent with the picture drawn in the earlier part of the chapter. By its omission we miss nothing of importance from the narrative, and the dramatic effect is heightened because the slaying of Agag follows directly on Samuel's oracle.

24–31. That the paragraph is an interpolation seems first to have been suggested by Stade (*G VI*². I. p. 221). The suggestion is adopted by Bu. both in *RS.* and in his edition of the text. The arguments are that the section is wholly superfluous and can be left out without disturbing the consistency of the narrative, and that it contradicts the assertion of v.¹¹ that Yahweh *repented* of having made Saul king — contrast the categorical statement that *he is not a man that he should repent* (v.²⁹).

24. Saul's confession: *I have sinned, for I have transgressed the command of Yahweh and thy word*] is not to be taken as hypocritical. The author means to teach that the most sincere repentance is of no avail when God has made his final decision. Christian commentators (Schm., for example), with New Testament ideas of confession and forgiveness, are obliged to suppose that the repentance here was feigned or insincere. Saul's excuse that he *feared the people* is the same already intimated, though it has not been explicitly stated. — **25.** *Now forgive my sin*] cf. Gen. 50[17], where Joseph's brothers ask his forgiveness for the injury done to him, and Ex. 10[17], where Moses is asked by Pharaoh to forgive his sin against Yahweh. The latter is evidently the model for the present writer. Samuel stands quite on the level of Moses. It is, perhaps, because the text seems to favour the Roman Catholic practice of confession that Schmidt paraphrases: *aufer, nempe apud Deum deprecando.* In Saul's further petition — *and turn with me that I may worship Yahweh* — it is implied that Samuel's presence is necessary to the validity of the service. — **26, 27.** The request is refused, and the sentence of rejection repeated. As Samuel turns to go away, Saul seizes the skirt of his robe to detain him, *but it rends.* The *me'îl* was the outer of the two garments ordinarily worn by the well-to-do. — **28.** The apparent accident is made the occasion of a renewed sentence: *Yahweh has rent thy kingdom from thee and given it to thy neighbour who is better than thou*] cf. 28[17]. The scene reminds us of Ahijah and Jeroboam, 1 K. 11[29-31]. — **29.** *Moreover the Victor of Israel will not lie nor repent, for he is not man that he should repent*] cf. Num. 23[19]. The contradiction to v.[11] is doubtless removed by the remark of Clericus that in one case the language is anthropopathic, in the other 'theoprepic.' But the Hebrew author was hardly so theologically schooled; and it remains improbable that the same writer should express himself anthropopathically in v.[11], and find it necessary to correct the anthropopathism a few verses later. — **30, 31.** Saul entreats for consideration *before the elders of the people and before Israel*] and the request is granted. The author is willing to leave him the semblance of the kingly office for the time being.

24. פי־יהוה] for the command of Yahweh Num. 3[16], al. The full expression עבר את־פי יהוה Num. 14[41], 22[18] (E). — [דבריך] the singular, which is represented in 𝔊, is more appropriate. It was a single message which Saul had

disobeyed.   On רבר for a command of God cf. BDB. s.v. II. 2. — **25.** ‏[ואשתחוה‏
should probably be pointed with the cohortative ending. — **26.** ‏[מהיות מלך‏
would perhaps favour the pointing מִמְּלֹךְ in v.²³. — **27.** ‏[כנף־מעילו‏ 24⁴·⁵· —
ויקרע‏] καὶ διέρρηξεν αὐτό ⅁.   But the scene is more impressive if human
agency is kept in the background. — **28.** ‏[ממלכות ישראל‏ for which τὴν
βασιλείαν σου ἀπὸ Ἰσραήλ ⅁.   The last two words are later addition to the
text of ⅁ (We.), which therefore had ‏ממלכתך‏ in their text, and this is so much
more forcible, and at the same time so much more likely to be expanded into
𝔅, that we must think it to be original; cf. also 1 K. 11¹¹. — **29.** ‏[ונם נצח ישראל‏
was read by ⅁ and Israel shall be rent in two, apparently = ‏ונם יחצה ישראל‏,
and this is accepted by Graetz (Gesch. d. Juden, I. p. 187).   But a prophecy
of the division of the kingdom is wholly out of place here.   We are obliged
therefore to retain the text of 𝔅.   נצו in one passage apparently means victory
(SS. referring to 1 Chr. 29¹¹), and in this place Jerome gives triumphator.
This tradition is the best within our reach.   We. decides for the Faithful One;
Dr. for the Glory; Ki. leaves a blank in his translation; Kl. emends freely and
gets: though we two were to protest to him, yet God is upright.

32–34. The fate of Agag.

— The original continuation of the
narrative, after the prophetic oracle v.²³, is found here, if what has
been advanced concerning vv.²⁴⁻³¹ is correct. — **32.** Samuel orders
Agag to be brought. — And Agag came to him trembling, and
Agag said: Surely death is bitter] the rendering is only provisional, as the meaning of one important word is uncertain, and the
text has apparently suffered. — **33.** The justice of Agag's fate is
asserted by Samuel: As thy sword has bereaved women, so shall
thy mother be bereaved above women] it is scarcely necessary to
explain the hyperbole by saying (as some have done) that Agag's
mother was bereaved of her son and her monarch at one stroke.
The most bereaved of women may be applied to any one sorely
bereaved.   And Samuel hewed Agag in pieces before Yahweh in
Gilgal] in fulfilment of the ban.   The act is strictly in line with
the law, Lev. 27²⁸ᶠ·.   It is the evident view of the author that Yahweh was pleased with the completion of the herem at his sanctuary.
It is somewhat remarkable that nothing further is said of the fatlings and lambs which the people had brought. — **34, 35.** Samuel
goes to his home in Ramah, and Saul to his in Gibeah. — And
Samuel saw Saul no more until the day of his death] the contradiction to 19²³ is obvious and shows the difference of the sources.
— For Samuel grieved over Saul] the reason for not seeing him
is that the grief would be thereby stirred afresh.   The last clause

of the verse, if it belongs here, must mean : *though Yahweh
repented*] and conveys a slight censure of Samuel. Probably,
however, it is a late insertion intended to round out this story.

32. מעדנת] must be an accusative expressing the manner in which Agag
came. This might be confident or defiant or cringing or cowardly. It is impossible to determine which is intended by the Hebrew word. The root
occurs in one passage (Neh. 9²⁵) as Hithpael, meaning *they lived luxuriously*.
So we might suppose here that Agag came *daintily*, as one who had fared
delicately; ἁβρός (Sym.), *pinguissimus* 𝕃, and ἀπὸ τρυφερίας (Aq.) point to this
meaning, the latter indicating מֵעֵדֶן; so מפנקא 𝕋. Aside from the intrinsic
improbability of a Bedawy chief being a luxurious liver, we must object to this
that it is a matter of minor importance. As the last clause of the verse shows,
the mental state of the captive is the important matter. 𝕲 therefore has a
claim on our attention when it gives τρέμων which might come from 𝕳 by a
change of pointing, first suggested by Lagarde (*Proph. Chald.* p. li) מְעַדְנִית,
from מער, *to totter;* he came *totteringly* would convey the idea of great fear,
and, as I am inclined to think, would be in accordance with the mind of this
writer, to whom Samuel was the imposing and even terrible embodiment of
the divine will. Others by metathesis make the word equivalent to מענדת,
in fetters (late Hebrew) — so Kimchi, followed by Grätz (*Gesch. d. Juden*, I.
p. 187). This is favoured by the curious ἐξ Ἀναθώθ 𝕲ᴸ, which might well
represent מֵענרות. If this meaning is adopted, it will be better to suppose the
original בענרה. The meaning *cheerfully* (Ew.) can scarcely be got from the
word, nor can the reason he gives — "the ancients held it to be a bad omen
when the sacrificial victim held back from the altar " — be verified in *Hebrew*
antiquity. The whole clause is lacking in 𝕾. Schm. combines two of the
meanings already considered : *virum delicatum et, quod concurrere solet, timi-
dum mortis*. Kl. substitutes אחוו for אגו and makes the clause mean *held
in chains.* — אכן סר מר־המות] the versions, except 𝕃, seem to have omitted
סר, whose resemblance to מר is such that duplication is easy. For אכן 𝕲
seems to have had הכן. For the rest of the clause πικρὸς ὁ θάνατος 𝕲 and
similarly 𝕾 and 𝕋. We. objects that this makes of that which is peculiar in
the narrative something quite trivial. But if it was the author's design to
impress the lesson of the *herem* and its awful character, he would quite as
appropriately make Agag lament his fate, as to make him self-confident or
defiant. The savage courage of Zebah and Zalmunna in meeting death, and
the arrogant temper of Adonibezek (Jd. 8¹⁸ 1⁷) would not adorn the tale,
where such a lesson is to be drawn. — **33.** אמך] 𝕲ᴸ adds υἱοῦ Ἀσηρ, which is
confirmed by l *filius doloris* (Cod. Leg.). As an אצר is found in the time of
Esau (Gen. 36²¹·³⁰), and as Amalek is brought into the same genealogy (Gen.
36¹²·¹⁶), it does not seem impossible for Agag to be addressed as 'Son of
Aser,' and the reading may be original. — וישסף] occurs in this place only.
The meaning is agreed upon by the versions and the commentaries. Possibly
we should read וישסע, cf. Jd. 14⁶, which, however, signifies *to tear in pieces* with

the hands. The change is advocated by Graetz (*Gesch. d. Juden*, 1, 188), and suggested, with a query, by Dr. — **34.** That Samuel's home is at Ramah is in accord with 1¹. — **35.** That Samuel *mourned for Saul* is taken up in the next chapter, and the statement here prepares the way for that. But the final clause ויהוה נחם וגו׳ does not fit well in this connexion. It is evidently a circumstantial clause, and in 16¹ is entirely in place. Here it must mean *though Yahweh had rejected him*, which may be justified by analogy, but would imply blame of Samuel. The connexion is better if it be stricken out. Budde begins the next section with it, but this does not seem natural.

1 SAMUEL XVI.–2 SAMUEL I. SAUL AND DAVID.

In the present arrangement of the Books of Samuel this is the second great division of the history. The introduction of David marks an epoch. There is no reason to doubt, however, that the same sources continue, for the death of Saul must have been related by both the authors who have given so much attention to his life. That various documents are combined in the history as it stands must be evident from the numerous discrepancies and duplicate accounts. Not improbably more than the two which have furnished the preceding history may be discovered here.

XVI. 1–13. The anointing of David. — Samuel is sent to Bethlehem, where, among the sons of Jesse, he is divinely directed to the choice of the right one, and anoints him as king. The tendency of the critics has been to make the section a late insertion. But several things indicate that it is the direct continuation of the preceding narrative. There seems to be nothing in the style or language which requires us to separate them. The rejection of Saul should logically be followed by the designation of his successor. In this author's view, the people should have a theocratic ruler. Saul was no longer such ; Samuel had retired. It seems impossible that the people should be left shepherdless. To this must be added the prominence which David had (in the later view) as a ruler especially chosen of Yahweh. It can hardly be supposed that this choice would not be made known in his youth. From the point of view of chapter 15, there is everything to make this section the natural continuation of that. Nor can I see that the position of Samuel is any different. His fear is introduced only to account for the secrecy of his movements.

1. The word of Yahweh comes to Samuel : *How long dost thou grieve over Saul, when I have rejected him from ruling over Israel ?* The circumstantial clause is quite in place here. — *Fill thy horn with oil*] as though the particular horn used in anointing Saul were to be used again. Possibly the author is influenced by the later conception of an anointing horn as part of the sacred furniture, as Solomon is anointed with the horn of oil taken from Yahweh's tent, 1 K. 1³⁹. — *And come, I will send thee to Jesse the Bethlehemite*] the name *Jesse* (Yishshai) belongs to this man alone in the Old Testament. Its etymology is obscure. Bethlehem, a well-known Judahite town five miles south of Jerusalem, still flourishes under its old name. — *I have looked me out a king*] Gen. 22⁸ 41³³ 2 K. 10³. — **2.** Samuel's objection is put in the form of a question : *How shall I go, since Saul will hear of it and kill me ?* The older commentators are somewhat exercised by Samuel's timidity in the face of a direct divine command, and extenuate it on the ground of natural human infirmity (Schm.). The narrator was more concerned to account for the privacy of the transaction. Hence the subterfuge : *Take in thy hand a calf and say : To sacrifice to Yahweh am I come*] the casuistry of the commentators attempts to justify Samuel's reticence, on the ground that he told one of the reasons for which he came. — **3.** *And invite Jesse to the sacrifice — I will tell thee what thou shalt do — and anoint whom I shall point out to thee.* — **4.** The command is carried out, and at Samuel's approach, *the elders of the city came trembling to meet him*] Samuel had the word of Yahweh, and therefore disposed of life and death : videtur fuisse consternatio orta ex improviso adventu tanti viri (Schm.). Hence their question : *Does thy coming betoken good, O Seer ?* 1 K. 2¹³. As Samuel's coming could hardly bring war, but might bring calamity, the translation *peace* is not appropriate. — **5.** Giving a reassuring answer and stating the ostensible object of his coming, he adds : *Purify yourselves and rejoice with me at the sacrifice*] which was of course a feast, 9¹³. The purification required was removal of ceremonial defilement. Samuel himself *prepared* (consecrated) *Jesse and his sons, and invited them to the sacrifice*] the ritual observances necessary in such case were, of course, best known to a priest-prophet. What follows seems to take place at the lustration, and we hear no more of the sacrifice. — **6.** When they came in order before him (as appears from the later verses), he was pleased with the eldest, Eliab, and said to himself: *Surely in the presence of Yahweh is his anointed*] 12³. A dialogue went on in the consciousness of the prophet. His own choice was moved by personal attractions, but Yahweh looked deeper. — **7.** *Look not at his person or the height of his stature*] though this had been emphasized (in the other document) in the case of Saul. — *For I have rejected him*] so far as the particular question now before us is concerned. — *For not as man sees doth God see*] the text is emended after 𝕲. — *For man looks at the appearance, but Yahweh looks at the heart*] the contrast is between bodily and mental endowments. — **8, 9.** A similar sentence is passed on Abinadab and Shammah. — **10.** *So Jesse made his seven sons pass before Samuel*] namely, the seven who were in the house, only to discover that *Yahweh had not chosen these.* — **11.** To Samuel's inquiry whether all had come, Jesse confesses: *There is still the youngest, and he is a shepherd with the flock*] 17³⁴. Samuel asks that he be sent for: *for we will not begin the sacrifice until he come hither*] the text is not altogether certain. — **12.** Jesse, in accordance with the command, sent and brought him: *And he was ruddy, a youth of fine eyes and goodly appearance*] nearly the same description is repeated 17⁴². Samuel receives the command to anoint him. — **13.** So he was anointed, *and the Spirit of Yahweh came upon David from that day onwards*] as had been the case with Saul, 10⁶·¹⁰. David has not been mentioned by name until this point. This is probably intentional, to heighten the effect. The narrative ends without further account of the proposed sacrifice, only adding after the anointing: *Samuel arose and went to Ramah.*

1. ולך אשלחך] generally we find לך followed either by another imperative, or by a finite verb with ו. But cf. לכה נא אקחך Num. 23²⁷; לכה איעצך Num. 24¹⁴. ישי, 'Ιεσσαί is found also in the form אישי (perhaps *man of Yahweh*).* —ראיתי] in this sense in E (passages are cited above). — **2.** ושמע] the perfect with *waw consecutive* continues the imperfect in any of its senses, so after particles which give a contingent sense, Dr., *Tenses*³, § 115, Davidson, *Syntax*, § 53 b, and the examples there cited, especially 2 S. 12¹⁸. The *pisqa* in the

---

* But שי seems to be one element of the name אבישי, 26⁶, etc. Hommel compares I-shai with I-chabod, I-thamar and I-ezer (*Altisrael Ueberlieferung*, p. 116).

middle of the verse indicates (as usual) a different mode of verse division.
— עֶגְלַת בָּקָר] Dt. 21³ Is. 7²¹. The expression indicates that עֶגְלָה might be
used of the young of other animals (? the camel). — בְּיָדֶךָ] cf. 14³⁴. —
3. בַּזֶּבַח] is a mistake for לְזֶבַח which is used with וַיִּקְרָא v.⁵ (erroneous anticipation of the בַּזֶּבַח in the latter verse). — אֲשֶׁר־אֹמַר אֵלֶיךָ] perhaps *whom I shall
command thee*, cf. כִּי אִם אָמַר לוֹ יהוה 2 S. 16¹¹. — **4.** לִקְרָאתוֹ . . . וַיֶּחֶרְדוּ] the constructio pregnans as often, Jd. 14⁵ 15¹⁴ I S. 21². — וַיֹּאמֶר] might be justified as
the indefinite *one said;* but as the elders are a distinct and limited body, it is
probable that we should read the plural, with the versions and 30 MSS. (DeR.).
— שָׁלֹם] read הֲשָׁלֹם. At the end of the verse 𝔊 adds ὁ βλέπων, that is הָרֹאֶה,
which can be construed here only as a vocative. The insertion by a scribe is
hardly probable, while the omission by one who thought the title not digni-
fied enough for Samuel is supposable. — **5.** הִתְקַדִּשׁוּ] the regular term for preparing oneself for approaching God, Jos. 3⁵. — וּבָאתֶם אִתִּי בַזֶּבַח] καὶ εὐφράνθητε
μετ' ἐμοῦ σήμερον 𝔊ᴬᴮ: *et state mecum et jocundimini* 𝕷 (Cod. Leg.). As 𝕳
is entirely commonplace and 𝔊ᴬᴮ is more vigorous, I have followed Th., al.,
in adopting the latter. — וַיְקַדֵּשׁ] is used of Moses when he consecrated the
priests, Ex. 28⁴¹ (P), but also when he prepared the people for the special
presence of God, Ex. 19¹⁴ (E); cf. also I S. 7¹. — **6.** The names of the three
sons here mentioned are repeated 17¹³. — וַיֹּאמֶר] the verb is frequently used
in the sense of *saying to oneself, thinking.* — אַךְ] is strongly asseverative. —
7. מַרְאֵהוּ] all that appears to the eye. — אֲשֶׁר יִרְאֶה הָאָדָם] the ellipsis is too
harsh and we must suppose a fault in the text. We., Dr., Bu. emend, after 𝔊,
to כַּאֲשֶׁר יִרְאֶה הָאָדָם יִרְאֶה אֱלֹהִים. Th. had proposed the same except that he
retained אֲשֶׁר. He is now followed by Ki., with the translation : *God does not
regard what man regards.* This is defensible, but if part of 𝔊 is taken, the
presumption is in favour of the whole. — לַעֵינַיִם] is difficult, because it does not
occur elsewhere in this sense — though nearly so in Lev. 13⁵ Num. 11⁷ (?)
cf. Lev. 13⁵⁵ cited by Dr. It must be contrasted with לַלֵּבָב; as the latter
must mean (Yahweh looks) *at the inner man* (cf. BDB. *s.v.*) we need an
expression meaning *at the outer man;* εἰς πρόσωπον 𝔊 may be only an attempt
to render 𝕳, but invites us to substitute לַפָּנִים, for which, however, there is no
analogy. — **8.** אֲבִינָדָב] the same name occurs 7¹. — **9.** שַׁמָּה] is apparently the
same with שִׁמְעָה, 2 S. 13³. — **10.** שִׁבְעַת בָּנָיו] means *his seven sons*, not *seven
of his sons*, which would be differently expressed. It is therefore inaccurate.
בָּחַר followed by בְּ seems to be Deuteronomic, Dt. 7⁶ 14² 18⁵ I S. 10²⁴. —
11. הֲתַמּוּ] supply לַעֲבוֹר as in Jos. 3¹⁷ 4¹¹ (JE). — שָׁאַר] seems to be lacking
in 𝔊 and the sense is good without it (Bu.). — וְהִנֵּה] is probably an abbreviated spelling of וְהִנֵּהוּ, though, as the subject immediately precedes, it is not
absolutely necessary that the suffix be expressed. — רֹעֶה בַצֹּאן] not *pasturing
the flock* but *acting as shepherd with the flock.* — נֹסֵב] κατακλιθῶμεν 𝔊ᴬᴮ;
ἀνακλιθῶμεν 𝔊ᴸ; discumbemus 𝕷. As ἀνάκλισις seems to represent מֵסַב in
Cant. 1¹² it is not certain that ᴸ had a different reading: κατακλίνομαι moreover does not anywhere render יָשַׁב. As סָבַב is used of going about the altar
as a part of the sacrificial worship, Samuel may mean *we will not begin the*

sacrifice until he come. 𝔖 seems to interpret אישוב.—**12.** עָס־יִפַת עינים] is impossible in spite of עָס־יִפַה מראה, 17⁴². In both passages we must restore עלם 20²² as was seen by Graetz and, independently of him, by Krenkel, *ZATW*. II. p. 309. Kl. proposes אדמוני שער, *red-haired*.—ראי] for מראה, here only. —**13.** וּתצלח] perhaps chosen with conscious reference to 10¹⁰. The accession of the spirit in the case of Saul was, however, spasmodic. The idea of the author seems to be that with David it was constant.—דוד] so written in Samuel and Kings; in Chronicles, Ezra, and Nehemiah דויד. The meaning of the name is unknown. Cf. BDB. *s.v.*—וּמעלה] of time as 30²⁵.

14–23. The first account of David's coming to court. — Saul is tormented by a divine visitation, apparently mental perturbation. Music being a known remedy, his courtiers recommend him to seek a skilful harper. On his approval of the plan, David is mentioned by one of the courtiers, and Saul sends for him. Coming to court, David speedily establishes himself in the favour of the king.

The affliction of Saul is ascribed to *an evil spirit from Yahweh* in v.¹⁴, the remainder of the account has *the Spirit of God*, twice with the adjective *evil* (vv.¹⁵·¹⁶), once in the current text without qualification. The difference in the use of the divine name probably shows that v.¹⁴ has been modified by the redaction. The rest of the paragraph is homogeneous except a slight insertion in v.¹⁹.

It is difficult to discover the exact idea of the Spirit of God in the mind of this author. There seems to be no trace of a belief in the existence of evil spirits, in our sense of the word, throughout the earlier period of Hebrew literature. And if the belief existed, the spirits could hardly be called *evil spirits of God*. In an instructive passage of the later history, 1 K. 22¹⁹⁻²³, we find *the Spirit* offering to be a spirit of deceit in the mouth of the prophets. From this we conclude that the Spirit thought of as the agency of evil was the same Spirit which stirred up men to good, and it is not improbable that the adjective *evil* is a later insertion in the account before us. The author's conception is certainly very different from that of v.¹³ in which the Spirit seems to be viewed as the constant endowment of a consecrated person.

14–23. In 14⁵² the author remarks that *whenever Saul saw a valiant man he attached him to himself.* This cannot be the conclusion of the history of Saul, and there is every probability that it was intended to introduce the history of David. The original connexion with the passage before us, however, has been obscured. In the body of the paragraph, Saul's affliction is ascribed to רוח אלהים. The original narrative must have used the same term at the first mention of the trouble. But we now find in v.14, רוח־רעה מאת יהוה, and as the opening part of that verse expressly declares that the *Spirit of Yahweh had departed from Saul* (with evident reference to his coming upon David, v.13) we conclude that v.14 has been composed for its present place. The critics are not agreed; Ku. (*HCO*2. p. 384 cf. p. 388) supposes something cut out for the insertion of 151–1613. Bu. (*RS*. p. 214) and Co. (*Einl*3. p. 102) find 1614 the direct continuation of 1452. Ki. supposes that this is the beginning of a new document — a life of David.

14. As now read, the verse says that *the Spirit of Yahweh departed from Saul and an evil spirit from Yahweh troubled him*] the verb means *fell suddenly upon* or *startled*. The affliction manifested itself in sudden or unreasoning fits of terror. Both mental and physical disease (but especially mental) were ascribed to the agency of evil spirits until very recent times, even in the most enlightened communities, cf. Schm. I. p. 549, Nevius, *Demon Possession* (1896). The wording of this verse may show that the author had such an idea, though, of course, he did not think of an organized kingdom of Satan, such as meets us in later times. He is careful, in fact, to show that this agent (or agency) was entirely subject to Yahweh by defining it as he does. The Arab idea that an insane person is possessed by a *jinn* is nowhere distinctly expressed in the Old Testament. Besides the lying spirit in the mouth of Ahab's prophets, we may cite here the evil spirit sent by God between Abimelech and his subjects in Shechem, Jd. 923. Possibly the spirit of jealousy mentioned in Num. 514 may be brought into the same category. The term used in the rest of this account shows a different conception. — **15, 16.** Saul's servants propose a remedy for his affliction : *An evil spirit of God is troubling thee ; let thy servants speak, and they will seek a man skilful in playing the lyre*] the instrument is one of those most frequently mentioned in the Old Testament. Music is associated with benign possession (by the spirit of God) in the case of the Prophets, 105 2 K. 315. Here it is expected to procure relief from obsession. A similar belief was held by the Greeks and Latins.*

---

* Ut ostendit Pythagoras apud Senecam, Schm. p. 551 citing Serarius, " qui addit plures autores atque exemplaria."

— **17.** Saul assents, saying : *Look out for me a man who plays well and bring him to me*] the king puts the qualification in somewhat higher terms than the courtiers. — **18.** One of the attendants mentions David as the very man for the place — *a musician, a man of valour, a soldier, judicious in speech,* and *a man of presence, and Yahweh is with him*] the panegyric is the recommendation of a friend at court, and must not be taken too literally. But it certainly implies that David had already had some experience in war, and had attained to man's estate. No supposition will enable us to harmonize this statement with the earlier part of this chapter, and with some parts of 17. — **19.** The result is that Saul sends messengers to Jesse, saying : *Send me David thy son*] that he is described as being *with the flock* is probably an afterthought of a scribe, though it was not by any means derogatory to a grown man to take charge of the flocks, as is seen in the cases of Moses and Jacob. — **20.** Obedient to the message, *Jesse took ten loaves of bread and a skin of wine and a kid*] the modest present of a farmer to his king, *and sent them by the hand of David his son to Saul*] it was not good form to approach the king without a present. — **21, 22.** David was taken into Saul's service *and Saul loved him and he became one of his armour-bearers*] the king surrounded himself with a body-guard of these squires. With the consent of his father, David was thus a permanent member of the court. — **23.** *And when the spirit of God came upon Saul, David would take the lyre and play, and Saul would breathe freely, and would be well, and the evil spirit would depart from him.*

14. ובעתתו] the perfect with waw consecutive has frequentative force. — רוח־רעה מאת יהוה] the spirit is nowhere else described with so much circumspection. In Samuel we find both רוח יהוה (10⁶) and רוח אלהים. The MSS. vary in 11⁶. In one instance 𝕳 has רוח יהוה רעה where 𝕲 found אלהים. The tendency of the scribes to substitute אלהים for the more sacred name makes it probable that in this case 𝕲 is secondary. Both רוח יהוה and רוח אלהים רעה רעה seem to me to be ungrammatical, and I suspect that the original was simply רוח אלהים throughout this paragraph. — **16.** יאמר־נא אדנינו עבדיך לפניך. יבקשו] is hardly possible (as is shown by We., Dr., and acknowledged by Bu.) though retained by Kl., and Ki., with a slight change. 𝕲ᴮ has εἰπάτωσαν δὴ οἱ δοῦλοί σου ἐνώπιόν σου καὶ ζητησάτωσαν which should probably be restored. 𝔖 omits after נא v.¹⁵ to אדנינו v.¹⁶ יאמר־נא. Probably the translators did not have אדנינו, as the omission then becomes a clear case of homeoteleuton. —

ירע מנגן] is in v.[18] ירע נגן. As there is no reason why the expression should vary in so short a space we should probably read ירע נגן in both cases, and this is favoured by 𝔊. On the כנור cf. Benzinger, *Hebr. Archäol.* p. 274. — אלהים] is lacking in 𝔊ᴮ𝔖. — נגן בידו] 18[10] 19[9], the variant of 𝔊 (*he shall play on his lyre*) is the substitution of a more obvious word. — **17.** מוטיב לנגן] Is. 23[16] Ez. 33[32] Ps. 33[3]. — ראו־נא לי] cf. ראיתי לי v.[1]. — **18.** ונכון דבר] *discriminating in speech.* — ואיש האר] generally we find יפה תאר, Gen. 39[6]. But in English we also speak of *a man of presence* instead of *a man of good presence.* — ויהוה עמו] the meaning is that he is prospered in what he undertakes, 10[7] Jd. 1[22]; cf. Gen. 39[2]. — **19.** אשר בצאן] is regarded as a harmonistic insertion by Bu. and Co. (*Einl*[3]. p. 102). The objection to it is that Saul has nowhere been told that David is *with the flock.* — **20.** חמור לחם] is contrary to analogy. Bread is always counted in loaves, and we should doubtless (with We., Dr.) correct to עשרה לחם, which is found in the parallel, 17[17]. עשרה was first corrupted to עמר which is represented in 𝔊ᴬᴮ, and then as that was seen to be absurdly small חמור was substituted. 𝔊ᴸ has expanded the text as has I— *asinum, et imposuit super gomor panis* (Cod. Leg.) — and this has been taken by Bu. into his text in the form חמור וישם עליו משא לחם. But this is one of the frequent cases in which the longer text is suspicious. — **21.** ויעמד לפניו] expresses the fact that David became one of the king's personal attendants, I K. 12[8]. — **23.** רוח אלהים] is corrected in all the versions to רוח רעה or רוח אלהים רעה. I suppose 𝔅 to be original, as the more difficult reading, and more likely to be emended by a scribe. — ורוח לשאול] Job 32[21], where Elihu declares that he must relieve himself by speech. The word would therefore favour 𝔊's understanding of Saul's malady as accompanied by fits of suffocation. But cf. רוחה, Ex. 8[11]. — רוח הרעה] can doubtless be justified by parallel instances, cf. Dr., *Notes*, p. 45 (on 6[18]). But I suspect the whole last clause to be a late addition, the sense being complete without it.

XVII. 1–XVIII. 5. The single combat of David with Goliath.

— The familiar story need not here be rehearsed. We may pass at once to the critical problems which it presents. The first fact which claims attention is that a large family of Greek MSS., represented by 𝔊ᴮ, omit considerable sections of the narrative, to wit, 17[12-31. 41] 17[55]–18[5]. The critics are still divided on the question which recension is original. Wellhausen in his study of the text decided for 𝔊, because harmonistic omissions imply a critical insight which we cannot suppose in the translators. This argument, though afterwards given up by We. himself, is still good. The universal rule in such cases is that the presumption is against the longer text. The argument is strengthened in this case by the phenomena observed in chapter 18, where also some sections are omitted by $\mathfrak{G}^B$. In that chapter it is generally agreed that the omission leaves a continuous, and therefore original, text. The probability that the same causes have been at work in the two contiguous chapters is very strong. In the present chapter, the shorter text is perfectly consistent with itself, and the omissions do not leave any appreciable hiatus. Whether the omitted sections also form a continuous narrative, as is claimed by Cornill, may, however, be doubted. Yet they have the appearance of parts of an independent document which has lost something in being fitted into another text.

We have had two accounts of David in the preceding chapter. Our first thought is that the two documents are continued in the present story, and that the lines of cleavage are indicated by the differences in the text. In fact, the omitted sections show affinity with 16^{1-13}. In both, David is the shepherd lad, the youngest of his father's sons. The natural sequence of the anointing by Samuel, is an exploit which will bring David to the notice of the people. More difficulty is encountered in making $17^{1-11.\ 32-40.\ 42-54}$ continue 16^{14-23}. In the account of David's coming to court, he is described as already an experienced warrior, while in our chapter he is called by Saul *a youth*. This objection is not perhaps decisive ; Saul might well call a younger man by this term, even though he had already reached years of discretion. Nor can we say that David's inexperience in the use of armour of proof is altogether inconsistent with what is said in 16^{18}. Even an experienced warrior might not be familiar with that sort of armament. And again, the use of the sling is not a sign of youth or inexperience. The weapon used by the Benjamites who could sling at a hair without missing, Jd. 20^{16}, and who are evidently regarded as a formidable corps, was not a plaything.

But when all is said, the incongruity of this account with what precedes is marked. Saul appears as a timid and irresolute man. The whole impression made by David is different from the description of him we have just had. The style of the narrator is more diffuse and less vivid than the parts of the Saul document which we have studied. For these reasons it seems impossible to make the identification proposed. Yet we need an account of an exploit on the part of David to account for Saul's outbreak of jealousy.   The author who makes him Saul's favourite armour-bearer in 16, and then makes Saul plot against him in 18, must give a motive for the change of mind.   He must, at least, make David very successful in battle and so arouse the king's jealousy. The fact that Goliath was slain by Elhanan 2 S. 21[19] would weigh somewhat against the present form of this narrative.   The natural conclusion is that in place of this chapter there was originally (as a continuation of 16[23]) a brief account of David's prowess against the Philistines.   This was later replaced by the present circum-stantial story, which, however, was first circulated without the addi-tions which we find in 𝕳 as compared with 𝕲.

On the critical questions the reader may consult, besides the usual authori-ties, W. R. Smith, *OTJC*[2]. pp. 120–124, 431–433; Cornill in the *Königsberger Studien*, I. pp. 25–34; and Bonk, *De Davide Israelitarum Rege* (Disserta-tion, 1891), pp. 17–27.   All these authors agree that the recension of 𝕲 has not arisen by omissions from that of 𝕳, but that a different document has been inserted in 𝕳.   WRS. argues for the original coherence of the narrative of 𝕲 with 16[14-23], which I have not brought myself to assert.   Yet there is nothing to prevent our supposing that there once stood here a brief account of David's exploit which did continue 16[14-23].

1–11. Fresh attack by the Philistines. — The enemy invade Judah.

The situation is described, the point of importance being the presence of a champion who challenges Israel. — **1.** The Philistines *gathered their forces for war*] a similar opening is found 28[1]. — *And gathered at Shocoh*] identified as "a strong position isolated from the rest of the ridge " west of Bethlehem, still bearing the name *Shuweikeh*.   An invasion of Judah in order to attack Saul is hardly probable, and an early author would make the Judahites call upon Saul for help.   The invading army *camped between Shocoh and Azekah*] mentioned in Jos. 15[35] in connexion with Shocoh.   From its name it seems to have been a stronghold, cf. Jer. 34[7]. — *In Ephes-Dammim*] as the situation is sufficiently described by the names of Shocoh and Azekah, this redundant statement is suspicious.   On the conjecture which emends it to *on the brink of the waters* see the critical note. — **2.** Saul with his army camped in the *Valley of Elah*] or *of the Oak*, cf. 21[10].   The present name *Wady es-Sant* resembles the ancient one in that *Sant* is also a tree. — *And arrayed the battle to meet the Philis-*

tines] 4² 2 S. 10⁹·¹⁰. — **3.** *And the Philistines were standing on the hill on this side, and Israel was standing on the hill on that side, and the valley was between them*] this is evidently meant to describe the situation at the time of the duel, and favours the shorter text, in which David's attack follows at once upon the challenge ; whereas in the section inserted by 刉 the challenge was repeated morning and evening for forty days. — **4.** *And there came out from the ranks of the Philistines a champion*] this is the only word we can use — the Hebrew term is obscure. — *Whose name was Goliath of Gath*] according to 2 S. 21²² he belonged to a family of giants. His height — *six cubits and a span* — would be at the smallest computation about ten English feet. — **5–7.** He was formidable not only by his size, but also by reason of his armour. The defensive armour is all of bronze — helmet and *breastplate of scales*] like the scales of a fish, plates overlapping each other and allowing free movement ; *whose weight was five thousand shekels of bronze*] say a hundred and fifty pounds avoirdupois. — *And bronze greaves upon his feet*] there seems to be no doubt of the meaning, though the word for greaves occurs nowhere else. — *And a bronze javelin between his shoulders*] the text is somewhat doubtful. A javelin was carried between the shoulders, at least sometimes, as Bochart shows from Homer (citation in Keil and Dr.). But the *bronze* seems to indicate a defensive weapon, and some Rabbinical authorities conjectured a *back plate*. — **7.** *And the shaft of his spear was like a weaver's beam*] in size, 2 S. 21¹⁹ 1 Chr. 11²³ ; *and the head of the spear was six hundred shekels of iron.* The principal object of the description is to show how impregnable the man seemed to be. Added to the enormous weight of his panoply, was his helper and squire — *and one carrying the shield went before him.* — **8.** The champion, having stepped forward from the ranks, *stood and cried out to the ranks of Israel*] it was, and is, the Arab custom for the warrior to vaunt his own prowess and to satirize his enemies, as a challenge to single combat. In this case the challenge is based upon the uselessness of a general engagement when the single combat would settle the whole matter ; *Why do you come out to form the line of battle ? Am not I a Philistine, and you servants of Saul ?* He offers himself as a sample of his nation. *Choose a* *man and let him come down to me!* The Israelites standing on the slope were above him. — **9**. The whole issue will be staked on the duel — *If he be able to fight with me and smite me, then we will become your servants*] and conversely. — **10**. In conclusion the champion renews the challenge : *I have taunted the ranks of Israel to-day — give me a man that we may fight together*] the challenge becomes a taunt, when no one is brave enough to accept it. It is possible, however, that some abusive language has been left out. — **11**. The only result in the ranks of Israel is fear, amounting almost to a panic. That the situation could not last forty days is evident. In the original narrative David, already a member of Saul's body-guard, steps forward at once and accepts the challenge — v.[32] is the immediate continuation of this verse.

1. The verse continues the preceding narrative as well as it joins to any of the preceding sections. — [ויאספו פ׳ מחניהב] cf. ייקבצו פ׳ את מחניהם, 28[1]. The second ויאספו is suspicious and may indicate that the text has been made up from two documents. — [שוכה] Σωχώθ ⑤. As Eusebius speaks of *two* villages, upper and lower, it is possible that the plural is original (We. who refers to Euseb. Onom. under Σοκχώ). Two separate places with this name are mentioned in Joshua 15[35. 48]. One of them was near Hebron, the other in the Shephela. Probably the latter is intended here. Ruins still bear the name *Shuweikeh* (Baed., *Palestine*,[2] p. 161, GAS., *Geog.* pp. 202, 227). — [באפס דמים] on the reading of certain MSS. of ⑤, Lagarde (*Uebersicht*, p. 76) restores בספר המים, cf. Buhl, *Geog.* p. 193 note. The overfulness of the text favours this, or something like it, and Buhl (*Geog.* p. 90) is inclined to adopt it, though it seems doubtful whether there was water enough in the wady to justify the language. *Pas-Dammim* occurs 1 Chr. 11[13] as the scene of a battle fought by David and his men. Possibly the text here is conflate. — **2**. On the *Wadi es-Sant*, Buhl, *Geog.* p. 18. — [אלה] *terebinth* or *oak*, cf. Moore, *Judges*, p. 121 *f.* with the references there given. — **3**. ערך לקראת, *to draw up the line of battle*, usually without מלחמה. The language of the account reminds us of the description of Michmash (מזה as 14[4]). — **4**. [ממחנות] the army has already been described as standing in order of battle, and it is plain that we should read ממערכת with ⑤ (Th., We., Dr., Kl., Bu., Ki.). Where ⑤[L] got its duplicate translation ἐκ παντὸς τοῦ λαοῦ τῆς παρατάξεως is not clear. — [איש־הבנים] has not been satisfactorily explained. ⑤ has ἀνὴρ δυνατός, 𝔏 *vir spurius*. The Hebrew is generally interpreted as *the man of the interspace* between two armies. But the space between two armies is not *two spaces* — except in the probably rare case where a watercourse divides it. There is, therefore, no reason for the dual. It is doubtful whether Josephus can be cited for this interpretation, though he describes Goliath as standing between the two armies. Kimchi in this interpretation (cited by Dr. and also by Schm.)

voices Jewish conjecture. Earlier Jewish tradition is represented by 𝔏 and a
fragmentary Targum (cited by Dr. from Lag.) according to which the words
mean *one born of mixed race* — the Targum adds that he was the son of Samson and of Orpah the Moabitess. Kl. conjectures חמשי, *heavy armed.* — [גלית
names of men have the feminine form not infrequently in Arabic. For *six*
cubits 𝔊 has *four*, which hardly makes the giant large enough to carry his
armour. — **5.** נחשה] some alloy of copper. As remarked by We., 𝔏 is consistent in making the defensive armour of this material, and the offensive
of iron. — **6.** קשקשות] also of the scales of the 'great dragon' Ezek. 29⁴. —
נחשת] *bronze and iron* 𝔊. — ומצחה] should be pointed as a plural, κνημῖδες
𝔊 — Th., We., al. — כירון] ἀσπίς 𝔊 everywhere except in this chapter translates
either מגן or צנה. Kl. conjectures כיור, which, however, is always a bowl or pan.
Possibly this clause has been interpolated from v.⁴⁵. — **7.** וחץ] *Kt.* is doubtless
to be corrected to ועץ *Qrê.* — מנור] occurs only in the phrase of the text. Cf.
Moore, *Proc. Am. Or. Soc.* 1889, p. 179, and *Judges*, p. 353. — צנה] seems to
have been the large shield, in distinction from the smaller מגן. — **8.** הפלשתי] for
which 𝔊 has ἀλλόφυλος without the article. The latter seems more vivid, as
though the champion in assumed modesty said : *I am one of many, make trial
of me and judge of the rest by the result.* — ברו] is unintelligible. Restore
בחרו with the versions, cf. 1 K. 18²⁵ (Dr. and Weir). — **9.** The regular hypothetical sentence beginning with an imperfect and carried on by a perfect with
waw consecutive, Davidson, *Syntax*, § 130 *a*. — **10.** חרפתי] can mean only
I have insulted or *taunted*, and must describe what the giant has already done.
As the preceding verses contain only the challenge to fight, we must suppose
that the unaccepted challenge was itself an insult, as indeed it was. But there
may have been some abusive language in the original document which a
scribe left out as blasphemous. — **11.** ויחתו] a strong word. They *were broken*
in spirit, *were dismayed*, cf. Dt. 1²¹ 31⁸ Jos. 1⁹.

12–31. David's coming to camp. — The narrative goes back
to the family of Jesse at Bethlehem. The three sons who are
named in 16⁶⁻⁹ are here said to have gone to the army. David,
the youngest, is called from the flock by his father to carry supplies to his brothers. He comes to the camp just as the Philistine utters his customary challenge. Inquiring more particularly
about the promised reward, he is taken to Saul, who consents to
his fighting.

The paragraph is lacking in 𝔊ᴮ and is marked with an asterisk
in some MSS. It is inserted in ᴬ and in ᴸ, but the differences are
such as to warrant us in saying that the two translations are made
by different hands. In the case of ᴬ also, the translator does not
appear to be the one from whom we have the rest of the Book,

12–16. The household of Jesse is described so far as is necessary to the present purpose. Jesse himself is too old to go to the war, and David is regarded as too young. Three of the sons are in the ranks. What has become of the other four is not told. — **12.** *And David was son of an Ephrathite of Bethlehem Judah whose name was Jesse, and who had eight sons. The man was in the days of Saul an old man, advanced in years*] such is apparently the intention of the ungrammatical or corrupt Hebrew. The adjective *Ephrathite* as applied to inhabitants of Bethlehem is found only here and in Ruth 1². — **13, 14.** The three sons, whose names are given, *had gone after Saul*] the tautology of the verses is intolerable. — *David was the youngest*] as already told. — **15.** The verse is a plain attempt to harmonize this account with 16¹⁴⁻²³. As it stands it can mean only that David's custom was to go to and fro between his home and the court. The improbability is obvious, and the contradiction with 16²² is not yet removed. — **16.** Another harmonistic verse, intended to give David time to reach the camp. As Bethlehem is only a few miles from Shocoh the author has been too generous : *The Philistine drew near morning and evening and took his stand, forty days.*

The present form of this paragraph seems to be due to the redactor. It cannot have continued 16¹⁻¹³ directly, but seems to be dependent on that. There would be no difficulty in making the author of 16¹⁻¹³ speak briefly of the Philistine invasion and add : *the three oldest sons of Jesse went after Saul to the war*, continuing by v.¹⁷.

12. הזה] if it be grammatical, the word must qualify David: *and this David, son of an Ephrathite.* But even then the sentence does not give a clear construction. The word is omitted by 𝔖, and was differently read by 𝔊ᴬᴸ — probably these point to an original הוא which would be in place. — בא באנשים] is unmeaning. The synonym of זקן is בא בימים /which should probably be restored here. 𝔊ᴸ𝔖 seem to point to בא בשנים against which nothing can be said, except that it occurs nowhere else. Dr., following Hitzig, strikes out בא as erroneous duplication of the two letters which follow. Kl. conjectures מבא באנשי המלחמה of which there seems to be a hint in 𝔗. — **13.** הלכו . . . וילכו] is redundant and impossible. One of the two verbs must be stricken out, and the last one is actually omitted by 𝔊ᴸ𝔖.

17–19. The mission of David. — He is commanded by his father : *Take to thy brothers this epha of parched corn*] parched corn is ears of wheat or barley plucked just before they are ripe, and roasted or singed in the fire. It is still eaten in Palestine, and is especially fitted for provision for travellers or soldiers, cf. 2 S. 17²⁸. The *epha* is something over a bushel. The army had of course no regular commissariat. To this provision were added ten of the round flat loaves of the fellahin. — *And bring them in haste*] 2 Chr. 35¹³. — **18.** David was also to take ten cheeses to the captain of the thousand, to ask his brothers of their welfare, and to *take their pledge.* What this means is uncertain, and no emendation yet suggested improves upon the text. Possibly some token had been agreed upon which they should send home in place of a letter. — **19.** Jesse concludes his command by indicating the locality in which they were to be found.

17. לחם הזה] read הלחם הזה, the ה has been lost after עשרה (Dr., Bu.). — **18.** חרצי החלב] although not found elsewhere, plainly means *cheeses.* Nothing else made of milk would be appropriate. Ancient tradition, as represented in the versions, agrees with this. — ערבתם] ὅσα ἂν χρήζωσιν (γνώσῃ) 𝔊ᴬ may point to צרכתם = *their need,* as was pointed out by Cappellus, *Critica Sacra,* p. 286, whereas *et cum quibus ordinati sunt* 𝔏 would favour ערכתם. But תקח would agree with neither of these. — **19.** That the verse is part of Jesse's speech is seen by Schm. and most of the recent commentators. Kl. dissents.

20–25. David's visit to the camp. — Rising early in the morning, *he left the flock in the hand of the keeper*] cf. v.²². After his journey of about twelve miles, *he came to the entrenchment just as the army was going forth to line of battle and shouting the war-cry*] lit. *shouting in the battle.* But the battle was not joined. The picture of the two armies going through this parade forty days in succession, only to hear the swelling words of Goliath, is ludicrous. — **22.** On discovering the situation, David *put off the vessels*] bags or baskets, we may suppose, *into the hand of the keeper of the baggage, and ran to the ranks*] the eagerness of a lad to see the battle needs no comment. The boys among Mohammed's followers at Medina wept when they were pronounced too young to go to war. As he had been commanded, *he came and asked his brothers of their welfare*] cf. v.¹⁸. — **23.** The champion appears * and speaks *according to these words*] the words

---

* Notice that the champion's name is given in full, as if he had not been named before.

given above. — **24**. *And David and all the men of Israel heard,
and when they saw the man, they feared greatly and fled before
him*. The received text puts the effect before the cause. The
language implies that the ranks were thrown into confusion. —
25. The universal talk was to this effect: *Have you seen this
man? To insult Israel he has come up. The king will greatly
enrich the man who shall smite him. He will give him his daughter
also, and will make his father's house free in Israel*] exempt from
exactions of service or of property.

20. שמר] is used of a keeper of sheep nowhere else. — וישא] without the
object is not common, and one is tempted to correct to ויסע. — המעגלה] the
same word (without the accusative ending) 26⁵·⁷. 𝕲ᴬ has στρογγύλωσις
here, which means something *round* or *rounded* — an entrenchment *around*
the camp? The Hebrew word is usually supposed to mean a wagon-barri-
cade. But we never hear of wagons in Saul's army, and the hill country in
which he marched was exceedingly unfavourable to them. — היצא] by omitting
the article we get a good circumstantial clause, as was already seen by Tanchum.
— במלחמה] may have been originally למלחמה (Th.). — **21**. ותערך] the feminine with a collective subject, cf. ותהי מואב, 2 S. 8². — **22**. ויטש] here in the
sense of *putting off* from one. — כלים] a word of wide signification — *the things*
which he had with him. — שומר] the guard left with the camp equipage. —
ויבא] is lacking in 𝕲ᴸ𝔖𝕷. — **23**. והוא מדבר] cf. Dr., *Tenses³*, § 166. ממערות
Kt. is evidently a scribe's error for ממערכות *Qrê*. — הדברים האלה] the reference
is to the words given in v.⁸. The present account, if once an independent
document, had a similar speech of Goliath either here or as a part of its introductory paragraph. — וישמע דוד] should, perhaps, be joined with v.²⁴, in which
case a ו should be prefixed to כראותם, so 𝕲ᴸ understands. — **24**. מאד ... וינס]
the two clauses are in the wrong order (logically), and I have therefore reversed them, with 𝕲ᴸ. But the whole verse accords ill with v.²⁵, and may be
a late insertion. — **25**. איש ישראל] is to be taken collectively. It was not one
man who was sent out with the offer of reward, but the reward was a matter
of common fame. — הראיתם] Ges.²⁶ 22 *s.* — העלה] is lacking in 𝔖 and superfluous. — עלה] is better pointed in the perfect tense.

26–31. David's desire to meet the Philistine. — He inquires
more particularly of the reward to be given, and thus brings upon
himself a rebuke from his brother. — **26**. Two questions are
reported, — the first concerns the reward: *What shall be done to
the man who shall smite yonder Philistine and take away reproach
from Israel?* The insult of the champion lies as a burden upon
the people until it is removed by the acceptance of the challenge.

David's estimate of the champion is manifested in a second question : *For who is this uncircumcised Philistine that he has dared to insult the soldiers of a living God?* The Philistines alone among the neighbours of Israel are stigmatized as uncircumcised, Jd. 14³ 15¹⁸ 1 S. 14⁶. The language of the question is taken from v.³⁶. The people reply *according to the word* just reported. — **28.** His brother Eliab heard the question, and was angry and questioned him : *Why is it that thou hast come down? With whom hast thou left that morsel of a flock?* The questions imply blame, which is now directly expressed : *I know thy self-will and the evil of thy heart, for to see the battle hast thou come*] the wilfulness of a headstrong boy. — **29.** The first half of David's reply is plain enough. The second half is more difficult : *Was it not but a word?*] which is generally accepted, is not satisfactory. David did cherish the intention, for which he was rebuked by his brother ; and it would be an evasion for him to plead that *as yet* he had done nothing but ask a question. *Is it not a matter of importance?* seems to be what we need, and probably the Hebrew will bear that interpretation. — **30, 31.** The earnestness of David is shown by his refusing to debate the matter with his brother, and *turning to another quarter*, where his inquiries are answered as before. His words — evidently those expressing contempt for the Philistine champion — were heard and reported to Saul, who *took him* to himself. Perhaps we should read *and they took him and brought him before Saul.*

26. הלז] may have a somewhat contemptuous force. — חרף] with the force of a subjunctive perfect; I have given a free translation. — אלהים חיים] Dt. 5²³. — **27.** כדבר הזה] is used to avoid repetition. — **28.** מעט הצאן ההנה] the sense is evident, though we cannot say in English *the fragment of those sheep*. — זדון] is the unrestrained impetuousness of a headstrong boy. — **29.** הלא דבר הוא] *was it not but a word* (from 𝕿 through Kimchi to most modern interpreters) would require the limitation in Hebrew as well as in English. *Was it not a command* of my father? which is Luther's idea, should also be more distinctly expressed. *Is it not an affair?* would certainly be an allowable translation for the passage. *Nonne res vera istud* (Schm.) is substantially the same, and *hat es denn keinen grund?* (Kl.) shows a similar apprehension. Kl. refers to Am. 6¹³. — **31.** ויקחהו] we should expect another expression, either *he called him,* or *they brought him before Saul.* 𝕲ᴸ has : *they took him and brought him before Saul.*

32–39. David volunteers to meet the Philistine. — The section joins immediately to v.[11], as any one may convince himself by reading them together : *Saul and all Israel heard these words of the Philistine and were terrified and feared exceedingly.   But David said to Saul : Let not my Lord's courage sink within him ! I will go and fight this Philistine.*   It is difficult to conceive a better connexion.   And although the general tenor of the narrative is against its direct coherence with 16[14-23], this particular opening is quite in harmony with the picture of David there presented. — **32.** A slight correction of the text is needed, and the translation already given is on this basis. — **33.** Saul objects that David is *a youth and he a man of war from his youth.*   The language is not necessarily inconsistent with 16[18], for to a seasoned warrior like Saul, David's comparative youth is in evidence.   Still, it hardly seems likely that the author of 16[18] would have put the objection in just this form. — **34.** David gives a chapter from his experience: *Thy servant was keeping sheep for his father*] this again is not inconsistent with 16[18] because the verb allows us to date the experience some distance in the past. — *And the lion and also the bear would come, and take a sheep from the flock*] the occurrence was repeated more than once.   The two animals mentioned are well-known enemies of the flock. — **35.** In such a case, *I would go out after him and smite him and deliver it from his mouth.*   The tenses indicate that this also was a repeated experience.   *And if he rose up against me, then I would seize him by the chin and smite him and slay him.* — **36.** The application to the case in hand : *Both lion and bear did thy servant slay, and this uncircumcised Philistine shall be like one of them.*   The next clause is like the conclusion of v.[26]. — **37.** The concluding sentence of David's speech is a profession of faith : *Yahweh who delivered me from the paw of the lion and from the paw of the bear will deliver me from the hand of this Philistine.*   The evidence of confidence is sufficient to convince Saul, who gives his consent with a prayer that Yahweh will be with David. — **38.** Saul's loan of his armour is comprehensible, even if David were already an experienced soldier ; for the occasion was no common one, and the king had, of course, the best armour. — He *clothed David with his garments*] is the author playing upon David's coming elevation to the throne?

Besides the *helmet of bronze* 頂 has a *coat of mail*, which is not confirmed by 𝔊ᴮ. — **39**. David *girded his sword over the coat*] his own sword is the natural meaning, so that in the opinion of the author he was already a warrior. Thus armed *he made a vain attempt to walk, for he had not proved them*] that is, these equipments. In contrast with the heavy-armed Philistine, his strength lay in ease and rapidity of movement. The armour was, therefore, given up.

32. אדם] 𝔊 renders ארני, which is appropriate, especially when we remember that David is in Saul's service (Th., We., al.). — עליו] refers to Saul himself, cf. Jer. 8¹⁸. It is difficult to find any other English rendering than *within him*, though the conception is, doubtless, that the heart weighs *upon* the discouraged man. — **34.** היה] might be used if David had just come from the flock, but it more naturally applies to a state which he has quitted some time in the past. — ובא] must be frequentative. — ואת־הרוב] is impossible. יאף הרוב, suggested by Graetz (*Gesch. d. Juden*, I. p. 197) on the ground of 𝔊, is appropriate, and probably original. It may indicate that the Syrian bear was a more formidable enemy than the Syrian lion — *even the bear*. זה, found in some editions, is only a modern error for שה. — **35.** The tenses continue those in the preceding verse, except ויקם, which is supposed by Davidson, *Syntax*, 54, R. 1, to be chosen to express a vigorous supposition. In fact, a break in the consecution is needed because we can hardly suppose that the animal always stood against him. — **36.** גם־הרוב] must be made גם את־הדרב to be grammatical. — מהם] 𝔊 adds: *Shall I not go and smite him and remove reproach to-day from Israel? For who is this uncircumcised* [that he should taunt the ranks of a living God]? The whole is modelled after v.²⁶. Possibly this verse originally ended with מהם. — **37ᵃ.** ויאמר דוד] superfluous, to our notion, but quite in accordance with Hebrew usage, which thus introduces concluding sentences of speeches. It is, therefore, original, though omitted by 𝔊ᴮ (retained by We., Dr., Bu., Ki.). The break in the sense is indicated by the space in the middle of the verse. In fact, a new paragraph begins with the second half verse. — **38.** מדיו] a plural in form, but as a singular מדו is attested by 2 S. 10⁴, it is possible that this is intended here; so 𝔊 understood. The garment intended is worn by warriors or officials, Jd. 3¹⁶ (Ehud), 2 S. 10⁴ (David's ambassadors), 1 S. 18⁴ (Jonathan), 2 S. 20⁸ (Joab). Kl., therefore, supposes that it was a coat of defence (made of leather?); the μανδύας 𝔊 was of sheepskin. But this is not certain. There seems no way of interpreting the language except to suppose that the author makes Saul recognize David's superior worth, and virtually abdicate to him by clothing him in the kingly garment. A later paragraph has the same idea when it makes Jonathan exchange garments with David, thus figuratively putting him in his place. — ונתי] is the wrong tense, and is omitted by 𝔊ᴮ. Kl. supposes the original to have been מדו יונתן. — קובע] is written כובע elsewhere, and by a number of MSS.

M

is so given here. — וילבש אתו שריון] found in 𝔥 is omitted by 𝔊ᴮ, and is probably a late interpolation. — **39.** ויאל ללכת] is impossible. ἐκοπίασεν 𝔊ᴮ renders וילא, cf. Gen. 19¹¹, *they wearied themselves to find the door*, that is, *they tried
unsuccessfully* to find it. The emendation is suggested by Schleusner, *Novus
Thesaurus* (1820), and independently of him by several others (Dr., *Notes*).
With this meaning of the verb, 𝔊 is consistent in adding ἅπαξ καὶ δίς. How
𝔊ᴸ came to ἐχώλαινε does not appear. — ויסרם דוד] should probably be read
ויסרכ with 𝔊ᴮ, for David had been clothed by others, who would also take
the garments off (𝔊ᴸ omits David's name, though it has the verb in the
singular).

40–54. The duel. — David goes out with the weapon to which
he is accustomed — the sling — taking pains to provide suitable
stones. After an exchange of speeches, he hits the target so successfully that the giant falls prostrate, and is despatched. The fall
of the champion is followed by the rout of the Philistine army.

40. *David took his club in his hand*] a very ancient weapon,
and still effective among the Bedawin. One of David's soldiers
used it successfully against an Egyptian champion, 2 S. 23²¹. —
*And chose five smooth stones from the bed of the stream and put
them in his scrip*] the word is probably a technical term for the
slinger's box or bag, in which he carried his ammunition. — *And
[took] his sling*] a well-known and formidable weapon, Jd. 20¹⁶.
— **41.** The verse is lacking in 𝔊 ; and as it breaks the connexion,
we may disregard it. — **42.** The Philistine *looked and saw David
and despised him, because he was a youth*] the rest of the description is identical with that given in 16¹². — **43, 44.** The Philistine's contempt and self-confidence : *Am I a dog, that thou comest
against me with a club ?*] that he adds imprecations *by his gods* is
only what we expect. With the threat to give David's flesh *to the
birds of heaven and to the beasts of the field*, cf. Dt. 28²⁶ Is. 18⁶
Jer. 15³. — **45–47.** David's reply begins with an allusion to the
Philistine's superiority in arms, as compared with the club to
which he has made scornful allusion. Yet as contrasted with the
sword and spear and javelin, David feels himself armed *with the
name of Yahweh Sebaoth, God of the ranks of Israel which thou
hast insulted this day*] the Massoretic division of verses is wrong,
and the words *this day* belong here. David's confidence overtops
that of the Philistine : *And Yahweh will deliver thee into my hand*

*and I will cut off thy head, and will give thy carcase and the car-
cases of the camp of the Philistines to the birds of heaven and to
the beasts of the earth*] the boast of the giant is thrown back at
him. The result : *all the earth shall know that Israel has a God*]
something of which the heathen are not yet convinced. The
immediate lesson to those present is indicated : *all this congregation shall know, that not by sword and spear doth Yahweh save,
for the battle is Yahweh's*] to dispose of according to his own
sovereign will. — **48–49.** There are indications that one of the
accounts here made the battle somewhat prolonged, David advancing and retreating according as the giant moved about in the
field. In the recension of 𝔊, however, the intention is to let
David finish the duel by a single blow, and this is consistently
carried out in what follows. Read therefore : *And the Philistine
rose and came to meet David*] joining immediately to what follows : *And David put his hand into the bag and took thence a stone
and slang it*] every movement is of importance to the historian
in a time like this — *and smote the Philistine in the forehead*] 𝔖
paraphrases by saying *between the eyes*. The force of the blow is
seen in the fact that *the stone sank into his forehead*] so that,
stunned, *he fell on his face to the earth*. — **50.** The verse is lacking in 𝔊ᴮ, and breaks the connexion. — **51.** *And David ran and
stood over the Philistine and took his sword and killed him*] in
this, which is the original form of one text, it was David's sword
which he used, and this agrees with the mention of his sword
above, v.³⁹. With the cutting off of their champion's head, the
Philistines realized the situation and fled. — **52.** *The men of Israel
and Judah rose and raised the war-cry*] the mention of Israel and
Judah separately has some colour here, because the battle was on
Judahite territory. The pursuit extended *to the entrance of Gath*]
so is to be read, *and to the gates of Ekron*] so that the corpses
were strewed all the way *from Sharaim*] in the vicinity of the
battlefield *to Gath and to Ekron*. — **53.** The pursuit was followed
by plundering the camp of the enemy. — **54.** The conclusion of
the account is evidently unhistorical.

40–54. The account is overfull, and is apparently the result of conflation.
The omissions of 𝔊 show this, but are not as complete a guide to the original
documents as in the early part of the chapter. —**40.** מקלו] in 2 S. 23²¹ the ·

weapon is called שבט. The oxgoad of Shamgar was essentially the same weapon.—בכלי הרעים אשר־לו] is evidently a gloss intended to explain ילקוט, a word which occurs nowhere else (We., Bu.).—ובילקוט] he would not have distributed the stones in two receptacles. The ו is therefore certainly wrong (omitted by $\mathfrak{S}\mathfrak{G}^L$). Omission of the preceding clause makes the sense clear. It should be remarked however that $\mathfrak{G}$ seems to have read אשר לו לילקוט = (the shepherd's bag) *which he had for a yalkut* (cartridge box).—וקלעו בידו] goes back to the verb at the beginning of the verse. I suspect that the earliest text had only ויקח דוד את מקלו וקלעו בידו.—41. The whole verse is lacking in $\mathfrak{G}^B$, the last clause lacking in $\mathfrak{G}^{243}$. It reads in $\mathfrak{P}$: *and the Philistine kept coming nearer to David, and the man bearing the shield was before him*. It is at least too early in the narrative, for the mention of the man with the shield is appropriate only when David is about to sling the stone. It emphasizes the difficulty he had in his attack. Probably the verse is a fragment of the same document, which is omitted by $\mathfrak{G}$ elsewhere.—42. ואדמני עם־יפה מראה] is borrowed from the description in 16¹², even to the textual error of עם for עלם. That David was *a youth* is sufficient reason for the Philistine's contempt, the rest is superfluous.—43, 44 are duplicates. One of the two speeches is sufficient to introduce David's reply, and this is apparently v.⁴³. In the feeling that David should reply to both, $\mathfrak{G}^B$ or its original inserted at the end of ⁴³, καὶ εἶπεν Δαυὶδ οὐχί, ἀλλ᾽ ἢ χείρω κυνός.—אלי] takes the place of עלי. The plural במקלות is out of place; read במקלת.—בהמת השדה] is more commonly ב׳ הארץ, which 21 MSS. (DeR.) have here, but cf. Joel 1²⁰.—46. היום הזה is connected with the preceding by $\mathfrak{G}^L$, and this involves the reading וסגרך for יסגרך. This is obviously correct (Th.), though rejected by We., Bu. That the fate of Goliath will be decided *this day* is plain without the express statement, both texts moreover have היום הזה later in the verse.—פגר מחנה] is defensible, taking פגר collectively. But with $\mathfrak{G}$ we should probably read פגרי פגרי מחנה, so Th., We., Bu.—חית הארץ] instead of the בהמת השדה of v.⁴⁴.—וירעו] as pointed, must give the purpose of the victory: *that all the earth may know*. It would be possible, however, to point וירעו, in which case the verb would simply carry on the narrative, cf. Ex. 14⁴·¹⁸ (P) Is. 49²⁶.—לישראל] $\mathfrak{G}\mathfrak{S}\mathfrak{L}$ seem to have read כישראל.—47. הקהל] is a late word, cf. Jd. 20².—ליהוה המלחמה] seems not to occur elsewhere.—48. והיה כי־קם] would seem to intimate that *as often as* the giant endeavoured to come to close quarters, David gave back, at the same time plying him with stones from the sling. An indication of the same view is seen in the המערכה near the end of the verse, for this would naturally mean the ranks of Israel. The whole second half of the verse from וימהר is lacking in $\mathfrak{G}^B$, which also reads at the beginning καὶ ἀνέστη. The shorter form thus presented is consistent with what follows, and I have adopted it.—49. אבן] is expanded into אבן אחת by Bu., following $\mathfrak{G}^L$, but this seems unnecessary.—ותטבע האבן] $\mathfrak{G}$ adds διὰ τῆς κεφαλαίας, which is favoured by We, and adopted by Bu. It seems doubtful whether one could say that the stone *sank through* the helmet, while it is entirely proper to say that it *sank into* the forehead.—50. The verse is evidently the concluding remark of one of the documents. *So David was stronger than the Philistine with the sling and with the stone, and smote the Philistine and slew him, though there was no sword in the hand of David*] the last clause is not an introduction to what follows (Th.), but emphasizes the simplicity of the shepherd boy's armament. Like the rest of this document, it is lacking in 𝔊B. — **51.** וישלפה מתערה] is lacking in 𝔊B, and evidently a redactional insertion intended to bring the verse into harmony with the preceding. — **52.** את־הפלשתים] ὀπίσω αὐτῶν 𝔊B, either form may be an afterthought, as the sense is good without either. — עד־בואך גיא] as the name of a town is expected we should read עד בואך גת with the original of 𝔊BL. — עקרון] is doubtless correct as compared with *Askalon* of 𝔊. — שערים] is evidently intended to be a proper name; and a town of this name is mentioned (Jos. 15³⁶) in immediate connexion with Shocoh and Azekah, therefore probably to be found in the vicinity of the battlefield. In order to make sense we must emend (with Kl.) to מדרך שערים, or better בדרך משערים, — that the wounded fell *all the way* from the battlefield to the two cities is information which is quite in place. The conjecture of We., adopted by Bu., which reads דרך השערים (with 𝔊), and understands by it the *roadway in the gates* of the two cities, falls to the ground on considering ועד, which follows. The wounded might fall in the gateway *at the cities,* but not *to the cities.* — **53.** מדלק] the verb is found with אחרי also, Gen. 31³⁶ (E). — **54.** ירושלים] is so evidently out of place here that we are forced to consider the clause an insertion of a late editor, in which case we shall regard the whole verse with suspicion. The mention of David's tent, however, is perfectly in accord with the narrative, 16¹⁴⁻²³, which makes him a member of Saul's staff.

XVII. 55–XVIII. 5. David's introduction to the court. — Saul professes complete ignorance of David and instructs Abner to make inquiries. Abner brings the young hero to the king, and Jonathan is especially drawn to him. A firm friendship is cemented between the two young men, and David is taken into the king's service.

The most ingenious harmonists have not succeeded in reconciling this paragraph with 16¹⁴⁻²³. As it is lacking in the original form of 𝔊, it must be judged like vv.¹²⁻³¹ above.

55. The narrative goes back a little : *And when Saul saw David going forth to meet the Philistine, he said to Abner, the general of the army : Whose son is the lad, Abner ?* There is no reason to take the question in any but the literal sense. It implied Saul's entire ignorance of David. The inquiry for his father was equivalent to asking, *who is he ?* The attempt of Keil to show that Saul's question did not imply ignorance of David is entirely

futile, and is refuted moreover by Abner's confession, which was :
By thy life, O king, I do not know] the Bedawy still swears *by the
life* of the person addressed. — **56–58**. Abner is commanded to
make inquiry, *and when David returned from smiting the Philistine, Abner took him and brought him before Saul, with the Philistine's head in his hand*] where he answered Saul's question. That
there was a more extended conversation which is not reported
seems implied by the following verse.

XVIII. 1. When David had finished speaking with Saul, *the
soul of Jonathan was bound up with the soul of David*] cf. Gen.
44^{30} (J). The manifestation of Jonathan's love is seen in the
covenant, v.^{3}. — **2**. Saul takes David into his service, *and did not
allow him to return to his father's house*] the parallel is 16^{22}. —
3. *And Jonathan made a covenant with David*] in the following
Jonathan alone acts, and hence the slight conjectural change here
adopted is desirable. The covenant between the two is also described (23^{18}), where Jonathan recognizes David as the future king,
and stipulates that himself shall be prime minister. A covenant
of brotherhood was made by Mohammed between the *Fugitives*
and the *Helpers*. Each Meccan was made brother to a Medinan,
and the bond was regarded as closer than blood brotherhood.
Something of the kind is intended here. — **4**. In making the covenant, Jonathan *stripped himself of the cloak which he had on*] the
garment mentioned is one worn by the well-to-do ; *and gave it to
David, and his accoutrements also, including his sword and his
bow and his girdle*] the simple shepherd lad is thus fitted to shine
at court. — **5**. Saul gave David a command in the army, in which
he showed good capacity — such is the order of the clauses in $\mathfrak{G}^{L}$.
So far from the promotion being offensive to the older soldiers,
it pleased all the people and also the servants of Saul] his court
officials. There seems no reason to dissociate this verse from the
·rest of the paragraph, as is done by Bu. The first clause of v.^{6} is
transitional, as is shown by its being lacking in $\mathfrak{G}^{B}$. The redactor,
by this clause, returns from the digression concerning David's pro-
motion to the main stream of the history.

XVII. 55–XVIII. 5. The paragraph is lacking in $\mathfrak{G}^{B\ etc.}$. The attempts to
harmonize the accounts are numerous. Schmid supposes that 16$^{14-23}$ belongs

chronologically after this. But consideration of that account shows that David was there unknown to Saul, which could not have been the case after the conflict with Goliath. — **55.** וכראות] cf. וכשוב at the opening of v.[57]. — בן־מי־זה] on the force of זה in such a question, cf. BDB. *s.v.* (4). — חי־נפשך] *by the life of thy soul*, cf. 20[3]. — המלך] is the vocative with the article — a common construction. — אם] after oaths, is negative. — **57.** וראש הפלשתי בידו] a circumstantial clause. — **XVIII. 1.** There seems to be some confusion in this and the following verse. That *Saul took him* seems to belong with v.[5], and v.[2] interrupts the account of Jonathan's friendship, begun in v.[1]. The form of the sentence, נפש ... דוד, also makes a difficulty. As it stands, it would naturally mean: *When David ceased speaking (since Jonathan's soul was bound up in the soul of David), then Jonathan loved him.* This, of course, is impossible. There is reason to suspect, therefore, that the parenthetical clause is an interpolation; and the explicitness of the last clause is an argument in the same direction. — ויאהבו] is probably a mistake for ויאהבהו, the regular form, which is substituted by the *Qrê.* — **3.** ודוד] is objected to by We., and omitted by Ki. (in Kautzsch). Bu., in his text, changes to לדוד, which relieves the difficulty. The received text may be due to the tendency to make David prominent, which manifests itself in 𝕲[L], where we find *David the king.* It should be noted, however, that כרת ברית ל usually means *to prescribe terms* as a conqueror does to the conquered, Jd. 2[2] Dt. 7[2] 1 S. 11[1]. On the meaning of the word ברית cf. Moore on Jud. 2[20] and reff. — **4.** את־המעיל] is what would be the second accusative in an active form of the verb, cf. Dav., *Syntax*, 74 c. — ומדיו] seems to include the weapons which follow. The *girdle* is much esteemed among the Orientals. — **5.** The order of the clauses adopted above from 𝕲[L] seems the only natural one. It is possible, however, that there has been corruption or interpolation of the verse. Kl. proposes to read: *And David came out, clothed with all that he* [Jonathan] *had put upon him, and brought him back to the men of war, and it pleased all the people and the servants of Saul.* Something like this may have been the original text, showing how fully Jonathan adopted the young warrior. — וישכיל] is justified by Dr., *Notes*, but וישכיל, suggested by We., certainly makes better sense. After ויצא we need to be told whither David went. The theory of Bu. (*R.S.* 219), that this verse (as it stands in 𝔐) belongs with 16[23], seems to be refuted by the fact that there is no reason for David's promotion, unless it be some feat of arms. That he successfully played the harp would be an argument in favour of keeping him in the vicinity of the king, instead of giving him a command in the field. The verse seems therefore to belong in its present environment.

XVIII. 6–30. Saul's jealousy of David.

— The eulogies of the women who greet the returning army, rouse the jealousy of Saul. He therefore removes David from service near his person, and appoints him over a band of soldiers in the field. David's activity and discretion are such that his hold on the people increases, which increases also Saul's fear. Michal, the younger daughter of Saul, falls in love with David, and Saul makes this an occasion for exposing David to new dangers. David's success adds to the king's dislike, which now becomes a settled hatred. This is the main stream of the narrative, which is preserved to us in the text of 𝕲ᴮ. It is interrupted in 𝕳 by inconsistent insertions. One of these (vv.¹⁰·¹¹) tells of Saul's attempt to murder David. Another (vv.¹⁷⁻¹⁹) gives the account of an unfulfilled promise of Saul to give his older daughter to David. Leaving these out, we find a consistent and well-planned story, of whose unity there can be no doubt. It belongs with 16¹⁴⁻²³. The *plus* of 𝕳 consists, in all probability, of fragments of another document, though their coherence is not so marked as in the case of the sections omitted by 𝕲 in the preceding chapter and the early part of this. As already pointed out, the consistency of the text of 𝕲 here is an argument for the originality of the same text in 17.

6–30. On the critical questions there is considerable disagreement. We. (*TBS.*) remarks on the consistency of the text of 𝕲ᴮ. Bu., in his text, assigns ¹²⁻¹⁹ to E, the rest of the chapter (except minute fragments) to J. I agree that the main narrative is connected with 16¹⁴⁻²³. But I cannot account for the text of Gᴮ, except by supposing that it represents one document and that the omissions represent another.

6–16. The original narrative seems to have consisted of ⁶ᵇ⁻⁸ᵃ· ⁹· ¹²ᵃ· ¹³⁻¹⁶, for this is all that is represented in one recension — that of 𝕲ᴮ. The interpolated section tells of Saul's attempt to transfix David with the javelin, an outbreak which comes too early here. A similar attempt is related farther on in the narrative.

6. The first part of the verse has already been remarked upon. The paragraph originally began : *And the dancing women came out from all the cities of Judah*] this would appropriately continue the account of the death of Goliath or any similar story. — *To meet Saul the king*] the prominence which David has in the history leads 𝕲ᴮ to read : *to meet David.* The women of the Bedawin still dance out with singing to meet the warriors returning from a foray.* — *With timbrels and with rejoicing and with cymbals*] the zeugma is awkward, and possibly the second word is corrupt.

---

* Doughty, *Travels in Arabia Deserta*, I. p. 452.

The timbrel [tambourine] was the instrument most frequently carried by the women when dancing, Ex. 15²⁰ Jd. 11³⁴. — **7**. The women sang antiphonally, as is still the custom in Eastern festivals :

> *Saul slew his thousands,*
> *And David his myriads.*

—**8**. *The incident was unpleasant to Saul*] as we can well understand : *To David they give the myriads and to me the thousands.* — **9**. The result : *Saul kept his eye on David from that day onward*] in suspicion and dislike.

[The interpolation vv.¹⁰·¹¹ is a duplicate of 19⁹ᶠ· and is here certainly out of place. It tells that *on the morrow the evil spirit of God came upon Saul and he played the prophet within the house while David was playing as was his custom. And Saul had the spear in his hand, and he raised the spear, saying to himself : I will smite it through David into the wall. But David moved away from before him thrice.* Saul's murderous impulse manifested itself in a similar attempt at a later stage of the history. There it is in place, because he had exhausted his indirect means of getting David out of the way.]

12, 13. Originally the verses read : *And Saul feared David and removed him from being near him, and made him captain of a thousand ; and he went out and came in at the head of the soldiers*] the meaning is obvious, and the connexion is good in itself, as well as with v.⁹. Saul's suspicion grew into fear, and he would no longer trust David in personal attendance (as armour-bearer, 16²¹) on himself. But, not wishing to insult the people's favourite, he gave him a post of honour which was also one of danger, keeping him on service in the field. The connexion is broken in the received text by the insertion of the loss of the Spirit (so we must interpret ¹²ᵇ·) as a motive for Saul's fear ; such a motive is here incongruous and unnecessary. — **14**. The result of the move was only to bring out David's virtues more conspicuously. — *In all his ways David showed wisdom, and Yahweh was with him*] to prosper him ; compare the case of Joseph, Gen. 39². — **15**. On perceiving this, Saul's fear was heightened — he *stood in dread of him.*

—16. In contrast with this was the affection of the people : *But all Israel and Judah loved David, because he went out, and came in before them.*

6. הפלשתי . . . בשוב] is coloured by Bu. as belonging to a different document from ויהי כבואם. In fact, one of the two verbs is superfluous. It would be equally easy to suppose בבואם the insertion of a scribe. The text of 𝕲ᴮ adopted above seems entirely to meet the necessities of the case. — הנשים] αἱ χορεύουσαι 𝕲 — possibly combining הנשים with יהמחלות, which comes later. But a change from המחללות is explicable, in case of a scribe who thought that word applicable to professional dancing women, and who wished to avoid making them the subject here, cf. Jd. 21²³. — לשור] (or לשיר *Qrê*) seems not represented in 𝕲ᴮ. — ובשמחה] the collocation seems awkward to us. We. cites I Chr. 13⁸ as parallel; but the parallel is not exact. The שליש is mentioned nowhere else. — **7.** המשחקות] is lacking in 𝕲ᴮ. — הכה ב׳] is generally *to smite among*, 6¹⁹ Num. 33⁴. The only exceptions that I find are this verse and the citations of it in 21¹² 29⁵. — באלפיו] should be read, with the *Qrê*. — **8.** ויחר לשאול מאד וירע בעיניו] is, doubtless, expanded from the simpler text, which is represented in 𝕲 וירע בעיני שאול. רבבות should doubtless be הרבבות 𝕲, to correspond with האלפים (We., Bu.). — ועור לו אך המלוכה] is lacking in 𝕲ᴮ. — **9.** עון] to be read עוין, with the *Qrê*. The verb occurs here only. Being a denominative, the form is probably intended to be a Poel participle (so Dr.), for מעוין. There are a few examples of such shortened forms. — **10, 11.** The verses are lacking in the same MSS. of 𝕲, which are without 17¹²⁻³¹. They contain another version of 19⁹ᶠ. There Saul's attempt is continued, even after David has once escaped. Here the attempt has no noticeable consequences, and everything goes on as if it had not been made. — ממחרת] must refer to the day after the triumphal entry. But this was too early for Saul's jealousy to have reached such a height, and David certainly would not have entertained thoughts of becoming the king's son-in-law after such an exhibition of hatred. — ויתנבא] the verb in this form ordinarily means *to prophesy.* The man possessed by the evil spirit acts in the same way as the man possessed by the good spirit — videtur spiritum hunc malum imitatum esse, ut simiam, Spiritum Sanctum, et ex Saule ineptum prophetam fecisse, Schm. p. 621. — והחנית] *the* lance which was the insignium of the chieftain, as is still the case with the Arabs. — **11.** ויטל] is pointed as though from טול, which occurs in 20³³, with the meaning *to hurl.* But here the spear seems not to have been actually hurled, and we should probably point ויטל from נטל, *he lifted up* — 𝕲ᴸᴬ 𝕿, Th., al. — אכה] is perhaps to be pointed אכּה, with 𝕿. — **12.** 𝕲ᴮ has only the first clause of the verse, and, as in the other cases, represents the original text. The other clause — *because Yahweh was with him while he had departed from Saul* — is an insertion on the basis of the verse 16¹⁴, which is itself an editorial construction. *Yahweh* and *the spirit of Yahweh* are interchangeable, Jd. 16²⁰. — **14.** לכל] read בכל with the versions (Th.), and read also דרכיו with the *Qrê*.

17–19. David and Merab. — Saul offers his older daughter, Merab, to David in marriage, on the vague condition that he be courageous and fight the enemies of Yahweh. The king was really moved in this by the hope that David would fall in battle. When this did not prove to be the event, he unscrupulously broke his word and gave his daughter to another.

The section is one of those lacking in $\mathfrak{G}^B$, and we naturally connect it with the others. In one of these we find that Saul's daughter was to be the reward of the man who should smite the Philistine champion, 17[25]. It is natural to suppose that the present paragraph is intended to show how Saul failed to carry out that offer. With this agrees the manner in which this section opens. Saul proposes his daughter without any evident occasion, unless it be that David has a claim on her already ; there is no question of a price to be paid. It seems evident, therefore, that this story is the sequel of 17[25]. On the other hand, it is quite irreconcilable with the following paragraph, which recounts David's marriage with Michal. As we shall see, the proposition there made is quite a new thing, and the form in which it is made shows entire ignorance of a previous similar proposal such as we have now before us.

17. Saul takes the initiative and offers Merab to David, with the stipulation (if such it can be called) : *Only be a valiant man, and fight the battles of Yahweh*] for the last phrase, cf. 25[28] and the title ' Book of the Battles of Yahweh,' Num. 21[14]. In this proposition, Saul's real thought was : *Let not my hand be upon him, but let the hand of the Philistines be upon him*] as is set forth also in the bargain struck for Michal. — **18**. David's reply is modest : *Who am I, and what is my father's clan in Israel, that I should be son-in-law to the king ?* It was the part of a gentleman to depreciate his own worth. Similar language is used by Saul himself when the kingly dignity is offered him. — **19**. The appointed time came, *but she was given to Adriel the Mehola-thite*] in the received text the same man is mentioned, 2 S. 21[8], but as the husband of Michal. The historical uncertainty is obvious. Saul's action as here represented is, of course, a deadly affront.

17–19. Budde and Kittel make the paragraph a part of the same document which immediately precedes. It seems to me that v.²⁰ continues v.¹⁶. The contrast between Saul's fear of David and the people's love of him (v.¹⁶) is heightened by the fact that even Saul's daughter loved him (v.²⁰). — **17.** הגדולה], like Leah, Gen. 29¹⁶, for which we find הבכירה 1 S. 14⁴⁹. Merab is mentioned only in this passage, and in 14⁴⁹ in ﬩. She is put in place of Michal (perhaps correctly) by 𝔊ᴸ in 2 S. 21⁸. — אמר] 14⁵² 2 S. 2⁷. — לבן־חיל said *to himself*, as not infrequently. — **18.** ומי חיי משפחת אבי] the *hayy* or Arab *kindred group* "was a political and social unity, so far as there was any unity in that very loosely organized state of society." The חי was therefore the same as the משפחה, and 𝔊ᴸ has only one of the two words here. We. and others suppose the original to have been חַיַי, which was afterwards explained by the insertion of משפחת אבי, and then misunderstood by the punctuators. I prefer to read ומי חי אבי with 𝔊ᴸ. The mention of one's *father* in such a connexion is natural, especially to an oriental. — **19.** בעת־תת] a time seems to have been set, Schm. 622. עדריאל is an Aramaic equivalent of עזריאל, Jer. 36²⁶, — *God is my help* seems to be the meaning of the word (Nestle, *Am. Jour. Sem. Lang.* XIII, p. 173). In 2 S. 21⁸ this Adriel is called *Son of Barzillai*. — המחלתי] a native of *Abel Meholah*, a place in the Jordan valley, cf. Jd. 7²² with Moore's note.

The same phenomenon shows itself here as in some earlier cases; two accounts are so similar that we suspect them to be variants of the same original. In this case the proposal of Merab is another form of the story of Michal. And as the former puts Saul's behaviour in a worse light than the latter, it is probably designed to take its place in the document which we have already seen to be prejudiced against Saul.

20–30. David marries Michal, Saul's daughter.

— The account shows no knowledge of the preceding paragraph. Michal is called *the daughter of Saul*, without reference to any other. Her affection for David comes to Saul as a welcome occasion to bring David into danger. He opens negotiations indirectly. All these indications point to the independence of the narrative. The step taken is the second of Saul's attempts to overthrow David, the first having been to give him service in the field, v.¹³.

20. Michal loved David, and when they told Saul, *the matter was right in his eyes*] 2 S. 17⁴. — **21.** The reason was that he thought to make use of her *as a snare*, or, more properly, *as a bait*, to lure him on to his destruction, so that *the hand of the Philistine should be upon him*] as above, v.¹⁷. The remainder of the verse is an interpolation. — **22.** It would be unbecoming in the king to make advances. He therefore commands his servants : *Speak to David privately*] after giving a favourable account of David's standing with the people, they were to advise : *now become son-in-law to the king*] the verb is used elsewhere of *intermarrying* with families or tribes, Dt. 7³. — **23**. David objects his lack of the qualifications : *Is it an easy thing, in your estimation, to become son-in-law to the king when I am poor and of no reputation ?* cf. v.¹⁸. — **24, 25**. When the reply was reported to Saul, he instructed his courtiers to meet the material objection, which was that David was too poor to pay the usual price for a king's daughter : *The king has no desire for a price*] the word is regularly used of the price paid by a man for a wife. Our word *dowry* conveys a wrong impression. Marriage by purchase can be traced in many regions. For example, *coemptio* seems to have been one method of marriage among the Romans. Old Testament examples are familiar, as Jacob, who paid the price in service. A sum of money is supposed to be given in the Book of the Covenant, Ex. 22¹⁶. *But* the king's desire is *for a hundred foreskins of the Philistines*. If the Philistines alone were uncircumcised among the inhabitants of Palestine, the kind of trophy chosen is explicable. The ostensible object was : *to be avenged on the king's enemies;* the real purpose was *to cause David to fall by the hand of the Philistines.* — **26, 27**. The proposition was acceptable to David, who *rose and went, he and his men, and smote among the Philistines a hundred men*] which the received text has made two hundred ; *and brought their foreskins and paid them in full to the king in order to become son-in-law to the king.* The king had, therefore, no pretext for further delay, *and gave him Michal, his daughter, to wife.* The original continuation of this verse seems to be 19¹¹. What follows here is an account of the mental, or moral, state of Saul, with a renewed panegyric of David. — **28**. *And Saul saw that Yahweh was with David, and that all Israel loved him*] the double favour (of Yahweh and of the people) increased Saul's dread. Vv.²⁸ᵇ·²⁹ᵇ·³⁰ are lacking in 𝔊ᴮ. See the critical note. — **29**. The climax of the chapter is here reached — *So Saul feared David yet more.* — **30**. A panegyric of David, such as we have had to superfluity. It simply says that as often as the Philistines made their incursions *David acted wisely above all the servants of Saul, and his name* *was exceeding precious.* It is intended to point the contrast afforded by Saul's conduct, as related in the following verse.

20. מיכל] the name appears as Μελχόλ in 𝔊 and as מלכיאל in 𝔖. It is possible therefore that the form is contracted (or mutilated) from מלכאל. Olshausen (*Gr.* § 277 f.) supposed it to be another form of מיכאל. — **21.** למוקש] Ex. 10⁷. The second half of the verse is an evident interpolation and is lacking in 𝔊^{B al.}. It breaks the sense, for Saul would not first make the proposition to David and afterwards insinuate it by his servants. As it stands, the sentence can only be an attempt to harmonize this narrative with the account of Merab. But what the editor meant by it is difficult to discover. The important word is בשתים, which can only mean *on two conditions* (shalt thou be my son-in-law), Pseudo-Hier *Questiones.* But what the two conditions are is not told, and this moreover would not harmonize the two accounts. We should expect something like the Jewish interpretation *by two* (so 𝔊^A) *i.e.*, by a double tie, or *by one of the two* (so 𝔗). But the former would be ironical, and the latter leaves the main word unexpressed. We are forced therefore to leave the problem unsolved. Kl. supposes בשנתים = *in two years,* but this does not help the real difficulty. 𝔊^L has ἐν ταῖς δυνάμεσιν (*in virtute* I), which probably represents only a conjecture. — **22.** בלט] of what is done stealthily, 24⁴. — התחתן] one is tempted to translate *propose yourself as son-in-law,* which the form would certainly bear. But this could not be carried through the passage, cf. v.²⁷. — במלך] probably shows the real force to be *ally yourself by marriage with the king.* — **23.** נקלה] is the exact opposite of נכבד, Is. 3⁵. — **25.** במהר] cf. Schm. p. 623; on Arab customs WRS. *Kinship,* p. 78. Greek examples are cited by Driver and Nestle (*Marginalien,* p. 14, citing *Il.* 9, 141 ff. 283 ff.). — כי] some good Hebrew MSS. have כי אם in the text — and this is the reading of the Babylonian school (Cappellus, *Critica Sacra,* p. 190; Baer, p. 118). — ערלות] We. refers to Dillmann, *Lex. Ethiop.* s.v. Josephus gives six hundred *heads* as the price, in order not to offend the taste of his Gentile readers. — **26.** ולא מלאו הימים] is lacking in 𝔊^B, inserted in 𝔊^A after the first word of the next verse. It is an interpolation, intended to magnify David's zeal (We., Dr.). — **27.** מאתים] is another change of the same sort. 𝔊 has *one hundred,* which is confirmed by 2 S. 3¹⁴. דוד after ויבא is lacking in 𝔊 𝔏. — וימלאום] should probably be read וימלאם, David being the subject. He alone could *pay in full to become the king's son-in-law.* The change to the plural was made to avoid the disagreeable picture of David presented by the word, one especially offensive to later ritual ideas — for which reason also it was omitted by 𝔊^B (We.).

Repeated consideration of the natural connexion of the narrative, forces me to the conclusion expressed above, that in the original story Saul's attempt to murder David in his house (19^{11ff.}) was made on his wedding night. Otherwise we have an incident, whose character stamps it as original, which we cannot fit into the history. In case this be correct, we should probably join 19¹¹ to 18²⁷ by taking two words from the end of 19¹⁰, and reading ויהי בלילה ההוא.

28. וידע] lacking in 𝔊^{BL}, is superfluous. — ומיכל בת־שאול אהבתהו] can be translated only parenthetically : ' Saul saw that Yahweh was with David (while Michal, Saul's daughter, loved him) and he feared.' But the effect is not harmonious, and we should doubtless restore the reading of 𝔊^{AB} וכי כל ישראל אהבו (𝔊^L combines the two texts). This gives an additional reason for Saul's fear, which is what we expect. — **29.** ויאסף] the *Qrê* substitutes ויוסף; the difference is only one of spelling. — לרא for לירא, cf. Ges.²⁶, § 69 n. The latter part of ²⁸ and the whole of ^{29f.} are lacking in 𝔊^B; they point out, superfluously, the contrast between Saul's attitude and that of David. The original opening of 19¹ may have been : *And Saul was hostile to David,* which is now read in 18²⁹.

Chapter XIX. Saul's attempts upon David. — The chapter is made up of four sections, which cannot be reconciled with each other.

1–7. Temporary conciliation of Saul. — Saul gives orders to slay David. Jonathan, after warning David, intercedes for him with success and brings him again before Saul.

The connexion of the paragraph is not plain. It appears to be another version of the story contained in 20^{1–39}. Its object is to account for David's continuance at court after Saul's hatred had become so pronounced.

1–7. The opening of the chapter would follow very well any of the statements of Saul's hatred contained in the preceding chapter. If the account is secondary, as compared with 20^{1–39}, we should probably refer it to the later of our two documents. Its object here is ι show why David is still found at court after Saul's hatred has become so pronounced. In this view of it, we might make v.^{1a.} join immediately to 18^{29a.} — *Saul feared David yet more, and gave orders to kill him.* The rest of the section would be an attempt to reconcile this command with the following paragraph, in which David is still the king's harper. That v.^{1a.} is by a different hand from what follows, is made probable by the difference in the form of Jonathan's name.

1. *Saul commanded Jonathan, his son, and all his officers to put David to death*] the writer seems not to have mentioned Jonathan's friendship for David earlier. Here he introduces it : *Yet Jonathan, Saul's son, delighted in David exceedingly.* — **2.** Jonathan warns David : *My father is seeking to put thee to death; now beware, in the morning*] the conversation is supposed to take place in the evening. — *Hide thyself and remain in a secret place*] this is the natural order, though not that of the received text. —

3. The proposition of Jonathan is : *I will go out and stand by the side of my father in the field where thou art*] so that David would overhear, and be informed without a direct communication from Jonathan, for which there might be no opportunity. The last clause of the verse : *and whatever I see I will tell thee*] does not seem to bear this out, and there may be interpolation. — **4.** Jonathan's panegyric is little calculated to soothe Saul's jealousy, and represents the author's view rather than that of Jonathan. The first point is : [David] *has not been at fault in regard to thee, and his actions towards thee are exceeding good*] this is appropriate to the object. — **5.** The next is not so certain to make a favourable impression : *And he risked his life*] 28²¹ Jd. 12³ ; *and smote the Philistine, and Yahweh wrought a great deliverance*] by him, as 𝔊ᴸ rightly interprets. The deliverance was in fact a reason for Saul's favour rather than his anger. Whether he was in a frame of mind to apprehend this, is not so certain. Still at the time he had *rejoiced,* as Jonathan reminds him. — *And why wilt thou sin in the matter of innocent blood in slaying David without cause ?* 25³¹ 1 K. 2³¹. — **6.** The plea was effectual and Saul gave his oath : *By the life of Yahweh, he shall not be put to death.* — **7.** Thereupon Jonathan *called David*] the evident implication is that he was not far away, as was planned in vv.²·³. — *And Jonathan brought David to Saul and he was in his presence as heretofore*] instead of being obliged to hide from him.

1. יונתן] in the rest of the chapter we find יהונתן. The form here may be due to a scribe. But elsewhere we observe considerable constancy in the usage of the different documents. — עבריו] of the officers of the king, as elsewhere. — **2.** אבי] is lacking in 𝔊ᴮ. But more probably it alone was expressed originally. — בבקר] is lacking is 𝔖. — וישבת בסתר] belongs after ונחבאת and this order seems to be indicated by 𝔊, as was pointed out by We. The vv.²·³ are supposed by Co. and Bu. to be an interpolation. In fact the sense is good without them. But if the whole paragraph has arisen under the influence of 20¹⁻³⁹, these verses belong to it; and if, on the other hand, that chapter is an expansion of this paragraph it is probable that the *hiding* here was the feature on which the author's mind took hold. Bu. proposed at first to strike out only 3ᵇ, while Ki. ascribes the whole of v.³ to the redactor. — **3.** The verse seems inconsistent with itself, as the only object of Jonathan's speaking with Saul *in the field* would be to avoid the necessity of communicating with him afterwards. And yet this communication is promised in the second half of the verse. — וראית מה] cf. ויהי מה = *whatever it may be,* 2 S. 18²². — **4.** מעשיו] is supposed by Dr. to be a singular. There seems no reason however why Jonathan may not make his affirmation *general*— to the effect that all David's actions are blameless. — ‏טוב־לך‎] the words seem to be transposed; possibly the second is an insertion, as it is not represented in 𝕲ᴮᴸ. — **5.** ‏בכפו‎] 𝕾 translates ' and he put his life in *thy* hands.' — ‏יהוה‎] 𝕲ᴸ adds δι’ αὐτοῦ, which is at least correct sense (represented also in 𝕾). — ‏לכל־ישראל ראית ותש‎] καὶ πᾶς ᾿Ισραὴλ εἶδον καὶ ἐχάρησαν 𝕲 (with slight variation)= ‏וכל יש׳ ראה וישמח‎. The decision between the two is not easily made. On the one side, the statement that Israel rejoiced at David's success seems calculated to stir up Saul's anger. But this is true of nearly all Jonathan's speech, and the reading of 𝕲 is quite in line with the rest of the speech. On the other side, the following ‏ולמה‎ is more forcible if connected directly with the statement of Saul's earlier attitude. For this reason I retain 𝕳. — **6.** ‏וישמע בקול‎] in the sense of hearing favourably Num. 21³ (J) Dt. 21¹⁸ Jd. 20¹³. — **7.** ‏ויגר־לו יהונתן‎] the subject is omitted by 𝕾𝕲ᴮᴸ 𝕷. The repetition of Jonathan's name three times in the same verse is in fact surprising, and shows the desire of the author (or perhaps the desire of a scribe) to call especial attention to Jonathan's nobility of character.

8–10. Saul attempts David's life. — The incident is a duplicate of that related in 18¹⁰ᶠ·, and the two accounts are possibly variants of one original. On the other hand, Saul seems there simply to have lifted the spear without throwing it, and it may be the idea of the author that David was saved by an unintentional turning away — led by the Spirit of God. It is possible therefore that the two accounts are intended to represent two successive attempts of the same kind, separated by the reconciliation 19¹⁻⁷. In both cases Saul's hatred is motived by David's success against the Philistines. — **8.** *And there was war again*] intimates that such had been the case before. As the account stands, the reference must be to the war in which Goliath was slain. — **9.** The evil spirit is here called (in 𝕳) *the evil spirit of Yahweh,* contrary to the usage of other passages. The emendation suggested by 𝕲 which brings them into conformity, is now generally adopted. The circumstances of the attack are given : *While he was sitting in his house with his spear in his hand, and David was playing with his hand.* — **10.** This time the frenzied king *sought to pin David to the wall with the spear*] if the account is by the same hand with the earlier parallel, 18¹⁰· ¹¹, we may say that it was the fixed idea recurring to the madman. — *But David slipped away from Saul's presence, so that he smote the spear into the wall*] the language is different from that used above. That David *fled and*

N

escaped is too strong language to use, if he simply went to his own house.

8–10. I cannot pretend to solve the riddle propounded by the interweaving of texts here. It seems to me probable however that one document gave the following order of events: (1) David's conquest of the Philistines; (2) Saul's first attempt with the spear; (3) Saul's command to Jonathan, followed by the temporary reconciliation; (4) the second attempt with the spear, followed by David's flight.

9. רוח יהוה רעה] cf. the note on 16¹⁴ (We., Dr., Bu., Ki. agree in the emendation here). — והוא בביתו] a circumstantial clause. — ביד] read בידו with four Hebrew MSS. and ⑤, so Th., We., al. — **10.** ובקיר] is lacking in ⑤ᴮᴸ, so that the meaning would be *to smite David with the spear*. The grotesque idea of pinning David to the wall is more likely original, in the account of a man possessed. — ויפטר] apparently *broke away* from what he was doing. — נס וימלט] cannot refer to David's escape from the immediate danger, which is sufficiently described by ויפטר. The words evidently mean that he left the court and city altogether. — בלילה הוא] belongs with the next verse.

11–17. The siege of David's house. — Saul sets watchmen about David's house, intending to kill him in the morning. Michal warns him of his danger and assists him to flee. She then supplies his place in bed with the Teraphim. Saul sends messengers to take David, and they bring back word that he is ill in bed. Thereupon he orders him to be brought as he is, and the deception is discovered.

The paragraph should begin with : *and it came to pass that night* from the end of v.¹⁰. The first question is : what night is meant? No reference has been made to a night at all. But the most natural interpretation is that David's wedding night is intended. Psychologically this is also what we should expect. Saul's growing fear has led him to promise David his daughter in marriage, in the hope that the price to be paid may bring David into danger and, in fact, remove him by death. The result has been only to increase David's reputation and Saul's fear. The crisis comes when the hated parvenu actually takes his bride to his house. This will be the time to strike ; David will be unsuspicious, his friends will have dispersed after the marriage feasting. Dramatically nothing could be more effective. To this should be added that the discrepancy with the preceding paragraph is as marked as could be conceived. In that section David has already

' fled and escaped.' In this he is unsuspicious of the king until warned by his wife.

11–17. The considerations urged above are perhaps sufficient to show the probability of the connexion of this passage with 18²⁷. That the account is old is conceded, but which document furnished it is not agreed upon by the critics. Co. is uncertain; Bu. puts it with E and makes it continuous with the preceding. Ki. also makes it continuous with the preceding.

11. *And it came to pass that night*] according to our construction the night of taking possession of the bride ; *that Saul sent messengers to the house of David to watch it, so as to kill him in the morning.* David was so unsuspicious that he had to be warned by his wife : *If thou do not deliver thy life to-night, to-morrow thou shalt be slain*] the fact that David is utterly unprepared for the information argues for the connexion suggested above. — **12.** The escape was effected in that she *let David down through the window*] similar instances are Jos. 2¹⁵, and the case of Paul in the New Testament, Acts 9²⁵. In 21²ᶠᶠ· we find David coming to the priest at Nob without arms and without attendants, which can be accounted for only by this verse. — **13.** In order to delay the discovery of David's flight, and so give him an opportunity to get away, Michal contrives to deceive the messengers. — *She took the Teraphim*] the household god, which is evidently presented as in human form ; *and placed it on the bed*] a plain couch, probably a rude frame covered with leather ; *and a cloth of goat's hair for his pillow*] the translation is only a conjecture. — *And covered it with the garment*] which regularly served for that purpose. The Israelite probably covered his head with a garment when sleeping, as is still done by the Arabs. — **14.** In the morning * *Saul sent messengers to take David and they thought him to be ill*] the stratagem was effective, so far as the first report of the messengers was concerned. — **15.** *And Saul sent to the house of David*] as we may conjecturally restore the reading : *saying : bring him on the couch to me that I may slay him.* — **16, 17.** The ruse is discovered, and Saul expostulates with his daughter : *Why hast thou deceived me thus ?* Her answer is a false plea, that her life had been threatened.

---

* Löhr calls attention to the fact that to enter the house of another in the night is contrary to oriental morals.

11. The verse should begin ויהי בלילה ההוא reading with 𝔊, so Th., We., al. The two words בלילה הוא are in 𝔐 connected with the preceding verse. Although precedents are found for בלילה הוא, it is better to read ב׳ ההוא as a ה may have easily dropped out on account of the recurrence of the same letter. — ולהמיתו] is an example of the reverse error. The initial ו has been duplicated from the preceding word (omitted by 𝔊). — ממלט את־נפשך] cf. 1 K. 1¹². — **13.** התרפים] cf. *ZWT*. 1881, 170 ff. κενοτάφια 𝔊 seems to imply *ancestral* images. The word is found always in the plural, but is here quite clearly applied to a single image; and this image is apparently of the natural human size. On the word cf. Moore on Jd. 17⁵ with the references there; cf. also the Lexx. with reff. and Schm. pp. 652, 659. — אל־המטה] one of the numerous cases where על and אל are confused. — כביר] occurs only in this passage and is not yet explained satisfactorily. 𝔊 read כבד, and Josephus expands this into a statement that Michal put a goat's liver into the bed, the palpitation of which (it being freshly killed is supposed) made the messengers of Saul think David was gasping with his illness. The objection is that Michal could hardly need such a device even if she had a freshly killed goat in the house. The reading of 𝔐 might readily be changed to כבד by a scribe unfamiliar with the word כביר. The cognate words כברה, *a sieve*, and מכבר, a metal *network*, as well as מכבר, 2 K. 8¹⁵, seem to indicate for this word something woven of goat's hair. יריעת עזים, Ex. 26⁷, is the goat's hair covering of the Tabernacle. The common interpretation of the present passage is that Michal put a mosquito net over the head of the image; so Schm. p. 653, Ew., *GVI*³. III. 107 f., E. Tr. III. p. 77. But is a net of this kind ever made of goat's hair? It seems more probable that she put a cushion as a pillow. מראשות is used of the pillow, Gen. 28¹¹·¹⁸. In 1 S. 26 and 1 K. 19⁶ מראשתיו means *at his head*, a phrase which would not naturally be used of a net put over the head. Whatever Michal used here was therefore probably placed as a pillow 𝔖. A living man would not need such, being accustomed to sleep on his arm. The Teraphim would lie too flat unless its head were supported by something of the kind.* But again, the image would be destitute of hair, and there is still a possibility that she took a bundle of goat's hair and made it simulate David's hair; so some of the Rabbis; cf. Schm. p. 653. All this shows the uncertainty that must attach to any translation. — **14.** ותאמר] but if the mere word of Michal was to be taken, there was no need of the elaborate precautions already related. We should read ויאמרו with 𝔊ᴬᴮ, making the messengers the subject. They came to take him, but seeing the bed thus arranged : *they said to themselves, he is ill.* — **15.** . . . . וישלח דוד] if the messengers had once seen David, as we have just supposed, it was superfluous to send them to see him again. Besides, as we learn from the latter part of the verse, their object was to fetch him; לראות is therefore cer-

---

* From the analogy of 1 S. 26, we might conjecture that she put *a skin of water* at the head of the bed, a sick man being feverish and thirsty; so נודא 𝔗, and Kimchi, *apud* Schm. p. 653. But there are several familiar words for waterskin, and we can think of no reason why so rare a word should be used in this case.

tainly wrong, and I propose to change it to לבית, or אל־בית. 𝕾^{AB} has only
καὶ ἀποστέλλει ἐπὶ τὸν Δαυείδ, which also would meet the requirement. —
17. למה אמיתך] on the idiomatic use of למה to convey a threat, cf. Dr., *Notes.*
The original continuation of this account seems to be 21², where David
comes to Nob to get provisions for further flight.

18–24. David's miraculous protection. — David flees to Ramah,
where Samuel presides over a choir of prophets. Saul sends for
him repeatedly, but the Spirit of God comes upon the messengers
so that they can do nothing but prophesy. At last Saul comes
himself and has the same experience. Hence arises the proverb.

The section is a late adaptation of 10^{10–13}, which explains the
origin of the proverb by Saul's experience at the outset of his
career. The present writer adapts the story to David's life, making its point his miraculous preservation from Saul's persecution.
In its emphasis of the divine care, it reminds us of the account
18^{11f.} where we suppose the original meaning to have been that
David turned from Saul's attempt *because Yahweh was with him.*
Because of this resemblance, we may conjecture that this paragraph was originally the sequel to the second attempt with the
spear — 19^{8–10}.

18–24. The critics agree that this piece is late, but are at a loss as to its con-
nexions. The theory advanced above gives its probable antecedent, whereas
its later continuation may plausibly be assumed to be David's flight to Achish,
21^{11ff.}. The appearance of Samuel shows the general stream of narrative to
which the story must be reckoned.

18. *But David fled and escaped*] resumes the narrative of
David's fortunes, after the diversion made by Michal's stratagem.
— *And came to Samuel at Ramah*] Samuel's home. The theory
of the author is that Samuel would be able to protect David.
After an interview, in which he told Samuel of his experiences
with Saul, *he and Samuel went and dwelt in . . .*] the place intended can no longer be made out. That it was some special
building in Ramah is the most probable conjecture — perhaps the
cloister (cœnobium) of the prophets. Such a dwelling or settlement existed at Gilgal in the time of Elisha, 2 K. 6^{1–7}. In 1 S.
10^5 it is implied that the prophets dwelt in the vicinity of the
sanctuary, and the sanctuary would be the proper place to seek the
supernatural protection which is here described. — **19, 20.** Saul is

informed of the fugitive's place of sojourn and sends messengers to take him : *And they saw the company of prophets prophesying with Samuel standing over them*] the religious exercises here described are evidently of the enthusiastic character of those in 10[5. 10]. *And the spirit of God came upon the messengers of Saul, and they also prophesied*] the contagion affected them, so that they were unable to carry out the king's command. — **21**. This was repeated with a second and with a third company of satellites. — **22**. At last, *Saul's anger was aroused and he also went to Ramah*] the opening of the verse is supplied from ⑤. — *In his progress, he came to the cistern of the threshing-floor which is on the height, and asked : Where are Samuel and David?*] the text is restored according to ⑤. — **23**. On being told, *he went thence, and the Spirit of God came upon him also and he marched along prophesying until he came to . . .*] the place mentioned is the same already named in v.[18]. — **24**. The manifestations in Saul, as in the others, are of an extravagant character : *He stripped off his clothes and prophesied before Samuel and lay naked all that day and all that night.* The resemblance to the ecstasy of the dervishes is striking. The *proverb* to which this gives rise has already been mentioned. The surprise which it expresses is far more in place in the earlier narrative than here, where Saul's possession has become a fixed fact.

18. ‏ורור ברח וימלט‎] as it stands may be the original conclusion of the preceding narrative (Bu.). — ‏בניות‎ *Kt.* : ‏בניות‎ *Qrê*] the word is entirely unknown. ⑤ adds here *in Ramah*, as 𝕳 does in vv.[20. 22f.]. But the addition there is necessary; here it is not, and the reading of ⑤ is the result of conformity. The Kethib is presumably to be pointed ‏נָיֹת‎, but no such word occurs elsewhere. A word ‏נוה‎ from a root meaning *to dwell* or *to sit quiet* is found, and in 20[1] this word is written ‏נוית‎ (by Baer only), which would be the plural of ‏נוה‎. ⑤ seems to have read ‏בנוַת‎ (ἐν Ἀυάθ[BL], corrected into ἐν Ναυιώθ in ᴬ). As pointed out by Dr. ‏נוה‎ " denotes in particular a pastoral abode," 2 S. 7[8]. That Samuel and David should have taken refuge in the sheepfolds is impossible to suppose. In 2 S. 15[25] David says to Zadok : " If I find favour in the eyes of Yahweh, he will bring me back and show me *his dwelling*," where the word ‏נוה‎ seems to designate the *tent* in which Yahweh dwelt. As the prophets in 10[5] come down from the *Bama* (which was the sanctuary) it does not seem remote to suppose the original here was ‏נות יהוה‎ or ‏נוה יהוה‎ which has been purposely obscured to conceal the fact that there was a sanctuary at Ramah (a fact which the later time could not rightly estimate). The precarious nature of the definitions given in this passage is well exposed by Driver in his *Notes*. For completeness I may add that Josephus gives a proper name Γαλβουάθ (*Ant.* VI. 221 = VI., XI. 5); the early Jewish tradition is represented by בית אולפנא of 𝔗; and that 𝔖 has יונת. — **20.** וירא] cannot be right and must be changed to ויראו with 𝔊. — להקת] is an unknown word. 𝔊𝔖 seem to have read קהל or קהלה (cf. Hoffmann, *ZATW.* III. 89). — נבאים] is lacking in 𝔊^B but is necessary to the sense. — עמד נצב] the two words together are impossible, and must be explained as the error of a scribe who wrote עמד from memory, and afterwards inserted the correct word נצב. Kl., followed by Bu., proposes מנצח on the basis of מליף 𝔗. But it must be remembered that 𝔗 throughout has the idea that Samuel was a rabbinical teacher, and its interpretation must be taken with allowance; moreover מנצח occurs only in Ezra, Chronicles, and the superscriptions to the Psalms (and Hab. 3). — **22.** וילך נם־הוא] καὶ ἐθυμώθη ὀργῇ Σαούλ, καὶ ἐπορεύθη καὶ αὐτός 𝔊 (with slight variation). The touch seems natural, and the loss of a single clause is not difficult to account for. — עד־בור הגדול] is ungrammatical. Restore עד בור הגרן with 𝔊^BL, and for בשכו read בשפי (ἐν τῷ Σεφεί 𝔊^B, ἐν Σεφί 𝔊^L). The שפי or *bare-topped hill* was the proper place for a threshing-floor. Kl. conjectures (with slight ground) *the threshing-floor on which Samuel was accustomed to sit in judgment.* — The second ויאמר means *one said*, as frequently. — ברמה] is here superfluous and probably to be omitted, with Bu. Saul is already in the immediate vicinity of Ramah when he makes the inquiry. — **23.** שם] error for משם (ἐκεῖθεν 𝔊^AB lacking in ^L). — הלך ויתנבא] I have no hesitation in restoring the regular הלך והתנבא which we should expect here. — **24.** נם־הוא] is omitted in both instances by 𝔊^BL, in the second instance only by 𝔖. One of the two can well be spared, and, if either, the latter. The older commentators (Theod.) saw in the stripping off of the clothes a sign of the loss of the kingdom.

XX. 1–XXI. 1. David's flight. — David complains to Jonathan of Saul's purpose to kill him. Jonathan reassures him, but offers to test his father's state of mind in any way David may suggest. David proposes to absent himself from the court under the plea of a family sacrifice. If Saul condones the breach of etiquette, they will know that all is well. If not, David's forebodings will be justified. The result is as David anticipated. Jonathan communicates the result of his test by a sign agreed upon, without personal communication with David. By grace of the redactor however they have a final interview, vv.[40-42]

It is evident that the piece does not agree with what immediately precedes. The hostility of Saul is as yet known only to David. Even Jonathan is ignorant of it. This points to a time before David's journey to Ramah, before the attempt frustrated by Michal, before even Jonathan's former intercession with his father. Had the author known of an earlier attempt at reconciliation, he would have made at least a passing allusion to it here. The difficulty into which we are brought by attempting to classify the paragraph with either of the two main sources of our narrative must be obvious. Yet it can hardly have been a stray leaflet which some scribe inserted after the double story was already completed. It has a bearing at least upon the life of David, for it prepares the way for his treatment of Jonathan's son Meribbaal. In the present state of our knowledge this is as much as we can say.

XX. **1**–**XXI**. **1**. On the critical questions consult the usual authorities and what is said above in the Introduction, § 5. As to the integrity of the piece itself, we may note that vv.[40-42] contradict the plain implication of what precedes — that it was dangerous for David and Jonathan to communicate directly. These verses are probably a later insertion. The rest of the chapter seems sometimes overfull and may have been interpolated. Budde's excision of vv.[4-17] as redactional however has not commanded any large measure of assent. Bonk gives a detailed analysis, which also lacks probability. Verses [11-17] may be from a different source from the rest of the chapter.

1–10. The first clause is the redactional suture. According to the rest of the verse David came and complained to Jonathan of the conduct of Saul. The older commentators, who accepted the historicity of the account as it stands, were much puzzled to account for David's behaviour. Why should he expose himself to further danger after having such unmistakable evidence of Saul's hostility as the preceding chapter furnishes? And how could Jonathan be so ignorant of Saul's temper after so public an exhibition? Attempts at conciliation (Schm., al.) are compelled to explain away the obvious force of language. David's complaint shows that Saul is not conceived of as having shown open hostility: *What have I done? What is my guilt, and what my sin before thy father, that he is seeking my life?* — **2**. Jonathan reassures David (or tries to reassure him): *Far be it! Thou shalt not die. My father does not even a small thing without letting me know, and why should my father hide this from me? Not so!* Jonathan's complete ignorance of Saul's state of mind could not be more strongly expressed. — **3**. David's reply suggests the reason of Jonathan's ignorance : *Thy father well knows that I am in favour with thee*] the standing phrase, elsewhere translated *have found grace in thine eyes*. Saul's thought is : *Let not Jonathan know this, lest he be pained*] possibly the original reason was *lest he make it known* or something equivalent. *Nevertheless, by the life of Yahweh and by thy life*] so the Bedawy swore " his tale was truth by the life of Ullah and by his son's life." * — *There is, as it were, a step between me and death*] either another step forward would plunge him into destruction, or else death was so close upon his track that in another step it would overtake its victim. — **4, 5.** To Jonathan's question : *What dost thou desire that I do for thee ?* David replies with his proposal : *To-morrow is the New Moon. But I shall not sit with the king to eat bread*] the plain implication is that David was expected at the king's table. His absence would be noted — evidence enough that there had been no open breach. The *New Moon* was a festival from the earliest times. To the present day the Arab of the desert greets the new moon with devout ejaculations, and the women ' chant their perpetual refrain of a single verse, and dance for an hour or two.' † We have every reason to suppose that the observance goes back to a time when the moon was an object of worship. The reason why David would not be at the table : *But thou shalt let me go and I will hide myself in the field until evening*] the politeness of David is manifested in asking Jonathan's permission. — **6.** *If thy father miss me, then thou shalt say : David asked leave of me*] it is doubtful whether Jonathan were empowered to act in the king's stead. But David designedly chooses to feign such a breach of etiquette as the king would easily condone if he were in a good mood. The permission was asked (ostensibly), *to run to Bethlehem his city, for there is a yearly sacrifice there for all the clan*] like Elkanah's, 2¹⁹. — **7.** If Saul should condone the slight : *then it is well with thy servant*] as to his standing with the king. Otherwise, *know that evil is determined upon by him*] that is, by *Saul*, cf. 25¹⁷. — **8.** David pleads the agreement already made between Jonathan and himself. *Thou shalt deal kindly with thy*

---

* Doughty, *Travels in Arabia Deserta*, I. p. 53.
† Doughty, *l.c.*, I. pp. 366, 455.

*servant because into a bond sanctioned by Yahweh thou hast brought
thy servant*] an agreement with divine sanctions between the two
is described 18³, and another was made later, 23¹⁸. *If there be
guilt in me, do thou slay me — to thy father why shouldst thou bring
me?* The strength of conviction shows itself in the form of the
protest. — **9**. Jonathan gives renewed assurance of his willingness
to serve his friend : *Far be it! If I know at all that evil is determined by my father to come upon thee, surely I will tell thee*] such
must be the meaning, although the present text expresses it awkwardly if at all (cf. the note). — **10**. David asks : *Who will tell
me if thy father answer thee harshly?*] the question implies that it
would not be safe for Jonathan to meet David personally. The
answer is given in v.¹⁸ᶠ. What comes between is not a part of the
earliest narrative.

1. ברמה . . . ‏[ויברח‎] is called the redactional suture above. It is possibly
however the original beginning of the account of David's flight to Achish,
where it would fit excellently instead of 21¹¹ᵃ. — ‏[ויבא ויאמר לפני יהונתן‎] is
rendered in 𝕲 as though it were ‏ויבא לפני יהונתן ויאמר‎, which is logically better.
Possibly however the division between the two documents is between the two
verbs, so that the original connexion was ‏ויאמר לפני יהונתן‎ ‏ודוד נס וימלט‎ —.
2. ‏לו־עשה‎ *Kt.*: ‏לא־יעשה‎ *Qrê.* The former intends to begin *if* my father *had
done*, but this is not suitable to the present context. We must therefore choose
the *Qrê*— my father *will not* do. — ‏[דבר גדול או‎] is lacking in 𝕲ᴮ and may
have fallen out by scribal mistake of the second ‏דבר‎ for the first. As the
shorter text makes good sense however, I have retained it. — ‏[יגלה אזני‎] cf. ¹². ¹³
and 9¹⁵. — ‏[אין זאת‎] a strong expression — *there is nothing of this*. — **3**. ‏וישבע‎
‏[עוד‎] as We. says, David has not sworn as yet, and does not swear now. 𝕲 has
only ‏וישב‎, which is all we need; ‏עוד‎ is a scribal expansion perhaps duplicate
of ‏דוד‎, and the duplication of its ‏ע‎ gave rise to the reading of 𝔚. The second
‏[ויאמר‎] means *says to himself*, as often. — ‏[פן־יעצב‎] the author of this passage
would seem to make Saul careful lest David should get information, rather
than lest Jonathan should be grieved, and traces of an original reading with
this force are found in 𝕲ᴮ, which has μὴ οὐ βούληται, which would represent
‏פן יעצה‎ (We.). 𝕲ᴸ has, with the same idea, ὅπως μὴ ἀναγγείλῃ τῷ Δαυίδ. It
is difficult to suppose however that ‏יעץ‎ was the verb here unless we read ‏פן‎
‏יעצו‎, *lest they take counsel together*, and we are obliged to decide for 𝔚, as
slightly more probable. — ‏[ואולם‎] strongly adversative to Jonathan's assertion
that there was no reason for David's suspicion. — ‏[חי־יהוה והי נפשך‎] cf. 14³⁹
and BDB. *s.v.* ‏חי‎. The ‏כי‎ is ‏כי‎ *recitativum*. — ‏[כפשע‎] *the like of a step* (Dr.);
‏פשע‎ occurs here only — the verb in one passage; 𝕲 seems to paraphrase.
— **4**. ‏[מה־תאמר‎] does not seem the word we need : τί ἐπιθυμεῖ 𝕲 points to
‏מה תאוה‎, which exactly fits the place. In that case we should point ‏ואעשה‎,

that I may do. — **5.** חרש] is frequently joined with the Sabbath as a day of religious observance, 2 K. 4²³ Is. 1¹³ Am. 8⁵. It was adopted by the Levitical legislation, Num. 10¹⁰ 28¹¹⁻¹⁵; cf. Dillmann, *Exodus und Levit.*, p. 578 f., Benzinger, *Hebr. Arch.*, § 69, Muss-Arnolt, *JBL.* 1892, pp. 73 f., 160 ff. — ואנכי ישב־אישב] is generally rendered *I should certainly sit.* But if David had meant that on that day he was confidently expected at the king's table, he would have expressed himself unambiguously to that effect. 𝔊 inserts a negative and this reading (ואנכי ישב לא אישב) has been generally adopted since We. — השלישית] is not expressed in 𝔊ᴮᴸ and is, in fact, superfluous. David did not know that he must remain in hiding until the third day. The word must therefore be dismissed. The only question is whether we should not also throw out the whole clause, which might easily be inserted by a scribe, in anticipation of what actually followed. — **6.** פקד] *first, to inspect* in order to see whether any is missing (13¹⁵ 14¹⁷), then *to discover* that some one is missing. — נשאל] with the proper Niphal force — *asked for himself*, Ges.²⁶ 51 *e*. — בית־לחם] for which 𝔊 read עד בית־לחם (adopted by We., Bu.). — **7.** ואם־חרה יחרה לו] καὶ ἐὰν σκληρῶς ἀποκριθῇ σοι 𝔊 (with slight variations). The latter seems on the whole more likely to have been substituted for the former than the reverse, it being more in conformity with what actually took place, v.¹⁰ (We.). — **8.** עָל] should evidently be עִם with 𝔊𝔖𝔗. (We., Dr., Bu.). — ברית יהוה] seems to be used nowhere else of a covenant between men, such as is alluded to here, but cf. Ex. 22¹⁰. — למה־זה] is rendered as a negative (which it is in intention) by 𝔖𝔏. — **9.** The difficulty is with the last clause of the verse : ולא אתה אגיד לך. It is possible to make the whole verse (from אם) an oath with the imprecation suppressed — so We. But in this passage, where the feeling is so strong, it would be unnatural to leave out so important a part of the asseveration. It is also possible to make the last clause an interrogation : *If I know . . . shall I not tell thee?* (Dr.) The difficulty would be relieved if we had instead of לא an emphatic particle like אכן. Such a particle exists in the form of לַ in Arabic and it is possible that it existed also in Hebrew. There are some traces of it aside from the present passage, as Ex. 8²², which is closely parallel to this : *If we sacrifice, . . . surely* the Egyptians will slay us. I have mislaid the reference to the article (in JAOS, if I remember correctly) in which the identification of this לא with the Arabic *la* was made, a few years ago. At the end of the verse 𝔊ᴸ adds εἰς τὰς πόλεις σου, which is also found, though differently placed, in 𝔊ᴬᴮ. The addition is difficult to account for; perhaps אתה was read אָרָה and was then supplemented by an adverbial clause inserted. Kl.'s adoption of the reading will hardly command assent. — **10.** או מה] ἐάν 𝔊 represents אם, which is doubtless original. A scribe took אם to be an abbreviation of two words, which he therefore restored. The received text might perhaps be justified by analogies (We., Dr.) but it seems simpler to correct it.

11–17. Jonathan's entreaty. — Jonathan gives renewed assurance of his fidelity and takes occasion to predict David's future

accession to the throne. With this in view, he entreats David's kindness for himself, or, in case he should not survive, for his children. The section interrupts the main thread of the narrative, and is characterized by a different tone. Instead of Jonathan's being the superior and David the suppliant, their position seems reversed.

11. The proposition of Jonathan is that they should *go out into the field*, where they would be free from observation. This proposition contradicts the plain intent of the main narrative, according to which it would be dangerous for them to be seen going together to the field. — **12, 13.** By somewhat radical treatment of the text we restore Jonathan's promise as follows: *Yahweh, God of Israel, is witness that I will sound my father about this time to-morrow, and if he be well disposed towards David, then I will send for thee to the field; but if there be evil*— *God do so to Jonathan and more also if I bring the evil upon thee; but I will uncover thine ear and will let thee go, and thou shalt go in peace.* The two alternatives are plainly put and the imprecation is joined with the appropriate one. The consciousness of the author that the latter alternative would be realized, shows itself in the concluding clause: *And Yahweh be with thee as he has been with my father!* — **14, 15ª.** The mention of David's future brings a request that his grace may be extended to Jonathan and his descendants. The writer has in mind the later account of David's treatment of Jonathan's son. — *And if I am yet alive, thou shalt show me the kindness of Yahweh; But if I should die, thou shalt not withdraw thy compassion from my house forever*] the two alternatives are completely stated, showing that the remainder of the verse belongs with what follows. — **15ᵇ, 16.** Should David forget the covenant, God would be the avenger: *But if, in Yahweh's cutting off the enemies of David from the face of the ground, Jonathan should be cut off with the house of Saul, then Yahweh will require it at the hand of David*] Jonathan is here put for *the house of Jonathan* and David for *the house of David*. The emphasis laid upon this matter makes us suspect that the house of Jonathan feared the ruling dynasty for a long time. — **17.** Jonathan continued to give assurances to David, *because with tender love he loved him*, cf. 18ª.

12, 13. The text has suffered in transmission, partly because the sentence is unusually long. As it stands, it is impossible to call it good Hebrew. After דוד we must restore עֵד, which has fallen out by reason of its similarity to דוד; so 𝔖 נסהד, while 𝔊 οἶδεν points to ידע, a corruption of the same original. Read therefore: *Witness is Yahweh*, cf. 12⁵. — [השלישית is superfluous here as in v.⁵, having been put into the text to make the promise conform to the event. — [והנה] should be והן equivalent to ואם; it is so read in 𝔖, while 𝔊ᴸ gives both: καὶ ἰδού, ἐάν. — [ולא־אז] the לא must be the same emphatic particle used above in v.⁹, here as there in the apodosis. — [וגליתי את־אזנך is lacking in 𝔊, which substitutes εἰς ἀγρόν (ᴬᴮ) or εἰς τὸ πεδίον. The latter seems more appropriate, for if Saul's mood was discovered to be good, Jonathan could send openly to the field and fetch David. At the beginning of v.¹³ 𝔊ᴸ has καὶ ἐὰν κακὸν ᾖ, which at any rate gives an appropriate meaning. I suppose the words [השדה ואם רעה] to have become illegible and to have been filled out by a scribe with a phrase from v.¹³, which fits in the context. — כי יוטב אל [אבי] is unintelligible; 𝔊ᴬᴮ ὅτι ἀνοίσω, 𝔊ᴸ ἐὰν μὴ ἀνοίσω. Both point to אבא for אבי and with אביא we must here read (in an oath) אם. The original אם אביא was miswritten אל־אבי, with which something had to be supplied. The original reading of Jonathan's oath I take therefore to be: עֵר יהוה אלהי ישראל כי אחקר את אבי כעת מחר והן טוב אל דוד ולא אז אשלח לך השדה: והן רע לו כה יעשה אלהים ליהונתן וכה יסיף אם אביא את הרע עליך. — **14.** The received text is here also corrupt. [ולא אם] is a duplication. ולא was written, and then, to make clear that לא was not meant, אם was added. — [ולא־תעשה] is represented by καὶ ποιήσεις 𝔊ᴮ, ποιήσῃς 𝔊ᴸ, showing that we should read again the emphatic particle in the apodosis. — [חסר יהוה] cf. 2 S. 9³. The third ולא should be read ולא and begin the next verse. — **15.** The first half of the verse, taken with the two preceding words, makes good sense. But the second half must be disconnected, and made the beginning of a third sentence. — [ולא בהכרית] will barely admit of connexion with the preceding (Dr.), but is better in every way when read ולא בהכרית. 𝔖 omits איש, perhaps rightly. — **16.** [ויכרת] εἰ ἐξαρθήσεται 𝔊ᴸ, rightly pointing יִכָּרֵת and connecting with the preceding ולא. Where 𝔊ᴮ gets εὑρεθῆναι is difficult to say. — [יהונתן] τὸ ὄνομα τοῦ Ἰωναθάν 𝔊ᴮ, the latter is adopted by Dr., Bu., but does not seem to improve the sense. — [עם־בית דוד] ἀπὸ τοῦ οἴκου Δαυείδ 𝔊ᴬᴮ, on the ground of which We., Dr., restore מעם. But what Jonathan requests is not that his house may continue *with* the house of David (as its dependants) but that it may not be cut off *by* them, which would not be expressed by מעם. 𝔊ᴸ μετὰ τοῦ οἴκου Σαούλ has some claims to be regarded therefore as original. — [מיד איבי דוד] cannot be right, as is evident; read מיד דוד. In some other cases איבי is inserted to avoid an imprecation on David. There is also a trace in one MS. of 𝔊 that the word was doubtful. — **17.** [להשביע את־דוד] Jonathan's love is no reason for his adjuring David. We are compelled therefore to read להִשָּׁבֵעַ אל־ר׳ with 𝔊. The main object of the interview was that Jonathan might assure David on oath that he would not betray him to Saul. — [כאהבתו אתו] has arisen by duplication of the following words. It is lacking in 𝔊ᴮ.

18-23. Jonathan describes more distinctly his plan for acquainting David with the state of Saul's mind. — **18.** The verse goes back to [10], in which David had inquired about the means of communication. First, a sketch of the situation : *To-morrow is New Moon and thou shalt be missed, when thy seat shall be vacant*] the sentence is no doubt tautological and perhaps the text has suffered. — **19.** What is intended by the opening of the verse is not clearly made out. David's course, however, is marked out for him : *Thou shalt come to the place where thou didst hide the day of . . .*] the day intended is no longer intelligible. — *And shalt sit down by the side of yonder stone heap*] the nature of the stone heap is not defined. — **20.** The general sense of the verse must be that Jonathan will choose some object by the side of David's hiding place *as a mark at which to shoot.* But it is impossible to construe the present text, and the evidence of the versions does not enable us to reconstruct it in better shape. — **21.** *And I will send the boy*] which one takes to recover the arrows when shooting at a mark : *Go find the arrow!*] the manner in which the boy is to be directed to the arrow is the token for David. — *If I say to the boy: The arrow is this side of thee, pick it up! — then, come! for it is well for thee, there is nothing the matter, by the life of Yahweh*] the sign is plain, and one that naturally suggests itself. — **22.** *But if I say to the lad: The arrow is beyond thee — then go! for Yahweh sends thee away*] the discovery of the mind of Saul will be an indication of God's will concerning David's course. — **23.** Jonathan's final word of confirmation : *And as for the word which we have spoken, thou and I, Yahweh is witness between me and thee forever*] Yahweh is a party to such solemn engagements, as we see in the case of Jacob and Laban, Gen. 31[50].

18. כי יפקר] is suspicious. But no better reading suggests itself. — **19.** ושלשת תרד מאד] gives no appropriate sense. 𝔊 substitutes תפקד for תרד, which is adopted by We., Dr., Bu., but does not seem satisfactory. That David would be more missed on the third day than on the second is true. But there was no reason to suppose that Saul's mind would not be discovered on the day following the interview. David should not wait until the third day to come to the place where he was to hide. I suspect that ושלשת at any rate (and perhaps the whole clause) is an insertion of the same hand which forced *the third day* into vv.[5. 12]; ואז תרד ובאת is what we expect. — ביום המעשה] the *day of the deed* is wholly unknown to us. There must be a reference to some former hiding on the part of David. But the only account of such a hiding preserved to us is in 19³, Jonathan's former intercession for David. On general grounds, we have already decided that that account was not known to the author of this narrative. It is difficult moreover to see how the day of that intercession could be called *the day of the deed*. We. supposes a reference to Saul's attempt with the spear (and refers to Job 33¹⁷). But David did not hide himself that day, so far as we know. We are in fact wholly in the dark. The versions — τῆς ἐργασίας 𝕲ᴸ, τῇ ἐργασίμῃ 𝕲ᴬᴮ, *qua operari licet* 𝕷, רחולא 𝕿, see in the word a designation of a working day in distinction from the festival day of the New Moon. But it is doubtful whether המעשה would be used to mark such a distinction — עבורה would be more natural. — [האבן האזל if correct can be only a proper name. But as pointed out by Th. 𝕲 (τὸ ἐργὰβ ἐκεῖνο 𝕲ᴮ, τῷ λίθῳ ἐκείνῳ 𝕲ᴸ) read both here and in v.⁴¹ the word ארגב, which would naturally mean *a heap of stones*, cf. the proper name *Argob* in Bashan, Dt. 3⁴ 1 K. 4¹³. We. therefore restores אצל הארגב הלז, which is generally adopted. — **20.** ואני שלשת החצים צדה אורה] would naturally mean : *and I will shoot the three arrows by the side of it*. But why *three* arrows? The later account speaks of only two, and it was not certain in advance that more than one would be needed. *The three arrows* are spoken of as if already mentioned, which is not the case. This half of the verse, moreover, in this wording does not fit the remaining words — *to send for me to a goal*. If this means anything it makes a complete tautology when taken with the preceding. 𝕲 reads שלשת as a verb — *and I will triple the arrows*, or *and I will use three arrows*, which does not seem to give any help. We., followed by Dr., Bu., reconstructs ואני אשלש בחצים = *and I on the third day* [will shoot] *with arrows*, which, if we can make שלש mean *to do on the third day*, somewhat relieves the difficulty, though the sentence is still awkward, and does not fit well with the latter part of the verse. I cannot help thinking that Kl. is on the right track in seeing in אורה a corruption of אראה. In that case Jonathan intended to say : '*I will choose* something near the stone heap *as a mark* at which to shoot.' But the original text is not discoverable. — **21.** [הנער] *the boy*, whom he would naturally have with him in practising archery. — [לך מצא the omission of לאמר is unusual. Possibly the original was simply למצא, which has been expanded under the influence of v.³⁶ where we have רץ מצא. [החצים] should probably be the singular in both instances. — [וכאה] must begin the apodosis, corresponding to לך in the next verse. But in this case the ו is abnormal and we should either read וכאת, or else with 𝕲ᴬᴮ omit the ו. The latter alternative is favored by the parallel in the next verse, the ו might readily have come from the end of the preceding word. — [דבר] is sufficient of itself without the addition of an adjective (*evil*) made by the versions. — **22.** [החצים the singular should be restored here also with 𝕲. The particular arrow which should give the sign was the one in Jonathan's mind all through the speech. The mistake of 𝕳 is probably because the form חצי (which occurs as an undoubted singular in v.³⁶) was taken for an abbreviated plural, the usual

singular being חיץ. — **23.** It seems necessary to insert עֵד (μάρτυς 𝕲) after
יהוה, or else to point the last two words of the verse עַד־עוֹלָם; cf. v.[12] as
amended above.

24–34. The discovery of the mind of Saul. — We may suppose that the interview just described took place in the evening.
The new moon had already been seen, so that the next day
(properly, the day had begun with the sunset) was the festival.
— **24.** David hid himself, and the festival day came, *and the king
sat at the* [sacrificial] *meal to eat.* The time of day is not given.
But, from the fact that Jonathan waited until the next morning
(after the second day) to carry his tidings to David, we may suppose it was late in the day. — **25.** The king's table companions
were only three. *The king sat on his seat, as usual, by the wall,
and Jonathan was opposite, and Abner sat by the side of Saul, and
David's seat was vacant.* The simplicity of the royal table is
evident. — **26.** The absence of David was not remarked upon at
this time, the king supposing a ritual reason : *For he said to himself : It is an accident : he is not clean because he has not been
cleansed*] the festival being a religious one, no one could eat of
the meal without being ritually purified. If David had neglected the proper rite of preparation, he had a sufficient excuse
for absence from the table. — **27.** The second day matters came
to a crisis. *Why has not the son of Jesse come to the table, either
yesterday or to-day ?* The known friendship of the two men made
it probable that Jonathan would be informed. — **28.** Jonathan
makes the excuse agreed upon : *David begged of me leave to run
to Bethlehem.* — **29.** Specific report of what David said in his
request : *Let me go, I pray, for we have a clan sacrifice in the city,
and that was what my brother commanded me.* The appearance
of the brother instead of the father has led to the supposition that
David's father was dead. Possibly we should read *my brethren*
(with 𝕲), and understand it of the members of the clan in general. Jonathan would then make the impression that David was
invited by the clan to be present at the festival, undoubtedly a
reason why he should seek to go, but not one that would conciliate
Saul. In Jonathan's further report of David's words is another
infelicity : *Let me slip away that I may see my brethren !* The
words must suggest to Saul that David was trying to escape from

him. — **30.** The wrath of Saul flames out upon his son : *Son of a rebellious slave girl !* Universal custom abuses a man by throwing opprobrium upon his parents. The son of a slave girl was of mean lineage ; and in case the mother were rebellious, her son might be suspected of being a bastard. Saul's anger did not allow him to reflect on the injustice of his abuse. *Do I not know that thou art a companion of the son of Jesse, to thine own shame and to the shame of thy mother's nakedness ?* To revile a man by the nakedness of his mother is still common among the Orientals (Doughty, I. p. 269). That a man may disgrace the womb that bore him is evident enough. But Saul in his excitement puts the thought into coarse language. — **31.** The reason for the anger is, that David is a rival for the throne : *For as long as the son of Jesse lives upon the earth, thy kingdom shall not be established*] the succession would naturally fall to Jonathan as the most capable, and probably the oldest of the sons of Saul. In the correct feeling that Jonathan will know where David is, Saul orders him to send and take him, adding : *for he is doomed to death*] cf. 2 S. 12⁵. — **32, 33.** At Jonathan's question why this should be, Saul's rage gets beyond control : *And Saul raised the spear at him to smite him*] as he had attacked David. — *So Jonathan knew*] more evidence could scarcely be expected, *that it was determined by his father to put David to death.* — **34.** *And Jonathan rose from the table in hot wrath and did not eat bread on the second day of the month because his father had reviled him*] the result of the inquiry was not simply the discovery of Saul's purpose towards David, but had brought unexpected insult to himself.

24. עַל־הלחם] is probably right. The sitter at the low Oriental table is decidedly *above* the food. The *Qrê* recommends אל, but the change is unnecessary. 𝕲 seems to have found על השלחן. — **25.** אל־מושב הקיר] is rendered by παρὰ τὸν τοῖχον 𝕲ᴸ, and אל הקיר is quite sufficient. — ויקם] why Jonathan should stand while the others sit is not clear. καὶ προέφθασεν 𝕲ᴮ, καὶ προέφθασεν αὐτόν 𝕲ᴸ, point to קדם, cf. 2 S. 22⁶ 2 K. 19³², which means *to confront*, generally in a hostile sense, but not necessarily so, Ps. 21⁴. The reading ויקדם in this place, suggested first (so far as I know) by Ewald, *GVI*³. III. 111, E. Tr. III. p. 80, is now generally adopted. — **26.** מקרה] various *accidents* might make one ritually unclean. — כי־לא טהור] is tautological. The pointing טֹהַר, suggested by 𝕲 (We.), relieves the difficulty to a certain extent only, but seems the best we can do. — **27.** ממחרת החדש השני] is impossible. We must have either ממחרת החדש, or else היום השני. 𝕲 has both, inserting היום. Probably the original was only ממחרת החדש. — הלחם] for *the table*, as in v.²⁴. — **28.** נשאל נשאל] implies an urgent request. — עד־בית לחם] I cannot persuade myself that the sentence is complete without a verb such as is supplied by 𝕲ᴸ δραμεῖν, or 𝕲ᴮ πορευθῆναι, or by 𝕿 למיזל, though the difference may show that the translators did not have either one in the text; לרץ seems to be the simplest. After *Bethlehem* 𝕲𝕾 add *his city*. — **29.** והוא צוה] the unusual order is perhaps due to an error. 𝕲 seems to have read simply ויצו. — ואראה] expressing the purpose of the request should be pointed וְאֵרָאֶה. — **30.** נעות המרדות] is made up of two words otherwise unheard of. Lagarde (*Mittheil*, I. p. 236 f.) makes the best of the present text, which might mean *one gone astray from discipline*. It seems better however, on the basis of 𝕲, to restore נערת (or נערה) instead of נעות. Only, as a man cannot be the son of more than one woman, the plural of 𝕲 is not allowable. The natural phrase would be נערה מֹרֶדֶת. A reflection on the chastity of Jonathan's mother is evidently intended, and מרד is used of Israel's rebellion against Yahweh (and adultery with other gods), showing that it would convey such a reflection. If נעות is original, we might suppose המרדות to be a gloss intended to explain its meaning — *son of perverseness* would fit the sense. — בחר אתה לבן] the verb does not go with the preposition; 𝕲 points to חֹבֵר or חָבֵר (adopted by Th. al.). — **31.** אתה ומלכותך] the אתה does not agree well with the meaning of the verb. It is lacking in 𝕲ᴬᴮ, and has evidently come in by the error of a scribe, who in writing תכן took it for the second person, and naturally put down אתה as its subject. Saul was not afraid for Jonathan personally, but for his succession to the throne. — בן־מות] already he is marked out by death as one of its children, cf. איש מות, I K. 2²⁶. — **33.** ויטל] as in the earlier case (18¹¹) should probably be pointed וַיָּטֶל, ἐπῆρεν 𝕲ᴬᴮ. — כלה היא] the lack of agreement is obvious. 𝕲 reads as in vv.⁷·⁹. But the particular *evil* is here defined in the clause להמית את־דוד. It will be sufficient therefore to correct כלה היא to כלתה, with We. al. — **34.** כי נעצב אל־ד׳] is lacking in 𝕲ᴮ, and is unnecessary. The wrath was fully accounted for by Saul's insulting language. — הכלמו] συνετέλεσεν ἐπ᾽ αὐτόν 𝕲ᴮ has arisen under the influence of כלתה, above. Here the absolute כָלָה עליו seems harsh, and 𝕳 is to be retained.

35–39. The warning given.

— As already agreed upon, Jonathan acquaints David of his danger. On the next morning: *Jonathan came into the field to the rendezvous with David, and* as agreed, he brought *a young lad with him*. — **36.** Jonathan starts the boy to find an arrow, and then, while he is running, shoots another *to fly beyond him*. — **37.** So when the lad came *to the place of the* [first] *arrow which Jonathan had shot, Jonathan cried after the lad and said: Is not the arrow beyond thee?*] this is in exact accordance with the agreement as worded above. — **38.** Jonathan gives an

additional message : *Hasten quickly, do not stop!* The words
spoken to the boy were intended for David's ear. *So Jonathan's
lad gathered the arrows and brought them to his master.* — **39**. The
writer reminds us that *the lad did not know anything* of the real
matter in hand, *but only Jonathan and David knew it.* This was
evidently the conclusion of the incident, except that he added
what we now find in 21¹: *David rose* from the place where he
was concealed *and departed,* while *Jonathan came into the city.*

35. למועד] the appointment naturally included both place and time.—
36. החצים] is to be corrected to the singular as above. Jonathan shot a
single arrow, and while the lad was running for it, he shot את־החצי, the particular arrow on which so much depended, so as *to pass beyond* the boy.—
37. הלוא] the whole line from this word to הנער in the next verse has fallen
out of 𝕲ᴸ. Possibly it made just a line in some early manuscript. A part of
the omission is supplied however after the word στῆς = תעמד.— **38.** מהרה
חושה] cf. Driver's note.— החצי *Kt.*] to be read as a plural (*Qrê*).— ויבא]
should be pointed וַיָבָא with 𝕲ᴬᴸ and the margin of ᴮ.

40-42. The verses give the account of a final interview, with
renewed expressions of affection. They stultify the whole preceding account, however, and must be regarded as an interpolation.
If it was so dangerous for Jonathan and David to be seen together
before Saul's mind was fully known, it was more so after the open
breach between him and his son. Jonathan's return to the city
without his arms, after sending back the lad, would be an invitation to suspicion. The interview is moreover without a purpose.
The solemn agreement had been made. The leave had been
taken. Two seasoned warriors cannot be supposed to have so
little steadiness of purpose that they must have one more embrace,
even at the risk of their lives. For these reasons we must regard
the paragraph as no part of the narrative just considered. Nor
does it agree with any earlier part of the book. Its allusions to
what took place in vv.³⁵⁻³⁹ are unmistakable. We must therefore
regard it as an editorial expansion, pure and simple.

40. The first thing is to get rid of the boy, and he is therefore
sent with Jonathan's weapons to the city. — **41**. David then *arose
from the side of the stone heap*] mentioned above as his hiding-
place, *and fell with his face to the ground, and prostrated himself
three times*] the occasion would not seem to admit of such exag-

gerated politeness. — *And each kissed his friend and each wept with his friend until . . .*] a point of time seems to have been given, but is not now discoverable. — **42**. Jonathan dismisses David with a reminder of their covenant: *As to what we two have sworn, in the name of Yahweh, Yahweh will be between me and thee, and between my seed and thy seed forever*. The Bedawy also says: There is none between us but Allah (Doughty, I. p. 267).

XXI. 1. As already remarked, this verse is the conclusion of this narrative, and must have stood after 20³⁹.

40. הביא] is lacking in 𝕲ᴸ, and is in fact superfluous. — **41**. מאצל הנגב] *from the side of the South Country* is of course impossible. Read מאצל הארגב corresponding to the emendation in v.¹⁹ (so 𝕲, and 𝕾 also has מן לות קיפא here). — עד־דוד הגדיל] *until David exceeded* (EV). But why David's victory in so curious a contest should be mentioned is impossible to conceive. 𝕲 has nothing to represent דוד, so that We. proposes עד הגדל; but this nowhere means *a great deal*, which is the only sense we can give it here. Kl. rightly remarks that what we expect is a point of time, and proposes עד יום גדול, which however does not seem sustained by usage. — **42**. לאמר] is the erroneous insertion of a scribe who supposed the words of the oath were to follow. — **XXI. 1**. ויקם] the subject seems necessary, and *David* is correctly added by 𝕲.

XXI.–XXVI. David an outlaw captain.

XXI. 2–10. David comes to Nob, where his appearance startles the priest. He excuses his lack of provision and of followers, and receives the sacred bread and also the sword of Goliath.

The brief narrative is well told. The natural question is whether it fits on to any of the preceding sections. The surprise of the priest indicates that David was accustomed to travel with a retinue. This is appropriate for a man who had attained prominence as a captain, and who had become the king's son-in-law. The condition in which he presents himself — without weapons and without food — is unusual, even for the ordinary traveller. This is inconsistent, not only with David's usual course, but even with the representations of the chapter just studied. For in that chapter David had ample time to furnish himself for the flight which he suspected would be necessary. The condition in which he appears before the priest is the natural sequel of only one preceding section, and that is the one where David is hastily let down through the window of his house at a time when guards were already posted, when there might be danger in the gleam or clash of weapons, and when in the sudden terror, bread would not be thought of. These reasons seem to justify the connexion immediately with 19^{17}.

2. The verse connects well with 19^{17} or 19^{18a}, which may be the original: *And David fled and escaped the night of his wed-ding, and came to Nob, to Ahimelech the priest*] Nob was a sanct-uary, as is evident from the continuation of this account. It was within the immediate jurisdiction of Saul, or he could not have dealt with it so summarily. A town of the name is located in Benjamin by Nehemiah (11^{32}), and the same is intended by Isaiah in his picture of the progress of an invading enemy from the north (Is. 10^{32}). From the latter passage, we learn that the town was in the immediate vicinity of Jerusalem. This situation would answer all the needs of our passage. David would natu-rally make his way southward from Gibeah so as to reach his own clan. He would stop for supplies at the first town in which he might have friends. Nob lay immediately on the way to Beth-lehem, and in his flight (late at night) he would reach it by the early dawn. Ahimelech the priest *came trembling to meet David*. In 16^4 the Sheikhs of Bethlehem tremble at the spiritual autocrat. Here the priest takes the same attitude in presence of the secular authority. The difference in the point of view is obvious. The priest is surprised at the way in which David comes. — *Why art thou alone, and no man with thee?*] the evident implication is, that David was usually accompanied by an escort. — **3.** David invents an excuse, to the effect that he is on a pressing errand from the king, and one that requires secrecy: *The king com-manded me a matter to-day, and said to me: Let no man know anything of the matter upon which I send thee*] the natural infer-ence is that he must not attract attention by travelling with a company. He intimates however that the troops had a rendezvous appointed: *And the young men I have appointed to meet me at a certain place.* — **4.** The haste of the departure is pleaded as a reason for asking provision : *And now if there be within thy reach five loaves of bread, give it me, or whatever may be at hand.* — **5**. The priest's objection to giving what bread he has, is : *There is no common bread within my reach, though there is sacred bread*] the latter, being consecrated, must be handled by consecrated persons only. This did not originally mean that only the priests could eat it. Like the sacrifices, it could probably be eaten by worshippers duly prepared liturgically. As a safeguard, such persons usually partook of the consecrated food within or near the sanctuary. But there seems to be no reason in the nature of things why it should not be taken away, if only proper care was exercised. — *If only the young men have kept themselves from woman*] *they might eat it,* is the natural conclusion of the sentence. As is abundantly clear from the Pentateuchal legislation, as well as from Arabic usage, the sexual act renders one unfit for any sacred ceremony until the proper purification has been undergone. — **6**. The obscurity of David's reply is probably due to our ignorance of the author's conception of holy and profane. In any case he gives assurance on the particular point of inquiry : *But women have been kept from us as always when I go on an expedition.* As war was a sacred work, abstinence from everything profane was David's habit in all his campaigns. — *And the arms of the young men were consecrated*] at starting, as we suppose was the custom in Israel, from the expression *consecrate war,* Jer. 6⁴ Mic. 3⁵. David makes his assurances so strong that he even says (to all appearance) that if the bread were common bread, it would become consecrated by contact with the consecrated vessel in which he proposed to carry it. The exact words in which he originally embodied this declaration are unfortunately lost to us. — **7**. The plea was effectual, *and the priest gave him consecrated* [food] *for there was no bread there except bread of the presence removed from before Yahweh, to place hot bread there, the day it was taken away.* According to later custom this was done once a week, Lev. 24⁸. — **8**. The verse is evidently designed to prepare for Doeg's betrayal of David later, 22⁹. Some have therefore supposed it to be an interpolation. But the later passage seems to presuppose this one. Doeg the Edomite, who is described as *Saul's muleherd,* was kept at the sanctuary by some religious (cere-

monial) obligation. — **9.** David asks further for spear or sword
since he has left his own weapons behind : *For the king's business
was urgent*] is his pretext. — **10.** The priest tells of the sword
of Goliath, *whom thou didst slay in the valley of Elah*] the language is used to indicate that David had a better title to the
sword than had any one else. It had been deposited by David
in the sanctuary, and was now *wrapped in a mantel, behind the
ephod*] the last phrase is omitted by 𝔊, perhaps because of dislike of the ephod, which here cannot be a garment or a breastplate. At David's desire, the sword is given him.

2. נבה] with an unusual form of the (locative) accusative ending, Ges.[26],
90 *i*; Stade, 132 (p. 102). Jerome (according to Buhl, *Geog.* p. 198) locates
Nob in the vicinity of Lydda. But there would seem to be no reason why
David should go westward, and into the country of the Philistines. Perhaps
Jerome was moved by the following account of David's coming to Achish.
But that is from a different document. The same line of argument is followed
by Schm. (p. 719 f.) to refute those who suppose David to have fled across the
Jordan to נבה (cf. Jd. 8[11]). — אחימלך] There seems to be no doubt that the
second half of the name is one of the names of Yahweh cf. Moore on Jd. 8[31].
We find an אחיה, 14[3], who officiated as Saul's priest, and he is probably the
same with our Ahimelech. 𝔊[AB] has *Abimelech* here. — לקראת דוד] 𝔊[AB] reads
לקראתו, which would be natural — but on that very account 𝔐 must be taken
to be original. — **3.** לאחימלך הכהן] 𝔊[AB] has לכהן simply. — דבר] 𝔊 adds
σήμερον, which is appropriate and forcible. The day began with the evening.
The command being received at or after sundown, to be carried out at once
would plausibly explain David's appearance in the early morning at Nob. —
מאומה] seems to be omitted by 𝔊[AB]. With the negative it has the force of
at all — here *let no man know at all of the matter*, Ges.[26], 137 *c*. — ואשר צותיך]
is redundant — perhaps a scribe's expansion. — יורעתי] might possibly be a
Poel form (Ges.[26], 55 *b*; Stade, 465). But the meaning is not so good as if
we had יערתי, which should probably be restored; 𝔊 διαμεμαρτύρημαι points to
העירתי, which was read as if from עור. But the form might equally be from
יער. If the original reading were יערתי it might give rise to both יורעתי and
העירתי. Kl. proposes נועדתי, Ex. 29[42] Job 2[11]. — פלני אלמני] 2 K. 6[8]. — **4.** [מה־יש
does not consist with the definite number of loaves asked for. We are
compelled therefore to read אם־יש with 𝔊[LA], εἰ εἰσίν (εἰ has dropped out
of 𝔊[B] owing to its resemblance to the beginning of the next word). —
או הנמצא] is a concise way of saying, *or whatever thou canst find.* — **5.** [חל
is the opposite of קדש. Of course we cannot judge the act of Ahimelech by
the later legislation which commanded that the bread of the presence should
be eaten by the priests only, and only in the sanctuary, Lev. 24[9]. There is no
evidence in this narrative that the priest did not take all the precautions

necessary. — אל־תחת] the אל is probably erroneous duplication of the preceding חל. — **6.** Confessedly a difficult verse, and one in which the versions give
us little help. For the religious ideas which lie at the basis of David's assurances, cf. WRS. *Religion of the Semites*, pp. 365, 436. — כתמל שלשם] cannot
mean that the privation has lasted *three days* (AV., cf. RV.), nor that it has
lasted *about three days* which would have been differently expressed. It
expresses a comparison : *as yesterday and the day before*, *i.e.*, as in former
times. David claims that his custom has always been to take care for ritual
purity on all his expeditions and that this is no exception. — ויהיו] must carry
on the description of what took place at the start : *Women were taboo . . .
and the equipments of the young men were consecrated.* This fully meets the
priest's scruples, and is emphasized in what follows. — והוא דרך חל] is unintelligible. David can hardly mean that he is upon a peaceable (and therefore
common) journey, for this is aside from the main purpose. There seems to be
no way of fitting the clause into the context, and the text is probably unsound.
From the clause which follows, we conclude that David meant to say that even
common bread would become consecrated by contact with the already consecrated vessels of his followers. Possibly the change of דרך to דבר might
enable us to get this meaning : והוא דבר חל = *and were it a common thing,
nevertheless it would become consecrated in the vessel* (in which it will be carried) cf. 𝕾ᴸ which favours this construction, though it retains דרך. — ואף כי]
would probably bear the construction just suggested ; 𝕾ᴮ seems to have read
כי only, while 𝕾ᴸ neglects the words altogether. — בכלי] διὰ τὰ σκεύη μου 𝕾
perhaps gives the original meaning. — **7.** המוסרים] the plural is probably due to
the accretion of a מ from the beginning of the next word (We.). — **8.** נעצר] as
the root is used above for that which is religiously forbidden (taboo), we may
suspect that it means here, *kept by a taboo*, or in accordance with later custom,
kept by a vow (so Schm. who compares the law of the Nazirite, Num. 6, but
this does not require a sojourn in the sanctuary). — אביר הרעים] νέμων τὰς
ἡμιόνους 𝕾 is restored by Lagarde (*BN.* p. 45, note) as אביל העירים, and as
אביר is not used of a *chief*, the latter (which is the more difficult reading)
should probably be adopted. Graetz suggests אביר הרצים (*Gesch. der Juden*,
I. 183), adopted by Dr., Bu., Ki. — **9.** ואין יש־פה] The form אין occurs
nowhere else. The punctuators wished to distinguish it from אַיִן and perhaps
to identify it with אם. 𝕾 has ἴδε εἰ ἔστιν ἐνταῦθα, which We. supposes to indicate ראה היש פה, though he finds the interchange of ה and נ unusual. As the
two letters are not unlike in the old alphabet we need not deny the possibility
of one being mistaken for the other. But if the original were אם we may
suppose 𝕾 to have avoided the aposiopesis by inserting ἴδε. I had already
suspected the original to be ואי יש פה, *and where is there*, before I saw Klostermann's conjecture to the same effect. It is to this question that Ahimelech
replies. — נחוץ] a supposed passive participle from נחץ. Kl. conjectures
נחרץ, *decisive, strict*, Dan. 9²⁶. More probable is נאוץ (from אוץ), or נחוש.
— **10.** The *Valley of Elah* is a reference to 17² or to the original account
from which that has been expanded. — לוטה] is the passive participle. —

בָּזֶה] is pointed in many editions בַּזֶה but this is incorrect.   At the end of the verse add καὶ ἔδωκεν αὐτὴν αὐτῷ 𝔊.

11–16. David at the court of Achish. — David escapes to the court of Achish king of Gath. There he becomes an object of suspicion, and feigns madness, whereby he preserves his life, and is allowed to go.

The paragraph is fitted into the narrative so that it seems to follow naturally on the preceding. On closer inspection we see that it does not. The opening verse indicates that David's flight was directly from the presence of Saul. In the presence of the Gittites, moreover, it would be an insane thing to carry the sword of Goliath. The linguistic marks of so short a piece are scarcely sufficient to identify it. It may be conjectured however that it originally followed the account of David's sojourn at Ramah (19^{24}).

11. Achish king of Gath is the same who was David's overlord in his later career. The present account seems to be an attempt to explain away the facts of history. — **12.** The servants (that is, officers) of Achish arouse his suspicions : *Is not this David, the king of the land?*] the conception of the author who could put the question into the mouth of the Philistines at this date is naïvely unhistorical. *Was it not to this man that they sang in dances saying : Saul has slain his thousands and David his ten thousands ?* It is curious however that Goliath's fellow-citizens should not adduce the death of their hero as a part of the charge against David. — **13, 14.** As David reflected on these words he feared, *and disguised his understanding, and raved in their hands, and drummed on the doors, and let his spittle run down upon his beard*] all signs of a maniac. Ewald cites the similar behaviour of Ulysses, and of Arabic and Persian heroes ; Schm. mentions Brutus and Solon. — **15, 16.** The king has no relish for this sort of company : *You see a madman, but why should you bring him to me ? Am I in lack of madmen that you should bring this to rave at me ? Shall this come into my house ?* From the implied assertion that Achish already had madmen enough, some have imagined that the members of his household were thus afflicted (Schm. p. 719, who cites no authorities).

11–16. The opening verse : *David rose and fled that day from the presence of Saul*, points to something earlier than the interview with Ahimelech. This verse, if originally following that interview, should read : *And David went thence.* That the general style of this section is similar to that of 19[18–24] is indicated by Bu., who prints the two in the same colour. I venture to think the point of view the same. In both, David is delivered without the aid of his prowess. Providence is his guide in both, and his escape, really miraculous in one case, is little short of that in the other. And if that account shows resemblance to 16[1–14] by the position it gives Samuel, this betrays a similar connexion by calling David *king of the land.* — **11.** אכיש] 'Aγχούς ⑮. — **12.** באלפו and ברכבו are written as in 18[7]. — **14.** וישנו] the form has perhaps preserved the original third radical. Else, it is a clerical error for וישנה or וישן (Stade, 493 *a*; Ges.[26], 60 *d*, 75 *bb*). The verb is used of changing one's clothes, 2 K. 25[29], and in the Hithpael, of disguising one's self, 1 K. 14[2]. טעם is the taste or flavour of a thing, applied figuratively to the character of a nation (Moab), Jer. 48[11], and to the understanding of a person, 1 S. 25[33]. The difficulty with the phrase here used (and in the form בשנותו את־טעמו Ps. 34[1] dependent on this passage) is that one does not change his understanding as he does his clothes. This is felt by ⑮ which renders καὶ ἠλλοίωσεν τὸ πρόσωπον αὐτοῦ. It is impossible to prefer this to the more difficult reading of 𝔐, but there is reason to suppose the obscurity due to early corruption of the text. The exegetical feeling of Schmidt (who adheres, of course, to the Massoretic text) leads him to see that the change of one's understanding is attributable to God alone. In fact, it is possible that God (or Yahweh) was the original subject here, so that the parallel with the deliverance at Ramah was once more striking than it now is. — ויתהלל] either *feigned himself mad*, or *raved* under the influence of fear, Jer. 25[16]. The next clause has a double translation in ⑮. — ויתו] ויתיו Qrê, is supposed to mean *make marks*, as we say *scribble.* But ⑮ καὶ ἐτυμπάνιζεν renders ויתף, as was pointed out by Cappellus, *Critica Sacra*, p. 261. Possibly ויתו is only a phonetic spelling of ויתף, Ew. *GVI*[3]. III. p. 116, E. Tr. III. p. 83. — **15.** הנה] one is tempted to restore הן — *if* you see a madman, *why* should you bring him to me? — איש משתגע] cannot be *the man is mad* (AV., cf RV.), but the words must be the object of the verb. — **16.** הסר] probably originally החסר (Kl.). — את־זה] used in contempt as 10[27]. — עלי] implies that the experience was burdensome to him.

XXII. 1–XXVI. 25. David as an outlaw. — The various localities in which he hid himself are mentioned, and the failure of Saul to seize him is shown. We have duplicate accounts of David's sparing Saul when he had him in his power. There are also other indications of compilation. But the separation of the documents is difficult, owing to the nature of the material. In any case, the

narrative consists of a string of adventures, each of which forms a unit of itself.

XXII. 1–5. David collects a troop of followers, and brings his father and mother into a place of safety. — **1.** The opening words would connect fairly well with 21^1 21^{10} or 21^{16}. From the general tone of the narrative, they agree better with 21^1 than with the others. After the signal given by Jonathan, therefore, David went, as was most natural, to his own clan, where he found safety *in the stronghold of Adullam*] the *cave*, which has become traditional, originated in the error of a scribe. *Adullam* is one of the Canaanite towns whose kings are said to have been conquered by Joshua, Jos. 12^{15}. It is mentioned in the Shephela, between Jarmuth and Shocoh, Jos. 15^{35}; in 2 Chr. 11^7 it comes in immediate connexion with Shocoh, and in Neh. 11^{30} it is one of the towns of Judah. These indications point to a location on the western edge of Judah and favour the identification with the present *Aid-el-Ma* ('*Îd-el-Mîje*, Buhl), twelve miles west by south from Bethlehem. The Judahite warrior probably already had friends there, and he was joined by his own clan. With David outlawed they would not be safe. — **2.** In possession of a stronghold, he soon became head of a band of soldiers or bandits : *There gathered to him all the oppressed*] those rendered desperate by the demands of their masters, *and every one who had a creditor*] a brutal exactor of debts who would not hesitate to sell the debtor's family into slavery, 2 K. 4^1; *and every embittered man*] according to 30^6 men who were angry because of some grievance. The case of David is similar to that of Jephthah (Jd. 11^3). The energetic man who is outlawed easily gathers such a force. They numbered, in David's case, *four hundred men ;* at a later stage of the history we find six hundred, 30^9. — **3, 4.** The verses are an interpolation, or at least from a different source. They tell how David entrusted his father and his mother to the king of Moab. The account has been found plausible on the ground that Ruth the Moabitess was an ancestress of David. But the fact that a young woman had married into the tribe of Judah, renouncing her own gods and leaving her father's house, would constitute a precarious title for her great-grandson in claiming protection. The *Mizpeh of Moab* here mentioned is not named again and cannot be identified. On the reading of David's request — *Let my father and my mother dwell with thee* — see the critical note. — **5.** The unexpected introduction of *Gad the prophet* shows that the verse is by a different hand from the one that wrote ¹·², and from the one that wrote ³·⁴. The purpose for which he comes is to warn David not to remain in Mizpeh, which being foreign ground is unclean, but to *come to the land of Judah*. In consequence of this advice *David came to the Wood of Hereth*. The location is unknown.

1. מערת עדלם] is also found 2 S. 23¹³ (and 1 Chr. 11¹⁵, which is dependent upon it). In both cases, the word is followed by a reference not to a מערה but to a מצדה (cf. v.⁴). On this account We.'s correction to מצדת here and in 2 S. 23¹³ is now generally accepted, cf. 23¹⁴. A cave might also be fortified as a stronghold, as were the caves in Galilee in the time of Herod. The tradition which identifies the cave of Adullam with the immense cavern of *Khareitun* is traced to the twelfth century of our era only (Baedeker, *Palestine*², p. 133). On the name Adullam cf. Lagarde, *BN.* p. 54 (from '*adula, to turn aside*). — **2.** מצוק] of the straits of the inhabitants of a besieged city, Dt. 28⁵³ Jer. 19⁹. — **3, 4.** Of the two theories concerning the relation of the verses to the Book of Ruth, it seems to me more likely that these are the original than the reverse (cf. Nestle, *Marg.* p. 14 and reff.). The Rabbinical conceit that David's father, mother, and brothers were slain by the Moabites after being entrusted to them (Schm. p. 743) has no foundation in the Biblical text. — יצא] does not suit the following אתכם. We should probably restore ישב as is read by 𝔖: *maneat* 𝔏 might be adduced as having the same force, but it probably goes back to γινέσθωσαν 𝔊 which We. would adopt (apparently reading יהי). (Th. prefers either יהיו or ישב to the reading of 𝔐.) Kl.'s attempt to retain יצא, changing אתכם to אליכם, is opposed by the following עד. — אתכם] παρὰ σοί 𝔊ᴮ, μετὰ σοῦ 𝔊ᴸ have the singular, which is to be preferred. — מה־יעשה־לי] probably in the sense what God will do *on my behalf*, cf. 14⁶ 25³⁰. — וינחם] pointed by the Massorites as though from נחה, read by 𝔊 as though from נחם, is really intended for וינחם, from נוח (We. confirmed by Dr., who cites 𝔖 and 𝔗 in favour of the reading). — במצרה] favours the reading מצודה above. 𝔖 however has במצפה here and in the following verse. — **5.** *Gad the prophet* is so called in only one other passage, 2 S. 24¹¹, and there the title seems to be a late insertion. Elsewhere he is *David's Seer*, 2 S. 24¹¹ (and the parallel 1 Chr. 21⁹), 2 Chr. 29²⁵. He belongs in the later history but not here. We should at least be told how he came to be with David. The object of his introduction is to get David by divine command from some place outside Judah back into his own country. Abiathar had not yet come down with the ephod; the oracle is therefore imported by a prophet. As Adullam was reckoned to Judah it is probable that for במצורה here we should read

במצפה (Bu. following Kl.). — יער] a rough region covered with thickets. 𝕲 reads here עיר. — חרת] possibly an Aramaizing form of חרש, 23¹⁵ (We. following a conjecture of Ewald, *GVI*³. III. p. 123). 𝕲 reads σαρείκ or σαρίχ.

6–23. The vengeance of Saul upon the priests. — Saul learns that Ahimelech has aided David. The priest is therefore summoned and questioned. He admits the act, but denies evil intent. But Saul is not satisfied and, at his command, the whole priestly clan is hewn down in cold blood. Only one — Ahimelech's son — escapes, perhaps because he was left behind in the journey to Gibeah. He flees to David with the ephod. David receives him and promises him protection.

6–23. As the section is plainly the sequel of 21²⁻¹⁰, there is no objection to supposing it originally continuous with that. We must however suppose that v.⁶ has been fitted to the present connexion. In fact the first half of the verse is irrelevant. The fact that David and his men were *known* has nothing to do with Saul's vengeance on the priests. The paragraph would be sufficiently introduced by ⁶ᵇ. The object of the author is evidently to show how the priestly oracle came to be with David instead of with Saul.

6. *And Saul heard that David and his men were known*] the author does not tell us how they were made known, and Saul in his speech betrays no knowledge of David's whereabouts. What moves his wrath is that none of his officers has told him of Jonathan's friendship for David, not that David has recruited a force of men. These considerations justify us in making this clause a redactional insertion. — *Saul was sitting in Gibeah under the Tamarisk*] perhaps a well-known tree like the Palm under which Deborah sat to administer justice, Jd. 4⁵. The locality is further described as on the *Bamah* (according to 𝕲) or sanctuary. Here he sat in state *with his spear in his hand*] in place of a sceptre. So the Argive kings and others (Sanctius cited by Schm.). — 7, 8. Saul appeals to his courtiers: *Hear, O Benjamites! The son of Jesse also will give you fields and vineyards, and will make you captains of thousands and captains of hundreds!* an ironical exclamation. ' It appears that you expect to gain as much from David who is of Judah, as you have already received from me who am of your own clan ! ' The absurdity of such an expectation is manifest. Yet it is only on this ground that their behaviour can

be explained : *For all of you have conspired against me, and no
one tells me when my son enters into a bond with the son of Jesse,
and none of you has pity upon me and tells me that my son has
abetted my servant against me as an enemy, as you see to be the
case*] a good statement of Saul's theory, only it is really an accusation against Jonathan rather than against David. — **9**. The part
of informer is taken by Doeg the Edomite who was *standing by
the officers of Saul,* though he was not one of the regular attendants at court. — **10**. After telling that he saw David come to Nob
he adds that Ahimelech *asked Yahweh for him*] as to the prosperity of his journey. The preceding narrative says nothing of
this, but the truth of the charge seems to be admitted by Ahimelech. He tells also of the *provision* given David, as well as of
the *sword of Goliath*, though the latter is thought to be a later
insertion.

6 ואנשים] should be corrected to והאנשים on account of the following אשר
(Kl., Bu.). — האשל] evidently a tree of some kind. But as the word occurs
only three times, the species is uncertain. That this was a sacred tree is not
improbable. Kl. conjectures that the enigmatical ἄρουρα of 𝕲 represents an
intentional substitution of אררה *the cursed* for the original name. — ברמה]
might be *on the height.* But 𝕲 has ἐν βαμά, which is the word for the village
sanctuary or *high place*, cf. 9¹². — **7**. בני ימיני] the plural of בן ימיני as in Jd.
19¹⁶. — וכ] Num etiam dabit quem admodum ego feci? (Schm.) The second
לכלכם must be an error. Read ונרכס with 𝕲ᴮ. — **8**. Saul says substantially
the same thing twice over, unless we suppose the two counts to state progres-
sive degrees of guilt : Jonathan *first* enters into a close agreement with
David, and *then* stirs him up to enmity against Saul. — חלה] *no one is sick for
me* sounds strangely, and we shall doubtless read חמל, cf. 23²¹; the emendation, suggested by Graetz,* is now generally adopted. — הקים] is generally used
of Yahweh's *raising up* either helpers or enemies, cf. 1 K. 11²³. — לארב] is
rendered by 𝕲 both here and v.¹³ as though it were לאיב, which is probably
to be restored. ארב would imply that David was *lying in wait* for Saul, which
even Saul's fancy could hardly find probable. — כיום הזה] implies that the
actual state of things was known to the courtiers. — **9**. האדמי] ὁ Σύρος 𝕲ᴮ. —
נצב על] is to be interpreted like the similar phrase in v.⁷. Doeg, in any case,
could not be said to be *placed over the servants of Saul* for these עברים were
the high officials. 𝕲 reads here ὁ καθεστηκὼς (ὁ καθεστάμενος) ἐπὶ τὰς ἡμιόνους.
The question comes whether we should have an explanation of Doeg's office
or of his presence at court. The latter seems to be more probable. The
author informs us that Doeg whose office would not naturally bring him to the

* According to Bu. *Books of Samuel* (*SBOT.*), but he gives no reference.

council of state was *standing by* the officers of Saul.   This makes it probable
that his office had been described before, and favours the originality of 21⁸.
נצב על, it may be remarked, is nearly always used of literal *standing*.—
10.   וישאל־לו ביהוה] by means of the sacred oracle.   That the consultation of
the oracle was lawful to the king alone, is a conceit of the Jewish expositors.
—ואת חרב ג' ה' נתן לו] is suspicious from the repetition of the words נתן לו.
It is therefore marked as secondary by Bu. in his text, and Co. agrees with him.
The verse is very short however without this clause, and the reference to the
sword in v.¹³ protects at least so much here.   Not impossibly the original had
only וצידה וחרב נתן לו.

11. Saul summoned Ahimelech and all his clan, *the priests who
were in Nob,* and they came. — **12, 13.** At Saul's address, Ahimelech answers obediently : *Here am I, my Lord !* Saul then makes
his accusation : *Why have you conspired against me, thou and the
son of Jesse, in that thou gavest him bread and a sword and didst
ask God for him, that he might stand against me as an enemy as
is now the case ?* If Saul knew that it was the sword of Goliath,
he would pretty certainly put the statement into the accusation.
— **14.** Ahimelech's answer is a defence of David : *And who
among all thy servants is like David, trusted, and the king's son-
in-law, and chief over thy subjects, and honoured in thy household ?*
The panegyric would be little calculated to quiet Saul's anger, but
it shows Ahimelech's honesty of intention. — **15.** Precedent moreover is on Ahimelech's side : *Is this the first time I have asked
God for him ?* The fact is not denied, but the intention of conspiracy — *far be it from me !* In his consciousness of innocence,
he prays that no guilt may be laid to the charge of himself or his
father's house. That these were under suspicion is manifest from
their being summoned before the king. — **16.** To Ahimelech's
protestation of ignorance and innocence Saul replies only with a
sentence of death on him and his whole clan. ' De innocentia tua
tecum nolo disputare, volo autem ut morte moriaris ; haec mea
voluntas est pro ratione ' (Schm.). — **17.** Saul commands the *runners standing about him*] the body guard of the king ran before
his chariot. They also acted as executioners. — *Turn about and
slay the priests of Yahweh*] we may picture the runners standing
near the king, the body of priests a little further back. In giving
the reason for his command, Saul accuses the priests of complicity
with David, giving no credence to the protest of Ahimelech : *For*

their hand also was with David] indicates that he has others in
mind as well as they — perhaps Jonathan only. The soldiers
refuse to carry out the command, owing to the sacred character
of the accused. — **18.** Doeg was less scrupulous, and at the king's
command he *turned and slew the priests*] Jd. 8²¹ 15¹² 2 S. 1¹⁵. The
victims were *eighty-five men who wore the linen ephod*] the characteristic garment of the priest 2¹⁸. — **19.** The verse tells that
Saul put the city of the priests to the sword in language closely
similar to the ban pronounced upon Amalek, 15³. For this reason
it is supposed by some to be an interpolation, and in fact it could
easily be spared from the narrative. We have no further information concerning the fate of Nob; and there is no parallel to the
wiping out of an Israelite city by Israelites, except in the very
late account of the destruction of Benjamin, Jd. 20 and 21.

13. אליו [אלו] *Qrê* is doubtless correct. — [וישאול] the infinitive absolute
continuing a finite verb, cf. Dav. *Syntax*, 88 *a*. — [אלי] another instance of
the confusion of אל and על. The latter alone is in place with קום in the hostile sense. — [לארב] must correspond with the word adopted in v.⁸; read therefore לאיב. A *lier-in-wait* does not *stand against* any one; he *lurks* for him.
— **14.** [וסר אל משמעתן] *and who turns aside to thine obedience* makes no sense
in this connection. סר is only another spelling for שר as is indicated by ἄρχων
𝔊; משמעת is the abstract for the concrete — *the subjects* of the king, Is. 11¹⁴
2 S. 23²³ (where however the text is doubtful). — **15.** [היום החלתי] is somewhat
difficult. It is necessary to read as a question, and the interrogative has probably dropped off before ה, unless we can suppose ההיום to become היום for
euphony. But what does the priest mean by asking: *Did I begin to-day to
ask?* The only plausible explanation seems to be that he means: *I have been
accustomed to consult the oracle for David on his other expeditions, with your
knowledge and consent; therefore you cannot charge me with it as a crime in
this instance.* — [בכל] read ובכל, 𝔊Ṥ. — **17.** [גם] is lacking in 𝔊. — [אזנו] אזני
Qrê is doubtless correct. — **18.** The name of the Edomite is here written דויג
instead of דאג. In pronunciation the two were probably alike. — [נשא אפור בר]
must mean *wearing a linen ephod*. 𝔊 omits בר.* — **19.** The similarity of the
language to 15³ is evident. Editorial insertions of this kind are not uncommon, so that Bu. and Co. are probably right in making the verse to be of
that class. — [לפי חרב] at the end of the verse is lacking in 𝔊 and superfluous.

---

* In addition to what was said above (on 2¹⁸) about linen as the material of
priestly garments in Egypt, it may be noted that in Babylon also the priests and
scribes wore linen clothing. This is pointed out by Gunkel, *Archiv für Religions-
wissenschaft*, I. p. 297.

20, 21. One son of Ahimelech escaped, whose name was Abiathar. His only refuge was with David, and to him he went, and told him *that Saul had slain the priests of Yahweh*] the commentators suppose that Abiathar was left in charge of the Oracle, while the other priests answered Saul's summons. There is nothing of this in the text however, and it is rather surprising that the Oracle is not mentioned in connexion with Abiathar here, and first comes into view in 23⁶. — **22.** David is not surprised at the news : *I knew that day, because Doeg was there, that he would certainly tell Saul.* He therefore accuses himself as accessory : *I am guilty of the lives of thy clan.* — **23.** He encourages Abiathar to stay with him and not fear ; *for whoever seeks thy life must also seek my life*] restoring the probable order of the words. — *For thou art a deposit with me*] the article deposited with one for safekeeping was sacred, and, as we know from an Arabic story, it was defended to the last by the one to whom it was entrusted.

20, 21. The evident point of this narrative is to show how the priest came to be with David instead of with Saul. But to the older view the priest was nothing without the Ephod. There is reason to suspect therefore that the original account of the slaughter of the priests inserted here the words : *and brought the Ephod with him.* The scruples of the later writer omitted the reference to the Ephod, whereupon it was inserted in 23⁶. — אביתר] on the name cf. BDB. and reff. — **22.** The somewhat awkward sentence must be rendered as above. Omitting שב with 𝕲ᴬᴮ, we might also omit the second כי and get simply כי דוע הגד יגיד which would be smoother. — סבתי] must be corrected to חבתי with 𝕲𝕾 Th. and most recent scholars (cf. Dr. *Notes*). — בכל־נפש] 𝕲ᴮ omits כל, whereas 𝕲ᴸ inserts it before בית. — **23.** נפשי and נפשך have become transposed in 𝕳. What David should say for the encouragement of Abiathar is not : *he who seeks my life is also seeking yours*, but : *whoever seeks your life must first take mine.*

XXIII. 1-29. **Saul seeks David.** — David delivers Keilah from the Philistines. Saul purposes to besiege him there. David, warned by the Oracle, leaves the city and dwells in the wilderness. The natives inform Saul, who makes another effort to capture him. At the critical moment however Saul is called away by a Philistine invasion. Between the two attempts, Jonathan visits David and encourages him, and the two make a bond of friendship. The original thread of the narrative has been disturbed by the

P

intrusion of the scene with Jonathan, and there are some minor fragments which seem to be interpolated.

1. The verse seems to connect well with 22². There David was in the stronghold of Adullam with four hundred men. Here he begins to use his power for the relief of his own people when oppressed by the Philistines. David is told: *the Philistines are fighting against Keilah*] a town which is reckoned to Judah, Jos. 15⁴⁴, though David's men had a different notion. If the identification with the present *Kila* be correct, the place lay only three miles south of Adullam. — *And they are plundering the threshing-floors*] a favourite act of robbery in a freebooting society. The treasure of the *fellahin* is easiest carried off at the time of threshing. Later it is apt to be hid in pits or stored in the strongholds. — **2.** David asked of the Oracle: *Shall I go and smite these Philistines?* The author does not deem it necessary here to explain how the Oracle came to be with David, and this is an argument against the originality of v.⁶, at least in the place in which it now stands. The answer to the question is an affirmative. — **3.** David's men however object. In other cases we find them not easy to control. — *Behold we are afraid here in Judah*] the distinction between *Judah* and the territory of *Keilah* is perplexing. Possibly Keilah was tributary to the Philistines, so that David's men thought of it as Philistine territory. On the other hand Keilah, like Carmel, may have been reckoned to Caleb or one of the other clans not yet absorbed in Judah. *How much more if we go to Keilah against the army of the Philistines!* The argument is *a fortiori*. — **4.** David therefore repeats his inquiry of the Oracle and receives a direct command and a promise: *Rise, go down to Keilah, for I give the Philistines into thy hand.* — **5.** In accordance with the command, *David and his men went to Keilah and fought against the Philistines, and drove away their cattle*] which they had brought in order to carry off the plundered grain. ⅁ᴮ inserts *they fled before him* before the last clause. In any case, *he delivered* the inhabitants of Keilah.

6. The verse is obviously displaced. Designed as it is, to show how David could consult Yahweh, it ought to come earlier. Or, if the author supposed the former response to have been given in some other way than by the Ephod, then the proper place for this verse is later, after v.⁹. The text has suffered in transmission, but may be plausibly restored so as to give the following meaning: *And when Abiathar son of Ahimelech fled to David, he came down to Keilah with the Ephod in his hand*] Keilah was the place to which he came down and he brought the Ephod, — these are data supplementary to the account of the slaughter of the priests.

1. קעילה] cf. Buhl, *Geog.* p. 193, who refers to the Tell-el-Amarna letters, *ZDPV.* XIII. 142; Guérin, *Judée,* III. 341 ff; GAS., *Geog.* p. 230. — **2.** האלך] the direct question is put to the Oracle as in the cases already noted. — **3.** אל־מערכת הפ׳] is perhaps an expansion. The original form of 𝕲 seems to have read simply *to Keilah of the Philistines* (pointed out by We.). The fact that מערכות does not correctly describe a plundering expedition need not weigh very heavily. David's men would naturally state the case strongly. — **4.** נתן] the participle is used of the immediate future, as frequently. — **5.** ואנשיו Qrê, is to be preferred. 𝕲ᴸ makes the order this: he *fought,* they *fled,* he *slew,* and *drove off the cattle.* — **6.** The commentators all remark on the impossibility of אפר ירד בידו. The simplest explanation of it seems to be that the first two words have been transposed. By inserting a ו we get a fairly good sense: קעילה ירד ואפור בידו. This is the actual text of 𝕲ᴸ and it calls attention to the fact that the place at which Abiathar found David was *Keilah,* and that the Ephod which is commanded a little later is the one from Nob.

7. Saul on hearing of David's place of sojourn said to himself: *God has sold him into my hand, for he has entrapped himself in coming into a city of doors and bars*] the king with a superior force would shut him in his cage as Sennacherib boasted afterwards that he had done to Hezekiah. — **8.** The royal summons was sent out and the whole people mustered *to besiege David and his men.* — **9.** David on hearing of the muster of the militia *knew that it was against him*] and not the Philistines as was ostensibly given forth (we may suppose) *that Saul was carving out an evil*] and he therefore prepares to consult God. — **10.** David recites the occasion of his anxiety. — **11.** The text of 𝕳 is evidently in disorder. The question at the opening of the verse receives no answer and is repeated later. Omitting it, we get: *Will Saul come down as thy servant has heard? Yahweh, God of Israel, tell thy servant!* To this question an affirmative answer is given. — **12.** The second question — *Will the burghers of Keilah give me*

and my men into the hand of Saul? — also receives an affirmative.
— **13.** David and his men *left Keilah, and wandered hither and
thither*] in consequence of which Saul abandoned his expedition.
The ingratitude of the men of Keilah is the subject of animad-
version by Schm., but the better part of valour is discretion, and
the town may not have been able to stand a siege. Whether it
owed allegiance to Saul however may well be doubted. — **14.** The
verse reads like a summing up of the history, so far as relates to
this part of David's life. It may have concluded the account of
his wanderings in one of the documents : *So David dwelt in the
Wilderness*] the Wilderness of Judah is meant, overhanging the
western shore of the Dead Sea. — *And Saul sought him continually, but Yahweh did not give him into his hand.* The allusion to
the Wilderness of Ziph is an intrusion.

7. נכר] gives no meaning proper to this context : *Deus abalienavit men-
tem ab eo* (Schm., p. 773) is without parallel. 𝕋𝔏 and the Jewish expositors
make the word mean *to deliver over*, but without support. 𝔊 has πέπρακεν,
evidently reading מכר, a verb often used of God's *handing over* his own into
the power of their enemies, Dt. 32³⁰ Jd. 2¹⁴ 3⁸ I S. 12⁹. It is safer to restore
this word, for which we have direct evidence, than to conjecture something
else. For סַגַּר Bu. adduces the following נסגר, which however, as Dr. points
out, argues the other way. If מסר were a good Hebrew word it would
exactly fit the place. — דלתים ובריח] the two gates locked by one great bar
across them. Probably small towns had but one entrance. — **8.** וישמע] cf.
15⁴. — לצור] a few MSS. have לצוד. But צור is the proper word for besieging
a fortress. — **9.** מחריש] the verb occurs in the Qal, Prov. 3²⁹ 6¹⁴, in the sense
of *planning*, as here. Saul was *brewing* evil is an English equivalent. Still
it is possible that the text is not sound. — **10.** לעיר] for the direct object. Dr.
cites a few instances, but possibly העיר should be read. — **11.** היסגירני ב'ק' בירו]
is in place in v.¹² where we find it repeated. A part of it is lacking in 𝔊 so
that the conjecture of We. is probable — that the whole was lacking in 𝔊, but
that owing to another error of that text היסגרני was inserted later. 𝔖 omits
all but the one question : *Will the Burghers of Keilah deliver me and my men
into the hand of Saul?* The reading of We. is adopted by Bu., who however
inserts ועתה from 𝔊. A scribe got the second question in the wrong place,
and left it there without erasure. From ירד at the end of the verse 𝔊ᴮ omits
to the last word of v.¹²; a clear case of homeoteleuton; the eye of the scribe
fell upon the second ויאמר יהוה instead of the first. 𝔊ᴸ has inserted the missing words though retaining the wrong reply to the first question. — **13.** כשש
מאות] where 𝔊 has *about four hundred.* It is difficult to decide between
them. 𝔊 may have been conformed to the statement in 22². — ויתהלכו באשר
יתהלכו] a genuine Semitic expression, cf. Koran 53¹⁶ : "Then covered the

Sidra tree that which covered it." — **14.** וישב בהר במדבר־זיף] is superfluous, and in fact contradicts the immediately preceding clause. Without this, the verse concludes an account of David's wandering. The clause originally stood at the opening of the next adventure, v.¹⁹.

15–18. Jonathan's visit. The verses are a distinct insertion. — **15.** *David feared because Saul had come out to seek him*] the sentence can refer only to some particular expedition of Saul, and therefore does not fit the immediately preceding statement which affirms Saul's continuous persecution. No more does it belong after v.¹³, which tells that David escaped. — *And David was then in the wilderness of Ziph*] the name still survives in *Tell Ziph* (GAS. *Geog.* p. 306 ; Buhl, *Geog.* p. 163), south from Hebron. Whether the *Horesha* of this passage is identical with *Khoreisa*, as suggested by Conder, is not certain. — **16.** Jonathan came to Horesha and *encouraged David in God*] by assurances of the divine protection. — **17.** Not only should David be protected from Saul, but he should also attain the kingdom, Jonathan contenting himself with the second place. — **18.** The *covenant* made is parallel to the two already spoken of, 18³ 20⁸.

15. The verse seems based on 26³. The author of the secondary account took a hint from the second clause of that verse, and built upon it a further instance of Jonathan's fidelity. — וירא] is intended (Ew., *GVI*³. III. p. 127, E. Tr. III. p. 92). David's *fear* is the proper introduction to Jonathan's consolation. — בחרשה] other cases of the preposition with the *He locale* are cited by Dr. In the following verse however חרשה seems quite clearly to be a proper name (so Kl., Bu., Ki.). *Wooded heights* do not exist in the Wilderness of Judah and probably never did exist there. The identification with *Khoreisa* seems to be adopted by GASmith and Buhl. Kl. supposes it to be the same with the יער חרת, 22⁵. — **16.** ויחזק את־ידו] cf. Jer. 23¹⁴ Ezek. 13²² Job 4³. — **17.** למשנה] cf. 2 Chr. 28⁷ Esth. 10³.

19–29. A narrow escape. — The Ziphites offer to conduct Saul to David. Saul therefore comes with a large force and has David and his men within his grasp. But at the critical moment he is called away by an invasion of the Philistines. The story is a local legend designed to explain the origin of the name given to one of the rocks in the region.

19. The verse continues ¹⁴ᵃ in its original form. The second half, however, is superfluous, and restoring the connexion we should read: *David dwelt in strongholds in the Wilderness of Ziph, and the Ziphites came to Saul and said: Is not David hiding himself in our region in strongholds?* Had they given the exact location, as now defined in the rest of the verse, it would have been unnecessary for Saul to urge them to discover David's hiding-place. — **20.** *And now according to thy heart's desire to come down, O king, come down; and it shall be our part to deliver him into the hand of the king*] possibly David's presence was burdensome, as it was felt to be by Nabal. — **21.** Saul expresses his gratitude because they have *taken compassion* on him. — **22.** He exhorts them: *Give attention still, and know the place where his foot rests!* The text cannot be called certain. According to 𝔥, a reason is added: *For I am told he is very cunning.* — **23.** The exhortation of the preceding verse is repeated in substance and Saul concludes: *Then I will go with you, and if he be in the land, I will search him out among all the thousands of Judah.* — **24.** The Ziphites went in advance of Saul at a time when David and his men were in the *Wilderness of Maon*] the place is mentioned along with Carmel and Ziph in Jos. 15⁵⁵, and still bears the name *Ma'in*. As the next verse tells that David on hearing of Saul's incursion *went and dwelt* in the Wilderness of Maon, there is reason to suspect the integrity of the text. — *In the Arabah to the south of Jeshimon*] is in fact sufficiently explicit. — **25.** *David went down to the crag which is in the Wilderness of Maon.* The idea seems to be that he fled down the mountain side without attempting a defence. — **26.** Saul was in hot pursuit — *David was going in hasty flight from Saul, and Saul and his men were about to fly upon David and his men, to seize hold of them*] the providential interference came just at the right moment. — **27, 28.** Saul is called off by the news of a Philistine invasion, and the place receives the name: *Rock of Divisions*. — **29.** The verse forms the transition to the following. *Engedi* is a well-known oasis in the wilderness of Judah, on the west shore of the Dead Sea.

19. As the verse stands it gives David's location tautologically: *in strongholds, in Horesha, in the Hill of Hachila*] but the indefinite *strongholds* is the only word which fits the situation, and it, as well as Saul's reply, is contradicted by the more exact locations which follow. These also seem inconsistent with each other unless we suppose Horesha to be located on the Hill of Hachila, which is unnatural. We are obliged therefore to strike out as later insertion all that follows במצדות. The last clause was put in under the influence of 26[1] and הריעה was inserted to reconcile this with the preceding. The location of the Hill of Hachila here however is given as *south* of the desert, whereas in 26[1] it is apparently east of it; cf. v.[14] (We.). — ההכילה] occurs only here and in 26[1. 3] (Glaser restores it by conjecture in 15[7] for חוילה); some copies have הכילה.—הישימן] is used of the Desert of Judah here and 26[1. 3], cf. Num. 21[20]. For a description cf. GAS., *Geog.* p. 313; also Robinson, *BR*[2]. I. p. 500 f. — **20.** לכל-אות] elsewhere בכל אות. Here we should expect בכל. For ולנו 𝔊 seems to have read אלינו connecting it with what precedes. ועלינו would be the regular form to express what we need in this context. — **21.** חמלתם] confirms the emendation made in 22[8]. — **22.** הכינו] supply לב, 1 Chr. 12[14]. The ellipsis does not occur elsewhere however, and perhaps we should read הבינו, De Rossi, with 6 MSS. Some editions prefix י. — וראו וודעו] one of the two words is superfluous, and 𝔊[B] has only ידעו. The words מי ראהו שם are inappropriate; Saul is not concerned with the particular man who shall discover David but with the discovery only. Besides, we should at least emend מי to ומי. 𝔊 has ἐν τάχει ἐκεῖ, on the ground of which Th. following a hint of Ew. reads המהרה — 'where his *fleeting* foot may be.' But the adjective is uncalled for. Ki. reads מהרה as an adverb: *know quickly*, but the order of the words renders this impossible. What the sense requires is a participle defining the condition of the subject — *where his foot is staying*. The original may have been רגיעה., cf. Is. 34[14], or מהלונו, Ps. 91[1]. But there is reason to suspect that the corruption is deeper, and that Saul really said: *spy out* (רגלו) *his resting-place* cunningly, because he is very sly. Something like this seems required by the concluding part of the verse. — כי אמר] *for one says* is perfectly good Hebrew. But it is surprising that Saul should give David's character by hearsay, so that this part of the verse also seems to have suffered in transmission. 𝔊 reads οὗ εἴπετε (εἴπατε) connecting with what precedes: *hasten where you say* (*he is*), adding *lest he play you a trick.* — **23.** The verse is so nearly a repetition of the preceding, that Kl. takes it to be an insertion from a different document. More probably it has been expanded by a scribe. 𝔊[B] omits מכל . . . אל-נכון, and what remains gives a satisfactory sense. — אל-נכון] probably we should read על (as so often). They were to return *resting on a certainty.* — מעון] identified by Robinson. The village lies not far south of Carmel. In this place 𝔊[L] has τῇ ἐπηκόῳ and Houbigant * conjectures therefore שמעון. But as the Ziphites were active in the matter, the Wilderness of Maon is appropriate enough.—בערבה] must mean in the valley of the Dead Sea. As the Jordan valley is called the Arabah, and the same valley extends south of the Dead Sea, this makes no difficulty. On Jeshimon cf. Num. 21[20] 23[28] and Dillmann's note. — **25.** לבקש] read לבקש with 𝔊𝕷𝕿 (Th.). — וישב] is inappropriate. 𝔊 had אשר which is evidently original (Th.). — **26.** שאול] add ואנשיו with 𝔊. — נחפז] cf. 2 K. 7[15] Kt. David was *putting himself into a*

---

* Cf. Josephus, *Ant.* VI. 280 (Niese, II. p. 54), ἐν τῇ Σίμωνος ἐρήμῳ.

panic in getting away. — עטרים] which is used of *protecting*, Ps. 5¹³, seems inappropriate here, so that the conjecture of Kl. who reads עטים is acceptable. — **28.** מרדף] on the Daghesh (Baer and Ginsb.) cf. Ges.²⁶ 22 *s.* — סלע המחלקה] the expositors are divided between the interpretations *Rock of Divisions* and *Rock of Escape*. The latter would be more appropriate if חלק could mean *to escape;* but this seems not to be the case. — **29.** The division of chapters and verses differs in the different editions, and Baer begins the next chapter with this verse — as do the majority of editions in circulation. Engedi still bears the name *Ain Jidi*, Robinson, *BR²*. I. p. 504, GAS. *Geog*. p. 269. For the older authorities, Reland, *Palaestina*, p. 763.

XXIV. 1–22. David's magnanimity. — Saul comes into David's power, but is spared and recognizes the generosity of his enemy.

The incident is similar to the one narrated in 26. In both cases Saul is at the mercy of David, and in danger of being slain except for David's restraint of his men. In both, David's motive is reverence for the Anointed of Yahweh. In the second of the two accounts, David makes no allusion to having spared Saul before, and Saul is equally silent. We have reason to think, therefore, that we have two versions of the same story. It is natural to suppose that one belongs with each of the two documents which make up the bulk of the narrative already considered. Almost the only clue to the relation of one of these stories to the other is that in this chapter Saul is brought into David's power, whereas in 26 David takes upon himself the danger of going into the enemy's camp. The slight preponderance of probability seems to me to be on the side of the latter representation (chapter 26) as more original.

1. As remarked above, the editions vary in the division of chapters. The only ones which agree with Ginsburg in making the dividing line the space which indicates a *Parasha*, are the very correct edition printed at Mantua 1742, and those printed by Plantin. I have followed this notation with the idea that Ginsburg's edition is likely to be widely current. — **2.** The force of *three thousand men* which Saul took with him reminds us of the standing army which he recruited at the beginning of his career, 13². The *Wild-goat's Crags*, on the face of which he sought David, are not yet identified, but the ibex (*bedn*) is still found in the region. — **3.** The *sheep folds* to which Saul came were possibly caves with a rough stone wall about the entrance, such as are still found in the

Wilderness of Judah.   Into one of these caves Saul went *to relieve
himself*, cf. Jd. 3²⁴, where the same euphemism is used as here.
This cave, however, was the one in which David and his men had
taken refuge.   They would naturally be unseen by Saul as he came
in from the daylight.   We need not insist that the whole of David's
force was in the one cave. — **4–7**.   The narrative does not follow
the natural order, and is perhaps interpolated. — **4**.   David's men
remind him of a promise of God : *This is the day of which Yahweh said: Behold I give thine enemy into thy hand, and thou shalt
do to him as thou pleasest.*   No such promise is recorded in the
preceding narrative.   The author probably had in mind later prophetic declarations.   According to the present text, David, without
replying to his men, secretly approached the king, *and cut off the
skirt of his mantle.* — **5**.   The feeling that his action was an indig-
nity gave him a twinge of conscience. — **6**.   The verse continues
the conversation between David and his men with no reference to
the skirt. — **7**. *So David restrained his men*]   the exact verb
intended is doubtful, see the critical note.

2. היעלים] cf. Buhl, *Geog.* p. 97 *note*.   𝔊ᴸ has τῆς θήρας τῶν ἐλάφων,
which possibly points to צור היעלים. — **3.** להסך] Ginsb. gives להסיך as the
reading of the Massora.   The phrase here used is found in only one other
passage, but the meaning seems clear.   A call of nature is the only adequate
reason for the King's going alone and unattended into a cave. 𝔊 also
speaks euphemistically, but Aq. rendered ἀποκενῶσαι (Theod. *Questiones*), and
Josephus describes Saul as ἐπειγόμενος ὑπὸ τῶν κατὰ φύσιν, with which compare *ut purgaret ventrem* 𝔏, and צורכיה למעבד 𝕮.   Only 𝔖 (which makes Saul
sleep) breaks the consensus of the ancient authorities. — בירכתי] indicates
a cave with branching recesses. — וישביב] describes the position in which
David's men were at Saul's entrance — they were *sitting down* in the recesses
of the cave (Dr.). — **4–7**.   According to the received text the order is as follows: (1) David's men point out his opportunity; (2) David rises and cuts
off Saul's skirt; (3) he repents of it; (4) he then replies to his men; (5) he
restrains them from bloodshed.   This is obviously an unnatural order, and Co.
and Bu. rearrange the clauses in the order ⁴ᵃ· ⁶· ⁷ᵃ· ⁴ᵇ· ⁵· ⁷ᵇ·   The narrative then
reads smoothly enough.   But it is difficult to see how the dislocation took
place.   It cannot be intentional, for there is no motive for it; the accidents
of transmission do not generally work in this way.   It seems simpler to suppose that the corruption has come in as so often by interpolation.   The earlier
account made no mention of David's cutting off Saul's skirt.   The fact that
Saul had been in David's power was sufficiently evident by their having been
in the cave together.   A later writer wanted more tangible evidence and so

introduced the incident of the skirt. Verse [7] joins directly to [4a], and what is between has been inserted. Verse [11] is inserted by the same hand and is as readily spared as [4b–6]. — 4. היום אשר] it would be grammatically correct to translate: *this is the day when Yahweh says*, in which case Yahweh speaks by his providential delivery of Saul into David's hand, and there is no reference to a prediction made at an earlier time. But it is unnecessary to describe Yahweh as *speaking* by such a providence, and the following words הנה אנכי נתן are in the regular prophetic form. I have therefore supposed such a reference here. The other view is defended by Dr., *Notes*. איבך *Qrê*, is correct. — 5. את־כנף] should have the article or be defined by a genitive. Th. proposes to insert המעיל. 𝔊 however reads τῆς διπλοΐδος αὐτοῦ instead of אשר לשאול, and the latter is suspicious from its conformity to v.[4]. Restore therefore את כנף מעילו. — 6. הלילה לי מיהוה] so in 26[11] I K. 21[3]. — 7. ויסע] the verb means to *rend* or *tear*, Jd. 14[6]. Even if we suppose a figure of speech, the action described by such a figure is too violent for the situation. 𝔊 καὶ ἔπεισεν may point to וישבע as conjectured by Cappellus (*Critica Sacra*, p. 330); it might also represent וישקט which would be appropriate here. Bu. proposes וימנע, citing 25[26. 34] which are not strictly parallel.

8. The verse division should be made to include the last clause of the preceding : *And when Saul rose from the cave and went on the road, David arose after him and went out*. As Saul turned at his call, David did the customary obeisance by prostration. — **9.** David's expostulation assumes that Saul is under the influence of evil advisers who slanderously say : *David seeks thy hurt*. — **10.** In contrast to this is the present experience : *To-day thine eyes see that Yahweh gave thee into my hand in the cave, but I refused to kill thee*] and the refusal is motived by his relation to Saul as his lord and as the Anointed of Yahweh. — **11.** David calls attention to the skirt as evidence ; *I have not sinned against thee though thou art aiming at my life, to take it*] repayment of evil with good. As already shown the verse must stand or fall with [4b–6]. — **12.** He leaves his cause in the hands of God, reiterating his refusal to lay his hand upon Saul. — **13.** The introduction of such a proverb as we here find is particularly infelicitous, for it intimates that the wickedness of Saul would be his destruction. There is good ground therefore for suspecting the verse to be an interpolation. — **14.** The unworthiness of Saul's effort is seen in the insignificance of the object. David compares himself to *a dead dog*, cf. 2 S. 9[8], or to *a flea*. — **15.** A prayer for vindication at the hands of Yahweh.

8. אחרי־כן] should apparently be אחריו as read by 𝔊^AB, and we should possibly omit ויצא with 𝔊^B. The reading of 𝔊^L is considerably shorter than either of the others — καὶ ἐξῆλθε Δαυὶδ ἐκ τοῦ σπηλαίου ὀπίσω Σαοὺλ λέγων omitting from one ὀπίσω to the other. — **10.** ראו עיניך] Saul's eyes had not seen anything in the cave, but the appearance of David made clear what his situation had been. We should retain the text therefore, instead of changing to ראה בעיניך with 𝔖. — ואמר] is irregular as pointed out by Th., We., Dr. The emendation to ואמאן suggested by We. on the ground of καὶ οὐκ ἠβουλήθην commends itself. Ki. adheres to 𝔐 translating *man sprach mir zu*, but the tense is wrong. 𝔏 reads ואמר = *and I thought to kill thee;* but it is scarcely possible that David would confess an intention of this kind. — ורהם] evidently requires עיני to be expressed as is actually done by 𝔏. On the ground of 𝔊 however we may restore ואהם (We.); the similarity of א and ה in the old-Hebrew alphabet is remarked upon by Ginsburg, *Introd.* p. 291. — **11.** ואבי] is curiously connected by 𝔊^L with the preceding: he is the Anointed of Yahweh *and my father.* 𝔊^B reads simply καὶ ἰδοὺ τὸ πτερύγιον. The diffuseness of this verse is an argument for its later insertion. What David wished to impress was sufficiently evident without so many words. — צדה] only here and Ex. 21^13. It there means *to intend* a thing. — **13.** The proverb of the ancients here introduced seems to mean that the destruction of the wicked will come from themselves — ' his violence shall come down upon his own head.' A reader might find this appropriate to Saul and insert it in the margin, whence it came into the text. We can hardly suppose the original author, who makes David show such deep respect for Saul, to put such an intimation into David's mouth. — הקדמני] should probably be plural — the following word begins with מ. — בך] should be בו which form alone is appropriate to the proverb. — **14.** The exaggerated humility with which David here speaks seems to me secondary, as compared with the vigorous language of 26^2). — **15.** וישפטני] in the meaning of freeing from one's enemies, as was done by the liberators of Israel in the Book of Judges.

16. Saul, overcome with emotion, *wept aloud* in oriental fashion. — **17.** Saul confesses that David is more righteous, in that he has repaid good for evil. — **18.** The present example is conspicuous proof : *To-day thou hast done great good to me in that Yahweh shut me up into thy hand and thou didst not kill me*] all David's acts towards Saul had been good, but this was the greatest. — **19.** Such an act is almost unheard of — *what man will find his enemy and send him on a good path?* Saul therefore predicts : *Yahweh will reward thee good for the good deed which thou hast done to me.* — **20.** Saul confesses his conviction that David is to come to the kingdom. — **21.** He therefore adjures David not to cut off his seed after him ; *and that thou wilt not destroy my name* *from my clan*] the blotting out of one's name by the destruction of his children was the gravest calamity, 2 S. 14⁷. — **22.** With David's compliance the interview ended ; *Saul went to his house and David and his men went up to the stronghold.*

16. דוד . . . ויאמר] is suspected by Bu. and is in fact doubtful. The same words occur in 26¹⁷ where they are in place and are followed by David's answer. — **18.** ואת *Kt.*] ואתה *Qrê.* — והגרת] the conjectural emendation of Kl. to והגדלת is accepted by Bu., Ki., and gives a much better sense : *To-day thou hast done the greatest thing which thou hast done to me in the way of good, namely* (את אשר): *Yahweh delivered me into thy hand,* etc. — **19.** וישלחו] is usually assumed to be a question and Dr. compares Ezek. 15⁵ᵇ. It seems easier however to emend with Kl., reading ומי instead of וכי (cf. 𝔏 *quis enim*), striking out איש. Otherwise we must assume an anacoluthon : *When a man finds his enemy and sends him on a good path — Yahweh will reward thee.* The author in this case intended to say : *Yahweh will reward him,* but changed the construction. — תחת היום הזה] is possible, but the following clause is difficult. We should probably read תחת הטוב הזה with Kl. — **20, 21.** These verses with the first three words of ²² are coloured by Bu. as a very late insertion (cf. ⋏.S. p. 229). The idea of this author however that David was to come to the kingdom might readily express itself by the mouth of Saul in this way.

XXV. 1. This notice of the death of Samuel has no connexion with what precedes or with what follows, but is duplicated in 28³. It may have followed immediately on 19¹⁸⁻²⁴ in a life of Samuel. The history as thus reconstructed told of David's preservation by the Spirit of Prophecy which fell upon Saul, and added that soon after that experience Samuel died, so that David took refuge in the Wilderness. Samuel was buried *in his house,* cf. 1 K. 2³⁴ (perhaps also 2 K. 21¹⁸ originally). Though other specific statements to this effect are not found, it is possible that burial in one's house was not uncommon. The fact that the sepulchres of the kings of Israel were in the palace (Ezek. 43⁷⁻⁹) would favour this view. There is a statement to the effect that the alleged bones of Samuel were transferred to Constantinople, A.D. 406. — *The wilderness of Paran* to which David is said to have gone is the extreme southern end of the Arabah. The historical improbability of David's going so far into the wilderness is not a sufficient reason for changing the text.

1. Schmid cites Serarius and Sanctius concerning the translation of Samuel's bones to Constantinople. He himself of course rejects that which the credulous and superstitious accept. — [מדבר פארן] known as the seat of Ishmael, Gen. 21²¹ and one of the stations of the Wandering, Nu. 10¹² 12¹⁶. On the ground of Μαάν 𝕲ᴮ most editors are disposed to emend to מעון here. But the change to this from the other on the ground of the next verse is more probable than the reverse.

XXV. 2–44. David and Nabal. — David takes the occasion of a festival, to ask a contribution from a wealthy Calebite named Nabal. His messengers are churlishly sent away empty, and David in his wrath vows to destroy the man and his family. Nabal's wife Abigail, on being informed of the way in which the messengers have been treated, suspects that mischief is brewing. Hastily taking a generous present she rides to meet David whom she pacifies. A few days later Nabal dies and David makes Abigail his wife.

The story presents a vivid picture of life in the land of Judah. It seems to be drawn from the source from which in subsequent chapters we have David's family history. The interest of the author is not in David's method with the wealthy sheep owners, but in the way he got a wife, and in the kind of wife he got. The connexion with what goes before is not plain, but as there is no trace in it of the persecution by Saul, we may suppose that it once followed directly on 23¹⁴, where the author disposes of Saul (so far as his history is concerned) by remarking that he sought David continually but that God did not deliver him into his hand. The close of the narrative joins directly to 27¹.

2–13. The provocation. — The situation is described : *There was a man in Maon*] a locality already mentioned 23²⁴ ; *whose business was in Carmel*] the only business which can be carried on in the region is that of the shepherd. Carmel, still bearing the name *Kurmul,* is directly south of Ziph. Nabal was wealthy in flocks, and at this particular time *he was engaged in shearing his flocks at Carmel*] the sheep shearing was a festival, like the harvest and the vintage. At such a time a large hospitality was customary ; the Sheikhs of the Bedawin still count on the generosity of the sheep masters (Robinson, *BR²*. I. p. 498). — **3.** The characters of the man and his wife are contrasted : *The woman was sensible and comely, but the man was rough and ill behaved*] as is borne out by the story. By race he was a *Calebite,* of the clan which possessed Hebron and the surrounding country. Apparently the clan still counted itself independent of Judah. — **4, 5.** *David heard in the wilderness* — perhaps in Horesha, 23¹⁵ — and sent ten men with a demand for protection money. The demand was entirely correct in form, bearing David's greeting — *ask him of his welfare in my name.* — **6.** The greeting is set forth at large, though the introductory words are obscure. — **7.** The basis of a claim is found in David's behaviour. He had refused to exercise the right of the strongest: *Thy shepherds were with us, and we did not jeer at them*] that the soldiers in such circumstances should refrain from provoking a conflict by biting words was an extraordinary instance of self-control. — *And nothing of theirs was missing*] scarcely less remarkable. — **8.** David's messengers appeal to the testimony of Nabal's own men, and to the fact that they have come *on a feast day*, and ask a present *for thy son David.* — **9.** The messengers deliver the message in the name of David. — **10.** Nabal's reply is an insulting one : *Who is David? And who is the Son of Jesse? Many are the slaves in these days who break away, each from his master*] the justice of the taunt in relation to many of David's followers gave it its sting. — **11.** Sarcastic reply to the request : *And I must take my bread and my wine and my flesh, which I have slain for my shearers, and give it to men of whom I do not know whence they are!* The answer is sufficiently plain. — **12, 13.** David's messengers bring their report, and David prepares to avenge the insult. Four hundred men are to go with him *and two hundred remained with the baggage*] an arrangement made also at a later time, 30¹⁰.

2. ואיש] we expect ויהי איש, and a case analogous to the text is difficult to discover. מעשה is used of the flocks and herds, the shepherd's *work*, as it is used of the crops — the *work* of the farmer, Ex. 23¹⁶. Similarly פעלה of the shepherd's flock, Is. 40¹⁰. — כרמל] on the site, Robinson, *BR²*. I. p. 495 f., GAS., *Geog.* p. 306, Buhl, *Geog.* p. 163. — גדול] *of great wealth*, like Barzillai 2 S. 19³³. — **3.** נבל] the word is not quite such a nickname as we think from the translation *fool*. It means *reckless* (cf. Is. 32⁶), and might be accepted as a compliment by a man like Nabal. — אביגיל] 𝔊 tries to make the word more euphonious by softening it to *Abigaia*. — קשה] Is. 19⁴ 2 S. 3³⁹. כלבו *Kt.* : כלבי *Qrê*. The former is possibly an attempt to be witty — *he was like* or *the name* was like (Kl.) *his heart ;* with an allusion to the well-known proverb ' as he thinketh in his heart.' The *Qrê* is doubtless right. ⑤ ἄνθρωπος κυνικός. On the clan Caleb cf. Moore, *Judges*, p. 30. — **6.** לחי] is unintelligible. The punctuators intend it to represent לְאֶחָי : *to my brethren*. But Nabal alone is addressed, so that we should at least make it a singular, *to my brother*. Even then the sentence is awkward and there is reason to suspect corruption, especially as the following ו is superfluous. The versions seem to have had no different reading. I suspect that כה is a corruption of לו (or רה) and that in לחי we have the חי or clan, to which I would join the ו from the next word, making ואמרתם לו ולהיו : *and you shall say to him and to his clan*. The whole sept would be gathered for the shearing. Houbigant suggests : ואמרתם כה לו אחי ארה. " R. Sal. et R. Levi: *sic fiat tibi post annum incolumi*. D. Kimchi: *sic fiat tibi per omnem vitam*. Et pro se citat *Chaldaeum*. Magis placet Tremellius, qui vertit post Luther : *Et dicite ei, si incolumis est*. Forte sic : *Et dicetis sic : Vivo* (h. e. Deo vivo vitae nostrae Domino te commendo) : *ut tu sit salvus*." Schm. p. 827. The embarrassment of the commentators is evident. — **7.** לא] read ולא with ⑤ℭℨ. The ו at the end of the preceding word is the occasion of the error. — הכלמנום] on the pointing cf. Ges.²⁵ 53 *p*. — **8.** יום טוב] elsewhere of a festival, Esth. 8¹⁷ and also in post-Biblical Hebrew. Cf. also מועדים טובים, Zech. 8¹⁹. — בנו] with loss of the א, Ges.²⁶, 72 *o*. — לעברידך ולבנך] ⑤ has only τῷ υἱῷ σου, which seems most appropriate. — **9.** וינוחו] most naturally means *and rested* from their weariness. Undoubtedly a considerable journey in the desert is presupposed, so that we may retain the reading. ⑤ reads ויקם and connects with the following, ⑤ᴸ giving the right order : καὶ ἀνεπήδησε Ναβὰλ καὶ ἀπεκρίθη. From the character given to Nabal we might expect some manifestation of anger, cf. 20³⁴, so that much may be said for this reading. — **10.** עברים] the article is necessary and is found in ⑤. — המתפרצים] perhaps, as Kl. suggests, *who play the robber*. — **11.** מימי] is scarcely possible. Water was indeed a scarce commodity in the desert. But David hardly expected his men to bring it to him from Nabal. Read with ⑤ ייני. Abigail did in fact take wine as part of her present.

14–19. Abigail's prompt action. — She was informed by one of the shepherd lads : *David sent messengers from the Wilderness to greet our master and he flew at them*] with insulting words. — **15, 16.** The claim of David as to his forbearance towards Nabal and his protection of the flocks is verified. His men had been *a wall* to the flocks against marauders. — **17.** The situation is critical, *for evil is determined upon our master*] cf. 20⁹. All depends upon Abigail, for it is impossible to approach Nabal : *he is such a son of Belial that one cannot speak to him*] the evil temper of the man makes him a terror to his household. — **18.** The hint was sufficient and the prudent woman took from the abundant stores provided for the shearers a substantial present for David.

Besides bread and wine, there were *five roasted sheep*] Gen. 18⁷˙ ⁸,
five measures of parched grain] 17¹⁷, *a hundred bunches of raisins
and two hundred cakes of figs*] that the bunches of raisins were
counted is evident from 2 S. 16¹. — **19.** The present was sent on
before, as in the case of Jacob's meeting with Esau, to make a
favourable impression.

14. הגיד] *had told* while the messengers were returning to David. — נער־
אחד מהנערים] is redundant. 𝕲 omits נער. (𝕲ᴸ has a double translation
of מהנערים). The conjecture of Kl. adopted by Bu. is attractive (reading
מהרעים). — ויעט בהם] means *he flew upon them* as the bird of prey swoops
upon its victim. Whether this fits the context is doubtful, for the anger of
Nabal could scarcely be compared to the eagerness of a rapacious bird. All
endeavours to correct the text are however unsatisfactory; καὶ ἐξέκλινεν ἀπ'
αὐτῶν 𝕲 implies ויט מהם. But Nabal had used insulting words as well as
turned from them. 𝔖𝕿 seem to render ויקט בהם, cf. Ps. 95¹⁰ = *and he was
disgusted at them*. But it was Nabal's expression of his feeling (not the feeling
itself) that gave offence. Of the conjectures, perhaps the best is ויבעט בהם
= *and he kicked at them*, cf. 2²⁹ Dt. 32¹⁵ (Tanch. cited by Th.). — **15.** בהיותנו
בשדה] 𝕲 prefixes καί and joins to the next verse. But the close of that verse
again gives a time determination, so that we must retain the reading of 𝕳. —
17. אל־אדנינו] the preposition should evidently be על. — מדבר] the מן of comparison : *he is more wicked than that one can speak to him ;* too wicked to speak
to. — **18.** אבוגיל and עישוח may show only the ease with which ו and י are inter-
changed, but there is reason to suppose that both are remains of forms once
current, cf. Ges.²⁶ 24 *b* 75 *v.* — סאים] according to Benzinger (*Archaeol.* p. 183 f.)
the *seah* was about twelve litres. The name still survives among the Bedawin
though the size of the measure has shrunk, Doughty, II. p. 113. 𝕲 seems to
have read *ephas* here. — ומאה] καὶ γόμορ ἕν 𝕲. We might expect raisins to
be measured rather than counted, but the reading of 𝕳 is protected by 2 S. 16¹.
We. conjectures that the translators read ומשא here and rendered καὶ γόμον
which is found in one codex (HP 236). — **19.** נבל] lacking in 𝕲ᴮ, should
probably be stricken out.

20. There was no time to spare : *She was riding on the ass,
and coming down the side of a hill while David and his men were
coming down towards her, and she met them*] came upon them
unexpectedly is the natural interpretation. — **21.** Before the meeting David had said : *Only for nought did I guard all that belongs
to this fellow in the Wilderness, so that nothing of his was missing.*
— **22.** As the text stands we read : *God do so to the enemies of
David and more also !* But, as was already seen by Kimchi, it
should be *God do so to David !* A scribe could not think of

David as forswearing himself, and so inserted a word which makes
the imprecation mean just the opposite of what the original narrator said.   A Lapide thinks that David used the language *more
vulgi*, as if most men hesitate to utter imprecations on themselves.
This however is not the case, and the parallel which he urges
(Dan. 4¹⁶) does not hold.   The oath was to the effect that David
would not leave alive of Nabal's household *a single male* — the
not very refined description is used also in 1 K. 14¹⁰ 16¹¹ 21²¹
2 K. 9⁸. — **23.** At the meeting, Abigail *alighted hastily* in order
to show respect, cf. Jd. 1¹⁴, *and fell upon her face before David*]
the customary obeisance to a superior. — **24.** *And she fell at his
feet and said: Upon me be the guilt*] 2 S. 14⁹.   In dissuading
David from carrying out his oath, she would take the responsi-
bility.   So Rebecca assumes the curse which Jacob anticipates,
Gen. 27¹³. — *Let thy maid speak in thine ears*] her humility is in
strong contrast with the arrogance of Nabal. — **25.** *Let not my
Lord give any attention to that good-for-nothing man!* The reason
is that his depravity has, in a sense, deprived him of judgment :
His name is Reckless, and recklessness dwells with him] as his constant companion.   We might paraphrase : " His name is *Brutus*
and he is a *brute*."   This is all that can be said — for herself
she can plead ignorance of David's embassy. — **26.** If the verse
belongs here it is a prediction that David's enemies shall become
like Nabal — equally foolhardy we may suppose — and so run into
destruction. — **27.** She prays that her present may be given to
the young men who accompany David. — **28.** She asks David's
indulgence, on the ground that his future success is assured, since
he *fights the wars of Yahweh*.   The argument is that the successful man can afford to be magnanimous.   The *secure house*
promised to David is his dynasty. — **29.** *And should a man rise
up to pursue thee and to seek thy life, then shall the life of my
Lord be bound in the bundle of the living, in the care of Yahweh
thy God*] the precious things are not left loose to be lost or
destroyed, but are carefully wrapped up and kept together, usually in the inner compartment, under the eye of the careful
housewife.   The reader will recall the ten pieces of silver of
the Gospel parable.   The idea is the same expressed later in
the declaration that the righteous are written in the book of the

Q

living, that is among those destined by God to long life. The
exact contrast is in the second half-verse : *But the life of thine
enemies he shall cast away with a sling*] a modern Jewish imprecation is : *may his life be bound in a bag full of holes*, and
thus quickly lost. The older commentators found in the two
expressions allusions to the future state of the righteous and the
wicked. But it is misleading to translate *nephesh* by the word
soul with our definition of that word. Abigail's view evidently
does not reach beyond the present life. — **30, 31.** The declaration which follows is to the effect that David will be happier in
future days, if he now restrains himself from taking vengeance on
Nabal : *When Yahweh shall have done what he has promised . . .
then thou wilt not have this as a qualm and as a reproach of heart,
that thou hast shed blood for nought, and that thine own hand has
delivered thee*] instead of waiting for the deliverance promised by
God. When that time comes, he will remember Abigail with
gratitude for her present action. — **32–34.** David's reply is a full
recognition of the providential nature of her mission, as well as a
tribute to her discretion. By her action she has *kept him back
from walking into blood-guiltiness*. Had she not acted, the
extermination of Nabal's house would have been complete.

---

20. והיה] has arisen erroneously from the following היא. The tense is
wrong as well as the gender. Read simply והיא (Bu.). — נס־ר] *in the shade
of the mountain* does not seem satisfactory. בסתר 𝕿 gives a good meaning —
on the side — but we have no other trace of a Hebrew word ס־ר in this sense.
𝕃 has *ad radices montis.* — **21.** אך] in the restrictive sense : *only to be deceived* have I done this. — לוה] is used contemptuously as elsewhere. —
22. לאיבי דוד] makes the whole imprecation nonsense. Kimchi says it is
a euphemism for לדוד. Clericus, following Abarbanel, makes the meaning to
be : *may God give David's enemies the wealth of Nabal*, but this is quite contrary to the uniform sense of כה יעשה אלהים. There seems to be no doubt that
the alteration was made to save David from false swearing, or possibly to
save the reader from imprecating a saint. — משתין בקיר] has been much discussed. The question is whether David means that he will not leave alive
a single male, or that he will not leave alive *even a dog*. The latter is favoured
by Isaaki, Kimchi, and A Lapide, as it was earlier by Procopius of Gaza, and
it is adopted by Schm. But it would hardly occur to an oriental to exterminate the dogs about his enemy's village, however natural it may be for a
Roman emperor to threaten the dogs of a besieged city (as was done by
Aurelian in a case cited by Clericus from Bochart). The other interpretation

which makes the words describe *every male* of the threatened family seems to
agree with the passages where the phrase occurs, in all which it is accompanied by words which apply to men and not to animals. Objections which
have been based upon oriental customs seem not to have a basis in fact. The
Targum in translating ידע מדע seems to understand *all who have reached years
of discretion,* while some expositors have taken the phrase in the opposite
sense of *young boys,* others interpreting of the lowest slaves. The question is
discussed at length by Bochart, *Hierozoicon,* I. II. 55. — **23.** [לאפי דוד על־פניה
the phrase has been confused by a scribe; restore על־אפיה (We.). —
24. [ותפל] is lacking in 𝔊ᴮ which makes the clause begin with the preceding
ותשתחו: *and she prostrated herself on the ground at his feet.* Repeated pros-
trations are in order however, and I have retained 𝔐 (Kl., Bu. read with 𝔊:
ותשתחו ארץ על רגליו). — [בי־אני] emphatic repetition of the pronoun, Davidson,
Syntax, § 1. — [העון] at the first blush it seems as if Abigail means to assume
Nabal's guilt. But the parallels, 2 S. 14⁹ Gen. 27¹³, show that the blame
which might fall upon the person addressed is assumed by the speaker, as
the Arab still says: may I be thy ransom! — [ותדבר] the conjunction is omitted by 𝔊𝔖𝔏, and the construction is quite as good without it. 𝔖 omits the
last three words of this verse and the opening words of the next, reading
only: *let thy maid speak in thine ears concerning this man Nabal.* As it is
difficult to see why a translator should thus shorten the text, it is possible that
we have here the earlier form of the sentence. — **25.** [הבליעל] lacking in 𝔖. —
[איש הבליעל] 2 S. 16⁷, cf. 20¹. — [על־נבל] lacking in 𝔊ᴮ, is more likely to be
inserted than to be omitted by a scribe. — **26.** The verse does not fit in the
context and is not clear in itself. It contains an oath of Abigail's, but to what
does she swear? The most natural connexion would be with what precedes:
Thy servant did not know . . . by the life of Yahweh! The strong assurance
that Yahweh had kept David back from bloodshed might perhaps be in place,
though the same theme is treated again in v.³¹ where it is more appropriate.
But even then the concluding part of the verse is enigmatic. Nabal was not
yet dead or stricken in any way. The wish that David's enemies should
become *like Nabal* is entirely premature. Besides this, the use of אשר instead
of כי is awkward and probably points to interpolation. I suspect the original
form of the sentence to have been: חי יהוה אשר מנעך מבוא בדמים . . . יהיו כנבל
איביך וגו׳. This was inserted in the text by a scribe who did not find Abigail's
language vigorous enough, and was itself interpolated by the insertion of the
current וחי נפשך which required the second יהוה. — **27.** ברכה in the same sense
Gen. 33¹¹ Jd. 1¹⁵ 1 S. 30²³. — [הביא] read הביאה. — **28.** The expressions put
into Abigail's mouth are the evident sentiments of one who knew David's
later career. It is not improbable that this extended speech is expanded from
a simpler form. — [בית נאמן] 2⁵⁵ 2 S. 7¹⁶ 1 K. 11³⁸ (all late passages). — מלחמות
יהוה] 18¹⁷. — [מימיך] cf. 1 K. 1⁶ Job 27⁶. — **29.** [ויקם] read וקם— hypothetical
(cf. Dr. *Notes*). — [את יהוה] the bundle is thought of as containing the precious things which the master of the house keeps in his immediate care —
with him. — [בתוך כף הקלע] we should expect the כ of comparison and then מן.

Still it is possible that the sling is thought of as the means of casting away — cast away *using the holder of the sling*, or *sling away with a sling*. — **30.** וצרר [לנגיד] 13[14]. — **31.** [לפוקה] the general intent of the passage is clear, though this word occurs only here. Either לך or לאדני is superfluous, and one must be stricken out. — [ולשפך] read לשפך with 𝕲 and five Heb. MSS. — [ולהושיע] add יד with 𝕲. *That one's own hand should save him*, is a standing phrase, Jd. 7[2]. — **34.** [והבאתי] a mongrel form, having both the preformative of the imperfect, and the ending of the perfect, cf. Ges.[26] 76 *h*, Nestle in *ZATW*. XIV. p. 319. The latter author supposes the form intended to give the reader his choice of two forms; Dr. suggests that it has been influenced by the following לקראתי, which seems to me more probable. — **35.** [ואישא פניך] the phrase is used in a bad sense, to describe the perversion of justice by favouritism. It seems to mean to give any one pleasure by granting his request, and so *to make the downcast face look up*.

36-44. The outcome. — Not long after this, Nabal is smitten by an act of God, and Abigail becomes David's wife. — **36.** Abigail comes home and finds her husband in no condition to receive an important communication — *He had a banquet like a king's and Nabal's heart was merry within him, and he was excessively drunken*] the effect is heightened by the contrast between his hilarity and the danger from which he had just escaped, and also by the contrast between the present revelling and the coming blow. — **37.** In the morning, when he had somewhat recovered from his debauch, the news was told him. — At the shock *his heart died within him and he became stone*] a stroke of paralysis is the natural explanation. — **38.** Ten days later, *Yahweh smote Nabal* with a second stroke which was fatal. — **39.** David recognizes that God has intervened : *Blessed is Yahweh who has pleaded the case of my insult received at the hand of Nabal*] a quarrel between men of the same blood should be referred to an arbitrator. One element of David's rejoicing is that Yahweh has so promptly assumed this office, the other is that *he has kept back his servant from evil*] that is, from violating customary law by shedding Israelitic blood. — **40.** David woos Abigail. Marriage of a widowed person soon after bereavement is still common in the East. — **41.** She is willing to be the lowliest of his servants — *a maid to wash the feet of his slaves.* — **43.** The account of Abigail is finished, but the author adds further information concerning David's family. First, David took *Ahinoam of Jezreel,* not the northern city of the name, but one in Judah. — **44.** In the second place, Michal, his first wife, had been given to *Palti ben Laish, of Gallim.* Saul regarded David's flight as a desertion of his wife, which brought her back under her father's power.

37. Instead of saying *when the wine had gone from Nabal,* 𝕲 renders *when Nabal had recovered from the wine.* — **38.** הימים] should perhaps be ימים, though the writer may have in mind *the* ten days (which actually elapsed in this case) as a known period. — **39.** מיד נבל] is connected with רב by Driver. The other construction חרפתי מיד נבל (preferred by Dr. Weir) seems to me more vigorous. — השיב יהוה בראשו] as in the case of Abimelech, Jd. 9⁵⁶. — וידבר באביגיל] seems to be parallel to Cant. 8⁸. In the latter however it evidently means to speak to a maiden's guardian for her hand. Abigail seems to have had the disposal of her own person. — **42.** ההלכת] the first ה has arisen by erroneous duplication. She *and the ten maids who followed her* did not ride — she rode and they *walked by her side.* — **43.** *Ahinoam* was also the name of Saul's wife, 14⁵⁰. — מיזרעאל] a Jezreel in Judah is mentioned Jos. 15⁵⁶ in the same group with Maon, Carmel, and Ziph. — **44.** There is no intimation that Saul was guilty of aggression in resuming the right to give his daughter to another husband. — פלטי] is פלטיאל in 2 S. 3¹⁵. — ליש] in 2 S. לוש, is rendered 'Aμεíς in 𝕲ᴮ and Iωás in 𝕲ᴸ. — מגלים] the only Gallim mentioned elsewhere, Is. 10³⁰, is evidently in Benjamin. 𝕲ᴮ has 'Ρομμά and 𝕲ᴸ Γολιáθ.

XXVI. Saul in David's power.

— Saul, at the suggestion of the Ziphites, again seeks David. When he is in the immediate neighbourhood, David goes into the camp at night. The whole army is overcome by deep sleep, but he refuses to allow his companion, Abishai, to slay Saul. To show what the situation has been, he carries away the king's spear and cruse of water. Arrived safely at a distance from the camp, he calls to Abner and reproaches him with neglect of duty. Saul recognizes David's voice and at David's expostulation confesses his wrong, after which each goes his way.

The section is obviously parallel to 24. And as there is here no reference to David's *repeated* acts of magnanimity, there is reason to think that both accounts go back to the same original. With this agrees the fact that the Ziphites are active in both. We have no hesitation, therefore, in assuming that one of them stood in one of the two histories of the period, the other in the other. Budde assigns this to E, the other (chap. 24) to J. Of the two, the present one seems to me to be nearer the event, and therefore to belong to the older of the two documents. The nearest historical parallel is Gideon's visit to the camp of the Midianites, Jd. 7[9-15], which is assigned by competent authorities to J.

XXVI. The identification of the narrative with E seems in this instance especially precarious. Budde (*RS.* 228) gives only the following marks: מרגלים which he does not allow to be a mark of E in 2 S. 15[10]; מעגל which occurs in this sense only once — 17[20]; מראשות 19[13] but also 1 K. 19[6], which can hardly be attributed to E; David's standing *on the top of the mountain* like Jotham, Jd. 9[7], in a section whose authorship is doubtful — to say nothing of the fact that so commonplace a phrase can hardly weigh much in an argument; אלהים אחרים, which is also common in D; הרע לי which occurs in J, Gen. 43[6] Ex. 5[22f.]; and, finally, Saul's confession, which can scarcely be called characteristic. The combined force of these indicia cannot be very great. They would probably be outweighed by the single word תרדמה which is characteristic of J, Gen. 2[21] 15[12]. Cf. also בני מות v.[16], found in 20[31] 2 S. 12[5] neither one of which is E.

1. The Ziphites bring Saul knowledge of David's whereabouts : *Is not David hiding himself on the hill of Hachilah on the face of the Desert*] the eastern front of the Desert, where it breaks down towards the Dead Sea is probably intended. The same locality is mentioned 23[19] in our present text. — **2.** Saul's force here consists of *three thousand men* as in 24[2]. — **3, 4.** On discovering that an invasion was on foot, David sent out spies, *and knew that Saul had come to*] some particular spot whose name is now lost. — **5.** He was able to make out the place where Saul was lying with the people camping about him. — **6.** David asks his two companions : *Who will go down with me to Saul, to the camp ?*] Abishai his nephew volunteers. — **7.** When they came into the camp, *Saul was lying asleep in the . . . and his spear was struck into the earth at his head*. The lance standing upright is still the sign of the Sheikh's quarters among the Arabs. Doughty, I. p. 221. WRSmith, *Kinship*, p. 271. — **8.** Abishai wishes to avail himself of the opportunity : *Let me smite him with his spear into the earth*] meaning to strike the spear through him into the earth. There may be a designed reminiscence of Saul's purpose to pin David to the wall, 18[11] 19[10]. One blow would be all that was needed. — **9.** David forbids him : *For who can lay his hand on the Anointed of Yahweh and be innocent ?*] the reverence for the

king is the same as in 24[6]; there more pronounced if anything.
— **10**. David's intention is to leave Saul in the hand of God —
either Yahweh shall smite him] by a direct stroke, as in the case
of Nabal, *or his day shall come and he shall die*] in accordance
with a decree already fixed, *or he shall go down into battle and
meet his end*. In any case, David refuses to take the matter into
his own hand. — **11**. Repeating his refusal, he directs Abishai to
take the spear and the jug of water. — **12**. With these trophies,
David and his lieutenant went their way, *and no one saw, and no
one knew, and no one awoke, for all of them were asleep, for a
deep sleep from Yahweh had fallen upon them*] like Adam's uncon-
sciousness, Gen. 2[21].

1. On reviewing 23[19] and its relation to the present verse it seems to me
not unlikely that the two were originally identical. That is: this account was
originally in direct sequence to 23[18], and has now been displaced by the
fuller (double) story contained in 23[19]–24[23]. — חכילה] a number of Heb. MSS.
have חבילה, and 𝔖 seems to have read חוילה. — **4**. אל־נכון] the name of a
place is expected, as was already evident to Schm. who translates *ad certum
(locum)*. 𝔊[AB] has ἐκ Κεειλά, 𝔊[L] εἰς Σεκελάγ, neither of which will do. Possibly we should read אל נכחו — *to the point just in front of him*. — **5**. 𝔊[AB]
omits the clause וירא . . . שאול by homeoteleuton. — מעגל] occurs also 17[20],
but what is meant is unknown. 𝔖 has here λαμπήνη, *a covered chariot*. It is
perhaps no objection to this that it would not fit 17[20]. But the fact that
Abishai wants to pin the king *to the ground* shows that he was not sleeping
in a chariot or on a couch. סביבתו *Kt.*: סביבתיו *Qrê* both here and in v.[7].
— **6**. ויען] David *answers* his own thought. — אחימלך] one of the numerous
foreigners who joined David's force — *a Hittite* like Uriah. On the Hittites
cf. Moore on Jd. 3[3]. — אבישי] from the analogy of other proper names, the
second member of the word should be the name of a god. — צרויה] the sister
of David, according to 1 Chr. 2[16]. If this be correct, we can account for the
designation of her sons by her name (rather than that of their father) only by
supposing that their father was a foreigner, and the marriage was one of those
in which the wife remained in her own clan and the children were counted to
that clan, cf. 2 S. 17[25]. — **8**. איבך *Qrê* is to be preferred. — בחנית וראי] as
pointed out by Krenkel (*ZATW.* II. p. 310) we should read בחניתו בארץ for
the fact that Saul's own spear was to be used is important. The conjunction
is not read by 𝔊𝔖, while 𝔖 renders חנית הזה אשר בארץ. — **9**. מי שלח] should be
followed by the reverse tense, not by ונקה as here. A י seems to have fallen
out after מי (cf. Dr., *Notes*) — this is favoured by 𝔊. — **10**. כי אם] cannot be
the adversative particle, nor can it introduce the substance of the oath after
חי יהוה for it would give a meaning the reverse of what David intends. The
כי therefore must introduce the substance of the oath, which is stated in three

possibilities, of which אם indicates the first, the others following with או. —
12. מראשתי] as suggested by We., a מ has probably fallen out before this
word, the preceding word ending with the same letter. The unusual termination is probably a corruption of the suffix — read ממראשתו striking out שאול.
The received text seems to be defended in Ges.²⁶ 87 *s*.

13. David *went across and stood upon the top of a mountain
far away*] the power of the orientals to make their voices heard
at a long distance has often been remarked by travellers. —
14. David calls Abner, making the greater impression upon Saul
by not directly addressing him. The reading of 𝔊ᴮ for Abner's
answer is, therefore, to be preferred : *Who art thou that callest?*
David had not called the king at all. — **15.** Having got Abner's
attention, David reads him a lesson : *Art not thou a man ? And
who is like thee in Israel ? Why then hast thou not kept guard
over thy Lord the king ? For there came one of the people to
destroy the king, thy Lord !* The sarcastic questions put the state
of the case with startling vividness. — **16.** Pronouncing them
deserving of death for their neglect, he calls attention to the fact
that the king's spear and water vessel are missing. This is evidence enough of the truth of what he is saying. — **17.** Saul recognizes David's voice, and the recollections called up by the sound
are expressed in his words : *Is this thy voice, my son David ?*
Evidently the old affection has been touched. — **18.** Having got
a hearing, David expostulates freely : *Why is it that my Lord is
pursuing his servant ?* The further questions are in reality assertions of his innocence. — **19.** Discussion of the cause of the king's
enmity follows. David can account for it only on the theory that
external influences have wrought upon the mind of the king.
These may be human or superhuman. On the one hand : *If
Yahweh has instigated thee against me*] as he afterwards instigated
David against Israel, 2 S. 24¹. The wrath of Yahweh against
David is conceived of as the cause of Saul's action. The theologians are compelled to explain Yahweh's causation as permissive,
Satan being the real instigator, as in 1 Chr. 21¹. *Let him inhale
an offering*] the sacrifice ascending in smoke was appropriated by
the deity through the sense of smell. Thus when angry he was
placated, as in the time of Noah, Gen. 8²¹ (J.). *But if they be
men, cursed be they before Yahweh*] the imprecation will fall upon

them and punish them. *For they have now driven me from union with the inheritance of Yahweh, saying: Go serve other gods!* The inheritance of Yahweh is the territory of Israel. Yahweh can be served only in his own land. The exile is compelled to serve the gods of the land in which he sojourns, Jer. 5[19]. — **20**. David prays that his blood may not be shed *away from the presence of Yahweh*] where it would not be avenged, for Yahweh is the avenger of wrong done to his servants. The reason for the prayer is that he is helpless against the superior might of Saul: *For the king of Israel is come out to seek my life, as the eagle hunts the partridge on the mountains*]. This emended reading gives a sense more in accord with the context than the traditional 𐤈. — **21**. Saul confesses his wrong and invites David to return. *I have done foolishly and have erred exceedingly.* — **22**. David does not notice the invitation, but only says: *Behold the spear, O king! Let one of the young men come over and take it.* — **23, 24**. Final repetition of the prayer: *May Yahweh reward each one's righteousness and fidelity*] in such a way that David's life may be treated as generously as he had treated Saul's life. — **25**. Saul prophesies David's success in general terms. There is no distinct allusion to the kingdom like the one in 24[21].

13. ההר] the particular mountain which was adapted for his purpose. — **14**. קראת אל־המלך] ὁ καλῶν 𐌰𐌱: ὁ καλῶν με; τίς εἶ, σύ; 𐌰𐌻. The shorter form is to be preferred. It was supplemented by a scribe who realized that the calling to Abner would affect Saul: *qui clamas et inquietas regem* 𐤋. — **15**. שמרת אל] we should read על as in the next verse. — **16**. בני־מות] cf. 20[31] 2 S. 12[5]. — ואת־צפחת] is corrected by Bu. to צפחת ואי. But it seems not unlikely that the governing force of the first אי was in the writer's mind so that he could use the accusative particle, Davidson, *Syntax*, 72, Rem. 4. — **17**. קולי] δοῦλός σου 𐌰𐌱. "The more courtly is less original" (We.). — **19**. מהסתפח] the verb is rare, but there seems to be no doubt as to the meaning, cf. the Niphal in Is. 14[1]. — **20**. פרעש אחר] is the same phrase used in 24[15]. There it is in place after the question *after whom*, etc. But here the thought is not the insignificance of David, but his helplessness. 𐌰𐌱 reads נפשי, which is also favoured by את, which is ungrammatical in the present text. — כאשר] the conjecture of Kl. who reads כנשר has everything in its favour. Only thus is the comparison fully expressed. — הקרא] the partridge is named from its loud clear note.* — **22**. החנית *Kt.*] the *Qrê* demands חנית, making

---

* Readers of Ginsburg's text will be puzzled by the word לאמר near the opening of v.[20]. It is a purely clerical error, the copyist having duplicated the word just

המלך the genitive. But the *Ktib* may be retained, making המלך the vocative
— **23.** ביר[is doubtless to be corrected to בידי with the versions.

1 Samuel XXVII.–2 Samuel I. David as Vassal of the Philistines.

XXVII. 1.–XXVIII. 2. David enters the service of Achish, King of Gath.

— Despairing of safety in the way in which he has been living, David resorts to Achish and is received by him. Finding life in the capital not to his taste, he begs a town for himself, which he may hold as an outpost of the kingdom. He receives Ziklag, and when settled there carries on constant warfare with the Bedawin. By representing that his raids are carried on against the Judahite clans, he gives his chief the impression that he has entirely estranged himself from his people. The confidence of the king is thereby so strengthened that when the Philistines muster their forces for an invasion of Israel, Achish summons David to follow and makes him the guardian of his person.

The paragraph evidently knows nothing of David's having once attempted to join the court of Gath, 21$^{11-16}$. It is remarkable for its silence concerning the oracle and the warning given to David to remain in the land of Judah, 22^5. It presupposes the marriage with Abigail, unless the mention of her in v.^{3} be an interpolation. It does not seem directly to continue 26, for David's experience there related was calculated to encourage rather than to discourage him. The only part of the preceding narrative which would naturally lead up to this is 23$^{19-28}$, where David is nearly captured by Saul and escapes only because Saul is called away by an invasion of the Philistines.

1. *David said to himself: Now I shall be destroyed some day by the hand of Saul; the only good thing is that I should escape to the land of the Philistines.* There, of course, he would be out of his enemy's reach; Saul would therefore despair of him and not seek him further. Schm. finds this move of David's a result of carnal lack of faith. — **2.** He therefore went with his band to

---

above in the next line, instead of giving ארצה which belongs here. The new and ostensibly most correct edition of the text has thus added a serious blunder to the list already known to us — and this in spite of the modern advantages of proofreading.

Achish ben Maoch, king of Gath] the accession of such a band would be welcome to a ruler whose territory was open to inroads from the Bedawin. We may readily suppose that David did not take this step without previous negotiations. — **3**. At first they resided in Gath itself, *each with his house*] the band was already becoming a clan. The number of people thus brought to Gath might be inconvenient to the king. — **5**. David represents to Achish the desirability of his having another residence *in one of the towns of the open country*] he might readily plead the advantage of such a situation in guarding the frontier. His own interest was, no doubt, to prevent amalgamation of his men with the Philistines. His language conveys the impression that it was too high an honour to dwell in the immediate vicinity of the king. — **6**. *Ziklag* is mentioned among the towns of Judah, Jos. 15³¹, and again in the list of Simeon, Jos. 19⁵. The indications are not sufficiently definite to enable us to identify the site. The second half of the verse tells us that *Ziklag has belonged to the kings of Judah until this day*. As we have no other instance of the phrase *kings of Judah* in the Books of Samuel, we may regard this sentence as an interpolation. It implies that Ziklag would naturally belong to the northern kingdom (as Beersheba did), but was kept by the family of David, whose title dated from the donation of Achish. — **7**. The time of David's sojourn is *four months* according to 𝔊, *a year and four months* according to 𝔥. Both seem too short according to Achish's own statement, 29³.

The section ⁸⁻¹² (according to We. ⁷⁻¹²) is in contradiction with the preceding, in that Gath is its scene. It is therefore thought by some to be an interpolation. On the other hand, the verses ⁵⁻⁷ may be the interpolation. Their excision leaves the narrative free from difficulty. But they are the necessary preparation for 30, so that we must suppose them a part of the document from which that chapter is taken.

1. אספה] cf. 26¹⁰. — יום־אחר] seems not to be used in this sense elsewhere, but is confirmed by 𝔊. — כי] we expect כי אם, and on the ground of 𝔊 we may assume that the original was כי אם אמלט in which the loss of אם is easily accounted for. — ממני] is not represented in 𝔊ᴬᴮ and can well be spared. — **2**. וישש־מאות] τετρακόσιοι 𝔊ᴮ. — **3**. הכרמלית] better read the masculine form to agree with נבל (𝔊). — **4**. ויוסף] read יסף with the *Qrê*. — **6**. צקלג] the identification proposed by Conder (cited by Buhl, *Geog.* p. 185) seems to have no sufficient ground. — **7.** The verse is said by Bu. (*RS.* p. 231) to be misplaced. It is possibly an interpolation like the most of such data. 𝕲𝕷 read *four months,* and the ימים may have arisen by duplication of the two letters preceding. 𝕲ᴬ renders ימי ארבעה ח', which shows how the reading might arise. That four months is too short a time for the actual duration of David's sojourn is evident, but so is a year and four months. — ימים] for a year, Jd. 17¹⁰ 2 S. 14²⁶.

Objection to the coherence of ⁸⁻¹² with the rest of the chapter is raised by Stade, *GVI.* I. p. 252 and by We., *TBS.* p. 140 (who includes v.⁷), cf. *Comp.* p. 253. The defence of the verses is undertaken by Kamphausen, *ZATW.* VI. p. 85 f., and he is supported by Kittel. The two parts of the chapter certainly do not fit well together, though both seem historically probable. The natural supposition is that we have two sources combined.

8. When settled in his new quarters, David *made raids upon the Gizrites and the Amalekites*] the *Geshurites* seem to have come into the received text by mistake. The Gizrites, being Canaanites, and the Amalekites, being Bedawin, were legitimate prey for both Philistine and Israel. But, owing to the location of Gezer, it seems better to substitute the Perizzites for the Gizrites in the text. — *For these tribes dwell in the land which stretches from Telam in the direction of Shur to the land of Egypt*] for justification of the reading, see the critical note. — **9.** *And David would smite the land*] *habitually* is implied in the form of the verb; *and not leave alive man or woman*] the method is too well known to excite surprise. That he *returned to Achish* seems to make Gath the starting point of the raids. — **10.** To the question of Achish : *Where have you raided to-day ?* David would return a misleading answer : *Against the Negeb of Judah, or against the Negeb of the Jerachmeelite, or against the Negeb of the Kenite*] the Negeb is the southern district of Palestine, bordering on the desert. David names Judah and two related clans — his friendly relations with them are indicated by his gifts, 30²⁹. Jerachmeel is, in fact, reckoned as one of the clans of Judah in 1 Chr. 2⁹·⁴². — **11.** The first part of the verse is really a parenthetical remark, explaining how David was not detected. The main narrative is taken up in the concluding portion : *Thus did David, and such was his custom all the days which he dwelt in the country of the Philistines.* — **12.** The result was that *Achish trusted David,* thinking that he had broken finally with Israel and would be his perpetual vassal. — **XXVIII. 1.** The previous narrative evidently leads up to the expression of confidence given by Achish when he commands David : *Be sure that thou shalt go out with me to the camp, thou and thy men.* That the occasion was embarrassing to David we may well believe. — **2.** His reply is designedly ambiguous. The author, who makes him so careful to spare Israel in his raids, certainly did not suppose that he would take part in the battle on the Philistine side. Achish understands David to promise great deeds, and says : *Therefore* [in case the promise is kept] *I will make thee keeper of my head forever*] that is, captain of the bodyguard.

8. הגשורי והגרזי] the *Geshurites* certainly do not belong here, and the second word is unheard of elsewhere. The *Qrê* substitutes והגזרי which would perhaps do, as Gezer was Canaanitish down to the time of Solomon, 1 K. 9¹⁶. But I suspect הפרזי (Dt. 3⁵) to be original — notice the resemblance of ג and פ in the older alphabet. 𝔊ᴮ has only one of the two names. Against Gezer is to be urged its location, too far north for David's forays (cf. Moore, *Judges*, p. 48). — הנה] must refer to the tribes just mentioned. The feminine plural in such cases is unusual but not unintelligible.— מעולם] does not fit in this context. We., Dr., correct to מטלם following a hint given by ten MSS. of 𝔊 (HP.). Telam, as shown above (on 15⁴), was a place on the southern border of Judah. — **9.** והכה] the tense indicates repeated or habitual action, whereas וישב calls attention to what took place in each single instance. — **10.** אל] should apparently be אן which is found in some MSS. of 𝔐 and sustained by 𝔖𝔗, whereas 𝔊𝔏 seem to render אל מי or אל מי.— **11.** לאמר כה עשה] it is highly unnatural to make דוד כה עשה the speech of the supposed fugitive and what follows the statement of the narrator. This לאמר should be stricken out, and the whole half verse made the narrator's statement. This is supported by 𝔏. Kl. supposes the first half of the verse to be a gloss, and this is not improbable. — **12.** הבאיש] Gen. 34³⁰ Ex. 5²¹. — בישראל] some MSS. and editions have ישראל.— **XXVIII. 2.** לכן] lacking in 𝔏, should perhaps be emended to אכן, though David's thought may be : *because of* this expression of confidence. For אתה read עתה with 𝔊𝔏. — שמר לראשי] the equivalent in 𝔊, ἀρχισωματοφύλαξ, is the title of the chief of the bodyguard at the court of the Ptolemies, cf. Deissmann, *Bibelstudien* (1895), p. 93.

XXVIII. 3–25. Saul's fate pronounced. — Saul in fear of the Philistines seeks divine guidance, but receives none by the appointed means of grace. In his despair he seeks out a necromancer, though he had formerly exterminated such from Israel, so far as was in his power. Informed of one, he visits her, and she

calls up the shade of Samuel.   But the spirit only denounces the
punishment in store for Saul.   Overcome by the sentence, Saul
falls prostrate to the earth, but is roused and induced to break his
fast by the woman whose guest he is.

The section breaks the connexion of the narrative and is undoubtedly from another document.   What that document is can
scarcely be doubtful from the position given to Samuel.   Although
dead, he appears as the same instrument of Yahweh's will who
appointed and dethroned Saul.   The last scene in Saul's life is the
last appearance of Samuel.   There is no need therefore to suppose
vv.[17. 18], which allude directly to Saul's disobedience, to be later
interpolation.   In a sense, the picture presented by chapter 15 is
not complete without this sequel.

3–25. The position of Samuel in this document is sufficient to identify it as
a part of the history from which chapter 15 is taken.   The secondary nature
of v.[17f.] is indicated by Bu. in his edition of the text, but can hardly be maintained when the connexion with 15 is seen.   It is also unfortunate that Bu.
should displace the section, ranging it between 30 and 31.   As part of a different document it must break the connexion wherever it is placed, and we
have no evidence that as a part of the Books of Samuel it ever occupied any
but its Massoretic position.   The reason urged is that the geographical situation is more advanced here than in chapter 29.   But this ignores the fact that
this account was written with the scene of Saul's death in mind, and that it
intended to ignore the history in which it is now imbedded.   On the critical
questions cf. Stade's review of Bu. (*ThLZ.* 1896, col. 8).   We. calls attention
to the resemblance to 15 (*Comp.* p. 254).

3. The verse prepares for the following narrative by telling,
first, that Samuel was dead — and so could not be consulted by
Saul except by calling up his shade.   The language — *Samuel
had died and all Israel had mourned for him and had buried him
in Ramah his city* — is in substance a repetition of 25[1].   The next
statement explains the difficulty Saul had in finding the means
of communicating with the shades — *he had removed the talismans
and necromantic charms from the land.*   This was in accordance
with the Deuteronomic law, Dt. 18[11].   That the magical or idolatrous apparatus is intended, rather than the persons who made use
of them, will be evident on considering the passages in point.
That the persons also were not spared is probably true.

3. וּבְעֵירוֹ] is superfluous; בְעֵירוֹ is read by 𝕲𝕷 and 4 MSS. of 𝕳. The word seems to represent בְּבִיתוֹ of 25¹, for which it was substituted in the transfer, to avoid scandal. — הָאֹבוֹת] the word has generally been understood of the familiar spirits who are (as alleged) subservient to the soothsayers; the derived meaning is supposed to be *the necromancers* who make use of such spirits. The Hebrew Lexicon of BDB. makes אוֹב always mean either *necromancer* or *necromancy*. Neither definition seems to fit all the cases. Not to speak of the difficulty in supposing the same word to designate both the spirit and the medium, or both the necromancer and his art, I would urge, first, the feminine form of the word, which makes it doubtful whether it can be referred to necromancers. It can hardly be claimed that these were so uniformly women that the gender of the word represents that fact. More significant is the fact that in the majority of cases אוֹב is classed not with persons, but with things — objects of idolatrous or superstitious practices. Thus in the familiar passage in Isaiah (8¹⁹) : *and when they say : Seek the* אֹבוֹת *and the* יִדְּעֹנִים *who chirp and mutter*, the contrast is drawn between these and God, and the most natural interpretation makes them some sort of idol. Again we are told (Is. 19⁸) that Egypt shall seek the idols (אֱלִילִים) and the אִטִּים and the אֹבוֹת and the יִדְּעֹנִים, where it is certainly not violent to interpret all the words as designating objects of the same class. The author of Kings (2 K. 23²⁴) tells us that Josiah destroyed the אֹבוֹת and the יִדְּעֹנִים and the *Teraphim* and the *idols* and the *abominations* — the last three are certainly objects of devotion, and the verb used (בְּעֵר) is more appropriate to the destruction of these than to the slaying of men. More significant is the assertion (2 K. 21⁶) that Manasseh *made* (עָשָׂה) an אוֹב and a יִדְּעֹנִי which could be said only of a talisman or fetish. There seems to be no passage which is inconsistent with this. Dt. 18¹⁰ᶠ· commands : *There shall not be in thee . . . a diviner, a soothsayer or an enchanter or a sorcerer or one who binds spells, or one that asks* אוֹב *or* יִדְּעֹנִי, *or one that inquires of the dead*, where the שֹׁאֵל אוֹב (not the אוֹב itself) is parallel with the soothsayers and enchanters. Should it be objected that a fetish cannot speak, we may reply that the Teraphim are declared to *speak falsehood* (Zech. 10²), a case which clearly refutes the objection. Many idols and fetishes are supposed to give revelations to their devotees. The prohibition to *go a whoring* after the אֹבוֹת and the יִדְּעֹנִים (Lev. 20⁶) is entirely in accord with my supposition, and so is the sentence pronounced upon man or woman *with whom is* an אוֹב (Lev. 20²⁷). Not much stress can be laid upon Jewish tradition in this matter, but it is significant that the Talmud makes a בַּעַל אוֹב one who *asks the skull* of a dead man (the citation is given by Levy, *NHWB.* s.v. אוֹב), and in another place the Teraphim of Laban are said to give him knowledge of the future, and to consist of a human head (that of Adam) cut off and preserved by means of spices (the citation from Elias Levita in Selden, *De Diis Syris*, Syntagma I. Cap. II.). In the same connexion may be mentioned the יְדֹעַ of Rabbinical tradition, which is defined to be an animal (or bird) whose bones the soothsayer took in his mouth, and they gave responses of themselves (Levy, *s.v.*). Bearing in mind the widespread use

of parts of the human body in magical rites, it does not seem too bold to conjecture that the אוב was a human skull (the root possibly means *to be hollow*)
which was prepared by superstitious rites for magical use. The owner of such
a talisman would be prepared to divine by it. The בעלת אוב of this chapter
would then be the sister of the בעלת כשפים of Nah. 3⁴; the figurative use of
the latter phrase does not interfere with the parallel. — הידענים] always mentioned in connexion with אוב, are something of the same nature. The reader
may consult Driver on Dt. 18¹¹ with his references; Nöldeke in *ZDMG.*
XXVIII. p. 667; Stade, *GVI.* I. pp. 425, 504; König, *Offenbarungsbegriff des
Alten Testamentes* (1882), II. p. 150.

4. The Philistine camp was at *Shunem*, at the west foot of the
ridge now called *Jebel Dahi*. Saul mustered his forces on Gilboa,
a ridge running southeast from the eastern end of the great plain.
The Philistines easily commanded the plain, the Israelites rallied
on the hills. — **5, 6.** Saul, terrified at the sight of the enemy's
force, *asked of Yahweh, but Yahweh did not answer him, either
by dreams, or by Urim, or by prophets*] all three are recognized
methods of divine communication in the Old Testament. The
Chronicler regards Saul's recourse to the necromancer as a refusal
to seek Yahweh, 1 Chr. 10¹⁴, and therefore a part of the sin for
which he is slain. But this is not the mind of the present writer,
to whom Saul is a man driven to desperation by the failure of
every attempt to ascertain the will of Yahweh. — **7.** In this strait
the king inquires for a woman *who possesses a talisman* of sufficient
power to summon the dead. The universality of the belief that
the shades can be summoned by the one who possesses the means
needs no comment. *Endor* (the fountain of Dor) still bears its
ancient name and is a poor village on the slope of *Jebel Dahi*. A
description of the locality is given by Stanley.* — **8.** Saul, for very
obvious reasons, *disguised himself*, cf. 1 K. 22³⁰. Coming to the
woman he makes his request: *Divine for me by the talisman and
bring up for me the one whom I shall say*] the power of the
woman to do what she was asked seems not to be doubted by the
narrator. — **9, 10.** In view of Saul's treatment of the necromancers, the woman suspects that her guest is *laying a snare for her
life*] expecting to inform against her. Saul reassures her by an
oath: *no guilt shall come upon thee for this thing.* — **11, 12.** Saul

---

* *Sinai and Palestine*, p. 337.

demands Samuel: *And the woman saw Samuel and cried out with a loud voice*] the more sober Protestant commentators see that it is unreasonable to suppose the souls of the departed subject to such calls, and therefore suppose the Devil to assume the form of the one invoked. But this is contrary to the assertion that the woman *saw Samuel.* For the method of the necromancer, which the narrator probably pictured with fidelity, it may be worth while to note that she alone saw the form, while Saul heard the voice. The first effect of the apparition on the woman was to reveal the identity of her guest: *Why hast thou deceived me, when thou art Saul?* The connexion of Samuel and Saul in earlier life is assumed to be known to her. — **13.** To Saul's question she replies: *I saw a god coming up out of the earth*] the worship of the Manes probably survived in Israel to a comparatively late date, so that her words must be taken in their literal sense. — **14.** On further inquiry she describes the apparition as *an old man coming up and he is wrapped in a cloak*] such as Samuel wore in his lifetime. Before the spirit, unseen by him, Saul prostrates himself in reverence.

4. *Shunem*, which is mentioned also Jos. 19[18] 2 K. 4[8] (cf. also the Shunammite, 1 K. 1[3]), still bears the name *Sulem*, Buhl, *Geog.* p. 217, who also mentions *Endor.* — קסומי] on the form, Ges.[26] 46 *e*. Methods of divination among the heathen Arabs are described by We., *Skizzen*, III. pp. 126 ff., 135 ff. — **9.** הוידעני] the plural should be restored; the final letter has been lost in the following מ. — **10.** ויקרך] the Daghesh is intended to guard the pronunciation of the emphatic letter, Ges.[23] 20 *h*. — **13.** אלהים ראיתי עלים] the plural participle would seem to indicate more than one ghostly figure. But only one is described in what follows, and we must suppose the agreement grammatical instead of logical. Similar instances of אלהים with a plural adjective are found Jos. 24[19] (E) Dt. 5[23] 1 S. 17[26. 36], etc. — **14.** זקן] ὄρθιον 𝔊 seems to represent זקף (We.). To this reading we may perhaps trace the Rabbinical conceit, referred to by Schm., that Samuel appeared standing upright, while in ordinary cases the shades present themselves feet upwards. The Greek expositors, to judge by Nestle's specimen (*Marginalien*, p. 15), saw in the word a declaration of Samuel's vigorous appearance.

15. The dialogue is begun by Samuel: *Why hast thou disturbed me in bringing me up?* The shades are at rest and prefer to remain so. Only on very rare occasions does Sheol itself rouse them, Is. 14[9]. The urgency of his situation is Saul's excuse: *I*

R

am in great straits, and the Philistines are warring against me, and God has turned from me and does not answer me more, either by prophets or by dreams] the absence of *Urim* here is perhaps a sign that it was not originally in v.⁶. — *So I have called thee, to tell me what I shall do*] consultation of the oracle is in order to right action, as we have seen in the case of both Saul and David. — **16.** Samuel refuses to answer the important question : *And why dost thou ask me, when Yahweh has turned from thee and become thine enemy ?* Reason enough why Samuel should refuse to help. —**17, 18.** The guilt of Saul in the matter of Amalek. The account of Saul's rejection in c. 15 would not be complete without this sequel. The punishment there denounced is here reaffirmed and declared to be close at hand. — **19.** The verse seems over-full. The first clause may be omitted with advantage. Correcting the remainder by 𝕲ᴮ we get : *And to-morrow thou and thy sons with thee shall fall, and Yahweh will give the camp of Israel into the hand of the Philistines.* — **20.** The message was heart-breaking enough ; *and Saul was overcome, and fell at full length upon the earth.* The fainting fit was accounted for partly by physical exhaustion — *he had not eaten bread all the day and all the night*] it may be supposed that morning was now approaching. — **21, 22.** The woman, coming to the prostrate Saul, appreciates the amount of his mental disturbance. She pleads her obedience to his request, even at the risk of her life, as a reason why he should now listen to her : *and let me set before thee a morsel of meat, and eat thou that thou mayest have strength and make thy journey*] a very sensible proposition. — **23.** Saul at first refused, *but his servants, as well as the woman, urged him.* At length *he rose from the earth and sat upon the couch*] one of the four articles of furniture in the ordinary house. — **24, 25.** *The woman had a fatted calf in the house*] and she also *baked unleavened cakes* for the entertainment of her guests. The similar description of Abraham's hospitality will occur to every one.

15. וָאֶקְרָאֶה] the pointing is anomalous and perhaps designed to allow the choice between וָאֶקְרָא and וָאֶקְרֶה (Nestle, *Marginalien*, p. 15). — **16.** עָרְךָ] is misspelled for צָרְךָ, probably by a scribe to whom the Aramaic form was familiar, or who wished to disguise the unpleasant thought that Yahweh could be one's enemy ; 𝕲 μετὰ τοῦ πλησίον σου points to עִם רֵעֶךָ which is adopted by Th.

and others, and favoured by 𝔖. But Saul's rival is mentioned later; *here* we expect an allusion to Saul's complaint that he is in *straits*. — **17.** לו] may be read as a dative of advantage. But it is better to restore לך with five MSS. of 𝔊, 𝔊^{AB}, and 𝔏. — **19.** Either the first clause or the last is superfluous. As Samuel would more naturally conclude what he has to say of Saul before passing on to the fate of Israel, I have omitted the opening clause of 𝔊 (We., Dr.). Stade, on the other hand, retains ᵃ and omits ᶜ. — עמי] *shall be with me* would seem to require the verb; 𝔊^{AB} found עמך נפלים which is restored by Th. — **20.** וימהר] seems to be the wrong verb. Perhaps by pointing וִיְמַהֵר with Kl. we can retain it. Comparison of 𝔊 here and in v.^{21} shows that it has the same verb in both places; We. therefore restores ויבהל here, conforming it to the other. But the argument seems precarious. — **23.** ויפרצו] the context requires ויפצרו. — אל] should be על with some MSS. — **24.** עגל־מרבך] a calf tied up in the house like the lambs which are stilled "crammed" by the women in Syria. — ותפהו] for ותאפהו, Ges.^{26} 68 *h.*

XXIX. 1–XXX. 31. David's homeward march, the capture of Ziklag by the Amalekites, and the recovery of the spoil. —

When the Philistine troops are mustered, the attention of the chiefs is drawn to David and his band. They inquire of Achish why he is there, and receive assurances of his fidelity. But they regard his presence as a danger, so that David, in spite of his protestation of fidelity, is sent away. Returning home, he finds that the Amalekites have taken revenge for his former incursions by attacking the undefended Ziklag and capturing its inhabitants, whom they have carried off as slaves. The spirit of mutiny shows itself among David's men, but he promptly finds them occupation in the pursuit of the enemy. His success is complete; besides recovering what has been carried away he takes great store of booty. This he uses to secure the attachment of the Sheikhs in the neighbouring districts.

The piece is a unit. Its interest in the fortune of David and in his legislative decision is plain. We may ascribe it without hesitation to the source which later gives us such copious details of David's life.

1. The camp of the Philistines was at *Aphek*, a locality unidentified, but which must have lain in the plain of Esdraelon. The Philistines probably wished to secure their possession of the Great Plain, and their communication with the Jordan valley, where we find them later in possession of Beth-shean, 31^{10}. — *Israel camped*

at the fountain in Jezreel] the phraseology implies that Jezreel is
not the town, but the valley. It is probable however that Saul
occupied the town, which lies just at the foot of Gilboa. He
would thus command the entrance to the valley, and would have
the high ground in his rear. — **2.** *The Tyrants of the Philistines*]
each with his army, *were marching by, by hundreds and by thousands*] referring to the troops in their different companies. There
seems to have been a review by the generals, in which David
marched in the rearguard with Achish. — **3.** The generals ask
what are these Hebrews?] discovering their characteristic dress
or arms. Achish replies in two particulars. David was first an
escaped *servant of Saul,* who would not want to return to his
harsh master. Secondly, he was a tried dependent of Achish:
*who has been with me these two years and I have not found any
fault in him from the day he fell to my lot until now.* The double
guarantee would seem to be sufficient. — **4.** The suspicious fears
of the generals break out in an angry demand: *Send back the
man to the place where thou hast stationed him*] as thy vassal;
lest he be an enemy in the camp] who will put hindrances in the
way of our success, and plot for our ruin. On a former occasion
the Hebrews in Philistine service had gone over to the enemy,
14²¹. — *With what should this fellow make himself acceptable to his
Master? Is it not with the heads of these men?*] pointing to the
Philistine soldiers. This is their reply to the plea that David is a
runaway slave. — **5.** The fact of David's former success against
the Philistines is an argument against his fidelity now. The
absence of any allusion to Goliath shows that the exploit of Chapter 17 was unknown to the author of this section.

1. On the locality cf. Miller, *Least of All Lands*, cited by GAS., *Geog.* p. 401.
Aphek is apparently the last station of the Philistines before advancing against
Saul's position at Jezreel, v.¹¹. This would naturally be somewhere in the
great plain of Esdraelon. This Aphek cannot therefore be *Aphek in Sharon.*
—**2.** סרני] the native name of the Philistine rulers, 5⁸, of whom Achish was
one.—**3.** The שרים I take to have been the military commanders in distinction from the סרנים, or civil rulers. The latter indeed marched to the war
and led their troops. But there must have been some sort of general staff. —
זה ימים או־זה שנים] is extremely indefinite — *some days or some years* would
hardly be the reply of a man who knew the situation: ἡμέρας τοῦτο δεύτερον
ἔτος 𝕲ᴬᴮ; ἤδη δεύτερον ἔτος σήμερον 𝕲ᴸ agree in making the time *two years,*

which would be simply זה שנתים (adopted by Bu.).—נפלו] add אלי with 𝕲𝕾𝕿𝕷.—**4.** The second שרי פלשתים is lacking in 𝕲𝕾𝕷.—במלחמה] read במחנה with 𝕲. The change was made under the influence of the preceding במלחמה (Kl.). Nestle (*Marg.* p. 15) calls attention to the contrast between the *Satan* here and the *angel of God* a little later; and also to the former experience of the Philistines with the Hebrews in their camp.

6. Achish breaks the news to David : *By the life of Yahweh*] this oath is not unnatural in the mouth of a Philistine when he is speaking to an Israelite. — *Thou art upright and it is right in my eyes that thou shouldst go out and in in the camp*] like any of the officers, 18¹⁵. — *But thou art not approved by the Tyrants*] the voice of the majority must be decisive. — **7.** Achish seems to fear David's anger, as he asks him *not to do evil in the eyes of the Tyrants.* — **8.** David utters a suspicion that Achish himself finds fault with him : *What have I done . . . that I may not go and fight against the enemies of my Lord the king ?* What David's real plan was is not disclosed. The author probably did not suppose he would fight against Israel. — **9.** He receives renewed assurance that he is blameless *as an angel of God* in the sight of Achish. — **10.** The command to depart at dawn the next day is repeated in detail, for we should read with 𝕲 : *Now rise early in the morning, thou and thy men who came with thee [and go to the place where I have stationed thee, and put no evil design in thy heart, for thou art good in my sight] but rise early in the morning and you shall have light, and go*] the clause in brackets has fallen out of 𝕳. It is assumed by Achish that the high-spirited warrior will feel insulted and be tempted to take revenge. — **11.** David therefore rose early *to return to the land of the Philistines*, but the *Philistines went up to Jezreel.*

6. צאתך] 𝕲 prefixes καί, meaning : *not only thou but also thy going out.* It cannot be denied that 𝕳 would be smoother if it read ישר בעיני אתה וטוב צאתך. But 𝕲 does not seem to have the better reading. — **9.** ידעתי] probably should be ידעך.—כמלאך אלהים] in the two other instances of the comparison, we find כמ׳ האלהים which should perhaps be restored here, 2 S. 14¹⁷ 19²⁸. The words are lacking in 𝕲ᴮ perhaps because they were thought to be incongruous with Achish's nationality. — **10.** The Hebrew, as it stands, puts two exhortations to *rise early in the morning* in immediate succession. The clause in 𝕲 which stands between them relieves the awkwardness. It is adopted by Th., We., Dr., Bu., Kl., Ki. As the cause of its loss, we can only conjecture that it filled just a line or just two lines in the archetype. For ועבדי אדניך which does not seem natural in the mouth of Achish, I restore אתה ונעריך with 𝔊ᴸ. The same recension reads at the end of the omitted clause ὡς ἄγγελος θεοῦ, which is perhaps original (adopted by Kl.).

XXX. The narrative is continuous with what precedes, following the fortunes of David. — **1**. When he and his men got home they found that *the Amalekites had invaded the Negeb and had smitten Ziklag and burnt it with fire*] the Bedawin had watched the departure of David and his men. — **2**. They had not followed David's method of warfare, for they had killed no one but *had carried captive the women and all that were in it, from small to great*] the fighting men were with David. The captives were probably destined to the Egyptian slave market. — **3, 4**. Finding the city burned, and their families carried away, David and his men *wept aloud until there was in them no more power to weep*] the fountain of tears was exhausted ; *consumptis enim lachrymis infixus tamen pectori haeret dolor.** — **5**. As it stands, the verse is a supplementary notice that should have come in at the end of v.². Probably it is a gloss. — **6**. *David was in great straits*] Gen. 32⁸ Jd. 2¹⁵ ; *for the people proposed to stone him*] popular indignation easily turns against the ruler in case of calamity. — *For the soul of every one was embittered*] 2 K. 4²⁷, where extreme grief is thus described. But the allied phrase *bitter of soul* is used also of *angry* men, Jd. 18²⁵ 2 S. 17⁸. In this case, the grief turned to anger. — *But David took courage in reliance on Yahweh his God*] as is shown by his prompt action. — **7, 8**. Commanding Abiathar to bring the Ephod, he asks : *Shall I pursue this band ? Shall I overtake them ?*] the double question is really one ; it were vain to pursue unless he could overtake. The answer was affirmative : *Pursue, for thou shalt surely overtake and shalt surely rescue.*

XXX. 1. [ועמלקי] cf. v.¹⁸, doubtless to be read ועמלק with 𝔊. — **2.** [אשר־בה] as it stands, refers to the women. But as we have later the express assertion that they had not killed a man, we should probably insert here with 𝔊 ואת־כל (Th.) which would include the old men and boys. — **3.** [והנה שרופה] the same construction in v.¹⁶. — **5.** The verse is supposed to be a gloss by Bu., and can

---

* Cicero, cited by Sanctius, Schm. p. 964.

in fact well be spared. — **6.** ותצר] Ges.[26] 67 *p.* The masculine form is used elsewhere except in Jd. 10[9], cf. Davidson, *Syntax*, § 109. — בנו] read בניו with the *Qrê*, cf. v.[22]. — ויהחזק וגו'] the clause reads like a later insertion; it is not exactly duplicated anywhere else. — **7.** Abiathar occurs 22[20] 23[9], probably from the same document. — **8.** ארדף] might be construed as the hypothetical introduction to the real question : *if I pursue*, shall I overtake? But 𝔊 reads interrogatively, and the answer רדף favours that reading — restore therefore האדרף (We.). — הגדור] cf. 1 K. 11[24] 2 K. 5[2] 6[23], and elsewhere, of marauding *banditti* as here.

9. David and his men came to the *Wadi Besor.* The name occurs only in this passage, and, as we have no knowledge of David's objective point, it is impossible now to identify this ravine. — **10.** *And there remained behind two hundred men who were too exhausted to cross the Wadi Besor, and David and four hundred men pursued*] the two halves of the verse have been transposed by mistake. — **11.** The party found *an Egyptian,* known by his dress or his features, whom they brought to David, and to whom they gave food. — **12.** After giving him water, *they gave him a cake of figs* cf. 25[18]. For a starving man this would be enough. — *His spirit returned to him*] he had been in appearance lifeless from his long fast. — **13.** To David's question concerning himself he replies : *I am an Egyptian lad, servant to an Amalekite, and my master abandoned me, because I fell sick, three days ago.* — **14.** His account of the expedition : *We raided the Negeb of the Cherethite*] a clan of the Philistines, Zeph. 2[5]. — **15.** The captive on being asked to act as guide, consents on condition that David will swear not to kill him, or to deliver him to his master. — **16.** Led by the slave, they come upon the enemy *spread over the face of the country, eating and drinking and dancing*] very possibly in a religiou feast — *on account of all the great spoil which they had taken.* — **17.** *And David smote them from twilight to evening*] the attack was sudden and soon decided, and the success was complete : *None escaped except four hundred young men who rode upon the camels and fled.*

9. הבשור] conjecturally identified with *Wadi Ġazze* (by Guérin, *Judée,* II. p. 213) * or with its branch *Wadi Sheri'a* (by Buhl, *Geog.* p. 88). — והנותרים עמדו] can only mean in its present connexion that the rest (besides the six hundred) stayed behind at Ziklag. But it is a constant feature of the tradi-

---

* I owe the citation to BDB. *sub voce.*

tion that David had only six hundred men with him, so that there were none to stay at Ziklag. We must treat the clause as an intruder (We.). Ew. (*GVI³*. III. 144, E.Tr. III. p. 105) proposes to insert a clause — *four hundred passed over, and the rest stayed*. But the next verse is then redundant. — **10.** The order is perverse, and the two halves of the verse should be transposed (We.). — פגרו] only here and v.²¹. The context indicates the meaning, cf. פגר *a corpse* from its limpness. — **11.** איש־מצרי] it would be more logical to describe him here as faint or starving, and to leave his race to be discovered later (Kl.). — ויהנו־לו לחם] it seems superfluous to tell us here that they gave him food, and then to add later that they gave him figs. However, we may account for the clause as a general statement — *they brought him to David and gave him food* — to be followed by the details. — **12.** ויני צמקים] lacking in 𝔊ᴮ, and not improbably the insertion of a scribe. It would not do to give a starving man much food at one time. — **13.** היום שלשה] 3 MSS. of 𝔐 add ימים which seems necessary, cf. 9²⁰. — **14.** נגב] the verb used is followed by אל in v.¹, and the preposition should be inserted here (We.). — הכרתי] the people so named are dwellers on the shore according to Zephaniah, who also associates them with the land of the Philistines as does Ezekiel (25¹⁶). Elsewhere they are mentioned with the פלתים as making up David's body guard, 2 S. 8¹⁸. Cf. E. Meyer, *Gesch. des Alterth.* I. p. 367. 𝔊ᴸ has χορρὶ here, reminding us of a similar confusion in 𝔐 in 2 S. 20²³: 𝔊ᴮ χολθεί. — ועל־איש ליהודה] the difference in the form of expression indicates that the phrase was inserted by a scribe who was surprised that Judah should not be mentioned. The Negeb of the Pelethite and the Negeb of Caleb would be enough territory for one raid. — **15.** At the end of the verse 𝔊ᴸ𝔖 agree in adding: *and he sware to him.* — **16.** החגים] the circuit of the sanctuary made at the feasts was undoubtedly a dance. That the Bedawin were here dancing before their gods, is the most natural interpretation of the scene. Arabic parallels are given by We. *Skizzen*, III. p. 106, with which compare Nöldeke's comments in *ZDMG*. XLI. p. 719. — **17.** ויכם דוד] 𝔊 seems to have had ויבא אליהם דוד ויכם which is adopted by Bu. But in such cases the shorter clause has the presumption in its favour. — מהנשף] it is still disputed whether the morning or evening twilight is intended. In the majority of cases נשף is certainly the early evening when the breeze begins to stir, and there seems no reason to interpret otherwise here. The enemy were wholly taken by surprise and seem to have made no serious resistance. To suppose that David spent the whole day in slaughter is difficult. — למחרתם] adds to the difficulty, for interpreted in the natural sense it would extend the slaughter over two whole days. The form moreover is abnormal. The ם can hardly be the pronominal suffix, and the adverbial ending is equally out of place. The text is probably corrupt. 𝔖 seems to have or to conjecture מאחריהם. The Bible Commentary suggests למחותם; We. להחרימם (adopted by Bu.); Kl. בכל מחניהם.

18, 19. David rescued all that had been carried away, *nothing was missing*] 2 S. 17²². — **20.** The meaning of the obscure verse must have been that, in addition to recovering his own, David captured a large amount of other property. — **21**. On the return, the two hundred who were left behind came to meet them, *and saluted them.* — **22**. The baser men among those who had marched in the pursuit propose to keep all the booty for their own company : *Because they did not go with us*] the present text reads *with me — we will not give them of the booty which we rescued*] the term *booty* shows that no previous title was to be recognized. All they would give would be : *to each man his wife and his children that they may lead them away and depart.* — **23**. David vetoes the proposition : *Do not do so after Yahweh has* [*wrought*] *for us and preserved us.* Injustice is a sin against God, and in this case the ingratitude is especially conspicuous. — **24**. The language of David continues in the couplet :

> *As the portion of the one who goes down into battle,*
> *So is the portion of the one who remains with the baggage.*

Early statutes (enactments or regulations) were put in rhythmical form for better retention in memory. The original couplet has here been increased by the added words : *They shall share alike.* — **25**. The author adds that *from that time on they made it a statute and a precedent in Israel.* David's decision in the matter became the *precedent* (משפט) ; it was a *statute* when he made it a general rule. Cf. Briggs, *Higher Criticism of the Hexateuch*[2], p. 248 f.

18. The two wives seem to be an afterthought, as in v.[5]. — **19**. ומשלל] seems to belong before ועד־בנים, and this is the order in 𝔊. Possibly however a word has fallen out; we should expect : מן נשים ועד־בנים. — **20**. The verse as it stands is unintelligible. Its object must be to tell us that in addition to the recovery of his own possessions David took a large amount of other booty : *ante pecus suum quod liberaverant duxerunt greges et armenta quae abstulerunt Amalekitis*, as Kimchi is rendered by Schmid. But this is not expressed by the present text. We.'s restoration, accepted by Dr., Bu., Ki., makes the people, out of gratitude, resign all the sheep and oxen to David as his share. But this is contrary to what follows, where the two hundred share in the booty with the others. I suspect the original to have been something like this : ואת־כל הצאן והבקר אשר נהגו עמלק לפניהם גם זה שלל דוד. — **21**. וישיבם] should probably be וישיבם, David being the natural subject, 𝔊𝕷. — וישאל] on the other hand is read as a plural by 𝔊𝕾. The men left behind would be the ones to ask for the welfare of those who had gone into the battle (We.); for

להם we should probably read לה (= לו). — **22.** כל] is lacking in 𝔖. — עמי] the singular form is no doubt thoroughly idiomatic. But if we retain it we should apparently change both נתן and הצלנו to correspond. It is easier therefore to read עמנו with 8 MSS. of 𝕳, and with 𝔊𝔖𝔏. — **23.** אחי את אשר] 𝔊 undoubtedly reads אחרי אשר which is to be preferred, because it makes all that follows a reason for the dissuasion. But in that case נתן is left without an object and must be replaced by another verb, as עשה, 14⁶. — **24.** הורד] of the *Ktib* is only a scribe's error. — **25.** לישראל] בישראל found in some copies and editions seems a little better here. — עד היום הזה] a frequent phrase, especially in late writers. It naturally implies that a considerable time had elapsed since the events narrated.

26. David uses the booty at his disposal to win the hearts of Judah. Mohammed's procedure after the battle of Honein will occur to every one. — *He sent of the booty to the elders of Judah and to his kinsmen*] reading with 𝔊. The enumeration of towns follows. All of them seem to have been in the South Country, none north of Hebron. — **27.** *Bethel,* as pointed out by We., the same with the *Bethuel* of 1 Chr. 4³⁰, there mentioned in connexion with Hormah and Ziklag; cf. also *Bethul,* Jos. 19⁴ (also with Hormah). *Ramoth-Negeb* one of the cities of Simeon, Jos. 19⁸. *Jattir,* Jos. 15⁴⁸ 21¹⁴ (with Eshtemoa). — **28.** *Aroer* was originally mentioned in Jos. 15²². The name still attaches to a ruin east-southeast of Beersheba. *Siphamoth* seems to be mentioned nowhere else. *Eshtemoa,* Jos. 15⁵⁰ 21¹⁴ identified by Robinson. — **29.** For the unknown *Racal* of 𝕳 we should probably read *Carmel* on the basis of 𝔊. — *The cities of the Jerachmeelite and the cities of the Kenite*] 27¹⁰. — **30.** *Hormah* Jd. 1¹⁷ Num. 21³. For *Bor-Ashan* we should probably restore the well-known *Beer Sheba* whose absence is inexplicable. — **31.** *Hebron,* the chief city of Judah, could not be left out when all the places were remembered *where David had sojourned, he and his men.*

26. לרעהו] καὶ τοῖς πλησίον αὐτοῦ 𝔊 seems preferable; 𝔖 ולחברהון has the conjunction like 𝔊. — **27.** בבית אל] written as one word by Baer; in Ginsburg's text two words connected by the Maqqeph. The name occurs in 𝔊ᴮ also in Jos. 15³⁰ (כסיל 𝕳) just before Hormah. In our passage 𝔊 has Βαιθσούρ which is favoured by Ew. and Th. For *Ramoth* 𝔊ᴮᴸ *Rama;* in Jos. 19⁸ where 𝕳 has רמת, 𝔊ᴸ has Ραθμούθ. — יתר] ἐν Γεθθόρ 𝔊ᴮ goes back to בעתר. Both names are found in the lists of Joshua (15⁴². ⁴⁸ 19⁷ 21¹⁴). Cf. *ZATW.* VI. p. 6. — **28.** ערער is the name of more than one place. The present one should be in the Negeb, and a ruin is pointed out in this region

called *Ar'ara* (Buhl, *Geog*. p. 183). In Jos. 15²² we now find עֲרָעְרָה for which
𝕲ᴮ has 'Αρουήλ. Probably עֲרָעֵר should be restored there (cf. Dillmann's
Commentary and Bennett's text in *SBOT*.). שִׂפְמוֹת of Ginsburg and the
common editions is written יְפֵמוֹת by Baer. In this verse 𝕲ᴮ has one more
than 𝕳, inserting 'Αμμαδεί which may be a corruption of 'Αροήρ (We.).
It does not seem to be a sufficient basis on which to restore עֵין־גֶּדִי (Ew.).
𝕲ᴸ seems to have read עָרֵי קֵין from v.²⁹. For שְׂפָמוֹת : Σαφεί 𝕲ᴮ, אִשְׁתְּמַע, cf.
Buhl, *Geog*. p. 163. — **29.** The verse is extended in 𝕲ᴮ perhaps by duplication
from the preceding. It agrees with 𝕲ᴸ in giving the name *Carmel*, which
Ewald substitutes for רֶכֶל. For the *Kenite*, 𝕲 has the *Kenezite*. Kenaz was
a clan of Judah, Jd. 1¹³, but the parallel 1 S. 27¹⁰ seems to decide for the
Kenite here. — **30.** *Hormah*, cf. Moore on Jd. 1¹⁷. — בְּבוֹר־עָשָׁן in the early
editions according to Baer; in many recent ones (Jablonski, etc.) בְּכוֹר־עָ׳. In
𝕲 it is represented by *Beersheba*. The absence of so prominent a place as
Beersheba is remarkable and the name is perhaps original. עָשָׁן however is
the name of a town in Judah, Jos. 15⁴² 19⁷. עָתָךְ occurs nowhere else in 𝕳.
It is suggested by Buhl (Ges. *HWB*¹².) that it is the same with עָתֶר noticed
above, which is twice named in connexion with עָשָׁן. I should substitute
Arad, Jd. 1¹⁶. The MSS. of 𝕲 differ widely.

XXXI. The death of Saul. —

Two accounts are given of the
death of Saul. In the one before us he is hard pressed in battle,
and, in despair, commits suicide. In the other (contained in
2 Sam. 1¹⁻¹⁰), he begs an Amalekite camp follower to slay him,
and thus meets his end. The two accounts seem independent,
and it is natural to suppose that they represent the two different
streams of tradition. In that case the chapter before us continues
the narrative of 28. It is, in fact, the natural sequel of that
chapter. For in that the shadow of the coming defeat already
falls. As there predicted, Saul sees Israel defeated and his sons
slain; and commits suicide in his sense of abandonment by Yahweh. It confirms this to notice that 2 S. 1 naturally continues
the history we have just followed, culminating in David's distribution
of the booty to Judah. Chapter 31 is unnecessary to that narrative, and in fact breaks the thread.

1. The account opens abruptly : *The Philistines fought against
Israel, and the men of Israel fled before the Philistines, and fell
down slain upon Mount Gilboa*] Israel was frequently defeated
in the plains. In this case the battle was fought on their own
ground — the high places. — **2, 3.** Three sons of Saul were slain,

and the fighting pressed hard upon Saul; the archers got him in range and he was wounded] the text is not certain. — **4.** Saul's command to his armour-bearer : *Draw thy sword and run me through with it*] the case of Abimelech Jd. 9⁵⁴ is closely parallel. There, it was to escape death at the hands of a woman. Here, it is *lest these uncircumcised come and make sport of me*] amuse themselves with the helpless but conscious warrior, Jd. 19²⁵. The armour-bearer *refused because he was much afraid*] whether the author means that he was in too great a panic to heed the command, or that he had too great reverence for his lord cannot be made out with certainty. The latter seems more probable. Saul then *took his own sword and fell upon it*] one of the very rare instances of suicide in the Old Testament. In view of it, the older commentators discuss the question of Saul's final salvation, generally with an unfavourable verdict.* — **5.** The armour-bearer would not survive his master. — **6.** The tragic element is pointed out in the fact that *Saul and his sons and his armour-bearer died together.* — **7.** The result was that the inhabitants of the cities in the Jordan valley deserted their cities, and the Philistines took possession of them. The recovery of the original text is difficult.

XXXI. The question of the place of the story can be fully considered only when we come to the following chapter. For the text we now have an additional source in the Chronicler who embodies this chapter in his work (1 Chr. 10¹⁻¹²).

1. נלחמים] Chr. נלחמו which should probably be restored. The author of Sam. changed to the participle to indicate that while David and his men were pursuing the Amalekites, the Philistines *were fighting.* — וינס איש] וינסו אנשי C. which is more idiomatic. — **2.** [וַיַּרְבִּקוּ 14²². — את] אחרי C. It is a question whether the original author did not write אל. The verb is generally used with ב. The names of Saul's sons show some variation in 𝕲. — **3.** אל] read על C. 𝕲𝕾. — המורים אנשים] seems impossible and C. leaves out אנשים. But המורים בקשת is redundant, and בקשת cannot be connected with וימצאוהו. Dr. proposes אנשים המורים בקשת meaning *some* of the archers, comparing Gen. 37²⁸ 1 S. 25¹⁰. It seems simpler to strike out אנשים בקשת as a gloss designed to define המורים. — ויחל מן־היורים] ויחל מאר מהמורים C. The words are generally taken to mean *he feared the archers exceedingly.* But we should expect מפני if that were the meaning. 𝕲 takes ויחל to be from חלל, καὶ ἐτραυματίσθη ᴬᴮ, καὶ ἐτραυμάτισαν ᴸ, and this gives a better sense, for the words of Saul to his armour-bearer are

---

* Schmid, p. 988.

the words of a man sore wounded. — מהמורים] εἰς τὰ ὑποχόνδρια 𝔊 would indicate במחש or במתנים. — **4.** The second ורקרני is lacking in C. doubtless
rightly. What Saul dreaded was that he should be alive to be mocked, not
that they should mutilate his body after his death. — **5.** מת] seems impossible
to reconcile with the following chapter. — **6.** For ונשא כליו C. has וכל ביתו, an
intentional exaggeration. — גם כל־אנשיו] lacking in C. 𝔊[B], is a similar exaggeration. — **7.** אנשי] C. כל־איש. For באשר בעבר הירדן * C. has simply
אשר בעמק, and this may be original, though it is difficult to see how it could
give rise to the present text. Probably we should read בערי העמק (Kl.). —
אנשי ישראל] is omitted by C. who was willing to throw the blame upon Saul
alone. — הערים] read עריהם with C. and 𝔊.

8. The next day the Philistines *came to strip the slain and
found Saul and his three sons fallen on Mount Gilboa*] the battle
had probably lasted until evening. — **9.** They sent the head of
Saul through the country of the Philistines *to bring good news to
their idols and the people*] perhaps the original author wrote *to
their gods and the people*. — **10.** His armour, as a trophy, came
naturally into *the house of Ashtoreth*] where this was we are not
told. — *And his corpse they exposed on the walls of Bethshan*] a
city in the Jordan valley at the entrance of the side valley which
comes down from the Great Plain. It still bears the name *Beisan*.
— **11.** The men of Jabesh Gilead, who had special reasons for
remembering Saul with gratitude (11^{1-11}), undertook to remove
the disgrace. — **12.** *All the men of courage rose up and marched
all night, and took the corpses of Saul and his sons from the wall
of Bethshan and brought them to Jabesh and burnt them there*]
although this was not Israelitish custom, there seems to be no
sufficient reason for departing from the received text. — **13.** The
bones were buried *under the tamarisk tree*] probably one well
known ; *and they fasted seven days*] in expression of their grief.

8. שלשת] omitted by C. — **9.** C. has a free reproduction of the first clause.
— בית] C. has את which is doubtless correct, and which seems also to be implied by 𝔊. — **10.** אשתרות] the singular form alone is in place. C. substitutes
אלהיהם. For תקע read הוקיעו (Lag. *Anm. zur Griech. Uebersetz. d. Proverbien*,
p. iiii), cf. 2 S. $21^{6.9}$. The Chronicler, thinking of the head and armour being
sent to Philistia, changes the last clause to: *and they stuck up his skull in the
house of Dagon.* On *Bethshan*, Moore, Jd. 1^{27} and reff. — **11.** אליו] lacking

---

* It is impossible to suppose that the Israelites *beyond the Jordan* deserted their
cities. The example of Jabesh Gilead is enough to show this.

in 𝕲ᴮ C. — **12.** וילכו כל־הלילה] lacking in C. which also changes the wording of the rest of the verse to accord with its own omission of Bethshan, v.¹⁰. — ויבאו] read ויביאום 𝕲 C. — וישרפו אתם שם] is lacking in C. On account of the lack of precedent, Bu. proposes to read ויספדו להם שם. The mourning however should be mentioned in connexion with the fasting at the end of the next verse. And the separate mention of the bones which follows (note ויקחו) is inexplicable with the proposed reading. — **13.** ויקברו . . . ויקחו] C. has only ויקברו. For האשל, C. has האלה, a more general word, or perhaps less obnoxious (if אשל is a sacred tree, as seems probable). The Hebrew name is reproduced in the modern Arabic name *athl*, applied to the Tamarisk, cf. Post. *Flora of Syria* (1896), p. 166.

2 Sam. I. 1–27. David's reception of the news of Saul's death.

— An Amalekite brings news to Ziklag and gives a circumstantial account of the death of Saul, in which he claims to have been instrumental. David and his men mourn for the death of Saul and his men, and the messenger is put to death for having laid hands on the Anointed of Yahweh. In addition to these marks of grief, David composes an Elegy which is inserted in the text, having been taken from the *Book of Jashar*.

The historical part of the chapter contains a separate and independent account of the death of Saul. In I. 31 we are told expressly that Saul met his death by his own hand. Here the Amalekite finds him suffering from extreme fatigue, but without a wound, v.⁹. It seems impossible to reconcile the two accounts. The easiest hypothesis is that the Amalekite fabricated his story. But the whole narrative seems against this. David has no inkling that the man is not truthful, nor does the author suggest it. The natural conclusion is that we have here a document different from the one just preceding. It strengthens our conviction to notice that this narrative, with a very slight change in v.¹, continues the account of David's experience at Ziklag without a break. It is highly dramatic that after David's severe contest with Amalek, an Amalekite should bring him the news of Saul's death. For this writer, whose chief interest was in David, the story contains all he cared to tell of the last days of Saul.

Budde in his text separates v.⁵ as a late insertion and vs.⁶⁻¹¹, ¹³⁻¹⁶ as belonging to a different document. He succeeds thus in producing a continuation of I. 31. But where the exscinded fragments belong it is impossible to see. They continue nothing that precedes, and they prepare for nothing that follows. They may be a mere editorial embellishment, but such a hypothesis should not be urged if we can get along without it.

1. The ambiguity of the data shows that the verse has been remodelled to make it connect this chapter with what precedes. The original author evidently made David remain in Ziklag two days *after his return from smiting the Amalekites.* The editor inserted the reference to the death of Saul. — **2.** *On the third day there came a man*] the Rabbinical commentators make him to have been Doeg, or his son, or the son of Agag. — *With his clothes rent and earth upon his head*] like the other bearer of bad tidings, I S. 4¹². — **3, 4.** On hearing that the man has escaped from the camp of Israel, David asks him : *How was the affair ?*] cf. I S. 4¹⁶. The reply is similar to that of the messenger at Shiloh : *The people fled from the battle, and many of the people fell, and Saul and Jonathan his son are dead*] the climax is reached in that in which the hearer is most interested. — **5.** David asks particularly concerning the death of Saul and Jonathan : *How dost thou know that Saul and Jonathan his son are dead ?* — **6.** As already pointed out, the reply contradicts the account already given of the death of Saul : *I happened to be on Mount Gilboa, and Saul was leaning on his spear, and the chariots and horsemen drew near him*] in 31³ it was the archers who got him in range. — **7.** *And he looked behind him and saw me*] Saul had been facing the enemy but now looked about for help. — **8.** After calling the stranger, Saul says : *Who art thou ?* To which the stranger makes the reply : *I am an Amalekite.* The contradiction has thus become more glaring ; Saul instead of appealing to his squire, who must have been near his person, finds only one person within call. Instead of shrinking from the abuse of the Philistine, he is willing to give himself to be despatched by an equally despised enemy, an Amalekite. — **9.** Saul's prayer : *Stand over me, I pray, and slay me, for dizziness has seized me*] the exhaustion of a man worn out with fighting. The following clause is obscure ; see the critical note. — **10.** *So I stood over him and slew him for I knew that he could not live after he had fallen*] an apology for his deed on the part of the murderer. He also took Saul's *crown and his armlet*] sev-

eral such are pictured on the arms of Assyrian monarchs.* For
the custom of kings to go into battle in their regalia, notice the
account of Jehoshaphat and Ahab in 1 K. 22[30] where Ahab's disguising himself is an exception to the rule. — *And brought them
to my lord here*] does not expressly state that the bearer regarded
David as the legitimate successor, but seems to imply it. —
11, 12. David and his men mourn for Saul and Jonathan *and for
the house of Israel*, with the customary signs of grief — rending
the clothes, fasting, and weeping. — **13.** To David's question concerning his origin, the messenger replies : *I am the son of an
Amalekite sojourner*] one who had taken up his residence in
Israel where he had the protection accorded to a client, but was
not in full citizenship. Of *proselytes* as we understand the word,
i.e., converts to the true religion, there is no trace in this early
period. — **14.** David's question shows his indignation at any one's
(we may suppose *a fortiori* at a stranger's) *putting out his hand
to destroy the anointed of Yahweh*] the sanctity of the king made
such an act sacrilege. The assassins of Ishbaal received similar
treatment to that recorded here, 4[10 f.], and for the reason here indicated. — **15, 16.** David has him slain by one of his soldiers and
justifies the act in the words : *Thy blood be upon thy head because
thine own mouth testified against thee*] the guilt of the man's
death rests upon himself because he deserves to die. Otherwise
it would rest upon David, cf. the case of Abner, 3[28] and also 1 K.
2[32. 33. 37].

1. The natural construction of the verse as it stands is to make ודוד שב וגו
a circumstantial clause and therefore parenthetical : ' It came to pass after the
death of Saul (David meanwhile had returned from smiting Amalek) that
David abode two days in Ziklag.' But it is doubtful whether this expresses
the sense of the author. What he means is that *after returning from Amalek,
David abode two days in Ziklag* before the message came. The infelicity of
the text shows editorial adaptation to the present context. The original beginning of the verse was probably ויהי אחרי שב דוד simply. In this case, there is
no reason why it may not have continued 30[31]. — העמלק] should be העמלקי
(so 6 MSS.) with 𝔖 or עמלק with 𝔊𝔏. — **2.** For Doeg as the messenger, Schm.
refers to Isaaki, and for the son of Agag to *Auctor Antiq. Bibl. qui falso
Philo fuisse dicitur*. Doeg is also given by Pseudo-Hieronymus, *Questiones*.
— מעם] is read by 𝔊 מעם, but 𝔐 is preferable (We.). — **4.** אשר־נס] another

* Nestle, *Marginalien*, p. 16.

case of אשר in the sense of כי, 1 S. 15²⁰, cf. Davidson, *Syntax*, § 146, R. 2. —
וימתו] is omitted by 𝔊ᴸ᪷, perhaps rightly; 𝔊ᴮ inserts: καὶ ἀπέθανεν καὶ Σαούλ.
— **6.** נקרא נקריתי] evidently the two forms are intended to be from the same
root, cf. 20¹. — ובעלי הפרשים] we read nowhere else of *masters of the horsemen*,
and 𝔊 omits בעלי here, unless οἱ ἱππάρχαι covers both words. Everywhere else
we find פרשים joined with רכב. Possibly some one started to write בעלי הצים
(Gen. 49²³) and afterwards discovered פרשים in his text. — הדבקתהו] strictly
means that they had already overtaken him. — **8.** ויאמר *Kt.*: ואמר *Qrê*. The
latter is necessary. — **9.** עלי] implies that Saul had sunk down — which ought,
however, to be distinctly expressed. — השבץ] occurs nowhere else, and the
meaning is doubtful: σκότος δεινόν 𝔊 possibly a corruption of σκοτόδινος =
dizziness.* The same idea seems to be expressed by צורנא ᪷ (cf. Nestle, *Marginalien*, p. 16 and reff.) : *angustiae* 𝔏, רתיתא 𝔗 suppose Saul overcome by
terror. Modern interpreters are represented by Th. who renders *cramp*, and
Kl. who accepts *giddiness.* Schmid supposes the sentence to mean *my
armour prevents me*, i.e., from carrying out my purpose to kill myself. This
interpretation is due to the theory that Saul had attempted suicide, but the
sword had been turned aside by his coat of mail, so that the blow was not
fatal. — כי־כל־עוד נפשי] is unusual. It is supposed to be by hypallage for
כי־עוד־כל נפשי (Ges. *HWB*¹². *s.v.* כל). But the only analogies cited are Job 27³
and Hos. 14³, the latter of which has a corrupt text. It is doubtful moreover
whether the sense supposed — *for yet my life is whole within me* — is appropriate. I think more likely that Saul means to give a reason for his dizziness,
in which case we might suppose כי כלתה נפשי : *for my strength is consumed*,
that is, *I am utterly exhausted*, cf. Ps. 84³, where, to be sure, the soul is consumed with desire. Graetz (*Gesch. d. Juden*, I. p. 224) proposes to read בל
for כל. — **10.** נפלו] on the pointing cf. Ges.²⁵ 61 *b*; the word must mean Saul's
falling to the earth, showing that he had sunk down in his exhaustion. — נזר]
of the royal crown 2 K. 11¹². — ואצעדה] occurs only here and Num. 31⁵⁾, but
צעדה, Is. 3²⁰, is another form of the same word. We. and Dr. propose to read
הצעדה here also, as the article seems required by the following אשר. Nestle's
objection that the king may have worn several bracelets does not remove the
difficulty, for *one of his bracelets* would not be expressed by the construction
in the text. — **11.** בבגדיו *Qrê*, is sustained by the following plural suffix. —
12. ועל עם יהוה ועל ב׳ ישר׳] is tautology and is relieved by 𝔊 which reads for
the first clause *and over the people of Judah.* But probably even then one
clause is an interpolation. — **13.** גר] cf. Bertholet, *Die Stellung der Israeliten
und der Juden zu den Fremden* (1896), pp. 1, 29. — **16.** For דמיך the *Qrê*
commands דמך as in 1 K. 2³⁷. The *Kthib* however is justified by 2 S. 3²⁸.
Cf. דמיו בו, Lev. 20⁹, etc., and רמו בו, Ezek. 33⁵.

17–27. David's dirge. — The author here inserts a poem on
the death of Saul and Jonathan which he ascribes to David, and

---

* Trendelenburg, cited by Schleusner, *Nov. Thesaurus*, V. p. 62.
S

which he avowedly takes from a book older than his own. The composition is just what it purports to be — a lament on the death of Israel's heroes. *How are the mighty fallen* is the refrain at the end of the opening tristich, which recurs also within the poem, and again at the close. After announcing his theme, the author deprecates the spread of news which will cause the enemy to rejoice. He then pronounces a curse upon Mount Gilboa, the scene of so cruel an event. With v.[22] he takes up the panegyric of the departed warriors — *swifter than eagles, stronger than lions.* He exhorts the daughters of Israel to lament over Saul, whose generosity they had often experienced in the distribution of the booty. And in conclusion he gives vent to his own personal bereavement in the loss of Jonathan.

There seems to be no reason to doubt the genuineness of the poem. One negative reason in its favour seems to be of over-whelming force : it has no religious allusion whatever. The strong current of tradition which early made David a religious hero, renders it improbable that any one should compose for David a poem which contains no allusion to Yahweh, to his relation to Israel, or to his care for Israel's king. A similar argument is the absence of any allusion to the strained relations which had existed between Saul and David. That David should show true magnanimity in the case is not surprising. But it would hardly be human nature for an imitator not to make at least a veiled allusion to David's experience at the court of Saul and during his forced exile. With these negative indications we must put the absence of any positive marks of a late date. There seems to be absolutely nothing in the poem which is inconsistent with its alleged authorship.

The text of the poem has unfortunately suffered in transmission, and in some parts it cannot be restored with certainty. For the most part it is written in verses of four accents. Its logical divisions are indicated in the outline already given.

17-27. A translation is given by Herder, *Geist der Ebräischen Poesie,* 3 Aufl. (Leipzig, 1825), II. p. 289 f. Justi inserts also in this edition his own translation, with a reference to his *Nationalgesänge der Hebräer* as well as his *Blumen althebräischer Dichtkunst,* neither of which I have seen. Translations are given also by E. Meier, *Poet. Nationalliteratur d. Hebr.* p. 123; Ewald, *Dichter des Alten Bundes,* I. p. 149 f.; Graetz, *Gesch. d.*

Juden, I. p. 224 f.; Stade, *GVI.* I. p. 259; GASmith, *Geog.* p. 404 f.   The consensus of recent scholars is in favour of the genuineness of the poem.

17. *David sang this dirge*] as he sang a dirge over Abner, 3³³; the same phrase Ezek. 32¹⁶. — **18.** The first half-verse is perfectly plain so far as the words are concerned, but in their present place they are wholly incongruous : *And he said to teach the children of Judah the bow*.   In the first place if the author meant that David *commanded* something he would have said so.   Secondly, the information that he commanded to teach *the use of the bow* (AV.) is irrelevant.   *The song of the bow* (RV.) is equally out of place unless it means *this song*, which some indeed suppose.   But it is a strange procedure for the author to tell us that David commanded to teach *the song of the bow* without letting us know that this means the song before us.   And why did he not say simply *this song* or *this dirge*, which would have been perfectly clear? We can do nothing with the text as it stands, and the efforts of the commentators only bring the difficulty more clearly into relief. The versions give only slight help.   The word rendered *bow* is omitted by ⅏.   But this does not heal the difficulty.   The only thing certain seems to be that the half-verse represents the opening words of the dirge with the introductory phrase : *And he said*. By a conjecture which will be discussed in the critical note, I suppose the next following words to have been : *Weep, O Judah !* The second half of the verse : *Behold it is written in the Book of Jashar*] is a marginal note which has crept into the text.   The Book of Jashar is mentioned Jos. 10¹³, and was possibly also cited in the original of 1 K. 8¹³, in both cases as authority for a poetical quotation.

18. ויאמר ללמד בני יהודה קשת] there is no reason why the author should not say ויצו if he meant that David commanded something.   We expect also את־הקשת instead of the simple קשת.   But the great difficulty is the irrelevancy of the passage in this connexion — between the announcement of the dirge and the dirge itself.   The Jewish expositors do not see the difficulty.   Isaaki says simply : " David said, now that the mighty men of Israel have fallen, it is necessary that the Children of Judah learn war and draw the bow."   Kimchi supposes that David encouraged his followers by reminding them that Judah was armed with the bow.   Among Christian commentators, Grotius interprets that the song was to be sung during the martial exercises of the soldiers; which of course has no foundation in the text.   Schm. translates ויאמר

inscripsitque, and makes the rest of the clause a title, similar to the titles of the Psalms. These ingenious examples show the impossibility of making anything of the present text. The versions seem to have had what we have, except that 𝔊 omits קשת; but this leaves us pretty much where we were before.

Ew. conjectures קשט for קשת translating, *he commanded to teach the children of Israel accurately.* Conceding that this translation is possible, it does not relieve the main difficulty, and the same is true of Th.'s emendation of the same word to קשב for which he cites Is. 21⁷. GASmith changes to קינות and regards the whole clause as a gloss. But why should a glossator get it into his head that David not only sang the קינה but that he had it *taught?* Such pains is unexampled, and the glossator can have supposed it possible only because there was already corruption of the text of which he had to make sense. Perles (*Analekten zur Textkritik,* p. 21) thinks קשת the result of abbreviation, קינת שאול having been shortened to קש׳ and then read קשת. He also supposes these words an insertion. We. has a theory to account for קשת. He thinks a glossator explained הפרשים in v.⁶ by putting in the margin בעלי קשת, and that one half of the gloss crept into v.⁶ and the other half into this verse, which may have stood in the corresponding line of the second column of the page. This is more ingenious than convincing.

Of all the authors I have found, Klostermann is the only one who seems to have made a start towards the right solution. He sees and says that ויאמר must introduce the poem; and as soon as this is pointed out, every one must recognize the correctness of the observation. Whatever we do with the rest of the verse, this must have been the original force of ויאמר — it immediately preceded the text of the poem. The second half of the verse is therefore a later insertion, which indeed its wording makes very probable. The words following ויאמר represent the opening verse of the dirge. Kl. (followed by Bu. in his text) supposes the original reading to have been ביני יהודה קשות which Kl. translates: *Receive, O Judah, cruel tidings.* But it is doubtful whether this is good Hebrew.

It is altogether probable that the word now represented by בני was originally parallel to the העצבי which (as we shall see) must be restored in the next verse. But if so the natural emendation is בכי. An entirely appropriate opening of the dirge would be

בכי יהורה
העצבי ישראל

After בכי had become corrupted to בני the other words may have been inserted to make some sort of sense. On the other hand, according to the measure which prevails throughout the poem, we should expect six words in this couplet instead of four, and the two words which we still find there may be corrupt representatives of the two which we desire. But, as to their original form, I have not any probable conjecture to offer.

19. The received text has : *The Gazelle is slain,* or : *The beauty is slain*] but either word is inappropriate. The gazelle is a fleet but shy animal, distinguished for a grace and beauty which we think of as feminine. Saul and Jonathan are later said to be *swifter* than eagles. But the eagle hastes to the prey, while the gazelle flees from the pursuer. One comparison is as inappropriate as the other is apt. Nor is the abstract *beauty* any better, for the word here used is never used of the *glory* which is given by strength. 𝔊 found a verb, and following its hint so far as to restore a verb here we may read: *Grieve, O Israel!* The next following words must then be made a clause by themselves: *On thy heights are the slain.* It is too long for the metre in the present text. The refrain — *How are the mighty fallen !* — recurs below, as has been already pointed out.

19. הצבי] is defended by Dr., though he finds it a little singular. In fact the word is nowhere used with reference to a man, and it would be strange if Saul's beauty were made his characteristic here, when we nowhere else hear of it. His manly strength indeed we might find it well to mention, but this would not be the term chosen. The *flower* of Israel's army might perhaps be described as here, though even this is without analogy. The *gazelle* is, of course, out of the question. Asahel is indeed compared to one of the gazelles, 2¹⁸, but we are expressly told that the point of the comparison is his swiftness of foot. 𝔊ᴬᴮ στήλωσον and 𝔊ᴸ ἀκρίβασαι both seem to render הציבי. On the ground of this, Kl. conjectures הַצְבִי which commends itself; the feminine form being chosen because Israel is the mother of the fallen heroes. במתיך should be pointed to agree with this. — חלל] rendered as a plural by 𝔊𝔏, is collective.

20. *Tell it not in Gath, make it not known in the streets of Ashkelon*] representative Philistine cities. The paronomasia of the first clause is repeated in Mic. 1¹⁰. — **21.** *Mountains of Gilboa ! May no dew descend ; and may no rain fall upon you, ye fields of death !* For the conjecture on which this translation is based see the note. The common text is unintelligible. — *For there was cast away the shield of heroes, the shield of Saul not anointed with oil*] the shield instead of being polished and cared for by its owner is left to rust or rot in the field. The text however is not free from difficulty.

21. הרי בגלבע] is suspicious because Gilboa was the name of the mountain ridge itself, not of the district. We should probably read הרי הגלבע, favoured by 𝔊ᴸ𝔏. Kl. proposes to restore חרבי גלבע *be desolate, Gilboa !* — an extremely attractive conjecture. אל־טל seems to require a verb, μὴ πέσοι 𝔊ᴸ : μὴ καταβῇ

𝕲ᴬᴮ; insert therefore ירד. The Arab poet also prays that no dew or rain may fall on the place where the heroes have fallen (We., *Skizzen*, I. p. 139). — ושדי תרומת] is unintelligible: *fields of offerings* have no place in the context, the ו is useless, and the form שדי suspicious. 𝕲ᴸ ὄρη θανάτου is probably right in reading the last three letters as the word מות. In that case, the simplest expedient is to restore the accredited שדות and to put the article for the two letters not accounted for — שדות המות is not very remote from the text and gives a satisfactory sense. Bu. conjectures שדה תרמות referring to Jd. 9³¹ which is however itself corrupt (cf. Moore on the passage). It would be better to read תרמות with Jer. 14¹⁴ *Kt.; fields of deceit* fit the context fairly well, and the same meaning is got by Kl. who proposes שדות רמות; GASmith reads ושדי מהומות; Graetz makes שדי תרומות, equivalent to מרומי שדה Jd. 5¹⁸. The variety of suggestions (and the number might easily be increased) shows the difficulty of the reading. — בלי משיח] is usually understood to apply to the shield, in which case we should read משיח which is found in 23 Heb. MSS. and some early editions. We. independently conjectured this to be the true reading. Graetz proposes כלי משיח: *the weapon of the anointed*. 𝕷 makes the words refer to Saul *quasi non unctus*, and this was adopted in AV. The reference to the shield was understood by 𝕲, and by some of the Rabbinical expositors. Budde makes a new verse begin with this clause, translating: *Not anointed with oil, but with the blood and fat of slain warriors, lies now the shield of Saul upon the battlefield.* See the note on the next verse.

22. Saul has been introduced by the mention of his shield in the preceding verse. This leads up naturally to a panegyric of him and his heroic son. The devouring sword of Saul is paralleled with the equally insatiable bow of Jonathan : *From the blood of the slain, from the fat of heroes, the bow of Jonathan turned not back, and the sword of Saul returned not empty*] the figure seems entirely appropriate ; and there seems, moreover, no reason to change the order of the clauses.

22. מדם חללים מחלב גברים] as noticed above, Bu. (and similarly Kl.) makes these words define the contrast between Saul's shield as it now lies, and its former state — instead of being carefully oiled and polished, it is smeared with the blood and fat of the slain. But with בשמן we should certainly expect כדם, and the change to another preposition is inexplicable. While we might allow the blood to smear the shield, it is hard to picture the *fat* of the slain as part of the polluting medium. On the other hand, the usual figure of the sword as a devouring monster certainly allows us to think of it as satiated with the fat as well as the blood of its victims. Retention of the usual connexion and order of the clauses therefore seems to be more satisfactory than any change yet suggested. — נשוג] an unusual spelling. The commoner form נסוג is found in some MSS.

23. The two heroes shared a common fate : *Saul and Jona-than, the beloved and the lovely*] cf. Cant. 1¹⁶. — *In life and in death they were not divided*] this seems to be the natural connexion and sense of the passage. — *They were swifter than eagles*] the speed of the bird of prey is noted elsewhere, Hab. 1⁸. The vehemence of its attack is the point of the comparison, cf. Jer. 4¹³. — *They were stronger than lions*] Jd. 14¹⁸.

23. אריות] this seems to be the usual plural for ארי, and does not mean *lionesses* as distinguished from *lions*.

24. The women of Israel are reminded of their loss and called upon to *weep over Saul.* As the women took the lead in public festivities on joyful occasions, so it was they who lamented the fallen when there was ceremonial mourning. They had special reason when a warlike prince had fallen, for from his hand they had received the spoil of the enemy : *who clothed you with scarlet and fine linen.* The two articles of luxury belong together, Luke 16¹⁹. For the *golden jewels* with which he decked them, cf. Jer. 4³⁰.

24. בכה with אל is not common, but cf. Ezek. 27³¹. We should perhaps read על with 10 MSS. — עם ערנים] *with dainties* is the natural meaning of the words, but the construction is harsh, and 𝔗 is obliged to insert ומוכיל לכם. It seems better to emend with Graetz (*Gesch. d. Juden*, I. p. 192) reading עם סרינים, cf. Jd. 14¹² Is. 3²³. עדי is collective as in Ex. 33⁶.

25. The lament over the fallen is followed by David's expres-sion of personal bereavement. Repeating the refrain : *How are the mighty fallen in the battle,* he makes special mention of Jona-than. Unfortunately, this half of the verse is hopelessly corrupt. The received text gives : *Jonathan on thy heights is slain.* But the pronoun must refer to Israel in order to make sense, and Israel has not been mentioned since the opening distich. No one of the various conjectures which have been brought forward seems free from difficulty.

25. If the first half of the verse stood alone we might suppose it to contain the lament which the women are to chant. For this reason Kl. emends by changing the words בתוך המלחמה into כלי מחמר ויאברו a variant of which he supposes now to stand at the end of the dirge (where 𝔊ᴸ reads ἐπιθυμητά for מלחמה). But if this be original, it is hard to account for the corruption.

Graetz corrects יהונתן to ישראל which would give a good sense in itself consid-ered. But the opening of v.²⁶ would then be very abrupt. We. points out that several Greek codd. read εἰς θάνατον ἐτραυματίσθη(ς) (𝕲ᴸ adds ἐμοί) which would allow us to restore למות חללת. Kl. goes further, suggesting: במותך חלית אני, *in thy death I too am wounded*, while Bu. reads in his text לבי במותך חלל, *my heart is wounded in thy death*. The last is less remote from the received text, but none can be regarded as convincing.

26. A burst of grief at the recollection of what Jonathan's friendship had been. It seems necessary to disregard the accents and arrange the words as a tristich :

> *I am in anguish for thee, my brother, Jonathan !*
> *Thou wert delightsome to me — exceedingly wonderful !*
> *Thy love for me was beyond the love of women.*

We thus conform to the metre of the rest of the composition. The *love of women* which the poet has in mind may be supposed to include both the love of the bride for her husband and the love of the mother for her son. — **27.** The refrain is here completed by the additional clause : *And the weapons of war perished !* The parallelism suggests that the *weapons of war* are Saul and Jonathan themselves (Dr. from Ewald).

26. נפלאתה] on the form as here pointed cf. Ges.²⁶ 75 *oo*. The text may not be sound, but no acceptable emendation has yet been proposed. Kl. points out that the termination would cause us to read נפלאתה, *thou wert wonderful*, an emphatic repetition of נעמת, and although this is without analogy, so far as I discover, it is probably the best we can do with the present text. Bu.'s נפלאת taken adverbially would require the מאד to follow. — **27.** המלחמה] ἐπιθυμητά is found in 𝕲ᴸ as noted above. It seems to be taken from Theodotion (cf. Field, *Hex. Origenis*).

The following translation is designed simply to embody the results of the foregoing inquiry.

I.

18. Weep, O Judah !
19. Grieve, O Israel !
On thy heights are the slain;
How are the mighty fallen !

II.

20. Tell it not in Gath;
Publish it not in the streets of Ashkelon !
Lest the daughters of the Philistines rejoice;
Lest the daughters of the uncircumcised be glad.

21. Mountains of Gilboa! May no dew descend
    Nor rain upon you, fields of death!
    For there was cast away the shield of heroes,
    The shield of Saul not anointed with oil.

22. From the blood of the slain,
    From the fat of heroes,
    The bow of Jonathan turned not back,
    And the sword of Saul returned not empty.

23. Saul and Jonathan, the beloved and the lovely!
    In life and in death they were not divided.
    They were swifter than eagles,
    They were stronger than lions.

24. Daughters of Israel, weep over Saul!
    Who clothed you with scarlet and fine linen,
    Who put golden jewels upon your clothing.
25. How are the mighty fallen
    In the midst of the battle!

III.
Jonathan   .   .   .   .   .

26. I am distressed for thee, Jonathan, my brother!
    Thou wert delightsome to me — exceeding wonderful!
    Thy love to me was beyond the love of women.
27. How are the mighty fallen,
    And the weapons of war perished!

2 SAMUEL II.–XXIV. DAVID THE KING.

This is the third part of the Books of Samuel, as now constructed. The composite nature of the history has been indicated
in the Introduction, as has the fact that the main source continues
into 1 Kings.

Chapters II.–IV. The Kingdom of Hebron. — The account
seems to continue immediately the story broken off (for the insertion of the Dirge) at 1^{16}.

II. 1–4a. David becomes king of Hebron. — *After this*, that
is, after receiving the news of Saul's death, *David asked of
Yahweh*] 1 S. 23^2 30^8. In the account here given, David's first

question is in the usual direct form, the second asks for a specific name. But probably the name was obtained by a process of exclusion like that used in discovering a person by lot. Hebron was in fact indicated by its position, and the oracle could hardly go astray. It was the well-known chief city of Judah, or rather of Caleb, Jd. 1[10. 20] Jos. 15[13]. The writer counts it to Judah, Caleb having already become a clan of that tribe. David *went up* to it from Ziklag which lay lower down. — **2, 3**. David brought up his household and his men with their families, *and they dwelt in the citadel of Hebron*] the received text has : *in the cities* of Hebron, which can hardly be correct. — **4**. *And the men of Judah came and anointed David there as king over the house of Judah*] the sovereignty would not be legitimate unless confirmed by the Sheikhs of the clans. How much choice they had in the matter is difficult to say. The master of a devoted band of seasoned soldiers was a dangerous man to reject. On the other hand, the public defence was likely to be well attended to by such a man, and David had always been well disposed towards his own people. That he continued to acknowledge the suzerainty of Achish seems almost certain, from the fact that the Philistines allowed him to extend his kingdom so far as he did.

1. The name חברון possibly means *confederacy*, and the other name given to the city — Kirjath-Arba — may indicate the fact that the town was originally settled by various clans who made an alliance; cf. Moore on Jd. 1[10] with his references. The cohabitation of various Arab tribes in Medina is a parallel instance. GASmith (*Geog.* p. 318) thinks the ancient city lay on a hill to the northwest of the present site. — **3**. ואנשיו] the suffix is superfluous; read והאנשים with 𝔊[B]. It is possible that the text of [2. 3] was originally shorter. — בערי חברון] is supposed to mean *in the towns* in the district of which Hebron was the centre. These dependent places however are called elsewhere חצרים, or else the *daughters* of the chief city, and there is no clear parallel to ערי חברון. It seems better therefore to read בעיר חברון and take עיר in its primary sense of *fort* or *citadel*, cf. 5[7. 9]. There is no reason why David's procedure at Hebron should differ from that at Jerusalem.

4b–7. David's message to the Gileadites.

— The fragment obviously presupposes 1 S. 31, and seems to continue that narrative directly, for 31[13] is abrupt in its ending and requires something further. In that case, this document had an account of David's anointing. — **4**. The Hebrew as it stands does not make sense.

They told David of the men of Jabesh Gilead, which is probably the intention of the author, would require a different order. — **5.** David blesses them because *they had done this kindness to their lord.* The burial of the dead is an act of piety. — **6.** In addition to invoking Yahweh's blessing on them, David promises : *I also will do you good because you have done this thing*] the text must be emended in a single word. — **7.** The times call for courage on their part : *For your lord Saul is dead and me the house of Judah have anointed king over them*] so that I am kept at a distance from you for the present, seems to be the implication.

4b. The sentence, as it stands, is incomplete : *They told David, saying : The men of Jabesh Gilead who buried Saul.* Precisely as in English, a predicate should follow; but the present text leaves us in the lurch. The English version : *The men of Jabesh Gilead were they that buried Saul* would require the insertion of המה at least. 𝕲ᴸ translates as if it had המה instead of אשר; 𝕲ᴮ transfers אשר, making it follow לאמר, while 𝕾 omits אשר. Bu. does the same on conjecture but does not profess to regard the resulting text as original. Kl. proposes to read על־ארת for לאמר, cf. Gen. 26³². I should think את־שמות equally appropriate — *they told David the names of the men.* But the insecurity of our footing is evident. — **5.** אנשי] 𝕲ᴮ has ἡγουμένους (ἡγεμόνας ᴸ) representing בעלי, cf. Jd. 9⁵¹ (𝕲ᴬ). For החסד הזה 𝕲ᴬ (ᴮ is lacking here) has τὸ ἔλεος τοῦ θεοῦ which is perhaps original; 𝕲ᴸ omits הזה. — **6.** הטובה הזאת] seems difficult. If it refer to the present embassy (perhaps with a gift) we should expect the verb to be in the other tense. Kl. makes אעשה a cohortative : *let me show you this friendliness.* But a king would hardly take this tone. It is best therefore to change הזאת to החת as is done by We. (Dr., Bu.). — **7.** וגם] naturally introduces a reason of the same kind with that which had preceded, and this can only be that the administration of Judah keeps David just now from coming to the assistance of Gilead.

II. 8–IV. 12. The reign of Ishbaal.
— Ishbaal, the only surviving son of Saul, becomes king over North Israel. The chief support of his throne is Abner, Saul's general. In the war carried on between the two Israelitish powers, David is the gainer. Ishbaal hastens his own downfall by his resentment at Abner's encroachments on the prerogative. Abner agrees to deliver the kingdom to David, but is murdered in blood revenge by Joab. Ishbaal, deprived of his chief officer, falls by the hand of assassins. But when these come to David expecting a reward, they are treated as the murderer of Saul had been treated.

The piece is homogeneous, except some brief interpolations which will be noticed in the course of the exposition. The most extensive is 3^{2-5}. The document from which the section is taken seems to be the same from which we have the full account of David's reign in 9–20.

8–11. Abner places Ishbaal on the throne. — The opening part of the paragraph is necessary to the understanding of what follows. Not so with ^{10a} and ^{11}, two chronological statements such as elsewhere belong to the final redaction of the book. — **8.** The verse follows 1 S. 31^{13}. After the death of Saul, we naturally inquire what became of his kingdom. As fitted to the present place it tells us that Abner *had taken Ishbaal and brought him over to Mahanaim*] the name Ishbaal has been mutilated to *Ishbosheth* to suit the squeamishness of the scribes. *Mahanaim*, an ancient sanctuary, was later David's refuge when driven out of his capital. It is mentioned in connexion with Jacob's wanderings, immediately after the treaty with Laban, Gen. 32^3. This account brings it into connexion with the Jabbok, and from 2 S. 18^{23} we infer that it cannot have been far from the Jordan valley. It is not yet clearly identified in any modern site. — **9.** Ishbaal's kingdom included nearly all Israel — all north of Jerusalem and all east of the Jordan : *Gilead*, the well-known transjordanic district, and the *Asherite*, north of the Great Plain, Jd. $1^{31f.}$, *and Jezreel, and Ephraim, and Benjamin, and* [in fact] *all Israel*. The original narrative continued by adding ^{10b} : *only the house of Judah followed David*. The extent of Ishbaal's kingdom is confirmed by the fact that the battle, an account of which follows, was fought at Gibeon, and further by the fact that a late writer would have reduced its proportions and have given more of it to David. The Philistine occupation of the country was maintained to an extent sufficient to secure their sovereignty, and it is probable that both Ishbaal and David were their tributaries.* That their vassals should weaken each other by war was, of course, according to the wish of the Philistines. — **10.** The first half-verse is an endeavour to introduce a scheme of chronology, like 1 S. 13^1. The data are suspicious. Ishbaal could hardly have been forty years old, and

---

* Cf. Kamphausen, " Philister und Hebräer," in the *ZATW.* VI. pp. 43–97.

it seems altogether likely that he reigned more than two years. —
11. Another insertion possibly occasioned by [10a], as though the
redactor in speaking of the length of Ishbaal's reign felt it necessary to add something concerning David. It could hardly escape
notice however that the two verses are inconsistent. The reign of
Ishbaal virtually coincided in length with David's reign at Hebron.
The hypothesis that Abner was five years in reconquering the territory of Saul is untenable, for in any case Ishbaal must count his
reign from the death of Saul, whose legitimate successor he was.
On the other hand, that five years elapsed after the death of Ishbaal before the tribes acknowledged David, is contrary to all the
indications of the narrative. The length of David's Hebron reign,
as given here, coincides with the datum in 5[5], and we have no
reason to doubt its correctness.

8. איש־בשת] *The man of shame* would be no name to give a son, especially a king's son. There can be no doubt that the original name is preserved
to us in the form אישבעל, 1 Chr. 8[33] 9[39]. We find traces of the original form
in some MSS. of 𝕲 and 𝕴 in this passage also. The reluctance of the later
Jews to pronounce the name Baal led to the substitution of בשת for it, even
in proper names. Another method was taken with this name in 1 S. 14[49].
As we see from Jerubbaal, the name Baal was, in the early period of Israel's
history, applied without scruple to Yahweh, cf. Moore, *Judges*, p. 195. —
מחנים] ἐκ τῆς παρεμβολῆς 𝕲: *per castra* 𝕴. That a proper name is intended
is certain. A number of transjordanic names have the (apparent) dual ending: Eglaim, Kirjathaim, and others. For the location we may note that
Jacob passed Mahanaim before he reached Penuel on his way from Syria to
Canaan, and that Penuel lay at the fords of the Jabbok. Josh. 13[26. 30] makes
Mahanaim a point on the boundary line of Gad and the eastern Manasseh.
But none of these indications are sufficient to identify the exact spot. *Mahne*
or *Mihne* mentioned by Buhl (*Geog.* p. 257) from Seetzen and Merrill (*Across
the Jordan*, p. 433 ff.) seems to lie too far from the Jordan valley to meet the
requirements of 2 S. 18. — **9.** האשורי] of a clan of this name we have a trace
in Gen. 25[3]. But they were evidently Bedawin and not likely to come under
Ishbaal. The Israelite tribe האשרי seems to fit the case. Th., following Ew.,
adopts הגשורי, which is supported by 𝕊 and some MSS. of 𝕴. It seems
doubtful however whether the *Geshurites*, who had a king of their own at
about this time, 3[3], could have been under Ishbaal. The tribe of Asher is
found in this verse by Pseudo-Hieronymus, *Questiones in Libros Regum.*
Notice the way in which אל and על are used together in this verse. The
original writer must have used על throughout. — **10, 11.** The authorities are
pretty well united in the supposition that [10a. 11] are redactional insertions.

12–17. The battle of Gibeon. — One of the battles between the soldiers of the two Israelite monarchs is related in detail. The reason for the choice of this particular one is its bearing on the later history — in its sequel. It is commonly assumed that Abner was the aggressor. But as the battle took place on Benjamite territory, where if anywhere Ishbaal's claim was valid, it seems more probable that David's men were acting on the offensive. David was seeking to extend his kingdom to the north of Judah. His piety towards Saul would not necessarily cause him to spare his successor. The account of the battle proper is very brief.

12. *Abner and the servants of Ishbaal*] that is, the standing army whose quarters were at the capital. — *Gibeon* was a well-known Canaanite city whose inhabitants had a treaty with the Israelites until the time of Saul. By the extermination of the Canaanite stock, Saul made the city Benjamite. A village on the ancient site still bears the name *el-Gib.* — **13.** *And Joab the son of Zeruiah*] who here appears for the first time as David's General, *and the servants of David went out*] from Hebron as 𝕲 correctly interprets. — *And met them at the pool of Gibeon*] a large reservoir which still exists. — **14.** Abner's proposition for a tournament is acceded to by Joab. Individual combats frequently precede the general engagement in oriental warfare. — **15, 16.** The tournament was held, with twelve champions for each side. Exactly what took place is not easy to make out, but the result was that they fell dead together. As in so many other cases the incident was commemorated by naming the place. The field was called *the Field of the Enemies.* — **17.** The battle which was thus introduced *was exceedingly severe.* But the result was in favour of David's men. The king himself does not seem to have been present.

12. וּבְעֹנָה] Γαβαώ 𝕲ᴬ. The place is five miles west of north from Jerusalem, cf. Robinson, *BR*². I. p. 455 f. — **13.** יוֹאָב] *Yahweh is father*, cf. אֲבִיאֵל and אֱלִיאָב. — יֵצְאוּ] 𝕲 adds ἐκ Χεβρών, adopted by Bu., but the insertion is more likely than the omission. — וַיִּפְגְּשׁוּם] does not necessarily mean (as Kl. supposes) that the meeting was unexpected, cf. Ex. 4²⁷. — יַהְדֹּו] is superfluous, and in fact impossible, after the suffix in וַיִּפְגְּשׁוּם. Probably it is a corruption of some word defining the circumstances — Kl. suggests חֹנִים, *camping.* — מִזֶּה

. . . ‏מזה‎] as in 1 S. 14⁴. — **14.** ‏וישחקו‎] used nowhere else of fighting. It seems plain however that the proposition was to have a combat of picked men as a prelude to the main battle. — **15.** ‏ויעברו‎] " of the individuals passing in order before the teller " (Dr.). — ‏ולאיש‎] omit the ‏ו‎ with 𝕲𝕾. — **16.** A difficult verse. The interpretation must proceed from ‏ויפלו יחד‎ which most naturally means *they fell all together*, i.e., the champions fell dead, not *the two armies came into conflict* as is supposed by Kl. The clause ‏ויחזק וגו׳‎ will then describe the action of the champions in the tournament: *Each took hold of the head of his fellow.* But who is meant by *his fellow?* We most naturally suppose it to be his next neighbour of his own party. But as this gives no suitable sense we are compelled to make ‏רעהו‎ refer to each one's antagonist. The next clause is difficult in either case: *and his sword in the side of his fellow.* A verb seems required, as ‏ויחזק‎ could not in itself mean that he struck his sword into his fellow, *defixit gladium* 𝕷. I suspect the corruption to be in ‏בראש‎ as is alleged by Kl., though I cannot accept his emendation. After ‏איש‎ 𝕲 inserts τῇ χειρί probably correctly. — ‏הצרים‎] might be *of the sharp knives* as is perhaps intended by the punctuation. The conjecture that 𝕲 τῶν ἐπιβούλων goes back to ‏הצרים‎, first broached by Schleusner, and accepted by Ew. and others, does not seem well founded. Ἐπίβουλος nowhere occurs for ‏צר‎ (or ‏צרה‎) but generally for ‏שטן‎, once for ‏צר‎. There is no question of *plotters* or *liers-in-wait*, but of determined *enemies*, which would be ‏הצרים‎.

18–23. The death of Asahel; a single incident of the battle, important for the prominence of the actors and for its sequel. — **18.** The three sons of Zeruiah, nephews of David, were foremost in the fight. Joab and Abishai have appeared in the earlier narrative. Asahel seems to have been the youngest. He is described as *swift of foot like one of the gazelles which are in the field*] the gazelle lives in the open country. Swiftness was a prime qualification for the ancient warrior, cf. what is said of Saul and Jonathan, 1²³. — **19.** Asahel's ambition was content with no less a prey than Abner himself whom he followed steadily. — **20.** Abner, overtaken by his pursuer, but conscious of his own superiority, is unwilling to fight with him. He first assures himself that it is Asahel as he supposed. — **21.** He then counsels him to be content with an antagonist of lesser rank: *Seize one of the young men and take his spoil*] trophy enough, without aspiring to the conquest of the general. — **22.** Abner makes a second attempt to dissuade his pursuer: *Why should I smite thee to the ground? And how [in that case] could I lift up my face to Joab thy brother?*] Abner fears the blood feud which must follow. — **23.** The only resource

was to strike : *And Abner smote him with a backward stroke in
the abdomen, and the spear came out at his back, and he fell there
and died in his place.* The remainder of the verse seems to be
an erroneous supplement, inserted as a reminiscence from the
similar passage 20¹² where alone such a standing still of the people
is in place.

18. עשהאל] similar names are עשיאל and עשיה. A similar ה in פרהצור Num.
1¹⁰. צבים the plural of צבי; the same word is used of the mature gazelle in
Arabic. — **19.** על־הימין] where we should expect אל. But על is repeated in
v.²¹. — **21.** נטה לך] the dative of advantage is frequent in such connexion, as
in סור לך of the following verse. — חלצתו] that which was stripped from the
slain. It was the natural law of war that the arms of the slain belonged to
the slayer. Such was Mohammed's ruling in his campaigns. The arms of
the hostile general would confer especial renown on their captor. — **22.** ואיך
אשא פני] a duplicate translation of 𝕲ᴮ goes back to ואיך זה פנה — obviously
the poorer text. — **23.** באחרי החנית] is supposed to mean *with the butt of the
spear*. It is doubtful however whether אחרים is so used, and it is further
doubtful whether the butt of the spear was ever so sharp that it would go
through a man, as here described. We. recognizes the difficulty, but has no
solution. Kl. proposes to read אחרנית which might describe the blow of a
man delivered backward, without turning to face his pursuer, but, of course,
with the point of the (reversed) spear. This is adopted by Bu. The concluding part of the verse disturbs the connexion and is regarded as an interpolation
by Kl., Bu. It also contradicts the account which follows.

24–III. 1. Conclusion of the battle. — A final stand is made
by the Benjamites, but when the attack is about to be made Abner
appeals for clemency, so that Joab draws off his men. — **24.** The
pursuit lasted until sundown when the contending parties reached
the Hill of Ammah, mentioned nowhere else and unidentified.
The author endeavours to give the exact location, but we are unable
to follow him. — **25.** There the Benjamites *collected behind Abner
and made themselves a phalanx*] a close *knot* like the bunch of
hyssop, Ex. 12²². That this was on the hill already mentioned is
evident, though not asserted in the present text. — **26.** Abner's
appeal : *Shall the sword devour forever? Dost thou not know
that the sequel will be bitter?*] is directed to the consciousness of
common blood in the pursuers. The Bedawin still shrink from
the extermination of a clan, even in bitter feuds. — *How long wilt
thou refrain from commanding the people to turn from the pursuit*

of their brethren ? The question is in effect a cry for quarter. —
27. Joab, though ruthless, is not altogether without conscience.
He would have kept up the pursuit all night unless Abner had
spoken, but now he will relent. — **28.** He therefore gives the signal and the fighting is stayed. — **29.** Abner and his men *marched
in the Arabah all that night and crossed the Jordan and went
through the whole Bithron*] or Ravine, doubtless the proper name
of one of the side valleys up which Mahanaim was situated. —
— **30.** At the muster of Joab's troops, *there were missing nineteen
men besides Asahel*] who receives special mention on account of
his prominence. — **31.** The loss on Abner's side — 360 men —
shows that the experienced warriors of David were opposed in the
main by untried men. Saul's old soldiers (of his body-guard) had
perished with their master. — **32.** The next day was occupied in
the march to Bethlehem, where Asahel was duly buried *in the sepulchre of his father*, and Joab continued his march through the
night so that *day dawned upon them in Hebron.* — **III. 1.** Concluding notice of this paragraph : *The war was prolonged . . .
but David kept growing stronger, while the house of Saul kept
growing weaker.*

---

24. The hill is described as על-פני גיח דרך, where גיח is obscure and probably corrupt : 𝔊ᴮ has Γαί which might represent גיא or עי. We. supposes גיח
to have arisen by the erroneous duplication of the two preceding letters together with ה from הדרך so that he restores על פני הר׳ which is adopted by
Bu. He also proposes to read במדבר for מדבר. He thus locates the hill *east
of the road in the wilderness of Gibeon.* Nothing better has been proposed,
but it is remarkable that after so complete a rout, the forces had got no further
than the wilderness (or pasture land) of Gibeon. The original reading was
probably different. — **25.** וגבעה אחת] as the mention of the Hill of Ammah is
superfluous unless the rally took place upon it, we should probably restore
האחרונה here with Ki., Bu. — **26.** באחרונה] I have ventured to read האחרונה
with 𝔊ᴸ. — וער] the ו is omitted by 𝔖𝔏, but not by 𝔊 as We. asserts. *How
long dost thou not command*, where we should say : *How long dost thou refrain
from commanding ?* — **27.** נעלה] the verb is used of giving up the siege of a
city, Jer. 37⁵·¹¹, cf. Num. 16²⁴·²⁷. In this place 𝔊 ἀνέβη seems to have read
יעלה; but the analogy of hypothetical sentences elsewhere favours 𝔋. —
28. The plain intimation is that the whole force was within hearing of the
commander's horn. — **29.** וילכו] the same verb with an accusative of the country traversed (as here) is found Dt. 1¹⁹ 2⁷. — **30.** ויפקרו] cf. 1 S. 20¹⁸. — ועשהאל]
is connected with the next verse by 𝔊ᴮ (or by the editor). It does not seem

T

natural to make Asahel prominent in this way, to the ignoring of Joab and Abishai, who must have been equally active in the combat. — **31.** באנשי] it is difficult to make out whether the author wishes to make two classes of the soldiers of Abner and the men of Benjamin. Probably not, in which case we should read without ו as 𝔊 does. — מהו] is incomprehensible, perhaps a marginal gloss which has crept into the text. 𝔊ᴸ omits it (so 𝔖 which inserts מת at the end of v.³⁰), while 𝔊ᴮ represents מאתו. — **32.** בית לחם] for which 9 MSS. (DeR.) have בבית ל and 𝔊 has ἐν B. — **III. 1.** ארכה] cf. Ez. 12²² Jer. 29²⁸. The word seems better than הרבה which was read by 𝔊.

III. 2–5. David's family.

— Before taking up the event which brought Israel into David's hands, the compiler inserts the names of the sons born to him in Hebron. They were six, from as many wives. — *Amnon* the first born, afterwards notorious, was the son of *Ahinoam* mentioned above, 1 S. 25⁴³. — *Chileab*, the son of Abigail, bears a name which reminds us of his mother's blood. — *Absalom's* mother was a daughter of *Talmai king of Geshur*, a small Aramaic kingdom, 15⁸. — *Adonijah* is well known in the later history, whereas *Shephatiah* is not again heard of. The same is true of *Ithream*, the son of Eglah, who is curiously described in the received text as the *wife of David*. This cannot be original, as all the others were equally wives of David. From the analogy of Abigail, we expect here the name of her former husband, but possibly the description was of a different kind.

2–5. The paragraph is placed by Bu. after 8¹⁴ and is followed in his text immediately by 5¹³⁻¹⁶. It is in fact probable that the notices of David's family belong together. Whether they ever stood at the end of 8¹⁴ is doubtful. — **2.** ויולדו] for which *Qrê* proposes ויולדו. The *Kt.* is probably for יולדו, cf. similar instances in Piel, Ges.²⁶ 69 *u.* — **3.** כלאב] may have some connexion with the tribe Caleb. — לאביגל] the form varies between אביגל and אביגיל. — נעור] is brought into connexion with Aram, not only 15⁸, but also 1 Chr. 2²³. It is contiguous to Bashan Josh. 12⁵. — **4.** אדניה 𝔊ᴸ has Ὀρνια; 𝔊ᴮ Ὀρνείλ. — **5.** אשת דוד] for which 1 Chr. 3³ has אשתו, is uncalled for. The name of a former husband would be in place. It is difficult to see how such a name could be replaced by David's, and it is possible that the woman was David's relative within the degrees afterwards regarded as prohibited, his half-sister for example. Such a marriage was regarded as regular so late as the time of the Elohistic author of the life of Abraham (Gen. 20¹²), and would have given no offence in the time of David. Read therefore אחות דוד. The sins of Jerusalem as enumerated by Ezekiel (22¹¹) include *the humbling of one's sister*, showing that such marriages were entered into down to the time of the Exile.

6–39. Abner's negotiation with David and his death. — Abner quarrels with his king on account of a concubine of Saul. He opens negotiations with David looking to the transfer of Israel's allegiance. To this end he visits Hebron. An agreement is reached in the absence of Joab. This officer, on learning of what has been done, recalls Abner and puts him to death in revenge for the death of Asahel. David shows by his lament for Abner, that he has no part in the murder.

The section seems to be generally regarded as homogeneous; only Bonk characterizes [12-16] as an interpolation. In fact the story is over full and there is reason to suspect that two accounts have been wrought into one. Verse [12] would join well to v.[1]. But the division comes more naturally after v.[19] than after v.[16]. One of the two accounts made Abner send to David by the hand of messengers; the other made him come in person. In the former document his motive was simply the conviction that David was the man of the future. The other gave the quarrel with Ishbaal as the occasion.

6–11. The quarrel with Ishbaal. — Abner was conscious of his own power, and trespassed upon the prerogative of the monarch. — **6.** While the war was going on, *Abner was overbearing in the house of Saul*] as is shown by the instance which follows. — **7.** *Saul had a concubine whose name was Rizpah*] cf. 21[8]. The custom of men of wealth and station to take wives of the second rank is abundantly illustrated from the time of Abraham down. — *And Abner took her*] missing in 𝔥, is necessary to the sense. It is preserved in 𝔊[L]. Ishbaal protested: *Why didst thou go in to my father's concubine?* He was fully in the right. The son inherited his father's wives with the rest of the estate. Abner invaded the rights of the king as truly as if he had seduced any one of Ishbaal's wives. To indicate assumption of the throne, Absalom takes possession of his father's concubines, 16[21], and the request of Adonijah for Abishag rouses the wrath of Solomon on the same grounds which provoke Ishbaal here. Arabic custom to the time of Mohammed is well known, and the same seems to have prevailed in Judah down to the Exile, cf. Ezek. 22[10]. — **8.** The reply of Abner is not a justification of his act but an assertion of his merits : *Am I a dog's head, I, who keep showing kindness to the house of Saul . . . and who have not delivered thee into the hand of David, that to-day thou findest fault with me about a woman?* The text is not altogether sound, but the thought is sufficiently clear. — **9, 10.** Abner swears to accomplish what Yahweh has sworn to David — *to transfer the kingdom from the house of Saul, and to establish David's throne over Israel and over Judah from Dan to Beersheba*] 1 S. 3²⁰. — **11.** The weak Ishbaal was not able to make any reply.

6. The first clause is an appropriate introduction to what follows. If it immediately followed v.¹ it would be superfluous, but that it did so follow is not certain. — מתחזק] the parallel cases of the verb with ב would favour the meaning *strengthened himself in the house of Saul*, that is, fortified his cause by dependence upon the house of Saul, 1 S. 30⁶. But the weakness of the house of Saul is against this rendering. It seems necessary therefore to interpret the words of Abner's arrogance towards the king whose throne was supported by him — *Abner regebat domus Saul* 𝕷. — **7.** בת־איה] an Edomite clan bore the name איה, Gen. 36²⁴. Before ויאמר 𝕲ᴸ inserts καὶ ἔλαβην αὐτὴν 'Αβεννήρ, and after the same word 𝕲 inserts the name of the king, as do 𝕾𝕷 and a few MSS. of 𝕳. On the son's marrying the wife of his father cf. W. R. Smith (*Kinship and Marriage*, p. 89 f.), who calls attention to Wellhausen's restoration of 1 Chr. 2²⁴, an emendation adopted by Kittel, in his edition of Chronicles (*SBOT.*). Wellhausen's emendation is in his dissertation *De Gentibus et Familiis Judaeis* (1870), p. 14, n. 1. Cf. also Driver on Dt. 23¹ (= 22³⁹). — **8.** הראש כלב] the expression is not used elsewhere, but seems intelligible without supposing a contemptuous reference to the clan Caleb. — אשר ליהורה] must qualify כלב, taking the place of an adjective — *Am I a Judahite dog's head?* But the construction of what follows is thus rendered more difficult, and there is reason to suspect that ליהורה, which is not represented in 𝕲, is not original. Its insertion may be the work of a scribe who interpreted the preceding word as referring to the tribe of *Caleb* as though Abner asked: *Am I a Calebite captain,* that is, *a turbulent freebooter?* Omitting ליהורה we get a fairly good sense. — אעשה] in the frequentative sense. The house of Saul is defined so as to include *his brothers* and *his comrades*. It is unnecessary to insert ו before אל־אחיו, as is done by some MSS. of 𝕳, by 𝕲 and 𝕷. The *guilt of a woman* (genitive of the object) is evidently regarded as a trifle. We should read אשה with 𝕲, so We., Bu., al. — **9.** אעשה־לו] + ἐν τῇ ἡμέρᾳ ταύτῃ 𝕲 is adopted by We. and others, though the sense seems good without it.

12–19. The return of Michal. — Abner sends messengers to David to treat for the submission of all Israel. David will enter

on the negotiation only on the condition of the return of Michal his wife. She is therefore brought back, and Abner speaks to the elders of Israel with a view to making David king.

12–19. As remarked above, the section does not altogether agree with what follows. In v.[21] Abner promises that he will go and gather all Israel, and they will make an agreement with David. It looks therefore as if Abner's visit (v.[20]) was the opening of negotiations, and there is no room for [12-19]. The latter is another representation of Abner's action, into which the narrator inserted the account of the return of Michal. This also presents difficulties. In v.[13] David stipulates that Abner shall bring her back. In v.[14] he sends for her to Ishbaal. In v.[16] Abner accompanies her as far as Bahurim, but apparently not to Hebron. It is not unlikely that this account (vv.[14-16]) was originally continued in such a form as to make Abner's visit to David the conclusion of the journey with Michal.

12. Abner sent messengers to David offering *to turn all Israel* to him, if David would make a definite agreement with Abner. The contents of the agreement are not told, but we may suppose that it included personal advantages to Abner, as well as immunity for past opposition. On some difficulties in the text, see the critical note. — **13.** David stipulates first of all that Abner should bring Michal when he comes to see him. The prohibition of the Law, which forbade a man to take back a wife who had been married to another, seems to have been unknown, cf. Deut. 24[1-4]. The scrupulosity of the Jews is shown by the Rabbinical fancy that Paltiel had not consummated his marriage with Michal. — **14.** David sends messengers to Ishbaal with the demand : *Give me my wife Michal, whom I bought for a hundred foreskins of the Philistines*] the reference to 1 S. 18[25, 27] is obvious, but the passage knows nothing of David's paying double the price demanded by Saul. — **15.** Ishbaal sends and takes her *from her husband, Paltiel ben Laish*] to whom she was given by Saul, 1 S. 25[44]. — **16.** Her husband followed her *weeping as he went* as far as *Bahurim*, a place near Jerusalem, 16[5]. Probably it was the last Benjamite village on the road they were travelling. Here at Abner's command he turned back. — **17.** The account should naturally tell of the completion of Michal's return. But it breaks off and tells of Abner's activity among the elders of Israel. In the present connexion we most naturally translate : *And Abner's word* *had been with the Sheikhs of Israel*] the implication is that he had taken measures to change the allegiance of Israel before his journey. — **18**. After reminding them that they had already some leanings towards David he adds the promise of God : *Now act! For Yahweh has said to David : By the hand of David my servant will I deliver my people Israel.* It is idle to inquire what particular promise is referred to. — **19**. The prominent mention of Benjamin is due to the fact that, as the tribe of Saul, it would be the most difficult to move.

---

12. תחתו לאמר למי ארץ לאמר] is unintelligible and certainly corrupt. 𝕲ᴸ has simply εἰς Χεβρὼν λέγων which looks like a conjectural emendation. 𝕲ᴮ has εἰς Θαιλὰμ οὗ ἦν παραχρῆμα λέγων, but what this represents is difficult to say. That David was in *Telam* at the time seems to be the intention, though elsewhere 𝕲 renders this name by Τελέμ. The other versions seem to have had the received text before them. All are compelled (like the modern expositors who try to make sense out of this text) to translate as though ארץ could stand for הארץ which is not the case. If Abner had meant to ask *whose is the land?* insinuating *in manu mea est terra ut ad te transferam,** he must have said למי הארץ. Even if this were the reading, the following לאמר would be unaccountable. Of the proposals to emend the text, Kl.'s deserves mention. He supposes the original to have been כל בית ישראל תחתי לתת למי ארצה לאמר, *all the house of Israel is under my hand to give to whom I please when I say.* The sentence would be an appropriate introduction to what follows. — **13.** כי אם־לפני] is redundant, and לפני is lacking in 𝕲, which also reads הבא, adopted by Th., al. On the Rabbinical theory of Paltiel's self-control cf. Schm. The text gives no indication that he was not Michal's rightful husband. David asserts his claim as one who had paid the purchase price, and to this extent he had suffered wrong. — **15.** איש] the reading אישה on the basis of 𝕲 is now generally adopted. The omission of the suffix may have been made intentionally by some legalistic scribe to disguise the fact that Paltiel is called her husband. — פלטיאל] the fuller form of the name which appears as פלטי 1 S. 25⁴⁴. — ל̇וٰש [ליש *Qrê* agrees with the form found elsewhere. — **16.** בחרים] elsewhere mentioned as on the road from Jerusalem to the Jordan valley, 17¹⁸. — **17–19**. The verses anticipate the account which follows. The intimation that the people had already for some time been seeking David as king and the reference to the promise of Yahweh, indicate a later hand than that to which we owe the main narrative. — הושיע] is to be changed to אושיע with 40 MSS. and the versions. — ובם־אבנר] must mean that, besides sending messages and messengers, Abner went in person to Benjamin and to David — wholly superfluous in view of what follows.

---

* Sanctius *apud* Schm., p. 111.

20, 21. As the narrative now stands, the verses form the conclusion of Abner's negotiation with David. Abner with a suitable escort came to David at Hebron, *and David made a feast to Abner and to the men who were with him*] the *feast* was an occasion for drinking rather than eating and is so named, like συμπόσιον. Abner agrees definitely : *I will gather all Israel to my Lord and they will make an agreement with thee*] by their Sheikhs or heads of the clans. The monarchy is established by consent of the tribes. So in the time of Rehoboam we find the tribes negotiating with the heir to the throne, before acknowledging him. — *And thou shalt rule over all which thou desirest.* The aspiration of David could hardly be less than the rule over all Israel. The promise of Abner seems to imply no more than that he will set about influencing the tribes, with the expectation of bringing them into allegiance to David.

20. ולאנשים] there seems no reason why we should not point with the article, which is in fact required by the following אשר. Read וְלָאֲנשים with Bu. — **21.** אקומה] 𝕲 seems to have added נא which however is not called for. — ויכרתו אתך ברית] καὶ διαθήσομαι μετ᾽ αὐτοῦ διαθήκην, 𝕲ᴮ : καὶ διαθήσομαι μετὰ σοῦ διαθήκην 𝕲ᴸ. The reading of 𝕳 seems the best, for Abner's promise looked to what afterwards occurred, 5³. — בכל] can hardly be *with all the conditions* that shall please thee (Th.), but *over all the people* that thou desirest. The main thing was that David should be acknowledged as king.

22–27. The murder of Abner. — Joab, David's general, was absent on an expedition when Abner made his visit. Not improbably David had so planned it. But *the servants of David*, that is, the mercenaries, *and Joab came from the raid*] in which they were then engaged, *and brought with them great spoil.* The booty of the surrounding tribes makes the revenue of such a monarchy to a considerable extent. The renewed assurance that David had dismissed Abner *and he had gone in peace* is intended to bring out more distinctly Joab's vindictiveness. — **23.** The information given to Joab does not indicate that Abner was planning to displace him. It was simply to the effect that the king had let Abner go in peace. By tribal morality, David as kinsman of Asahel was bound to take blood revenge as much as Joab himself. — **24.** This is the first point of Joab's expostulation with David — that he did not smite Abner while he had him in his power. — **25.** The second ascribes to Abner treacherous motives : *Dost thou not know Abner the son of Ner, that he came to deceive thee*] under pretence of friendly negotiation ; *and to know thy going forth and thy coming in, and to know all thou art doing?*] in order to make a later attack upon the person of the king. Joab was unable to conceive of Abner as anything but an enemy of Judah. The freedom with which Joab expostulates shows the position which he occupied both as kinsman and as officer of David. — **26**. Joab, without David's knowledge, promptly *sent messengers after Abner and they brought him back from the Cistern of Sirah*] unknown to us except from this passage. — **27**. Abner turned back, doubtless under the impression that the king had sent for him, *and Joab turned him aside to the side of the gate to speak to him quietly*] the ostensible purpose is given without comment. — *And he smote him there in the abdomen*] cf. 2²³. *So he died for the blood of Asahel the brother of Joab.* The curious thing is not that Joab should take blood revenge, but that Abner should be so unsuspicious. We can account for his conduct only by supposing that he had a distinct safe conduct from David.

22. באֹ] as generally recognized, the true reading is באים (Ginsb. gives באו in the margin) the ם having disappeared in the מ of the next word. — רב] is omitted by 𝔊ᴸ and is in fact superfluous; how much booty they brought with them does not concern us here. — **24**. הלוֹך] throws emphasis on the fact that Abner had been allowed to *go away* at all. 𝔊 has ἐν εἰρήνῃ conforming to the clause in v.²³. — **25**. 𝔊 and 𝔖 read הלוא at the beginning of the verse and this word is probably to be restored (Th.). — את־אבנר] τὴν κακίαν ᾿Αβεννήρ 𝔊 is attractive (Kl.). — מבואך] is changed by the punctuators to מובאך for the sake of the paronomasia. — **26**. הסרה] is called by Josephus Βησηρά. The translation of Josephus in Bohn's Library speaks of '*Ain Sarah* near Hebron, of which I find no other trace. — **27**. For תוך read ירך with 𝔊 (Th.). — החמש] always elsewhere we find אל החמש which is found here also in 13 MSS. and is favoured by 𝔊. — אחיו] is awkward, so that Bu. restores אחי יואב with 𝔊ᴮ. I suspect however that וימת is an intrusion. The sense is perfectly good without it.

28-32. David declares his innocence of the crime. — **28**. *I and my kingdom are innocent before Yahweh*] who avenges those slain without cause, Ps. 9¹³. — **29**. *Let it come upon Joab and upon all his clan*] the imprecation strictly interpreted would affect David himself, but the following clauses show that David is thinking of

Joab's descendants.   Among these he prays that there may always be *one that has an issue and one that is a leper*] two diseases which involve continual defilement ; *and one that holds the spindle*] effeminate and unfit for manly occupations. — **30.** An editorial note or later interpolation excusing the deed of Joab : *But Joab and Abishai had lain in wait for Abner because he had killed Asahel.*   Strictly speaking, it contradicts v.[27], where Joab alone is the slayer. — **31, 32.** As further evidence of his innocence, David commands all the people to show the customary signs of mourning, *rending the clothes and putting on haircloth.*   He himself honoured the dead by following the bier, and by weeping at the grave.

28. מעם יהוה] one is free *from* an obligation, Gen. 24[8], or from the guilt incurred by violation of it, Nu. 5[31], or from the one who has a claim based on the obligation or the violation, Jud. 15[3].   In this case Yahweh has the claim, for innocent blood cries to him for vengeance.   The double מן — I am innocent *towards* Yahweh *of* the blood — does not seem to occur elsewhere.   The original reading of 𝔊 was מעתה ו instead of מעם יהוה. — מדמי] 𝔊[L] represents רמי which it makes the beginning of v.[29]. — **29.** יהלו] the verb is used twice of the tempest, as whirling upon the head of its victims, Jer. 23[19] 30[23], and once of the sword Hos. 11[6].   It does not seem appropriate to the blood which is the subject here; 𝔊[L] omits the verb altogether and it is possible that it read simply יהיה elsewhere used in similar context. — ואל] read ועל with 10 MSS. and the versions. — מחזיק בפלך] as shown by Dr., it is better to adhere to the established meaning of פלך, *a spindle.*   In contrast with the warrior Joab, an effeminate descendant would be a curse.   Still, *a cripple* who supports himself by a staff or crutch seems more suitable in this context, and it is possible that the text has suffered.   According to Theodoret, Aquila read *one blind*, perhaps because a blind man feels his way with his staff. — **30.** The verse interrupts the narrative, and can be understood only as a later insertion.   For הרגו read ארבו as suggested by Ew. (*GVI*[3]. III. p. 160, Eng. Tr. p. 117) on the basis of 𝔊. — **31.** שקים] the clothing of mourners.   Schwally (*ZATW.* XI. p. 174) compares the ihrâm of the Moslem, which however is not of haircloth. — המטה] the couch on which a man lay was also used as a bier.

33–39. The burial of Abner. — David expressed his grief in an impromptu dirge :

33. *Must Abner die as dies the fool ?*
34. *Thy hands were not bound,*
Thy feet were not brought into fetters :
As one falls before ruthless men, thou didst fall.

The fool brings an early death upon himself by his reckless conduct, Prov. 7²²ᶠ. Abner had not even the honour of being made a prisoner of war, or of suffering death after being overpowered in battle. — **35**. After the burial, the people came *to cause the king to eat bread while it was yet day*. David showed that he was in earnest in mourning by swearing not to taste anything until sundown, when of course a new day began. — **36, 37**. All the people *took notice* and knew that David had no part in the matter *and were pleased*. His relationship to Joab laid him open to suspicion. — **38**. *Know you not that a prince and a great man has fallen to-day in Israel?*] reason enough for mourning. — **39**. As the verse now stands, it contains David's confession of his own weakness and inability to punish Joab. Such a confession so early in his career seems improbable. The original reading, which can be restored only conjecturally, seems to have said that although Abner was uncle and high official of a king, the sons of Zeruiah had treated him as harshly as they would a common man. Tribal morality being on their side, David did not attempt to punish them, but contented himself with a prayer that Yahweh would *requite the* doer of evil according to his evil.

33. הכמות] the verbal form is infinitive. — נבל] the name of *Nabal* is rendered by ⑤. But the death of Abner could not be compared in any way with the death of Nabal. — **34**. נחשתים] of a pair of bronze fetters as in Jd. 16²¹. — כנפל] is probably to be pointed as a participle (Kl.). — **35**. לחברות] cf. 13⁵. The verb occurs only in the document of which this chapter is a part. — **36.** בכל] ⑤ reads כל, making it the subject of the preceding וייטב and omitting טוב at the end of the verse. This is favoured also by ⑤ and ⑫, and is preferred by We., who is obliged, however, to strike out בעיני כל־העם also. Would it not be better to strike out the whole half verse as a gloss? — **38.** וגדול] 7⁹; for שר וגדול however, ⑤ᴮ has שר גדול. For בישראל ⑤ and some MSS. of ⑫ have מישראל. — **39.** רך] the word means *tender in years*, or *delicately nurtured*, Gen. 33¹³ Dt. 28⁵⁴. Neither meaning is appropriate to David, who was certainly a mature man and who had been brought up in hardship. It is moreover difficult to connect the word with what follows: *tender though anointed king* is perhaps possible, but how does it apply to the situation? Following a suggestion of We., Bu. emends to רך ויח ממלך, *too tender and lowly for reigning*. But it is not likely that David would openly express this, even if it were his thought. ⑤ᴸ makes the clause apply to Abner and translates συγγενὴς καὶ καθιστάμενος ὑπὸ τοῦ βασιλέως, and with this agree many MSS. of ⑤, only reading καθεσταμένος. The original would apparently be

והוא דוד ופקיד למלך, *though he were relative and officer of a king (yet these sons of Zeruiah were too strong for him* is the continuation, reading ממנו for ממני). For other conjectures see Kl.

IV. 1–12. The assassination of Ishbaal. — The death of Abner removed the main support of the throne at Mahanaim. Two of the king's officers therefore seize an opportunity, when the king is unguarded, to murder him. They bring his head to Hebron in the hope of reward. But David treats them as he had treated the confessed assassin of Saul.

The piece is an evident continuation of the preceding narrative and is homogeneous except for a single (or double) interpolation, [2b-4].

1. *When the son of Saul heard that Abner had died in Hebron, his hands were limp*] he lost courage ; *and all Israel was thrown into confusion*] showing that Abner was not only the stay of the king, but also the administrator of the kingdom. — **2.** Ishbaal had two captains of guerilla bands whose names were *Baana* and *Rechab*. The fact that in [5] they are mentioned in the reverse order indicates that the present clause is part of the redactional note. They are described as *sons of Rimmon the Beerothite, of the Benjamites*] Beeroth was a city of the Gibeonites, Jos. 9[17], but is reckoned to Benjamin Jos. 18[25]. According to Robinson it occupied the site of the present *El-Bireh*, nine miles north of Jerusalem. An editor or scribe now explains why a Beerothite should be called a Benjamite. But he does not tell us why Beeroth should *not* be reckoned to Benjamin. The fact which he finds surprising seems natural to us. — **3.** The Beerothites *fled to Gittaim*] also a city of Benjamin, Neh. 11[33], *and have been clients there until this day*] they did not attain full citizenship. If the author means that this is the way in which they came to be Benjamites, he has expressed himself obscurely. On the other hand, if he means that though Benjamites, they preferred clientage in another clan to their blood right, we must suppose this Gittaim to be somewhere else than in Benjamin. — **4.** The verse is another interpolation. The design seems to be to show how reduced was the house of Saul — the heir to the throne was a cripple. After the battle of Gilboa his nurse fled in such trepidation that the

child fell from her arms and became lame. The correct form of
his name, preserved in Chronicles, is Meribbaal. In the text of
Samuel it has been purposely mutilated to Mephibosheth. —
5. The two assassins came to the house of Ishbaal while he was
taking his noon sleep — the *siesta* which is general in hot countries. — **6.** As it stands in 𝕳 the verse is superfluous and perplexing. The very different reading of 𝕲 is now generally adopted :
*And the doorkeeper of the palace was cleaning wheat, and she grew
drowsy and slept; so Rechab and Baanah his brother slipped in*]
the modest establishment of Ishbaal afforded only a maid servant
as porter, and she was obliged to do other work while keeping the
door. — **7.** Ishbaal was *lying upon his bed in his sleeping room*]
and therefore an easy victim. The murderers cut off his head
and, with this evidence, travelled *the road of the Arabah all night.*
— **8.** They present the head of their murdered king to David
with the remark : *Yahweh has avenged thee on Saul and his seed*]
the apparent hypocrisy which made Yahweh a partner in their
bloody crime called forth the indignation of the older expositors.
But such language is second nature to an oriental. — **9, 10.** David's
reply is a reference to a precedent : *As for the one who told me,
saying : Saul is dead — though I regarded him as a bringer of
good tidings — I seized him and slew him in Ziklag to give him the
reward of good tidings.* The sense is clear : Even though the
tidings of Saul's death were welcome to David, that did not hinder
him from punishing the messenger. — **11.** *How much more when
wicked men have slain a righteous man in his house and upon his
bed; shall I not seek his blood at your hand and destroy you from
the land?* Otherwise the land itself would suffer on account of
unavenged blood. — **12.** The murderers are put to death, their
hands and their feet cut off and hung up over the pool at Hebron,
where they would be seen by all the city, and the head of Ishbaal
is buried in the tomb of Abner his relative, so that he is joined to
his kin in his burial.

1. בֶּן־שָׁאוּל] is proper without the insertion of אִשְׁבַּעַל made by 𝕲𝕾. — אבנר]
the addition of בֶּן־נֵר, made by We. and Bu., is not favoured by the best MSS.
of 𝕲. — **2.** בֶּן־שָׁאוּל] is here impossible and we must insert לְאִשְׁבַּעַל with 𝕲.
The identification of Beeroth and *El Bireh* is objected to by Buhl (*Geog.*
p. 173) on the ground that Jos. 9[17] indicates a place southwest of Gibeon, and

that Eusebius locates it (*OS.* p. 233) on the road to Nicopolis. But cf. Robinson, *BR*[2]. I p. 452; Baedeker, *Palestine*[2], p. 212. — על] is evidently for אל. — **3.** ויברחו] the meaning seems to be that though the Beerothites were reckoned to Benjamin, yet they preferred to become clients at Gittaim rather than to retain their blood rights. But as Benjamites could hardly become clients of Benjamites (at Gittaim), we suspect the true state of the case to have been that the Beerothites, originally Canaanites, sought protection at Gittaim and thus were reckoned to Benjamin. Bertholet (*Stellung d. Israeliten*, p. 47) supposes the clientage sought because of Saul's attack on the Gibeonites, in which case the murder of Ishbaal was an act of revenge. — **4.** The second half of the verse is removed by Bu. and inserted after 9[8], but it is doubtful whether it belongs there. — מפיבשת] the name has been changed like איש־בשת to avoid pronouncing the word Baal. We find מריב בעל, 1 Chr. 8[34] 9[40], and along with it מרי־בעל, 9[40]. From the analogy of Jerubbaal we naturally interpret מריב בעל, *Baal is a warrior*. This was changed by the ingenuity of the scribes to מפיבשת, *who puffs at the shameful thing* (We. *TBS.* p. 31); other conjectures are cited by Nestle, *Israelitische Eigennamen*, p. 120 f.). 𝔊[B] calls him Μεμφιβόσθε, the name which it has also for Ishbaal, whereas 𝔊[L] has Μεμφιβάαλ. This indicates that the name has undergone two transformations; first it was made *Mephibaal* and then *Mephibosheth*. — **5.** משכב הצהרים] 𝔗 has, curiously, *the sleep of kings*. — **6.** The opening word as pointed in 𝔐 is unintelligible; the repetition of the subject towards the close of the verse is unmotived; and the whole verse anticipates the following account. Welcome relief is given by 𝔊 which introduces an entirely new feature; καὶ ἰδοὺ ἡ θυρωρὸς τοῦ οἴκου ἐκάθαιρεν πυροὺς καὶ ἐνύσταξεν καὶ ἐκάθευδεν (καὶ ὕπνωσεν[L]). This is adopted as original by Ew., Th., We., and later commentators, though they differ somewhat in the retroversion : והנה שערת הבית סקלת חטים ותנם ותישן is given by We. and adopted by Dr., Bu., whereas Kl. rejects both texts and constructs a new one on conjecture. — נמלטו] generally means *to slip away, to escape*. The only analogy for the sense required here is 1 S. 20[29], and even there it is doubtful whether the writer had not the usual meaning in mind. — **7.** The second את־ראשו is omitted by 𝔊[L]𝔗. — **10.** כי] introduces the substance of the oath. — בעיניו] ἐνώπιόν μου 𝔊 is probably original. The point is that the Amalekite was punished in spite of the nature of his tidings. — אשר לחתי לו] can be justified; but (since We.) אשר is generally thought to be an erroneous insertion; the clause is then sarcastic. — **11.** את־איש־צדיק] is unusual though not entirely without parallel, Ex. 21[28] Nu. 21[9], cf. Davidson, *Syntax*, 72 R. 4, Ges.[26] 117 *d*. — הלא] is lacking in 𝔊, but the question is more vigorous than the direct assertion.

V.–XXIV. David's rule over all Israel.

V.–VIII. The establishment of the kingdom. — The tribes make David king, and he establishes his capital at Jerusalem. He is attacked by the Philistines but conquers them. His next

step is to bring the Ark from Baale-Judah.   The progress is interrupted by an untoward incident, but after some delay the palladium is safely settled in a tent pitched for it.   David proposes to
build a house for Yahweh but is forbidden, though he receives a
promise for his own house.   The next chapter contains an account
of several successful wars, closing with a summary which evidently
marks the conclusion of a section of the narrative.

In this division of the book various hands are discernible, as
will appear in the course of the exposition.

V. 1–5. David is anointed king over all Israel, and the length
of his reign is given.   The anointing is a natural sequel of the
preceding narrative.   But the speech of vv.[1.2] seems later than
the simple statement of v.[3]. — **1.** *All the tribes of Israel came to
David*] by their representatives, claiming kinship with him. —
2. Moreover, they recognize that he had been the actual leader
while Saul was king ; and further, Yahweh had promised that
David should shepherd the people. — **3.** *All the Sheikhs came to
Hebron*] as they were already there in v.[1], it is probable that this
is a different document. — *And the king made an agreement with
them*] cf. 3[21].   We may conjecture that there was some definite
understanding of rights and duties on both sides. — *And they
anointed David as king over Israel*] the Chronicler adds : *according to the word of Yahweh by the hand of Samuel*.   But this
agrees with v.[2] rather than v.[3]. — **4, 5.** One of the chronological data frequent in the Books of Kings.   This seems to
be late, as it is not copied by the Chronicler who appropriates the
rest of the chapter.   There is, however, no improbability in the
numbers, as David evidently had a long reign, and the life he led
would make him an old man at seventy.

1–5. All that is required by the narrative is v.[3] which alone I suppose to
be from the earlier document.   The vv.[1-3] are repeated substantially in 1 Chr.
11[1-3]. — **1.** ויבאו כל־שבטי ישראל] Chr. has כל ישראל ויקבצו because the people
were in his view a homogeneous whole. — ויאמרו] is lacking in Chr. and 𝔏,
whereas לאמר is omitted by 𝔊. — **2.** עלינו] lacking in Chr. — הייתה מוציא] *Kt.*
corrected in the margin to היית המוציא, which is of course correct; notice
המבי(א) which follows. — **4.** ארבעים] the versions and 17 MSS. have וארבעים.
— **5.** שלשים ושלש 𝔊[L] thinks it necessary to make the exact sum of forty years,
and puts *32 years and six months* here.

Budde removes vv.⁴· ⁵ from this position and inserts them in connexion with 3²⁻⁵, 5¹³⁻¹⁶ after 8¹⁴. But it is clear that this does not restore a text that ever existed. These verses are a redactional insertion, but they never stood in any other connexion than their present one. In fact they are in place at the beginning of David's reign over Israel.

6–16. The capture of Jerusalem. — David captures the fortress of Jerusalem and makes it his capital. His prosperity is evidenced by the attention of the king of Tyre and by the increase of David's harem.

The section is an apparent unit, but does not fit well in the present context, for the attack of the Philistines, v.¹⁷ evidently came before the capture of Jerusalem. The union of all Israel under a single crown was in fact sufficient reason for the Philistines to bestir themselves. Probably the campaign of the Philistines made David feel the necessity of possessing Jerusalem. While in the hands of the Canaanite, this city really cut his kingdom in two. When he took it, it became the natural capital of the country, and its strength in the Jebusite period was equally marked after David took possession of it.

6. *The king and his men*] his regular soldiers are evidently intended, *went to Jerusalem against the Jebusite, the inhabitant of the land*] the same phrase is used elsewhere of the Canaanite (Gen. 50¹¹) and the Amorite (Jos. 24¹⁸). The remainder of the verse is obscure. Apparently, the Jebusites say to David : *Thou shalt not come in hither for the blind and the lame shall keep thee back*] but this cannot be got out of the present text, and no emendation that is convincing has yet been suggested. There is no reason for taking *the blind and the lame* in any but the proper sense. In derision, the walls were manned by cripples. The explanatory clause : *meaning that David cannot come hither,* is unnecessary and probably a later insertion. — **7**. *David took the stronghold of Zion*] undoubtedly the eastern ridge of the two now covered by the city of Jerusalem. — **8**. Another case of corruption. As it stands, the verse seems to give the reason why the blind and the lame are shut out of the sanctuary. But this clause is perhaps an afterthought. Two theories are held as to the first half of the verse. One makes it give the city over to sack, the other makes it a command to spare the lame and the blind.

Neither is satisfactory. From the form of the introductory phrase, the verse should contain a reflection of David on his successful capture of the city. — **9.** *David dwelt in the fortress*] which he had just taken, *and built it round about from Millo*] the fortification or retaining wall mentioned also among the works of Solomon 1 K. 9^{15}, and rebuilt by Hezekiah, 2 Chr. 32^5. — **10.** Concluding remark — *David kept on growing great and Yahweh was with him.*

6. Budde ingeniously prefixes 6^1 to this verse, and thus makes David levy thirty thousand troops for the siege of Jerusalem. But there is no reason to suppose that any such number was necessary. The Jebusites confided in the strength of their citadel, and this was captured by the bravery of a few led by Joab. This would indicate that David's band of trusty veterans did the greater part of the work. The Chronicler indeed makes *David and all Israel* the subject, but this can hardly weigh. — ירושלם] here as elsewhere is made a dual by the punctuators, with no apparent reason. The city is named in the Tell-el-Amarna tablets which show that it was a dependency of Egypt before the Israelite invasion of Palestine; cf. Winckler's edition, $180^{25. 46}$ 183^{14}. The *Jebusites* are named as one of the nations of Canaan, but seem to have possessed no more territory than the city of Jerusalem. כי אם־הסירך העורים = *but the blind will have removed thee*, is inappropriate. The tense is wrong, the verb should be plural, and הסיר is not used of *repulsing* an enemy. We.'s emendation, הסירך, meets two of the objections but not the third. It has been proposed therefore to correct to הסירת — the English Version tacitly does so — with the meaning *except thou have removed* (Kl.), which is faultless so far as the form of the verb is concerned, but would naturally be followed by the accusative sign. I suspect that the adversative כי אם is not original and that the conjunction is כי. The אם הסירך then represents a verb with the object — say ימנעו אתך or יקדמונך; ἀντέστησαν 𝕲 would favour the latter. *The blind and the lame* are taken by some of the Rabbinical expositors to mean the gods of the Jebusites, an interpretation suggested by Ps. 115^{5-7} (on the theory that it was composed by David). Another conceit of the same kind sees in the blind and the lame, images of Isaac and Jacob, on which the Jebusites had written the covenant made by Abraham with Abimelech their ancestor (?), on which covenant they relied for protection (so Levi ben Gerson). Equally forcible is the theory of a modern scholar that the blind and the lame "are the dreaded guardian spirits, the protecting deities of Jerusalem, called thus either by the people or by the late scribes of Judea, while in fact they were the 'watchers' = עירים and the פוסחים, 'threshold crossers or leapers' of the Jebusites" (Kohler in *Am. Jour. Theol.* I. p. 803). It is enough to notice that the words must have the same sense here and in $v.^8$. The Chronicler omits all after the first הנה, perhaps by homeoteleuton. —

7. ציון] later a poetical name for Jerusalem itself. Robinson's identification of Zion with the southwestern quarter of modern Jerusalem is now generally

given up. — [היא עיר דוד] is superfluous along with v.⁹ᵇ. — **8.** [כל־מכה יבסי]
naturally means *whoever smites a Jebusite*, and we expect as the apodosis either
a permission to take his spoil, or the promise of a reward for the deed, or the
threat of punishment. Neither one can be got out of ויגע בצנור, though the
form of the verb is correct. צנור occurs in only one other passage and is not
certain even there. In later Hebrew the word means a *canal* or *pipe*, and so
it has been interpreted here of the eaves-trough of the citadel, or of the sewer
under the city, as though David offered a reward for whoever should smite the
Jebusite *and get up to the pinnacle* of the castle, or, on the other hand, for
whoever should *climb up through the sewer* or *reach the moat*. The precarious
nature of the proposed interpretation is obvious, and is emphasized by the
fact that the sentence so construed is left incomplete, and that the lame and
the blind who follow are equally without intelligible connexion. By reading
ויע Ewald makes the storming party *cast into the moat* the lame and the
blind who defended the walls. The Chronicler departs from the text of this
verse, perhaps because he found it unintelligible. Conjectures of Th., Kl., Bu.
give no real help. 𝔊 sees in צנור *a dagger*, Aquila *a watercourse*, and Symmachus *a battlement.* — [ענאו] for which *Qrê* שנאי : 𝔊ᴮ καὶ τοὺς μισοῦντας. —
[הבית] 𝔊 interprets correctly when it renders οἶκον κυρίου. — **9.** [ויבן] read
ויבנה with 𝔊 (We.). — [המלוא] the word occurs in the name of a fortress (?)
Beth-Millo, Jd. 9⁶. — [וביתה] may be *and inwards*, Millo being the external
limit of his building, or *towards the house* which would naturally be the sanctuary, as in v.⁸.

11. *And Hiram king of Tyre*] the prominent commercial city
of the Phoenicians ; *sent messengers to David*] it is altogether
probable that the Philistines were the common enemy of both
parties. The superiority of the Phoenicians as builders is well
known from the history of Solomon. — **12.** *David knew*] apparently by the evidence of the Phoenician embassy. The natural
conclusion is that the embassy came soon after his occupation of
Jerusalem. The chronology makes it doubtful whether Hiram
came so early to the throne, but this may be the fault of the chronology. — **13.** The increase of the harem increases the prestige
of an oriental ruler. — **14.** From the occurrence of the name *Solomon*, who was born some years after the occupation of Jer., we
conclude that this list gives the name of all David's sons known
to the author. — **16.** Eljada was originally Baaliada, as we discover
from the parallel in Chronicles, and as is indicated also by 𝔊.

11. [חירם] probably a shortened form of אחירם. According to Josephus
(*Ant.* VIII. 3, 1) Hiram's eleventh year was the year of Solomon's accession,
which would of course be inconsistent with an embassy early in David's reign,

U

The artisans sent by Hiram were probably his slaves. — קיר] lacking in 𝔊ᴮ, is in fact superfluous. — **12.** נשׂא] is active — Yahweh *had exalted* his kingdom. נשׂאת, that is, a Niphal, is read by 𝔊 and Chr. — **13.** פלנשׁים] omitted by Chr. The action of David shows no acquaintance with the Deuteronomic law, Dt. 17¹⁷. The Rabbinical ingenuity which interprets the law as forbidding more than eighteen wives, and which shows that David had just that number, is set forth in Schmid, p. 222. — מירושלם] בירו' 1 Chr. 14³. — **14–16.** The list of David's sons is repeated in 1 Chr. 3⁵ff. and 14⁴ff.. By duplicating אליפלט and inserting נגה (duplicate of נפג) the number is there increased to thirteen instead of eleven. אלידע is בעלידע in both places in Chr.; Βααλειμάθ 𝔊ᴮ and Βααλιλαθ 𝔊ᴸ show that the same form was once found in the present passage.

17–25. Two battles with the Philistines. — In two encounters David defeats the Philistines. The time is before the capture of Jerusalem, so that we have here an insertion from another document. — **17.** The occasion was that *they had anointed David king over Israel*] the Philistines might readily suppose that David was growing too powerful. His behaviour indicates that he had not given them direct provocation. — *He went down to the stronghold*] the verb makes it sufficiently plain that the citadel of Zion is not intended. — **18.** The Philistines came and *plundered* (Jd. 15⁹) in the *Valley of Rephaim*] now generally identified with the valley that extends southwestward from Jerusalem. — **19.** David asks counsel of the oracle and receives a favourable answer. — **20.** *Yahweh has broken down my enemies before me like the breaking of waters*] through a dam. *Baal Perazim* is possibly referred to as Mount Perazim Is. 28²¹. — **21.** *They left their gods*] as we should probably read, *and David and his men carried them away.*

17. וירד אל המצודה] although the citadel of Jerusalem has been called a מצורה v.⁹, it cannot be intended here. If this incident were later in time than the capture of Jerusalem, David would not have needed to go to that stronghold, for he resided there. Usage does not allow us to say, either, that one *went down* to Jerusalem. The allusion must therefore be to one of his earlier resorts, perhaps Adullam. — **18.** הרפאים] τῶν Τιτάνων 𝔊. Robinson, who makes the identification (*BR²*. I. p. 219), gives no reasons except the declaration of Josephus. The location however answers the needs of Jos. 15⁸ 18¹⁶, and would be a natural route for the Philistines, cf. Buhl, *Geog.* p. 91. — **19.** האעלה] confirms what was said about the stronghold. — **20.** פרץ] of the breaking down of a wall, 2 Chr. 24⁷ Ps. 80¹³. בעל frequent in the names of places, the town being named from its patron deity, as modern names are often taken from the patron saint or his church. — **21.** עצביהם] for which Chr. has אלהיהם. The latter, which was also read by 𝔊 here, is doubtless original.

A late scribe hesitated to call the idols *gods*. The Chronicler adds that David burned them with fire, and a similar addition is made by 𝔊ᴸ. But this seems to have been an addition to accord with the views of later times.

22. A similar situation, perhaps a part of the same campaign. — **23.** In answer to his inquiry he is directed not to make a direct attack. — *Go about to their rear and come upon them opposite the Balsams*] the word is treated like a proper name. — **24.** Specific directions giving an omen : *And it shall be when thou hearest the sound of marching in the tops of the balsams, then thou shalt act promptly, for then Yahweh will have gone forth before thee to smite the camp of the Philistines*] it is scarcely possible to suppose that the incident is not based upon the sanctity of the trees in question. — **25.** David's obedience was rewarded with a victory *and he smote the Philistines from Geba*] the place is doubtful, *to Gezer*] in the border of the Philistine territory.

23. הסב] the Hiphil is uncalled for and we may either read a Niphal, or, with Dr., strike out the ה as erroneous duplication from the preceding word. — הבכאים [בכאים Chr.: בוכים 𝔖. Some derivative of בכה is indicated by τοῦ κλαυθμῶνος 𝔊, so that the *Bochim* of Jd. 2⁵ was in the mind of both translators. But the location does not seem suitable. — **24.** בשמעך [כשמעך is preferred by Qrê. — צעדה] the article should probably be prefixed with Chr. — תחרץ] *look sharp* is our colloquial equivalent. — **25.** מגבע] ἀπὸ Γαβαών 𝔊 agrees with מגבעון Chr. But both Geba and Gibeon are too far from the valley of Rephaim for the pursuit to begin at either one. The mention of Gibeon and Perazim together by Isaiah does not prove anything as to these two events. — גזר] on the location cf. GASmith, *Geog.* p. 215 f.

VI. 1–23. The bringing up of the Ark. — David attempts to bring the Ark to the citadel, but an untoward incident prevents the accomplishment of his purpose for a time. After three months a second attempt is made, this time with success. David's religious zeal, or its violent expression, brings upon him a rebuke from his wife Michal, and this results in a permanent estrangement.

There seems no reason to question that the story belongs to the main narrative of the life of David. The Chronicler, who borrows it, makes considerable changes in the opening section, to accord with his point of view.

1. David gathered the warriors of Israel, thirty thousand in number. As Yahweh is a God of War such an escort is appropri-

ate. Numerical data however are generally open to suspicion. —
2. They went to *Baal Judah*] the name indicates that it was a
seat of the worship of Yahweh. The present narrative does not
necessarily presuppose the account of the Ark in 1 S. The Ark
is described as that *which is called by the name of Yahweh Sabaoth
who thrones upon the Cherubim*] cf. 1 S. 4⁴. The whole clause
however looks like a later insertion (We.). — **3.** They *made the
Ark of God ride on a new cart*] a *new* cart so as to avoid the
possibility of defilement. The method was evidently the same
used by the Philistines. The house of Abinadab from which they
took it is described as *on the hill*, cf. 1 S. 7¹. — *And Uzzah and
Ahio the sons of Abinadab were driving the cart*] the last word
of the verse, with the first six words of the next verse, is erroneous
duplication. — **4.** The verse is confused by the error just noted,
but seems originally to have said that *Uzzah walked by the side of
the Ark while Ahio went before it.* — **5.** *David and all the house
of Israel were dancing before the Ark*] in religious exaltation, *with
all their might; and with songs and with harps and with lyres and
with drums and with rattles and with cymbals*] the instruments
intended correspond approximately to those still used.* — **6.** *They
came to the threshing-floor of Nachon*] the location is unknown. —
*And Uzzah stretched out his hand to the Ark of God and took hold
of it for the oxen stumbled*] or *shook it* (cf. 𝔊 below). The
stumbling of the oxen would shake the cart and threaten to make
the Ark fall to the ground. — **7.** *And the wrath of Yahweh was
kindled against Uzzah*] as though he were affronted by the action,
and God smote him there] there seems to be no reason for the
change of the divine name, and the text may have been interpolated. — *And he died there in the presence of God*] for the reading
see the note below. The question why Uzzah should be smitten
was not a puzzle to the older commentators, so much as the question why everybody else was not involved in the same fate. For
the whole transaction was contrary to the provisions of the Law
which gives specific instructions for the transport of the Ark. The
Ark was first to be covered by the priests (Num. 4⁵ᵇ) ; it was then

---

* Some ancient oriental musical instruments are figured (from the Assyrian
monuments) in Wellhausen's translation of the Psalms (*SBOT*. N. Y., 1898),
Appendix, entitled " Music of the Ancient Hebrews."

to be taken up and carried by the Levites (4¹⁵). The palpable violation of these provisions would seem to be a reason why the whole procession should come to grief. But the fact is, as now generally conceded, that the method of David shows his ignorance of the Levitical regulation. Uzzah gave offence by his too great familiarity in laying hold suddenly of the sacred emblem. This is all that is implied in the text. The wrath of Yahweh was but momentary, as is evinced by his treatment of Obed-Edom. — **8.** The temper of Yahweh was reciprocated by David who *was angry that Yahweh had brought destruction upon Uzzah*] literally, *had broken a breach*, such as gives a city into the hands of the enemy. — **9.** The unaccountable conduct of Yahweh when David was preparing him a new residence and new honours, gave rise to fear as well as anger. David's question: *How shall the Ark of Yahweh come to me ?*] is the expression of his fear to have it come at all, not an inquiry as to the best way of bringing it. — **10.** He *was not willing to remove the Ark of Yahweh to the city of David*] to the citadel. It was to all appearance already within the town of Jerusalem. — *He turned it aside to the house of Obed-Edom the Gittite*] one of several Philistines in David's service.

1. Bu. prefixes this verse to 5⁶, making the gathering of all Israel to be for the purpose of taking Jerusalem. He then makes v.² follow directly on 5¹², as though David's bringing up of the Ark was because he knew that Yahweh had established him as king over Israel. The present section however reads well as it stands, the *people* of v.² referring evidently to the *young men of Israel* of v.¹. ויאסף for ויסף, cf. Dr. and Schm. — עוד] is superfluous and probably an erroneous insertion. For 30,000 𝕲 has 70,000. — **2.** [מבעלי] would naturally define the people with David as *the burghers of Judah*, and is so understood by 𝕲. But in that case we have no indication of the place where they were to find the Ark. That place is called by the Chronicler בעלה, so that it is easy to correct here to בעל יהודה, the י having been duplicated (We.), or to בעלת יהודה. Both 1 Chr. 13⁶ and Jos. 15 identify the place with Kirjath Jearim. — שם שם] one of the two words is superfluous, lacking also in 𝕲. — **3.** [אשר בגבעה] is possibly corrupt, as it seems unnecessary to describe the location so exactly, and it is omitted by Chr. — עזא] here is for עזה. — ואחיו] is naturally read as אָחִיו or אֶחָיו. But it seems strange that his brother should not be named as well as Uzzah. אחיו, as another form of אחירו, is a possible proper name so that I have retained it. — [העגלה חדשה] is an obvious case of disagreement, and it seems clear that the eye of the scribe wandered from העגלה, which he had just written, to עגלה early in the verse so that he

repeated חדשה . . . בנבעה before he discovered his mistake. — עִם ארון האלהים]
makes no sense, either with what precedes or without it. We are compelled
to suppose that in his confusion over his error the scribe omitted something.
What is needed is simply an affirmation that *Uzzah walked* by the side of the
Ark. — **5.** בכל עצי ברושים] is unintelligible — *cypress trees* certainly have no
place here, and to make the words mean *with all manner of instruments made
of fir wood* (EV.) is to insert the main idea into the text. Nor is it known
that fir (or cypress) wood was used in the manufacture of musical instruments.
With most recent editors, therefore, we should correct to the reading of Chr.
— בכל עז ובשירים — the first two words occur again in v.¹⁴. 𝕲 has a double
translation, one half of which confirms this restoration, the other half consists
of the words which represent בכל־עז in v.¹⁴. כנענעים seem to be *sistra* (the
word is rendered σείστροις by Aq. and Sym. according to Field), instruments
used in the worship of Isis. — **6.** נכון] evidently a proper name; the endeavour
of some of the commentators to make it mean indefinitely, a *certain* threshing-
floor, is not sustained by usage, nor is Th.'s interpretation *fixed* or *permanent*
in distinction from a temporary floor used only for a particular field or during
one season. Whether Nachon is the correct name, or whether we should read
כידון with Chr., or Νωδάβ with 𝕲ᴮ, cannot be determined. 𝕲ᴸ reads Ορνὰ τοῦ
᾿Ιεβυσαίου, an evident correction, intended to make the Ark select its permanent abode thus early. — וישלח] requires את ירו which is read by all the
versions and by Chr. (which however changes the order of what follows) but
has accidentally dropped out of 𝔥. — ישמטו] is a rare word and the passages
in which it occurs throw little light upon its meaning here. In 2 K. 9³³ it is
used transitively of throwing a person out of a window. It would be natural
to interpret here therefore *the oxen cast it down*. But the object would pretty
certainly be expressed if this were the meaning. Another meaning of the
verb is to *release* a debt, and we might conjecture that the oxen *slipped*, losing
their foothold. Bochart (*Hierozo.* I. II. Cap. 37) cites Arabic analogy which
would make the verb mean *were mired*. 𝕲 περιέσπασεν αὐτήν seems to find
the object expressed — שמטו — and so with 𝔗 מרגוהי. *Calcitrabant* 𝔏 seems
to be a conjecture only. — האלהים] after the יהוה expressed above is superfluous. — על־השל] is lacking in 𝕲ᴮ and therefore suspicious. There is no Hebrew
word של known to us: ἐπὶ τῇ προπετείᾳ 𝕲ᴸ: *super temeritate* 𝔏: *pro igno-
rantia* 𝕴: על ראשתלי 𝔗 seem to go back to a common source which interpreted
the word by the Aramaic. The present tendency (We., Dr., Bu., Ki.) is to
regard the phrase as the mutilated remains of the words of the Chronicler:
:.ל אשר שלח ידו על הא'. More likely they represent an attempt to give the
exact location, now unintelligible. Kl. conjectures על השלב which he supposes
to mean *on the side beam* of the cart on which Uzzah sat. But this is precarious. — עִם ארון אלהים] for which Chr. has לפני אלהים as has 𝕲ᴸ. The latter
is probably original, for it would be more likely to be corrected into the other
phrase. 𝕲ᴮ combines the two readings. — **8.** ויקרא] must be 'impersonal'
as in similar instances — *one called* the place, etc. — **10.** עבד־אדם] the second
part of the name is probably the name of a god, and the whole corresponds to

יבריה. That the man was a Gittite, and therefore a Philistine, is purposely ignored by the Chronicler, who takes pains to enroll him as a Levite and put him among the doorkeepers. Of course, as a follower of David and a resident in the land of Israel, he was a worshipper of Yahweh.

11–19. The second attempt. — **11.** During the three months of the Ark's sojourn, *Yahweh blessed Obed-Edom and all his house*] whether with riches or with children we are not told, probably with both. — **12.** The blessing conferred upon Obed-Edom is the reason why David renews his effort. This is concealed by the Chronicler, who supposes David to have a fixed purpose during all the three months. ⑤ᴸ correctly interprets when it inserts : *and David said : I will turn the blessing to my house.* — **13.** *When the bearers of the Ark had marched six paces*] and it was thereby evident that Yahweh was willing to go, *he sacrificed an ox and a fatling*] David is undoubtedly the subject. The change from the cart to the shoulders of men was prompted by the fact that the cart had proved unfortunate on the previous occasion. This author shows no suspicion that the former was the legal, or even the traditional, method. Practical considerations may also have weighed, for the ascent to the citadel was probably steep and possibly winding. There is no indication that more than one sacrifice was made during the progress. — **14.** *And David was dancing*] the word occurs only in this passage and seems to mean *whirling*, like the devotional dancing of the dervishes. — *And David was girded with a linen ephod*] such as the priests wore, 1 S. 2[18]. We should probably think of this as a strip of cloth like the *izar* of the Moslem. Religious vestments are survivals of earlier costume. The scantiness of this dress, as contrasted with the long robe appropriate to a king, is the ground of Michal's contempt. — **15.** The procession continued *with shouting and the sound of trumpet*] as we might say *with shouting and blare*. Making a loud noise was an act of worship as late as the time of the Psalmist. — **16.** The verse is designed to prepare for the scene at home, v.[20f.]. As it breaks the thread of the narrative, and is introduced awkwardly, it is perhaps a redactional insertion. Correcting the opening word, the verse says : *And the Ark of Yahweh was coming into the city of David when Michal the daughter of Saul looked through the window and saw King*

David leaping and whirling, and she despised him in her heart]
the dignity of a king had been no better observed by Saul when
he lay down naked in the company of the prophets. But this she
chose to forget. — **17**. The successful conclusion : *They set the
Ark in its place, in the tent which David had pitched for it*]
and the rites of sacrifice were observed. — **18**. At the conclusion
of the sacrifices *David blessed the people in the name of Yahweh*]
that he acted as priest seems evident. — **19**. David distributed to
the people bread, raisins, and (apparently) other victuals.

11. The conjectures of the Rabbis on the blessing of fruitfulness conferred
upon Obed-Edom are given by Schm., p. 277. The Chronicler inserts here
the account of Hiram's embassy, of David's family, and of the preparation
of the Levites for the coming procession. — **12.** האלהים] + καὶ εἶπε Δαυίδ
Ἐπιστρέψω τὴν εὐλογίαν εἰς τὸν οἶκόν μου 𝔊^L which is represented also in I
(Cod. Germ. 7 apud Sabatier, et Cod. Leg. Goth. apud Vercellone). It may
be original, having been omitted by 𝔥 on account of its frank egoism. —
13. For the first clause 𝔊 has : *and there were with him* [or *with them*] *seven
bands.* The reading seems to have arisen by corruption of 𝔥. — **14.** מכרכר]
the word occurs only here and v.[16]; Chr. omits it in his reproduction of this
verse and substitutes משחק for it at its second occurrence. It was either obso-
lete in his time, or he thought it undignified. — **15.** בית] is omitted by 𝔊^L𝔖
and 3 MSS. of 𝔥. — **16.** והיה] is certainly the wrong tense, as the Chronicler
shows by correcting it to ויהי. Even with the correction, the verse reads awkwardly; it is unnecessary also, for Michal's remarks are self-explanatory and
the situation need not be described in advance. — שׁפז] this stem occurs here
only, the Qal in Gen. 49[24] only. — **19.** למאיש] is sustained by some analogous
passages, I Chr. 27[23] Ex. 11[7] Jer. 51[62]. — אשׁפר] is entirely unknown. The
versions only conjecture, as is shown by Dr., and no suitable emendation has
yet been suggested, cf. also Lag. *Mittheilungen*, I. p. 213 ff.

20. On David's return to his house, his wife Michal greets him
with the sarcastic exclamation : *How glorious was the king of
Israel as he exposed himself to-day to the eyes of his servants'
maids !* The comparison which follows indicates that it was inde-
cent exposure which moved her wrath. — **21, 22.** The retort reminds her of the fallen fortunes of her family : *Before Yahweh I
was dancing ; Blessed be Yahweh who chose me above thy father
and above all his house !* The change in the text will be defended
below. The words *to command me as prince over the people of
Yahweh* seem intended to point the contrast between Abigail's
appreciation and Michal's contempt. The last clause of v.[21] be-

longs with the following verse : *And I will sport before Yahweh, and will be yet more lightly esteemed than this, and will be lowly in thine eyes. But of the maids of whom thou hast spoken I shall surely be held in honour*] the king trusts the sense of the common people to understand his religious zeal. As for Michal's opinion he does not value it. — **23.** The natural understanding is that the estrangement was the reason for Michal's childlessness — not that she was stricken with barrenness by Yahweh, as some have supposed.

20. אמהות עבדיו] would be the lowest maidservants, cf. the phrase *a servant of servants*. — כהגלות נגלות] two forms of the infinite construct. Probably one is an erroneous insertion; else conflation of two readings has taken place. — הרקים] is used of wild and reckless men from whom, of course, decency cannot be expected. 𝕲 seems to have read הרקדים, but we have no evidence of a class of *dancers* in Israel who could give point to such a comparison. — **21.** לפני יהוה] needs to be completed by an affirmation of some kind, which we find in 𝕲 which reads: ὀρχήσομαι· εὐλογητὸς Κύριος. If this were original we see how the scribe omitted the words, his eye falling upon the second יהוה instead of the first. It seems probable therefore that we should restore the whole, reading לפני יהוה אנכי מרקד ברוך יהוה. The participle מרקד seems the most natural form. — לצות אתי נגיד] cf. 1 S. 25³⁰. — **22.** ונקלתי] 𝕲 reads ונגלתי which is perhaps original. — בעיני] read with 𝕲 בעיניך, for this alone gives the appropriate sense. — **23.** That Michal was stricken with barrenness by God is said by Schmid to be *communis sententia.* But there is in the text no indication of a divine judgment. — ילד] the Orientals read ולד.

VII. 1–29. The promise.

— David is exercised by the thought that Yahweh has only a tent, while the king himself dwells in a house. He lays this before Nathan with the evident purpose of building a temple, if the prophet should approve. The latter at first consents but afterwards is directed to veto the plan. But the message is accompanied with a promise on God's part to build David a house, that is, to establish his dynasty forever. The conclusion of the account gives David's prayer of gratitude, which becomes a prayer of intercession for Israel.

The chapter bears marks of a comparatively late date. It shows what we know as the Messianic expectation, which pictured the perpetual rule of the house of David. But this expectation was not fully formulated until the time of the Exile, when the loss of their dynasty made the pious Israelites value it the more. Various expressions in the text show at least Deuteronomistic influence, so that we are warranted in making the chapter a part of the Exilic redaction.

VII. Cornill (*Einl*[3]. p. 104) contents himself with the seventh century as the date of the chapter, and this is also Budde's idea. The former says: "The destruction of the people and its dynasty seems to lie outside the horizon." But it is a question whether the Exile was ever regarded by believing Israelites as a *destruction* either of people or dynasty. An unequivocal allusion to the capture of the city is indeed not found. But some expressions seem at least to hint at it.

1, 2. *When David had taken possession of his house*] apparently the new one built by the Phoenicians : *Yahweh moreover had given him rest round about from all his enemies*] the circumstantial clause indicates that this author did not dwell much upon the successive wars which filled the greater part of David's reign. The verse is continued immediately by the following, and is incomplete without it — *then David said to Nathan*] the court prophet who appears several times in the history. — *I dwell in a house of cedar while the Ark of God dwells in a curtain*] the statement of the fact which the king finds unbecoming, is enough to indicate the purpose he has formed. — **3.** The prophet encourages David to do as he has planned. — **4.** This was however not the mind of God : *it came to pass the same night that the word of Yahweh came to Nathan*] the revelation coming in the night is probably to be understood as a dream. — **5.** The question : *Shalt thou build me a house to dwell in ?*] is equivalent to a negative. It is so reproduced by Chr. 𝕊. — **6.** The reason is that such a procedure would be contrary to precedent. Yahweh had never dwelt in a house : *but I have sojourned in a tent and in a tabernacle*] the Mosaic Tabernacle is not necessarily intended. — **7.** No command had ever been given for the building of a house nor had one of the Judges of Israel been reproached for not building it.

1. הניח־לו מסביב מכל־איביו] Dt. 12^{10} 25^{19} Jos. 23^1. The Chronicler omits the second half of the verse, possibly because he wishes to locate the promise in the early part of David's reign. He also changes כי־וישב into כאשר ישב with the intention of making this the immediate sequel of the bringing up of the Ark. — **2.** נתן] doubtless a shortened form of נרניה or נתנאל, cf. also נתן־מלך 2 K. 23^{11}. — **4.** ויהי דבר־יהוה] 1 S. 15^{10}; the phrase is frequent in

Jeremiah and Ezekiel. — **5.** האתה] לא אתה Chr. The former is probably original because the change from it to the other reading is more probable than the
reverse. — **6.** באהל ובמשכן] 𝔖 renders only במעון. Chr. has מאהל אל אהל
וממשכן which should evidently be completed by adding אל מישכן. On the
whole, it seems better to retain the text, as it might be expanded into the
reading of Chr., while the reverse process is hardly likely. מישכן is used of
the tent of Korah, Num. 16²⁴, and of the dwellings of the Bedawin, Ezek. 25⁴. —
7. הדבר דברתי] seems more vigorous if we point הֲדַבֵּר — *have I at all spoken ?*
It is so rendered by 𝔊. — יבטי] is to be corrected to יפטי Chr., for it was the
Judges who had been commanded to shepherd Israel, cf. v.¹¹.

8–16. The prophet is sent with a message of promise to David,
prefaced by a recital of the benefits heretofore conferred upon
him. The oracle shows traces of the rhythmical structure so frequent in prophetic composition, though it cannot be made strictly
metrical without emending the text in many places. — **8, 9.** First
the rehearsal of Yahweh's benefits :

> *Thus saith Yahweh Sebaoth*
> *I took thee from the pasture*
> *To be chief over my people ;*
> *And I was with thee wherever thou didst go*
> *To destroy thine enemies before thee.*

The remainder of the verse does not fit well in the context. As
it stands, it begins the promise : *And I will make thee a name, like
the name of the great in the earth.* But it seems more logical to
begin the promise with the next verse. — **10.** The verbs must refer
to the future :

> *And I will give a place to my people Israel,*
> *And will plant them and they shall dwell in their place ;*
> *And they shall no more be disquieted*
> *And violent men shall no more oppress them.*

So far, we come out fairly well with the metre. But the two clauses
now added : *As in former times, from the day when I set judges
over my people Israel,* cannot be forced into a couplet. It does
not seem violent to suppose them an addition to the original text.
The author of the verse ignores the fact that David had already
been given rest from his enemies, and we must suppose that in his
time the national existence was again threatened. According to

the received text, the promise to David now begins. But it is difficult to make sense of the present wording : *And I will give thee rest from all thine enemies, and Yahweh will make known to thee that Yahweh will make thee a house.* The objections to this are obvious. The change of person is without motive ; the repetition of the name Yahweh is superfluous ; it is to tell this very thing that the prophet has come. What we expect is something like this : *And now thus saith Yahweh : Thou shalt not build me a house, but I will build thee a house.* For this is the point of the whole message. For various attempts to improve the text, see the critical note. — **12.** The metre changes and the flow of the words is better :

> *And it shall be when thy days are filled out,*
> *And thou shalt lie down with thy fathers,*
> *That I will raise up thy seed after thee,*
> *Which shall come forth of thy body,*
> *And I will establish his kingdom.*

This explains the sense in which Yahweh is to build a house for David. The filling out of one's appointed days is parallel to Gen. 29[21]. One's children *come forth from his bowels*, an expression which is softened by Chr., but which occurs Gen. 15[4]. — **13.** The verse alludes to David's desire to build a temple, and promises that Solomon shall fulfil that desire. But as David's *seed* in the preceding verse means his whole dynasty, and as the dynasty is also the subject of what follows, this verse distinctly breaks the connexion and must be regarded as an interpolation. — **14.** This continues the main thought :

> *I will be to him a father,*
> *And he shall be to me a son ;*
> *When he goes astray*
> *I will correct him with the rod of men,*
> *And with stripes of the sons of Adam.*

The opening words are applied to Solomon 1 Chr. 22[10] 28[6]. But the idea is adopted in many Messianic passages, as Ps. 2, to express the relation existing between Yahweh and the Messiah. The rod of men is such as men use for each other — not such as the divine anger would naturally choose, for that would annihilate

the object of the chastisement. — **15.** The verse gives renewed
assurances :

> *And my kindness will I not turn from him,*
> *As I turned it from him who was before thee.*

Our text inserts the name of Saul, but this is an interpolation. —
16. The promise is for all time to come :

> *Thy house and thy kingdom shall stand firm,*
> *Forever in my sight,*
> *Thy throne shall be established forever.*

Cf. 1 S. 2^{35} 25^{28} 1 K. 2^{45}. — **17.** Up to this point we have heard
the commission which Nathan received. The present verse simply
adds that he carried it out.

A study of this passage in its relation to the general subject
of Messianic prophecy is given by Prof. Briggs in his *Messianic
Prophecy* (1886), p. 126 ff.

8. [מן־הנוה מאחר הצאן] $\mathfrak{G}^B$ has simply ἐκ τῆς μάνδρας τῶν προβάτων. For
מאחר some MSS. have מאחרי. — [על־ישראל] we should probably omit על with
some MSS., $\mathfrak{SL}$. — **9.** [ועשתי] does not fit in the context, as it is in the wrong
tense. It might be allowed however to read the preceding verb as the mood
of purpose, pointing וְאַכְרִיתָה and translating : *And I was with thee in order
to cut off thine enemies,* and then to make this continue that construction —
and in order to make thee a name. But parallels are not frequent, and it
seems simpler to suppose an expansion of the original text. — [גדול] should be
stricken out with Chr. $\mathfrak{G}^B$. — **10.** [לישראל] read ישראל with some MSS., $\mathfrak{S}$. —
[בני־עולה] cf. 3^{34}. — **11.** [ולמן] read למן with $\mathfrak{G}^B$. For לך Ew. proposes לו, and
to correspond makes אביך into אביו (GVI^3. III. p. 179, E. Tr. III. p. 132).
This is accepted by We., Dr., Bu., and is necessary if the clause belongs with
what precedes. But in the evident corruption of the rest of the verse, this is
not certain. — [והגיד לך יהוה] is difficult. It can be understood only in the
sense : *and Yahweh will tell thee.* But the prophet is sent for the purpose
of telling him now and the future is out of place. Chr. reads ואגד לך, which
$\mathfrak{G}$ saw to be ואגדלך, *and I will magnify thee.* This goes well enough with
what precedes, but the transition to what follows is awkward. What we
expect is an explicit introduction of the promise on the part of the prophet, a
phrase like *and now, thus saith Yahweh.* The most plausible reading yet suggested seems to be Bu.'s והנני מגיד לך with omission of יהוה. Even thus the hurt
seems only slightly healed. יהוה at the end of the verse is corrupted from והיה
at the opening of the next verse. — **12.** והיה should introduce the verse as in
Chr. and $\mathfrak{G}$. — [ימלאו] מלאו Chr. is equally good, and perhaps more likely to be
changed into our reading than the reverse. — **13.** The verse is regarded as a

later insertion by We. (*Comp.* p. 257) and Bu. — כסא ממלכתו] Chr. and 𝔊 have כסאו. — **14.** The latter half of the verse is omitted by Chr., who probably applied it to the Messiah and would not admit that he could go astray. — **15.** יסור] should be אסיר according to Chr., 𝔊𝔖𝔏. — מעם שאול אשר הסירתי Chr. has simply מאשר היה לפניך and as we can think of no reason why he should hesitate to mention Saul in this connexion, we must suppose he shows the text of the passage as he read it, and that the present reading is due to scribal expansion; 𝔊 moreover found מאשר although it has הסירתי. Three stages of the text are therefore represented in Chr., 𝔊, 𝕳. — **16.** וממלכתך] is supposed by Prof. Briggs to be an interpolation. — לפניך] cannot be right, and should be changed to לפני with 𝔊𝔖 — Chr. changes the wording of the whole verse. — כסאך] the conjunction is prefixed by 𝔖𝔏 and also by 𝔊, which however reads *his* throne as it does *his house* and *his kingdom.* — **17.** חזיון] חוז is preferred by Chr.

18. David's gratitude is shown by his appearing in the immediate presence of Yahweh. *Sitting* is not the usual attitude of prayer in the Old Testament, and has caused the commentators some perplexity. But that the oriental mind does not see anything inappropriate in it is proved by the Mohammedan ritual where it is one of several postures, as it is in the worship of some orders of dervishes, and in that of the Copts. The prayer begins with an implied confession of unworthiness : *What am I, and what is my house, that thou hast brought me thus far ?* — **19.** So far as the verse is intelligible, it says : *And this was little in thine eyes, my Lord Yahweh, and thou hast* [now] *spoken concerning thy servant for distant times.* The remaining clause which reads : *And this is the instruction of man, O Lord Yahweh,* gives no adequate sense in the present connexion. It cannot mean : *and this is the manner of man,* or : *and is this the manner of man ?* Conjectural emendation has got no farther than to show that the original may have read *and hast shown me the form* . . . . — **20.** *And what shall David say more to thee, seeing that thou knowest thy servant, O Lord Yahweh ?* The heart of the worshipper is known to God without much speaking. — **21.** *To glorify thy servant hast thou promised, and according to thy heart hast thou done, in showing thy servant all this greatness*] this translation is based on a reconstructed text. — **22.** The author glides into general expressions of praise, not especially appropriate to David's situation. — *Therefore thou art great*] the logical conclusion from Yahweh's dealings with his people. — **23.** The confused sentence seems originally to have read : *And who is like thy people Israel; [is there] another people in the earth which a god went to redeem for himself as a people, to make himself a name, and to do for them great and terrible things, in driving out a people and its gods before his people ?* As remarked by Geiger,* on whom later scholars depend, the scribes found even the supposition that another god could do what Yahweh had done, offensive or unthinkable, and so endeavoured to make the whole refer to Israel; hence the confusion. — **24.** A contrast between Yahweh and the false gods who had not elected a people : *But thou didst establish thy people Israel as a people for thyself forever]* the well-known covenant relation. — **25.** Prayer that Yahweh would carry out the word spoken to David. — **26.** *That thy name may be great forever]* that Yahweh acts for his name's sake is a frequent thought in the later books of the canon. — *In that men say: Yahweh Sebaoth is God over Israel]* seems to be the meaning of the next clause, which however may be scribal expansion. — **27.** Because of the revelation made to him, David *has found courage to pray this prayer.* — **28, 29.** The theme is repeated in slightly varying language, an indication of how much the heart of the author was concerned for the house of David. — *Thou art God and thy words are faithfulness]* the abstract noun for the adjective.

18. וישׁב] the unusual attitude has occasioned prolix discussion on the part of the commentators, as may be seen in Schm. p. 350 f. — ומי ביתי] cf. 1 S. 18¹⁸ 1 Chr. 29¹⁴. — **19.** למרחק] is used of distant times in the past 2 K. 19²⁵, here of distant times in the future. — וזאת תורת האדם] the sentence seems to have been unintelligible to the Chronicler, who replaces it with וראיתני כתור האדם המעלה, which however is equally obscure. The versions seem to have no other text unless 𝕮 (חזיא) reads מראה for תורת. The mystery of the incarnation was found here by Luther : *this is the manner of the man who is God the Lord,* a rendering which is defended by Calov, but rejected by the sound sense of Schm. The latter scholar however does not succeed in his own rendering, nor can the paraphrase of Grotius : *familiariter mecum agis quomodo homines hominibus agere solent* be justified by Hebrew usage. On the basis of the reading in Chr., Ewald (*GVI*³. III. p. 180, E. Trans. III. p. 132) conjectures the text to have been והראיתני בתור האדם למעלה, *and hast made me look upon the ranks of men onwards.* But תור in this meaning is not found elsewhere, and the author could hardly have expressed this sense in wording so

---

* *Urschrift und Uebersetzungen,* p. 288.

obscure. We. gets substantially the same meaning by restoring והראני דרות
האדם, *and hast shown me generations of men.* But it was not the generations
of men that interested David so much as the generations *of his descendants,*
and this he would have brought out distinctly. Bu. adopts We.'s conjecture,
adding לעלם of his own motion (suggested by המעלה Chr.). Oettli in his commentary on Chr. suggests וראיתני כתורת אדם, *und siehst mich an so gütig als
wärest du meinesgleichen.* But would this Hebrew sentence express this
meaning? I suspect that the corruption is beyond cure, but that והראני is a
part of the original and that it was followed by האר, possibly with the suffix;
and hast shown me thy beauty Lord Yahweh would be appropriate in the context, and אדם may be erroneous duplication of the following אדני.— **21.** בעבר.
בעבר עבוד [דברך Chr.: διὰ τὸν δοῦλόν σου 𝕲ᴮ. The originality of עבדך seems
established, and Nestle (*Marginalien,* p. 16) restores לכבד עבדך דברת following an indication given by Chr. in the verse preceding.— [הגדולה] as shown by
Dr., the word does not fit in the present position, and I have adopted his transposition (from Reifmann).— **22.** על־כן גדלת [ἕνεκεν τοῦ μεγαλυθῆναί σε 𝕲ᴸ
joined with the preceding verse. The reading of 𝕲ᴸ is at least equally good.
— יהוה אלהים [Κύριε, κύριέ μου 𝕲 points to אדני יהוה which we find elsewhere
in this chapter.— **23.** ישראל [כישראל Chr. 𝕲. The כ comes from the end of
the preceding words, *ZATW.* VI. p. 212.— אחד [ἄλλο 𝕲 evidently אחר. For
הלכו Chr. has הלך confirmed by the following לו and also by 𝕲ᴮ. 𝕲ᴸ on the
other hand has carried through an emendation reading הלכת and לך.— [לעם
עם Chr. 𝕲 and 𝕿.— לשום [ולשום Chr. 𝕲.— לו [לו Chr. and 𝕲.— [ולעשות לכם
omitted by Chr.— לכם [להון 𝕿 with which agrees 𝕃, whereas 𝕾 renders לו.
For הגדולה read גדלות with Chr.— לארצך [לגרש Chr. and 𝕲.— עמך [although
the authorities agree, must be changed to עמו. The next clause is contained
in the versions, but seems to be an insertion, in the line of the other changes
made. Still it is possible that the original author at the end of his long sentence
resumed the direct address.— [ואלהיו] is omitted by the Chronicler, to whom
the false gods were naught. The extent of the change made in the verse is
shown by the number of variants just given. The original text as we pick it
out of this material was: ומי כעמך ישראל גוי אחר בארץ אשר הלך אלהים לפדות־לו
[וחכנן לך.— **24.** לעם לשום לו שם ולעשות להם גדלות ונראות לגרש מפני עמו גוי ואלהיו
ותחן Chr.— **25.** [ועשה 𝕲ᴮ seems to have read ועתה, joining the clause to the
following verse.— **26.** 𝕲ᴮ omits from לאמר. It looks as if the verse had been
expanded, for the first half is optative while יהיה נכון of the last clause can
hardly be so understood. Is not this a case where the Chronicler made an
insertion which afterwards affected the text of Samuel?— **27.** כי־אתה [is lacking in 𝕲ᴮ.— את־לבו [is absent from Chr. The phrase מצא את־לב seems to
occur nowhere else.— **29.** [הואל וברך with coördination of the verbs, instead
of subordination of the second, the construction found in 1 S. 12²² and in the
parallel to the present passage, 1 Chr. 17²⁷. Cf. Davidson, *Syntax,* 83.

VIII. 1–18. David's wars. — David conquers in succession the
Philistines, Moab, Zobah, Damascus, and Edom. The brief

account of these wars is supplemented by a list of his officials.
The chapter is apparently from a document other than the one
which gives us Ch. 10, for the wars here enumerated are, in part
at least, the same recounted there. The tone of the whole chapter is the tone of a summary — the author would give us a brief
sketch of David's wars and pass on to something more important.

1. *David smote the Philistines and subdued them*] Dt. 9³ Jd. 4²³,
cf. Jd. 3³⁰. The author adds that he took something from the
hand of the Philistines, but what he took cannot now be made out
with certainty. — **2.** *And he smote Moab and measured them off
with a line making them lie down upon the earth*] two-thirds (of
the males we may suppose) were thus put to death. The question
as to the cruelty of this proceeding seems to be raised unnecessarily, when we consider how frequently the whole population was
'devoted' in war. The Chronicler however seems to have had
some compunctions in this case, for he leaves out the notice. The
tribute afterwards exacted is disguised under the name of a *present*, as so often in oriental governments. As in the time of Mesha,
it probably consisted of sheep and wool, 2 K. 3⁴. This writer
seems to have no knowledge of David's obligation to Moab, as
indicated in 1 S. 22³. — **3.** The next conquest was that of *Hadadezer son of Rehob, king of Zobah*] a small Aramaean kingdom in
the neighbourhood of Damascus, cf. 1 S. 14⁴⁷ 1 K. 11²³. According to 2 S. 10⁶ the provocation was given by Hadadezer's aiding
the Ammonites against David. — *When he went to lay his hand
upon the River*] the phrase *to lay hand upon* recurs Ezek. 38¹². The
River is, here as elsewhere, the Euphrates. Whether David or
Hadadezer is the subject is not clear, but probably David. The
fact that David never actually possessed so much territory does
not prove that this author did not believe him to have possessed
it. — **4.** The original seems to have said that *David captured a
thousand chariots and slew twenty thousand footmen*. As chariots
were of no use in the hill country of Palestine, he *hamstrung the
chariot horses, leaving only a hundred*] for purposes of state we
may suppose. — **5.** *Syria* of Damascus for *the Syrians* of Damascus. The country north of Palestine seems to have been cut up
into a number of petty kingdoms. Damascus, a well-known city

x

of great antiquity, was always an important place. The aid of the Damascenes is given to Zobah because they are threatened with a common danger. — **6**. David reduced them to the position of tributaries, putting garrisons in their country. — **7**. David took the *golden shields*] the meaning is not altogether certain, *which were on the officers of Hadadezer*] an addition to the verse in 𝔊 identifies them with those carried off by Shishak 1 K. 14²⁶. — **8**. *And from Tibhath and from Berothai*] places not certainly known to us, *David took much bronze*] copper mines seem to have been worked in the region of Lebanon. 𝔊 and Chr. add that this bronze was used by Solomon for the vessels of the Temple — an addition to be judged like that to v.⁷.

1. אֶת־מֶתֶג הָאַמָּה] *the bridle of the cubit* is obscure. From its being taken *from the hands* of the Philistines we infer that it was some tangible possession, probably a piece of territory. אֶת גַּת וּבְנֹתֶיהָ Chr. would therefore be entirely in place. The reason for suspecting it, is the difficulty in supposing so easy a phrase corrupted into the reading of 𝔐. The versions give no help: τὴν ἀφωρισμένην 𝔊, possibly reading הַמֻּגְרָשׁ or הַגְּבוּל; τὸν χαλινὸν τοῦ ὑδραγωγίου Aq. points to the text we have: τὴν ἐξουσίαν τοῦ φόρου Sym. is the original of *frenum tributi* (מֶתֶג הַמַּס?) 𝕷: תִּקּוּן אַמְחָא 𝕿 represents the tradition known to Aq.: רָמַת גַּמָּא 𝕾 seems to be a proper name. The expositors have generally felt it necessary to find an equivalent for *Gath and its dependent towns* given us by Chr. They have done this by making אַמָּה equivalent to אֵם as sometimes used in Hebrew for a city (*metropolis*). *The Bridle of the Metropolis* would then conceivably have been the citadel which commanded the town and so commanded the district. But it is difficult to see why so figurative a phrase should be used in a prose passage. On the other hand, from the fact of the *bridle* or *rein* denoting power (as the *leading string* sometimes in English) some have concluded that David is here represented as taking the suzerainty from the hand of the Philistines, either that he assumed the supreme power over them or else that he threw off *their yoke*. Why this again should be so obscurely expressed, it is impossible to see. The older commentators are excerpted by Pole. Among the recent scholars Ewald (*GVI*³. p. 202, E. Trans. III. p. 148) decides for the Philistine sovereignty over Israel, which David wrested from them. Keil supposes *the metropolis* to be meant, so that the phrase is equivalent to Gath, whose king he supposes to be overlord of the Philistines,* and in this he is followed by Erdm. whose American editor however leaves the meaning undecided. Th. conjectures *the border;* We. retains the text, which he supposes to mean *the authority over the*

---

* Isaaki discovered that the only one of the Philistine cities which had a king was Gath.

metropolis, in which he is followed by Dr., while Bu. leaves a blank in his text. — **2.** בחבל] is put in the plural by 𝔊ᴮ. — השכב] on the use of the adverbial infinitive cf. Davidson, *Syntax*, 87. — ומלא החבל] *the contents of one line :* 𝔊 gives the proportion *two* and *two*, and 𝔏 gives it *one* and *one*. — **3.** הדרעזר] Chr. has הדרעזר and 𝔊 'Αδρααζαρ. Some MSS. have the same form in this chapter. The name is evidently similar to אליעזר, אביעזר, and יועזר, and the first element is the name of the god Hadad. That it is *Hadad* and not *Hadar* seems evident from the names Benhadad 1 K. 15¹⁸, and Hadadrimmon Zech. 12¹¹, as well as from the Aramaic and Assyrian parallels. Cf. BDB. and reff., especially Baethgen, *Beiträge zur Semit. Religionsgeschichte*, p. 67 ff., also Schrader *COT.* p. 190 f. The god Hadad (*Addu*) is met in the Tell-el-Amarna Tablets (Winckler, 149¹⁴ 150⁷), in Arabia (We. *Skizzen*, III. p. 51), and apparently in Edom, Gen. 36³⁵. — רחב] 𝔊 'Ρααβ ('Ραφφ) reminds us of *Rahab*, Jos. 2¹ and רחביה, 1 Chr. 23¹⁷. — צובה] known as *Subit* to the Assyrians according to Meyer, *Gesch. d. Altertums*, p. 347, and Schrader, *COT.* I. p. 171. The Chronicler is probably mistaken in locating the battle at Hamath which is too far north. — להשיב ידו] is objected to by Th., Dr., as meaning necessarily to *bring back* the hand where it had once been. But the passage in Ezekiel (38¹²) seems to show that it may denote simply extending one's power, for Gog, who is there addressed, had not yet possessed the countries which he was expecting to plunder. 𝔊 ἐπιστῆσαι does not imply that the translators read להציב with Chr., cf. Is. 1²⁶ 𝔊. — בנהר] is sufficiently explicit without the addition of פרת (Qrê, Chr. and 𝔊). — **4.** אלף ושבע-מאות פרשים] as the chariots are alluded to immediately after, it is probable that they were mentioned here. Chr. and 𝔊 agree in אלף רכב ושבעת אלפים פרשים, the first part of which meets the requirements of the case. The 7000 horses or horsemen are out of proportion to the chariots, so that probably the text is corrupt. It is surprising that if David took the foot soldiers prisoners we should not be told what he did with them, which is another reason for supposing that the original text is lost. עקר as in Arabic: *he cut the hock tendon of an animal* thus making it useless for riding. — הרכב] must here mean *the chariot horses.* — **5.** ותבא] the country is thought of as feminine. — **6.** נצבים] cf. 1 S. 13³. — **7.** שלטי] χλιδῶνας 𝔊 would apparently make them *bracelets* or *armlets.* None of the passages in which the word occurs can be said to be decisive, but the identification in 𝔊 with the מגנים of 1 K. 14²⁶ would favour *shields.* In Ez. 27¹¹ the same word is rendered by 𝔊 *quivers* which Symmachus has in the present text, whereas Aquila has here *collars,* cf. Field's note, *Hexap. Origenis*, I. p. 558. — אל] read על. — ירושלם] + καὶ ἔλαβεν αὐτὰ Σουσακεὶμ κτλ. nearly all MSS. of 𝔊 and 𝕴. The addition is in line with some other notes which have found their way into the text of 𝔊, and is probably not original. — **8.** מבטח] Chr. מבבחת: 𝔊ᴸ Ματεβάκ (of which 𝔊ᴮ Μασβάκ is probably a corruption) seems to confirm the reading of Chr. — ומכון Chr.: καὶ ἐκ τῶν ἐκλεκτῶν 𝔊 perhaps reading ומבחורי. The name here reminds us of *Beirût.* — מאר] + בה עשה שלמה את-ים וגו Chr., contained also substantially in 𝔊 and 𝕴. The interest of the Chronicler in all things that pertain to the Temple accounts for his insertion of the sentence, and it has probably come from Chronicles into the Greek of Samuel.

9. *Tou, king of Hamath*] an important city on the Orontes, probably capital of the Hittite kingdom. — **10.** *Hadoram his son*] seems to be the more probable form of the name. The dignity of the ambassador shows the degree of honour paid by the mission. — *To greet David and to congratulate him*] for his success, *for Hadadezer had been an enemy of Tou*] probably seeking to establish an independent kingdom in a country once tributary to Hamath. The ambassador brought an appropriate present of jewels and objects of art. — **11.** *These also the king dedicated to Yahweh*] quite in accord with antique custom. — **12.** *From Edom*] is probably to be read. The other countries named in the verse we have already met.

9. חעי] with Chr. we should probably read חעו : 𝔊ᴮ Θοου, *Thou* 𝔏; but Θαεί 𝔊ᴬᴸ. — **10.** יורם] in which the first element might be the name of Yahweh. Chr. however has הרורם and 𝔊 Ἰεδδουράν which confirms Chr. to a certain extent, for 𝔊ᴮ has Ἰδουράαμ in Chr. — [איש מלחמות חעו cf. אנשי מלחמתך Is. 41¹² (Ezek. 27¹⁰ is different). — **11.** גם] indicates that other things had been spoken of as *dedicated*, which is not the case in our narrative. It is not unlikely therefore that this and the following verse are a late insertion (Bu.). — **12.** מארם] מאדום Chr. and 𝔊𝔖 besides 11 MSS. of 𝔥. As Aram is covered by the last clause of the verse, and as Edom belongs with Moab and Ammon, we should correct the text here accordingly. The fact that the conquest of Edom is narrated later, is only another evidence that these verses are an insertion from another document.

13. The verse is obscure, and as the Chronicler makes the first part of it refer to Abishai instead of David, we cannot be sure what he read. That the account refers to *Edom* seems quite certain. By slight emendation we may get: *And David made a name on returning, in that he smote Edom, in the Valley of Salt*] the location is brought into connexion with Edom again in 2 K. 14⁷ Ps. 60². — **14.** The treatment of Edom was the same as that of Aram. The remark that *Yahweh delivered David wherever* he went is evidently intended to conclude this account of his wars.

13. בשבו מהכותו] but the reputation was not made on his return but by the smiting. 𝔊 connects ויעש דוד שם with what precedes and then goes on : καὶ ἐν τῷ ἀνακάμπτειν αὐτὸν ἐπάταξεν = ובשבו הכה. The difficulty in supposing this to be original arises from the simplicity of הכה which could hardly be cor-

rupted into מהכותו. I suspect therefore that we should read בשבו בהכותו.
Others have conjectured that a clause has fallen out after ארם. Grätz (*Gesch.*
I. p. 255) makes a conflate text from this and the Chronicler. Th. inserts
ויך את אדום which is adopted by Erdm. and Keil, cf. also Köhler (*Gesch. A T.*
II. p. 288) who calls this the common hypothesis. We. adopts the reading of
𝔊. —ארם] read אדום with Chr. 𝔊𝔖, 6 MSS. of 𝔥.

15–18. The administration. — David himself acted as chief
executive and constantly *administered judgment and justice to all
his people.* In connexion with what follows this can mean only
that David acted as chief justice, and was accessible to the people
as a monarch should be. — **16.** Joab was over the army, *and
Jehoshaphat son of Ahilud was the Recorder*] hardly *the Chronicler*
who wrote the annals of the reign ; more likely *the king's Monitor*
who kept him informed of the course of public business. —
17. The priests here mentioned are evidently regarded as officers
of the court. *Zadok* is not mentioned earlier, but Abiathar, whose
name we should read in the second place, was the companion of
David's wanderings, 1 S. 22²⁰. *Sousa* seems to have been the
name of the scribe. — **18.** *And Benaiah son of Jehoiada was over
the Cherethites and the Pelethites*] that is, the body-guard. — *And
David's sons were priests*] there seems no reason to change the
plain meaning of the word.

16. מזכיר] on the meaning of the word cf. Jacob, " *Beiträge zu einer Einleitung in die Psalmen,*" *ZATW.* 1897, p. 76. — **17.** צדוק is called here בן־
אחיטוב. Possibly the genealogy is based on the succession. We.'s conjecture,
which leaves Zadok without a father, is not supported by any document. The
same may be said of the transposition of אחימלך בן־אביתר which however seems
necessary, for Abiathar acted as priest until the reign of Solomon. — אחימלך]
אבימלך Chr. is perhaps based on the difficulty just noted. — שריה] 'Ασά 𝔊ᴮ :
Σαραίας 𝔊ᴸ : שיא 20²⁵ (where we find 'Ιησοῦς 𝔊ᴮ : Σουσά 𝔊ᴸ) : שושא 1 Chr.
18¹⁶. The reading שושא accounts most naturally for all the variations. Perhaps we should make the next word הסופר. — **18.** והכרתי] read with the parallel על הכרתי. 𝔊 in order to make sense inserts σύμβουλος. The endeavour to
retain the received text, by taking ו in the sense of עם (Kimchi, Schm.), is
unsuccessful. The Cherethites are known to us as Philistines from 1 S. 30¹⁴.
The Pelethites who are mentioned only in connexion with the Cherethites
cannot be certainly identified. That they constituted the body-guard of the
king is apparently the mind of the Targum which translates *archers and
slingers.* Cf. Josephus, *Ant.* VII. 11, 8. The Rabbinical expositors show their
lack of historical sense when they find here the Sanhedrim or the Urim and

Thummim (Isaaki and Kimchi cite this from *our Rabbis* but do not themselves approve it).   More excusable is the theory of Jewish expositors that two clans of Israelites are intended (Isaaki, Kimchi, LbG.).   But 1 S. 30¹⁴ Ezek. 25¹⁶ Zeph. 2⁵ seem conclusive as to the Philistines.   We hear also of Gittites in David's service, and the custom of enlisting foreigners for the king's body-guard has prevailed down to recent times in many countries, for obvious reasons. — כהנים] the traditional exegesis has difficulty in supposing David's sons to be *priests* in the proper sense, for by the Levitical code none could be priests except descendants of Aaron.   For this reason the Chronicler changes his text, substituting הראשנים ליד המלך.   Cf. also αὐλάρχαι 𝔊.   But there is no reason for departing from the plain meaning of our text.

IX.–XX. David's court life. — We come now to a homogeneous and continuous narrative of David's experiences from the time when he was firmly settled on the throne until near the close of his life. The author is evidently well informed and has an interest in presenting the history without bias. That he was not very remote in time from the events which he narrates is evident. The unity and integrity of the section, except some minor interpolations, is generally conceded.

IX. 1–13. David's fidelity to Jonathan. — David inquires whether Jonathan has left any children. He learns of one son whom he brings to court and makes his companion, besides restoring to him the family property.

1. The opening of the verse is lost, or misplaced.   Perhaps it should be taken from 7¹ : *It came to pass when David was established in his house, that he said : Is there left of the house of Saul any to whom I may show kindness for the sake of Jonathan ?* The question is as appropriate after the death of Ishbaal as after the revenge of the Gibeonites. — **2.** Information is sought from a *servant of the house of Saul,* apparently a feudal dependent, whose name was *Ziba.* — **3.** The king puts the question even more distinctly than at first : *Is there not a man belonging to the house of Saul ?*] and he avows his object more distinctly : *that I may show the kindness of God*] that to which he was bound by his solemn engagement, cf. 1 S. 20¹⁴. Ziba informs him of a son of Jonathan who was lame. — **4.** To the king's further question Ziba says that he is *in the house of Machir son of Ammiel, in Lo-Debar*] a man of wealth and prominence, as we gather from 17²⁷. The place was beyond the Jordan, probably not far from Mahanaim. — **5, 6.** In response to the king's command *Meribbaal*] on the name see the note on 4⁴, *came to David and fell upon his face*] the customary act of obeisance. — **7.** Meribbaal has reason to fear, but is reassured by David, who not only gives a general promise of kind treatment, but a specific one : *I will restore to thee all the land of Saul thy father*] whether this property was in possession of David as successor in the kingdom, or whether it had been seized by some one else, we are not told. Besides this, Meribbaal was made a member of the king's household : *thou shalt eat at my table continually*] this special mark of favour is the more noteworthy on account of Meribbaal's physical imperfection. — **8.** The recognition is sufficiently humble to satisfy even an oriental : *What is thy servant that thou shouldst turn thy face to a dead dog such as I am ?*] the man had doubtless been made to feel that he was a useless member of the family, and was all the more grateful for kind treatment. — **9, 10.** David arranges that Ziba shall cultivate the land and bring its produce to Meribbaal for his support — presence at court would rather increase than diminish his expenditure. The extent of the estate is indicated by the force needed to cultivate it — Ziba's fifteen sons and twenty servants. — **11.** Ziba promises to obey all that the king commands. The second half of the verse cannot be correct as it stands. It seems originally to have been, in the form preserved by 𝕲, the author's concluding remark : *So Meribbaal ate at David's table like one of the sons of the king.*

12, 13. The verses seem to be an appendix, giving further information as to the line of Saul. It was represented by Meribbaal's son *Micha.* The glossator feels that he must again assure us that Meribbaal ate continually at the king's table *though he was lame in both feet.*

1. By an ingenious conjecture, Kl. prefaces this chapter with 21¹⁻¹⁴, and this is adopted by Bu., so that in his edition we read the account of the famine and the consequent vengeance of the Gibeonites on the house of Saul, and then the story of David's remembrance of his obligation towards Jonathan. At first view this seems natural, and the impression is strengthened by the fact that we have an unusual אחרי כן at the end of 21¹⁴ which is easily made ויהי אח׳ כן. and appropriately introduces 9¹. But on reflection the probability of this being the original order is reduced. It seems doubtful whether David would wait until the evidently late date of 21 before making inquiry for the family of Jonathan. Budde, in order to his theory, is obliged to strike out 21⁷ which otherwise seems entirely in place. Finally, it is difficult to see how 21¹⁻¹⁴ if it were ever the prelude to this chapter came to be dislocated. For these reasons it is not safe to accept the reconstruction here in mind; and we are compelled to seek another connexion for this chapter. By striking out the insertions from another document we find 9¹ following immediately on 6²³. At the first blush this seems not to be appropriate. David's quarrel with Michal would seem to stir up any but good thoughts towards the house of Saul. On the other hand we must remember that the author may have intended to show that the foolish words of a woman could not make David forget his obligations to Jonathan. And it would be psychologically probable that the unsympathetic behaviour of Michal should recall the contrasted character of Jonathan her brother, and so put David on the thought of Jonathan's family. If this be the original order, it is probable that the opening phrase of 7, ויהי כי ישב המלך בביתו once formed the introduction to the present section. — **2.** [עבדך] it is not necessary to add the pronoun, as is done by 𝔊ᴮ. — **3.** [חסר אלהים] cf. הסר יהוה 1 S. 20¹⁴. It is difficult to suppose the meaning to be *kindness such as God shows*. More probably, it is the kindness imposed by God in the obligation of the oath. At the end of this verse, Bu. inserts 4⁴ᵇ which gives the cause of the lameness. It is doubtful however whether the verse ever stood here, as the brevity of Ziba's answers seems characteristic. — **4.** [לו דבר] Λαδαβάρ 𝔊, is called in 17²⁷ לא דבר and (as it appears) in Jos. 13²⁶ is called לדבר. — **6.** [מפיבשת] 4⁴. The mutilation of the name has been already commented on. — [וישתחו] in 𝔊ᴸ placed before ויפל. — **8.** [שלחני] 1 S. 20²⁹, cf. Jud. 1⁷ and Moore's note. — **10.** [לבן־אדניך] εἰς τὸν οἶκον τοῦ κυρίου σου 𝔊ᴸ is an attractive emendation; with it goes καὶ φάγονται for ואכלו. By adopting this we avoid the awkwardness of 𝔐. That the *family* of Meribbaal should eat of the produce of his land is quite in order. — **11.** The sentence ומפיבשת וגו is entirely unintelligible as a part of Ziba's response to the king. The change of שלחני to *mensam tuam* made by some MSS. of 𝔏 would allow us to interpret it as a part of Ziba's answer. But in his mouth it is wholly superfluous. It seems best therefore to restore the reading of 𝔊ᴬᴮ ἐπὶ τῆς τραπέζης Δαυείδ (τοῦ βασιλέως 𝔊ᴸ), and regard the sentence as a remark of the author. Such a remark is the natural conclusion of the account, and what follows must be an afterthought. — **12.** [מיכא] the spelling makes it difficult to suppose the name contracted from מיכיהו. It seems to be of the same form with ציבא v.², cf. also עירא 20²⁶. Jastrow (*JBL*. XIII. p. 112) cites Jerome's suggestion that the name signifies *humilitas*, from מוך. — **13.** [והוא פסח שתי ר׳] the fact that we have a change from נכה רגלים of v.³ is additional evidence that these two verses are a later addition.

X.–XII. The Ammonite war and David's adultery. — On

occasion of a change in the throne of Ammon, David sends an

embassy to the new monarch. Their reception is anything but
agreeable, and the insult offered in the ambassadors to their
monarch is naturally followed by war. The war is made more
serious by the engagement of the Syrians on the side of Ammon.
Joab successfully repulses the Syrians and lays siege to Rabbath
Ammon. David remains in Jerusalem, where, under sudden
temptation, he commits adultery with the wife of Uriah, one of
the knights of his army. In order to conceal his crime he
sends for Uriah, and after consulting him about the state of the
army, sends him to his house. Uriah however refuses to indulge
in luxuries not suited to a soldier, and twice spends the night in
the open air. The straits into which David is brought lead him
to order the indirect murder of Uriah. His commands are carried out by Joab, and he takes Bathsheba as his wife. The birth
of her son is followed by a visit from the prophet Nathan, who
rebukes David for his sin and announces the punishment. In
truth the son born of adultery is taken ill, lingers awhile and dies.
The author also tells us of the birth of Solomon from the same
mother. The siege of Rabba is concluded by David in person.

The section is suspected of expansion in the Nathan speeches,
and shows some indications of compilation from two sources.

X. 1-5. The insult. — Nahash, *king of the Children of Ammon*,
is the same we have met above, 1 S. 11[1]. As we do not know the
length of Saul's reign, nor at what time in the reign of David his
death took place, it is impossible to predicate extraordinary length
of his life. — **2.** David, recognizing what Nahash had done for
him, sent to condole with Hanun concerning his father. Possibly
Nahash, as an enemy of Saul, had given aid to David in his early
struggles. — **3.** The princes of Ammon, with Bedawish scorn for
the peasant king, provoke the suspicions of their chief: *Dost thou
think that David is honouring thy father that he has sent bearers
of condolence?* The interested motive is found in the office of
these messengers as spies. David's treatment of Moab and Edom
gave colour at least to the suspicion of his ambitious designs. —
4. With the lack of seriousness so often seen in a youthful prince
(as in the case of Rehoboam) Hanun was ready to act upon these
suspicions. He took the messengers *and shaved half their beard*]

the person of an ambassador should be inviolate. Moreover the
beard is held in especial honour in the East : *and cut their robes
in two to their buttocks*] the long flowing robes of the ambassadors were thus reduced to less than decency required. — **5.** The
news reached David and he judiciously advised them to remain at
Jericho, the frontier city, until the growth of their beards should
allow them to return without being subject to annoyance.

1. מלך בני עמון] the Chronicler prefixes נחש which we should certainly
expect at the beginning of the account. Chr. (19¹) on the other hand omits
חנון. It seems to me the name is required in both cases. 𝕲 however has the
same text with 𝔚. — **2.** על אביו [אל־אביו] Chr. is more in accord with usage,
cf. Jer. 16⁷. — **3.** *Is David honouring thy father in thine eyes?*] the meaning
is : *Does it seem to thee that David is doing this for his alleged purpose?* On
the participle, Dr. *Tenses*³, § 135, 4. — בעבור חקר את־העיר] as the fortified
city was of great importance, it is here put in the foreground. Chr. makes a
general reference to the *land.* — **4.** Instead of *half their beards,* 𝕲 puts *their
beards.* — ער־שתותיהם] the shameful nakedness of captives is described in the
term חשופי־שת Is. 20⁴. — **5.** וישבתם] the regular consecution after the imperative, Davidson, *Syntax*, § 55 *a*.

6–14. The opening of the war. —

The Ammonites saw *that
they had made themselves of bad odour with David*] as we readily
conceive. — They therefore *hired the Syrians of Beth Rehob*] a
city in the Lebanon (Antilebanon) region, Num. 13²¹, near Dan
Jd. 18²⁸. *Zobah* is known to us from 8³. It is possible that
Hadadezer was originally mentioned in this verse as he is there.
Maacah another small kingdom in the same region, Dt. 3¹⁴ Jos.
13¹¹. *Tob* is probably the country mentioned in Jd. 11³, but has
not been identified. — **8.** The Ammonites formed their order of
battle before the gate — we naturally suppose the gate of Rabbah
— while the Syrians drew up *by themselves in the open country*]
Joab was thus between two fires. — **9.** Discovering this, he felt
that the defeat of the Syrians was the important point, and with a
picked force he threw himself upon them. — **10.** The bulk of the
army he put under the command of Abishai, and they drew up
facing the Children of Ammon. — **11, 12.** Joab encourages his
brother with the promise of mutual help, and exhorts him to show
himself strong *for the sake of our people and for the cities of our
God*] the latter phrase is unusual. — **13, 14.** The plan was that

Joab should make the first attack while Abishai held the Ammonites in check. The onset was successful; the Syrians fled: *The
Ammonites saw that the Syrians had fled, and they fled and
entered the city*] they had kept a place of retreat open. The
conclusion of the verse: *And Joab returned from the Ammonites
and came to Jerusalem*] marks the close of this campaign.

6. נבאשו בדוד] cf. 1 S. 13⁶. 1 Chr. 19⁶ substitutes התבאשו עם דויד. Moore
(*Judges*, p. 399) conjecturally identifies *Beth Rehob* with Paneas. The fact
that *Hadadezer* is mentioned in v.¹⁶ without any introduction favours Budde's
theory (*RS.* p. 250) that he was originally named in this verse, and further
probability is given by the mention of the *king* of Maacah. — טוב] can hardly
be *Taiyyibeh* in Gilead (GASmith and Buhl). The small number of troops
sent from Maacah leads We. to suppose איש אלף to be an interpolation and
he thus gets *the king of Maacah and Ishtob*. Kl. makes a further change by
striking out the conjunction, and so finds the name of the king to be Ishtob.
There seems however no sufficient reason for departing from the text. The
Chronicler makes the unheard-of force of *32,000 chariots and the king of
Maacah and his people*. He also adds that the allies *came and camped before
Medeba* which is adopted without sufficient reason by Kl.; v.⁸ is decidedly
against it. — **7.** כל־הצבא הגברים] we might perhaps allow the apposition: *the
army, the heroes*. But this is an unusual construction, and here especially
suspicious because *all the army* naturally means the militia in distinction from
the veteran force of גברים. Chr. has צבא הגבורים כל which is evidently intended
for *all the army of heroes*, though the punctuators perversely read צָבָא. 𝔊ᴸ also
has πᾶσαν τὴν στρατιὰν τῶν δυνατῶν with which agree 𝔖𝔗𝔏. I suspect however that either הצבא or הגברים is a later insertion. Grätz conjectures הצבא
והגברים. The subsequent account shows that more than the standing army
was engaged. — **8.** פתח העיר [פתח השער Chr. 𝔊ᴸ. Such substitutions are not
uncommon. — **9.** בחורי בישראל] the construct before a preposition undoubtedly occurs, Davidson, *Syntax*, 28, R. 1, but as the Chronicler has בחור בישראל
it seems proper to correct our text accordingly. 𝔊ᴸ seems to point to בחור בני
ישראל whereas 𝔊ᴮ renders בחורי ישראל. — **10.** אבישי] here only, in Samuel. —
ויערך] the plural is found in Chr. and 𝔊ᴮ, but is not necessary. It would
be proper in English also to say *Abishai drew up before the Ammonites*. —
12. ערי אלהינו] occurs nowhere else and is inappropriate here, for the cities of
Yahweh were not in danger. There is ground therefore for Kl.'s conjecture
(adopted by Bu.) that the *Ark of our God* originally stood here. The Ark
went with the army on a subsequent campaign as we know. — **13, 14.** The
account is very brief and was probably once fuller.

15–19. A second campaign. — Our present text contains the
account of an effort on the part of the Syrians to retrieve themselves. The paragraph breaks the sequence of the narrative how-

ever, and is possibly from another source. There seems no room
for it in the time at our disposition, and the bringing in of the
Syrians from beyond the river shows a conception of the situation
different from anything we have met above.

15, 16. The consciousness of defeat caused the Syrians to take
joint measures — *they gathered together, and Hadadezer sent and
brought out the Syrians beyond the River*] the Euphrates is meant.
The face of the narrative indicates that his authority extended
into Assyria, unless we suppose that he simply applied for assistance to the king of that country. — *They came to Helam*] the
place, which is mentioned again in the next verse, is unknown. —
17. David musters all Israel and takes the offensive. — **18.** The
result was a decisive defeat for the Syrians.   It is difficult to
suppose that the clause *he slew seven hundred chariots* is original,
though perhaps it may be justified by the analogy of 8[4] where
David is said to have *hamstrung all the chariots*.   The enormous
number of 40,000 horsemen is suspicious, especially in view of the
fact that this author does not speak of footmen at all, while Chr.
has 7000 chariots and 40,000 footmen. — **19.** This verse, by speaking of *all the kings, servants of Hadadezer*, implies that Hadadezer
was chief ruler, having subject monarchs.   This is in contradiction
to 8[9] where his sovereignty is limited by the kingdom of Hamath.
— *They made peace with Israel*] cf. Jos. 10[1, 4].

15–19. The later insertion of the paragraph is affirmed by Winckler (*Gesch.
Israels*, p. 139).   More exactly, he believes that v.[19b] joins directly to v.[14]. —
16. The presence of Hadadezer, which has not been intimated before, is
another argument for the separate origin of the paragraph.   The current
editions of the text have *Hadarezer* here, as in Chr.   But the Mantua edition
of 1742 (with the *Minchath Shai*), Baer, and Ginsburg have *Hadadezer* as
elsewhere in Samuel. — חילם] rendered *their army* by Thenius is doubtless the
same proper name which occurs just below — so 𝕲𝕾𝕿.   If Cornill is correct
in restoring the same name in Ezek. 47[16], it was on the boundary line between
the territories of Hamath and Damascus.   On the other hand, it has been
identified by Hoffmann (*Phön. Inschriften*, p. 39) with Aleppo (Haleb).   For
שובך Chr. has שופך. — **17.** הלאמה] a different spelling of the name.   It is
omitted by Chr. — **18.** ויהרג] the objects of this verb seem always to be things
that have life — the *vine* Ps. 78[47] is no exception.   The 7000 chariots of the
Chronicler are in line with some other exaggerations of his. — וישלמו את־ישראל]
as in Jos. 10[1, 4], whereas Chr. substitutes עם for את, like 1 K. 22[45].   The clause

and they feared to deliver the Ammonites seems superfluous after the Syrians have become subject to Israel, and was possibly the original conclusion of v.[14].

XI. 1–5. David's sin. — The author has enclosed the account of David's sin between portions of the history of the Ammonite war, 11[1] being continued by 12[26]. The time and the circumstances agree so well, that we must suppose him to follow the actual order of events. — **1.** The time seems to be fixed at a year after the embassy to Hanun. The return of the season was a fitting time to refresh the king's memory of the insult. Joab and the army therefore *laid waste the Ammonites* in the well-known method of oriental warfare, where the growing crops are eaten off by the invaders. The campaign in this case was more than a raid, for the Israelites *laid siege to Rabba* the chief city of Ammon. The ruins (or town, it has recently received a Circassian colony, according to GASmith, *Geog.* p. 20) still bear the name *Amman;* cf. Burckhardt, *Travels in Syria*, p. 356; Baedeker, *Palestine*[2], p. 185 f. The site is about twenty miles east of the Jordan, east by north from Jericho. The siege of a walled town was a tedious matter, so that David can hardly be blamed for remaining at Jerusalem. — **2.** One afternoon David *arose from his siesta and walked on the roof of the palace*] which, being on the highest point of the city, commanded a view of the courts of the surrounding houses. Thence he saw *a woman bathing.* — **3.** To his inquiry *one said: Is not this Bathsheba, daughter of Eliam*] according to 23[34] he was a son of the well-known Ahitophel; *the wife of Uriah the Hittite*] one of the foreigners in David's service. — **4.** David sends for her and gratifies his passion, *for she was cleansed from her impurity*] the remark is added to show why conception followed. — **5.** She relied upon the king to find a way out of the difficulty.

1. המלאכים] is vocalized as though it were המלכים and so read by Chr. (1 Chr. 20[1]) and the versions. The clause is then supposed to mean *eo tempore quo solent reges ad bella procedere* 𝔏. But if this be the meaning, it is obscurely expressed, for the *ad bella*, which gives the point, is not represented in 𝔐. The interpretation seems especially unfortunate, in that the example of David shows that kings did not regularly go out to war, but sometimes sent their armies. We might suppose indeed that there is a covert condemnation of David for not doing as kings (on this theory) usually do. But this seems far fetched. The supposition of Kimchi therefore claims attention which is that the time designated is *the season of the year when the kings* [of Syria] *made their invasion.* If however we go so far, it is better to accept the *K'tib* המלאכים and understand *at the season of the year when the messengers of David first went forth.* This interpretation was suggested by Grätz (*Gesch. d. Juden*, I. p. 254) and is adopted by Kl. — **2.** מעל משכבו] it is assumed that he usually took an afternoon sleep. — ויתהלך] Gen. 3⁸. — Bathsheba is called in 1 Chronicles, 3⁵, בת־שוע בת עמיאל, where the ב has been softened into ו,* and the two elements of the name אליעם have been transposed. — אוריה] we naturally interpret the name as meaning *Yahweh is my light.* If that be the sense, we may suppose that the Hittite adopted a new name or modified his old one, on entering David's service. On such names, cf. Jastrow, *JBL.* XIII. p. 122. — **4.** והיא מתקדשת מטמאתה] cannot mean *and she purified herself by ablution* after coition, which would require ותתקדש. The participle indicates what had just been accomplished by the bath at her house — ritual cleansing after the periodic sickness (Isaaki, Kimchi). That such a time was favourable to conception was known to the Arabs at an early day, cf. WRSmith, *Kinship*, p. 276. The conceit of the Rabbis that David's men divorced their wives before going on a campaign, is a device to minimize David's guilt.

6–13. The attempt at concealment. — David sent to the army for Uriah. — **7.** And when Uriah came, David asked about Joab and the army and the war, as if he had sent for him in order to be informed about the campaign. — **8.** At the end of the interview, David commands : *Go to thy house and wash thy feet*] refresh thyself after thy journey. — *And there followed him a portion from the king*] Gen. 43³⁴. — **9.** But Uriah lodged at the gate of the palace *with his lord's servants*, that is, the body-guard. — **10, 11.** Uriah, on being questioned, gives the chivalrous answer : *The Ark and Israel and Judah are camping in booths, and my lord Joab and my lord's servants are camping in the open fields, and I should go to my house to eat and to drink and to lie with my wife !* The statement of the supposition is enough to show its absurdity. But he adds his oath. It is altogether probable that women were *taboo* to soldiers in active service, 1 S. 21⁶. This is the only intimation that the Ark was carried in David's campaigns, but from the fact that the priests start to carry it in the train which

---

* On the other hand it is possible that שוע, which we find in some other proper names, is the original form ; notice *Shua, Abishua, Elishua*, and *Jehoshua*. These names seem to indicate that שוע was the name of a divinity, and this would account for the change.

leaves Jerusalem at Absalom's invasion, taken in connexion with this passage, we may infer that the practice was not uncommon. — **12.** Another attempt must be made, so Uriah is kept another day. — **13.** This time the king *invited him and he ate in his presence and drank, so that he made him drunk*] in the hope that the wine would cause him to forget his resolution. But the sturdy soldier was not so to be overcome : *In the evening he went out to lie on his couch with the soldiers*] egregius sane miles et constantissimus (Schm.).

6. After אל־יואב ⅖ inserts לאמר perhaps correctly, though the presumption is in favour of the shorter text. — **7.** ולשלום המלחמה] seems a little odd. But it shows how שלום had taken a very wide meaning. — **8.** משאת המלך] *the king's present* in this case was, no doubt, a dish from the royal table. — **9.** כל] lacking in ⅖ᴮ, is superfluous. — **10.** Uriah's house lay at a lower level than that of the king, hence his *going down* to it is spoken of. — **11.** סכות] are rude shelters, huts or booths, made of branches of trees. For an instance of devotion among Mohammed's followers similar to that of Uriah, I may be allowed to refer to my *Bible and Islam*, p. 19. — חיך וחי נפשך] is tautological, and perhaps one of the phrases is an error for חי יהוה. — **12.** וממחרת] is by most recent expositors connected with what follows, in agreement with ⅖ᴸ. But I cannot see the necessity. Only two nights are spoken of. The principal meal was in the evening, as we gather from v.⁸. There is no reason why David should not invite Uriah that day. — **13.** ויקרא] continues the narrative without pause : *Uriah remained . . . and the king invited him.*

14–27. The murder. — Despairing of accomplishing his object, David plans the death of Uriah. — **14, 15.** He writes a letter in which he commands Joab : *Set Uriah in face of the heaviest fighting and retreat, leaving him in the lurch, that he may be smitten and die.* — **16.** Joab, in posting the besiegers, *set Uriah where he knew there were valiant men*] according to the command given. — **17.** A sortie was made *and there fell some of the soldiers of David, and Uriah the Hittite died also*] the device was successful at the first attempt. — **18, 19.** Joab sends a verbal report. He anticipates that the general news will not be pleasing to the king. Possibly the king's prudence had before this come into conflict with Joab's rashness. — **20, 21.** Joab is made to put a somewhat extended speech in the mouth of David, which reflects the opinion of the narrator rather than that of Joab or of David. There seems no reason to suppose however that the verse is a later inter-

polation.   Our author may well have been acquainted with the
story of Abimelech, which belongs to one of our oldest documents.
The example of his death may have been proverbial among Hebrew soldiers, and have given a rule concerning the attack on
walled towns.   These are only possibilities, but, so far as they go,
they favour the originality of [21a].   *Did not a woman throw a mill-
stone upon him from the wall?* cf. Jd. 9[53].   Joab realizes that the
news of Uriah's death will appease the king and, according to 𝔥,
takes no special care to disguise the fact from the messenger.   𝔊[L]
has here the whole of the messenger's reply as given in [23f.], which
does in fact disguise the main point; see the critical note. —
22.   The text of 𝔥 has been shortened to avoid repetition.   This
is in accordance with the taste of a later time.   The older writers
did not hesitate to repeat themselves.   Restore therefore in accordance with 𝔊 : *And the messenger of Joab went to the king in Jerusalem, and came and told David all that Joab commanded him, all
the news of the war.   And David's anger burned against Joab,
and he said*] there follow the exact words anticipated by Joab,
which need not be repeated. — **23.**   The reply of the messenger :
*The men were bold against us and came out to us in the field, and
we drove them back to the entrance of the gate. —* **24.**   Continuation
of the account :   The soldiers of David in the heat of the pursuit
came within range of the archers on the wall, *and there died of
the king's servants about eighteen men, and also thy servant Uriah
the Hittite is dead*] thus expressed, the mention of Uriah comes
quite naturally, as he was a prominent soldier.   The *eighteen men*
are given in only one recension of 𝔊, but seem to be original. —
25.   David is relieved by this statement, and he commands the
messenger to encourage Joab : *Let not this matter displease thee,
for the sword devours thus and thus*] so we must translate on the
ground of Jd. 18[4] 1 K. 14[5].   The meaning seems to be : *now one
and now another* falls, so that this is only the common experience.
At the end of the verse the received text has *and strengthen him,*
that is, *encourage Joab.*   The word is possibly a scribe's afterthought. — **26.**   The woman observed the usual period of mourning for her husband.* — **27.**   As soon as this was over, *David sent*

---

* Seven days according to Schwally, *ZATW.* 1892, 153.

and brought her to his house, and she became his wife. Marriage
very soon after the death of a consort is common in the East, so
that this haste did not violate the conventions. The case of Abigail is similar. The last clause of the verse : *But the thing which
David had done was evil in the eyes of Yahweh* belongs with what
follows.

15. הבו] here apparently used like תנו. But the original may have been
הבא (Kl.) : εἰσάγαγε 𝕲ᴮ. — **16.** בשמור] not *in observing* the city, but *in keeping guard* over it, which was the work of the besiegers. We hear nothing
of battering-rams or mines, so that we conclude the city was to be reduced by
starvation. — אל־העיר] את־העיר which is found in some MSS. seems better, but
עלי־ה' would be better still. — **21.** ירבשת] another instance of the mutilation
of a name because it contained the word *Baal*. 𝕲ᴸ has 'Ιεροβοάλ which
𝕲ᴮ has corrupted to 'Ιεροβοάμ. — ואמרת] Instead of the brief reply *Uriah also
is dead,* 𝕲ᴸ inserts here the whole explanation of the situation as given in
23. 24 : *the men were bold against us, etc.* The case is similar to that in v.²²,
where 𝕲 inserts David's speech as Joab expected him to make it. The arguments for the originality of the *plus* here seem to be the same as there, except
that the outward attestation is weaker. On the whole the probability seems
to be on the side of 𝕲ᴸ. — **22.** For המלאך : ὁ ἄγγελος 'Ιωὰβ πρὸς τὸν βασιλέα
εἰς 'Ιερουσαλήμ 𝕲. — יואב] πάντα τὰ ῥήματα τοῦ πολέμου. καὶ ἐθυμώθη Δαυεὶδ
πρὸς 'Ιωάβ κτλ. 𝕲. The genuineness of this additional matter is recognized
by Th., We., Dr., Bu., Kl., Ki. — **23.** וגברו עלינו] can hardly be so strong as
prevailed over us. The garrison had made a sally. That they had mustered
up courage to do this is the point of the story.—ונהיה עליהם] seems to mean
we drove them back : συνηλάσαμεν 𝕲ᴸ. Possibly the original reading was different, but if so it cannot certainly be recovered. We should expect at least
אחריהם.— **24.** ויראו המוראים] confusion of ירא and ירה, cf. Ges. ²⁶, 75 *rr.* —
מעבדי המלך] 𝕲ᴸ adds ὡσεὶ ἄνδρες δέκα καὶ ὀκτώ. It is difficult to see why any
one should insert the words if they were not original, while a scribe who was
concerned with the fate of Uriah alone might leave them out. — **25.** את־הדבר]
grammatically the nominative to ירע; but the speaker has in mind the logical
force of the phrase, in which הדבר is the object of the emotion indicated in
the verb, Ges. ²⁶, 117 *l,* Davidson, *Syntax,* 72 *R* 4. — וחזקהו] comes in awkwardly after the command to Joab, and is lacking in 𝕲ᴸ as well as a number
of MSS.

XII. 1–15ᵃ. The rebuke of Nathan. — The prophet, being sent
to David by Yahweh, puts his conduct before him by recounting a
feigned case of trespass. David is convicted of sin and professes
repentance. He is assured of forgiveness, but at the same time
the evils which are to come upon him for his sin are predicted.

It is doubtful whether the piece is of the same origin with what precedes and follows. If we leave it out, we get a very good connexion, joining 11²⁷ᵇ directly to 12¹⁵ᵇ : *The thing was evil in the sight of Yahweh, and Yahweh smote the child which the wife of Uriah bore to David.* There is nothing unreasonable in supposing that the early narrative was content with pointing out that the anger of Yahweh was evidenced by the death of the child. A later writer was not satisfied with this, but felt that there must be a specific rebuke by a direct revelation. It is possible also that the incident of Nathan has itself been worked over, as will be seen in the course of the exposition.

1. Nathan appears ostensibly with a case for the king's judgment, a flagrant case of oppression of the poor by the rich. — **2, 3.** *The rich man had many sheep and cattle, but the poor man had nothing but one little ewe lamb which he had bought; he fed it and it grew up with him and with his children*] such pet lambs are frequently seen in the houses of the poor in Syria. *It used to eat of his morsel and drink of his cup and lie in his bosom*] the preciousness of the single pet made it, in fact, *like a daughter.* — **4.** The occasion of the tragedy was the coming of a traveller. The duty of hospitality is imperative. But the rich man spared his own, *and took the lamb of the poor man and prepared it for the man who had just come*] similar cases were doubtless common enough, and a part of the king's work is to judge the cause of the oppressed. — **5.** The statement of the case was enough : *By the life of Yahweh the man that did this is worthy of death*] it does not appear that David would actually sentence him to death, 1 S. 20³¹ 26¹⁶. — **6.** *And he shall restore the lamb sevenfold*] reading with 𝔊ᴮ.

1. נתן] 𝔊𝔖 and 3 MSS. of 𝔥 add הנביא. The insertion of such explicative words is generally secondary, but at the opening of this section the word seems necessary. After לו 𝔊ᴸ adds: Ἀπάγγειλον δή μοι τὴν κρίσιν ταύτην, which is represented also in 𝔩, whence it passed over into many MSS. of 𝔏. It is not necessary to the sense (as is affirmed by Kl.) and can be explained as a scribe's insertion, though it is adopted by Ew. and Kl. — ראש] another case of irregular insertion of א. — **2.** לעשיר] There seems to be no reason for this punctuation; the article is necessary to the sense, as we see from ולרש of the next verse. — **3.** ויחיה] as in Is. 7²¹. — תאכל] the tense in this and the two following verbs expresses customary action. — **4.** הלך] as We. points out, the parallel is close to the use of our word *visit* — there came *a visit* to the rich man. — [לָאִישׁ הֶעָשִׁיר] there are cases enough of the anarthrous noun in such a phrase to justify the punctuation. — [לַעֲשׂוֹת] the same verb is used of Abraham's preparing a calf for his guests, Gen. 18⁷. — **6**. [אַרְבַּעְתָּיִם] ἑπταπλασίονα ⑮ᴮ ᵃˡ.. The change to 𝔐 was made to bring David's ruling into line with the law of theft, Ex. 21³⁷ (Th.). — [וְעַל אֲשֶׁר לֹא־חָמַל] Schill proposes (*ZATW*. XI. p. 318) to change לֹא to לוֹ, making the sense: *and spared his own*. The received text however seems to make fairly good sense.

7. The application : *Thou art the man*] for the sake of distinctness ⑮ adds *who has done this*. But the shorter text is more vigorous. The following speech sets forth the obligation imposed by Yahweh's benefits. David was the rich man. — **8**. *I gave thee thy master's house and thy master's wives into thy bosom*] we have no other indication that David possessed the *harem* of Saul. But, according to the law of succession, they were his by right. *And if this were too little I would add as much again*] the reference is evidently to the wives, first from the form of the pronoun, secondly because it was the abundance in wives which formed the contrast between David's wealth and Uriah's poverty. — **9, 10**. *Why hast thou despised Yahweh*] the giver of so much good, *in doing that which was evil in his eyes*] Yahweh is the protector of the oppressed. The logical ending of the question is the last clause of v.¹⁰ : *and hast taken the wife of Uriah the Hittite to be thy wife ?* This is the crime that is set forth in the parable. The present text has been expanded by a double reference to the murder of Uriah, and by the threat *that the sword shall not turn from David's house forever*, an inappropriate prediction. — **11**. The prophetic discourse takes a fresh start, denouncing a punishment in kind : *I will take thy wives before thine eyes and will give them to thy neighbour*] the evident reference is to Absalom's conduct in taking possession of his father's concubines. — **12**. The punishment should be as public as the crime had been secret. — **13**. David, convicted by the prophet's presentation, confesses his guilt. He is assured : *Yahweh has caused thy sin to pass away*] it is misleading to translate *has forgiven*. The sin rested upon David and would work death for him. Yahweh took it away so that he should not die, but it wrought the death of the child. — **14**. *Nevertheless, because thou hast scorned Yahweh in this thing,* *the child that is born to thee shall surely die*] the text has been altered to avoid reading an offensive expression. — **15ª.** The visit of Nathan, or rather the account of it, is concluded.

7. [האיש] ὁ ποιήσας τοῦτο is added by 𝔊. — [כה־אמר יהוה] Bu. supposes these words with what follows to the word בעינו in v.⁹, to be a later expansion, so that the original connexion was: *Thou art the man! Uriah the Hittite hast thou slain.* But this spoils the parable. It was not the murder that was the point of the parable, but the rape of the neighbour's darling. It is indeed explicable that this should be lost sight of in a measure when the author interposes a rehearsal of Yahweh's benefits. Had he proceeded at once to the specification of the crime, he would have put the adultery in the foreground. But while this accounts for the order of the clauses in the text, it would not justify omission of the adultery from the accusation. — **8.** [את־בית אדניך] τὰ πάντα τοῦ κυρίου σου 𝔊ᴸ : בנת מריך 𝔖. It is possible that there was originally a reference to Michal, the daughter of Saul, as is supposed by Kl. — את־בית [ישראל ויהורה] as כהנה at the end of the verse palpably refers to the wives of David, there is strong reason to think that 𝔖 has here preserved the original reading, *the daughters of* Israel and Judah. David had not been slow to take of these as wives and concubines. Geiger classes this among the intentional changes of the scribes, and We.'s protest seems to be based on modern rather than ancient feeling. — **9.** [את דבר יי'] probably we should read את יי' with 𝔊ᴸ and Theodotion (Nestle). At the conclusion of the speech we expect the crime which is set forth in the parable to be most prominently mentioned. The received text gives however: *Uriah thou hast slain with the sword, his wife thou hast taken as thy wife, and him thou hast slain with the sword of the Ammonites.* This is confusing from its double mention of the murder, as well as its reversal of the true order. As the next verse comes back to the crime with the emphasis upon the rape, I suspect that verse to have preserved to us the original ending of this one in the words יתקה וגו', which would be the proper continuation of v.⁹ after בעינו. — **11, 12.** The punishment here threatened does not seem to be within the plan of the original author of this section. He saw the punishment of David's sin in the death of the child. This was inflicted even after David's repentance. It is surprising therefore that after the repentance this punishment (Absalom's insult) should not be alluded to. Either it also should be made a part of the exemplary chastisement, or it should be remitted. The inconsistency of the present recension is obvious, and I suspect that vv.¹¹·¹² are a later insertion. The original train of thought dealt somewhat mildly with David: he had indeed taken his neighbour's wife, and by his own judgment deserved death; but his repentance secured his reprieve; the sentence was commuted to the death of the child. This was too mild for a later editor, who worked over ⁹⁻¹² as already shown. — **14.** נאצת [את־איבי יהוה] The verb nowhere means *cause to blaspheme.* The only sense appropriate here is indicated by the בזחני of v.¹⁰. The insertion of איבי was made to prevent repetition of an apparently blasphemous phrase in the public reading (Geiger, *Urschrift*, p. 267), cf. a similar instance 1 S. 25[22].

15ᵇ–25. The death of the child. — The well-known account needs but little comment.   As already indicated, the half verse ¹⁵ᵇ seems to have joined originally to 11[27] : Yahweh was displeased with the thing which David had done, *and smote the child . . . and it became sick.* — **16**. David does not show any indication that the doom of the child had been pronounced by the prophet : *David besought God for the boy and fasted strictly*] the afflicting oneself was to move the pity of Yahweh.   During all the time of the illness, *he came in and lay on the earth*] we naturally suppose *in sackcloth* as 𝔊ᴸ reads, and we naturally suppose also that it was *before Yahweh,* though this is rendered doubtful by v.[20]. **17**. His courtiers, *the elders of his house, stood over him* as he lay on the ground *to raise him up*] the Sheikhs of the family naturally had large influence with the king. — **18**. On the seventh day the crisis of the disease was reached, and the child died. — *And the officers of David were afraid to tell him*] by a very natural course of reasoning : *how shall we say : the child is dead, so that he will do some harm ?*] something *desperate,* as we may paraphrase. — **19**. The effect was not what they anticipated : *David saw that his courtiers were whispering together and perceived that the child was dead.* — **20**. The fact that *he came to the house of Yahweh and worshipped* after changing his clothes indicates that his fasting had not been there. — **21**. The officers find his conduct strange : *While the child was yet alive thou didst fast and weep, but when the child died thou didst rise up and eat bread*] the fullest expression of grief (fasting and weeping) generally comes when death has occurred. — **22**. The explanation is that by fasting and weeping he hoped to move Yahweh : *Who knoweth whether Yahweh will have mercy and so the child will live ?*] where we should say in English : *whether Yahweh may not* have mercy. — **23**. But the event has declared itself : *Why is it that I should fast?   Am I able to bring him back ?   I am journeying to him, but he will not return to me*] some sort of continued existence in Sheol seems to be implied. — **24**. Bathsheba bears a second child who receives the name Solomon.   Whether the name means *the peaceful* is impossible to say. From this narrative we should rather conjecture *recompense,* the child which replaces the one taken away. — **25.** The verse should include the last two words of v.²⁴ : *And Yahweh loved him and sent by the hand of Nathan the prophet and called his name Jedidiah*] that is : *the Beloved of Yahweh.* The phrase at the end of the verse is probably to be corrected to : *by the word of Yahweh.*

16. ובא] the tense indicates his constant custom during this period. — וילן ושכב] 𝔊ᴮ has only one of the two verbs, whereas 𝔊ᴸ (with a number of Greek MSS.) has καὶ ἐκάθευδεν ἐν σάκκῳ = וילן בשק. The same reading is probably that of 𝕴 because Ambrose gives *in cilicio jacuit* (cited by Sabatier), and the Codex Legionensis has *et dormivit in cilicio.* This ancient attestation makes the reading important, and its internal probability is evident. — **21.** בעבור הילד חי] is retained by Dr. who translates *on account of the child when alive.* We. had however acutely conjectured that the original reading was בעור ה׳, nd this is confirmed by 𝔊ᴸ and 𝕿, as well as by the following verse. — **22.** יחנני] the correction of the *Qrê* (וחנני) is unnecessary, as remarked by Dr. — **24.** ותקרא [ויקרא *Qrê* is unnecessary. — **25.** בעבור יהוו] can hardly be correct. We must read בדבר יהוה with 𝔊ᴸ and one Hebrew edition (Cappel, *Critica Sacra*, p. 265). 𝕊𝕿 add אהבו.

26–31. The account of the siege of Rabba is resumed. — **26.** Joab takes the *water city*] apparently a fortification built to protect the fountain which still flows at Amman. — **27, 28.** Joab, in sending the news, prefers that his king should have the glory : *Gather the rest of the people and camp against the city and take it, lest I take the city and it be called by my name*] as Jerusalem had received the name *City of David.* — **29.** The advice is carried out, and David captures the city. — **30.** *And he took the crown of Milcom*] the chief god of the Ammonites, *from his head,* and the *weight of it was a talent of gold*] the weight is sufficient to show that it could be worn only by a statue. — *And upon it was a precious stone and it* (the stone) *came upon David's head*] a parallel in the crown of the Delian Apollo is cited by Nestle (*Marginalien,* p. 17). The name of the god is disguised by the punctuators partly from reluctance even to pronounce the name of the abomination, partly from unwillingness to admit that David's jewel had once been contaminated by contact with the idol. — **31.** There has been some controversy over this verse, the question being whether David tortured his captives, or whether

he put them at hard labour.   For the former might be argued
that he had received special provocation, both in the insult offered
his ambassadors and in the obstinate resistance to the siege.   But
the theory cannot be consistently carried through without straining
the meaning of the words.   The most probable interpretation is
that he brought out the people *and set them at the saws and the
picks and the axes and made them work at the brick-moulds*] their
lot, which could be compared to that of the Israelites in Egypt,
was to the Bedawy, and scarcely less so to the peasant, the most
wretched that could be conceived.

26. עִיר הַמְּלוּכָה] is called just below עִיר הַמָּיִם, which should be restored
here.   Rabba itself was the *royal city*.   On the interchange of מלכה and מים
cf. We.   Cheyne conjectures עִיר מלכם meaning the citadel, *Ex. Times*, 1898,
p. 144. — **30.** מלכם] is vocalized as though it meant *their king*.   But the
crown of 130 pounds' weight could never have been worn by a man, and the
king would certainly not have sat in state while David approached and took
the crown.   It seems quite certain therefore that the idol of the Ammonites is
meant, whose name is given as מִלְכֹּם 1 K. 11⁵.   𝔊 has here Μελχόλ, Μελχόμ,
Μολχώμ and other forms, in the various MSS., while 𝔊ᴸ conforms to the reading of the punctuators. — ואבן] Chr. has וכה אבן which I have adopted, as it is
confirmed by 𝔖𝔗 here.   The received text would assert that the whole crown
was placed on David's head. — **31.** וישם] 1 Chr. 20³ has וישר which means *he
sawed them*.   But while he might saw them with saws, the other instruments
here mentioned would be without an appropriate verb.   The reading has crept
into 𝔊ᴸ. — והעביר אותם במלכן] is unintelligible.   The *Ktib* is probably right in
reading במלבן.   The מלבן is however not the *brick kiln* but the wooden form
in which the clay is pressed into shape.   We are compelled in accordance
with this to change העביר into העביד with Chr.   So Grätz (*Gesch.* I. p. 256),
and Hoffmann, *ZATW.* II. p. 53 ff.

XIII. 1–XIV. 33. The violation of Tamar and the conse-
quences. — The story is well known ; the violation of his sister is
avenged by Absalom and he is obliged to flee the country.   By a
device of Joab the king is induced to pronounce in favour of his
recall.   The history throws much light upon the social condition
of the people.   It is from the old and good source from which we
have so much of David's history, and it has suffered comparatively
little in transmission.

1–7. A stratagem is suggested by Jonadab whereby Tamar will
be brought into the power of her brother. — **1.** Tamar, own sister

to Absalom, was beautiful like her brother. — *And Amnon son of David*] the author so describes him to show that he was only a half brother to Tamar. From 3² we learn that he was the oldest son. — **2.** *And Amnon was so distressed that he grew sick*] on account of the apparent hopelessness of his passion — *for she was a virgin*] so that he thought it impossible to make any approaches. — **3.** Jonadab his cousin and intimate friend was a *very wise man*, though in this case his wisdom was put to base uses. — **4.** The inquiry: *Why art thou thus weak, O Prince, morning by morning?* On hearing the cause the adviser has a device ready. — **5.** Amnon was to feign himself sick and when the king should visit him, to say: *Let Tamar my sister come and give me to eat and prepare the food in my sight, that I may see it and eat from her hand*] the sick fancy was likely to be indulged by the king. — **6.** At the visit Amnon asks specifically that Tamar may *make two cakes* for him. — **7.** The expected result came about. David commanded Tamar: *Go to the house of thy brother Amnon and prepare him food*] we suppose that each of the adult sons of the king had his own establishment; Amnon's house and servant are mentioned in this account.

1. אמנון] proper names not infrequently end in ון; Gideon, Abdon, Eglon, and others are examples, cf. König, *Lehrgebäude*, II. p. 153. **2.** להתחלות] is used just below in the sense of *feigning oneself sick*. It is therefore strange to find it used here in another meaning, and it is possible that the text has suffered. Ew. proposes to read להתדלות = *to grow weak*, and Kl. להתהלל = to become insane. The latter is attractive. The reason given why Amnon despaired of any attempt is that she was a virgin; the implication being that the virgin had less freedom than the married woman or widow. — **3.** It is somewhat surprising to find Jonadab called a *wise* man. — יונדב] ⅏ᴸ calls him *Jonathan* which is the name of another son of Shimeah, 21²¹. — **5.** ויתחל] it is not necessary in this passage to read ויתהלל (Kl.); the capricious appetite of a sick man would claim the indulgence of the king quite as readily as the delirium of one who feigned himself mad. — **6.** The request for two *heart-shaped* cakes is not intended as a play on the situation.

8. Tamar came to the house, *and took dough and kneaded it and made cakes as he looked on, and baked the cakes*] all as Amnon had desired. — **9.** The verse interrupts the narrative and makes insoluble difficulties. It is probably therefore an interpolation. — **10.** At Amnon's command she brings the food to him *in the inner room.* The house probably had only a public room and a chamber. — **11.** He solicits her to unchastity. — **12.** She refuses: *Do not force me, my brother*] Jd. 19²⁴, *for it is not so done in Israel*] the implication is that such practices were known among the Canaanites. — **13.** The clear-minded maiden sees the character of the deed, and its consequences both to herself and to him: *As for me, whither could I carry my shame? And thou shouldst become as one of the fools!* And yet she would not refuse an honourable life with him: *Now speak to the king, for he will not withhold me from thee*] it is impossible to suppose that this is a subterfuge, an attempt to gain time. It must have plausibility even if it were only that. We are forced to conclude that marriage with a half-sister was allowed in Israel at this time, as is indeed evident from Ezek. 22¹¹, cf. what was said above, on 3⁵. — **14.** He overpowered her and accomplished his purpose. — **15.** The deed was followed by a revulsion of feeling: *the hatred with which he hated her was greater than the love with which he had loved her*] he therefore bids her begone. — **16.** The sense has been best preserved to us in 𝔊ᴸ which reads: And she said; *No, my brother; for greater is the second wrong than the first which thou didst me, in sending me away.* The received text can be translated only by violence. — **17.** The sentence begins with the last words of ¹⁶: *And he would not listen to her, but called his lad that served him and said: Put this wench forth from my presence*] the language is the language of contempt and injury. — **18.** The verse originally told only that the servant obeyed the order. — **19.** *Tamar put ashes on her head and rent the long-sleeved tunic which she wore, and put her hand upon her head*] all signs of intense grief, cf. Est. 4¹ 2 K. 5⁸ Jer. 2³⁷. — **20.** Absalom meets her and perceives the trouble: *Has Amnon thy brother been with thee?*] possibly Amnon's reputation was not of the best. The family ties however prevent summary vengeance; there is nothing for it but silence: *Now, my sister, be silent, for he is thy brother; do not lay this thing to heart!* The sooner we can forget the family disgrace, the better. *So Tamar dwelt, a desolate woman, in the house of Absalom her brother.* — **21.** Although David was angry, *yet he did not vex the soul of Amnon his son* [by chastisement], *for he loved him, because he was his first-born*] the sentence, which is necessary to the sense, must be completed from 𝕲, a part having fallen out of 𝔥. — **22.** Absalom, though filled with hatred for Amnon from that time on, did not betray his feeling in any way.

8. ‏ותבשל‏] the verb generally means *to boil.* — **9.** ‏המשרת‏] occurs only here. Kl. followed by Bu. proposes to read ‏ותקרא את־המשרת‏, *and she called the servant,* cf. v.[17]. But in any case, there is a contradiction* between this and the following verse. Whoever placed the cakes before Amnon, it is clear that if they were already there he could not command them to be brought to him. That he himself (the sick man) moved into the chamber after they had once been put before him is improbable, and is not intimated in the text. The simplest supposition is that this verse has been inserted by some one who supposed that it was necessary to clear the room. — **12.** ‏יעשה‏] Gen. 34[7]; the tense indicates customary action. Sins of this kind are elsewhere called ‏נבלה‏ as here. — **14.** ‏ויחזק מ׳‏ cf. 1 S. 17[50]. — ‏אתה‏] should be pointed ‏עמה‏: ‏אָתָּה‏: 3 MSS.: μετ' αὐτῆς 𝕲. — **16.** ‏אל־אורת‏] is not found elsewhere. ‏על אורת‏ occurs with the meaning *because of.* But this requires to be completed by the following words; and while we might suppose such a sentence as: *and she said to him because of this great evil,* we are at a loss to continue. There seems no doubt therefore that the text is corrupt and that we should restore ‏אל אחי כי‏ with 𝕲[L] (We., Dr., Bu.). The presumption being thus in favour of 𝕲[L] we should probably adopt its further reading: μεγάλη ἡ κακία ἡ ἐσχάτη ὑπὲρ τὴν πρώτην, though some propose to read ‏גרולה הרעה הזאת מאחרת‏ which is a little nearer 𝔥. — **17.** ‏את־נערו משרתו‏] as the verb which follows is plural it is not improbable that we should read ‏נעריו‏: 𝕲 has τὸ παιδάριον αὐτοῦ τὸν προεστηκότα τοῦ οἴκου. ‏זאת‏ is contemptuous and ‏מעלי‏ intimates that her presence was burdensome to him. — **18.** The first half verse is explanatory of the term ‏כתנת כסים‏ in v.[19]. It interrupts the narrative here, and is probably a marginal gloss which has been inserted in the wrong place. — ‏מעילם‏] should be ‏מעולם‏ (We.). The whole verse is lacking in 𝔖. ‏ונעל‏ is incorrect, it should be ‏וינעל‏. — **19.** ‏אפר‏] for putting on the head in grief ‏עפר‏ is more common, cf. Ez. 27[30]. ‏כתנת הפסים‏ is here rendered τὸν χιτῶνα τὸν καρπωτόν by 𝕲[B], but these words are given as the rendering of Aq. by Theod.: τ. χ. τ. ἀστραγαλωτόν 𝕲[L] seems to be the true reading of 𝕲. Josephus combines the two: *having sleeves and reaching down to the ankles.* — **20.** ‏אמינון‏ which occurs nowhere else has been conjectured to be a diminutive of contempt. The analogies in Hebrew are so uncertain that it seems safer to assume a mere clerical error. Kl. conjectures ‏האמנם‏: *has indeed* thy brother been with thee. — ‏ושממה‏] χηρεύουσα 𝕲[B] seems to omit the conjunction, 𝕲[L] has a duplicate translation. — **21.** The verse is incomplete in 𝔥, while 𝕲 has an apt conclusion: καὶ οὐκ ἐλύπησε τὸ πνεῦμα Ἀμνὼν τοῦ υἱοῦ αὐτοῦ, ὅτι ἀγάπα αὐτόν, ὅτι πρωτότοκος αὐτοῦ

---

* As pointed out by Stade, *ThLZ.* 21, 6.

ἦν, adopted by Th. and others. The occasion of its omission is its beginning
with ולא like the next verse. — 22. It is a question whether the mention of
Absalom's hate belongs here. His motive for silence would seem to be rather
a desire that his designs should not be suspected.

23–29. Absalom avenges his sister's wrong. — 23. Two years

later, Absalom had *shearers;* the sheep shearing was a time of
feasting, cf. 1 S. 25[4]; *in Baal Hazor near Ephraim*] the place
has been identified with some probability about 20 miles north of
Jerusalem. To the festival *he invited all the sons of the king.* —
24. The invitation is made to include *the king and his officers.*
— 25. The king declines, lest the multitude be burdensome to
Absalom, and on being urged *gives him his blessing* as an indication that enough has been said. — 26. *Then if not, let Amnon my
brother go with us*] the request seems to have aroused some suspicion. — 27. On further urging, all the princes were allowed to
go. — 28. *Absalom made a feast like the feast of a king*] a clause
accidentally lost from 𝕳. The servants were ordered to kill
Amnon as soon as he was under the influence of the wine. —
29. The order was carried out, *and all the king's sons rose and
each mounted his mule and fled.* That Absalom intended to
secure the throne for himself by massacring all competitors
would be a not remote inference.

23. בעל חצור, cf. Buhl, *Geog.* p. 177. — עם־אפריכ] the preposition indicates
that a place is intended and not the tribe. 𝕲[L] Γοφράιμ indicates that the first
letter should be ע. And as we know of an *Ephron* in Benjamin, we may
restore it here. — 24. The invitation is here made more extensive than is intimated in the preceding verse. This, with the almost incredible *naïveté* with
which Absalom insists upon the presence of Amnon, makes me suspect that
vv.[24-27] are a later expansion of the account. — 25. ויפרץ] 1 S. 28[23] (Bu. ויפצר).
— ויברכהו] can be intended only as a termination of the interview, which is
prolonged only because Absalom modifies his request. — 26. ולא] is to be
understood as in 2 K. 5[17]. Similar construction in the affirmative form (ויש)
are Jd. 6[13] 2 K. 10[15] (We.). It is not necessary therefore to point ילֹא, though
that also would make good sense (Th.). The mention of Amnon alone here,
when in fact all the sons went, emphasizes the incongruity of these verses with
the main narrative. — 28. We must insert with 𝕲 ויעש אבשלום משתה כמשתה המלך
(Th.). The words have been lost by homeoteleuton.

30. Rumour exaggerated the calamity, reporting that Absalom
had slain all the princes, without exception. — 31. *The king rent*

his clothes and threw himself on the ground, and all his officers who were standing by him rent their clothes] for the slight emendation of the text see the critical note. — **32**. Jonadab was in the counsel of Absalom, or else shrewd enough to suspect the true state of the case : *Let not my Lord think they have slain all the young men, the king's sons, for Amnon alone is dead*] this he was able to conclude from Absalom's mien, *from the day of the violation of Tamar.* — **33**. The conclusion drawn by Jonadab is that *Amnon alone is dead.* — **34**. The opening words are corrupt beyond restoration. What we expect is a temporal phrase such as : *While Jonadab was yet speaking,* continued by the statement : *the watchman lifted up his eyes.* The rest of the verse has in 𝔐 lost a sentence which is preserved in 𝔊. Restoring it we read : *The watchman lifted up his eyes and saw, and behold, much people were coming [on the Beth-Horon road, on the descent; and the watchman came and told the king, saying : I see men coming] from the Beth-Horon road on the side of the hill*] the words in brackets were omitted by a scribe, owing to similarity of ending to what precedes. The watchman being on the tower, it is necessary that he should come and tell the king. — **35**. Jonadab sees in this the confirmation of what he has said. — **36**. The arriving party and those who had been looking for them join in loud lamentation, cf. Jd. 21² — **37, 38**. The text is confused. First, we have a statement of Absalom's flight, then we are told that the king mourned for his son continually, then we are told again of Absalom's flight. Besides this, a perpetual mourning is contradicted by v.³⁹ which speaks of David's being comforted. The accepted solution of the difficulty is to throw out ³⁸ᵃ as a later insertion and arrange the rest in the following order : *And he mourned for his son continually. But Absalom fled and went to Talmai, son of Ammihud, king of Geshur, and was there three years*] the emendation originated with Böttcher and is adopted by We., Dr., Bu. On the other hand, Kl. supposes the *continually [all the days]* to refer to the three years of Absalom's banishment and therefore puts : *and the king mourned for his son all that time* after v.³⁸. It is possible that neither conjecture has restored the original. Absalom's mother was a daughter of Talmai, 3³. — **39**. The verse forms the transition to what follows. Emending by 𝔊ᴸ we read :

And the spirit of the king longed to go out to Absalom his son, for he was comforted for the death of his son Amnon.

31. וכל־עבדיו נצבים קרעי בגדים] means: *while all his servants stood with rent clothes.* But as pointed out by Th. (We., Dr.) this is not to the point. 𝔊ᴮ renders וכל־עבדי הנצבים עליו קרעו את בגדיהם which fits the rest of the verse. — **32.** בני־המלך] is superfluous and probably an insertion. — כי־על־פי אב׳ היתה שימה] is obscure: *for on the mouth of Absalom it was set — his death* is to be supplied if we retain the text. But Absalom had not betrayed his intention in speech, even if we can accept שימה as a passive participle. It seems more likely that שימה is a noun meaning *a scowl* (as argued by We., Dr.), or that it is a corruption. Ginsburg reads שומה. Ew. proposes שטמה: — *enmity.* Even in this case we should expect על־פני instead of על־פי. According to oriental custom Absalom would show his anger in his face, even when trying to avoid an open quarrel. — **34.** ויברח אבשלום] confirmed by 𝔊, is nevertheless difficult to place. The most plausible thing to do if the words are to be retained is to make them the conclusion of Jonadab's address: *Amnon alone is dead and Absalom has fled* (so that he will not inflict further damage). But even thus the statement is unnecessary. The words may have crept in by a simply stupid error of a scribe whose thought anticipated v.[37]. But it is more probable that they are a corruption of something which can only be conjectured. A plausible conjecture is that of Kl., adopted by Bu. in the shape ייתר אחיו שלום. My own conjecture is that the author wrote והוא עוד מְדַבֵּר or something equivalent. The report of the murder cannot have long preceded the coming of the princes. — הלכים] after this word, 𝔊 has preserved for us a line, also originally ending with הלכים which has fallen out of 𝔥. It is restored by Th., We., Dr., Bu., Kl., in substantially the same form, to wit: בדרך חרנים במורד ויבא הצפה. ויגד למלך ויאמר ראיתי אנשים הלכים. The second הלכים is not represented in 𝔊, but it was probably in the original 𝔥 because without it the following מדרך is harsh, and its presence alone fully explains the error of the scribe. For מדרך אחריו it is evident that 𝔊 had מדרך חרנים, 𝔊ᴮ ἐκ τῆς ὁδοῦ τῆς ᾽Ωρωνήν (Σωράιμ 𝔊ᴸ). The Beth-Horon road comes down from the north. — **37, 38.** On the restoration cf. Dr. who (following We.) supposes that a scribe erroneously began the paragraph with גשור . . . ואבשלום and then discovered that he had omitted ויתאבל וגו׳. He inserted the omitted words, and then to get a proper connexion repeated [37a] in a shortened form.* עמיחור *Kt.* is made עמיהוד *Qrê,* which is favoured by 𝔊. — **39.** ותכל דוד המלך] cannot be construed. 𝔊ᴸ evidently read ותכל רוח המלך. For כלה in the sense *to be consumed with desire,* cf. Ps. 84³ 143⁷. It does not seem to be necessary to change לצאת (Bu. reads לראת, Kl. לשאת) — for the king's longing might easily be described as a longing to *go out* to Absalom, though his pride would not let him go.

---

*It is possible that originally David was said to mourn over both his sons — the dead and the banished.

XIV. 1–11. Joab devises a fictitious case by which to appeal to the king. He knew that *the king's heart was towards Absalom.* — **2.** He sent to *Tekoah*, a town in Judah, *and took thence a wise woman*] probably one already known to him by reputation. He directs her to play the mourner : *Put on mourning garments, and do not anoint thyself, and become like a woman now many days mourning for one dead.* — **3.** In this plight she was to present herself as a suppliant for justice before the king. — **4.** *And the Tekoite woman came,* and after the customary prostration cried : *Help, O king, help!* — **5.** To the king's question : *What ails thee?* she replies : *Verily I am a widow, and my husband is dead*] a pleonasm which may well be excused in the circumstances. — **6.** The case is this : the family being reduced to two brothers, *these two quarrelled in the field when there was no one to interfere and one smote the other and killed him.* — **7.** The result is the probable extirpation of the family, for : *The whole clan has risen up against thy servant and say: Deliver up the smiter of his brother, that we may slay him for the life of his brother whom he has killed, and we will destroy the* [only] *heir.* In the flow of her speech the woman gives the result as part of the purpose of the avengers. The procedure is quite in accordance with clan custom, and yet the result will be a calamity : *They will quench my remaining coal so as not to leave my husband name or remnant on the face of the ground.* Extremum jus extrema injuria. The extinction of a family is dreaded as one of the chief misfortunes. — **8.** David gives a promise to see that the woman and her son are protected. — **9.** She is not satisfied with this : *Upon me, my lord the king, be the guilt and upon my father's house; and the king and his throne shall be innocent*] the insinuation is that David has simply put her off with a promise, because he does not wish to involve himself — his defence of the guilty son would make him partaker of the guilt. — **10.** David makes a more distinct decree, empowering the woman to bring her prosecutors into the royal presence : *Him that speaks to thee, bring before me and he shall not touch thee again.* — **11.** This is enough if only it can be made sure, and the petitioner therefore asks an oath : *Let the king name Yahweh thy God, not to let the avenger of blood destroy, and they shall not exterminate my son.* The king swears accordingly : *By*

the life of Yahweh a hair of thy son shall not fall to the ground]
the object of this importunity is to make sure that David's mind
is fully made up, before the application is made to the case of
Absalom.

1. עַל־אַבְשָׁלוֹם] the interchange of עַל and אֶל has already been remarked.
With עַל we should expect a verb; reading אֶל we get a tolerable sense. —
2. תְּקוֹעָה] the location was recovered by Robinson (*BR.*² I. p. 486), two
hours south of Bethlehem. — **4.** וַיֹּאמֶר] of most editions is a careless scribe's
mistake for וַתְּבֹא, which is found in 40 MSS. of 𝕳, as in 𝕲𝕾𝕿𝕷. At the end
of the verse 𝕲 adds a second הוֹשִׁיעָה, which seems original (Th.). — **5.** אֲבָל]
as in 1 K. 1⁴³. — **6.** וַיִּכּוּ] ought of course to be the singular. A scribe had in
mind the phrase *they strove one with another*, in which case the plural would
be allowable. — אֶת־הָאֶחָד] τὸν ἀδελφὸν αὐτοῦ 𝕲ᴸ is attractive and perhaps
original. — **7.** וְנִשְׁמִירָה] for which 𝕾 renders as though it found יִישָׁמִירוּ, is supported by 𝕲 and is probably correct (We., Dr. al.). — **10.** וַהֲבֵאתוֹ] for וַהֲבֵאתְהוּ,
and therefore to be read וַהֲבִאתִיו (We.). — **11.** אֱלֹהֶיךָ] θεὸν αὐτοῦ 𝕲ᴮ. The
more difficult is to be preferred. — מֵהַרְבִּית] the pointing is difficult to account
for. Kl. conjectures מֵהַרְפָא, which fits the sense.

12–20. The application. — The woman first asks and receives
permission to say a word. — **13.** Her rebuke of the king is expressed in a question : *And why dost thou devise against the people
of God a thing like this — and the king in speaking this word is as
one guilty — in order that the king may not bring back his banished?* The *people of God* are in her own case ; the heir is likely
to be cut off. David in his treatment of Absalom is devising
against them just what the Thekoites were devising against the
plaintiff in the case alleged. — **14.** The first half of the verse is
plain : *For we die and are as water spilled upon the ground which
cannot be gathered*] the point is that Amnon is dead and cannot
be brought back by any harshness towards Absalom. The rest of
the verse is entirely obscure. Conjecturally the conclusion is an
exhortation to the king *not to keep his banished* son in perpetual
banishment. The conjecture of Ew., accepted by most recent
scholars, makes the whole second half of the verse mean : *And
God will not take away the life of him who devises plans not to
banish from him a banished one.* But it can hardly be said that
this is much encouragement to David. — **15.** The woman excuses
herself for appearing before the king : *For the people made me
afraid.* She still talks as though her suit were the main purpose

of her visit. — **16**. *For the king will hear, to deliver his servant from the hand of the man who seeks to destroy me and my son from the heritage of Yahweh*] this is a part of the reflection which induced her to come before the king. — **17**. The woman concludes her speech : *The word of my lord the king will be a comfort*] literally, *a resting place*. The reason is the wisdom of the king : *for like the angel of God is my lōrd the king to hear good and evil*] and to discern between them, is of course implied. — *And Yahweh thy God be with thee*] is evidently her parting blessing. — **18**. The king does not let her go until his curiosity is satisfied on one point, and so asks her *not to conceal* that one thing. — **19**. The question concerns the agency of Joab, and the answer is an admiring testimony to the king's shrewdness : *By thy life, my lord the king, I cannot turn to the right or the left from all that my lord the king has spoken*. His question contains an affirmation, and the affirmation is correct. — **20**. *In order to change the face of the affair*] that is, the affair of Absalom — *did thy servant Joab this thing*] an excuse for Joab and his instrument. The final compliment to the wisdom of the king is intended to say that his decision is certain to be right.

13. ‏ומדבר‎] pointed as though a Hithpael, with assimilation of the ‏ח‎, Ges.[26], § 54 *c*. The last clause is explanatory of ‏כזאת‎ (We., Dr.), which refers to the case of the woman herself as just alleged. 𝕲[L] (following Theodotion) had a different text, which however cannot be restored with certainty. — **14.** ‏כי־מות‎ ‏נמות‎] 𝕲[L] makes the point more plain by rendering ὅτι τέθνηκεν ὁ υἱός σου, meaning Amnon. — ‏ולא־ישא אלהים נפש‎] the clause as it stands is incomprehensible. Taken with what follows, it might be forced to mean : *and God does not take away life, but devises plans that his banished be not banished from him* (so substantially RV.). In this case the long suffering of God, in not taking away the sinner until he has had opportunity to repent, would be set forth as an example to David. The objections are obvious. The assertion that *God does not take away a life before doing so and so* is entirely too sweeping. Common observation shows that this is not his rule. Moreover, the statement that *God devises devices that his banished be not banished* is obscure and without Old Testament analogy. The most obvious conjecture is to read ‏והשיב‎ for ‏וחשב‎ and, joining it with the preceding, render *And God does not take away a soul and then return it,* that is : death is irrevocable. We are then left without a connexion for what follows. 𝕲[B] omits ‏לא‎ : καὶ λήμψεται ὁ θεὸς ψυχήν, καὶ λογιζόμενος τοῦ ἐξῶσαι ἀπ᾽ αὐτοῦ ἐξεωσμένον, which does not give any help. 𝕲[L] which seems to have the translation of Theodotion (Field) gives us: καὶ οὐκ ἐλπίζει ἐπ' αὐτῷ ψυχή, which connects well with what precedes — *and no one hopes for it* (? the water, some MSS. have αὐτῶν). This evidently substitutes אליהם or אליו for the אלהים of 𝕳 and makes נפש the subject of the verb. In view of the difficulty we find in understanding the received text, this seems acceptable. On the same authority the last clause means: *Yet the king devises a plan to keep away from him one banished!* (The exclamation is an intimation that this ought not to be), reading המלך for לבלתי, and לנדח for ידח. We. objects to the phrase *banish a banished one*, but it does not seem difficult. Ew. changes והשב in the received text to הושב, and is followed by We., Dr., Bu., Ki. — **15.** אשר] omitted by two MSS. of 𝕳, is in fact redundant. But the author is reproducing the speech of a woman of the people. — המלך אדני] is not the usual order and אדני is lacking in 𝕲ᴸ. — **16.** האיש] add המבקש with 𝕲 (Th. al.). — אלהים] 𝕲ᴸ 𝕿 seem to have read יהוה, which is better. — **17.** שפחתך] restore האשה with 𝕲ᴮ, for this is evidently the concluding part of the woman's speech. — למנחה] a resting place, something in which one may feel secure. — כמלאך האלהים] we find the same comparison in 19²⁸, where also the point is the ability to discern the right, cf. v.²⁰ לדעת. — **19.** אם־אש] usually taken to be for אם־יש in the meaning *it is not possible*. The form however is unusual — the text is suspicious in the only other case of its occurrence, Mic. 6¹⁰. The conjecture of Perles (*Analekten zur Textkritik des Alten Testamentes*, p. 30) is therefore plausible, that we should read אשוב, for which also 𝕾 סטית may be cited.

21–24. Absalom is brought back but not received at court. — **21.** Joab, as a high officer of the court, was standing by the king during the woman's plea. David turns to him and says: *Behold I have done this thing*] the thing asked is granted, and so in purpose is already accomplished. — **22.** Joab expresses his thanks in language that shows how much the matter lies on his heart. Why Joab should have such an interest in Absalom is not apparent. — **23, 24.** Joab brings Absalom back, but the king commands: *Let him turn aside to his own house, and my face he shall not see*] the return was therefore not a restoration to the favour of the king.

21. עשיתי] the Qrê in some editions is עשיתָ and so 20 codd. in DeRossi. But the best editions point according to the consonantal text. — **22.** עברו] the Qrê perversely commands עבדך, which is found in 16 codd., but not sustained by the versions.

25–27. The author or the redactor inserts a panegyric of Absalom's personal beauty, and an account of his family. The latter contradicts 18¹⁸, and the whole breaks the connexion of the narrative. There seems no reason however to put the paragraph at a

z

very late date, unless it be the mention of the standard weight as
the *royal* weight; and this seems difficult to date exactly. The
fact of Absalom's personal beauty may have been a matter of early
tradition. The author emphasizes a similar fact in the case of
Adonijah 1 K. 1⁶. — **25.** *No man in Israel was so praiseworthy
as Absalom; from the sole of his foot to his crown there was no
blemish in him*] David also seems to have had great personal
beauty. — **26.** The main sentence is: *and when he shaved his
head, he would weigh his hair, two hundred shekels by the king's
weight*] the shaving of the head had some religious signification,
as we see in the Nazirites. The specification of the *king's* weight
points to a time when Assyrian or Babylonian measures had begun
to be used in Palestine (We.). The main sentence is interrupted
by a parenthesis telling that the shaving of the head took place
once a year. — **27.** The verse gives Absalom three sons and a
daughter. The harmony of this with 18¹⁸ is secured by supposing
that all the sons died in infancy. But if this were so, the author
would have mentioned it here. 𝔊 adds at the end of the verse
that Tamar *became the wife of Rehoboam, the son of Solomon, and
bore to him Abia* (Abiathar, in 𝔊ᴮ).

25. יפה is omitted by 𝔊ᴮ, and כל by 𝔊ᴸ, while 𝔖 omits both. As the
shorter text has the presumption in its favour and as איש בישראל להלל gives a
perfectly good sense we should probably read so, throwing out both the
inserted words. — להלל] in the sense *to be praised* is good Hebrew, cf. Dav.
Syntax § 93. 𝔊 however may have found מהלל, which it read מְהֻלָּל. — **26.** On
the construction see Dr. *Notes.* For 200 shekels, Th., followed by Koehler
(*Bibl. Gesch. des A. T.* II. p. 345), conjectures twenty; 𝔊ᴸ has 100. — **27.** תמר]
Μααχά 𝔊ᴸ ⅃ (Cod. Leg.). The addition at the end of the verse is found in
nearly all MSS. of 𝔊 and in ⅃. It apparently comes from 1 K. 15², where
Abijah's mother is called *Maacah daughter of Absalom.*

28–33. Absalom secures recognition at court. — After dwelling
in Jerusalem two years without seeing the face of the king, Absalom *sent for Joab to send him to the king*] evidently to expostulate
concerning the situation. Joab, however, *was not willing to come*
even after a second summons. He probably felt that he had done
enough in procuring Absalom's recall. — **30.** Absalom's imperious
temper shows itself in the means taken to secure Joab's attention.
He said to his servants: *see Joab's field next to me where he has*

barley; go and set it on fire] the standing grain when fully ripe burns readily, as is seen in the experiment of Samson with the foxes. At the end of the verse (or at the beginning of the next) 𝕲 insert : *And the servants of Joab came to him with rent clothes and said: the servants of Absalom have set the field on fire.* The sentence may be original. — **31, 32.** To Joab's question, Absalom thinks it sufficient answer to say that he had sent for him. The king's son treats Joab as a servant. He will send to the king the message : *Why have I come from Geshur? It would be better for me still to be there*] the half recognition which he has received is more galling than exile. Without further explanation of his arson, he goes on : *And now let me see the face of the king, and if there be guilt in me, let him kill me.* — **33.** The appeal made by Joab was successful, and Absalom was received by his father, who *kissed him* in token of full reconciliation.

30. והוצתיה] for which the *Qrê* commands והציתוה. The form הוצית seems to occur nowhere else, so that the *Ktib* here is most easily accounted for by supposing it to be the blunder of a scribe, cf. Ges.²⁶ § 71. The insertion of 𝕲 is accepted by Th., Kl.; rejected by We., Bu. The transition is abrupt without it, and its omission may be accounted for by homeoteleuton, so that the probability is rather in its favour.

XV. 1.–XIX. 44. The usurpation of Absalom. — After due preparation, Absalom has himself anointed king at Hebron. At his approach to the capital, David retires to the Jordan valley. Absalom is for some time in possession of the capital, while David finds support in transjordanic Israel. By a decisive battle, the cause of Absalom is lost, he himself being slain. The grief of the king at the loss of his son is as great as if he had lost his kingdom. The feeling between Judah and Israel breaks out again in the return of the monarch, and the sequel is the rebellion of Sheba ben Bichri.

This is one of the most vivid pieces of narrative in the Old Testament, and evidently belongs to an old and well informed source. This source is apparently the same from which we have had the account of Amnon and Absalom which immediately precedes.

XV. 1–6. Absalom plays the demagogue. — First he assumes the state befitting the heir apparent : *He procured a chariot and* *horses and fifty men to run before him*] the chariot was an unaccustomed luxury. The fifty retainers would form a body-guard for the young prince. In the absence of precedent for the settlement of the throne, such preparations indicated that the prince was putting himself forward with a claim to the succession. We have no evidence that David had as yet made any provision in favour of Solomon. Primogeniture has never been the rule in the East, and Absalom, being of royal blood on both sides, may well have regarded himself as the best fitted for the throne. — **2.** Absalom now made it his habit to *rise early and stand at the gate*] of the city, the place of public concourse. — *And every man that had a case to come before the king for judgment Absalom would call to himself*] and show interest in him, first by asking him about his home. — **3.** Then came an insinuation that the king was careless about the administration of justice : *Thy pleadings are good and right, but there is no one to hear thee on the part of the king*] we may suppose that the man was encouraged to state his case before this was said. — **4.** Suggestion that Absalom himself had the interest of justice at heart : *Oh, that one would make me judge in the land, and to me should come every man who has a case, and I would give him justice!* The public good is represented as his main interest. — **5.** He would not allow the customary obeisance, but would place men on the level of friendship : *When a man came near to do obeisance he would put out his hand and take hold of him and kiss him.* — **6.** The result is not surprising : *He stole the understanding of the men of Israel*] he deceived them, cf. Gen. 31²⁰.

1. רצים לפניו] such runners formed a part of royal state in very early times, and have continued to the present in the East. — **2.** כל־האיש] should probably be כל איש: πᾶς ἀνήρ 𝔊. The answers of the men would be different; the author puts a general answer for the different specific ones : *Thy servant is from one of the tribes of Israel;* as if he had said : *the man answered : I am from this or that tribe.* — **4.** מי־ישמני] cf. the expression מי־יתן also expressing a wish, Jer. 8²³. — ומשפט] is lacking in 𝔊ᴸ𝔏. — **6.** ויגנב א׳ את־לב] cannot mean *he won their affection*, but must be interpreted by the similar phrase, Gen. 31²⁰, where the only meaning allowable is *Jacob deceived* Laban. So Absalom *stole the brain* of Israel, *befooled* them. The heart is the seat of the intellect, cf. BDB. s.v. לבב and לב, and especially Delitzsch, *System der Bibl. Psychologie*² (1861), p. 248 f. where the parallels are cited.

7–12. The usurpation. — The site chosen is Hebron where we may suppose there was more or less dissatisfaction at the removal of the capital to Jerusalem. The time seems to be four years after Absalom's restoration to favour. The pretext was a vow made to the Yahweh of Hebron. — **8.** *For thy servant vowed a vow when I dwelt in Geshur in Aram saying: If Yahweh bring me back to Jerusalem, I will serve Yahweh in Hebron*] the nearest parallel seems to be the vow of Jacob Gen. 28^{20-22} (E), and like that, this vow calls for personal appearance before God with sacrifice, Gen. 35^{1-7}. It is evident, as in the case of Baal, that the Yahweh of a particular place assumed a distinct personality in the common apprehension. Although the Ark was at Jerusalem, David did not find it strange that Absalom should want to worship at Hebron. The Yahweh of Hebron would be the special God of Judah. — **9.** David gives the desired permission. — **10**. At the time of his departure *Absalom sent emissaries into all the tribes of Israel, saying: When you hear the sound of the trumpet, then say: Absalom has become king in Hebron*. It is evident that much more elaborate preparation was made than appears on the surface of this concise narrative. The signal was expected to go from village to village, and enough men were distributed to declare the coronation an accomplished fact. — **11.** Besides his own party, *Absalom took two hundred men from Jerusalem who were invited*] as guests to the festival. — These *went in their innocence*] being ignorant of the plan. But as members (we may suppose) of the leading families they would be hostages in Absalom's hands, or if convinced, as they might easily be at Hebron, that Absalom's cause was the winning one, they would exert a powerful influence in his favour. — **12.** As it stands, the verse does not fit the context. It says that *Absalom sent Ahithophel from his city,* but whither (which is here the most important point) we are not told. There is authority for correcting to: *Absalom sent for Ahithophel,* or to: *Absalom sent and brought Ahithophel.* But from the later narrative we conclude that Ahithophel was the soul of the rebellion, and we have reason to suspect therefore that the original text contained something to the effect that Ahithophel fomented the conspiracy from Giloh, while Absalom was carrying on the sacrificial feast at Hebron. This alone would account for the fact that the *conspiracy was strong and the people with Absalom kept increasing in number*.

7. ארבעים שנה] has given the scholars trouble. The Rabbinical expositors count from the time when the Israelites demanded a king (Isaaki, Kimchi), or from David's first anointing by Samuel (LbG.), or again from the slaying of the priests at Nob (Pseudo-Hier.), as though the rebellion were a punishment for David's deception. The natural reckoning would be from the coronation of David at Hebron (Cler.), but it is unlikely that the usurpation took place in the last year of David's life, The most obvious way out of the difficulty is to correct the *forty* to *four*, which is favoured by 𝔊ᴸ, Josephus, Theod., and, if we may judge from the MSS. of 𝔏, also by I. — **8.** וישב] is erroneous duplication of the verb which follows. The punctuators try to make the best of it by reading וישׁב, which however cannot be the adverbial infinitive of שׁוב. For the latter, which is read by 𝔊, we must restore הישׁב or שׁוב (Th. al.). At the end of the verse 𝔊ᴸ adds ἐν Χεβρών, which seems necessary (adopted by Kl., Bu.), and which may have been left out because it emphasizes the distinctness of the Yahweh of Hebron. — **10.** מרגלים] generally *spies*, but here a little broader in meaning. — **11.** ולא ידעו כל־דבר] a strong expression — *they did not know anything* of the matter. — **12.** וישלח אבשלום את־א׳] it is evident that this is wrong. The only emendation suggested by the versions is to read וישלח אב׳ ויקרא or ויקרא אב׳ which are supported by various Greek Codices; or else to insert ויבאהו with 𝔖. Neither one seems to go far enough, for it remains inexplicable that Ahithophel should not be invited until the very last moment. The reconstruction of Kl. lacks probability. — הגילני] from גילה like השׁילני from שׁילה. *Gilo* is enumerated among the towns of the hill country of Judah. It is not yet certainly identified, but a *Beit Jala* and a *Jala* exist in the vicinity of Bethlehem, Buhl, *Geog.* p. 165.

13–16. David, taken by surprise, flees the city. The first news he receives is that *the heart of the men of Israel has gone after Absalom*] there must have been widespread dissatisfaction to justify the report, or even to make it plausible to David. — **14.** The citadel in which he had established himself could not protect him — evidently he feared disaffection in his household. It is perhaps not without reason that 𝔊ᴸ reads : *lest the people come upon us*. That David wished to spare the city the horrors of a siege (Kl.) is not indicated in the text. It seems rather that he was convinced that his only safety was in flight. — **15.** The officials of the court consent. — **16.** *So the king went out and all his household with him*] literally, *at his feet*. The only exception was *ten concubines* who were left in charge of the house.

14. ‏[פן ימהר‏] μὴ φθάσῃ ὁ λαός 𝕲ᴸ. — 15. ‏[הנה עבדיך‏] is sustained by 𝕲, though we rather look for a verb; 𝕾 adds ‏עבדין‏.

17, 18. The text has suffered, but we are able to make out that *the king and all the people who followed him went out and stood at Beth Merhak*] a place otherwise unknown, possibly the last house on the Jerusalem side of the Kidron wadi. The reason for the king's making a halt here is that he might inspect his party. They defile before him : *all his officers and the Cherethites and the Pelethites*] the veteran body-guard. With them was a recent re-cruit, Ittai the Gittite, who was apparently once mentioned here, as he is addressed by David in the next verse. He was, we may judge, a soldier of fortune who had just enlisted in David's service with a band of followers. There is no analogy in Hebrew antiq-uity for regarding him as a Philistine hostage.* — 19. David gen-erously advises Ittai to seek his fortune with the new king, rather than with himself (who could hardly offer much in the way of pro-motion) : *Why wilt thou also go with us ? Return and dwell with the king, for thou art a stranger and an exile from thy place*] one seeking a home and who thought he had found it. — 20. *Yesterday was thy coming, and to-day shall I make thee wander with us ?* The question, which is indicated by the inflection of voice, is rhe-torical. The hardship of such a course is indicated in the circum-stantial clause which follows : *when I am going hither and yonder*] literally ; *when I am going where I am going;* David himself did not know where, cf. 1 S. 23¹³. He therefore advises : *Return and take thy brethren with thee, and Yahweh show thee kindness and faithfulness*] David's thoughtfulness for others shows itself in this incident, at a time when he might be excused for consulting his own interest. — 21. Ittai solemnly declares : *Wherever my lord the king shall be, whether for death or for life, there will thy ser-vant be !* — 22. At this protestation of fidelity David commands him to march on, so he marched by with a train which embraced his men and their families.

17. ‏[העם‏] two codd. have ‏עבדיך‏ and this is also the reading of 𝕲ᴮ. The original seems to be 𝕳 which means *the people of the household.* — ‏[בית המרחק‏] *the house of Distance* might possibly be the furthest house from the centre

---

* Which is Thenius' hypothesis, retained by Löhr, *Th*³. p. 172.

of the city. But this is precarious. The reading of 𝔊 seems to have been
זית המדבר, which however has been corrected in the chief MSS., cf. Field,
Hex. Orig. I. p. 569. — **18**. The text of 𝔊 has suffered by conflation but its
fulness does not help to restore the true reading. The difficulty with 𝔒 is
that it makes *all the Gittites* to have followed David from Gath. Had the
author meant to say that the troops were those who had followed David from
Ziklag he would have said so. The sudden introduction of Ittai in the next
verse seems to prove that he was once mentioned here, and the consequence
is easily drawn, that these Gittites were his men. For וכל־הגתים therefore, Bu.
with Kl., Ki., following a hint of We., proposes to read וכל אנשי אתי הגתי.
The objection to this is that it makes these Gittites a force of six hundred men.
But the Cherethites and Pelethites were only six hundred in number, and it is
unlikely that a fresh band of the same size would be enlisted while the veterans
were faithful. Ew. (*GVI*[3], III. p. 243, E. Tr. III. p. 179) changes הגתים into
הגברים which does not relieve the sudden introduction of Ittai in the next verse.
— **19**. למקומך] might perhaps stand: *an exile as to thy place;* but the versions
seem to have read ממקומך, 𝔊𝔖𝔏 and one Hebr. cod., whereas 𝔗 inserts איזל.
— **20**. 𝔊[B] has a double translation of the opening part of the verse. One
part of this seems to have read with the interrogative באת התמול. אנוער *Kt.*,
is doubtless to be corrected to the *Qrê.:* אניעך, unless we go further and read
אנירך. At the end of the verse חסר ואמת are unattached and we should doubtless insert with 𝔊 ויהוה יעשה עמך which fell out after the preceding עמך (Th.).
— **21**. כי אם is not in place, nor is the אם alone, which in an oath has a negative force. Nothing is left to us but to suppose that a scribe made a blunder
— as was already discovered by the punctuators. — **22**. חטף] cf. Ex. 10[10]. 𝔊[L]
inserts *the king* here through a misapprehension of Ittai's position (as leader).

23. The condition of things at the particular moment when the
Ark appeared was this : *All the people were weeping with a loud
voice, while the king stood in the Kidron wadi, and the people passed
by before him on the road of the Wilderness Olive*] the Kidron is
the well known valley east of Jerusalem. The road taken was
probably the one on the south slope of the Mount of Olives, the
same which is still travelled to Jericho and the Jordan valley. —
And behold Zadok . . . bearing the Ark of God] the present text
inserts *and all the Levites with him*. But as the Levites are unknown to the Books of Samuel, this is obviously a late insertion.
Probably the original was *Zadok and Abiathar*. They now *set
down the Ark* to allow the people to pass by. As the Ark went
on the campaigns of David, it was a natural thought to take it at
this time. — **25**. The king commands the Ark to be taken back :
If I find favour in the eyes of Yahweh, he will bring me back and

will show me it and his dwelling. — **26.** If on the other hand
Yahweh has no pleasure in him, he resigns himself to the divine
will. — **27, 28.** At the same time, David is not unmindful of the
advantage of having friends in the city : *Thou art returning to the
city in peace and with you are your two sons, Ahimaaz thy son and
Jonathan the son of Abiathar ; see, I am going to delay at the fords
of the Wilderness until word comes from you to inform me.* —
29. The Ark is accordingly returned to its place.

23. The text has suffered. The central point seems to be עבר בנחל which
is suspicious, for the road did not (probably) follow the course of the wadi,
but crossed it. In the following, also, the king seems to be still reviewing his
company. We.'s conjecture that we should read עמד בנחל is therefore generally adopted and has much to recommend it. We have further two assertions
that the people were passing along, one of which is superfluous, and I have
therefore stricken out the first וכל־העם עברים. Again, for על־פני we should
read על פני with 𝔊L, and finally דרך את־המדבר is an impossible expression and
must have been דרך זית המדבר : κατὰ τὴν ὁδὸν τῆς ἐλαίας τῆς ἐν τῇ ἐρήμῳ GL
probably represents this, and it is not necessary to reconstruct literally דרך
הזית אשר במדבר as is done by Dr., Bu. — **24.** וכל הלוים אתו] is easily accounted
for, as the insertion of a later scribe, whose point of view was that of the
Chronicler. A similar insertion is ברית which betrays itself by its difference
of position in the MSS. of 𝔊. — האלהים] Κυρίου 𝔊B which also adds ἀπὸ Βαιθάρ
which if original can only represent מביתו. The verb ויצקו is probably for
ויציגו. The enigmatical ויעל אביתר may possibly mean *and Abiathar offered*
(sacrifices) as David had done on another journey of the Ark. But we should
expect the object to be expressed, and as the words are omitted by 𝔊L, they
are probably due to an attempt to readmit the displaced Abiathar into the
text. — **25.** העיר] 𝔊L adds וישב במקמו adopted by Bu. But it is not necessary
to the sense, and insertion is more likely than omission. — והראני] ὄψομαι 𝔊L.
— **27.** הרואה] is obscure. It is taken by Ew. as an address to Zadok, as if he
were a *seer*, which does not appear to be the fact. 𝔊B reads ראו which is suspicious from its recurrence at the beginning of v.28. We. supposes an insertion
הכהן הראש which has been corrupted into the present text. It is impossible to
decide with certainty. For שבה, I am inclined to read שָׁב (the participle) —
the ה having come from the following word. — **28.** בעברות המדבר] is probably
correct. The *Qrê* substitutes בערכות המ׳ which is tautological. 𝔊L finds a
reference to the same *Wilderness Olive* mentioned above. — **29.** וישבו] probably וישב 𝔊B, the Ark being the subject.

30. David now takes up his march, going up the ascent of
Olivet with his head covered and his feet bare, both signs of grief.
The people also covered their heads *and went up, weeping as they*

went. — **31**. On hearing of the defection of Ahithophel, David prays : *Turn the counsel of Ahithophel to foolishness, O Yahweh!* As remarked above, Ahithophel, the grandfather of Bathsheba, had a special reason to seek the destruction of David. — **32**. As David was *coming to the hill top where one worships God*] sanctuaries on the hills are too well known to need remark. — *There met him Hushai the Arkite the friend of David, with his tunic rent and earth upon his head*] the place or family from which he got his name is unknown. — **33, 34**. David sees in Hushai an instrument for counteracting the influence of Ahithophel : *If thou go with me, thou shalt be a burden to me ; but if thou return to the city and say to Absalom : I am thy servant, O king . . . then thou canst bring to nought for me the counsel of Ahithophel*] the sentence is a little complicated by the length of the speech which Hushai is to make to Absalom. The apparent sense of it is : *Thy servant will I be, O king ; thy father's servant was I formerly, and now I am thy servant.* But as the Hebrew is awkward, it is possible that the text has suffered. 𝕲 certainly read something quite different in part of the sentence : *Thy brothers have gone away and the king thy father has gone away after* [*them*] *; now I am thy servant, O king! let me live ; I have been thy father's servant heretofore, and now I am thy servant.* — **35, 36**. David instructs Hushai to keep Zadok and Abiathar informed, and to send word by their sons as has already been planned, cf. v.[28]. — **37**. As a result of this advice, Hushai returns to the city, reaching it about the time of Absalom's arrival.

---

30. חפו איש ראשו] we find חפו ראשם in Jer. 14[3] where also it is a sign of grief. — **31**. וּרוּד] read וּלרוד with 𝕲[L] and 3 MSS. of 𝔥. It is unnecessary however to change the verb to הגר (Bu.). — **32**. הארכי] ὁ ἀρχιέταιρος Δαυείδ 𝕲 as in 16[16]. The original 𝕲 was ὁ Ἀρχὶ ἑταῖρος Δαυείδ, of which we have traces in a few MSS. The friends or boon companions of the king were a special class of courtiers, as it would seem. The Arkites are mentioned Jos. 16[2] between Luz and Ataroth. — **34**. The difficulties with the received text in the middle of the verse are these : אהיה is in an unusual position and separated by המלך from its subject אני; both ואני have the ו of the apodosis which is certainly extreme (Dr.) ; and the clause ואני עברך repeats the first. At the opening we should expect a salutation of the king. 𝕲 has (with slight variations) : διεληλύθασιν οἱ ἀδελφοί σου, καὶ ὁ βασιλεὺς κατόπισθέν μου διελήλυθεν ὁ πατήρ σου to which it adds the reading of 𝔥 in a second translation, only rendering אהיה by ἔασόν με ζῆσαι. It is not impossible that the original had some such reference as this: *thy brother has passed away, and the king thy father has passed away after him* (Kl.). The assumption that David was as good as dead would be flattering to Absalom. The *let me live* seems to us "too currish" (We.), but it might not so strike an oriental.— **36.** הנה] 19 codd. have והנה which is also read by 𝕲ᴸ. At the end of this verse 𝕲ᴸ inserts a repetition of what Hushai was expected to say to Absalom.— **37.** רֵעֶה] the pointing is unusual, cf. Ges.²³ 93 *ll.* —יבא] on the tense cf. Davidson, *Syntax*, 45, *Rem.* 2, Dr., *Tenses*³, 27 γ.

XVI. 1. The account follows the fortunes of David. When he had got a little beyond the summit, *Ziba the servant of Meribbaal met him*] having come from the city, it would seem, by another road ; *with a pair of asses saddled, and two hundred loaves of bread and a hundred bunches of raisins*] cf. 1 S. 25¹⁸. The *two hundred fruits* were probably figs, Am. 8¹. — **2.** To the king's question Ziba replies that this is provision for the king's household. — **3.** A further question concerning his master brings out the reply : *He remains in Jerusalem, for he thinks : To-day will the house of Israel give me back my father's kingdom*] it is possible that Meribbaal had the idea that the popular disturbance would bring the house of Saul again to the front. But it is hardly likely that he, a cripple, should expect to be their choice for the throne. The excuse given later by Meribbaal himself accounts sufficiently for his remaining behind, and we must suppose Ziba's accusation slanderous. — **4.** The king believes in the man who has done him a kindness, and without waiting to hear the other side gives him all Meribbaal's property. Ziba acknowledges the gift by obeisance and a prayer for the king's continued favour.

1. צמד] Kl. conjectures ועמו, and in fact two asses seem insufficient for the occasion. — קיץ] is translated by 𝕲ᴮ φοίνικες, but by 𝕲ᴸ παλάθαι; the other versions seem to favour the latter. — **2.** ולהלחם *Kt.;* והלחם *Qrê.* The latter seems to be correct. — **3.** ממלכות] as indicated above (on 1 S. 15²⁸) probably a false spelling of ממלכת. — **4.** השתחויתי] *I bow myself* in gratitude.

5. The next incident was less agreeable. — *The king came to Bahurim*] the village already mentioned in the account of Michal's return, 3¹⁶. It seems to have been on distinctly Benjamite territory. *There came out a man of the clan of Saul whose name was Shimei son of Gera, cursing as he came.* — **6.** His hostility was made known by his actions as well as his words : *He stoned David and all his officers and all the people and all the soldiers at his right hand and at his left*] this represents the king surrounded by his body-guard. — **7, 8.** Shimei's words were : *Get thee gone, get thee gone, vile and cruel man ! Yahweh has brought back upon thee all the blood of the house of Saul*] this temper was probably not uncommon in Benjamin. We could condone it if the owner had not shown such obsequiousness at a later date. — *Behold thee now in thy calamity !*] a spectacle to all men. — **9.** Abishai is ready to avenge the insult : *Why should this dead dog curse my lord the king ?* cf. 9⁸. — **10.** David denies that he has anything in common with the violent temper of the sons of Zeruiah : *When Yahweh has said to him : Curse David ! then who shall say : Why hast thou done so ?* The infliction was of divine ordering, and must be borne patiently. — **11.** A second remark on the same subject: *My son who came from my bowels seeks my life, how much more this Benjamite*] is excusable. — **12.** *Perchance Yahweh will look upon my affliction and repay me good for his cursing this day*] Nestle (*Marginalien*, p. 18) compares the Qoran (68³²), where the owners of the blasted garden say : " Perhaps our Lord will *give us in exchange* a better than it." — **13.** As David continued his journey, *Shimei went along on the side of the mountain parallel with him, cursing as he went, and threw stones and dust*] more as an expression of hatred than with the expectation of inflicting bodily injury. — **14.** So the king and the people came to (? some place the name of which is lost) *and he refreshed himself there.*

5. וּבָא] is the wrong tense, and should be corrected to וַיֵּבָא, so apparently 𝔊. We should however expect the order וְהִמֵּ׳ דוד בא. *Shimei* is the name of several men in the history of Israel. The Benjamite clan *Gera* is mentioned Gen. 46²¹ Jd. 3¹⁵. — **6.** מִימִינוֹ וּמִשְׂמֹאלוֹ] as the Benjamites are elsewhere represented as ambidextrous (Jd. 20¹⁶) one is tempted to make this describe Shimei as *throwing* with his right hand and with his left. But in usage מִימִין almost always means *at the right hand* of a person or a thing. — **8.** וְהִנְּךָ בְּרָעָתֶךָ] καὶ ἔδειξέ σοι τὴν κακίαν σου 𝔊ᴸ is probably only a free translation, though it may possibly imply וְהֶרְאֲךָ רָעָתֶךָ. — **10.** כִּי יְקַלֵּל] the Qrê כֹּה יְקַלֵּל does not seem to help. It is awkward to join with what follows: *when he curses and when Yahweh says : curse.* I suspect that Kl. is right in reading here as below, favoured also by 𝔊, הַנִּיחוּ לוֹ וִיקַלֵּל: *let him curse ! When Yahweh has said,* etc. — וְכִי] כִּי *Qrê.* — **11.** The verse is supposed by Kl. to be a paraphrase of the preceding. There seems no reason, however, why the king may not have made more than one remark on the same subject. — **12.** בעני] is doubtless for בעיני. Rabbinical subtlety sees here one of the *Tiqqune Sopherim*, supposing the original reading to have been בעינו: *with his eye*, which was changed to avoid anthropomorphism (Geiger, *Urschrift*, p. 325). The *Qrê* reads בעיני which is intended to mean *upon my tears*. But such a meaning for עין is without parallel. בעיני with the genitive of the object, *the sin committed against me*, is contrary to analogy. — קללתו] is the reading of Baer and Ginsburg, whereas the majority of printed editions have קללתי in the text, with קללתו *Qrê*. — **13.** הלוך ויקלל] is not the usual form of such a phrase, and it is possible that הלוך is an erroneous insertion; it is lacking in 𝔖. — לעמתו] the second time is awkward: ἐκ πλαγίων αὐτοῦ 𝔊^B: ἐπ᾽ αὐτόν 𝔊^L 𝔖 may be conjectural renderings only, but show the difficulty of the word. — **14.** עיפים] we expect the name of the place, and it is possible that עיפים represents such a name; otherwise one has dropped out: παρὰ τὸν Ἰορδάνην 𝔊^L looks like a conjecture. In 15²⁸ David expects to lodge at the המדבר ערבות, and in 17¹⁶ we find him at what is intended to be the same place. Possibly this name once stood here. — וינפש] cf. Ex. 23¹².

15. The narrative now leaves David, in order to show how things are going at Jerusalem. Absalom had taken possession without opposition. The populace seem to have been on his side, if we may judge by the assertion that *the men of Israel* made his train. — **16.** *And when Hushai the Arkite, the friend of David, came to Absalom and said: Long live the king, Absalom said: Is this thy friendship for thy friend?* Such seems to be the construction of the sentence. — **18.** The questions of Absalom imply that Hushai should have gone with David, to which implication he replies: *No! For whom Yahweh and this people and all Israel have chosen — to him will I belong and with him will I dwell*] the combination of God's will and the will of the people overrules all else. The flattery is obvious. — **19.** *And in the second place: Whom should I serve? Should it not be his son?*] that is, the son of the friend just alluded to. The speaker endeavours to show that the friendship is best manifested by turning to the son: *As I have served thy father, so will I serve thee*] the fine words suffice for the occasion.

15. וכל־העם איש יש׳] καὶ πᾶς ἀνὴρ Ἰσραήλ 𝔊^B. The latter seems original. — **16.** יחי המלך] is given only once in 𝔊. The apodosis seems to begin with v.¹⁷. — **18.** לא] the second time is corrected by the *Qrê* to לו, which is essential. — והעם הזה] refers to the people there present: καὶ ὁ λαὸς αὐτοῦ 𝔊^L in connexion with what follows is tautological.

20. Absalom asks advice concerning the first step. — **21.** Ahithophel is prompt with his reply : *Go in to thy father's concubines which he left to keep the house, and all Israel will hear that thou hast made thyself abhorred of thy father ; and the hands of all who are on thy side will be strengthened*] the breach would thus be made incurable, and on Absalom's side would be the determination of men who know this. The act advised, however, is not a mere act of wantonness. The successful usurper took possession of his predecessor's *harem* as a matter of right, as we have seen in the case of David himself. Absalom's act was only the public affirmation of the logic of the situation. — **22.** *They pitched the tent*] the bridal tent of the Semites which has survived, in the canopy of the Jewish wedding ceremony, to our own day. Absalom thus took possession of the king's rights, *before the eyes of all Israel.* Had this author known of Nathan's denunciation of this punishment for David's adultery, he would have made some allusion to it here. — **23.** That the advice thus acted upon was just what the occasion demanded is indicated by the author in his panegyric : *The counsel of Ahithophel which he counselled in those days was as though one inquired of the word of God.*

20. הבו לכם] addressed to the whole circle of counsellors. — **21.** בוא אל] frequently used of the consummation of marriage. — נבאשת את] the combination occurs nowhere else, and it is possible that the Hiphil was originally written : κατῄσχυνας τὸν πατέρα σου 𝕲. — **22.** האהל] cf. the חפה of the bridegroom, Ps. 19⁶; also WRSmith, *Kinship*, p. 168 f.; Wellh., *Muhammed in Medina*, p. 178. — **23.** The *Qrê* bids insert איש after ישאל, which is certainly smoother.

XVII. 1–14. Ahithophel and Hushai. — In a debate as to the next step to be taken, Ahithophel counsels an immediate pursuit of David. Hushai by an elaborate argument counteracts the impression made by Ahithophel, and secures delay. The debate was held the day of the arrival in Jerusalem, apparently after the appropriation of the concubines was decided upon, but before it was consummated.

1. Ahithophel is himself ready to take the field against David : *Let me choose twelve thousand men, and I will arise and pursue David to-night.* — **2.** The time was favourable : *And I will come upon him when he is exhausted and weak, and I will throw him*

*into a panic, and all the people with him will flee and I will smite
the king alone.* The picture drawn has a good deal of probability.
David was weary and discouraged ; the company with him would
easily be thrown into a panic ; and in the confusion the king
might be slain with little loss of life otherwise. — **3**. Reading with
𝕲 we translate : *And I will bring back all the people to thee as the
bride returns to her husband ; only one man thou seekest — and all
the people shall be at peace*] the figure is flattering to Absalom, as
well as the intimation that David alone is a disturber of the peace.
— **4**. The advice commended itself to Absalom and the assembled
Sheikhs. — **5**. He desires however to get all possible light and so
orders Hushai to be summoned : *that we may hear what is in
his mouth also.* — **6**. The case is laid before Hushai : *Thus has
Ahithophel spoken ; shall we carry out his word ? If not, do thou
speak !* In case of disagreement only would it be necessary to
make a speech. — **7**. Hushai, who knows that delay will work for
David, pronounces against the scheme. — **8**. The argument : first,
David and his men are old soldiers, and of angry temper *like the
bear robbed of her cubs.* The Syrian bear was formidable, as
indeed it is still. 𝕲 adds here : *and like the wild boar of the
plain.* Secondly, David is too shrewd to spend the night where
he is likely to be surprised ; he *is a man of war and will not lodge
with the people*] the hope of a panic is likely to be frustrated. —
9. The danger of an attack on such a man is evident : *Now he
has hidden himself in one of the caves or in one of the places*] an
indefinite word is chosen, in order to suggest that a great variety
of such places exists — *and when some of the people fall at the first
attack, the report will spread*] literally, *the hearer will hear and
say — there is a slaughter among the people who are with Absalom.*
The plausibility of this cannot be denied. Among the suddenly
levied troops of Absalom a panic was more likely to arise than
among the seasoned soldiers of David. — **10**. The result can
easily be foreseen : *Even the valiant man, whose heart is like the
heart of a lion, shall utterly melt away*] in fear, *for all Israel
knows that thy father is a hero, and valiant men are they who are
with him.* — **11**. So far the refutation of Ahithophel ; now comes
the counter-proposal : *But I counsel*] the tense indicates that the
plan has been fully matured in his mind ; *let all Israel be gathered*

*to thee from Dan to Beersheba as the sand which is by the sea for
multitude, with thy Majesty marching in the midst of them*] the
picture of the monarch in the midst of such an army was calculated to impress the imagination of Absalom. The language
moreover contains an insinuation that the expedition proposed
by Ahithophel, and under his leadership, could not be as effective
as if Absalom himself were the general. — **12.** In this case the
destruction of David is certain : *We will come upon him in one of
the places where he has been discovered*] by that time we shall be
in no uncertainty as to his whereabouts : *and we will light upon
him as the dew falls upon the ground, and there will not be left of
him and the men who are with him even one.* — **13.** An objector
might say that the king will thus have time to get into a fortified
place. But if so : *all Israel will bring ropes to that city, and we
will drag it to the wadi*] on which it may naturally be supposed
to be situated, *until there is not found there even a pebble*] the
hyperbolical language is calculated to make an impression. —
14. The oratory of Hushai carried the day, in accordance with
the divine ordering : *Yahweh had commanded to bring to nought
the good counsel of Ahithophel in order that Yahweh might bring
calamity upon Absalom*] hence the blindness of Absalom to his
real interest.

1. אבחרה־נא is followed by the dative of advantage here as elsewhere
according to 𝕲 : ἐμαυτῷ. — שנים־עשר] the δέκα χιλιάδας of 𝕲ᴸ seems more
natural to us, but is suspicious for that very reason. — **2.** והחרדתי] of throwing
into a panic (stampede) by a sudden attack, Jd. 8¹². — **3.** כשוב הכול האיש
אשר־אתה מ'] is unintelligible, as any one may see in the attempt of the AV,
adopted without remark by the Revisers. 𝕲 had a different text, which since
Ew. (*GVI*³. III. p. 247, E. Trans. III. p. 183) has been generally adopted in
the form : כשוב הכלה לאישה אך איש אחר אתה מבקש. The only difficulty is that
if Ahithophel compares himself to the groomsman who brings the bride to her
husband, he should use a different verb from שוב. Schill (*ZATW*. XII.
p. 52) proposes כשובי מהכות האיש וגו', which also gives a fairly good sense, but
does not explain the origin of 𝕲. — כל] read וכל with 𝕲. — **5.** קרא] read קראו
𝕲. — נס־הוא] emphasizes the pronominal suffix which precedes. Davidson,
Syntax, 1. — **6.** On the question whether we should translate as above, or
(as is also possible, disregarding the accents) : *shall we do as he says or not ?
Speak thou*, cf. Dr. *Notes*. For אס־אין 𝕲ᴸ has ἤ πῶς. Probably we should
read ואם־אין, the ו having fallen out after דברו. — **8.** בשרה] 𝕲ᴮ adds : καὶ ὡς
ὗς τραχεῖα ἐν τῷ πεδίῳ. The fierceness of wild swine is sufficient to justify

this comparison (cf. Nestle, *Marginalien*, p. 18), but as the comparison is nowhere else actually made in the Old Testament, the presumption is against it here. — את־העם] the point seems to be that David will arrange the camp so that his own person will be guarded from surprise. — **9.** והנה עתה] seems not to be hypothetical: *and suppose now* that he is hidden (Kl.), but to draw the conclusion from what has just been said: *being a man of war, David has certainly hidden himself.* — הפחתים] cf. 18¹⁷. For בהם we may restore בעם with 𝕲ᴸ. — **10.** והוא] not to be corrected to והיה with 𝕲ᴸ (Kl.) for that makes a difficulty with the following verb; but the reference is not to be limited to השמע which precedes (Dr.). The speaker explains what he means by the next following words: *And he* (I mean *even the valiant man*) *shall melt away.* — ימס] in the thought of the speaker *the heart* is the subject. — **11.** כי יעצתי] seems perfectly good, but cf. We. — ופניך] *and thy countenance,* of the personal presence of the monarch. — בקרב] means *into the war.* But קרב in this sense is a late word, and 𝕲𝕷 read here בקרבם which should be restored (Th.). — **12.** ונחנו] evidently from נחו, not to be confounded with the pronoun. Perles, *Analekten,* p. 32, proposes ונחנה (so 𝕲ᴮ). — נוחר] with recession of the accent on account of the following monosyllable. The verb is taken by some to be a jussive form instead of the cohortative, Ges.²⁶, § 109 *d.,* Davidson, *Syntax,* § 63, Rem. 1. There is no need to assume an anomaly, as the Niphal perfect makes good sense: *and there will not* [by that time] *have been left one.* — **13.** והשיאו] the Hiphil is rare, and does not seem natural here. 𝕲ᴮ καὶ λήμψεται may represent והביאו which seems to fit the case. — הנחל] as the towns were generally on the hills it was fair to assume that there would be a wadi in the vicinity. — צרור] from Am. 9⁹ the meaning *pebble* seems assured.

15-22. David receives the news of his danger.
— Hushai at once informs the priests of the discussions in the council. As he could not be certain which would be adopted he advises David to put the Jordan between him and the enemy: *Do not lodge to-night in the Araboth, but cross over*] the place is the same at which David has told them he could be found, 15²⁸. The danger is: *lest the king and all the people with him be swallowed up.* — **17.** The two young men were waiting at *En-Rogel,* now generally identified with the *Well of Job* (for *Joab?*) at the junction of the two valleys of Kidron and Ben Hinnom. If they *should be seen to come into the city* after having started out with David, it would awaken suspicion. — **18.** A lad saw them, however, and reported. Discovering themselves to be pursued, they took refuge *in the house of a man in Bahurim*] so that we may suppose not all the inhabitants to have been of the same mind with Shimei. *The well in his court* was a good place of hiding. — **19.** The woman of the

house *took and spread a cloth over the mouth of the well and strewed fruit upon it*] as if the fruit were drying. — **20**. The reply of the woman to the question of the pursuers is probably designed to be enigmatical. It is completely so to us. — **21, 22**. The messengers come to David and bring Hushai's advice, *and David arose and all the people who were with him and crossed over the Jordan*] the Jordan, a swift-flowing stream, is troublesome either to ford or to cross by ferry. On this account immediate pursuit need not be feared when once on the other side. *By morning, there was not one left behind*.

16. כערבות] Baer and Ginsburg have no *Qrê* here, and it seems difficult to suppose that the fords could be called *fords of the wilderness*. I have therefore rendered as a proper name. — יכלע] the so-called impersonal construction, Davidson, *Syntax*, § 109. — **17.** עין־רגל is mentioned in the boundary line of Benjamin and Judah, Josh. 15[7], evidently at the foot of the valley of Ben Hinnom. For a description of the present *Bir Eyyub* cf. Robinson, *BR*[2]. I. p. 332. Buhl's objection that this is a well, and not a fountain, is met by the fact that water flows in the well, sometimes even coming over the top, so that it might well receive the name *Spring*. — השפחה] the article indicates only the particular one who was sent on this message; we should say *a maid*. The tense of the verbs seems to require the translation : *the maid was to come and tell them, and they were to go and tell David*. — **19.** הרפות] is unknown. The Targum has דקילין, *dates*, and it seems most probable that fruit of some kind would be the thing exposed for drying; 𝕲[L] has παλάθας which also means fruit. 𝕲[B] seems to transfer the Hebrew word, ἀραφώθ. Aq. and Sym. have πτισάνας which is taken by 𝕃. This word means *hulled* or *crushed* barley, and something of the same kind is intended by 𝕾 רושא. The tradition represented in 𝕿 should have a good deal of weight in a case of this kind; cf. Nestle, *Marginalien*, p. 18, who also favours *fruit*. — **20.** מיכל] is a word which occurs nowhere else, and even its derivation is uncertain. The Arabic and Assyrian parallels which are alleged are not convincing. 𝕲[B] has μικρόν; 𝕲[L] σπεύδοντες omitting המים, and 𝕃 *gustata paululum aqua; festinanter* seems to come from I. We might conjecture that an original נבהלים or ממהרים has been corrupted into מיכלימים, but this is no more than a possibility. — **22.** עד־אור הבקר] is connected by the punctuation with what follows; 𝕲 however joins to the preceding. The more vigorous sense seems conveyed by the former construction. — אחד] the punctuation is anomalous, Ges.[26], § 96.

23. A verse is added to show the fate of Ahithophel. Convinced that a wrong start was made and that the outcome would be failure, *he saddled his ass and rose and went to his house, to his city*] here added to show that his house in Jerusalem was not meant. — There *he gave command concerning his house*] testamentary disposition of his estate, *and strangled himself*. Cases of suicide are not common in the Old Testament. The most prominent is that of Saul. There is no evidence that the Biblical writers found it especially abhorrent. Ahithophel was not refused burial in the sepulchre of his father.

23. אל־עירו] the change to ואל־ made by some MSS. seems unnecessary.

24–29. David's settlement at Mahanaim. — As though the temper of transjordanic Israel was more conservative than that of the tribes west of the river, David found refuge and support among the same people who had clung to Ishbaal. The paragraph begins to tell of Absalom's preparations for battle, and then breaks off to tell of the reception provided for David by the leading men of Gilead. Vv.²⁷⁻²⁹ belong logically after ²⁴ᵃ.

24. David came to Mahanaim, and Absalom also crossed the Jordan, *he and all the men of Israel with him*. Some time probably was required to summon the militia, but we do not know how much. — **25.** The general of Absalom's army was Amasa, who is described in 𝔐 as *son of a man whose name was Ithra the Israelite*. The statement is surprising, because it is superfluous to call a man an Israelite who dwelt in the land of Israel. Only in case he were a foreigner is it natural to add his gentilic description. Furthermore, the Chronicler knew him as *Jether the Ishmaelite*, 1 Chr. 2¹⁷. It is highly probable that the latter is correct; a scribe would have every reason to correct *Ishmaelite* to *Israelite*. No motive can be discovered for the reverse process. The language which is used further: *who came to Abigail daughter of Nahash sister of Zeruiah*] is explicable only on the theory that we have to do with a *çadîqa* marriage, that is, one in which the wife remains with her clan and the children become members of that clan. For *Nahash*, the Chronicler substitutes *Jesse*, and a number of Greek codices have the same name here. But the Greek reading may have arisen from the desire to harmonize this passage with Chronicles. It seems impossible to get at the truth of the case. It is quite in accordance with custom that Absalom should appoint his kinsman to high office, as David did in the case of Joab. — **27.** At Mahanaim David received material help

from *Shobi ben Nahash*] whom, as representing the old royal
family, he had probably made viceroy over Ammon, *and Machir
ben Ammiel of Lo-Debar*] the protector of Meribbaal, 9⁴, *and
Barzillai the Gileadite of Rogelim*] the name is evidently Aramaic.
The place is mentioned only here and 19³². — **28**. These friends
brought couches and rugs and bowls and pottery] in order to furnish the houses occupied by the fugitives. Besides this, provisions in abundance : *wheat and barley and flour and parched
grain and beans and lentils*] these the vegetable products. —
29. The enumeration goes on with another class of edibles : *honey
and curds and sheep and calves*. These they set before David and
his people, knowing that they would be *hungry and weary and
thirsty in the desert.*

25. בן־איש ושמו יתרא הישראלי] the form of the sentence is puzzling. We
expect the order to be איש יש׳ ושמו יתרא, We. Why should a man's name be
called *Ithra the Israelite ?* His name was Ithra and he was an Israelite, but
in Israel itself *Israelite* would be no distinguishing mark. In case of a foreigner it would be different: *Uriah the Hittite* was in a certain sense the
name of David's soldier. This consideration certainly favours the restoration
of *Ishmaelite* here in accordance with Chr. 𝔏 makes him a Jezreelite. The
latter is read also in this place by two Greek codd. (III. and 55 of Parsons),
but probably no great weight can be given to this testimony. — אשר־בא אל אבי]
the sentence would be unnecessary except in case of a * çadîqa* marriage, on
which cf. WRSmith, *Kinship*, Chap. 3. — בת־נחש] as the Chronicler makes
Abigail a daughter of *Jesse*, the Jewish expositors make Nahash here to be
another name for Jesse. But this is very improbable. Schm. and others make
him the first husband of Zeruiah's mother. 𝔊ᴸ and a number of codd. read
'Ιεσσαί, which however may be due to harmonistic tendency. To the theory
that Nahash and not Abigail was the sister of Zeruiah, which would be a possible construction of the text, We. objects that Nahash is not a woman's name.
But of this we cannot be certain. It is not impossible that בת־נחש has come
in under the influence of בן־נחש in the verse below. — **27**. ושבי] καὶ Σεφεει
𝔊ᴸ, 'Ουεσβεί 𝔊ᴮ. It is possible that a verb once stood here. — מרגלים] ἐκ
Ρακαβείν 𝔊ᴸ. — ברזלי] doubtless the first element is בן = בר, Nestle, in *Am.
Jour. Sem. Lang.* XIII. 3. — **28**. The missing verb is put by 𝔊 here and
would better be restored in the form הביאו. For משכב : δέκα κοίτας καὶ ἀμφι-
τάπους 𝔊. The δέκα is עשרת, but by a slight change we get ערשת which makes
excellent sense. With this change (Kl. and Nestle) the text of 𝔊 is adopted
above. — קלי] is erroneously duplicated in the text. It seems to belong with
קמח. — **29**. ושפות] is obscure. 𝔊ᴸ seems to have understood *calves*, and so
𝔏; and this fits the immediate context. 𝔊ᴮ does not translate, while 𝔖𝔗
make the word mean *cheese*. Possibly there is an error in the text.

XVIII. 1–8. The battle. — David's army sets out from Mahanaim to meet the force under Absalom. David offers to go himself, but yields to the entreaties of the soldiers that he stay in the
city. He charges the captains to spare Absalom. — **1.** The king
in person reviews the army and appoints officers. — **2.** The three
generals are Joab, Abishai, and the newly recruited Ittai. — *I also
will go with you*] the form of the offer indicates that the king did
not feel strong enough to assume the chief place. — **3.** The
soldiers dissuade him ; if they should be defeated, the enemies'
object would not be attained so long as David should remain
alive : *For thou art equal to ten thousand of us*] a common estimate of a valued leader. — And besides *it is good that thou be a
help to us from the city*] by sending out the reserves in case of
necessity. — **4.** The troops march past the king as he stands in
the gate. — **5.** The charge to the generals : *Gently for my sake
with the lad Absalom!* To his father he was still but a boy.
That *all the soldiers heard* is intended to prepare for v.¹². —
6. The battle took place *in the jungle of Ephraim*] not otherwise
known to us. — **7.** Absalom's party was defeated with the loss of
20,000 men. — **8.** The battle became a rout ; *scattered over the
face of the country, and the jungle devoured more than the sword*]
the rocky thickets were fatal to those who attempted to flee.

2. וישלח] καὶ ἐτρίσσευσε 𝕲ᴸ points to וישלש, which is more likely to be
original because the less common word. — **3.** כי־עתה כמנו] there seems to be
no doubt that we should read אתה for עתה, with 2 codd., 𝕲ᴮ, 𝔖, 𝔏 and Sym.
(Cappel, *Critica Sacra*, p. 309, Th. al.). The sentence still does not seem
quite correct, and the original may have been simply ואתה כמו עשרה אלפים.
𝕲ᴸ has ὅτι καὶ νῦν ἀφαιρεθήσεται ἐξ ἡμῶν ἡ γῆ; which Kl. supposes to point to:
for then the earth would bring forth [ten thousand times] *more than we.* But
this seems forced. — לעזיר] לעזוֹר Qrê. The latter is to be restored (as the
Hiphil is uncalled for) unless indeed we conjecture לעֹזֵר. — **5.** לאט־לי] 𝕲 has
a verb: φείσασθέ μου (μοι) possibly חמלו. But there seems no reason for departing from the received text, cf. Is. 8⁶. — **6.** אפרים] 𝕲ᴸ reads מחנים, obviously a correction of the editor, cf. GASmith, *Geog.* p. 335 *n.* — **7.** Omit the
second שם 𝕲, which has come in from the verse below. At the end of the
verse add איש with 𝕲. — **8.** נפצות] is to be corrected to נפוֹצת with Qrê.

9–18. The fate of Absalom. — In the general flight Absalom
happened upon the servants of David] that is, the body-guard. —
His mule *came into the thick branches of a great oak, and his head*

caught fast in the oak, and he was hung between heaven and earth]
being left there as the mule kept on her way. — **10, 11.** To the
young man who told him, Joab said : *Thou sawest him! And
why didst thou not smite him to the ground? And my part would
have been to give thee ten shekels of silver and a girdle*] the girdle
was often richly wrought, and so worn as an ornament. — **12.** The
soldier's reply : *And if I were weighing in my hand a thousand
pieces of silver, I would not put forth my hand on the king's son*]
for the reason of the king's charge : *Take care of the young man
Absalom.* — **13.** Further argument of the case : *Had I wrought
deceitfully against his life, nothing would have been hidden from
the king, and thou wouldst have stood aloof.* This seems to be the
best that can be made of the present text. — **14.** Joab breaks off
the conversation, takes three darts in his hand : *and thrust them
into the heart of Absalom yet alive in the midst of the oak.* We
think of the oak as a mass of thickset branches in which Absalom
was struggling. — **15.** The three darts must put an end to the
already exhausted man, and it is a work of supererogation on the
part of Joab's armour-bearers to smite him and kill him again.
It is probable therefore that the verse is an interpolation. —
16. Joab calls off the pursuit, knowing that the end has been
attained. — **17.** They cast Absalom's body *into the great pit*] the
article seems to indicate that it was one well known. — *And they
raised over him a great heap of stones*] Jos. 7²⁶ 8²⁹. — **18.** Another
monument had been erected by himself in the vicinity of Jerusalem.

9. ויקרא] is probably correct, though we might expect another verb. —
ויתן] καὶ ἀνακρεμάσθε 𝕲ᴸ: ואיתלי 𝕿: ואתתלי 𝕾, all pointing to ויתל, which
alone is in place, notice תלוי in the next verse. — **11.** ועלי לתת] an obligation
rests *upon* one. 𝕲ᴮ has simply καὶ ἐγὼ ἂν δεδώκειν, in favour of which Th.
urges that there was no obligation in the matter. But surely it is the commander's duty to reward valour in his soldiers. — **12.** ולא] is, of course, ולוא.
— שקל] We. proposes to make a passive, because the recipient does not tell
the money, but the payer. The soldier however seems to mean : *if* I were to
feel the weight of that money paid into my hand. — מי] is unintelligible; read
לי with the versions and 2 codd. — **13.** או] may possibly do, but it is better
to correct it to אם. 𝕲 connects the whole clause with the preceding verse,
making it a part of David's exhortation. Take care of the young man Absalom, *lest any one work injustice to his life.* But the present verse seems to
need the words. The only real difficulty is in the word שקר. The killing of
Absalom would not be *deceit.* — בנפשי] בנפשי Qrê. The latter is read also by

𝕲ᴸ. — **14**. שבטים] *clubs* are not thrust into one's heart, so that we should probably read שלחים with 𝕲 βέλη (Th.). — **15**. For the reason above given, We. regards the verse as an interpolation (*Comp.* p. 261). Th., followed by Ki., begins the sentence with the preceding clause: *But as he was yet alive in the heart of the oak, ten of Joab's armour-bearers compassed him.* But for this we should at least have והוא עוד instead of the bare עורנו. For this reason it seems best to regard the verse as an interpolation except וימיתהו at the end; this word, pointed וימֹיתֻהו, will readily join to the end of v.¹⁴. The ingenious construction of Kl. which makes Joab simply release Absalom from the tree so that he is really slain by the armour-bearers, lacks basis in the text. — **18**. On מצבת, We., *TBS.* The statement seems to conflict with 14²⁷. Of the two, this seems more likely to be original, as it is quite in place to explain why Absalom had a monument *in the king's dale.* The location is unknown. Josephus puts it two stadia from Jerusalem (*Ant.* VIII., X. 3). — הזכיר] cf. *ZATW.* XI. p. 178, XVII. p. 74; and Schwally, *Leben nach dem Tode* (1892), pp. 28, 58. The indications are in favour of worship of the dead, as the motive for the erection of such a monument.

19–32. The news is brought to David by two runners. The first is Ahimaaz, already known to us, 15²⁷. He asks permission to bring the king tidings: *that Yahweh has pronounced for him as against his enemies.* — **20**. Joab at first refuses permission because he knows that the king will be grieved at Absalom's death; and to bring bad tidings would not be of advantage to Ahimaaz. — **21**. Joab then calls a negro (naturally, a slave) and commands him: *Go tell the king what thou hast seen*] a message of grief by a despised messenger. — **22**. Ahimaaz again begs permission: *However it may be, let me run*] the motive is not very clear — whether a desire to break the news more gently than the slave would, or simply an ambition to carry the tidings. Joab dissuades him: *Why is it that thou wilt run, my son, seeing that no reward will be given thee?* — **23**. Ahimaaz is still insistent, and Joab gives the desired permission: *And Ahimaaz ran by the way of the [Jordan] valley, and outran the negro*] the direct way was probably across the hills, but the roughness of the country made that way more difficult. — **24**. Meanwhile *David was sitting between the gates*] that is, in the building which was both gateway and tower. The watchman had *gone up to the roof of the gate;* thence he saw *a man running alone.* — **25**. To the news, the king said: *If he be alone, tidings are in his mouth.* Were he a fugitive from the battle, others would appear scattered over the plain. —

26. Seeing another runner : *the watchman on the gate cried : Another man running alone !*] to which the king made answer : *This also is a bearer of tidings.* — **27.** The watchman recognizes the foremost : *I see that the running of the first is like the running of Ahimaaz ben Zadok*] so Jehu is known at a distance by his manner of driving. The king judges the character of the message from the character of the messenger : *He is a good man and a good message he will bring.* — **28.** *And Ahimaaz drew near and said to the king : Peace*] the customary salutation, followed by the customary prostration. The news is conveyed in a pious ejaculation : *Blessed is Yahweh thy God who has delivered over the men who lifted up their hand against my lord the king !* The words give certain information of the victory, and contain a hint of the fate of Absalom. — **29.** The king asks directly concerning his son, and receives the reply : *I saw the great tumult when Joab sent thy servant but I do not know what it was.* It seems evident that this is false. — **30, 31.** The negro's arrival and greeting : *Let my lord the king receive tidings : for Yahweh has avenged thee*] cf. v.¹⁹. — **32.** The question about Absalom receives this time an unmistakable answer : *May the enemies of my lord the king, and all who rise up against thee for evil be as the lad is !*

19. שפט יהוה מיד איביו] the *constructio pregnans* like 1 S. 24¹⁵. — **20.** [על־כן is to be read with the *Qrê*. כן has fallen out owing to its similarity to בן. 𝕲ᴸ represents כי only, cf. Jd. 6²². — **21.** It is an old question whether כושי is to be taken as a proper name or as an appellative. As the form used is nearly always הכושי, the latter is more probable. The *Cushites* were properly the Nubians, but probably the name was extended to cover all natives of Africa beyond Egypt. The trade in slaves brought them to Asia. The first occurrence of the word here should be without the article לכושי, the second on the other hand should have the article supplied—הכושי. — **22.** [ויהי מה] *let it be what it may*, is an answer to Joab's objection in v.²⁰. — [מצאת] is obscure. We. proposes מצאת, *brought forth*, which is adopted by Bu. But the phrase is even then not very clear. Possibly the word is a corruption of ויאמר which is needed in the next verse. — **23.** At the beginning insert ויאמר with 𝕲𝕾𝕷. — הככר] is the Jordan valley, Gen. 13¹² Dt. 34³. — **26.** [אל־השער] Before, the watchman had cried directly to the king, and so, if we may judge by the king's reply, he does here. Read therefore על השער with 𝕲ᴸ 𝕾 : *in culmine* 𝕷 seems to mean the same; אל השער of 𝕲ᴮ will hardly do. After the second איש add אחר with 𝕲𝕾. — **27.** [ואל־בשורה טובה יבוא] it seems more natural to read ואף בשורה טובה יביא which is favoured by 𝕿, and cf. 𝕲ᴸ οἴσει. — **28.** [ויקרא 𝕲ᴸ

renders ויקרב, which was conjectured also by We. before the publication of
that edition. — אישר־נשאו] traces of a Greek reading point to an original: *who
hate* (שנאו) *the hand* [or *power*] of my lord the king. — **29.** It seems necessary
to read השלום with 15 codd. — את־עבד המ׳] is superfluous and grammatically
in the wrong place; it should be stricken out, reading את־עברך for ואת־ע׳ (Bu.
following We.). מה should perhaps be followed by שם 𝔊, or היא. — **30.** [ויעמד
𝔊ᴸ adds ὀπίσω αὐτοῦ. — **31.** הכושי] the second time is omitted by 𝔊ᴮ 𝔖𝔏 and
is in fact superfluous.

XIX. 1–9ᵃ. David's emotion and Joab's rebuke. — The king
was shocked] having hoped against hope to the last. — *He went
up to the chamber over the gate*] a common feature in city gate-
ways. *And thus he said in his weeping: My son Absalom! My
son, my son Absalom! Oh that I had died for thee, Absalom, my
son, my son!* The fondness which had shown itself in early
indulgence, here breaks out in uncontrolled grief. — **3.** The victory *was turned to mourning that day, because the people heard:
the king grieves for his son.* — **4.** Instead of the triumphal march,
*the people stole away to the city as people steal away who are
ashamed of having fled in battle*] the approval of the king had
been their incentive. There seemed now no hope of this. —
5. The king on his part *wrapped up his face and cried aloud:
My son Absalom! Absalom, my son, my son!*] oblivious of everything but his grief. — **6, 7.** Joab rebukes David: *Thou hast shamed
to-day the face of all thy servants, who saved thy life and the life of
thy sons and daughters, and the life of thy wives and concubines,
by loving thine enemies and hating them that love thee*] the hard-
headed warrior told a wholesome truth. The throne of David
would not have been secure so long as Absalom lived. The conduct of the king said in effect: *that princes and officers are nothing
to thee*] in comparison to Absalom. *For I know that if Absalom
were alive, and all of us were dead this day, then thou wouldst be
pleased.* — **8.** The occasion calls for action: *Rise, go forth and
speak to the heart of thy servants*] speak a word of encouragement,
Is. 40¹. Should he not do this, the people would desert — an
oriental army quickly melts away under discouragement: *And
this will be worse to thee than all the evil that has come upon thee
from thy youth until now*] the nature of the threatened evil is not
given, but probably the thought is that the kingdom will fall to

pieces. — **9.** The last four words belong to the following paragraph. David sees the force of Joab's words, commands himself, comes down and sits in the gate, and receives the people.

1. וירגז] the verb seems to mean *to tremble* under strong emotion. — בלכתו] ἐν τῷ κλαίειν αὐτόν 𝕲ᴸ pointing to בבכתו. In spite of We.'s commendation of 𝔅, the alternate reading seems to me better. — **2.** The verse logically belongs after v.⁵, unless the author means that news was carried to Joab while still in the field. — **3.** The second ביום ההוא is superfluous and perhaps erroneous. — **4.** במלחמה] is lacking in 𝕲ᴸ. — **5.** לאט] for לָט, the vowel written *plene*, as in ראש 12¹. — המלך] the second time, is probably to be omitted with 𝕲ᴸ 𝔖𝕷. — **6.** הבישת] from בוש, Ges.²⁶ § 78 *b*. — ונפש פלגשיך] 𝕲ᴮ omits נפש:, bringing this clause into line with the preceding. The insertion was probably made to prevent too close association of the concubines with the wives (Nestle). — **7.** כי אין לך] the parallels give the meaning *thou hast no* princes. But here the sense seems to be like that of כאין נגדו Is. 40¹⁷. — כי־אז] the כי simply resumes the former כי (Dr.). — **8.** אינך יוצא] is the protasis. The אם which follows is the אם of the oath, cf. Davidson, *Syntax*, § 132, *R* 3. — ער] some copies have וער. — **9.** לפני המלך] 𝕲ᴸ adds אל השער.

9ᵇ–15. Proposals are made for the recall of David. — *Israel had fled, each to his tent, and the people expostulated in all the tribes of Israel*] the intimation seems to be that the common people were vexed at the slowness of the leaders. — **11.** The recollection of David's former benefits, with the fact of Absalom's death, prompts the question : *Why do you delay to bring back the king?* This word of theirs came to the ears of David (for the correct text, see the note). — **12.** With genuine oriental love of his own clan he incites Judah not to be behind the other tribes, working by means of his friends the priests : *Say to the Sheikhs of Judah : Why should you be the last to bring back the king to his house?* The reason was, of course, that they had been the leaders in the rebellion. — **13.** The bond of blood is urged as a reason why they should not be backward. — **14.** Amasa, as one of the most influential, is to be won by the promise of the chief command in place of Joab. — **15.** *And Amasa turned the heart of all the men of Judah as one man*] so that they sent for David to return with all his retainers.

10. נדון] would mean *were in a state of mutual strife* (Dr.). But as the Niphal occurs nowhere else, we should perhaps read נלון with 𝕲ᴸ. — והוא] is emphatic. — **11.** At the end of the verse, 𝕲 adds the clause which in 𝔅 comes at the end of v.[12], omitting it there: ודבר כל־ישראל בא אל־המלך. As shown by Th., the words belong here and not there. — **12.** The end of the verse should be at the Athnach, the rest having come in by transposition, and having been increased by erroneous addition of אל־ביתו from the line above. — **13.** The opening words seem the most proper introduction to the speech, and it is possible that they belong immediately after the second לאמר of the preceding verse, all between being erroneous duplication. — **14.** תמרו] for ־אמרו, Ges.[26], 68 *h*. — **15.** וישׁ] 𝔊[L] is probably correct in its interpretation when it inserts *Amasa* as the subject. Quite as good is the reading of 𝔗: וישׁ לבב.

16–24. The return of the king. — So David *returned* marks the transition, closing the account of the negotiations and opening the narrative of his journey. Judah came down to Gilgal, the well-known sanctuary in the Arabah, *to go to meet the king.* It seems hardly consistent with this to add : *to bring the king over the Jordan.* The latter seems to have been the work of Ziba. — **17.** The verse should include the first four words of v.[18] : Shimei *went down to meet the king with the men of Judah, and a thousand men of Benjamin with him*] the account is continued in [19b]. — **18.** The zeal of Ziba is described in a parenthetical sentence which includes [19a]. He, with his fifteen sons and twenty servants, *rushed through the Jordan before the king*] the meaning of the verb is uncertain. — **19.** *And they kept crossing the ford to bring the household of the king over, and to do what would please him.* The Jordan, though not a large stream, is swift and treacherous. The women and children would need the help of strong and experienced guides. The latter part of the verse returns to Shimei, who *fell down before the king as he crossed the Jordan*] at the very ford. — **20.** Shimei's prayer is : *Let not my lord charge guilt to me ; and do not remember what thy servant did perversely . . . that the king should pay attention to it*] he attempts no justification, as indeed grounds for justification were none. — **21.** He now realizes that he sinned, and confessing it pleads his present zeal : *I am come to-day, first of all the house of Joseph*] Benjamin is not reckoned to Joseph in the genealogies — this must be a more ancient conception. — **22.** Abishai is strenuous, as before, to put Shimei to death : *because he cursed the anointed of Yahweh*] the divinity that doth hedge a king made his crime blasphemy. — **23.** David again disclaims fellowship with the sons of Zeruiah who would be his *adversary,* hindering him from doing what he would. *To-day* *shall a man be put to death in Israel?* Evidently conciliation was to be the order of the day, for the king had the confidence that he was fully restored to his throne. The acclaim of the people had moved him to this generosity. — **24**. He therefore gives Shimei the sworn assurance that he shall not die. We should be better pleased with Shimei had he taken his punishment like a man, for his reviling of the king no doubt expressed his real mind.

16. להעביר וגו׳] It would be more appropriate to say *when he had crossed*, and perhaps something of that kind was the original text. — **17, 18**. The verse division here and in the following two verses is confused (We.). Divide at מנ‍נימן, at לפני המלך, and at בעינו. — וחמשת] on the form Ges.[26], § 97 *e.* — וצלחו] the tense seems wrong and we should probably strike off the initial ו; notice the preceding word. The meaning of צלח is elsewhere *to come violently upon, to take violent possession of*, generally used of the Spirit's coming upon a man. The only reason for its use here is that it describes the energy with which Ziba acted. — **19**. ועברה העברה] is taken traditionally to mean that *a ferry-boat went over*. But this meaning for עברה is without confirmation. The word elsewhere means *ford*. The verb here must be the plural ועברו, and the tense indicates the repeated action. The band of experienced men went back and forth, carrying the children and leading the riding animals of the women. It is unnecessary therefore to correct according to 𝔊 to ויעברו העברה (Kl., Bu.). — לעביר] for להעביר, Ges.[26], § 53 *q.* — The extraordinary points over the word יצא indicate that the Scribes wish to suggest יצאת (Ginsburg). — בעינו] to be read with *Qrê* בעיניו. — **20**. הֵעֲוֵה] cf. 7[14]. — **23**. לישפן] in 1 S. 29[4] the Philistines contemplated the possibility of David's becoming a שטן, *a traitor in the camp;* in much the same light David views the sons of Zeruiah here. — היום] the second time, is probably to be read ההיום, Lag. *Proph. Chald.* p. li. — ידעתי] οἴδατε 𝔊[L] is perhaps more forcible — *do you not know that I have the right to decide as king?*

25. The next incident was the coming of Meribbaal *ben Saul*, as he is called by 𝔥. — *He had not dressed his feet*] his lameness made some special attention to them advisable. — *And had not trimmed his moustache and had not washed his clothes*] neglect of the person is a sign of mourning. — **26**. As Meribbaal's home was Jerusalem, he came *from Jerusalem* to meet the king. The king naturally inquires why he had not gone with the household at the coming of Absalom. — **27**. The reply is: *My lord the king, my servant deceived me. For thy servant commanded him: Saddle the ass that I may ride upon her and go with the king*] the sufficient explanation why he was powerless to do more is his lameness, which he therefore mentions. — **28.** *But he slandered thy servant to my lord the king*] the case is sufficiently clear, and he leaves it to the decision of the king. — **29.** *For all the house of my father were deserving only of death before my lord the king, when thou didst set thy servant among those who eat at thy table*] the undeserved kindness of the king was a reason why he should now be contented with his decision : *And what further claim have I to cry to the king?* The resignation is a little forced. — **30.** The king is impatient : *Why wilt thou go on talking? I have decided: Thou and Ziba shall divide the land*] undoubtedly the zeal of Ziba in serving the king was the reason for this decision. Possibly there was also some suspicion that Meribbaal had not been as prompt as he might have been in endeavouring to follow David. — **31.** Meribbaal is content even that Ziba should have the whole : *since my lord the king has come home safe and sound.*

25. בן־שאול] υἱὸς υἱοῦ Σαούλ 𝕲B : υἱὸς Ἰωναθὰν υἱοῦ Σαούλ 𝕲L are evident expansions. — ולא־עשה רגליו] had the author meant simply that he had not *washed* his feet, he would probably have used another verb. In Dt. 21¹², עשה is used of trimming the nails, but the nails are named. — למן־היום לכת] the article is surprising, but perhaps due to the mistake of a scribe; Dr. cites Ex. 9¹⁸. — **26.** ירושלם] should be מירושלם (Ew. *GVI*³. III. p. 259, E. Trans. III. p. 191). — **27.** After עבדך insert לו, and for אהבשה read חבשה, so 𝕲𝔖, for Meribbaal was not able to saddle her himself. And the fact that he had given command to Ziba put the crime of the latter in a stronger light. — עליה] should possibly be עליו, as חמור is generally the *male*. — **28.** וירגל] here only of going about as a slanderer. — **29.** In 𝕲L the second half of the verse is: *And from whose hand shall I receive justice? And he cried further to the king.* This may be original, as the next verse intimates that he is talking too much. — **30.** תרבר] 𝕲L seems to read תרבה.

32–40. The parting with Barzillai.

— It is not certain that the author follows the exact order of events. We suppose that the parting from Barzillai took place before the meeting with Meribbaal. The plan is to recount the meeting with Ziba, Shimei, and Meribbaal in connexion, and then to take up the parting scene.

32. Barzillai came down from his home, *and went with the king to bid him good-bye at the Jordan*] it was the part of politeness to accompany a departing guest the first stage of his journey. — **33.** The old man *had nourished the king in his exile at Mahanaim*, a thing which his wealth enabled him to do. — **34.** David

invites him to become a member of the court. — **35.** Barzillai
declines on account of his years. — **36.** Age had blunted his senses
so that he did not *know good from evil*] the sense in which he
intends this is indicated by his further questions : *Can thy servant
taste that which I eat and that which I drink ?*] the inconsistent
use of the pronouns in such sentences is not uncommon. — *Or
can I hear the voice of singers, men or women ?*] the pleasures of
the court have no attractions for him. — **37.** *For thy servant will
go a little ways with the king, and why should the king give me this
recompense ?*] depreciation of his own services in accordance with
politeness. — **38.** His only desire is to return home *and die near
the sepulchre* of his father and his mother. But the favour which
he declines for himself he will accept for Chimham his son. —
39. The king willingly consents to take Chimham with him : *and
all thou shalt choose to lay upon me I will do.* — **40.** With this,
David dismisses his host, standing at the Jordan.

32. הירדן] (first) is superfluous, Bu. (at any rate *accus. loci*, Kl.). —
את־בירדן] cannot be right of course. And as we must emend, it will be best
to follow 𝕲^L ἐκ τοῦ Ἰορδάνου. Barzillai parted from him at the Jordan, *from
that point* he dismissed him. The emendation of Kl., adopted by Bu., which
finds here a mention of Chimham, seems to me too bold. — **33.** בשיבתו] is
rendered by 𝕲 ἐν τῷ οἰκεῖν αὐτόν (so 𝔖). It is quite likely however that the
author intended בשביתו, as the stay across the Jordan was a real *exile.* —
34. אתך] τὸ γῆράς σου 𝕲 indicates שיברך (possibly a reminiscence of the שיבתו
in v.³³), adopted by Ew. and others. — **35.** כמה] the question is : *Is my age
such that it is proper for me to go to court ?* — **36.** עור] is twice lacking in 𝕲^L.
Such words are easily inserted and also easily omitted. — **37.** כמעט] ὅτι ὀλίγον
𝕲^L is certainly smoother. — את־הירדן] is probably to be stricken out, as the
verb was taken by a scribe to mean *cross over.* If retained, it must be changed
to אל הירדן. — **38.** כמהם] Nestle (*Am. Jour. Sem. Lang.* XIII. p. 173) suggests
that the name is derived from כמה, *he has weak sight.* — **39.** הבחר עלי] *constructio pregnans.* — **40.** והמלך עבר] It seems unnecessary that Barzillai should
cross and then recross the river. 𝕲^L is probably right therefore in reading
עמד for עבר here : *All the people crossed the Jordan, but the king stood still;
and the king kissed Barzillai and bade him good-bye.*

XIX. 41–XX. 3. The strife between Judah and Israel. — The
king *passed by Gilgal, Chimham being with him, and all the people
of Judah were marching along with the king, and half the people
of Israel*] the mark which divided Judah and Israel shows itself

on every such occasion. The king's conduct in this matter rather accentuated than obliterated it. — **42**. The men of Israel apparently realize that Judah has been favoured by an invitation from David : *Why have our brethren the men of Judah stolen thee and brought the king and his house over the Jordan?* The conclusion of the verse seems to mean : *when all the men of David are* [equally] *his people*] the wrong was in David's giving the preference to his kinsmen. — **43**. The answer of Judah : *Because the king is near* of kin *to me*. And *why is it that thou art angry at this thing? Have we at all eaten of the king? or has any thing been carried away by us?*] the insinuation is that Israel has interested motives, suspecting that Judah is claiming offices and emoluments. — **44**. The retort : *I have ten shares of the king*] out of the twelve which all Israel might claim, *and I am the first born rather than thou*. Elsewhere, Judah is supposed to have succeeded to the birthright in default of Reuben. *Why hast thou treated me with contempt — was not my word first to bring back my king?* The fact was as they claimed. But in spite of all, the men of Judah were more strenuous in the strife. — **XX. 1**. The result was a new rebellion : *There happened to be there a vile man whose name was Sheba ben Bichri, a Benjamite*] the feelings of men had become so inflamed that any bold leader might stir up a revolt. He started the cry :

> *We have no share in David,*
> *And we have no part in the Son of Jesse;*
> *Each to his tents, O Israel!*

The exhortation is to leave their allegiance, and resume the old tribal independence. — **2**. The men of Israel deserted the train of David, *but the men of Judah clave to their king from the Jordan to Jerusalem*] the blood was the bond.

3. Further account of the rebellion is interrupted by this verse, which tells how David treated the ten concubines on whom Absalom had demonstrated his possession of the royal power. These he put *in a house of guard*] where they would be under surveillance, *and supported them, but did not go to them*] as a husband. — *So they were shut in until the day of their death*] the last two words are obscure and probably corrupt.

41. כמהן] occurs here only, elsewhere כמהם.—ויעבירו] *Kt.*: העבירו *Qrê.*
Better than either is עברים 𝕲ᴮ.—**42.** וכל־אנשי דוד עמו] the clause, in the pointing of 𝔐, reads like an afterthought and is superfluous in the context. But
if we point עמי, we get the assertion that *all David's men are his people,* which
bears directly on the subject. It seems to me enough to make this slight
change. Kl. proposes וכל איש ישראל עמו. But in this passage where the distinction is made between Israel and Judah, this would be misleading.—
43. נשאת] is grammatically and syntactically difficult. Grätz (*G. d. Juden,*
I. p. 287) proposes to read משאת, *or has a portion* [from his table] been carried
away for us? This in connexion with the previous clause makes good sense
and seems favoured by 𝕲. The Judahites say: we have neither eaten of the
king's table nor received presents from it. Dr. proposes to read נשא (the infinitive absolute).—**44.** ברור] read בכור with 𝕲 (Th.).—ולא] is difficult and probably to be emended to הלא. The second question is plainly required by the sense.
The second לי is difficult, and has probably arisen by erroneous duplication of
ל at the beginning of the next word.—**XX. 1.** איש בליעל] 𝕲ᴸ inserts בן,
whereas 𝕲ᴮ has בן בליעל. We find ימיני for *Benjamite* only here and in Esth.
2⁵.—**3.** נשים] lacking in 𝕲ᴸ.—ואליהם] the masculine for the feminine—6
codd. have ואליהן, but this is probably a correction of the scribes.—אלמנות חיות]
is unintelligible, and as the sense is complete without it, possibly a gloss. But
the meaning of the glossator is obscure; חיות occurs only here but might mean
life: *a widowhood of life* however would not mean *a life-long widowhood.*
𝕲 χῆραι ζῶσαι seems to read אלמנות חיות — *living widows* however is so self-
evident that it could not need to be expressed. *A widowhood during the
lifetime of the husband* or *widows whose husband was living* (We.) would be
otherwise expressed.

XX. 4–13. The murder of Amasa.

— Joab shows the same
conscienceless rigour in dealing with Amasa as he showed in the
case of Abner — more unscrupulous in fact, because in Abner's
case he had the excuse of blood revenge.

4. The king has already appointed Amasa chief of the army,
for he commands him (and not Joab) to call together the men
of Judah within three days. — **5.** Amasa, however, lacked the
energy of Joab *and delayed beyond the time which he had appointed him.* — **6.** David sees that time works for the rebels and
orders Abishai to take *his lord's servants,* that is, the body guard,
and pursue him, lest he find fortified cities and escape from us. —
7. The original reading seems to me to be : *And there went out
after Abishai, Joab and the Cherethites* and the others. — **8.** *They
were by the great stone in Gibeon when Amasa came leading the
people*] meaning *the soldiers* whom he had levied. As Amasa was

raising the men of Judah, it is difficult to see how he could be at
Gibeon, unless he overtook Abishai there, and we may interpret
this language accordingly. The second half of the verse is designed to show how Joab prepared himself for his attack in such a
way that Amasa's suspicion was not aroused. Unfortunately, it is
impossible to discover from the present text how he did it, and
the versions give little help. That Joab's sword *was girded on his
loins* is so much a matter of course that the author probably intended to tell us more. — **9.** As Joab greets Amasa, he stretches
out his right hand to take hold of Amasa's beard *to kiss him*] the
common salutation of kinsmen. — **10.** *But Amasa was not ware
of the sword which was in Joab's hand*] if it was in his *left hand*
the fact should have been stated here. One is led to think that
it was concealed (in the sleeve?) in the outstretched hand. — *So
he smote him with it in the abdomen, and shed his bowels to the
ground, and he did not give a second blow*] the experienced slayer
of men knew the most effective stroke. The work done, he proceeded with the order of the day. — **11.** A man was stationed by
the body to urge the passing soldiers to follow Joab. — **12.** Amasa
was wallowing in blood in the midst of the highway] the con-
vulsive throes of one dying may well be so described. It is not
to be wondered at that people stopped to look. Hence the removal from the highway into the field, and the throwing of a garment over him, because the sentinel *saw that every one who came
to him stood still.* — **13.** The removal from the highway had the
desired effect ; *all men went on after Joab.*

4. שלשת ימים] the temporal clause should be closely joined with what follows — *in three days stand thou here.* — **5.** ויוחר [וייחר] *Qrê.* Some form of
אחר seems to be intended, whether וייחר for ויאחר, or ויוחר for ויאחר seems impossible to make out — the *Qrê* of course intends the latter, cf. Ges[26], § 68 *i.*
— [יעדו + דור 𝕲[L] (Bu.). — **6.** For *Abishai*, 𝕾 substitutes Joab, which We.
supposes to be original. But as Joab is in disgrace it seems more natural that
Abishai should be called upon. Joab apparently accompanied the expedition
in a subordinate position. But his energy and habit of command made him
the real leader. — [עינו] the difficulties in the word are disposed of by reading ממנו with 𝕲[L]. Bu. proposes ונצל לעינינו. — **7.** אחריו אנשי] that the second
word is a corruption of אבישי is indicated by 𝕲[AB], which however retains the
suffix of אחריו. As this does not agree with what precedes, it seems obvious
that we should read אחרי אבישי (Graetz). — **8.** לפניהם] may be for לפני העם, a

2 B

mistake which occurs elsewhere. If this were the original reading, it meant that Amasa with his troops had reached Jerusalem just after the departure of the body guard and had pushed on after them, overtaking them at Gibeon. The rest of the verse reads, so far as we may attempt to translate it: *And Joab was girded as to his garment, his clothing, and upon him* [or *it*] *was a sword-girdle bound on his loins in its sheath, and he went out, and it fell.* The impossibility of such a sentence is obvious. If the key to the situation is that *the sword fell,* the author should at least tell us that Joab took it up before he reached Amasa. 𝔖 has a clue perhaps when it says his sword *rested on his hips like a dagger.* In this case, we may suppose that Joab had arranged his sword in some unusual way in order to this emergency, but how this was, we cannot clearly make out. The same version renders ותפל: *and his hand fell upon his sword,* which again might help us if we could suppose it to be original. But the testimony of 𝔖 alone is hardly sufficient to establish this. — ויאב] Bu. inserts a clause *and Joab ran to meet him,* which is without support in any document. — מדו לבש] is redundant, and the second word is possibly inserted to explain the first. Kl. conjectures with some plausibility חרב בידו instead of חגור מדו, and מתחת לבשו for the simple לבשו. The second חגור is pointed חגור by 𝔊B. — מצמרת] ἀμφηκῆ 𝔊L. — והוא יצא] 𝔊B has a double translation, καὶ ἡ μάχαιρα ἐξῆλθεν, καὶ αὐτὴ ἐξῆλθεν. Both of these indicate that *the sword* is the subject of the verb, which should therefore be יצאה. Kl. proposes והוא הוציא: *and he took it out.* But that the sword *fell* has as little place in the narrative as it had before all these emendations. That Joab had one sword (or dagger) concealed under his clothing in his left hand, while he ostentatiously let his usual weapon fall to the ground to disarm suspicion (Kl., Dr.) is certainly very obscurely stated in the emended text. — **9.** ותחז] for ותאחז like ויוחר of the *Qrê,* v.⁵. — **12.** מתגלל] πεφυρμένος 𝔊B does not seem to indicate a different text. 𝔊L inserts τεθνηκὼς καί, evidently reading מת as a separate word. That וימת is said above is against the insertion; on the other hand the statement that he *died* would not preclude the assertion that he still moved convulsively where he lay. — כל־הבא עליו ועמד] is quite regular. But it is possible that the ו of the last word is erroneous duplication of the preceding ו. In this case it is better to connect עליו with the following: *every comer stood over him,* so 𝔊L. Bu. thinks the whole clause, from כאשר, to be a later insertion, while Kl. supposes it to belong earlier in the verse. — **13.** כאשר] we should probably prefix ויהי with 𝔊L. — הגה] most satisfactorily accounted for as Hiphil of יגה, and probably with the suffix, for הוגו (הונגהו).

14–22. The death of Sheba. — As might be expected, the rebellion was of short duration. Sheba seems to have had comparatively little following, and with his death peace was restored. — **14.** *He went through all the tribes of Israel to Abel Beth Maacah*] as the coming of the army of Joab is told in the fol-

lowing verse, the subject is probably Sheba. The city was one of the most northerly possessed by Israel. It is identified by Robinson with the present *Abil* or *Abil el Kamh* in the upper Jordan valley. The rest of the verse is obscure. It seems intended to assert that Sheba's following was made up of his own clan. — **15**. Here he was besieged : *they raised a mound at the city, and it stood with the wall*] that is, *even with it*, to the same height. It was a favourite device in ancient sieges to raise a mound of earth to the same height with the besieged wall. This gave the besiegers command of the wall, and allowed them to throw a bridge to it. The earth was brought in baskets and *poured out* to make the mound. In addition, *all the men of Joab were devising to throw down the wall*] by the various methods which, as experienced warriors, they knew. — **16**. A *wise woman* asks a conference with Joab. — **17**. The interview is opened. — **18, 19**. *They used to say formerly : Let them ask in Abel and in Dan whether what the faithful in Israel established has come to an end?* The question implies that in these cities Israelitic custom was maintained if anywhere. The reproach upon Joab is evident if he will now wipe out such *a city and mother in Israel*] that is, a city looked up to with the veneration which a mother should receive. The text has suffered, but can be restored with a good degree of probability. — **20, 21**. Joab disclaims the purpose ascribed to him, but sets forth the cause of the siege. If Sheba alone were given up, the siege should cease. The woman promises that his head shall be *thrown out through the wall*. — **22**. The woman persuades the people, Sheba is put to death, and the siege terminates.

14. ויעבר] it seems almost necessary to read עבר והוא making the reference to Sheba. — ובית] as only one city is besieged we should read בית here as in v.¹⁵, Ew. *GVI*³. III. p. 264, E. Trans. III. p. 195. On the site of Abel, cf. Robinson, *BR*². III. p. 372; Baedeker, *Palestine*², p. 263. The town lies on a hill in the fertile valley west of *Tell el Kadi*, in which the springs of the Jordan have their rise. — וכל־הברים] we have no trace of *Beerites* who belong in this connexion. 𝔊ᴮ seems to have read וכל־בכרי : 𝔊ᴸ וכל־עיר: another group of MSS. represent וכל־העדים: *omnesque electi* 𝕃 and Arm., would render וכל־הבחורים. The last is accepted as the original reading by Th. and others, whereas Kl. on the ground of 𝔊ᴮ reads וכל־הבכרים, that is, Sheba's own clan. — ויקלהו] ויקהלו *Qrê*. The latter is favoured by the versions.

But the *Ktîb* also has claims. If it means *and they treated him with contempt*, it would account for the small strength which he showed in the sequel. — אף] is lacking in 𝔊. *And as for all the Bichrites, they gathered and came in* [to Abel] *after him* (Dr.) is perhaps the best that can be done, but is not entirely satisfactory. My own conjecture is that ויבאו וגו is duplication of the first clause of verse [15] and that the original stated that *all the young men esteemed him lightly* (הקלוהו) *and came and besieged him*, that is: the people had already taken measures to defeat him before the coming of Joab. But this is probably as subjective as the other conjectures. — **15.** ותעמד בחל] seems plainly to mean *and it stood with the wall*, so that it is unnecessary with Keil to make חל the *moat*. But We., Kl., Bu., make it refer to the wise woman and prefix משחיתים] *were laying waste*, which is the ordinary meaning, does not fit well here. Ew. proposes to make it denominative from שחת: *were digging a pit*, that is, *were undermining* the wall. — מתעשתין 𝔗 seems here to agree with 𝔊 ἐνοοῦσαν (ἐνενόουν) which We. supposes to represent מחשבים (adopted by Kl., Dr., Bu.). — **16.** אשה חכ׳ מן־העיר] is transferred by Kl. (Bu.) to the verse above, where ותצא is prefixed to it. The text thus constructed undoubtedly makes good sense, but it is difficult to see how it could have been changed into what we have. — העיר] + ואמר 𝔊𝔖. — **18.** לאמר] is superfluous, and is lacking in 𝔊[L]. — דבר] λόγος 𝔊 is probably correct: they used to have *a proverb*. The contents of the proverb are obscure in 𝔥: *let them ask in Abel, and so they ended* must mean that people sought wisdom in Abel. But the commendation of the wisdom of the town would have no special influence with Joab. With this text moreover we have difficulty in the following verse. From the duplicate translation of 𝔊 we easily extract one which makes a better sense. For the words extending from וכן in this verse through ישראל, v.[19] substitute ובכן הָתַמּו אשר שמו אמוני ישראל since Ew. (III. p. 264) generally adopted. The proverb will then mean that the two neighbouring cities of Abel and Dan knew what tradition had established; they were the seats of genuine Israelitic life. Such cities Joab might well hesitate to destroy. — אתה] should probably be ואתה 𝔊[L]. — להמית] should be לשחת as pointed out by Nestle (*Marg.* p. 20) on the ground of אשחית at the end of the next verse. — **22.** העם] 𝔊 inserts καὶ ἐλάλησεν πρὸς πᾶσαν τὴν πόλιν which seems necessary to the sense. The resemblance of העם and העיר may account for the omission.

23-26. The officers of the administration are here repeated, with some variations from 8[16-18], or, more probably, are original here and copied in the other document. The names of Joab, Benaiah, Jehoshaphat, Zadok, are the same in both lists. *Seraiah* there is represented by *Sheya* or *Shewa* here; probably both are corrupted from a common source. *Abiathar* in this passage is more in accordance with what we know of the history than is *Ahimelech ben Abiathar* of the other. New in this passage, as compared with the other, is *Adoram* (Adoniram), who is said to have been *over the forced labour*, the *corvée* which is inseparable from an oriental monarchy, cf. Jd. 1²⁸ and Moore's note. As we can conceive of a reason for the omission of this *datum*, in the desire to shield David from the imputation of tyranny, we may suppose it original here. The other discrepancy is in substituting *Ira the Jairite* as *priest* in the place of *David's sons*. The author or editor in putting this list here evidently designed it to mark the close of the account of David's reign. The main narrative, which is continued in 1 K. 1, goes on to the accession of Solomon, the coronation of Adonijah being simply a prelude to the reign of his brother.

23. אל] should of course be על, as in 8¹⁶ 1 Chr. 18¹⁵. In both those passages we have simply הצבא instead of כל הצ׳ ישראל. The latter is ungrammatical and ישראל should be stricken out — it is lacking in 12 MSS. of 𝔊 (Parsons). — הכרי] for the more common הכרתי, possibly simply a textual error. The form הכרי occurs in 2 K. 11⁴·¹⁹. But as the author of 2 Sam. always uses הכרתי it seems better to restore that form here with *Qrê* and 𝔊ᴮ (Χελεθθεί), ᴬ (Χερεθθεί). — **24.** וארדם] as 𝔊ᴮ reads *Adoniram* here, and an officer of Solomon named Adoniram was also *over the forced labour*, it is natural to identify the men and the names. — **25.** ושיא *Kt*, ושוא *Qrê*, see on 8¹⁷. 𝔊ᴮ has ᾽Ιησοῦς here, 𝔊ᴸ Σουσά. — **26.** עירא] two of David's mighty men bear the name, 23²⁶·³⁸. One of them is possibly the same person with this one. He is called however in 23³⁸ 1 Chr. 11⁴⁰ היתרי. 𝔊ᴸ reads ὁ ᾽Ιέθερ here and 𝔖 has רמן יחיר. There is no intrinsic difficulty in the way of reading *Jairite* however, and the identity with the Jetherite (or Jathrite) of 23³⁸ is only a conjecture.

XXI.–XXIV. Four chapters are here inserted which break the connexion of the narrative, for this once made 1 K. 1¹ follow immediately after 20²⁶. It seems as if the compiler threw together the fragments which were left after completing the main narrative and put them here, because they belonged in the reign of David, and he did not know where else to put them. Examination shows however that they were probably inserted at different times. First an editor put in 21¹⁻¹⁴ and 24, two narratives of calamity which belong together. The two were then forcibly separated by the list of exploits and heroes which occupies 21¹⁵⁻²² 23⁸⁻³⁹. And this again was cut in two by the two Psalms 22 and 23¹⁻⁷. We have nowhere a better illustration of the complexity of the process by which our books reached their present form.

XXI. 1–14. The famine and the expiation. — The narrative seems to be old and good. But it is not in its proper place chronologically. There is reason to suppose that it was omitted by the author of 9–20, because he had enough unfavourable features without it. We may be glad that a succeeding editor found the story and transcribed it, for few sections of the Old Testament show more clearly the religious ideas of the time. We see how Yahweh as the avenger of a broken covenant requires from the children of the offender the blood that has been shed.

1. The famine was a mark of Yahweh's displeasure, *and David sought the face of Yahweh*] to inquire the occasion. The reply is : *there is blood upon Saul and upon his house because he slew the Gibeonites*] the blood of a murdered man rests upon the murderer Dt. 19¹⁰, cf. Jd. 9²⁴ 2 S. 1¹⁶, and the case of Lady Macbeth. — **2.** The narrative is interrupted by a parenthesis. Whether such an explanation as the parenthesis gives was needed by the first readers of the story is doubtful. If an explanation were necessary, moreover, the author would put it after the first mention of the Gibeonites and not when David's speech has been introduced. For these reasons the verse (after the first five words) is now generally regarded as a gloss, including also the first three words of v.³. It should be noticed however that the interpolation makes no mention of Joshua, so that probably the glossator had no knowledge of the narrative which now stands in Jos. 9. — *The Children of Israel had sworn to them*] such covenants were very common during the process which ended in the establishment of Israel in Canaan. — *But Saul sought to smite them in his zeal for the Children of Israel and Judah*] as in some other places, Judah seems to be an afterthought. — **3.** David's inquiry is : *what shall I do to you, and wherewith shall I make expiation*] the verb is used of the (priestly) work of removing Yahweh's anger, generally by an offering. The result would be : *that ye may bless the heritage of Yahweh*] that is, bring a blessing on Israel. — **4.** The reply of the Gibeonites consists of two parts. For one thing, they will not accept blood money — it is not a question of silver and gold between them and Saul. On the other hand, they are not so bloodthirsty as to require victims from Israel at large. David

inquires further : *What do you say that I shall do for you ?* —
5, 6. The expiation shall be made by the family of the murderer :
*As for the man who consumed us and who thought to destroy us
that we should not remain in all the border of Israel, let seven of
his sons be given us and we will expose them before Yahweh*] that
the sins of the father should be visited upon the children is a
matter of course. The expiation was to be made *in Gibeon in the
mount of Yahweh*] as we learn from the history of Solomon, a
celebrated sanctuary existed at Gibeon. The received text has
corrupted the original reading to *in Gibeah of Saul, the chosen of
Yahweh*. — **7**. A note to the effect that David screened Meribbaal his client from the vengeance that would otherwise have
overtaken him. — **8**. The victims actually taken were two sons
of Rizpah, the concubine who was the occasion of Abner's revolt,
and the five sons of Merab] so we should read, for it was Merab
who was given to Adriel, 1 S. 18[19]. The name of Michal's husband was Paltiel. — **9**. The Gibeonites exposed the seven as they
had determined, *and the seven of them fell together*] the verb is
hardly appropriate if the victims were suspended above the
earth. The time of the year was harvest, which comes in April
or May.

1. אל־שאול ואל־בית הדמים] the preposition is to be changed to על, the
accents are to be disregarded, and the ה is to be made the suffix of בית; read
therefore על ביתה דמים, so 𝕲 (We.). — **2.** האמרי] as in some other passages, a
comprehensive name for the early inhabitants of Canaan. — בקנאתו] cf. 1 K.
19[10. 14]. — **3.** וברכו] the imperative is used to express the purpose of the preceding verb, cf. 1 S. 12[17]; Dr. *Tenses* [3], § 65; Davidson, *Syntax*, § 65 *d*, Ges.[26]
§ 110 *i*. — **4.** לי] is changed unnecessarily to לנו by the *Qrê*. — עם־שאול] the
assertion that they *have no silver and no gold in possession of Saul* only says
that they will not put forward a claim for material damages. The *blood-wit*
was forbidden by the later legislation, Num. 35[31], but is evidently regarded as
allowable in our text. — ואין־לנו איש להמית] *and we have no man to slay* does
not seem appropriate. 𝕲[L] transposes two words, איש להמית, which is smoother.
— מה־אתם אמרים אעשה לכם] as pointed out by Dr., the present text must be
translated as above. 𝕲[L] seems to have read ואעשה which would then be the
apodosis : *whatever you say I will do.* — **5.** נִשְׁמַדְנוּ] cannot be used in this
form. It would be possible to point נִשְׁמַדְנוּ as is done by one of the renderings found in 𝕲. This would require a change in the pointing of דמה. It
seems also that the apodosis begins with ינתן of the next verse. The probability
therefore favours a change of לנו נשמדנו into להשמידנו (We. adopted by Bu.).

The construction would then be parallel to Jd. 20⁵. Ew. proposed לישמרנו apparently retaining לנו.—**6.** וינתן] the *Qrê* changes to a Hophal without apparent cause.—והוקענום] the verb is used Num. 25⁴ of some form of execution, precisely what is difficult to determine. 𝔊ᴮ has here ἐξηλιάσωμεν and the other Greek versions use words meaning *to impale* or *to hang*. W. R. Smith supposes it to mean *cast over a precipice*. 𝔗 also makes it mean *to hang* or *crucify*. But this is contradicted for this passage by ויפלו below.—בגבעת שאול]
ἐν Γαβαὼν Σαούλ 𝔊ᴮ. Two MSS. omit the name of Saul. The narrative is favourable to Gibeon as the site of the expiation. Saul has come in by mistake.—בחיר יהוה] in v.⁹ we find that the men were exposed כהר לפני יהוה.
It is therefore probable that בהר יהוה was original here (We., Bu.).—**8.** The name of one of Rizpah's sons appears in the distorted form given to the son of Jonathan.—מיכל] two codd. of 𝔐 have מרב which is represented also in 𝔊ᴸ𝔗. The latter alone agrees with the statement 1 S. 18¹⁹.—**9.** ויפלו]
is changed by Kl. into ויתלו, on the supposition that ויקיעם means they *hung* them. שבעתם is to be read, as indicated in the margin. The *Qrê* also demands והמה for יהם, but this does not seem necessary. The last clause drags awkwardly and is perhaps a scribal expansion, בראשנים is lacking in 𝔊ᴸ.—
תחלת] is perfectly intelligible as the accusative of circumstance, without the preposition which is prefixed by the *Qrê*.

10. The devotion of Rizpah is seen in her watching the bodies day and night : *and she did not permit the birds of the heaven to rest upon them by day, nor the wild beasts by night*] the last clause naturally implies that the bodies were not suspended above the ground, but rested on the earth. That this continued for some time is indicated by the pains taken to say that it lasted *from the beginning of harvest until water was poured out upon them from heaven*. But whether this means until the beginning of the regular autumn rains is impossible to say. So long an exposure of corpses is in glaring inconsistency with Dt. 21²²ᶠ, all the more that it is here done to propitiate the Deity.—**11, 12**. When David was told of the fidelity of Rizpah, *he went and took the bones of Saul and of Jonathan from the citizens of Jabesh Gilead who had stolen them*, as narrated above.—**14.** These with the bones of the exposed— that the bones alone remained shows that the exposure had lasted a considerable time—*he buried in Zela in the sepulchre of Kish his father*] the locality is unknown. That *God was propitiated toward the land after this* is the conclusion of this narrative. The propitiation was not wrought by the burial but by the execution of the men.

10. השׂק] *the* cloth which she would naturally wear as a mourner. This *she spread upon the rock*, to lie upon, we must suppose. — אל] for עַל as often. — קציר] 𝔊 adds κριθῶν, which is perhaps original. — **11.** At the end of the verse 𝔊^{AB al.} adds: καὶ ἐξελύθησαν, καὶ κατέλαβεν αὐτοὺς Δὰν υἱὸς Ἰωὰ ἐκ τῶν ἀπογόνων τῶν γιγάντων. 𝔊^L has the same words at the end of v.¹⁰. They seem to have wandered hither from v.¹⁶. — **12.** תלום] Why the Qrê should want to substitute תלאים is incomprehensible. — שׂם הפלשׁתים] the Qrê assumes that the division of words is wrong, but again without internal probability. — **14.** ויקברו] perhaps we should read ויקברם: *and he buried them with the bones of Saul.* 𝔊 inserts after Jonathan, *the bones of the exposed.*

15–22. The fate of four Philistine champions. — The section is part of a summary containing the exploits of David and his men. It seems to belong with 5¹⁷⁻²⁵, though that passage relates victories over the Philistine army, while this gives exploits of individual soldiers. — **15.** War broke out, and David and his men *went down* — from Hebron apparently. There was war *again*, indicates that this is taken from a more extended history. — **16.** The text is corrupt. It gave originally the name of a Philistine who was one of the Rephaites. The name is now lost, and even the description given of him is unintelligible. All we make out is that *he thought to slay David.* — **17.** Abishai delivered his captain, and David's men took an oath that the king should not go to battle with them any more *and quench the light of Israel.* Compare *the coal that is left* of the Thekoite woman. — **18.** That there was war *again* in Gob implies that the preceding war had been in the same locality. The place is mentioned nowhere except in this chapter. — *Sibbechai the Hushathite*] a Bethlehemite family is named Hushah, 1 Chr. 4⁴. — **19.** In another campaign *Elhanan ben Jair the Bethlehemite slew Goliath the Gittite*] the harmonistic purpose of the Chronicler in making the victim *the brother of Goliath* is evident. — **20.** Still another *tall man* with the curious physical deformity of six fingers on each hand and six toes on each foot is mentioned as belonging to the same family. — **21.** His challenge to Israel brought upon him the fate of his brothers. — **22.** The verse sums up the paragraph — four champions of one family were slain by David and his men.

15. ויעף דוד] is suspicious and probably corrupt; 𝔊^B reads καὶ ἐπορεύθη Δαυείδ. Had the Philistine attacked him when weary, a more explicit statement would have been made. — **16.** ‏[ויישכו בנכ]‏ ‏(ויישבי‏ *Qrê*) cannot be a proper name. Taking the words by themselves, we should naturally connect them with the preceding verse in the sense, *and they dwelt* (that is, *camped*) *in Nob*, only for the name of the place we should read *Gob* as in v.¹⁸. This is adopted by We., Dr., Bu., who agree in inserting the words after ‏עמו‏ of the preceding verse — perhaps the best we can do, though the displacement is difficult to account for. It is possible that in ‏בנכ אשר‏ we have ‏בן‏ with a mutilated proper name; 𝔊ᴸ reads καὶ Δαδοῦ υἱὸς Ἰωάς where the first name seems a corruption of ‏דור‏. For ‏בילירי‏ we should probably read ‏מילירי‏. The name ‏הרפה‏ is apparently an eponym. — ‏[קינו]‏ would be *his lance*, but it is more probable that the weight of some other piece of armour would be given, as 1 S. 17³⁸ where we find the helmet, ‏קובע‏, which therefore may be restored with some probability here (Kl., Bu.). ‏משקל‏ seems to be an error for ‏שקל‏. The clause *and he was girded with a new* is of course unintelligible without the name of the piece of armour which he had on; 𝔊ᴮ gives κορύνην, *a club*, which however is not girded on like a sword; 𝔊ᴸ and Theodotion παραζώνην. Lagarde conjectures ‏רשנה‏ (the form of the clause naturally points to David as the subject, Kl.). — **17.** ‏[לו]‏ after ‏דור‏ is probably to be omitted, with 𝔊. — **18.** For ‏נב‏ here many codd. have ‏ננ‏, whereas 𝔊ᴮ and 𝔖 read *Gath*, 𝔊ᴸ Γαζέθ, and the parallel, 1 Chr. 20⁴ has ‏גזר‏. In this confusion it seems best to retain the reading of 𝔐, which is more likely to have been replaced by a well-known name than the reverse. — **19.** ‏[יערי ארגים]‏ is hardly a man's name and the ‏ארגים‏ has plainly crept in from the line below. For ‏יערי‏ it seems better to restore also ‏יעור‏ or ‏יעיר‏ with Chr. — **20.** ‏[איש מדין]‏ (‏מדון‏ *Qrê*) is probably intended to mean *a man of strife*. But from the context we infer that ‏איש מדה‏ of Chr. is original. On six-fingered persons, the commentators refer to Pliny, *Hist. Nat.* XI. 43. — ‏[מספר]‏ read ‏במספר‏ (Kl.). — **21.** ‏[שמעי]‏ ‏שמעא‏ *Qrê* is also the reading of Chr. The same person is called ‏שמעה‏ in 13³. — **22.** On the use of the accusative sign with the subject of passive verbs, cf. König, *Syntax*, § 108 f., Davidson, *Syntax*, § 79.

XXII. David's song of triumph.

— A psalm is here introduced which is found also in our Psalter (Ps. 18). It there has a title which seems adopted from this place, and the indications point to this as the earlier place for it. The text has suffered in the copy now before us (as we might expect) more than in the Psalter.

The poet begins with an expression of trust in Yahweh, vv.²⁻⁴. He then recounts his experience of calamity and deliverance, ⁵⁻²⁰. He affirms his uprightness, which he believes to be the reason why he enjoys the divine favour, ²¹⁻³⁰. He praises God as the source of his strength and success, ³¹⁻⁴⁶, and closes with a doxology, ⁴⁷⁻⁵¹. Allusions to specific events in the life of David cannot be discovered. The description of misfortune is conveyed in general terms, such as any one might use who had been in deep trouble. The theophany which brings deliverance is set forth in terms not unlike those used by the other Old Testament poets. Where the poet speaks of his own deserts it is impossible to suppose that he has David's experience in mind. The impression made by the Psalm is that it is the utterance of a man speaking for the company of the faithful and embodying their experience in words. For these reasons it is difficult to suppose the composition to be David's own.

As many excellent commentaries on the Psalter are accessible to the student, it is unnecessary to give here any extended exposition of this psalm, or a translation of it. I shall content myself with notes on the various readings which are discovered by comparing this text with that of Ps. 18.

1. The title here begins with וידבר דוד. The compiler of the Psalter, in accordance with his custom, prefixed למנצח לעבד יהוה לדוד and was then obliged to change to אשר דבר. For ומכף he reads ומיד, which is certainly no improvement.

2. The psalm here opens with יהוה סלעי, while Ps. 18 prefixes a clause ארחמך יהוה חזקי, and the same is found in 𝔊ᴸ. The insertion seems to weaken the force of the opening, so that in this instance our text seems original. That a psalmist took the liberty of expanding his text is only what we should expect from the history of hymnology. — לי] is lacking in Ps. and is in fact superfluous. It is a question whether מפלטי ought not also to be stricken out. The metre and the sense are complete without it :

> *Yahweh is my rock and my fortress ;*
> *My God is my crag in whom I trust.*

3. אלהי] should probably be pointed אלהי; Ps. reproduces the word in the form אלי, which is unmistakable. From ומנס Ps. omits, and apparently with good cause, for the clause is quite out of keeping with the rest of the verse.

5. כי] lacking in Ps. and 𝔊ᴸ, is therefore suspicious. משברי is clearly to be preferred to חבלי Ps. — **7.** אקרא] in the second clause is intolerable : אשוע Ps. is far better. After ושועתי add חבא from the לפניו תבא of Ps. — **8.** ותגעש] Kt. and Ps., evidently has הארץ for its subject. The Qrê ויתגעש perhaps intends Yahweh as subject : *He shook himself* (with wrath) and the earth trembled; in this case however another verb would probably have been chosen, as יתגער, Nestle, *Marginalien*, p. 21. — ומוסרי הרים [ומוסדות השמים Ps. The latter is to be preferred, for the *foundations of heaven* are nowhere else mentioned. —

11. וירא] וידא Ps.; the latter is far finer, cf. Dt. 28⁴⁹. — **12.** After חשך insert סתרו Ps., and read סכתו for סכות. We thus get a good parallelism:

וישת חשך סתרו
סביבתיו סכתו

The word חשרת is obscure; חשכת Ps. is favoured by 𝕲ᴮ σκότος while 𝕲ᴸ ἐφείσατο seems to have read חשׂך. — **13.** The verse as it stands consists of but one member, whereas Ps. has two. The latter is doubtless original, except that בערו is to be retained instead of עָברו.

14. וירעם] Ps. 𝕲ᴸ and 𝕾 unite in prefixing ו. — **15.** The second member is too short; Ps. has וברקים רב ויהמם. I conjecture וברקים רמה ויהמם. There seems to be no reason for the Qrê ויהם. — **16.** ויגלו] the form ויגלו Ps. agrees better with the sense in this verse. The tense changes in v.¹⁷ in order to a more vivid presentation of the actual deliverance. — **18.** עז] מאיבי is difficult to construe. Apparently כי has dropped out after מאיבי. — **19.** משען] read למשען with Ps. and codd. mult. — **23.** משפטיו Qrê is favoured by Ps. and the parallelism. — ממנה] is difficult after the plural and probably to be read ממני (מני Ps.), and this involves the reading אסיר (Ps.): οὐκ ἀποστήσεται ἀπ' ἐμοῦ 𝕲ᴸ: οὐκ ἀπέστην ἀπ' αὐτῶν 𝕲ᴮ. — **26.** ונבור] is certainly out of place: גבר Ps. is confirmed by 𝕲. — **27.** תתבר] is an evident error for תתברר Ps. One ר has dropped out. — תתפל] תתפתל Ps., a similar case of carelessness. — **28.** The second clause gives no suitable sense. For ועיניך על־רמים read ועינים רמות Ps.

29. The assertion *Thou art my torch* seems to have been too bold for the Psalmist, who changes into: *Thou lightest my torch.* The probability seems in favour of our text. In the second member however read ואלהי for ויהוה. — **30.** The second half of the verse speaks of leaping a wall. It seems clear that the parallelism requires גדר instead of גדוד, and this calls for אָרִץ (Lag., *Proph. Chald.*, p. xlvi) instead of ארוץ. — **31.** The second clause is perhaps an interpolation, as it breaks the parallelism (Kl.).

32. For the second מבלעדי, Ps. substitutes זולתי which many codd. have here. The dissimilation is more elegant. — **33.** מעוזי חיל] seems to give no suitable sense, whereas המאזרני חיל Ps. is excellent. — ויתר] seems to be a corruption of ויתן Ps., and דרכי Qrê is to be adopted. — **34.** רגלי Qrê and Ps. is correct. — **35.** ונחתה] ונחתה Ps., neither one giving a suitable sense. The passage seems to require *and makes my arms like a bow of bronze.* ויתן will hardly do, for the same verb follows immediately — perhaps וישת would meet the conditions. — **36.** וענתך] the word seems to be nowhere else applied to God, and is incongruous in this passage; καὶ ἡ ὑπακοή σου 𝕲ᴮ: καὶ ἡ παιδεία σου 𝕲ᴸ if taken to mean *and thy discipline* [obedience to thee] *brought me up* would be appropriate, but both מוסרך and תוכחתך are somewhat remote in form from the word in the text. Other conjectures are unsatisfactory. — **39.** ואכלם] is doubtless erroneous duplication of the preceding word (lacking in Ps.). — **40.** ותחזרני] another spelling for ותאזרני Ps. — **41.** תתה] has lost its נ — a case of simple carelessness like some others in this chapter. — **42.** וישעו] *they looked* would be possible, but יִשָׁעֵנִי Ps. is confirmed by 𝕲. — **43.**]אדקם ארקעם one of the two words is superfluous. The reading has come about by conflation, as is shown by אריקם Ps. and codd. אדקם alone fits the context. — **44.**]עַמִי is hardly appropriate; עָם Ps. is better, but still better would be עַמִים, parallel with גוים. For תשמרני substitute תשימני Ps. 𝕲ᴸ has a very different sense for this verse. — **45.** Ps. inverts the order of the clauses (also 𝕲ᴸ), which is better. — **46.**]יבלו as pointed, gives a strained sense. The conjecture of Kl. יובלו לי, adopted by Bu., has everything in its favour. —]ויחגרו is equally unfortunate, but corrected by Ps. ויחרגו.

47.]צור is superfluous and omitted by Ps. 𝕲ᴸ, while 𝕲ᴮ seems to have read נצר. — **50.** אזמרה Ps. is the better form. — **51.**]מגדיל there seems to be no reason for the *Qrê.*

XXIII. 1–7. David's last words. — The psalm here introduced is intended to give David a Testament like that of Jacob and Moses. The contents however are obscure and the text is corrupt. Both vocabulary and thought show it to be a comparatively late production.

1. After the title we have the ostensible author's introduction of himself:

> *Oracle of David ben Jesse,*
> *Oracle of the man set on high,*
> *The Anointed of the God of Jacob*
> *And the Joy of the songs of Israel.*

2, 3ᵃ. A second introductory stanza, assuring the hearer that what is spoken is divinely inspired:

> *The Spirit of Yahweh spoke in me,*
> *And his word was on my tongue;*
> *The God of Jacob said to me,*
> *The Rock of Israel spoke:*

3ᵇ, 4. The oracle now follows, and is evidently intended as a panegyric upon the just ruler:

> *One ruling over men, a righteous man,*
> *Ruling in the fear of God;*
> *Like the light of the morning shall he rise,*
> *The sun of a cloudless morn,*
> *Making the green earth brilliant after rain.*

5. The poet reflects on the divine revelation just vouchsafed :

> *Verily, sure is my house with God,*
> *For an eternal covenant he made with me,*
> *Set in order in all things, and he will keep it,*
> *For all my salvation and all my delight are in him.*

The text has suffered, and the last clause is quite unintelligible. The above restoration is only provisional.

6, 7. Some violence is needed to get a sense out of the present text. By conjecture we may restore the following :

> *But vile men shall not flourish,*
> *They are like thorns of the desert, all of them,*
> *Which are not harvested by the hand,*
> *Nor doth a man labour for them.*
> *Though armed with iron and spear*
> *They shall be utterly consumed with fire.*

The subject of the last couplet is no longer the thorns, but the wicked men, of which they are a type.

1. The versions differ extraordinarily in their understanding of the Psalm, and their apprehension is usually a misapprehension. — נאם] is used of a divine communication nearly if not quite always. — ונאם] I have omitted the ו with 1 cod. of 𝔐, also 𝕷𝕲L and 𝔖. — הקם] is for הוקם, which is found in a number of codd. — הקם על] the construction is difficult, the only parallels to this use of על being Hos. 7¹⁶ 11⁷, both corrupt passages : ὃν ἀνέστησεν ὁ θεός 𝕲L (κύριος 𝕲B) may point to הקים עליון. The last clause can hardly mean the *sweet singer of Israel.* — **3.** For the first *Israel* I have substituted *Jacob* with 𝕷 and 𝕴. It is possible that לי should be supplied before מושל (ו), so that Yahweh would say *I have a ruler,* that is, *I have found a ruler.* — ויראת] a number of codd. interpret correctly in writing ביראת. — **4.** וכאור] the ו is omitted by 𝕲L𝔖𝕷; it is however quite in place as introducing the sequence. — מננה] should be a participle, perhaps a Piel, though that form does not occur elsewhere. Otherwise read מַגִּיחַ. Kl. proposes מצמיח, מחיה or מְנֹבֵב; the last is adopted by Bu. — ממטר] 𝕲𝕷 seem to have read כמטר, which would better be adopted if we change the preceding word to מנבב — *like rain making the green of the earth to spring.* The influence of a beneficent ruler is elsewhere likened to *showers that water the earth.* — **5.** כי־לא־כן] gives just the opposite of the desired meaning. I see in לא the strongly affirmative particle לָא, which we have met occasionally elsewhere. — וישמרה] is pointed as a passive participle by 𝔐 : καὶ φυλάξει αὐτήν 𝕲L seems to be better. — ישעי] it does not appear what 𝕲L has in mind in translating τὸν ἀντίθετόν μοι : adversantem mihi 𝕴. — חפץ] should be חפצי apparently. — כי לא יצמיח] as above remarked, is unintelligible. Kl. proposes to read כי־לו־יצמח, making the whole sentence a promise of God: *all my help and all my good pleasure shall spring up for him* (that is, for David). It seems to me better to throw out the לא יצמיח, as having strayed in from another place (Nestle, *Marginalien*, p. 22), and to close the verse with וכל־חפצי בו. — **6.** 𝕲ᴮ begins the verse with כי לא יצמיח from the end of the preceding, and this agrees better with the rhythm. — ובליעל] omit ו 𝕲ᴮ. — מנד] does not seem appropriate; read מדבר with Kl., Bu. For קוץ, Perles (*Analekten*, p. 53) proposes קֹץ, in which case we should read כמוץ מרה. For יקחו, I propose ילקטו — the worthlessness of the thorns is seen in the fact that no one cares to gather them. — **7.** The reading just given naturally carries with it the reading ייגע instead of יגע (confirmed by 𝕲), and makes this clause parallel to the one preceding. — ימלא] is incomprehensible: ἐὰν μή 𝕲ᴸ points to אם־לא. But the negative does not fit, and I conjecture אם־לו or perhaps better אם למו — *if they have iron* as their defence. — חנית] διακόψῃ αὐτούς 𝕲ᴸ, perhaps חצב in some form. — בשבת] which is quite superfluous, has come in by error from the next verse.

8–39. The catalogue of David's knights.

The author throws together a list of the men who distinguished themselves in David's wars and who in consequence were enrolled in a special band. The section agrees in tenor with 21¹⁵⁻²² and seems to be a part of the same document. It is copied in 1 Chr. 11¹¹⁻⁴¹ᵃ where the text is in a number of cases better preserved.

8. First mentioned is *Ishbaal the Hachmonite chief of the Three*] that is, of the distinguished band which ranked above all except the commander in chief. — *He swung his spear over eight hundred slain at one time*] cf. v.¹⁸. — **9.** *And after him was Eleazar ben Dodo the Ahohite*] an Ahoah is mentioned among the Benjamite clans, 1 Chr. 8⁴. — *He was with David at Pas-Dammim and the Philistines gathered there*] the text is that of the Chronicler. *Pas-Dammim* is the *Ephes-Dammim* of 1 S. 17¹. — **10.** Beginning the sentence with the last clause of the preceding we read: *And the men of Israel retreated, but he stood and smote the Philistines until his hand was weary and clave fast to the sword*] the muscles became so stiff that he could not relax them. So in our own times, an Arab champion boasted: "The Kusman perished before me until the evening, when my fingers could not be loosed from the handle of the sword."* — **11.** The third is *Shammah ben Agee the Hararite*. His exploit was when *the Philistines gathered*

---

* Doughty, *Travels in Arabia Deserta*, II. p. 28.

at Lehi] cf. Jd. 15⁹. — *And there was a plot of ground full of len-
tiles*] a well-known crop, for which however the Chronicler here
substitutes *barley*. — **12.** *He stationed himself in the middle of the
field and defended it*] literally *delivered it.* The account of these
three was to all appearance originally concluded by ¹⁷ᵇ : *These
things did the three heroes.* The connexion is now broken by the
following paragraph which relates the joint deed of three of the
heroes.

8. וישב בשבת] has not the appearance of a proper name : ישבעם בן Chr.:
'Ιεβόσθε 𝕲ᴮ : 'Ιεσβάαλ 𝕲ᴸ. From the last reading we suspect the original to
have been ישבעל (אשבעל) which some scribe corrected in well-known fashion
to ישבשת which gave rise to the reading of 𝕳. Chr. mutilates by changing the
last letter only. — חכמוני [תחכמני Chr. The latter looks more like the original; the ת of the former probably represents the article : ὁ Χαναναῖος 𝕲ᴮ : υἱὸς
Θεκεμανεί 𝕲ᴸ. It is possible, as supposed by Bu., that the name of the man's
father has dropped out and that we may supply it from 1 Chr. 27² where we
find ישבעם בן־זבריאל. But as in 1 Chr. 27³² we find another man called also
בן־חכמני, this is not certain. — ראש השלשי] would naturally be *the third captain,* that is, next in rank to Joab and Abishai. Chr. has however ראש השלישים,
chief of the Thirty, or ר׳ השלישים Qrê, *chief of the picked men.* We are wholly
helpless in the endeavour to decide between these readings. To them 𝕲ᴮ
adds ἄρχων τοῦ τρίτου, *captain of the third* (division ?), 𝕲ᴸ πρῶτος τῶν τριῶν :
We. conjectures ראש השלשה, that is *chief of* this first *three;* while Kl. supposes a statement that he was *a Shalishite,* that is a native of *Rosh* (elsewhere
Baal) *Shalisha.* Marquart in a somewhat extended discussion of this list
(*Fundamente Israelitischer und Jüdischer Geschichte,* 1896) adopts ישבעל
בח־חכמני ראש השלשה. The unmeaning collocation of words הוא עדינו העצנו is
not helped by the Qrê העצני. The original reading of 𝕲 seems to be preserved in 𝕲ᴸ : οὗτος διεκόσμει τὴν διασκευὴν αὐτῶν, hic adornavit adornationem
suam Ɩ (*Cod. Goth. Leg.*). This may represent הוא ערך את־כליו, or possibly
הוא עדר מערכם, compare 1 Chr. 12³⁹. But this does not help us in connexion
with what follows, and we are forced to adopt the parallel, 1 Chr. 11¹¹ : הוא
עורר את־חניתו. For שלש : שמנה Chr. The latter seems to have been purposely
changed, so as not to give Ishbaal more than Abishai. — **9.** דרי [רורו Qrê.
The latter form occurs also v.²⁴ Jd. 10¹ and 1 Chr. 11¹²⋅²⁶. On the other hand
we find דודי in 1 Chr. 27⁴ and as this is the natural contraction of דודיה it
may be original here (Marquart). — האחוחי [בן אחוחי Chr. which recurs in
v.²⁸ 1 Chr. 11²⁹ and 27⁴. Marquart (*l.c.*) conjectures בית־הלחמי. But the consensus of the four papers seems to me to favour the received text. בחרפם
בפלישתים, *in their bandying insults with the Philistines* is not bad in itself;
but the שם which follows indicates that the name of a place has preceded :
בפס דמים Chr. supplies one. This requires the insertion with Chr. of הוא היה
before שם. Marquart conjectures בעמק רפאים. In any case the following word

requires us to read והפלשתים Chr. for בפלשתים. The following clause, *and the men of Israel went up*, is unmeaning. Probably the author intended to continue the preceding *and overpowered the men of Israel;* καὶ ἀνεβόησεν ἀνὴρ Ἰσραήλ 𝔊ᴮ may be no more than a corruption of καὶ ἀνέβησαν ἀν. Ἰσ. 𝔊ᴸ and so not an independent witness. On the other hand it may conceivably represent ויצעקו which points to an original ויצעקו (Marquart). — **10.** Chr. omits from ויעלו v.⁹ to לחיה v.¹¹. — הוא] should be והוא. — **11.** ואחריו] ואחריו Qrê. — הררי] in v.³³ (1 Chr. 11³⁴) we have another *Hararite* and we should prefix the article here as there. 𝔊 however points to הארכי in this verse (Marq.). Kl. supposes this hero to be identical with שמעה בן אלא 1 K. 4¹⁸. — לחיה] is evidently intended as a proper name, in which case we must see in it the *Lehi* well known from the history of Samson. Ew. conjectured this (*GVI*³. III. p. 192, E. Tr. III. p. 141), and is confirmed by 𝔊ᴸ ἐπὶ σιαγόνα. — **12.** ויתיצב] Chr. deprives Shammah of his glory by making this and the two following verbs plural.

13–17ª. An exploit of three of the heroes is inserted here, because they were supposed to be the three just mentioned. The terms in which they are introduced does not however indicate this. — **13.** *Three of the Thirty*] implies that the Thirty have been mentioned, and shows the original place of the section. — They *came down to the mountain top, to David to the fortress of Adullam when a clan of the Philistines was encamped in the Valley of Rephaim*] the well-known scene of several battles. — **15.** David had a longing for the water he used to drink in his boyhood : *Oh, that one would give me to drink from the well of Bethlehem!* That there is now no well in the town does not prove anything for earlier times. — **16.** The three heroes *broke through the camp of the Philistines* to accomplish David's desire. He however would not drink the water *but poured it out to Yahweh*] as too precious for any other use. — **17.** *Yahweh forbid that I should do it ! This is the blood of the men who went at the risk of their lives*] the value thus put upon it shows David's appreciation of his knights quite as well as if he had drunk their present.

13. שלשה [שלשים Qrê, Chr. 𝔊, no doubt correctly. — ראש] it is difficult to suppose that the Thirty are all called chiefs in this connexion. If we change קציר to הצור it would be most natural to read ראש הצור, and suppose the intervening words the insertion of a scribe who connected ראש wrongly with what precedes. Chr. has only ראש על הצר. — אל-קציר] they certainly did not come *unto the harvest;* הצר Chr. 𝔊ᴸ is doubtless correct, and to be consistent we must make מצדת for מערת, confirmed by the next verse. — **14.** Possibly a gloss, as it is entirely unnecessary to the sense. This does not invalidate the **argu**ment just based on במצרה for it still shows that the glossator found מצרת in v.¹³. — **15.** מי ישקני] the question expresses a wish, as often. באר is naturally a well of living water — only such would account for David's desire. Perhaps because no well was known in later times, the margin substitutes בר here, and is followed by Chr., cf. Robinson, *BR²*, I. pp. 470, 473. — **17.** מאלהי [יהוה Chr. points to מיהוה which is found in many codd., and which is the more usual construction. — הרם] is difficult, because the question does not contain a verb. The Chronicler supplies the verb, but makes an awkward sentence which can hardly be original. Probably הרם is corrupted from זה דם or הוא דם (Bu.). The last clause of this verse appears to belong after v.¹², as already noted.

18, 19. The received text confuses the Three and the Thirty so as to contradict itself. It seems plain that the narrative knows only the two bands ; were there a *Second Three* it must be designated. Bearing this in mind and correcting the text accordingly, we may read of Abishai : *He was captain of the Thirty — he swung his spear over three hundred slain, so he got a name like that of the Three. He was more honourable than the Thirty and became their captain, but to the Three he did not attain.*

18. השלשה [השלשי *Qrê.* Neither of these can be right and it is necessary to read השלשים with two MSS. (We.). — ולו־שם בשלשה] there is no way in which Abishai could have a name among the Three without being enrolled among them, which is expressly denied in the next verse. Chr. and some MSS. read ולא for ולו, on the ground of which Marquart proposes ולא שים בש׳ which is the same thing stated at the end of v.¹⁹. I have conjectured ולו שם כשלשה which does not seem inappropriate, and departs very slightly from the text. — **19.** The first השלשה must be corrected as in the other case to השלשים. For הכי, We. substitutes הנו, but הוא is simpler and answers the purpose.

20–23. *Benaiah* is next described as *a man of valour, a doer of great deeds.* His home was the Judahite town Kabzeel. — *He smote the two sons of Ariel in Moab*] unless indeed towns or sanctuaries are intended. — *And he used to go down and smite the lions in the pit on snowy days*] when he could track them easily. — **21.** Moreover, *he smote a tall Egyptian who had in his hand a spear ; he went against him with only a club and snatched the spear from the Egyptian's hand, and killed him with his own spear*] the better weapon did not avail. — **22.** The result was a reputation *like that of the Three.* — **23.** He too received an important command, for *David set him over his servants*] by which the bodyguard seems intended, 1 S. 22¹⁴.

20. חיל [בן־איש־חי Qrê is doubtless correct (so Chr.). But what concerns us is not the character of Benaiah's father or grandfather, but his own. It is probable therefore that we should read simply איש חי (Ew.) : ἀνὴρ αὐτός 𝔊ᴮ indicates איש הוא which however seems unnatural. Kabzeel is named among the towns of Judah in Jos. 15²¹. — [אראל] is unintelligible, and as בני אראל אראל is witnessed by 𝔊, that emendation seems obvious; הכה indicates that men and not sanctuaries are intended. — [ירד והכה] the consecution is awkward and we should perhaps read ירד, in which case we should have the account not of a single exploit, but of the man's custom. — **21.** [אשר] read איש Qrê and Chr. — [מראה] should be מרה with Chr. — **22.** [בשלשה] Bu. has already conjectured כשלשה which seems plausible, and which confirms a similar conjecture of mine above. According to this the Heroes included the Three, the Thirty, and two who were unclassed but who ranked above the Thirty and below the Three. — **23.** [אל] read על with Chr. — [משמערו] 𝔊ᴸ τὴν φυλακὴν αὐτοῦ may possibly have read משמרתו.

24–39. Catalogue of the Thirty. — That the names are more than thirty in number need cause no surprise, as we may suppose the corps to have been kept full after losses in war. — **25.** *The Harodite*] probably from Harod in the Great Plain, Jd. 7¹. — **26.** *The Paltite*] very uncertain. — *The Tekoite*] already known to us by the Tekoite woman. — **27.** *The Anathothite*] from the town which was afterwards the home of Jeremiah, situated a short hour northeast of Jerusalem. *The Hushathite* has already appeared, 21¹⁸. — **28.** *Netophathites* are mentioned elsewhere ; the town in connexion with Bethlehem after the Exile, Ezr. 2²² Neh. 7²⁶. — **30.** *Pirathonite*, cf. Jd. 12¹⁵. The *Wadies of Gaash* may be connected with *Mount Gaash*, Jd. 2⁹. — **31.** For *Abi-Albon* we should perhaps read *Abibaal* (We.) ; his town may be identified with Beth-Arabah, Jos. 15⁶. — **32.** The *Shaalbonite*, possibly from Shaalbin, Jos. 19⁴² (Shaalbim 1 K. 4⁹). — **34.** Eliphalet was from Beth Maacah, 20¹⁴. — **39.** The total of 37 does not agree with the names given. The Chronicler (1 Chr. 11⁴¹⁻⁴⁷) adds a number of others.

24. [בית לחם] read מבית לחם Chr. 𝔊ᴸ and some codd. — **25.** [אליקא הה׳ is omitted by Chr. and 𝔊. — **26.** [הפלטי] הפלוני Chr.: ὁ Κελωθεί 𝔊ᴮ: ὁ Φαλγονί 𝔊ᴸ. In the conflict of testimony it is difficult to put much confidence in any one of the forms. — **27.** [מבני] would naturally be read מִבְּנֵי and is so read by 𝔊ᴮ. But Chr. in two places has a proper name סככי which is also represented in 𝔊ᴸ. — **28.** [האחחי] cf. v.⁹. — **29.** [חלב] חלד 1 Chr. 11³⁰, and 21 codd. here, besides 𝔗 (Cod. Reuchl.) : חלרי 1 Chr. 27¹⁵. — **30.** [הרי] חורי Chr. is confirmed

by several codd. of 𝕲, Field, *Hexapl.* I. p. 586. — **31.** אביאל [אבי־עלבון הערבתי
הערבתי Chr.: 'Αβιὴλ υἱὸς τοῦ 'Αραβωθίτου 𝕲ᶜᵒᵈᵈ·. On the basis of these Kl.,
followed by Bu., has restored אבי־בעל בית הערבתי — הברחמי [הבחרומי Chr. is
probably gentilic of בחרים. — **32.** בני ישן יהונתן [בני ישן יהונתן gives no good sense. בני־ישן
is probably corruption of a proper name, in which case it is most natural to
suppose יהונתן corruption of a gentilic: Βασαὶ ὁ Γωυνί 𝕲ᶜᵒᵈᵈ·. Chr. connects
יהונתן with the following by a בן, as do the Greek Codd. used by Field. —
33. ההררי and האררי are different spellings of the same word. — **34.** בן המעכתי]
probably to be corrected to בית־המעכתי (Kl.). — **35.** חצרו *Kt.* is confirmed by
Chr. הארבי should perhaps be הארכי (Dr.). — **38.** היתרי possibly from *Yattir*
(Kl.). — **39.** The only way in which we can make a total of 37 is to count
בני ישן as two. The number was computed after the corruption took place.

XXIV. The census and its results. — Incited by Yahweh,
David orders a census and insists upon it against the remon-
strances of Joab. No sooner is the work done than he sees its
sinfulness and repents. He is given his choice of three calamities
and chooses the pestilence. After ravaging the country, the destroying angel reaches Jerusalem but is bidden to stay his hand.
David receives the command to build an altar on the place where
the angel had stood when the plague was stayed. He therefore
purchases the site and offers sacrifices upon it.

There seems no reason to doubt that the section is from the
same source with chapter 21¹⁻¹⁴, and once followed that paragraph
without a break. The possibility of secondary insertions however need not be denied.

1–9. The census. — 1. *Yahweh was again angry with Israel*
must be a reference to the account of the famine. There seems
to be no other instance of Yahweh's wrath against Israel in our
present history of David. — *And instigated David against them*]
to do them harm, 1 S. 26¹⁹. The language leaves no doubt of
the author's theory that God incites men to do that for which he
afterwards punishes them. *Go, number Israel and Judah.* Why
this should be a sin we are not told, but it was doubtless regarded
as such by popular opinion — as we see from Joab's protest. —
2. The command is given *to Joab and the captains of the army
who were with him*] this was especially appropriate, as the number of fighting men was the point in mind. *Go about in all the
tribes of Israel . . . and muster the people and let me know the*

number of the people. — **3.** Joab's protest : *May Yahweh thy God add to the people a hundred times as many as they are, while the eyes of my lord the king are looking on !*] that is, during David's lifetime. *But why should my lord the king take pleasure in this thing ?* The protest is evidently as strong as the servant of an absolute monarch can make it. It is explicable only on the theory that this was a new and unheard-of step. — **4.** The command is too positive to be evaded and the work is undertaken. — **5.** The beginning was made in the country beyond the Jordan — *from Aroer and from the city which is in the midst of the Wadi*] so we must emend the text. The same places are mentioned in Dt. 2³⁶ as forming the southern boundary of the territory taken by Israel from Sihon. The ruins of Aroer still bear the name *'Arā'ir*. The first objects of the survey were *the Gaddites unto Jaazer*] the town marked the boundary of the first district on the north, cf. Num. 21²⁴ ⅁. Both Aroer and Jaazer are mentioned in the list of towns belonging to Gad, Num. 32³⁴⁻³⁶. — **6.** It is impossible to make sense of the received text. Three points are clear however : *They came to Gilead*] which lay next in order as they went northward ; *they reached Dan*] the most northerly point of Israel's actual possessions, *and there they turned towards Sidon,* as we should expect. The intervening clause seems to have said that they came *to the land of the Hittites to Hermon.* — **7.** *The Fortress of Tyre* to which they next came would naturally be a post on the boundary of the Phoenician territory. — *And all the cities of the Hivvites and the Canaanites*] as they worked their way southward these marked the boundary of their operations. The Hivvites were the original inhabitants of Shechem and Gibeon. — The end of their journey was the *Negeb of Judah, at Beer-sheba*] well known from the history of Abraham, and as the southernmost town in Judah. — **8.** The time occupied was *nine months and twenty days.* — **9.** As in so many other cases, the numbers are not to be relied upon. For the 800,000 of Israel the Chronicler has 1,100,000, and for the 500,000 of Judah he gives 470,000.

1. Bu. removes the first clause to the margin and begins the section ויסת יהוה. This is in accordance with his theory that 21¹⁻¹⁴ originally followed this chapter. If we deny this supposed original order the reason for modifying the verse falls to the ground. — ויסת] as is well known, the Chronicler could not conceive of Yahweh's inciting David to sin, and he therefore begins the account (1 Chr. 21¹) ויעמד שטן על ישראל ויסת. This conception of Satan was entirely unknown to the older writer. Ewald's proposal to correct Sam. by Chr. is motived by a theological prejudgment. — כהם] seems to make no difficulty, though objected to by Bu. — **2.** שר־החיל] 𝔊ᴸ seems to have read ואל שרי החיל which is favoured by v.⁴ and by the paraphrase, ואל שרי העם, 1 Chr. 21³. — שוט] probably to be corrected to the plural with 𝔊ᴸ. For the tense in וידעתי cf. Dr., *Tenses*³, § 112. — **3.** ויוסף] it seems best to omit the ו with 𝔊ᴸ and Chr., but cf. Davidson, *Syntax*, § 136, *R*, 1, *d.* — כהם] *the like of what they now are.* — **4.** לפני] read מפני with 𝔊ᴸ. — **5.** ויחנו ב׳] is suspicious, as the surveying party did not have to stay long in one place: καὶ ἤρξαντο ἀπὸ Ἀροήρ 𝔊ᴸ has doubtless the correct reading ויחלו מערוער (conjectured by We. apparently without knowledge of this recension of 𝔊). This requires the emendation of ימין to ומן. On the site of Aroer, Burckhardt, *Travels in Syria*, p. 372; G. A. Smith, *Geog.* p. 559. The town is mentioned by Mesha, line 26. — הגד] the article is suspicious; probably הגדי should be restored with 𝔊ᴸ in which case the ו of the next word may be stricken out. The location of Jaazer is given by Jerome (Eusebius) as ten (or eight) miles from Philadelphia and fifteen from Heshbon, *OS.* pp. 86, 131. Conjectural identification with the site now called *Sar* is given in Buhl, *Geog.* p. 263 f. — **6.** תחתים חדשי] cannot be the name of a place. The reading of 𝔊ᴸ was evidently תחתים קדשה, *to the land of the Hittites to Kadesh.* As the Hittites occupied the region of Lebanon they make no difficulty, but Kadesh on the Orontes is too far away, and Kedesh of Naphtali has nothing to do with the Hittites. The conjecture of Ew. (*GVI*³. III. p. 220, E. Tr. III. p. 162) is therefore attractive, that for חדשי we should read חרמן (better חרמנה). The clause יען וסביב also makes difficulty. It seems to conceal ושם סכבו or its equivalent. We., Bu. read ומדן סכבו. — **9.** The separate enumeration of Israel and Judah can hardly be evidence of late date. We have already had occasion to notice indications of their separate feeling. The numbers given are increased for Israel by some Greek MSS. to 900,000 while those of Judah are diminished to 400,000.

10–16. The punishment. — As the account now stands, David's repentance comes before his denunciation, which hardly seems natural ; v.¹⁰ is probably an insertion. — **11, 12.** *Gad, David's seer,* had received a revelation during the night, commanding him to say from Yahweh : *Three things I lay before thee : Choose one of them that I may do to thee*] what the three are is not stated here but in the following verse. — **13.** The choice offered is : *three years of famine in thy land, three months fleeing before thine enemies while they pursue thee, or three days' pestilence*] it has been supposed that as the three years of famine were actually inflicted in the matter of the Gibeonites, so the three months' flight repre-

sents David's experience in the rebellion of Absalom. But of
this there is no evidence. — **14.** David's choice is motived by the
thought that Yahweh is more merciful than man. — **15.** The more
graphic text of 𝕲 gives us : *So David chose the pestilence. And
when the days were the days of wheat harvest, the plague began
among the people and slew of the people seventy thousand men*] *the
days of wheat harvest* explain how Araunah came to be at his
threshing-floor. The fact that the plague had only begun when
Yahweh stayed the angel's hand justifies David's confidence in his
mercies. — **16.** The angel comes to Jerusalem, when Yahweh
repents, and commands : *Enough, now stay thy hand!* The exact
locality which he had reached was *the threshing-floor of Araunah.*
The reason why Yahweh repented is his affection for Jerusalem.

10. In favour of treating the verse as an intruder is the use of ספר instead
of מנה v.¹. After כן insert כי with 𝕲ᴸ (Kl.). — **11.** ויקם דוד בבקר is apparently
a part of the interpolation. — [הנביא] is omitted by Chr. and is superfluous. —
12. [הלוך] on this use of the infinitive Davidson, *Syntax,* § 88 *b.* — [נוטל] read
נטה with Chr. — **13.** For שבע, Chr. has שלש which makes the offer more
symmetrical. — [צריך] should evidently be צרך to agree with what follows;
the word is to be taken collectively. We. prefers וחרב רדפך to והוא רדפך.
— **15.** The reconstruction of the verse by We. adopted by Dr. and Bu. is the
one reproduced above. The reading of 𝕳 *and Yahweh sent a pestilence upon
Israel from the morning until an appointed time* is obscure, but seems to imply
that the threatened three days were fulfilled. 𝕲 has a double reading, a second translation of 𝕳 being inserted in the original rendering. Cutting out
this insertion we have left : καὶ ἐξελέξατο ἑαυτῷ Δαυειδ τὸν θάνατον, καὶ ἡμέραι
θερισμοῦ πυρῶν, καὶ ἤρξατο ἡ θραῦσις ἐν τῷ λαῷ. This evidently represents a
good Hebrew text. — [ויומת] is perhaps to be pointed וַיְמֻת. It seems violent
however to introduce המלאך המכה (Bu.). — [מדן ועד־באר שבע] is lacking in Chr.
and probably an interpolation. — **16.** [וישלח ידו המלאך] the order of the words
is unusual. But it seems impossible to get along without המלאך unless we
insert it in the preceding verse. Bu. inserts v.¹⁷ after לשחתה, which gives a
plausible text. — [האורנה] the article with the proper name is impossible and
must be stricken out. The original form of the name cannot be recovered :
אורנה *Kt.,* ארונה *Qrê;* ארניה *Kt.,* ארונה *Qrê* v.¹⁸; elsewhere in this chapter
ארונה or ארניה, in Chr. uniformly ארנן. 𝕲 has 'Ορνά both here and in Chr.

17–25. The commemorative altar. — The first verse is either
an interpolation or displaced, as ¹⁸ joins immediately to ¹⁶. As it
stands, it asks that Yahweh will spare the people but punish David
and his house. Neither in what follows nor in v.¹⁶ is any notice

taken by Yahweh of this prayer. — **18.** The place where Yahweh
reveals himself becomes a sanctuary and properly receives an
altar. — **20.** Araunah *looked down* from the elevation on which the
threshing-floor was placed, and seeing the king and his servants
crossing over to him, he went to meet them and showed the customary reverence. — **21.** In accounting for his mission, David
speaks of building an altar, *that the plague may be stayed from
the people*] he is apparently not certain that it has actually been
checked. — **22.** Araunah's reply considers the first object of the
altar, the sacrifice, and offers the material which he has at hand :
*Let my lord the king take and offer what he pleases ; see the oxen
for the burnt offering and the threshing sledges and the implements
for wood*] the yokes and goads are *the implements of the oxen.*
We are reminded of 1 S. 6¹⁴, where the cart which brought the
Ark furnishes the wood for the extemporized altar and the kine are
the burnt offering.   Threshing sledges were heavy boards with
stones set in the under side, and they were dragged over the grain,
as is still the custom in the East. — **23.** *The whole has thy servant, my lord the king, given to the king*] the usual response of
the oriental to the expression of desire for something in his possession.   On the text, see the note.   The conclusion of the verse
is a prayer for the success of the sacrifice : *Yahweh thy God accept
thee !* — **24.** After refusing to offer that which cost him nought,
David buys the field and the cattle *for fifty shekels of silver*] the
Chronicler expands these to six hundred shekels of gold. —
25. The altar was built and the sacrifices offered, *and Yahweh
was entreated for the land and the plague was stayed from
Israel.*

17. Against the originality of the verse is the fact that Gad's message
makes no allusion to it.   If stricken out, the connexion is perfect. — **20.** עליו]
naturally to be corrected to אליו (Bu.).   Immediately after it we should perhaps insert וארונה דש חטים from Chr., though the Chronicler has treated the
verse very freely. — **23.** ארונה המלך] has given rise to much speculation, as
though Araunah had been king of the Jebusites before the conquest of the
city.   It is evident however that if this had been the case (its intrinsic
improbability need not be dwelt upon) the author would have taken pains
to inform us.   In ארונה here we have a corruption of ארני as was recognized first
by Böttcher (We.).   The subject to נתן then must be עבדך which has fallen
out. — **25.** 𝔊 adds at the end of the verse that *Solomon added to the altar*

later because it was small. This assumes what was also the mind of the Chronicler, that the site now fixed became the site of Solomon's Temple. But of this we cannot be certain. The site of Solomon's Temple was fixed by the location of the palace, of which it was the sanctuary. It is not likely that this was anywhere except in the citadel where both David and Solomon resided.

The division of books here is quite artificial, as the history of David is continued in 1 Kings with the account of Abishag and the revolt of Adonijah. That the division is not very early is probably indicated by 𝕲ᴸ which begins its Third Book of Kings with 1 K. 3 of the received text, and numbers the two chapters which intervene 25 and 26 of our book.

APPENDIX

———◆———

I. THE CRITICISM OF THE OLD TESTAMENT TEXT

THE foregoing commentary was in the hands of the printer before I received the third edition of Thenius' Commentary edited by Professor Löhr. Careful examination of this volume shows, to my surprise, a serious divergence from Thenius' own work in respect to the treatment of the text. As the position taken by Professor Löhr indicates how far we are from uniting upon even the most elementary questions of Old Testament science, an examination of his argument will be in place here. Thenius opened the way to a rational treatment of the text in his exposition of the Books of Samuel. His results have been widely accepted, and all recent inquiry has been based more or less distinctly upon his work. Yet now the editor who claims to continue his work attempts to discredit a considerable part of it and announces a principle which would be repudiated by the original author.[*] Such a phenomenon deserves study.

The position of the author (by which I mean Professor Löhr) is stated as follows : " The aim of Old Testament textual criticism is (if indeed we wish to retain common ground and a sure footing)[†] a philologically correct edition of the Massoretic Text." The first remark suggested by this language is that *common ground* is not at present attainable. The prejudgment which made the Massoretic Text unassailable to scholars of the seventeenth century has not yet died out. Those who are affected by it can have no

---

[*] This was written before I saw Bertholet's review of Löhr (in ThLZ. XXIII, 529 ff.), which agrees with my criticism of this part of the book.

[†] Wenn anders wir *einen gemeinsamen und sicheren Boden* unter den Füssen behalten wollen; Thenius,[3] p. xc.

common ground with those who believe that the received text of the Old Testament has suffered from the accidents of transmission, and who seek to improve it by every resource known to textual criticism.

What we know as the Massoretic Text is the text common to all Jewish copies of the Old Testament. It is well known that this has been transmitted with great care for some centuries — though we must not suppose that the rules for the Scribes, intended to secure perfect copies for the public service, were applied to those intended for private use. The praise which we cheerfully accord to this extraordinary diligence should not blind us to the fact that no scrupulosity could cure errors already in the text. And that the original to which this diligence was applied was not the autograph, but an extremely defective copy — this must be evident to any unprejudiced observer.

Where and when this archetype of our Hebrew copies was settled upon we do not know. But it seems probable that after the revolt of Bar Cochba, the Jewish scholars united upon some one manuscript as a standard, and guarded its propagation. It is not impossible that they were reduced to a single manuscript, for the marks sedulously preserved to us (extraordinary points, suspended letters, unusual orthography) are marks which we should expect to find in a single imperfect manuscript.* Had the text been edited even rudimentarily, these would have disappeared. But even if we suppose (as tradition seems to affirm) that the authorities had three or more MSS. at their disposition, we shall not thereby increase our confidence in the received text. Textual criticism is a science of recent growth. We have no reason to suppose that the scribes of A.D. 200 either had adequate material for a really critical edition of the Old Testament, or that they were able to make intelligent use of such material as they had. Three manuscripts or a dozen, if of the same family or type, could not correct each other's errors except in minor particulars.

In this condition of things it seems misleading to call the Massoretic Hebrew Bible a *recension*. By recension we mean an edition

---

* This seems to have been first declared by Lagarde in the preface to his *Anmerkungen zur griechischen Uebersetzung der Proverbien* (1863), reprinted in *Mittheilungen*, I. p. 19 ff.

revised and corrected by a single hand with a definite purpose and according to some fixed principle. To choose a single manuscript, because it happens to be accessible, and to make it the parent of numerous copies is not to make a recension. And the reverse is true — to reconstruct a codex which happens to be the parent of a large family of derived manuscripts is not to recover a distinct recension of the text. The eccentricities of the recovered copy are not the result of editorial purpose, but are the accumulated errors, misunderstandings, attempts at correction, of all the scribes who have had a hand in the whole preceding line of transmission.

The philologically correct edition of the Massoretic Text which is desiderated by Professor Löhr is no more than the recovery of the single defective codex upon which the judgment of the Scribes (or perhaps their necessity) settled in the time of Hadrian. It forms no natural stopping place in the history — or at least it forms no stopping place at which the exegete can say 'this is the goal of my labours.'

The example of Professor Löhr is instructive, because it shows the difficulty of fixing any point short of the earliest attainable text as the end of critical effort. What this scholar actually adopts in his commentary is not a philologically correct edition of 𝔥. He is forced to have recourse to 𝔊 for frequent emendation. The only result of his self-limitation is that he makes a half-hearted use of this version, accepting it where he is obliged to, rejecting it where he thinks it goes too far.

It has already been pointed out (Introduction, § 7) that serious difficulties meet us in attempting to make systematic use of the versions for correction of the text. Confining ourselves to 𝔊 for the present, we must see that these difficulties are no reason for despair. If we could attain the original form of this version, it would be practically equivalent to a Hebrew MS. of the second century before Christ. Greater age is not always a guarantee of greater correctness, but as the corruption of the Hebrew text probably went on actively during just the period which elapsed between the translation of 𝔊 and the choice of 𝔥, the presumption is that in this case the older copy would be more valuable. Even if it were not, the experience of the critics shows that the poorest copy will sometimes enable us to correct a better one.

As 𝕲 lies before us, we have not this original. We have
instead, widely different copies, some of which represent clearly-
marked recensions.   What makes these variant copies valuable is
that they represent additional MSS. of the Hebrew.   For one
object of the editors in making their different recensions was to
bring their Greek nearer to the Hebrew in their hands.   In the
various Greek copies we have therefore testimony to Hebrew
MSS. of different dates, but probably all of them as old as the
archetype of our 𝔥, some of them older.

Now we cannot doubt that there was an autograph of the Books
of Samuel, from which all these copies both of 𝕲 and 𝔥 are ulti-
mately derived.   Their differences show corruption of this autograph.   The textual critic cannot be called over-ambitious, if he
sets as his goal the restoration of the earliest reading attainable,
that is, the reading of the autograph.   Professor Nöldeke says (as
cited in the book under discussion) : "To introduce single more
or less certain corrections into a connected text of a later recension gives in any case a *bizarre* result — a text which has never
existed in this form even approximately, and which makes my
philological taste shudder."

It is unfortunate that the great name of Professor Nöldeke
should give weight to such an argument.   Philological taste,
indeed, hardly constitutes an argument, tastes being proverbially
not subject to discussion.   So far as argument is discernible behind
the sentence just quoted it seems to be to this effect : Because 𝔥
has been current for so many centuries, we should refuse to correct it until we can restore the autograph in its integrity.   This
would reduce the labour of the textual critic to the task of restoring the most accurate form of the Massoretic text.   But this is
not the real meaning of Professor Nöldeke or of Professor Löhr.
Neither one supposes that we are to comment on 𝔥 as the seventeenth century scholars did, without trying to correct its most obvious errors.   For in the Books of Samuel, with which we are now
concerned, it is evident that the Massoretic text swarms with errors.
Whether we call it a recension or not, its present constitution is
due to the accumulated mistakes of centuries.   It is dotted all
over with impossible collocations of words, glosses, lacunae, false
readings.   The bizarre effect at which the philological taste must

shudder is already there. It remains true that to remove part of the errors while leaving others, is to reproduce a text which never existed. But this is incident to all textual criticism. The material in hand is never sufficient to enable us to retrace the exact steps of transmission and remove the errors in the order in which they came into the text. Restoration of a lost autograph is always approximate, the degree of approximation being determined by the amount of evidence at hand. To stop at a certain amount of correction when the material is not exhausted, is to be unfaithful to our opportunity.

The reaction in favour of 𝕳 represented by Professor Löhr seems therefore unjustifiable. This comes out clearly in his own statement. For he formulates his principles of textual criticism in a series of theses, and it will not be out of place to reproduce them here.

" 1. Where 𝕳 and 𝕲 show an equally good, *i.e.* grammatically unobjectionable, text, there is no reason for changing the reading of 𝕳."

The argument is fallacious. It is well known that a grammatically unobjectionable text often arises by deliberate alteration on the part of a scribe. In fact, the most dangerous corruptions of ancient documents have come in where a scribe attempted to substitute a smoother reading for one which was to him obscure or ungrammatical. The well-known dictum that the more difficult reading is to be preferred derives its force from this fact. No doubt the dictum has sometimes been abused ; but, rightly understood, it is the foundation of sound criticism. The grammatical correctness of 𝕳 is no argument for its originality, and our rule should read : *Where 𝕲 and 𝕳 show variant readings, both being grammatically intelligible, they have* prima facie *equal claims to attention, and the decision between them must be made on the ground of internal probability*. In the nature of the case the frequent verdict must be *non liquet*.

" 2. Where 𝕳 shows a younger reading, that is, one based on correction, this may be remarked according to 𝕲 ; but we must not change the text of 𝕳."

If the author wishes to publish an edition of the Massoretic text, there is no objection to his doing so, and we cannot hold him to more than his avowed object. If he sets out to remove only the grammatically unintelligible readings, he has a right so to limit himself. But if he is endeavouring to understand the Books of Samuel (and that is the object of a commentary), there is no reason why he should retain a reading which he believes to have come into the text by the " correction " of a scribe.

" 3. Where 𝕲 shows a *plus* as compared with 𝕳, this must be accepted only where the connexion compels us. But even here we must remark :

" (*a*) The inserted sentence of 𝕲 may have been interpolated, and so we cannot be certain that we do not accept with it matter which did not belong to the text.

" (*b*) Often the *plus* of 𝕲, even though (according to our ideas of style) it fits smoothly in the context, lies under the suspicion of being an addition of the translators ; and if it is that, it cannot come into consideration."

To this it should be remarked that the longer text is always open to suspicion. Observation shows that an ancient document is more likely to be interpolated than to be abbreviated. But this rule should not be turned against 𝕲 alone ; it should be made general : *The* plus *of either text is suspicious unless we discover probable cause of accidental omission.* The most probable cause of omission is, of course, homeoteleuton, and this is as likely to affect 𝕳 as to affect 𝕲. Several cases where it has undoubtedly affected 𝕳 are noticed in this commentary. It cannot be shown that the translators of 𝕲 made insertions in their text. All the evidence goes to show that they tried to render the text before them. The danger of taking over interpolated matter from 𝕲, with a genuine reading, can scarcely be called considerable. The text of 𝕲 has itself suffered from the ordinary accidents of transmission, is all we need to say.

" 4. 𝕲 comes into consideration only where 𝕳 has really been corrupted, and even then only :

" (*a*) In case 𝕲 had not itself the corrupt reading before it.

" (*b*) In case 𝕲 does not show a correct, but wholly divergent, text.

" (*c*) In case 𝕳 cannot be emended from its own resources."

The rule thus formulated proves useless in practice. The task of the critic is precisely to discover when his text has really been corrupted (*entstellt*). The most dangerously corrupt passages are those which seem to read with perfect smoothness. The great value of 𝕲 is that it calls our attention to just such passages. The limitation of our use of 𝕲 to the cases 'where 𝕲 had not itself the corrupt reading before it' is also useless in practice. The critic must always bear in mind the possibility that 𝕲 tried to render the text which we find in our copies. This is so much a matter of course that it is needless to state it. Textual criticism is always more or less subjective ; in many cases that arise, opinions will differ. Some will suppose the rendering of 𝕲 to be based on a divergent text, where others see in it an attempt to translate our 𝕳. We are compelled to make allowance for this difference, with the hope that there will be a growing consensus of judgment as time goes on.

When 𝕲 has a ' correct but wholly divergent text,' its testimony is of the highest value. It may have preserved for us a reading which became illegible in one of the ancestors of 𝕳, and which was then filled in on conjecture by a scribe. Or it may show where a text, really original, has been purposely obscured so as not to offend later religious susceptibilities. Or again, it may show a gap which has been differently filled in, in the different copies. In none of these cases is it right to refuse the help of 𝕲.

What is meant by emending 𝕳 from its own resources (*aus sich heraus*) is not clear. The phrase might describe emendation from Hebrew MSS., and it is evident that these must not be neglected. Our trouble is that they are entirely inadequate — they do not suggest a remedy for the most desperate passages in the Books of Samuel. Even where they seem to give us help they may be simply proffering ingenious conjectures of the scribes. In any case they cannot claim the antiquity which certainly belongs to the text of 𝕲.

But emending 𝕳 *aus sich heraus* may possibly mean constructing a text by analogy, on the basis of parallel passages, or according to known Hebrew usage. But this is simply conjectural emendation. We cannot do without conjecture, but it should be our last resort, and it should not be put in the same class with

2 D

emendation on the basis of evidence, even the evidence of a version.

Our conclusion is that the exegete cannot consistently set his aim short of the earliest attainable text.

II. LUCIAN AND THEODOTION

As has been pointed out (Introduction, p. xxxi), a distinct recension of the Greek Old Testament is preserved for us in the edition of Lagarde. This recension has been identified by Lagarde himself with that of Lucian, of which we are informed by Jerome. What is actually established about it is that it represents the text current in Constantinople in the fourth century.

The existence of two such divergent texts as are embodied in this (^{L}) and in the Codex Vaticanus (^{B}) presents some problems which are yet far from solution, but to which the attention of the reader may be directed.

To begin with, we are unable to say when and where the Greek translation of the historical books of the Old Testament was made. The traditional account of the origin of the Septuagint is concerned with the Pentateuch alone, and, even if it were trustworthy, it could throw no light upon the translation of the historical books. It is natural to suppose that various attempts were made for these, and that our copies represent the mingling of these various translations. We have internal evidence that two distinct versions of the Book of Judges were current,* and that they have been confounded in our editions of 𝔊. The conditions which invited to independent attempts at translation are the same for the Books of Samuel as for the Book of Judges. Even if there were one version which served as a substratum for all the copies, the scribes of that day, so far as they had some knowledge of Hebrew, would feel at liberty to alter or expand their archetype, so that there would soon appear to be " as many versions as there were copies," as was afterwards the case with the Latin Bible.

The state of things when Christian scholarship began to interest itself in the Biblical text is made known to us by the labours of

---

* Moore, *Judges*, pp. xliv–xlvi.

Origen. These labours are visibly illustrated by a recently recovered fragment of the Hexapla,* as well as set forth in the descriptions of the Fathers. They interest us here because they make known to us a number of different translations of the Old Testament into Greek. Besides what he supposed to be the original Septuagint, Origen had in his hands Aquila, Symmachus, and Theodotion. Besides these four, he was acquainted with portions of a fifth, sixth, and seventh. But it is not necessary to suppose that all the Greek translations then in existence were known even to this indefatigable scholar. The contrary is the case, for one of the two translations of the Book of Judges seems to have escaped his notice.

It is necessary for us therefore to exercise caution in treating the Greek material in our possession. We should not confuse ourselves by assuming that all our MSS. or recensions are influenced by one or another of the versions known to Origen. It seems especially undesirable to postulate various forms of these versions, as though we could distinguish a first, second, and third edition of Symmachus, as many of Theodotion, and so of the others.

That this caveat is not uncalled for is illustrated by Mez in his essay on the Bible of Josephus.† In this book the author gives a very instructive comparison of Josephus with the historical data of Judges and Samuel. The statements of the *Antiquities* are set side by side with those of our 𝕳 and with those of the different recensions of 𝕲. His conclusion is that Josephus follows the text of Lucian. The necessary inference is that the text of Lucian is older than Lucian — for Josephus wrote two centuries before the time of Lucian. "There were two Greek Bibles before the time of Origen, the text of [B] and its congeners, probably native to Egypt, and a Syro-Italian Bible, best preserved in the so-called Lucian text " — this is the conclusion of Mez, and it is one which we may provisionally accept.

Doubt begins to assert itself at the next step in the argumentation. Our author goes on to point out that Origen knew a Greek Old Testament, which he called by the name of Theodotion. On

---

* Klostermann, " Die Mailänder Fragment der Hexapla," *ZATW*. XVI. p. 334 ff.
† *Die Bibel des Josephus untersucht für Buch V–VII der Archäologie.* Basel, 1895.

the basis of certain resemblances between our Lucian and the fragments of Theodotion, he concludes that the two were allied in some way. He formulates his conclusion in the words: "The primitive Lucian has become a primitive Theodotion;" by which he means that ^{L} is only a copy of Origen's Theodotion, and that an earlier copy of the same version was the Bible of Josephus. The proposition is sufficiently important to warrant examination.

In order not to confound things that differ, we should avoid assuming that there were other Lucians than the Lucian known to us, or other Theodotions than the Theodotion whose fragments have been preserved to us. Our two known quantities are the recension of ^{L} in the edition of Lagarde (or the MSS. on which that edition is based), and the fragments of Theodotion collected by Field in his edition of the Hexapla. Our task is to compare these known and tangible entities, and not to confuse ourselves with their unknown predecessors. Predecessors they doubtless had, but these are as yet out of our reach.

Bringing the text of ^{A} and ^{B} into the comparison,* the relevant facts are as follows:

1. Of 144 instances adduced by Mez, there are *twenty-five* in which Josephus agrees with the text common to the three Greek witnesses ^{ABL}. There are *eighty-eight* in which he agrees with neither one of the three. Out of the remainder we discover *seventeen* in which he may be fairly counted for ^{L}, in *seven* he agrees with ^{AB}, in *four* with ^{BL}, in *two* with ^{AL}, while in only one can he be said to go with ^{B} as against the other two witnesses.

The result is a negative one. The large number of instances in which Josephus agrees with neither one of our three forms of text shows that his Bible cannot be identified with either one of these. But as between these, his Bible appreciably resembled ^{L}, whereas it seems to have had no connexion with the type of text preserved in ^{B}. Although negative, this result is an important one. It indicates that the Josephus text should be counted as a separate recension of $\mathfrak{G}$.

2. Comparison of the two Greek texts shows that ^{L} is noticeably fuller than ^{B}. In the first six chapters of Samuel, about one

---

* The inquiry is confined to the Books of Samuel.

tenth of the words in ^L are not in ^B — over 4400 in one, to about
4000 in the other. The disproportion in other parts of the Book
is not so marked. But it seems safe to say that they differ by seven
or eight per cent, the *plus* being almost uniformly on the side of ^L.

3. Examination into the nature of this additional matter shows
that a part of it is due to a desire to make good Greek. Thus,
the most frequent insertion is that of the definite article, which is
needed by the Greek idiom but is not expressed in Hebrew (and
is consequently omitted by ^B). For κυρίῳ ^B we find τῷ κυρίῳ ^L, for
κιβωτὸς κυρίου ^B, ἡ κιβωτὸς τοῦ κυρίου ^L. The shorter form is here
more exactly representative of the Hebrew, the longer is better
Greek. For the same reason, we find a preposition used in ^L
which is lacking in ^B; in a few cases the conjunction is inserted,
and in a rather larger number the subject or object of the verb,
unexpressed in 𝔥 and ^B, is supplied in ^L. In saying that such
words have been *supplied* in ^L, or in calling them *insertions*, we
must be careful to guard our words, for we do not mean to imply
that ^B is the earlier text which forms the basis upon which ^L supplied what was lacking, or into which it inserted these additional
words. The number of these additional words is such that we
can hardly think of an editor going through a previously existing
text and inserting them into it. They are entirely consistent with
the theory that the translator of ^L was independent of any predecessor, and that he was less slavishly bound to his text than the
translator of ^B. If Lagarde's canon be correct, that the more
exact conformity shows later date, we should argue for the priority
of ^L.

4. There are, however, indications that the *plus* of ^L is sometimes due to interpolation of a shorter text. One of the first
examples we meet is 1 S. 1³, where 𝔥 has ליהוה צבאות. In ^B this
is rendered by τῷ κυρίῳ θεῷ σαβαώθ, whereas we find in ^L τῷ κυρίῳ
σαβαώθ θεῷ παντοκράτορι. It is evident that σαβαώθ and παντοκράτορι represent the same Hebrew word, and therefore that ^L has
been interpolated. But it does not follow that its original was the
text of ^B. In fact it seems pretty certain that its earliest form was
τῷ κυρίῳ θεῷ παντοκράτορι, which is a complete translation of 𝔥
or rather of a variant Hebrew text, and that σαβαώθ was injected
into this by a scribe familiar with the Hebrew phrase. In some

cases the argument is not so clear, and it is undoubtedly true that
ᴸ has sometimes been expanded by insertion of a new translation
alongside of the old.   But it seems impossible in any large proportion of the variations to prove that ᴮ was the original on which
ᴸ is fashioned.

5. One point of considerable importance seems demonstrable :
the Theodotion of Origen is not identical with our ᴸ. This is
established by more than one line of argument :

a. According to Field (*Hexapla Origenis,* I. p. xxxix f.), one
mark of Theodotion is leaving Hebrew words untranslated, trans-
ferring them in Greek letters.   This editor gives a list of such
words, *six* of which occur in the Books of Samuel.   Out of these
six only *one* is found in ᴸ, namely, ἐξ ἀναθώθ for מערנת, 1 S. 15^{32}.

b. Origen's diacritical marks give us a criterion.   It may not be
superfluous to remind the reader that in the Hexapla the text of 𝕲
(what Origen regarded as the original Septuagint) was emended
to conform to the type of Hebrew then current.   Where it was
deficient, words and phrases were inserted.   These inserted words
and phrases had prefixed to them an asterisk (made in the Greek
form ※), and, what especially interests us here, they were generally taken from Theodotion.   Although the greater part of these
marks are no longer preserved to us (for the Books of Samuel),
yet we have occasionally in Greek MSS. some words *sub asterisco,*
and it is fair to assume that these asterisks for the most part go
back to Origen.   Their testimony is exhibited by Field, and in
1 Samuel we find 29 asterisks.   In fourteen cases the asterisked
words are found in ᴸ ; in six cases the same matter is found in ᴸ,
but in different words.   In the remaining nine the insertions are
not made in ᴸ at all.   The conclusion seems not remote.   Our ᴸ
cannot be a faithful representative of Theodotion.   The cases in
which the additional matter is inserted *in other words* seem inexplicable if ᴸ was in any sense dependent on Theodotion.

c. The early Fathers sometimes directly cite Theodotion, and
the MSS. also sometimes designate his reading by the initial letter
of his name.   This testimony also is conveniently reproduced for
us by Field.   In the first fifteen chapters of Samuel I find 49
words or phrases assigned to Theodotion.   *In only three cases* is
the reading found in our ᴸ.   Two of these are the insertion of the

single word ἐκάθητο, 1 S. 1⁹ 4¹³· The word is lacking in ᴮ, but it must be evident that the insertion is one that could be made by different editors in entire independence of each other's labours. In the third case (1 S. 2³¹ᶠ·) where we find a sentence ascribed to Theodotion which we now find in ᴸ, there is room to doubt the accuracy of the ascription, for Theodoret, who is one of our best authorities on the various Greek renderings, says nothing of Theodotion in this connexion. In general, we must view the testimony of these scholiasts with some reserve. It is always conceivable that by some blunder a reading of Theodotion has been wrongly labelled. But all the weight of this testimony, which is the best we have, is against the identification of Theodotion and ᴸ; for it must be evident that three cases out of forty-nine cannot establish influence of one recension on the other. Out of this same list we find three cases where Aquila and Theodotion agree, two where Symmachus and Theodotion agree, and two where Aquila, Symmachus, and Theodotion agree. Yet the independence of these three Greek translators is universally acknowledged.

For the Books of Samuel, therefore, we must conclude : (*a*) that the recension of Lucian cannot be treated as a descendant or near relative of Theodotion; and (*b*) that the type of text used by Josephus must be classed by itself, though showing features of resemblance to our ᴸ, rather than to the recension represented by the Codex Vaticanus.

III. THE LITERARY PROCESS

Professor Löhr in his Introduction to the Commentary already mentioned (Thenius³, 1898), gives a useful *conspectus* of the recent literary criticism of the Books of Samuel. He puts in four parallel columns the analyses of Budde, Cornill, Kittel, and Wellhausen. The practical unanimity of these four authorities is thus brought forcibly to view. In the additions or corrections which he offers, I am glad to say that he frequently agrees with opinions which I had reached independently — as, for example, in denying the coherence of 1 S. 7, and 12 with E, and in asserting the Deuteronomic character of these chapters.

It is a matter for congratulation that the agreement in the critical analysis is so marked. The separation of the different sources may be taken as virtually settled. The further question of how they came to be united still needs discussion, though here also some points are practically agreed upon. I can best indicate the points of agreement and the points of divergence by a sketch of what I suppose to be the actual process. What really took place in the literary history of Israel ?

1. There was an author who undertook to write a history of the rise of the monarchy in Israel with an account of the reign of David. Whether he included the life of Solomon also does not concern us here. He wrote soon after the death of Solomon, and his work (which I call Sl.) included the following sections of our Hebrew Bible :

(*a*) A brief life of Saul beginning with his genealogy (1 S. 9¹), recounting his search for the asses and the meeting with Samuel (9. 10¹⁻¹⁶), the battle with Nahash which brought him to the throne (11), and his campaign against the Philistines (13. 14).

(*b*) An account of David at the court of Saul, where the interest already turns more distinctly to David. It included his coming to court (1 S. 16¹⁴⁻²³), an adventure with the Philistines now lost to us, Saul's jealousy (18⁶⁻¹³·²⁰⁻²⁹ᵃ 19¹¹⁻¹⁷), David's flight (21²⁻¹⁰) and his life as an outlaw captain (22. 23¹⁻¹⁴ 25–27. 29. 30), ending with the death of Saul (31).

(*c*) David's reign, embracing 2 S. 2–4. 7. 9–20, the history being originally concluded by the account of Solomon's coronation and the death of David (1 K. 1. 2).

For the most part Professor Löhr agrees with this statement, and he seems to represent the consensus of recent opinion. A difference however emerges into view at the next step of the reconstruction. My own theory is as follows :

2. A writer with a theocratic bias was dissatisfied with the comparatively worldly view of David presented in the history just defined, and also with its lack of serious condemnation of Saul — for he argued that the rejection of Saul must be accounted for by something in his character. This author therefore rewrote the history, making use, for the most part, of the data given by Sl., though he seems to have had some other source at his command. His design was to show how Samuel was the ruler of Israel by

divine right until the choice of David. His work, which I call Sm., included:

(a) For the life of Samuel; an account of his early life and the fall of Eli's house (1 S. 1–6), the deliverance from the Philistines (7), the demand for a king and its answer by the sacred lot (8. 10^{17-25}), the farewell address (12), and the rejection of Saul (15).

(b) For the early life of David; his anointing (16^{1-13}), his exploit with Goliath (17 in some form), the consequent introduction to court (18^{1-5}), the jealousy of Saul and the insult in the matter of Merab (18^{14-19}), various attempts upon David, his flight to Samuel, to Achish, and to Moab (18^{30}–19^{10}. 19^{18-24}. 21^{11-16}. 22^{3-5}), his generosity to Saul (23^{19}–24^{26}), concluding with Samuel's last appearance (28) and the death of Saul (2 S. 1).

(c) For the reign of David he was content with mentioning the coronation by all Israel, some account of the capture of Jerusalem and the removal of the Ark, and the detailed Messianic promise (2 S. 7), with a summary of David's wars. Probably he gave also some additional matter now lost to us, the Redactor having found that it too obviously duplicates what has been preserved from the other document.

3. The union of these two accounts into one history would give us substantially our present Books of Samuel, and the process is so much like what actually took place in the Pentateuch, that we may claim analogy as an argument in its favour. The alternate theory sees in the sections which I have classed together, fragments of different origin inserted into the framework of Sl. at different times. Löhr's statement is:

"Interpolations are: (a) 1 S. 15 and 28 — Saul's rejection, dating from the prophetic period; (b) 2 S. 7 — the prophecy of the eternal continuance of David's house, later than the preceding but preëxilic; (c) 1 S. 10^8 13^{7-15} — a parallel to 15, older than the reception of the younger source into 7–12, and dating from the Exile.

"Additions are: (a) 1 S. 1–3 — an account of the youth of Samuel, probably taken from some outside history, here intended as an introduction to 7–12; (b) 1 S. 4–6 — an ancient narrative of the experiences of the Ark, adopted with the intention of showing the straits of the Philistines; (*c*) 1 S. 23^{14}–24^{23} 2 S. 1$^{6\text{ff.}}$ 1 S. 16$^{1-13}$ 19$^{18-24}$ 21$^{11-16}$ — these are late, even very late, sections; (*d*) 1 S. 17–20 — these chapters are seriously reëlaborated or intermixed with material from other sources."

The theory thus stated seems to be a revival, or survival, of the now discredited *supplement-hypothesis*. The process which it supposes is unlike anything with which we are acquainted elsewhere in the Old Testament. As we now know, the complicated process by which the Pentateuch (Hexateuch) received its present form was not of this kind. The repeated redactions to which this work was subject were the putting together of documents already complete in themselves. They were not the injecting of diverse sections by successive interpolations, into one history. The Books of Chronicles cannot be adduced in favour of Professor Löhr's theory, for they are to all appearance the work of a single author, making copious use of the previously existing history.

For these reasons, the hypothesis already advanced in the Introduction to this commentary seems to stand.

INDEX

ABBREVIATIONS

SIGNATURES FOR THE HEBREW TEXT AND VERSIONS OF THE OLD
TESTAMENT

𝕳 The received consonantal text of the Hebrew Bible.

𝔐 The Hebrew text with vowels and accents — Massoretic.

𝕲 The Greek version in its various recensions — see Introduction, § 7.

𝕴 The Old Latin, derived from some form of 𝕲.

𝕷 The Latin version made by Jerome.

𝕾 The Syriac version, ordinarily called the Peshiṭta.

𝕿 The Targum.

AN INTRODUCTION TO

The Literature of the Old Testament

By Prof. S. R. DRIVER, D.D., D.Litt.

Canon of Christ Church, Oxford
New Edition Revised

Crown 8vo, 558 pages, $2.50 net

" It is the most scholarly and critical work in the English language on the literature of the Old Testament, and fully up to the present state of research in Germany."—Prof. PHILIP SCHAFF, D.D.

" Canon Driver has arranged his material excellently, is succinct without being hurried or unclear, and treats the various critical problems involved with admirable fairness and good judgment."
—Prof. C. H. TOY.

"His judgment is singularly fair, calm, unbiassed, and independent. It is also thoroughly reverential. . . . The service, which his book will render in the present confusion of mind on this great subject, can scarcely be overestimated."—*The London Times.*

"As a whole, there is probably no book in the English language equal to this 'Introduction to the Literature of the Old Testament' for the student who desires to understand what the modern criticism *thinks* about the Bible."—Dr. LYMAN ABBOTT, *in the Outlook.*

" The book is one worthy of its subject, thorough in its treatment, reverent in its tone, sympathetic in its estimate, frank in its recognition of difficulties, conservative (in the best sense of the word) in its statement of results."
—Prof. HENRY P. SMITH, *in the Magazine of Christian Literature.*

" In working out his method our author takes up each book in order and goes through it with marvelous and microscopic care. Every verse, every clause, word by word, is sifted and weighed, and its place in the literary organism decided upon."
—*The Presbyterian Quarterly.*

" It contains just that presentation of the results of Old Testament criticism for which English readers in this department have been waiting. . . . The whole book is excellent; it will be found helpful, characterized as it is all through by that scholarly poise of mind, which, when it does not know, is not ashamed to present degrees of probability."—*New World.*

" . . . Canon Driver's book is characterized throughout by thorough Christian scholarship, faithful research, caution in the expression of mere opinions, candor in the statement of facts and of the necessary inferences from them, and the devout recognition of the divine inworking in the religious life of the Hebrews, and of the tokens of divine inspiration in the literature which records and embodies it."—Dr. A. P. PEABODY, *in the Cambridge Tribune.*

THEOLOGY OF THE NEW TESTAMENT.

By GEORGE B. STEVENS, D.D.

Professor of Systematic Theology, Yale University.

Crown 8vo, 480 pages, $2.50 net.

"In style it is rarely clear, simple, and strong, adapted alike to the general reader and the theological student. The former class will find it readable and interesting to an unusual degree, while the student will value its thorough scholarship and completeness of treatment. His work has a simplicity, beauty, and freshness that add greatly to its scholarly excellence and worth."—*Christian Advocate.*

"Professor Stevens is a profound student and interpreter of the Bible, as far as possible divested of any prepossessions concerning its message. In his study of it his object has been not to find texts that might seem to bolster up some system of theological speculation, but to find out what the writers of the various books meant to say and teach."—*N. Y. Tribune.*

"It is a fine example of painstaking, discriminating, impartial research and statement."—*The Congregationalist.*

"Professor Stevens has given us a very good book. A liberal conservative, he takes cautious and moderate positions in the field of New Testament criticism, yet is admirably fair-minded. His method is patient and thorough. He states the opinions of those who differ from him with care and clearness. The proportion of quotation and reference is well adjusted and the reader is kept well informed concerning the course of opinion without being drawn away from the text of the author's own thought. His judgments on difficult questions are always put with self-restraint and sobriety."—*The Churchman.*

"It will certainly take its place, after careful reading, as a valuable synopsis, neither bare nor over-elaborate, to which recourse will be had by the student or teacher who requires within moderate compass the gist of modern research."—*The Literary World.*

THE CHRISTIAN PASTOR AND THE WORKING CHURCH

By WASHINGTON GLADDEN, D.D., LL.D.

Author of "Applied Christianity," "Who Wrote the Bible?" "Ruling Ideas of the Present Age," etc.

Crown 8vo, 485 pages, $2.5o net.

" Dr. Gladden may be regarded as an expert and an authority on practi-
_al theology. . . . Upon the whole we judge that it will be of great
service to the ministry of all the Protestant churches."—*The Interior.*

" Packed with wisdom and instruction and a profound piety. . . .
It is pithy, pertinent, and judicious from cover to cover. . . . An exceedingly comprehensive, sagacious, and suggestive study and application
of its theme."—*The Congregationalist.*

" We have here, for the pastor, the most modern practical treatise yet
published—sagacious, balanced, devout, inspiring."—*The Dial.*

" His long experience, his eminent success, his rare literary ability, and
his diligence as a student combine to make of this a model book for its purpose. . . . We know not where the subjects are more wisely discussed
than here."—*The Bibliotheca Sacra.*

" This book should be the *vade mecum* of every working pastor. It
abounds in wise counsels and suggestions, the result of large experience
and observation. No sphere of church life or church work is left untreated."
—*The* (Canadian) *Methodist Magazine and Review.*

" A happier combination of author and subject, it will be acknowledged,
can hardly be found. . . . It is comprehensive, practical, deeply
spiritual, and fertile in wise and suggestive thought upon ways and means
of bringing the Gospel to bear on the lives of men."—*The Christian Advocate.*

" Dr. Gladden writes with pith and point, but with wise moderation, a
genial tone and great good sense. . . . The book is written in an excellent, business-like and vital English style, which carries the author's point
and purpose and has an attractive vitality of its own."—*The Independent.*

" A comprehensive, inspiring, and helpful guide to a busy pastor. One
finds in it a multitude of practical suggestions for the development of the
spiritual and working life of the Church, and the answer to many problems
that are a constant perplexity to the faithful minister."
The Christian Intelligencer

A HISTORY OF

CHRISTIANITY IN THE APOSTOLIC AGE

BY

ARTHUR CUSHMAN McGIFFERT, Ph.D., D.D.

Washburn Professor of Church History in the Union Theological Seminary, New York

Crown 8vo, 681 Pages, $2.50 Net.

" The author's work is ably done. . . . This volume is worthy of its place in the series."—*The Congregationalist.*

" Invaluable as a résumé of the latest critical work upon the great formative period of the Christian Church."—*The Christian World* (London).

" There can be no doubt that this is a remarkable work, both on account of the thoroughness of its criticism and the boldness of its views."
—*The Scotsman.*

" The ability and learning of Professor McGiffert's work on the Apostolic Age, and, whatever dissent there may be from its critical opinion, its manifest sincerity, candid scholars will not fail to appreciate."
—Dr. George P. Fisher, of Yale University.

" Pre-eminently a clergyman's book; but there are many reasons why it should be in the library of every thoughtful Christian person. The style is vivid and at times picturesque. The results rather than the processes of learning are exhibited. It is full of local color, of striking narrative, and of keen, often brilliant, character analysis. It is an admirable book for the Sunday-school teacher."—*Boston Advertiser.*

" For a work of such wide learning and critical accuracy, and which deals with so many difficult and abstruse problems of Christian history, this is remarkably readable."—*The Independent.*

" It is certain that Professor McGiffert's work has set the mark for future effort in the obscure fields of research into Christian origin."
—*New York Tribune.*

" Dr. McGiffert has produced an able, scholarly, suggestive, and constructive work. He is in thorough and easy possession of his sources and materials, so that his positive construction is seldom interrupted by citations, the demolition of opposing views, or the irrelevant discussion of subordinate questions."—*The Methodist Review.*

" The clearness, self-consistency, and force of the whole impression of Apostolic Christianity with which we leave this book, goes far to guarantee its permanent value and success."—*The Expositor.*

History of Christian Doctrine.

BY

GEORGE P. FISHER, D.D., LL.D.,

Titus Street Professor of Ecclesiastical History in Yale University.

Crown 8vo, 583 pages, $2.50 net.

" He gives ample proof of rare scholarship. Many of the old doctrines are restated with a freshness, lucidity and elegance of style which make it a very readable book."—*The New York Observer.*

"Intrinsically this volume is worthy of a foremost place in our modern literature . . . We have no work on the subject in English equal to it, for variety and range, clearness of statement, judicious guidance, and catholicity of tone."—*London Nonconformist and Independent.*

" It is only just to say that Dr. Fisher has produced the best History of Doctrine that we have in English."—*The New York Evangelist.*

" It is to me quite a marvel how a book of this kind (Fisher's 'History of Christian Doctrine') can be written so accurately to scale. It could only be done by one who had a very complete command of all the periods."—PROF. WILLIAM SANDAY, *Oxford.*

"It presents so many new and fresh points and is so thoroughly treated, and brings into view contemporaneous thought, especially the American, that it is a pleasure to read it, and will be an equal pleasure to go back to it again and again."—BISHOP JOHN F. HURST.

" Throughout there is manifest wide reading, careful preparation, spirit and good judgment."—*Philadelphia Presbyterian.*

" The language and style are alike delightfully fresh and easy . . . A book which will be found both stimulating and instructive to the student of theology."—*The Churchman.*

" Professor Fisher has trained the public to expect the excellencies of scholarship, candor, judicial equipoise and admirable lucidity and elegance of style in whatever comes from his pen. But in the present work he has surpassed himself."—PROF. J. H. THAYER, *of Harvard Divinity School.*

" It meets the severest standard; there is fullness of knowledge, thorough research, keenly analytic thought, and rarest enrichment for a positive, profound and learned critic. There is interpretative and revealing sympathy. It is of the class of works that mark epochs in their several departments."—*The Outlook.*

" As a first study of the History of Doctrine, Professor Fisher's volume has the merit of being full, accurate and interesting."
—Prof. MARCUS DODS

" . . . He gathers up, reorganizes and presents the results of investigation in a style rarely full of literary charm."
—*The Interior.*

Christian Ethics,

By NEWMAN SMYTH, D.D., New Haven.

Crown 8vo, 508 pages, $2.50 net.

"As this book is the latest, so it is the fullest and most attractive treatment of the subject that we are familiar with. Patient and exhaustive in its method of inquiry, and stimulating and suggestive in the topic it handles, we are confident that it will be a help to the task of the moral understanding and interpretation of human life."
— *The Living Church.*

"This book of Dr. Newman Smyth is of extraordinary interest and value. It is an honor to American scholarship and American Christian thinking. It is a work which has been wrought out with remarkable grasp of conception, and power of just analysis, fullness of information, richness of thought, and affluence of apt and luminous illustration. Its style is singularly clear, simple, facile, and strong. Too much gratification can hardly be expressed at the way the author lifts the whole subject of ethics up out of the slough of mere naturalism into its own place, where it is seen to be illumined by the Christian revelation and vision."—*The Advance.*

"The subjects treated cover the whole field of moral and spiritual relations, theoretical and practical, natural and revealed, individual and social, civil and ecclesiastical. To enthrone the personal Christ as the true content of the ethical ideal, to show how this ideal is realized in Christian consciousness and how applied in the varied departments of practical life—these are the main objects of the book and no objects could be loftier."
— *The Congregationalist.*

"The author has written with competent knowledge, with great spiritual insight, and in a tone of devoutness and reverence worthy of his theme."
— *The London Independent.*

"It is methodical, comprehensive, and readable ; few subdivisions, direct or indirect, are omitted in the treatment of the broad theme, and though it aims to be an exhaustive treatise, and not a popular handbook, it may be perused at random with a good deal of suggestiveness and profit."
— *The Sunday School Times.*

"It reflects great credit on the author, presenting an exemplary temper and manner throughout, being a model of clearness in thought and term, and containing passages of exquisite finish."—*Hartford Seminary Record.*

"We commend this book to all reading, intelligent men, and especially to ministers, who will find in it many fresh suggestions."
—PROFESSOR A. E. BRUCE

CHRISTIAN INSTITUTIONS.

By ALEXANDER V. G. ALLEN, D.D.

Professor of Ecclesiastical History in the Episcopal Theological School
in Cambridge.

Crown 8vo, 577 pages, $2.50 net.

"Professor Allen's Christian Institutions may be regarded as the most important permanent contribution which the Protestant Episcopal Church of the United States has yet made to general theological thought. In a few particulars it will not command the universal, or even the general assent of discriminating readers; but it will receive, as it deserves, the respect and appreciation of those who rightly estimate the varied, learned, and independent spirit of the author."—*The American Journal of Theology.*

"As to his method there can be no two opinions, nor as to the broad, critical, and appreciative character of his study. It is an immensely suggestive, stimulating, and encouraging piece of work. It shows that modern scholarship is not all at sea as to results, and it presents a worthy view of a great and noble subject, the greatest and noblest of all subjects."—*The Independent.*

"This will at once take its place among the most valuable volumes in the 'International Theological Library,' constituting in itself a very complete epitome both of general church history and of the history of doctrines. . . . A single quotation well illustrates the brilliant style and the profound thought of the book."—*The Bibliotheca Sacra.*

"The wealth of learning, the historical spirit, the philosophic grasp, the loyalty to the continuity of life, which everywhere characterize this thorough study of the organization, creeds, and cultus constituting Christian Institution. . . . However the reader may differ with the conclusions of the author, few will question his painstaking scholarship, judicial temperament, and catholicity of Christian spirit."—*The Advance.*

"It is an honor to American scholarship, and will be read by all who wish to be abreast of the age."—*The Lutheran Church Review.*

"With all its defects and limitations, this is a most illuminating and suggestive book on a subject of abiding interest."—*The Christian Intelligencer.*"

"It is a treasury of expert knowledge, arranged in an orderly and lucid manner, and more than ordinarily readable. . . . It is controlled by the candid and critical spirit of the careful historian who, of course, has his convictions and preferences, but who makes no claims in their behalf which the facts do not seem to warrant."—*The Congregationalist.*

"He writes in a charming style, and has collected a vast amount of important material pertaining to his subject which can be found in no other work in so compact a form."—*The New York Observer.*

Apologetics;
Or, Christianity Defensively Stated.

By the late ALEXANDER BALMAIN BRUCE, D.D.,

Professor of Apologetics and New Testament Exegesis, Free Church College, Glasgow; Author of " The Training of the Twelve," "The Humiliation of Christ," " The Kingdom of God," etc.

Crown 8vo, 528 pages, $2.50 net.

Professor Bruce's work is not an abstract treatise on apologetics, but an apologetic presentation of the Christian faith, with reference to whatever in our intellectual environment makes faith difficult at the present time.

It addresses itself to men whose sympathies are with Christianity, and discusses the topics of pressing concern—the burning questions of the hour. It is offered as an aid to faith rather than a buttress of received belief and an armory of weapons for the orthodox believer.

" The book throughout exhibits the methods and the results of conscientious, independent, expert and devout Biblical scholarship, and it is of permanent value."— *The Congregationalist.*

" The practical value of this book entitles it to a place in the first rank."— *The Independent.*

" A patient and scholarly presentation of Christianity under aspects best fitted to commend it to 'ingenuous and truth-loving minds.' "— *The Nation.*

" The book is well-nigh indispensable to those who propose to keep abreast of the times."— *Western Christian Advocate.*

"Professor Bruce does not consciously evade any difficulty, and he constantly aims to be completely fair-minded. For this reason he wins from the start the strong confidence of the reader."— *Advance.*

" Its admirable spirit, no less than the strength of its arguments, will go far to remove many of the prejudices or doubts of those who are outside of Christianity, but who are, nevertheless, not infidels."— *New York Tribune.*

" In a word, he tells precisely what all intelligent persons wish to know, and tells it in a clear, fresh and convincing manner. Scarcely anyone has so successfully rendered the service of showing what the result of the higher criticism is for the proper understanding of the history and religion of Israel."— *Andover Review.*

" We have not for a long time taken a book in hand that is more stimulating to faith. . . . Without commenting further, we repeat that this volume is the ablest, most scholarly, most advanced, and sharpest defence of Christianity that has ever been written. No theological library should be without it."— *Zion's Herald.*

The International Critical Commentary.

" A decided advance on all other commentaries." — THE OUTLOOK.

DEUTERONOMY.

By the Rev. S. R. DRIVER, D.D., D.Litt.,
Regius Professor of Hebrew, and Canon of Christ Church, Oxford

Crown 8vo. Net, $3.00.

"No one could be better qualified than Professor Driver to write a critical and exegetical commentary on Deuteronomy. His previous works are author-ities in all the departments involved; the grammar and lexicon of the Hebrew language, the lower and higher criticism, as well as exegesis and Biblical the-ology; . . . the interpretation in this commentary is careful and sober in the main. A wealth of historical, geographical, and philological information illus-trates and elucidates both the narrative and the discourses. Valuable, though concise, excursuses are often given." — *The Congregationalist.*

"It is a pleasure to see at last a really critical Old Testament commentary in English upon a portion of the Pentateuch, and especially one of such merit. This I find superior to any other Commentary in any language upon Deuter-onomy." — Professor E. L. CURTIS, of Yale University.

"This volume of Professor Driver's is marked by his well-known care and accuracy, and it will be a great boon to every one who wishes to acquire a thorough knowledge, either of the Hebrew language, or of the contents of the Book of Deuteronomy, and their significance for the development of Old Tes-tament thought. The author finds scope for displaying his well-known wide and accurate knowledge, and delicate appreciation of the genius of the Hebrew language, and his readers are supplied with many carefully con-structed lists of words and expressions. He is at his best in the detailed examination of the text." — *London Athenæum.*

"It must be said that this work is bound to take rank among the best com-mentaries in any language on the important book with which it deals. On every page there is abundant evidence of a scholarly knowledge of the litera-ture, and of the most painstaking care to make the book useful to thorough students." — *The Lutheran Churchman.*

"The deep and difficult questions raised by Deuteronomy are, in every in-stance, considered with care, insight, and critical acumen. The student who wishes for solid information, or a knowledge of method and temper of the new criticism, will find advantage in consulting the pages of Dr. Driver." — *Zion's Herald.*

"We believe this series to be of epoch-making importance."
— The N. Y. EVANGELIST.

JUDGES.

By Dr. GEORGE FOOT MOORE, D.D.,

Professor of Theology, Harvard University.

Crown 8vo.   Net, $3.00.

"The typographical execution of this handsome volume is worthy of the scholarly character of the contents, and higher praise could not be given it."
— Professor C. H. TOY, *of Harvard University.*

"This work represents the latest results of 'Scientific Biblical Scholarship,' and as such has the greatest value for the purely critical student, especially on the side of textual and literary criticism." — *The Church Standard.*

"Professor Moore has more than sustained his scholarly reputation in this work, which gives us for the first time in English a commentary on Judges not excelled, if indeed equalled, in any language of the world." — Professor L. W. BATTEN, *of P. E. Divinity School, Philadelphia.*

"Although a critical commentary, this work has its practical uses, and by its divisions, headlines, etc., it is admirably adapted to the wants of all thoughtful students of the Scriptures.   Indeed, with the other books of the series, it is sure to find its way into the hands of pastors and scholarly lay-men." — *Portland Zion's Herald.*

"Like its predecessors, this volume will be warmly welcomed — whilst to those whose means of securing up-to-date information on the subject of which it treats are limited, it is simply invaluable." — *Edinburgh Scotsman.*

"The work is done in an atmosphere of scholarly interest and indifference to dogmatism and controversy, which is at least refreshing. . . .   It is a noble introduction to the moral forces, ideas, and influences that controlled the period of the Judges, and a model of what a historical commentary, with a practical end in view should be." — *The Independent.*

"The work is marked by a clear and forcible style, by scholarly research, by critical acumen, by extensive reading, and by evident familiarity with the Hebrew.   Many of the comments and suggestions are valuable, while the index at the close is serviceable and satisfactory." — *Philadelphia Presbyterian.*

"This volume sustains the reputation of the series for accurate and wide scholarship given in clear and strong English, . . . the scholarly reader will find delight in the perusal of this admirable commentary." — *Zion's Herald.*

The International Critical Commentary.

The Books of Samuel

BY

REV. HENRY PRESERVED SMITH, D.D.,

Professor of Biblical History and Interpretation in Amherst College.

Crown 8vo, Net $3.00.

"Professor Smith's Commentary will for some time be the standard work on Samuel, and we heartily congratulate him on scholarly work so faithfully accomplished."—*The Athenæum.*

"It is both critical and exegetical, and deals with original Hebrew and Greek. It shows painstaking diligence and considerable research."—*The Presbyterian.*

"The style is clear and forcible and sustains the well-won reputation of the distinguished author for scholarship and candor. All thoughtful students of the Scriptures will find the work helpful, not only on account of its specific treatment of the Books of Samuel, on which it is based, but because of the light it throws on and the aid it gives in the general interpretation of the Scriptures as modified by present-day criticism."—*The Philadelphia Press.*

"The literary quality of the book deserves mention. We do not usually go to commentaries for models of English style. But this book has a distinct, though unobtrusive, literary flavor. It is delightful reading. The translation is always felicitous, and often renders further comment needless."—*The Evangelist.*

"The treatment is critical, and at the same time expository. Conservative students may find much in this volume with which they cannot agree, but no one wishing to know the most recent conclusions concerning this part of sacred history can afford to be without it."—*Philadelphia Presbyterian Journal.*

"The author exhibits precisely that scholarly attitude which will commend his work to the widest audience."—*The Churchman.*

"The commentary is the most complete and minute hitherto published by an English-speaking scholar."—*Literature.*

"The volumes of Driver and Moore set a high standard for the Old Testament writers; but I think Professor Smith's work has reached the same high level. It is scholarly and critical, and yet it is written in a spirit of reverent devotion, a worthy treatment of the sacred text."—PROF. L. W. BATTEN, of P. E. Divinity School, Philadelphia.

The International Critical Commentary.

" We deem it as needful for the studious pastor to possess himself of these volumes as to obtain the best dictionary and encyclopedia."
— THE CONGREGATIONALIST.

ST. MARK.

By the Rev. E. P. GOULD, D.D.,

Late Professor of New Testament Exegesis, P. E. Divinity School, Philadelphia.

Crown 8vo. Net, $2.50.

"In point of scholarship, of accuracy, of originality, this last addition to the series is worthy of its predecessors, while for terseness and keenness of exegesis, we should put it first of them all." — *The Congregationalist.*

"The whole make-up is that of a thoroughly helpful, instructive critical study of the Word, surpassing anything of the kind ever attempted in the English language, and to students and clergymen knowing the proper use of a commentary it will prove an invaluable aid." — *The Lutheran Quarterly.*

"Professor Gould has done his work well and thoroughly. . . . The commentary is an admirable example of the critical method at its best. . . . The Word study . . . shows not only familiarity with all the literature of the subject, but patient, faithful, and independent investigation. . . . It will rank among the best, as it is the latest commentary on this basal Gospel." — *The Christian Intelligencer.*

"It will give the student the vigorously expressed thought of a very thoughtful scholar." — *The Church Standard.*

"Dr. Gould's commentary on Mark is a large success, . . . and a credit to American scholarship. . . . He has undoubtedly given us a commentary on Mark which surpasses all others, a thing we have reason to expect will be true in the case of every volume of the series to which it belongs." — *The Biblical World.*

"The volume is characterized by extensive learning, patient attention to details and a fair degree of caution." — *Bibliotheca Sacra.*

"The exegetical portion of the book is simple in arrangement, admirable in form and condensed in statement. . . . Dr. Gould does not slavishly follow any authority, but expresses his own opinions in language both concise and clear." — *The Chicago Standard.*

"In clear, forcible and elegant language the author furnishes the results of the best investigations on the second Gospel, both early and late. He treats these various subjects with the hand of a master." — *Boston Zion's Herald.*

"The author gives abundant evidence of thorough acquaintance with the facts and history in the case. . . . His treatment of them is always fresh and scholarly, and oftentimes helpful." — *The New York Observer.*

The International Critical Commentary.

" It is hardly necessary to say that this series will stand first among all English serial commentaries on the Bible."

— THE BIBLICAL WORLD.

ST. LUKE.

By the Rev. ALFRED PLUMMER, D.D.,

Master of University College, Durham. Formerly Fellow and Senior Tutor of Trinity College, Oxford.

Crown 8vo. Net, $3.00.

In the author's Critical Introduction to the Commentary is contained a full treatment of a large number of important topics connected with the study of the Gospel, among which are the following : The Author of the Book — The Sources of the Gospel — Object and Plan of the Gospel — Characteristics, Style and Language — The Integrity of the Gospel — The Text — Literary History.

FROM THE AUTHOR'S PREFACE.

If this Commentary has any special features, they will perhaps be found in the illustrations from Jewish writings, in the abundance of references to the Septuagint, and to the Acts and other books of the New Testament, in the frequent quotations of renderings in the Latin versions, and in the attention which has been paid, both in the Introduction and throughout the Notes, to the marks of St. Luke's style.

"It is distinguished throughout by learning, sobriety of judgment, and sound exegesis. It is a weighty contribution to the interpretation of the Third Gospel, and will take an honorable place in the series of which it forms a part." — Prof. D. D. SALMOND, in the *Critical Review*.

"We are pleased with the thoroughness and scientific accuracy of the interpretations. . . . It seems to us that the prevailing characteristic of the book is common sense, fortified by learning and piety." — *The Herald and Presbyter*.

"An important work, which no student of the Word of God can safely neglect." — *The Church Standard*.

"The author has both the scholar's knowledge and the scholar's spirit necessary for the preparation of such a commentary. . . . We know of nothing on the Third Gospel which more thoroughly meets the wants of the Biblical scholar." — *The Outlook*.

"The author is not only a profound scholar, but a chastened and reverent Christian, who undertakes to interpret a Gospel of Christ, so as to show Christ in his grandeur and loveliness of character." — *The Southern Churchman*.

"It is a valuable and welcome addition to our somewhat scanty stock of first-class commentaries on the Third Gospel. By its scholarly thoroughness it well sustains the reputation which the INTERNATIONAL SERIES has already won." — Prof. J. H. THAYER, of Harvard University.

This volume having been so recently published, further notices are not yet available.

The International Critical Commentary.

" For the student this new commentary promises to be indispensable." — The METHODIST RECORDER.

ROMANS.

By the Rev. WILLIAM SANDAY, D.D., LL.D.,
Lady Margaret Professor of Divinity, and Canon of Christ Church, Oxford,

AND THE

Rev. A. C. HEADLAM, M.A., D.D.,
Principal of King's College, London.

Crown 8vo. Net, $3.00.

"From my knowledge of Dr. Sanday, and from a brief examination of the book, I am led to believe that it is our best critical handbook to the Epistle. It combines great learning with practical and suggestive interpretation." — Professor GEORGE B. STEVENS, *of Yale University.*

"Professor Sanday is excellent in scholarship, and of unsurpassed candor. The introduction and detached notes are highly interesting and instructive. This commentary cannot fail to render the most valuable assistance to all earnest students. The volume augurs well for the series of which it is a member." — Professor GEORGE P. FISHER, *of Yale University.*

"The scholarship and spirit of Dr. Sanday give assurance of an interpretation of the Epistle to the Romans which will be both scholarly and spiritual." — Dr. LYMAN ABBOTT.

"The work of the authors has been carefully done, and will prove an acceptable addition to the literature of the great Epistle. The exegesis is acute and learned . . . The authors show much familiarity with the work of their predecessors, and write with calmness and lucidity." — *New York Observer.*

"We are confident that this commentary will find a place in every thoughtful minister's library. One may not be able to agree with the authors at some points, — and this is true of all commentaries, — but they have given us a work which cannot but prove valuable to the critical study of Paul's masterly epistle." — *Zion's Advocate.*

"We do not hesitate to commend this as the best commentary on Romans yet written in English. It will do much to popularize this admirable and much needed series, by showing that it is possible to be critical and scholarly and at the same time devout and spiritual, and intelligible to plain Bible readers." — *The Church Standard.*

"A commentary with a very distinct character and purpose of its own, which brings to students and ministers an aid which they cannot obtain elsewhere. . . . There is probably no other commentary in which criticism has been employed so successfully and impartially to bring out the author's thought." — *N. Y. Independent.*

"We have nothing but heartiest praise for the weightier matters of the commentary. It is not only critical, but exegetical, expository, doctrinal, practical, and eminently spiritual. The positive conclusions of the books are very numerous and are stoutly, gloriously evangelical. . . . The commentary does not fail to speak with the utmost reverence of the whole word of God." *The Congregationalist*

"This admirable series."—THE LONDON ACADEMY.

EPHESIANS AND COLOSSIANS.

By the Rev. T. K. ABBOTT, B.D., D. Litt.

Formerly Professor of Biblical Greek, now of Hebrew, Trinity College, Dublin.

Crown 8vo. Net, $2.50.

" The latest volume of this admirable series is informed with the very best spirit in which such work can be carried out—a spirit of absolute fidelity to the demonstrable truths of critical science. . . . This summary of the results of modern criticism applied to these two Pauline letters is, for the use of scholarly students, not likely to be superseded."—*The London Academy.*

" An able and independent piece of exegesis, and one that none of us can afford to be without. It is the work of a man who has made himself master of his theme. His linguistic ability is manifest. His style is usually clear. His exegetical perceptions are keen, and we are especially grateful for his strong defence of the integrity and apostolicity of these two great monuments of Pauline teaching."—*The Expositor.*

" It displays every mark of conscientious judgment, wide reading, and grammatical insight."—*Literature.*

" In discrimination, learning, and candor, it is the peer of the other volumes of the series. The elaborate introductions are of special value."— Professor GEORGE B. STEVENS, of Yale University.

" It is rich in philological material, clearly arranged, and judiciously handled. The studies of words are uncommonly good. . . . In the balancing of opinions, in the distinguishing between fine shades of meaning, it is both acute and sound."—*The Church.*

" The exegesis based so solidly on the rock foundation of philology is argumentatively and convincingly strong. A spiritual and evangelical tenor pervades the interpretation from first to last. . . . These elements, together with the author's full-orbed vision of the truth, with his discriminative judgment and his felicity of expression, make this the peer of any commentary on these important letters."—*The Standard.*

" An exceedingly careful and painstaking piece of work. The introductory discussions of questions bearing on the authenticity and integrity (of the epistles) are clear and candid, and the exposition of the text displays a fine scholarship and insight."—*Northwestern Christian Advocate.*

" The book is from first to last exegetical and critical. Every phrase in the two Epistles is searched as with lighted candles. The authorities for variant readings are canvassed but weighed, rather than counted. The multiform ancient and modern interpretations are investigated with the exhaustiveness of a German lecture-room, and the judicial spirit of an English court-room. Special discussions are numerous and thorough."—*The Congregationalist.*

The International Critical Commentary.

"A decided advance on all other commentaries."—THE OUTLOOK.

PROVERBS

By the Rev. CRAWFORD H. TOY, D.D., LL.D.
Professor of Hebrew in Harvard University.

Crown 8vo. Net, $3.00.

"In careful scholarship this volume leaves nothing to be desired. Its interpretation is free from theological prejudice. It will be indispensable to the careful student, whether lay or clerical."—*The Outlook.*

"Professor Toy's 'Commentary' will for many years to come remain a handbook for both teachers and learners, and its details will be studied with critical care and general appreciation."—*The Athenæum.*

"The commentary itself is a most thorough treatment of each verse in detail, in which the light of the fullest scholarship is thrown upon the meaning. The learning displayed throughout the work is enormous. Here is a commentary at last that does not skip the hard places, but grapples with every problem and point, and says the best that can be said."—*Presbyterian Banner.*

"Professor Toy's commentary on Proverbs maintains the highest standard of the International Critical Commentaries. We can give no higher praise. Proverbs presents comparatively few problems in criticism, but offers large opportunities to the expositor and exegete. Professor Toy's work is thorough and complete."—*The Congregationalist.*

"This addition to 'The International Critical Commentary' has the same characteristics of thoroughness and painstaking scholarship as the preceding issues of the series. In the critical treatment of the text, in noting the various readings and the force of the words in the original Hebrew, it leaves nothing to be desired."—*The Christian Intelligencer.*

"A first-class, up-to-date, critical and exegetical commentary on the Book of Proverbs in the English language was one of the crying needs of Biblical scholarship. Accordingly, we may not be yielding to the latest addition to the International Critical Series the tribute it deserves, when we say that it at once takes the first place in its class. That place it undoubtedly deserves, however, and would have secured even against much more formidable competitors than it happens to have. It is altogether a well-arranged, lucid exposition of this unique book in the Bible, based on a careful study of the text and the linguistic and historical background of every part of it."—*The Interior.*

"While this commentary is called 'critical' and is such, it is not one in which the apparatus is spread out in detail; it is one which any intelligent English reader can readily use and thoroughly understand."—*The Evangelist.*